Relational Database
Writings
1985 - 1989

Relational Database Writings 1985-1989

C. J. Date

with a special contribution by
Andrew Warden

ADDISON-WESLEY PUBLISHING COMPANY

Reading, Massachusetts • Menlo Park, California • New York •
Don Mills, Ontario • Wokingham, England • Amsterdam • Bonn •
Sydney • Singapore • Tokyo • Madrid • San Juan

Library of Congress Cataloging-in-Publication Data

Date, C. J.
  Relational database writings, 1985-1989/by C. J. Date; with a
special contribution by Andrew Warden.
      p.   cm.
  Includes bibliographical references.
  ISBN 0-201-50881-8
  1. Data base management.   2. Relational data bases.   I. Warden,
  Andrew.   II. Title.
QA76.9.D3D3725   1990
005.75'6—dc20   89-17571
                                                               CIP

Programs presented in this text are printed from
camera-ready material prepared by the author.

ABCDEFGHIJ-MA-89

This book (like its predecessor)
is dedicated to the desert

Preface

This book can be regarded as a sequel to my book *Relational Database: Selected Writings* (Addison-Wesley, 1986). Like that earlier book, it consists of a collection of papers on the general topic of relational database technology—basically all those of my papers from the period 1985-1989 that seem to me to be worth preserving in this more durable form, together with a group of papers by another specialist in the relational field, Andrew Warden (see below). Some of the papers were originally published in various technical journals (and I am grateful to all concerned for permission to republish them in this fashion), others were previously unpublished.

The rationale for the book is as follows. It is undeniable that relational technology has started to take off in a big way, not only in the academic world but (at last) in the commercial marketplace also. A broad understanding of that technology is finally beginning to permeate the DP industry at a variety of levels. However, there are numerous specific relational topics that can certainly stand some extended explanation or elaboration or clarification—in particular, aspects that display some subtleties or depths, the ramifications and consequences of which are not always immediately apparent. Such topics typically do not fit well into a basic database textbook. Nor, individually, do they possess enough substance to require a whole book of their own (for the most part, at any rate, although in one or two cases this claim might be less than fair—an entire book probably could be devoted to the topic of foreign keys, for example). Thus, the idea of bringing together into a single volume a collection of papers that deal with such matters seemed to be a useful one. Hence this book.

The book overall is arranged into five principal parts, the first four of which are deliberately intended to correspond directly to the four parts of its predecessor:

I.   Relational Database Management
II. Relational vs. Nonrelational Systems
III. The SQL Language
IV. Database Design
V.   Adventures in Relationland
     (by Andrew Warden)

Part I (the longest) consists of a collection of papers on relational technology and relational systems in general. Part II consists of a single paper that addresses certain aspects of the difference between relational and nonrelational systems. Part III contains a number of papers—mostly of a somewhat critical nature—having to do with the relational language SQL (now both a de facto and an official standard). Part IV (like Part II) contains just one paper, this one on some problems in the area of relational database design. Finally, Part V is a "special guest" part: It consists of a sequence of seven short papers by Andrew Warden that present some of the basics of relational systems in a highly original (and, I believe, enlightening) manner.

A couple of general remarks on the technical content of the book are in order at this point:

- As mentioned above, the language SQL has become the standard for interacting with relational systems. For this reason, SQL is used almost exclusively throughout the book as the basis for examples, even when SQL per se is not the main topic of the particular paper in question. The dialect of SQL used (where it makes any difference) is usually that of the IBM product DB2.

- Several of the papers in this book (and in its predecessor also) argue that the problem of *nulls*—i.e., the missing information problem—is still very far from being completely understood, and that current proposed solutions to that problem should be regarded as preliminary at best. (In particular, the "solution" provided in current SQL is just plain wrong.) Other papers in the book, however, for which the nulls problem is not the major point at issue, simply make the assumption that nulls are indeed understood, and are supported by the system, and generally are considered to be A Good Thing. Those latter papers will need some minor revision if it is ever decided to do away with nulls alto-gether, or if—a more optimistic wish—a satisfactory solution to the missing information problem is ever found.

It goes without saying that the opinions expressed in the papers are all my own (or Warden's, of course—but I completely subscribe to the opin-ions in Warden's papers, which is why I wanted to include them in the book in the first place). However, it is only fair to warn readers that some of those opinions might be regarded as a trifle heretical, in the sense that they are in conflict with the way most current systems actually work and with the published opinions of various authorities in the field. In particular, there are a few issues on which I find myself in disagreement with Ted Codd. Since Ted is of course the originator of the relational model, I do not take such disagreements lightly; but I naturally feel a responsibility to tell the truth as I see it. Readers will have to examine the issues and make up their own minds on such matters.

Finally, a brief note on the structure of the book: Since each chapter was originally intended to stand alone as an independent paper, each one typically contains sections, figures, and references whose numbering is unique only within the chapter in question. A few even have their own ap-pendixes. To a very great degree, I have preserved the independence of in-dividual papers (editing out only the worst of the overlaps); thus, all references within a given chapter to (e.g.) Section 3 or Fig. 2 or Appendix A are to be taken as references to the indicated section or figure or appendix of the chapter in question. There are no explicit cross-references at all, ex-cept in Chapters 5 and 6, which are really two halves of a single paper anyway, and in the chapters of Part V, which form a coherent series and are definitely intended to be read in sequence.

ACKNOWLEDGMENTS

Most of all, I would like to thank my friend Hugh Darwen (alias Andrew Warden) for his major contribution to this book, for his critical reviews of my own chapters, and for numerous helpful discussions. I would also like to acknowledge the helpful comments I received on earlier drafts of some of the chapters from several friends and colleagues, especially Nagraj Alur, Charley Bontempo, Ted Codd, Mike Ferguson, Nat Goodman, Rob McCord, Roger Miller, Mike Stonebraker, Diann Trautwein, Sharon Wein-berg, Colin White, Paul Winsberg, Gabrielle Wiorkowski, Ed Wrazen, and Bob Yost. I am particularly indebted to Nat Goodman for his contributions to Chapter 8. My thanks also to my long-suffering family and friends, as always. As for my editor, Elydia Davis, and the staff at Addison-Wesley:

After working with them on so many projects, I am beginning to run out of new ways to express my appreciation. I think the best I can do is to say that their assistance has been as friendly, obliging, and professional as it always is, and as I have come to expect.

Saratoga, California   C. J. Date
1989

About the Authors

C. J. DATE

C. J. Date is an independent author, lecturer, and consultant specializing in relational database systems. He is a cofounder, with Dr. E. F. Codd (the originator of the relational model), of the well-known consulting company *Codd and Date International* and various subsidiary companies. He was previously a database specialist at the IBM Santa Teresa Laboratory in San Jose, California, where he was involved in technical planning for the IBM relational products SQL/DS and DB2.

Mr. Date is best known for his books, in particular *Relational Database: Selected Writings* (the predecessor to the present book) and *An Introduction to Database Systems*, Volume I (currently in its fourth edition), which is the standard text in the field.

ANDREW WARDEN

Andrew Warden is the pen name of Hugh Darwen, a computer professional who has been involved in software development since 1967 as an employee of IBM UK Ltd. He has been active in the relational database arena since 1978.

Mr. Darwen was one of the chief architects and developers of an IBM relational product called Business System 12, a product that faithfully embraced the principles of the relational model. It was in studying the feasibility of building a SQL interface to that product that he found the many flaws in SQL that militated against such an interface. Those flaws are described in his contribution to this book.

Mr. Darwen is currently active in the UK working group that is participating in the formulation of SQL2, the likely successor to the existing SQL standard.

Contents

PART I   RELATIONAL DATABASE MANAGEMENT

CHAPTER 1
Why Relational?   **3**
      Abstract   3
      Comments on Republication   3
  1. Introduction   4
  2. Simplicity   4
  3. Simple Data Structure   6
  4. Simple Operators   7
  5. No Frivolous Distinctions   9
  6. SQL Support   10
  7. The View Mechanism   11
  8. Sound Theoretical Base   12
  9. Small Number of Concepts   13
10. The Dual-Mode Principle   14
11. Physical Data Independence   15
12. Logical Data Independence   16
13. Ease of Application Development   17
14. Dynamic Data Definition   18

15. Ease of Installation and Ease of Operation   19
16. Simplified Database Design   20
17. Integrated Dictionary   20
18. Distributed Database Support   21
19. Performance   22
20. Extendability   23
21. Conclusion   24
   References and Bibliography   24

CHAPTER 2

What Is a Domain?   **27**

Abstract   27
Comments on Publication   27
1. Introduction   28
2. The Basic Idea   29
3. Some Common Misconceptions   32
4. Data Value Atomicity   35
5. Aspects of Domain Support   38
6. A Domain Is a User-Defined Data Type   43
7. Support for User-Defined Data Types   48
8. Summary and Conclusion   50
   Acknowledgments   52
   References and Bibliography   52
   Appendix A: User-Defined vs. "Extended" Data Types   54

CHAPTER 3

Defining Data Types in a Database Language   **59**

Abstract   59
Comments on Republication   59
1. Introduction   60
2. Preliminaries   61
3. Basic Data Elements   62
4. Conversions   66
5. Comparisons   68
6. Computational Operations   68
7. Builtin Functions   69
8. Assignment   70
9. Literals   70
10. Variables   72
11. Operators and Expressions   74
12. Input/Output Formats   79

13. Implementation Issues   79
14. Summary   80
    Acknowledgments   81
    References and Bibliography   81

CHAPTER 4
Why Duplicate Rows Are Prohibited   **83**
    Abstract   83
    Comments on Publication   83
1. Why Duplicates Are Good (?)   84
2. Why Duplicates Are Bad (I): The Fundamental Issue   84
3. Why Duplicates Are Bad (II): The Question of Meaning   89
4. Why Duplicates Are Bad (III): Miscellaneous Points   93
5. Conclusion   96
    Acknowledgments   97
    References and Bibliography   97

CHAPTER 5
Referential Integrity and Foreign Keys Part I:
Basic Concepts   **99**
    Abstract   99
    Comments on Publication   99
1. Introduction   100
2. Examples   101
3. A Relational Model of Data for Large Shared Data Banks   107
4. Extending the Database Relational Model to Capture More Meaning   107
5. Referential Integrity   110
6. Domains, Keys, and Referential Integrity in Relational Databases   113
7. A Proposal   116
8. Foreign Key Rules   119
9. Benefits of Foreign Key Support   125
    References and Bibliography   127
    Appendix A: Syntax Summary   130

CHAPTER 6
Referential Integrity and Foreign Keys Part II:
Further Considerations   **133**
    Abstract   133
    Comments on Publication   133

10. Some Outstanding Questions   134
11. Why Every Table Should Have Exactly One Primary Key   136
12. Why Foreign Keys Should Match Primary Keys, Not Alternate Keys   138
13. Why Foreign Keys Are Not Pointers   140
14. Why Key Declarations Should Be Special-Cased   141
15. Why Conterminous Referential Paths Should Be Treated with Caution   143
16. Why Primary Key Values in Base Tables Should Not Be Wholly or Partly Null   147
17. Why Composite Foreign Key Values Should Not Be Partly Null   148
18. Why Overlapping Keys Should Be Treated with Caution   152
19. Why Noncomposite Keys Are a Good Idea   159
20. Why a Single Target Table Is a Good Idea   163
21. Some Operational Considerations   165
22. Conclusion   167
    Acknowledgments   167
    References and Bibliography   167
    Appendix A: Referential Integrity in the SQL Standard   170
    Appendix B: Referential Integrity in DB2 and SQL/DS   172
    Appendix C: Why "Update Cascades" Is Desirable   181

CHAPTER 7

A Contribution to the Study of Database Integrity   **185**

    Abstract   185
    Comments on Publication   185
 1. The Basic Idea   187
 2. Integrity vs. Recovery vs. Concurrency vs. Security   188
 3. Integrity Rules   190
 4. A Classification Scheme for Integrity Rules   194
 5. Domain Rules   194
 6. Single-Row Rules   197
 7. Multi-Row Rules   200
 8. Aggregate Function Rules   204
 9. State vs. Transition Rules   205
10. Immediate vs. Deferred Rules   206
11. Combinations of the Foregoing   208
12. Special Cases   208
13. Miscellaneous Considerations   209
    Acknowledgments   214
    References and Bibliography   214

CHAPTER 8
NOT Is Not "Not"!
(Notes on Three-Valued Logic and Related Matters)   **217**
    Abstract   217
    Comments on Publication   217
  1. Introduction   218
  2. Types of Null   219
  3. The Three-Valued Logic Approach   223
  4. Some Important Tautologies   232
  5. Examples   233
  6. Some Questions   239
  7. Miscellaneous Issues   239
  8. Conclusion   241
    Acknowledgments   243
    References and Bibliography   243
    Appendix A: The Default Value Approach   245

CHAPTER 9
Further Relational Myths   **249**
    Abstract   249
    Comments on Republication   249
  1. Introduction   250
  2. Myth 27: Updating Must Be Record-at-a-Time   252
  3. Myth 28: Relational Systems Cannot Handle Bill-of-Materials   253
  4. Myth 29: Building Intermediate Result Tables   255
  5. Myth 30: Foreign Keys Undermine Data Independence   256
  6. Myth 31: Relational Systems Have No Dictionary   257
  7. Myth 32: Top-Down Design vs. Normalization   258
  8. Myth 33: The Relational Approach Is Just a Fad   260
  9. Myth 34: There's No Such Thing as a Relational Database   264
 10. Conclusion   265
    Acknowledgments   265
    References and Bibliography   265

CHAPTER 10
What Is a Distributed Database System?   **267**
    Abstract   267
    Comments on Republication   267
  1. Background   268
  2. A Fundamental Principle   270

3. Rule 1: Local Autonomy   274
4. Rule 2: No Reliance on a Central Site   275
5. Rule 3: Continuous Operation   276
6. Rule 4: Location Independence   277
7. Rule 5: Fragmentation Independence   280
8. Rule 6: Replication Independence   282
9. Rule 7: Distributed Query Processing   285
10. Rule 8: Distributed Transaction Management   287
11. Rule 9: Hardware Independence   290
12. Rule 10: Operating System Independence   290
13. Rule 11: Network Independence   290
14. Rule 12: DBMS Independence   291
15. Summary and Conclusions   295
    Acknowledgments   297
    References and Bibliography   298

PART II   RELATIONAL VS. NONRELATIONAL SYSTEMS

CHAPTER 11
Support for the Conceptual Schema:
The Relational and Network Approaches   **301**

Abstract   301
Comments on Republication   301
1. Introduction   302
2. The Conceptual Schema   302
3. Some Criteria for the Conceptual Schema   304
4. The Relational Approach   307
5. The Network Approach   308
6. Conclusion   317
References and Bibliography   317

PART III   THE SQL LANGUAGE

CHAPTER 12
What's Wrong with SQL?   **325**

Abstract   325
Comments on Republication   325

1. Introduction   326
2. What's Wrong with SQL Per Se   327
3. What's Wrong with the SQL Standard   331
4. Application Portability   333
5. Conclusions   336
   Acknowledgments   336
   References and Bibliography   336

CHAPTER 13
EXISTS Is Not "Exists"!
(Some Logical Flaws in SQL)   **339**
   Abstract   339
   Comments on Publication   339
1. Introduction   340
2. An Example of a Contradiction   342
3. A Problem of Interpretation   345
4. Transforming All-or-Any Comparisons into Existence Tests   348
5. Another Anomaly . . .   351
6. . . . and Another   353
7. Conclusion   355
   Acknowledgments   356
   References and Bibliography   356

CHAPTER 14
Dates and Times in IBM SQL:
Some Technical Criticisms   **357**
   Abstract   357
   Comments on Publication   358
1. Introduction   358
2. Data Types   359
3. Literals   361
4. Column Definitions   362
5. Conversions   363
6. Durations   366
7. Special Registers   370
8. Arithmetic Operations   370
9. Assignments   373
10. Comparisons   373
11. Summary and Conclusion   375
    Acknowledgments   376
    References and Bibliography   376

CHAPTER 15
SQL Dos and Don'ts   **379**
    Abstract   379
    Comments on Publication   379
  1. Introduction   380
  2. Advantages and Benefits   381
  3. General Recommendations   382
  4. Database Design Recommendations   390
  5. Data Definition Recommendations   393
  6. Data Manipulation Recommendations   401
  7. Conclusion   422
    Acknowledgments   423
    References and Bibliography   423

PART IV   DATABASE DESIGN

CHAPTER 16
A Note on One-to-One Relationships   **427**
    Abstract   427
    Comments on Republication   427
  1. Introduction   428
  2. What Does "One-to-One" Mean?   428
  3. The (Zero-or-One)-to-One Case   431
  4. The (Zero-or-One)-to-(Zero-or-One) Case   435
  5. The Genuine One-to-One Case   437
  6. Conclusions   449
    Acknowledgments   450
    References and Bibliography   450

PART V   ADVENTURES IN RELATIONLAND
(by Andrew Warden)

An Introduction
(by C. J. Date)   **453**

Preface   **456**

CHAPTER 17
The Naming of Columns   461

CHAPTER 18
In Praise of Marriage   467

CHAPTER 19
The Keys of the Kingdom   475

CHAPTER 20
Chivalry   483

CHAPTER 21
A Constant Friend   493

CHAPTER 22
Table_Dee and Table_Dum   501

CHAPTER 23
Into the Unknown   509

POSTSCRIPT
Is SQL Getting There?   521

Index   523

Publishing History

Why Relational?
  Originally published in two parts in *The Relational Journal,* No. 4 (August 1988) and No. 5 (November 1988).

Defining Data Types in a Database Language
  Originally published in *ACM SIGMOD Record* 17, No. 2 (June 1988).

Further Relational Myths
  This paper is based on material from two separate papers, "Relational Database: Further Misconceptions Number One" (originally published in *InfoDB* 1, No. 1, Spring 1986) and "Relational Database: Further Misconceptions Number Two" (originally published in *InfoDB* 1, No. 2, Summer 1986).

What Is a Distributed Database System?
  Originally published in two parts in *InfoDB* 2, No. 2 (Summer 1987) and No. 3 (Fall 1987). A shorter version of the paper appeared earlier under the title "Rules for Distributed Database Systems" in *Computerworld* (June 8, 1987).

Support for the Conceptual Schema: The Relational and Network Approaches
> Originally published (in somewhat different form) as Chapter 28 of the book *An Introduction to Database Systems* (3rd edition), by C. J. Date, Addison-Wesley (1981).

What's Wrong with SQL?
> Originally published (in somewhat different form) in *Datamation* 33, No. 9 (May 1, 1987), under the title "Where SQL Falls Short."

Dates and Times in IBM SQL: Some Technical Criticisms
> Originally published (under a slightly different title) in *InfoDB* 3, No. 1 (Spring 1988).

A Note on One-to-One Relationships
> Originally published in *InfoDB* 3, No. 4 (Winter 1988/89).

Adventures in Relationland (by Andrew Warden)
> Originally published as a series of articles in *The Relational Journal,* beginning with Number 3 (March 1988).

All other papers in the book are previously unpublished.

PART I

RELATIONAL DATABASE MANAGEMENT

1

Why Relational?

ABSTRACT

There has been a need for some time for a paper that provides a succinct yet reasonably comprehensive summary of the major advantages of the relational approach. This paper is an attempt to meet that need.

COMMENTS ON REPUBLICATION

In my teaching and consulting activities I have frequently been asked for a reference to a document that provides in one place a succinct yet reasonably comprehensive answer to the question "Why relational?" So far as I was aware in early 1988, no existing document really did a satisfactory job of answering that question; I therefore decided to try and produce such a paper myself. No doubt the paper that follows is not entirely satisfactory either—the list of advantages of the relational approach could probably go on for ever, or at least for a very long time—but at least it is an attempt. It should be taken in that spirit.

Originally published in two parts in *The Relational Journal,* No. 4 (August 1988) and No. 5 (November 1988). Reprinted by permission.

1. INTRODUCTION

As noted in the Abstract, there has been a need for some time for a paper that provides a succinct but comprehensive summary of the major advantages of the relational approach. This paper is an attempt to meet that need. The material it contains is thus definitely not new—much of it has previously appeared in references [4,8,12,13] or elsewhere—but I am not aware of any other paper that gathers it all together into a single place as this one does. Also, please note the objective of succinctness; every one of the advantages identified herein could easily be discussed at much greater length, but such is not the aim of the present paper. (Even so, the paper is much longer than originally planned!) Please note too that the paper is primarily concerned with technical advantages, not business or economic advantages. Of course, what business and economic advantages exist do all stem from the technical advantages in the first place.

The reader is assumed to have at least a slight acquaintance with the basic capabilities and concepts of relational systems. A comprehensive description of those capabilities and concepts can be found in reference [4].

2. SIMPLICITY

If the advantages of the relational approach must be summed up in a single word, that word is *simplicity*—where by "simplicity" I mean, primarily, simplicity for the *user*. Strong evidence in support of this claim can be found in reference [3], where a sample application (a machine shop scheduling application) is coded in both CODASYL (DBTG) COBOL and a relational language. For full details of the example, the reader is referred to the original paper [3]; here I content myself with simply listing a few comparative statistics.

	CODASYL	*relational*
statements	> 60	3
GO TO	15	0
PERFORM UNTIL	1	0
currency indicators	10	0
IF	12	0
FIND	9	0
GET	4	1
STORE	2	1
MODIFY	1	0
MOVE CURRENCY	4	0
other MOVEs	9	1
SUPPRESS CURRENCY	4	0

The relative simplicity of the relational solution is very striking.

> *Aside:* In fact, the relational solution could have been reduced even further to just two statements, a GET and a STORE—the MOVE is not strictly necessary. What is more, the CODASYL "solution" (which was taken from another source, not created by the authors of reference [3]) included at least two bugs! *End of aside.*

The example thus clearly shows that relational systems can provide tremendous simplifications in the area of *data manipulation.* And of course (although the table above does not illustrate the point directly) comparable simplifications can be achieved (and normally are achieved) in the areas of *database design, database definition, database installation,* and so forth. No wonder that users of relational systems have reported anywhere from 5- to 20-fold increases in productivity. In particular, applications become feasible in such systems that would not have been feasible with an older-style system because of difficulty of installation, or cost of operation, or lack of an ad hoc query facility, or for many other reasons.

To repeat, then: The overall advantage of the relational approach is simplicity. Simplicity, in turn, translates into *usability* and *productivity:*

- Usability means that even comparatively unskilled users can use the system to do useful work; that is, it is often possible for end-users to obtain useful results from the system without having to have the DP department create a COBOL program for them. (The machine shop scheduling example illustrates this particular point very clearly.) In this way a major potential bottleneck can be bypassed entirely.

- Productivity means that both end-users and DP professionals can be more productive in their day-to-day activities. As a result, they can between them make significant inroads into the well-known application backlog problem (see Section 13 later in this paper).

There are numerous subsidiary advantages that contribute to the overall simplicity of relational systems. I give below a list of such advantages, for purposes of reference, then go on to discuss each one in detail. *Note:* I make no claim that the list is complete in any sense. Also, of course, the various items in the list are not all independent of one another but are interrelated in numerous ways. I apologize in advance for any repetitiveness in the paper that may be caused by this latter fact.

- Simple data structure
- Simple operators

- No frivolous distinctions
- SQL support
- The view mechanism
- Sound theoretical base
- Small number of concepts
- The dual-mode principle
- Physical data independence
- Logical data independence
- Ease of application development
- Dynamic data definition
- Ease of installation and ease of operation
- Simplified database design
- Integrated dictionary
- Distributed database support
- Performance
- Extendability

3. SIMPLE DATA STRUCTURE

The first contributor to the simplicity of the relational approach is, of course, the simple logical data structure. Relational databases are perceived by the user as *tables* (and nothing but tables); and tables are a very simple and familiar structure—indeed, tables have been used as a means of keeping records (on paper, etc.) for literally hundreds of years. What is more, tables are *sufficient,* in the sense that there is no known data that cannot be represented in tabular form. This is one reason why tables are the *only* data structure provided in relational systems. One of the problems with older-style, nonrelational systems is that they typically provide several different data structures—several different ways, that is, of representing data—which means that (a) the user interface to those systems is more complex, and (b) there are generally no good objective criteria by which the user can choose the "right" way to represent some given piece of data.

Note: By "data structure" in the foregoing paragraph, of course, I mean "data structure *at the logical level*" (only). Other structures will certainly be desirable (and will certainly be provided) at the physical level. But those physical-level structures will not (or at least should not) be visible to users.

4. SIMPLE OPERATORS

The second contributor to relational simplicity is the relational operators. Relational operators, such as SELECT, UPDATE, etc., in the relational language SQL (see Section 6 below), are *set-level*—i.e., they operate on entire sets of values, not just on one value at a time. As a consequence, they are both powerful and easy to understand (and use); users do not have to write program loops in order to repeat some operation over and over on every record in some set. In other words, users simply specify *what* they want to do, not in detail *how* to do it. Suppose, for example, that we are given the following two tables (with the obvious interpretation):

```
EMP     ( EMP#, ENAME, DEPT#, SALARY )
        PRIMARY KEY ( EMP# )

DEPT    ( DEPT#, LOCATION, BUDGET )
        PRIMARY KEY ( DEPT# )
```

Then a user needing to know (for example) employee numbers and names for employees who work for a department that is located in San Jose can simply issue the following more or less self-explanatory SQL statement:

```
SELECT EMP#, ENAME
FROM   EMP
WHERE  DEPT# IN
     ( SELECT DEPT#
       FROM   DEPT
       WHERE  LOCATION = 'San Jose' ) ;
```

The result might look like this:

```
EMP#    ENAME
----    -----
E02     Berg
E05     Haydn
E09     Ives
E13     Elgar
```

   The set-level nature of the operation is evidenced by the fact that the result is a set (actually a table—a table can be regarded as a set, namely a set of rows). The SELECT statement issued by the user can be regarded as just a stylized *description* of that desired result—it is *not* a detailed prescription or *procedure* for the system to follow in order to compute the result set. The system (actually a system component called the *optimizer*—see further discussion in Section 19, later) will *convert* that description into an appropriate procedure. Thus, the system will decide what loops to execute and how to "navigate" through the physical storage structure on the disk in order to build the result set. For this reason, relational systems are frequently described as "automatic navigation" systems. By contrast, systems in which users have to do that navigation for themselves—i.e., nonrelational systems—are known as "manual navigation" systems.

Note too that automatic navigation does not apply only to retrieval operations. Here is an update example ("change the color of all red parts in table P to orange"):

```
UPDATE P
SET     COLOR = 'Orange'
WHERE   COLOR = 'Red' ;
```

Again this is a set-level or multiple-row operation, in general.

By taking the burden of navigation off the user's back in this way, the relational system is freeing the user to concentrate on solving the real problem—e.g., finding an answer to the query, in case of the SELECT example above, and using that information for whatever purpose it is needed in the outside world. In the case of end-users, in fact, it is automatic navigation that makes it possible for the user to use the system in the first place. It is not difficult to find a simple SQL operation for which an equivalent COBOL program would be ten or twenty pages long, and writing—and debugging—that program would be out of the question for most users (and maybe not worth the effort involved even when not).

> *Aside:* It was of course the set-level nature of the relational language that accounted for the reduction (or at least, most of the reduction) in code size in the machine shop scheduling example mentioned in Section 2, earlier. In other words, the set-level nature of the operators is a major source of the increase in productivity that relational systems can provide. *End of aside.*

The SELECT example above also serves to illustrate another point. As already explained, the result of that SELECT is a set (a set of rows). More precisely, the result is a *table.* The example thus illustrates the well-known (and very important) relational *closure* property—that is, the value of any relational expression, such as the SELECT statement above (which can be regarded as just a specific relational expression), is always another relation or table.

The relational closure property is important for many reasons. Most of those reasons are beyond the scope of the present paper, but two obvious ones can be pointed out here:

- First, the user in a relational system is always operating in the same simple tabular framework, a very nice unifying feature of such systems.

- Second, because the *output* from a relational operation is the same kind of object as the *input* (they are both tables), that output can become input to another operation—which means in turn that relational operations can be *arbitrarily nested*. (This latter point is important for exactly the same kind of reason that it is important to be able to nest *numeric* expressions in ordinary arithmetic. Numbers are closed under the ordinary arithmetic operations, just as relations are closed under the relational operations.)

To conclude this section, there are a few additional factors regarding the relational operators that deserve to be called out explicitly:

- Relational operators do not involve any notion of "current position." It is worth mentioning that the two bugs in the CODASYL version of the machine shop scheduling example both had to do with the CODASYL concept of current position.

- Data in a relational system can be requested in any order desired; i.e., the user is not limited to some predefined order that might not happen to suit the requirements of the particular problem at hand.

- Certain commonly required computational functions—e.g., counting, totaling, averaging, etc.—are provided directly in most relational languages, instead of having to be programmed. SQL in particular includes such functions.

- Relational operations do not depend on predefined "links" between tables, but rather allow the user to exploit arbitrary, value-based, cross-table connexions in a totally dynamic fashion. In effect, the relational user is not limited to following static, predefined access paths in the database (as in a hierarchic or network system), but rather can dynamically *impose* such paths (hierarchic or otherwise) on the database at execution time—whatever paths may be needed for the particular problem at hand.

Finally, of course, all of the foregoing advantages apply to application programmers as well as to end-users. Application programmers too can be more productive in a relational system.

5. NO FRIVOLOUS DISTINCTIONS

The operators described in the previous section can be combined together in various well-defined ways to form relational *expressions*—i.e., expressions whose value is a relation. Those expressions, in turn, serve a variety of different purposes. The following is a list (based on a list given in reference [5]) of some of the applications for such expressions:

- Retrieval—i.e., defining the set of data to be retrieved as the result of a query;

- Update—i.e., defining the set of data to be inserted or modified or deleted via an update operation;
- Virtual data—i.e., defining the set of data to be visible through a view (see Section 7 below);
- Access rights—i.e., defining the set of data over which authorization of some kind is to be granted;
- Stability specifications—i.e., defining the set of data that is to be the scope of a locking or other concurrency control operation;
- Integrity constraints—i.e., defining some specific rule that the database must satisfy at any given time;

and certainly others besides. It follows that similar functions involve similar actions on the part of the user in a relational system. For example, the actions of (a) formulating a relational query, and (b) defining a relational view, are essentially identical so far as the user is concerned, and indeed are essentially identical at a fundamental level also. In other words, there are—or should be—"no frivolous distinctions" in a relational system. As a result, relational systems mean less to learn, less to remember, fewer decisions to make, etc. (see Section 9 later for further discussion of these points).

6. SQL SUPPORT

There is absolutely no question that the relational language SQL ("Structured Query Language") represents a major advance over older database languages such as the DL/I language of IMS or the DML and DDL of CODASYL. Furthermore, there is now an industry standard version of SQL [9], and almost every DBMS vendor has either implemented or promised to implement some dialect of the language. (Though the reader should be warned that at the time of writing, at least, very few vendors, if any, actually support the standard dialect per se—vendor publicity to the contrary notwithstanding.)

The arguments in favor of standards are well known:

- They can reduce training costs.
- They can increase application portability.
- They can increase application longevity.
- They can serve as a basis for intersystem communication.
- They can simplify customer choice.

On the other hand, it has to be said that the SQL standard is not a particularly *good* standard (i.e., there are some disadvantages also). The reader is referred to reference [9] for a comprehensive discussion of the standard and of some of its potential disadvantages.

7. THE VIEW MECHANISM

I have already said that the user perception of the database in a relational system is very simple, consisting as it does just of tables. The relational *view* mechanism allows that perception to be simplified still further: In effect, it allows the database to be (logically) tailored and rearranged and restructured to meet the specific requirements of some specific user, as follows.

Basically, a view is a *virtual table*—i.e., a table that does not exist in its own right but is instead defined in terms of one or more real or "base" tables (and/or other views). A view is not represented by its own, separate, distinguishable stored data; instead, it is represented by a *definition,* which is stored in the system dictionary (see Section 17, later). That definition consists essentially of a relational retrieval expression (a SELECT statement, in SQL terms). Here is an example, based on the departments-and-employees database shown earlier:

```
CREATE VIEW SJ_EMPS AS
      SELECT EMP#, ENAME, DEPT#, SALARY
      FROM   EMP
      WHERE  DEPT# IN
           ( SELECT DEPT#
             FROM    DEPT
             WHERE   LOCATION = 'San Jose' ) ;
```

In principle, any table that can be retrieved by a relational retrieval operation can alternatively be defined as a view. However, no retrieval is actually performed at the time the view is defined (at least, this statement is—again—true in principle, though it may not be true in all systems). Instead, when the user issues an operation against the view, that operation is logically combined with the view definition to yield a modified operation, and the modified operation is then executed. For example, suppose the user issues the following SELECT operation against the view SJ_EMPS:

```
SELECT EMP#
FROM   SJ_EMPS
WHERE  SALARY > 50000 ;
```

The operation actually executed (i.e., the modified operation) is:

```
SELECT EMP#
FROM   EMP
WHERE  DEPT# IN
     ( SELECT DEPT#
       FROM    DEPT
       WHERE   LOCATION = 'San Jose' )
AND    SALARY > 50000 ;
```

The advantages of views include the following:

- They can be tailored to individual user requirements, thus simplifying the user's perception of the database and hence simplifying access operations also. For example, a view might consist of some combination (e.g., a relational join) of two base tables, so that the user can deal logically with one table instead of two. In effect, views thus provide a shorthand, rather as macros do in a programming language.

- Different users can have different views of the same data; moreover, different users can be accessing those different views all at the same time.

- Views can also be used to hide sensitive information, thus providing one (important) form of data security.

- Finally, views are crucial in the provision of *logical data independence* (see Section 12 later for more discussion of this point).

8. SOUND THEORETICAL BASE

The point cannot be emphasized too strongly that, compared to other database approaches, *relational really is different*. It is different because it is not ad hoc. Older systems *were* ad hoc; they may have provided solutions to certain important problems of their day, but they did not rest on any solid theoretical base. Relational systems, by contrast, do rest on such a base, namely the *relational model* [1]; and the relational model, in turn, is based on certain fundamental mathematical disciplines, namely set theory and predicate logic—which means that it is *rock solid*.

Thanks to this solid foundation, relational systems behave in well-defined ways; and (possibly without consciously realizing the fact) users have a simple model of that behavior in their mind, one that enables them to predict with confidence what the system will do in any given situation. There are (or should be) no surprises. This predictability means that user interfaces are easy to understand, document, teach, learn, use, and remember.

Note: It cannot be denied that many relational systems today do nevertheless display rather ad hoc and unpredictable behavior in certain areas. To take a concrete example, consider the treatment of view updating in the IBM relational product DB2 [12,15], which does display a certain amount of unpleasant arbitrariness. But such arbitrariness tends to occur precisely at those points where the system in question has departed from the underlying theory. For example, a crucial component of the relational model is the concept of *primary key*. However, DB2 does not fully support that concept,* and it is that omission that is the direct cause of the arbitrariness just referred to. DB2 is not the sole offender in this regard, of course—similar criticisms apply to most other systems at the time of writing—but it does serve to illustrate the undesirable consequences of disregarding the prescriptions of the underlying theory.

Incidentally, I was tempted to make "existence of a sound theoretical base" the very first point in the paper—it is so important, and so fundamental. And yet it is common to find people, even today, who still decry theory—indeed, many critics of relational systems in the past have actually objected to the fact that they are based on theory [5,6]! The objection seems to be that only theoreticians are capable of understanding, or need to understand, something that is based on theory. My own position is exactly the opposite: Systems that are not based on theory are usually very difficult for *anyone* to understand. It cannot be stated too strongly that "theoretical" does *not* mean "not practical." On the contrary, considerations that are initially dismissed as being "only theoretical" [sic] have a nasty habit of becoming horribly practical a few years later on.

9. SMALL NUMBER OF CONCEPTS

The relational model is notable for the small number of concepts it involves. For example:

(a) As explained in Section 3 above, there is one and only one way to represent data: All data in a relational database is represented as column values within rows within tables.

(b) As a consequence of (a), one and only one operator is needed for each of the four basic manipulative functions "retrieve," "insert," "change," and "delete." For this reason, all relational languages have basically four manipulative operators (verbs). In SQL, for example, the four operators are SELECT, INSERT, UPDATE, and DELETE; in QUEL [8], they are RETRIEVE, APPEND, REPLACE, and DELETE.

By contrast, nonrelational systems fundamentally require 4*n* manipulative operators, where *n* is the number of ways that data can be represented in the system under consideration. In CODASYL-based

---

*Support for primary keys was added to the DB2 product after this paper was first written. However, it is still true at the time of writing that DB2 does not support the primary key concept *fully*. For example, it still allows tables to exist that do not have a primary key, and it still does not make use of the semantics of primary keys in deciding which views are updatable.

systems, for example, where data can be represented either as records or as "links" between records, we typically find a STORE operator to create a record and a CONNECT operator to create a link; a MODIFY operator to change a record and a RECONNECT operator to change a link; an ERASE operator to delete a record and a DISCONNECT operator to delete a link; and so on. (Actually, CODASYL systems usually provide not just two but five or six different ways of representing data—and so the foregoing argument applies with even more force—but records and links are easily the two most important ways.)

(c) For exactly the same reason (i.e., the fact that there is only one way to represent data), fewer operators are also needed in a relational system for all of the other functions—data definition, authorization control, integrity control, exception handling, mapping to storage, etc.—that are required in a general-purpose DBMS. In the case of authorization specifically, it is the simplicity and regularity of the data structure that makes possible the sophisticated data protection mechanism that is typically found in relational systems—a mechanism in which value-dependent, value-independent, context-dependent, and other security constraints can be easily defined and conveniently enforced.

A separate but related point is the following: In the relational model, distinct concepts are cleanly separated, not bundled together. By contrast, the CODASYL link construct mentioned above bundles together several fundamentally distinct notions: It is simultaneously a representation of a one-to-many relationship, an access path (or collection of access paths), a mechanism for enforcing certain integrity constraints, and so on. As a result, it becomes difficult to tell exactly what purpose a given link is serving (and it may be used for a purpose for which it was not intended). For example, a program may come to rely on an access path that is really a side effect of the way the database designer chose to represent a certain integrity constraint. If that integrity constraint needs to be changed, then the database will have to be restructured, with a strong likelihood that the program will then have to be rewritten—even if that program is completely uninterested in that integrity constraint per se.

10. THE DUAL-MODE PRINCIPLE

In most relational systems the same language (typically SQL) is used for both programmed and interactive access to the database. This is the *principle of dual-mode access* (dual-mode principle for short). The dual-mode principle has at least three immediate consequences:

1. Different categories of user—system administrators, database administrators, application programmers, end-users from any number of different backgrounds—are all "speaking the same language" and are thus better able to communicate with one another.

2. The same function has the same syntax no matter what interface it is part of (again, there are no "frivolous distinctions" between interfaces). This fact makes it easy for one person to switch roles—e.g., to perform data definition (administrative) functions on one occasion and ad hoc query (end-user) functions on another.

3. Application programmers can easily debug the database portions of their programs (i.e., embedded database statements) through the interactive interface. That interface thus serves as a powerful and convenient program debugging facility.

11.   PHYSICAL DATA INDEPENDENCE

Physical data independence (abbreviated to just "independence" in the present section) is the independence of users and user programs from details of the way the data is physically stored and accessed. It is critically important for at least two reasons:

1. It is important for application programmers because, without it, changes to the physical structure of the database would necessitate corresponding changes to application programs. Note that changes to the physical structure are frequently necessary in practice for a variety of reasons—performance, growth, new installation standards, new application requirements, etc.

2. It is important for end-users because, without it, direct end-user access to the database would scarcely be possible at all. Physical data independence and very high level languages such as SQL go hand in hand.

In the absence of such independence, one of two things happens: Either it becomes almost impossible to make required changes to the database because of the investment in existing applications, or (more likely) a significant portion of the application programming effort is devoted purely to maintenance activity—maintenance activity, that is, that would be unnecessary if the system had provided the necessary independence in the first place. Both of these factors are significant contributors to the application backlog problem mentioned earlier in this paper.

Of course, physical data independence is not an absolute—different systems provide it in differing degrees. To put it another way, few systems if any provide no physical data independence at all; it is just that some systems provide more than others. But relational systems do typically provide more than nonrelational ones, thanks to *the strong separation between the logical and physical levels* in relational systems. In other words, physical-level details have no place in user programs or terminal activities in a relational system (see the discussion of "automatic navigation" in Section 4 of this paper).

> *Note 1:* The separation between the logical and physical levels just referred to is one of the most significant features of the relational approach. It is also one of the most widely misunderstood! Most of the many misconceptions that exist regarding relational systems [5,6] stem from a basic confusion of the two levels and a lack of appreciation of this basic point. Further discussion of those misconceptions is beyond the scope of this paper, however.

> *Note 2:* The previous point notwithstanding, it has to be admitted that existing relational systems are unfortunately still not perfect in this area. For example, it is unfortunate that most systems currently bundle the logical notion of enforcing uniqueness with the physical notion of an index or other access path. Nevertheless, it is still fair to say that existing relational systems are superior to nonrelational ones in the degree of logical/physical separation they provide.

12. LOGICAL DATA INDEPENDENCE

The term "data independence" really covers two somewhat distinct notions—physical data independence (discussed in the previous section) and logical data independence. As explained above, physical data independence means that users and user programs are independent of the physical structure of the database, and hence that the physical structure can be changed without invalidating existing user programs or terminal activities. Logical data independence, of course, means that users and user programs are independent of the *logical* structure of the database (as tables and columns), and hence that the logical structure can also be changed without invalidating existing user programs or terminal activities. For example, it should be possible to split an existing table into two tables, either horizontally (by rows) or vertically (by columns), without having to rewrite existing programs.

Relational systems today do support a certain degree of logical data independence by means of the relational view mechanism. For instance, if table T is logically replaced in some way by two tables T1 and T2, then logical data independence can be preserved by defining T as a view of those replacement tables T1 and T2. *Note:* It is unfortunately true that most systems today support this notion in a less than 100 percent manner, owing to the fact that (as indicated earlier) their support for views is also less than 100 percent (details beyond the scope of this paper); but the potential for full support is there.

One last remark on the general topic of data independence: Data independence (of both varieties) was one of the major original objectives for the relational approach [1]. Older systems are notoriously weak in this whole area. Support for data independence (of both varieties) is important, because it translates into *protection for the application investment.*

13. EASE OF APPLICATION DEVELOPMENT

Relational systems facilitate the application development process in a variety of significant ways. In fact, a relational DBMS is the ideal base on which to construct a well-integrated, easy-to-use, efficient, and flexible application development system, and several vendors have indeed provided such a system. (By "application development system" here, I mean a system that provides all the necessary facilities for the development of user applications.) Consider the following:

1. First, relational systems typically provide a comprehensive and well-integrated set of frontend products—ad hoc query subsystems, report writers, business graphics, spreadsheets, application generators, natural language interfaces, and so forth—all of them having a relational "flavor" (to a greater or lesser extent). These frontends are a particularly strong feature of the better systems available today: They are easy to learn, easy to use, effective, and well integrated with the base DBMS and with each other. Together, they illustrate very clearly the point that the relational model is *not* meant to be seen as an end in itself; rather, the ideas of the model are intended to serve as a foundation for, and a powerful unifying force in, the design and construction of still higher-level interfaces—interfaces that are well engineered and truly usable by a wide variety of human users who have neither the time nor the inclination to delve into the intricacies of the DBMS per se.

   The availability of such frontends means that it may not be necessary to develop an application program (in the traditional sense of the term) at all. The importance of this point can scarcely be over-emphasized.

2. Second, the availability of application generators in particular means that if specialized applications are needed, then they can be developed

quickly and easily, still without any programming in the conventional sense.

3. Third, the high degree of data independence provided (both physical and logical) and the high level of the relational programming interface (typically embedded SQL) together mean that when it *is* necessary to write a conventional program, then that program is easier to write, requires less maintenance, and is easier to change when it does require maintenance, than it would be in an older, nonrelational system.

4. Last, and largely as a consequence of the previous three points, the application development cycle can involve a great deal more *prototyping* than it used to: A first version can be quickly built and shown to the intended users, who can then suggest improvements for incorporation into the next version, and so on. As a result, the final application should do exactly what its users require it to; the overall development process is far less rigid than it used to be, and the application users can be far more involved in that process, to the benefit of all concerned.

14.   DYNAMIC DATA DEFINITION

In a relational system, data definition operations can be executed at any time, without having to halt the system or interrupt other operations in any way. This fact makes relational systems very flexible. Nonrelational systems are much less so. For example, adding a new type of object (such as a new record type or a new index or a new field) in a nonrelational system is an operation not to be undertaken lightly, involving as it typically does all of the following:

- Bringing the system to a halt (and by the way, many installations these days simply cannot afford to halt the system—they require round-the-clock operation);
- Unloading the database;
- Revising and recompiling the database definition; and finally
- Reloading the database in accordance with that revised definition.

In such a system, it becomes highly desirable to get the database definition—and therefore, much more significantly, the database *design—complete* and *correct* once and for all, before starting to load and use the data. This fact in turn means that

(a) The job of getting the system installed and operational can quite literally take months or even years of highly specialized people's time, and

(b) Once the system is running, it can be difficult and costly, perhaps prohibitively so, to remedy early design errors.

In a relational system, by contrast:

- It is possible to create and load just a few tables and then to start using the database immediately.

- It is possible to add new tables and new columns later in a piecemeal fashion, without having any effect on existing users of the database.

- Physical data independence means that it is possible to experiment with the effects of having or not having particular indexes or other access paths, again without affecting existing users at all (other than in performance, of course).

- Logical data independence means that it is even possible, under certain circumstances, to rearrange the logical structure of the database—e.g., to move a column from one table to another—and still not affect the logic of existing programs.

In a nutshell, it is not necessary to go through the total database design process before any useful work can be done with the system, nor is it necessary to get everything right the first time. The system is *forgiving*.

15. EASE OF INSTALLATION AND EASE OF OPERATION

The ability to create new definitions at any time without having to bring the system to a halt (discussed in the previous section) is really only part of a larger overall objective, which is to eliminate the need for *any* planned system shutdown. Thus, for example, it should be possible to invoke utilities from an online terminal, and those utilities should be able to run in parallel with production work; e.g., it should be possible to take an image copy of the database even while transactions are simultaneously updating it. Ideally, the system should have to be started exactly once, when it is first installed, and should then run "forever." (I am not claiming that this objective has yet been fully achieved.)

Eliminating the need for planned shutdowns is, in turn, part of a still larger objective, which is simply to make the system as easy to install and easy to operate as possible. Various features of the system, some of them touched on in previous sections, contribute to the achievement of this objective. Details of such features (other than details already given) are beyond the scope of this paper, but it is worth pointing out explicitly one very important consequence of them, namely the following: It requires only a comparatively small population of DP professionals (administrators, system programmers, system operators) to provide database services to a very large population of users (application programmers and end-users). Relational systems are extremely cost-effective.

16. SIMPLIFIED DATABASE DESIGN

Database design in a relational system is generally easier than in a nonrelational system; in simple situations, in fact, it can be almost trivial. Note that this latter claim *must* be true, or the whole idea of "personal" database systems on PCs and workstations just would not be feasible. (However, it is also true that there are still likely to be some difficult decisions to be made in complex design situations.)

Here are some of the reasons why database design tends to be easier in a relational system:

- First, the decoupling of logical and physical levels means that logical and physical design problems can be separately addressed. (The "right" way to do database design is to get the logical design right first, then map that logical design into physical storage structures as a follow-on activity. Such a clean separation is very hard to achieve with a nonrelational system.)

- Second, at the logical level, the data structure is just about as simple as it possibly can be, which obviously helps in the logical design process.

- Third, there are some sound theoretical principles (basically the principles of normalization) that can be brought to bear on the logical design problem.

- Last, the dynamic data definition feature and the high degree of data independence (both physical and logical) mean that it is not necessary to do the entire design all at once, and neither is it so critical to get it right first time.*

A comprehensive logical design methodology for relational databases that uses a combination of the principles of normalization with a top-down (entity-based) approach is described in some detail in reference [7].

17. INTEGRATED DICTIONARY

A true relational system provides an online, inline, user-extendable, relational dictionary (or catalog) that is completely integrated with the rest of

---

*Perhaps a more accurate statement is that the consequences of making a mistake in database design in a relational system are *not so disastrous* as they typically are in a nonrelational system.

the data—integrated, in the sense that it is represented in the same way (by means of tables) and can be queried in the same way (by means of the user's normal query language, typically SQL). In other words, there is no artificial and unnecessary distinction between database data and dictionary data, or between data and "data about the data" ("metadata," as it is sometimes called). This integration brings with it a number of benefits, among them the following:

1. There is only one interface to document, teach, learn, remember, etc. Looking something up in the database and looking something up in the dictionary are one and the same process. To see the advantage here, consider the analogy of looking something up in a book and looking something up in the table of contents for that book. It would be very annoying if the table of contents appeared somewhere other than in the book itself, in a format that required some different manner of access (for example, if the table of contents was in Spanish and was stored on a set of 3-by-5 cards, while the text of the book itself was in English). The role of the dictionary with respect to the database is precisely similar to that of the table of contents with respect to a book.

2. The process of creating generalized (i.e., metadata-driven) application programs is considerably simplified. For example, consider what is involved in creating a generalized data entry application, which accepts as initial input the name of a table and then displays the names and data types of the columns of that table on the screen, so that the end-user can proceed to enter data for rows of that table. The ability to access the dictionary is clearly crucial to such an application.

18. DISTRIBUTED DATABASE SUPPORT

Distributed database systems look set to be the next major breakthrough in the database marketplace [11]. Indeed, a few products have already begun to appear that provide some degree of genuine distributed database support (as opposed to distributed *processing* support, which is technically easier to provide but requires more involvement on the part of the user). True distributed database support means that an arbitrary collection of relations, from an arbitrary collection of databases, on a variety of different machines, running a variety of different operating systems, and connected by a variety of different communication networks, can function as if they were all stored in a single database on a single machine. The user is completely insulated from all details of the distribution.

From the standpoint of the present paper, the significant point is the following: *All known general-purpose distributed database systems, both research prototypes and available products, are relational.* In fact, there are several reasons why all those systems *have* to be relational; relational technology is a prerequisite to distributed database technology [2,11]. Some of the reasons for this state of affairs are as follows:

- Relational requests have high semantic content
- Relational responses are multiple-record
- Relational requests are optimizable
- Fragmentation support is feasible
- Fragmentation independence is feasible

This is not the place to rehearse all the relevant arguments in detail; the reader is referred to references [2,11] for detailed discussions. The point I wish to make here is simply that relational products are well placed to take advantage of the next big advance in database technology, and nonrelational products are not.

19. PERFORMANCE

Historically, relational systems have always suffered from the reputation of being poor performers. The reader may therefore be surprised to hear that performance is (potentially) a *strength* of relational systems! Of course, it is always difficult to make definitive statements regarding the performance of DBMSs in general, or even of some specific DBMS in particular; performance is dependent on so many variables, including machine type and size, operating system, buffer parameters, number of users, and of course transaction mix. But one general point that can be made is the following: In a nonrelational system, system performance depends heavily on the quality of the application programmer; in a relational system, by contrast, it depends much more on the quality of the system *optimizer*. (And which would you prefer to trust, in the long run?)

As a matter of fact, it can be argued with some justification that a relational system with a good optimizer might *out*perform a nonrelational system, for at least the following reasons:

1. The optimizer has a wealth of information available to it that an application programmer typically does not have. To be specific, it has certain statistical information, such as the size of each table, the number of values in each column, the number of times each different value occurs in each column, and so on. As a result, the optimizer is able to make a more accurate assessment of the efficiency of any given strategy for implementing a particular request, and is thus more likely to choose the most efficient implementation.

2. Furthermore, if the database statistics change significantly (e.g., if the database is physically reorganized), then a different choice of strategy may be desirable; in other words, reoptimization may be required. In a relational system, reoptimization is trivial—it simply involves a reprocessing of the original relational request by the system optimizer. In a nonrelational system, by contrast, reoptimization involves rewriting the program, and will probably therefore not be done at all.

3. Third, the optimizer is a *program,* and therefore by definition is much more patient than a typical application programmer. The optimizer is quite capable of considering literally hundreds of different implementation strategies for a given request, whereas it is extremely unlikely that a human programmer would ever consider more than three or four.

4. Fourth, the optimizer can be regarded in a sense as embodying the skills and services of "the best" human programmers. As a consequence, it has the effect of making those skills and services available to *every-body*—which means, of course, that it is making an otherwise scarce set of resources available to a wide range of users, in an efficient and cost-effective manner.

Finally, of course, relational systems with performance comparable to the fastest of nonrelational DBMSs are now an established fact; see, e.g., reference [14].

20. EXTENDABILITY

Almost all research in database systems is founded upon a relational base, and indeed has been so ever since the first widespread dissemination of Codd's original ideas in 1970 [1]. As a consequence, users of today's relational systems are in a much better position to take advantage of the fruits of that research as and when they appear (where by "better" we mean, of course, "better than if they were users of some other kind of system"). Distributed database support (see above) is a case in point. Other examples include the following:

- Incorporation of additional semantics
- Improved integrity support
- Improved optimization
- New storage structures and access methods
- New hardware technology (e.g., parallel processors)
- Higher level interfaces
- More sophisticated builtin data types (e.g., images, text)

- User-defined data types
- User-defined functions
- Expert database systems (inferential services)

21. CONCLUSION

As stated in the Abstract, the aim of this paper has been to provide a succinct yet reasonably comprehensive summary of the major advantages of the relational approach. To my mind, those advantages are overwhelming. Surely nobody can disagree that, so far as database management is concerned, relational technology is the technology of choice, and relational systems are here for good (pun intended).

REFERENCES AND BIBLIOGRAPHY

1. E. F. Codd, "A Relational Model of Data for Large Shared Data Banks," *Communications of the ACM* 13, No. 6 (June 1970). Republished in *Communications of the ACM* 26, No. 1 (January 1983).

2. E. F. Codd, "Why Distributed Systems Are Relational" (tentative title). In preparation.

3. E. F. Codd and C. J. Date, "Interactive Support for Nonprogrammers: The Relational and Network Approaches," in C. J. Date, *Relational Database: Selected Writings* (Reading, MA: Addison-Wesley, 1986).

4. C. J. Date, *An Introduction to Database Systems: Volume I,* 4th edition (Reading, MA: Addison-Wesley, 1986); *An Introduction to Database Systems: Volume II* (Reading, MA: Addison-Wesley, 1982).

5. C. J. Date, "Some Relational Myths Exploded," in C. J. Date, *Relational Database: Selected Writings* (Reading, MA: Addison-Wesley, 1986).

6. C. J. Date, "Further Relational Myths" (in this volume).

7. C. J. Date, "A Practical Approach to Database Design," in C. J. Date, *Relational Database: Selected Writings* (Reading, MA: Addison-Wesley, 1986).

8. C. J. Date, *A Guide to INGRES* (Reading, MA: Addison-Wesley, 1987).

9. C. J. Date, *A Guide to the SQL Standard,* 2nd edition (Reading, MA: Addison-Wesley, 1989).

10. C. J. Date, "What's Wrong with SQL?" (in this volume).

11. C. J. Date, "What Is a Distributed Database System?" (in this volume).

12. C. J. Date and Colin J. White, *A Guide to DB2,* 3rd edition (Reading, MA: Addison-Wesley, 1989).

13. C. J. Date and Colin J. White, *A Guide to SQL/DS* (Reading, MA: Addison-Wesley, 1988).

14. Tom Sawyer, "Tandem Enters the Relational World," *InfoDB* 2, No. 3 (Fall 1987).

15. IBM Corporation, *IBM DATABASE 2 Version 2 SQL Reference.* IBM Document No. SC26-4346-3 (1988).

16. ANSI X3H2 / ISO/IEC JTC1/SC21/WG3, ISO-ANSI (working draft) SQL2. Document ISO DBL SYD-2 / ANSI X3H2-88-259 (July 1988).

2

What Is a Domain?

ABSTRACT

We present a systematic and reasonably comprehensive tutorial on the relational domain concept—an area in which there is considerably more than meets the eye at first glance, and also one in which there seems to be a certain amount of confusion in the existing literature.

COMMENTS ON PUBLICATION

As the Abstract suggests, this paper is an attempt to provide at least the beginnings of a "definitive statement" on what the relational domain concept is all about. It was my opinion at the time I wrote the paper (late 1988) that existing papers on the subject were not particularly clear (to say the least) and really did not do justice to the importance of the concept. It seemed to me, therefore, that there were at least three arguments in favor of trying to produce such a "definitive statement" at that time:

- It would serve as a convenient single-source reference in which to find a comprehensive answer to the question "What is a domain?" (hence

---

Previously unpublished.

the paper's title), and also as a convenient single-source tutorial on the subject.

- In particular, it would make readers aware that domains are much more than the simple pools of values they are usually considered to be.

- It would also (I hope) serve to prevent vendors from producing half-baked implementations. While I accept that a full implementation of the domain concept would probably be a major undertaking, any partial implementation should at least be upward compatible with an eventual full implementation. (I do believe that a full implementation is ultimately desirable.) I am concerned that, in certain respects, the existing literature points in the wrong direction, and that there is therefore a risk that vendors will produce implementations that will be a little off base and will be difficult to extend correctly in the future.

In regard to this last point (which criticizes the existing literature), I find that—in all humility—I must take issue with a number of Codd's published remarks on this subject. In particular, I feel that his most recent paper on the topic (reference [5]) contains several statements that I cannot really agree with, and also (rather surprisingly) that it fails to do full justice to the concept. My criticisms were originally documented in reference [13] and are elaborated in the paper that follows.

Note: Almost none of the material in the paper is really new; however, most of it (I believe) has not previously appeared in database publications per se (or at least, not in database publications that have received wide circulation), but rather in programming language publications. As the paper makes clear, it is my contention that the domain concept of database management is basically identical to the *user-defined data type* concept of programming languages. Indeed, I am touching here on a wider theme, which is that database management and programming languages share a lot of common ground, and accordingly that the database community and the languages community have a lot to learn from one another. For some reason, however, the database community seems to have been somewhat reluctant in the past to make use of ideas from the languages community (on occasion, in fact, it seems even to have deliberately ignored such ideas). Domains happen to provide a particularly obvious case in point, but they are not the only one.

1. INTRODUCTION

It is well known that domains represent one of the most fundamental components of the relational model [1]. So far as I am aware, however, no commercially available DBMS fully supports the domain concept at the time of writing (vendor claims to the contrary notwithstanding); the SQL standard in particular does not include any domain support at all at the present time, and nor do most SQL implementations. What is more, the concept seems to be surrounded by a certain amount of confusion—it is not even totally clear from the existing literature what full support for domains would entail. The purpose of this paper is to try to shed a little light on the subject.

2. THE BASIC IDEA

Let me begin by briefly reviewing what "everyone knows" regarding domains:

- A domain is a *conceptual pool of values,* from which one or more columns (in one or more tables) draw their actual values. A given domain contains *all permitted values* of some particular type. For example, in the familiar suppliers-and-parts database (see, e.g., reference [7]), we have the following domains, among others:

supplier numbers (S#)	— providing values for columns S.S.# (in table S) and SP.S# (in table SP)
part numbers (P#)	— providing values for columns P.P# (in table P) and SP.P# (in table SP)
city names (CITY)	— providing values for columns S.CITY (in table S) and P.CITY (in table P)

  In this example, the domain called S# contains all possible legal supplier number values, the domain called P# contains all possible legal part number values, and so on. The set of values actually appearing in column S.S# at any given time must be some subset of the set of values appearing in the S# domain; likewise, the set of values appearing in column SP.S# at any given time must also be some subset of the set of values appearing in the S# domain;* the set of values appearing in column P.P# at any given time must be some subset of the set of values appearing in the P# domain; and similarly for all the other columns and domains in the database.

---

*Of course, columns SP.S# and S.S# are also subject to an additional constraint—namely, the constraint that, at any given time, the set of values appearing in SP.S# must be some subset of the set of values appearing in S.S#—owing to the fact that column S.S# is a primary key and column SP.S# is a matching foreign key (with "nulls not allowed"). Although somewhat peripheral to the main topic of the paper, this remark does illustrate the point that a primary key and any matching foreign key should be defined on the same domain [10].

Note: There is no requirement that a given column and its underlying domain have the same name, but as a general rule it is a good idea if they do. We have followed this convention in the example above and will generally continue to do so throughout this paper. See reference [12] for further discussion of this point.

- The values in a domain are generally assumed to be "atomic"—i.e., they have no internal structure so far as the DBMS is concerned (but see Section 4 below). Note carefully, however, that the relational model does *not* specify the permissible data types for those values. In an early paper [2], Codd talked in terms of integers and character strings only, but he did also remark that the model could easily be extended to include "other primitive types."

  Incidentally, one "primitive type" that would seem almost a sine qua non—though very few systems in fact support it today—is the type "logical" (or "Boolean"), with values *true* and *false*. I will assume the existence of such a type for the remainder of this paper.

- There is no requirement that domains be physically stored in the database (assuming that the system supports the concept at all, that is); in most cases, in fact, they would probably *not* be physically stored, because most domains will contain a very large number of individual values, most of which are not actually being used in any table at any given time. (Remember that a given domain contains *all possible* values of a particular type.)

- However, domains should certainly be *declared* as part of the database definition (assuming, again, that the system does support the domain concept), and column declarations should include a specification of the relevant underlying domain. For example (pseudoSQL):

```
CREATE DOMAIN S#    CHAR(5) ;        /* supplier numbers */
CREATE DOMAIN P#    CHAR(6) ;        /* part numbers     */
CREATE DOMAIN CITY CHAR(15) ;        /* city names       */
CREATE DOMAIN  ..........  ;         /* ..............   */
 .....

CREATE TABLE S                       /* suppliers        */
      ( S#     DOMAIN ( S# ),
        .....,
        CITY  DOMAIN ( CITY ),
        PRIMARY KEY ( S# ) ) ;

CREATE TABLE P                       /* parts            */
      ( P#     DOMAIN ( P# ),
        .....,
        CITY  DOMAIN ( CITY ),
        PRIMARY KEY ( P# ) ) ;
```

```
CREATE TABLE SP                        /* shipments        */
     ( S#     DOMAIN ( S# ),
       P#     DOMAIN ( P# ),
       ..... ,
       PRIMARY KEY ( S#, P# ),
       FOREIGN KEY ( S# ) REFERENCES S ... ,
       FOREIGN KEY ( P# ) REFERENCES P ... ) ;
```

Now the system knows that (for example) columns S.CITY and P.CITY are defined on the same domain, whereas (for example) columns S.S# and P.P# are defined on different domains.

Note, incidentally, that the question as to what domains exist in a given database is a *database design* question [12]. In other words, it is the database designer who decides that (for example) supplier cities and part cities are the same kind of object and hence share a common domain, whereas supplier numbers and part numbers are different kinds of object and hence are drawn from different domains.

- Two values can normally be compared with one another only if they come from the same domain (because such a comparison is comparing "apples and apples"—i.e., it is comparing like with like). Conversely, two values normally *cannot* be compared with one another if they come from different domains (because such a comparison is comparing "apples and oranges"—i.e., it is not comparing like with like). Thus, for example, a comparison such as

```
SP.S# = S.S#
```

makes sense. By contrast, a comparison such as

```
SP.P# = S.S#
```

does not make sense (even though supplier numbers and part numbers are both character strings); any attempt to perform such a comparison probably represents a silly mistake on the part of the user, and the DBMS should reject it.*

- In particular (and as a direct consequence of the previous point), the DBMS should normally reject any attempt to perform a join, or a union, or a divide . . . (or indeed any relational operation) in which there is a comparison, explicit or otherwise, between values from differ-

---

*Of course, it is entirely possible that some user will come up with a legitimate reason to compare supplier numbers and part numbers, even though the database designer might originally have decided at design time that supplier numbers and part numbers are different things. Such a query, if reasonable, must naturally not be prohibited. See the discussion of "domain check override" in Sections 5 and 6 of this paper.

ent domains. For example, the following SQL operation should clearly be rejected (though most DBMSs at the time of writing will accept it):

```
SELECT  S.S#
FROM    S
WHERE   NOT EXISTS
      ( SELECT  SP.P#
        FROM    SP
        WHERE   SP.P# = S.S# ) ;
```

Note: The example is deliberately a trifle complicated. It is meant to be an attempt to find supplier numbers for suppliers who do not supply any parts. However, the user has made a mistake (probably just a typing error) in the last line: "SP.P#" in the inner WHERE clause should have been "SP.S#". Unfortunately, most DBMSs will not catch the error but will simply produce the wrong answer.*

To summarize, therefore: "Everyone knows" that DBMS support for domains would enable the system to catch silly mistakes on the part of users, and hence would make the system safer than it would otherwise be (in the sense that it would be able to prevent the occurrence of certain errors in the use of the database). However, there are quite a few additional aspects of domains and domain support that are not captured by this simple characterization. The remainder of this paper is concerned with some of those additional aspects.

3.   SOME COMMON MISCONCEPTIONS

Before we go any further, there are a few common misconceptions that need to be cleared up. The first concerns a lack of understanding of the distinction between domains and columns. Section 2 above should have made it clear that the two concepts *are* distinct: A given domain is a set of possible values, a given column represents a *use* of a given domain within a given table. Indeed, a column and its corresponding domain will in gen-

---

*Just as an aside, incidentally, it is not clear when the requirement that comparisons be "domain-constrained" in this manner first surfaced. In his original paper [1], Codd did little more than hint at the idea (in his discussion of join—". . . suppose we are given two binary relations, which have some domain in common . . . "). And in a subsequent paper, in fact [2], he explicitly indicated that comparands need *not* always come from the same domain (". . . [two distinct] domains are [compatible for comparison purposes] if both are domains of integers or both are domains of character strings"). By 1974, however, he was taking a harder line: "If [columns] A, B are defined on distinct domains, it is normally (though not always) nonsensical to make comparisons of A,B for equality" [3]. Of course, the issue is basically one of *user-defined data types* and *type compatibility,* as those concepts are understood in the world of programming languages; see, e.g., the ALGOL 68 Report [19]. We will return to this point in Sections 5 and 6, later.

eral have different *names* (although we did recommend in the previous section—as a good design discipline [12]—that they should have the same name wherever possible).

Despite the foregoing, however, it is not uncommon to encounter statements to the effect that the term "domain" is just a relational term for what more conventionally would be referred to as a data item or field (i.e., a column). Even today, in fact, there are unfortunately some relational systems—perfectly good systems in many other respects—that refer to columns as domains.*

Second, it is sometimes suggested that a domain is basically just a special case of a relation (specifically, a unary relation, i.e., a relation of degree one)—admittedly a relation that is being used to serve a certain special purpose, but a relation nonetheless. However, there is a definite and important distinction to be drawn between the two concepts, namely as follows: *Domains are static, relations are dynamic* (loosely speaking). In other words, the content of a relation typically changes over time, whereas the content of a domain does not (remember once again that a given domain contains *all possible* values of a particular type).

> *Aside:* Of course, it is not 100 percent true to say that domains are totally static; the set of values in a domain can change over time, just as the set of values in a relation can change over time. The point is, however, that a change at the domain level is *different in kind* from a change at the relation level. A change at the domain level is really a *definitional* change. For example, a change in the set of all possible supplier numbers means a change in the definition of what it is that constitutes a legal supplier number. It is a little bit like changing the definition of supplier numbers from CHAR(5) to CHAR(7). By contrast, a change at the relation level is just a regular update to the database (and must abide by the constraints implied by the existing domain definitions—see Section 5 below). *End of aside.*

---

*Honesty compels me to confess that I might be partly to blame for this confusion: In the first edition of my book *An Introduction to Database Systems* [6] (though not in the second or subsequent editions), the term "domain" was frequently used where the term "attribute" (the formal term for column) would have been clearer—for example, ". . . the primary key of a relation may involve any number of domains" (p. 44). In my own defense, however, let me add that even the first edition of the book did try to make the distinction between the two concepts clear—for example, ". . . the single domain of the divisor must be the same as the right-hand domain of the dividend" (in a discussion of relational division, p. 90). In other words, the *concepts* were not confused, though the terminology could have been better. In any case, that terminology was in fact just taken direct from Codd's original paper [1]; that paper also used "domain" throughout where "attribute" would have been more accurate (e.g., "Such a domain . . . is called a primary key"). The term "attribute" did not appear in that paper at all. So the blame, if blame there is, should at least be shared!

Third and last, it is perhaps not as widely recognized as it ought to be that the relational model permits both simple and compound (or composite) domains [2,8]. A simple domain is a domain of atomic values (once again, however, see Section 4 below for further discussion of what it means for a data value to be atomic). We have been tacitly assuming throughout this paper so far that all domains are simple (where it made any difference). A composite domain is basically just a combination of simple domains— where by "combination" we really mean *Cartesian product*. For example (pseudoSQL again; we assume for the sake of the example that there is no builtin DATE data type):

```
CREATE DOMAIN MONTH CHAR(2) ;
CREATE DOMAIN DAY   CHAR(2) ;
CREATE DOMAIN YEAR  CHAR(4) ;

CREATE DOMAIN DATE  ( MONTH DOMAIN ( MONTH ),
                      DAY   DOMAIN ( DAY ),
                      YEAR  DOMAIN ( YEAR ) ) ;
```

The composite domain DATE has three *components* MONTH, DAY, and YEAR, each defined on the domain of the same name. (In general, however, note that a component name and the corresponding domain name could be different—for example, consider the case of the composite domain COMPLEX_NUMBER, which has two components, REAL and IMAGINARY, both defined on the domain REAL_NUMBER.)

If the set of MONTH values is 1–12, the set of DAY values is 1–31, and the set of YEAR values is 0–9999 (for simplicity let us limit ourselves to A.D. dates only), then the set of DATE values is

```
 1    1     0
 1    2     0
 1    3     0
 .    .     .
 1   31     0
 2    1     0
 .    .     ..
 .    .    ...
12   31  9999
```

(a total of 12 * 31 * 10,000 = 3,720,000 values). Of course, not all of those 3,720,000 values are legal dates; we would probably want to specify some domain-level integrity constraints in order to prohibit illegal values. See Section 5 below or reference [9] for further discussion of this possibility.

Columns in turn are simple or composite depending on whether the domain they are defined on is simple or composite. For example:

```
CREATE TABLE EMP
      ( EMP#     DOMAIN ( EMP# ),
        ..... ,
        HIREDATE DOMAIN ( DATE ),
        ..... ,
        PRIMARY KEY ( EMP# ) ) ;
```

HIREDATE here is a composite column. Relational operations should be able to refer both to that column in its entirety and to its components MONTH (HIREDATE), DAY (HIREDATE), and YEAR (HIREDATE) individually, using the component names MONTH, DAY, and YEAR as *component selector functions*. For example (pseudoSQL again):

```
SELECT ...
FROM    EMP
WHERE   EMP.HIREDATE = '010184' ;

SELECT ...
FROM    EMP
WHERE   YEAR ( EMP.HIREDATE ) < '84' ;
```

A couple of asides: First, the only comparison operators that would be defined for a composite domain—in many cases—would be "equals" and "not equals" (though in the particular case of DATEs we would probably want to define "less than" and "greater than" also [11]). Second, of course, the components of a composite domain or column should be allowed to be composite in turn, in general.

The foregoing discussions notwithstanding, it is usual to take the terms "domain" and "column" to refer specifically to *simple* domains and columns, barring any explicit indication to the contrary. We will follow this convention for the remainder of this paper.

4. DATA VALUE ATOMICITY

As indicated in Section 2, it is normal to assume that all domain values are *atomic*—i.e., they are nondecomposable so far as the system is concerned.* For brevity, I will refer to this assumption as "the atomic value assumption." Relations constructed on the basis of this assumption are said to be *normalized* [1], or equivalently to be in *first normal form*. Such relations satisfy the property that, at every row-and-column position within the relation, there is always exactly one data value, never a set of multiple values. In other words, first normal form just means *no repeating groups* (loosely speaking).

The arguments in favor of normalized relations are well known, and include the following:

(a) First, of course, there is the point that normalized relations can be visualized as tables [1]. In many ways, it is this familiar tabular representation that makes relational systems easy to use and understand, and makes it easy to reason about the way such systems behave.

---

*Some programming languages (e.g., PL/I) use the term "scalar" to denote the same concept.

(b) Second, normalization permits a simpler data naming and addressing mechanism than would otherwise be necessary. Every individual value in a relational database can be addressed by specifying the name of the containing table *plus* the name of the containing column *plus* the primary key value of the containing row [4]. In other words, the row-and-column structure of a normalized relation constitutes a kind of *coordinate system* by which every individual value in the database can easily and unambiguously be referenced.

(c) Third, a normalized relation is a simpler structure, mathematically speaking, than an unnormalized one; *all* data is represented in one and only one way, namely as explicit values within rows within columns within tables. As a consequence, the operators needed to deal with normalized relations are simpler too, and there are fewer of them [7].

(d) Finally, there is a solid body of theory (dependency theory, also known as further normalization theory) available for use in designing databases that are based on normalized relations [18]. So far as I am aware, there is no comparable theory for unnormalized relations.* Moreover, there is no comparable theory (again, so far as I am aware) that indicates when an unnormalized design is more appropriate than a normalized one.

But does the atomic value assumption really stand up under close scrutiny? Let us consider this question. First, the fact that the relational model does permit values to be composite (i.e., it supports composite domains and columns) does *not* seem to me to present any problem in regard to that assumption. Composite values of the kind referred to can be seen merely as a convenient shorthand—they do not invalidate any of the arguments (a)–(d) sketched above (at least, not to any significant extent, though it is true that they do lead to a need for some slight refinement to the tabular representation convention and to the data naming and addressing mecha-

---

*An unnormalized relation is a relation that does *not* satisfy the property that every row-and-column position contains exactly one data value. It can be thought of as a relation that includes one or more repeating groups. More precisely, an unnormalized relation is a relation for which at least one of the underlying domains is *relation-valued*. A relation-valued domain (called a *nonsimple* domain in reference [2]) is a domain whose elements are themselves relations. Note carefully that relation-valued domains should not be confused with *composite* domains: The elements of a composite domain are merely concatenations of simple values, one from each of the constituent simple domains; i.e., the elements of a composite domain are *tuples* (see Section 3). By contrast, the elements of a relation-valued domain are *sets* of tuples, or in other words relations. Furthermore, those relations may themselves be unnormalized in turn (etc., etc.).

nism). But the existence of composite values is not the only reason to question the atomic value assumption. Consider the following additional points:

- First, note carefully that the term "atomic value" means only that the data value in question has no internal structure *so far as the system is concerned.* It does *not* necessarily mean that the value has no internal structure, period. For example, there is nothing to stop a user from defining a given column as "character string" but using that column (tacitly) to contain structured values of any degree of complexity (e.g., a repeating group). In other words, there is really no way to *enforce* the atomicity requirement. What is more, several systems provide certain operators (e.g., SUBSTR and LIKE in SQL) that could be regarded as actively encouraging such subversive behavior, inasmuch as the provision of such operators amounts to an implicit recognition of the fact that data values might have some internal structure even though the system does not know what it is. The meaning of "atomic value" begins to get a little fuzzy in such a system.

- Moreover, several systems include support for one or more builtin data types that are quite definitely *not* atomic, but rather do have an internal structure that is known to the system. Dates and times provide an obvious example; names and addresses provide another; complex numbers provide yet another. In such cases, the system usually (and of course quite rightly) also provides operators that allow disciplined access to the various component pieces of those nonatomic values (e.g., MONTH, MINUTE, etc., in the case of dates and times). Codd himself is on record as agreeing that such facilities might sometimes be desirable for "certain kinds of values" [5].

- In fact, it is not clear that there is any *fundamental* reason why data values need be atomic, even if it is generally agreed that such atomicity represents a good discipline for (e.g.) database design. Indeed, it is widely accepted that in application areas such as CAD/CAM that stray outside the comparatively narrow confines of traditional business data processing, such atomicity becomes something of a millstone, and several research projects are under way at universities and elsewhere that are examining (among other things) the possibility of relaxing this particular requirement of the relational model. See, e.g., references [14,15,16,17].

In sum, therefore, we see that data value atomicity cannot truly be regarded as a hard and fast requirement, but only as a laudable objective in many situations (not all). Indeed, in Sections 6 and 7 below we will argue that, in general, domain values should be allowed to have an internal structure of arbitrary complexity.

5.   ASPECTS OF DOMAIN SUPPORT

We have now (at last) covered enough of the basics of domains to begin to explore the question of exactly what full support for domains would involve. It should be clear by this time that there is a lot more to such support than just domain-constrained comparisons; in fact, it is my position (argued in detail in the next section) that a domain is nothing more nor less than a *user-defined data type,* and hence that *100 percent support for domains equals 100 percent support for user-defined data types.* Before attempting to justify this position, however, let me first list a few specific items that would have to be included in any such "100 percent support" for domains:

- First, the system must provide a way to define new domains. This purpose is served by the hypothetical CREATE DOMAIN statement shown in our earlier pseudoSQL examples, of course. Such a statement must allow the user to specify at least all of the following:

  - a name for the new domain

  - the underlying data type*

  - any domain-level integrity constraints that apply to the domain [9]

  For example:

  ```
  CREATE DOMAIN COLOR CHAR(6)
        CHECK  COLOR IN ('Red','Yellow','Blue','Green') ;
  ```

  In the case of composite domains, of course, the user must also be able to specify the components of that composite domain (component name plus underlying domain name).

- Not all comparison operators make sense for all domains. In the case of the COLOR domain above, for example, the operator "=" certainly does make sense, but the operator "<" probably does not— "Red" is neither less nor greater than "Yellow," except in the trivial sense of alphabetic ordering.† (As pointed out in Section 3, an analo-

---

*Which might be another domain, of course. See Section 6.

†This remark might be too strong. In some cases, we might indeed wish to define a "<" operator for colors, based on (e.g.) wavelength. Here (once again) we are beginning to move into the area of user-defined data types, with all that that concept implies. See Sections 5 and 6, later.

gous remark probably applies to most composite domains.) The CREATE DOMAIN statement therefore needs to provide a means for the user to define the operators that do apply to the domain in question (see Section 6).

- The previous paragraph touches on another interesting point, namely that there are really two different " < " operators, which we might refer to as *semantic* " < " and *lexical* " < " respectively. In SQL terms, the semantic " < " applies to the WHERE clause and the lexical " < " applies to the ORDER BY clause. All domains are presumably subject to a lexical " < " (it must always be possible to impose *some* kind of ordering on the output from a query), but—as the COLOR example above illustrates—not all domains are subject to a semantic " < ". If the semantic " < " does make sense for a given domain, then that same operator can probably be used as the lexical " < " also, but in general the system should allow the domain definer to specify both. Note, incidentally, that the lexical " < " should still be regarded as a logical operator, not a physical one; lexical ordering should not depend on quirks of the underlying implementation such as character code collating sequence.

- The system must also provide a means for the user to specify the relevant domain for each column in each named table (base table, view, etc.).

  - Incidentally, this point serves to illustrate one specific benefit of domain support, namely that it provides a mechanism for *global column definition*. For example, a geographic database might contain 100 columns all defined on the domain of "geographic position" (latitude and longitude). It is obviously desirable in such a case to be able to define "geographic position" just once, and then allow that definition to be inherited in some way by the 100 columns (much as certain programming languages permit the definition of variable B to be inherited from that of variable A by specifying that B is "LIKE" A). Quite apart from anything else, such a facility saves keystrokes. It also prevents two columns that ought to have the same definition from inadvertently being given different definitions.

- Operations must also be provided to DROP and ALTER domains. Note, however, that these operations are likely to be subject to certain restrictions on their use. For example, altering an existing domain to change the underlying data type from INTEGER to FLOAT (say) might easily imply a massive reorganization of the database. On the other hand, there can be no denying that such operations are occasionally necessary, and domains provide the appropriate conceptual basis for dealing with them.

■ By definition, the values that can legally appear within any given column are limited to the values appearing in the corresponding domain.
For example, given the COLOR domain as defined earlier in this section, any attempt to introduce a value other than "Red", "Yellow",
"Blue", or "Green" into a column defined on that domain is clearly
an error, and the system should reject it. Thus full domain support
implies (among many other things) certain limited support for data
value integrity checking [9].

Note: A given column might be subject to one or more additional
constraints that apply just to that specific column (i.e., "column constraints" [9]), over and above the applicable domain constraint. For
example, in the suppliers-and-parts database, the part color column
P.COLOR (which we assume to be defined on the COLOR domain as
defined above) might have the additional constraint that "Yellow" is
not a valid color for a part. Of course, any such additional constraint
can only *reduce* the set of legal values for the column, not increase it
(in other words, such constraints must logically be "ANDed" on to the
applicable domain constraint).

There are several ways in which the user might be able to specify
the set of values appearing within a given domain, and hence to specify
the integrity constraints that are implied by that domain:

- by specifying the underlying data type (e.g., DECIMAL(6))

- by actually enumerating the values (as in the COLOR example
above). *Note:* This is probably the one case in which the set of values
constituting the domain *will* be physically stored in the database
(more precisely, in the database catalog).

- by specifying one or more value ranges (e.g., "1..100", to use the
syntax of Pascal)

- by specifying a template or pattern or "picture" (e.g., "999-99-9999"
would be an appropriate template for the domain of social security
numbers, at least in the USA)

- by specifying a simple conditional expression (e.g., "MOD
(ACCOUNT#,9) = 0"—meaning that account numbers must be di-
visible by nine)

- by specifying a checking procedure (i.e., an exit routine) that is to be
invoked every time a value is introduced into a column defined on
the domain

Refer to reference [9] for further discussion of each of these possibilities.

- The system must obviously provide appropriate catalog or dictionary support for everything identified in the foregoing paragraphs. At the very least, the catalog should include a system table that describes all domains (together with their definitions—underlying data type,* whether logical "<" applies, etc.), and the system table that describes all columns should itself have a new column showing the underlying domain for each column described.

- Finally, we come to what is probably the best-known aspect of domain support, namely domain-constrained comparisons. As explained in Section 2, it is generally the case that two values can legally be compared only if they come from the same domain; thus (to repeat the example from Section 2), the expression

```
SP.S# = S.S#
```

is legal, whereas the expression

```
SP.P# = S.S#
```

is not. In his "twelve rules" paper, however [4], Codd also suggested that the system should support "semantic override" versions of certain of the relational operators, namely theta-select, theta-join, outer theta-join, and divide. "Semantic override" means that the relevant operation should be performed even if it does involve comparisons between values from different domains. Such a capability is needed to cater for the fact that, as pointed out in Section 2, there will be occasions (albeit rare occasions) on which the user needs to ask a query that was not foreseen by the database designer at design time—for example, a query that does compare supplier numbers and part numbers, even though supplier numbers and part numbers are normally regarded as not being comparable. Note, however, that Codd was careful to suggest that "semantic override" operations should be separately authorizable, and furthermore that such authorization should be granted only in very exceptional cases.

Note: It is not clear why union and difference (etc.) were excluded from the list of "semantic override" operators; orthogonality would clearly require that it be specifiable in all contexts in which it makes sense. The point is not very important, however, because we will argue in Section 6 below that "semantic override" per se is not the appropriate concept anyway and should not be supported. Also, note that Codd

---

*Or underlying domain (see Section 6).

subsequently replaced the rather general term "semantic override" by the more specific term "domain check override" [5]. From this point on we will use the latter term.

We are now very definitely beginning to stray into the realm of user-defined data types and what the programming language community refers to as "strong typing." In fact, all of the aspects of domain support identified above really belong to this realm. As a simple example, consider the following definitions (which would be legal in Pascal):

```
TYPE MONTH = ( 1..12 ) ;
VAR  HIREMONTH : MONTH ;
```

Here we have a user-defined data type called MONTH and a variable called HIREMONTH that is defined to be of that data type (and is hence constrained to the corresponding set of values). The situation is obviously analogous to a relational database in which we have a *domain* called MONTH and a *column* called HIREMONTH that is defined on that domain. Furthermore, there are in fact some languages (e.g., SIMULA 67, MODULA-2, Ada, though however not Pascal) that support some or all of the other aspects of domains identified above, such as the ability to specify which operators are legal. Essentially, therefore, we claim that a domain is just a data type, and a column is just a variable that is defined to be of some specified type (i.e., to draw its values from some specified domain).

Since the idea that a domain is really just a data type is in fact the most important overall message of this entire paper, we devote a separate section to it (Section 6 below), and we deliberately defer detailed discussion of the ideas introduced above—domain-constrained comparisons, domain check override, and related matters—to that section.

One last point before we conclude the present section: Since a domain *is* basically just a data type, it is after all not quite fair to say that current DBMSs provide no domain support at all. The fact is, even SQL (for example) does support domains in a very primitive sense, inasmuch as it does provide certain builtin primitive data types (INTEGER, FLOAT, etc.). But when we talk about domain support in the context of relational systems, we really mean more than this primitive level of support—we mean that the system should provide a facility by which users can define their own, more sophisticated, data types, such as "supplier numbers," "part numbers," "city names," "colors," etc., etc., with all that such a facility implies. For the rest of this paper, therefore, we will normally take the term "domain" to mean, very specifically, a *user-defined* data type.

6.   A DOMAIN IS A USER-DEFINED DATA TYPE

We begin by discussing the idea of domain-constrained comparisons in a little more detail. At first sight, that idea seems to be a very straightforward one—and indeed it *is* straightforward, so long as we restrict our attention to simple comparisons of the form

```
comparand-1   comparator   comparand-2
```

where "comparand-1" and "comparand-2" are both simple column references such as S.S#, SP.S#, etc., and "comparator" is a simple scalar comparison operator such as "=", "<", etc. On the basis of our discussions of this topic prior to this point, we can readily agree that (e.g.) the expression

```
S.CITY = P.CITY
```

is legal, whereas (e.g.) the expression

```
S.S# = P.P#
```

is not. However, given that the supplier number and part number domains are both defined to be of type character string (refer back to the definitions in Section 2 of this paper), we would presumably also agree that the expressions

```
S.S# = 'X4'
```

and

```
P.P# = 'X4'
```

are both legal. (Note that we *must* agree on this point, for otherwise there would be no way to compare any column with a simple literal.) Suppose further that both of these expressions evaluate to *true* for some S and some P—i.e., the value "X4" currently appears in the database as an existing supplier number *and* an existing part number (which is certainly possible, of course). We are thus led to the seemingly absurd conclusion that there can exist three values—call them *a, b, c*—such that *a* and *b* are both equal to *c* but are not equal to each other.*

Before we attempt to resolve this apparent paradox, let us consider another example. The suppliers-and-parts database includes two further columns, P.WEIGHT (part weight) and SP.QTY (shipment quantity), that

---

*More precisely, *a* and *b* can both be compared with *c* (and are both equal to *c*), but they cannot be compared with each other.

will obviously both be defined on numeric domains. Equally obviously, those domains will be distinct (weights and quantities are clearly different things). Thus we can surely agree that the expression

```
P.WEIGHT > SP.QTY
```

is illegal. But what about the following expression, which is logically and semantically equivalent to the previous one?

```
P.WEIGHT - SP.QTY > 0
```

And what about the following?

```
P.WEIGHT > SP.QTY + 25

P.WEIGHT - SP.QTY > 25
```

Clearly, we would like all of these expressions to be rejected as illegal also. But the concept of domain-constrained operations, as that term is usually understood, is just too weak to deal with anything more complex than expressions of the "simple comparison" form identified at the beginning of this section. Something more is needed.

Let us consider the expression

```
S.S# = 'X4'
```

once again. This expression is an example of what is known in programming language circles as a *mixed-mode* expression—in other words, it is an expression involving operands of different types (a supplier number and a character string, in the example; of course, we are assuming here that the system does recognize "supplier number" as a valid data type). Any language that permits such expressions must include a set of *implicit type conversion rules,* by which one of the operands in such an expression can be implicitly converted ("coerced") to the type of the other. (*Note:* We can restrict our attention to expressions involving just two operands without loss of generality, of course, so long as we simultaneously restrict our attention to binary operations only.) In the example, the character string literal must be coerced to the type "supplier number." To invent some more pseudoSQL syntax, it is as if the original expression had been written as follows:

```
S.S# = S#('X4')
```

The term on the right-hand side of the " = " sign is intended to represent a literal of type "supplier number." In other words, the necessary conversion of the character string "X4" to type "supplier number" has now been shown explicitly. Note, incidentally, that any system that does support user-defined data types really *should* provide some explicit syntax for specifying literals of such types.*

So we see that there actually is no paradox; the two expressions

```
S.S# = 'X4'                and                P.P# = 'X4'
```

are really shorthand for the following two expressions, in which the conversions have been shown explicitly:

```
S.S# = S#('X4')            and                P.P# = P#('X4')
```

And of course the converted values S#('X4') and P#('X4') are not equal to one another; in fact, the expression

```
S#('X4') = P#('X4')
```

is illegal, because there is no coercion rule that will convert a supplier number to a part number or vice versa.

We turn now to the WEIGHT and QTY examples. The first example, to repeat, was:

```
P.WEIGHT - SP.QTY > 0
```

Again this is a mixed-mode expression. The types of the three operands, reading from left to right, are "weight," "quantity," and "integer," respectively. If we assume (as is usual) that the operator " $-$ " is of higher precedence than the operator " $>$ ", then we can concentrate our attention first on the subexpression

```
P.WEIGHT - SP.QTY
```

(which is also mixed-mode). Once again the system's coercion rules come into play. Assuming, however, that the system is taking the business of data types seriously, there will not *be* any coercion rule that will convert a weight to a quantity or a quantity to a weight. The subexpression will thus be illegal (and hence the overall expression will be illegal also).

A similar analysis shows that the expression

```
P.WEIGHT > SP.QTY + 25
```

is illegal also, for a similar reason: First, the "25" is (presumably successfully) coerced to type "quantity," and the subexpression SP.QTY + 25 is evaluated to produce a new quantity. But then the attempt to compare a

---

*By the syntax shown in the example, we are effectively proposing that each user-defined data type name also be usable as a user-defined *function*. An invocation of such a function has the effect of converting its argument to a value of the applicable type.

weight with that new quantity fails (no coercion rule).* A similar argument shows that the expression

```
P.WEIGHT - SP.QTY > 25
```

is also illegal.

> *Aside:* To return for a moment to our earlier claim that even SQL does support domains in a very primitive sense: Notice that SQL does also include some simple (system-defined) coercion rules. A comparison between a DECIMAL value and a FLOAT value, for example, causes the DECIMAL value to be coerced to FLOAT. Likewise, an "IN comparison" (meaning a comparison between a scalar and the elements of a set) also involves some coercion, since the elements of the set in question are not themselves scalars but rather 1-tuples that *contain* scalars. *End of aside.*

Note carefully that all of the foregoing examples illustrate the point that the idea of "domain-constrained operations" cannot be limited to comparison operations only—it must take arithmetic operations into account also, and indeed all scalar operations supported by the system. What is more, it is neither necessary nor sufficient that the two operands in a binary operation be drawn from the same domain (i.e., be of the same data type). For example, given the two domains (data types) VELOCITY and TIME, it clearly makes no sense to add a VELOCITY value and a TIME value together; however, it definitely does make sense to multiply two such values, and furthermore the domain (data type) of the result is DISTANCE.

Thus we see that full support for the domain concept would require at least all of the following (this list is taken from reference [7]):

- The ability to specify the complete set of domains, D say, that apply to a given database. Note that D would have to be a closed set, in the sense that any element-level operation supported by the system (such as $-Z$ or $A + B$ or $X > Y$) would have to yield a value that belonged to some domain of the set D. Note in particular that D would have to include the domain of Boolean (logical) values, because many expressions (e.g., the expression $X > Y$) yield a truth-value as their result.

- The ability to specify, for every domain Di in the set D, exactly which unary operators apply to values di from that domain Di.

---

*A sophisticated implementation will catch the error at compile time, of course—it should not be necessary to wait until run time and actually evaluate the subexpression SP.QTY + 25 before discovering the error.

- The ability to specify, for every pair of domains Di and Dj (not necessarily distinct) in the set D, exactly which binary operators apply to pairs of values di and dj from those domains Di and Dj. Similarly for every set of three domains, every set of four domains, etc., etc.
- The ability to specify, for every legal combination of operator and domain(s), the domain of the corresponding result.

Let us now try to pull the foregoing ideas together. What we are really talking about is a system that supports *user-defined data types,* together with *strong typing.* We can define strong typing (a little loosely) as follows: A given system is said to support strong typing if and only if:

- Each variable (i.e., column) is defined to be of a single specific type (i.e., domain).
- The only legal expressions in the system are such that, whenever two values are combined together in some operation, then either the two values are of the type(s) required for that operation, or there exists an appropriate coercion rule for implicitly converting either or both of the values to the required type(s).

What are the implications of all of the foregoing for Codd's concept of "domain check override"? Again, it is the data type paradigm that is the key to understanding what is really going on here. Instead of having either

(a) Special versions of the relational operators ("domain check override theta-join," etc.), or

(b) Special versions of the scalar comparison operators ("domain check override greater than," etc.),

what is really needed is *an appropriate set of coercion rules.* Another way of saying this is that in certain cases—not all—*domains need to be able to inherit the operators that apply to the domain they are defined on** (which might just be a builtin, system-defined "domain" such as INTEGER, of course).

Let us consider an example. Suppose our database includes *employee birthdates* and *product announcement dates,* and suppose that the database designer has decided that BIRTH_DATE and ANNOUNCE_DATE are different domains, both of them however defined on the same underlying data type (domain) DATE. Suppose now that a user wants to ask the query:

---

*I am indebted to Hugh Darwen for helping me to clarify my thinking in this area. The DATE example discussed subsequently is taken from a private memo from him to myself.

"Which products were announced on their owners' birthdays?" This query involves a comparison between BIRTH_DATE and ANNOUNCE_DATE, a comparison that the database designer did not foresee the need for at design time. (Actually, the comparison involves only the MONTH and DAY components of the dates concerned, but we will ignore this detail for simplicity.) Thus, the user will write a query that looks somewhat as follows:

```
SELECT ...
FROM   ...
WHERE  EMP.BIRTH_DATE = PROD.ANNOUNCE_DATE ... ;
```

At this point, the system could either reject the query on the grounds that it is attempting a cross-domain comparison, or—provided, of course, that the user is appropriately authorized—it could effectively translate it into the following form:

```
SELECT ...
FROM   ...
WHERE  DATE ( EMP.BIRTH_DATE ) = DATE ( PROD.ANNOUNCE_DATE ) ... ;
```

In this translated form, the BIRTH_DATE and ANNOUNCE_DATE values are being explicitly converted to the underlying DATE data type; in other words, the effect of the translation is to coerce both of those values to type DATE, so that DATE-type operations can be performed on them. The equality comparison can thus now legitimately be performed.*

However, I certainly agree with Codd that the use of any such automatic coercion facility needs to be very carefully controlled.

7. SUPPORT FOR USER-DEFINED DATA TYPES

This is not the place to go into full detail on what is required on the part of a system that allows users to define their own data types; a comprehensive discussion (with an extensive example) can be found in reference [11]. However, it is probably worth summarizing the major points here. Basically, the

---

*A very primitive method of forcing certain coercions is provided in some programming languages today. PL/I, for example, provides a function called UNSPEC, which returns the *internal machine representation* of its argument, essentially as a string of bits. In PL/I, therefore, a comparison between a birthdate and an announcement date might look like this:

```
UNSPEC ( BIRTH_DATE ) = UNSPEC ( ANNOUNCE_DATE )
```

The HEX function provided in the IBM products DB2 and SQL/DS is somewhat analogous. However, UNSPEC and HEX are really too undisciplined. Indeed, I once heard it suggested, with some justification, that UNSPEC was "the first dirty word to be included in a high-level language" (I regret that, to my chagrin, I cannot remember who was responsible for this pointed observation).

process of defining a new data type involves several distinct but interdependent steps, as follows:

- Deciding the required semantics
    - what is required in intuitive terms?
    - basic data objects
    - conversion operations
    - comparison operations
    - computational operations
    - builtin functions
    - assignment operations
- Deciding syntactic details
    - literals
    - variables
    - operators and expressions (including coercions)
    - input/output formats
- Deciding implementation details
    - underlying representation (data type)
    - operator implementation
    - host language interfacing

It is important to understand that user-defined data types can have an internal structure of any degree of complexity. (Indeed, part of the point of the user-defined data type idea is precisely to provide a systematic and disciplined means of dealing with objects that do have a complex internal structure.) For example, we might define a data type called POLYGON, whose internal structure includes an ordered list of (x,y)-coordinates representing the vertices of the polygon in question. Operators for that data type might include an operator to test whether a given point is inside a given polygon, an operator to compute the area of a given polygon, an operator to test whether two given polygons overlap (have any internal points in common), etc., etc.

In regard to the question of internal structure, incidentally, it is worth stating explicitly—although we have alluded to the point several times in the paper already—that the system should allow the underlying representation for a user-defined data type to be any data type (or sensible combination of data types), *builtin or user-defined,* already known to the system. The system should also provide a simple mechanism by which the operators available for a given data type can easily be inherited from the operators that apply to the underlying representation.

A couple of final points:

- First, some authorities draw a distinction between *user-defined* and *abstract* data types. To such writers, what we have been describing in this paper would be *abstract* data types, and a user-defined data type would be essentially just a simple special case—basically either an *enumerated* type (e.g., the set of colors "Red," "Yellow," "Blue," and "Green") or a *subrange* type (e.g., the range of integers 1..100). Of course, this is merely a matter of terminology; it does not invalidate any of the ideas we have been discussing in any way.

- Second, there has been much interest over the past few years in *object-oriented* database systems [20]. Now, it is a little difficult to say exactly what the term "object-oriented" means in this context (there does not seem to be any true consensus), but some authorities, at least, would probably agree that an "object" is (again) exactly what we have been calling a user-defined data type in the present paper. Thus, this paper might reasonably be regarded as an introduction to some of the ideas behind object-oriented database systems also.

8.   SUMMARY AND CONCLUSION

In this paper, we have discussed the question of what it means for a system to provide full support for the relational domain concept. We have concluded that domains are really data types, and hence that domains provide an example (one of several, in my opinion) of a field in which the database community could learn and profit from the experience of the programming languages community. Existing database literature is less than fully satisfactory in this area, and I am concerned that it will lead to product implementations that are less than fully satisfactory also if we are not careful. The present paper can be seen in part as an attempt to avoid such a situation.

By way of conclusion, let me summarize some of the advantages that can accrue if the system does provide full support for domains.

- The first and overriding point is that domains certainly *exist* in an abstract sense, regardless of whether the system actually provides any support for them. Identifying the underlying domains is a crucial step in the process of database design [12]. More specifically, domains provide the *glue* that holds the database together, in the sense that they show exactly where the relationships are that logically connect the tables together—relationships exist at precisely the points where the tables in question share a common domain.* Given that all of these points are true, it would obviously be nice if the system were to provide direct support for the concept and enforce the associated discipline.

- The definition of a given domain provides an obvious "hook" or central point of control for the specification of a variety of features that are common to all columns that use the domain—the underlying data representation, whether the semantic " < " operator has meaning, other applicable operators, any relevant domain-level integrity constraints, etc. Taken together, these points add up to the "global column definition" advantage discussed earlier in this paper (in Section 5).

- Domains provide a basis for a systematic, comprehensible, human-factored *column naming convention*—to wit, columns should normally be given the same name as their underlying domain, wherever possible (as recommended in Section 2 of the present paper and elaborated in reference [12]). That naming convention, in turn, might well be exploited by the system also at some future time to simplify the formulation of certain join, union, and other operations [21].

- Domains also provide a basis for dealing with certain kinds of database redefinition and reorganization operations in a systematic manner.

- The strong typing feature is a (partial) guarantee of *correctness*—it provides for safer use of the database, because the system can detect and reject data type violations ("domain-constrained operations"). It also provides for greater efficiency, because such type violations can be caught at compile time.

- System support for the domain concept provides a simple, foolproof, and application-independent method—using the system catalog—of locating all uses of a given domain, no matter where they may be in the database.

- The user-defined data type mechanism provides a systematic and controlled discipline for dealing with objects of arbitrary complexity (see Section 7).

- The user-defined data type mechanism also provides a basis for defining extensions to the system in (again) a systematic and controlled manner.

---

*Elsewhere (e.g., in reference [7]) I have stated that foreign keys are "the glue." As indicated above, however, it is really domains that provide this function; foreign-to-primary-key matching is merely a special case (a very important special case, of course) of a more general mechanism—namely, the matching of any two columns that happen to be defined on the same domain.

▪ Finally, domains could be used as a basis on which to define a variety of *domain-based access paths.* A domain-based index, for example, would contain an entry for each individual value of the relevant domain currently existing in the database, together with a pointer to each corresponding stored record (no matter what stored table that record belonged to). A domain-based access path would provide good performance for certain domain-based operations, such as natural join or referential integrity enforcement or cascade delete. *Note:* Certain products today do already support cross-table indexes, in fact, though they typically do so without providing much (if anything) in the way of domain support per se. CODASYL-style links can likewise be regarded as a limited form of domain-based access path; again, however, they do not provide any support for the domain concept per se.

ACKNOWLEDGMENTS

I am grateful to Hugh Darwen for his careful review of an earlier draft of this paper and for several helpful discussions, which served to clarify my ideas and enabled me to improve the presentation considerably; also to Nat Goodman for his comments and useful suggestions.

REFERENCES AND BIBLIOGRAPHY

1. E. F. Codd, "A Relational Model of Data for Large Shared Data Banks," *Communications of the ACM* 13, No. 6 (June 1970). Republished in *Communications of the ACM* 26, No. 1 (January 1983).

2. E. F. Codd, "Relational Completeness of Data Base Sublanguages," in R. Rustin (ed.), *Data Base Systems,* Courant Computer Science Symposia Series, Vol. 6 (Englewood Cliffs, NJ: Prentice-Hall, 1972).

3. E. F. Codd, "Understanding Relations (Installment No. 5)," *FDT* (previous title of *SIGMOD Record,* bulletin of the ACM Special Interest Group on Management of Data) 6, No. 4 (1974).

4. E. F. Codd, "Is Your DBMS Really Relational?" *Computerworld* (October 14, 1985); "Does Your DBMS Run by the Rules?" *Computerworld* (October 21, 1985).

5. E. F. Codd, "Domains, Keys, and Referential Integrity in Relational Databases," *InfoDB* 3, No. 1 (Spring 1988).

6. C. J. Date, *An Introduction to Database Systems: Volume I,* 1st edition (Reading, MA: Addison-Wesley, 1975).

7. C. J. Date, *An Introduction to Database Systems: Volume I,* 4th edition (Reading, MA: Addison-Wesley, 1986).

8. C. J. Date, "Some Relational Myths Exploded," in C. J. Date, *Relational Database: Selected Writings* (Reading, MA: Addison-Wesley, 1986).

9. C. J. Date, "A Contribution to the Study of Database Integrity" (in this volume).

10. C. J. Date, "Referential Integrity and Foreign Keys. Part I: Basic Concepts; Part II: Further Considerations" (in this volume).

11. C. J. Date, "Defining Data Types in a Database Language" (in this volume).

12. C. J. Date, "SQL Dos and Don'ts" (in this volume).

13. C. J. Date, "Domains" and "Data Types" (private communications to E. F. Codd, January 22, 1988).

14. D. Batory et al., "GENESIS: A Reconfigurable Database Management System," Tech. Report TR-86-07, Dept. of Comp. Sci., U. of Texas at Austin (March 1986).

15. M. J. Carey et al., "The Architecture of the EXODUS Extensible DBMS," *Proc. ACM Object-Oriented Database Workshop* (1986).

16. Mark A. Roth, Henry F. Korth, and Abraham Silberschatz, "Extended Algebra and Calculus for Nested Relational Databases," *ACM Transactions on Database Systems* 13, No. 4 (December 1988).

17. Michael Stonebraker, "Inclusion of New Types in Relational Data Base Systems," Memorandum No. UCB/ERL M85/67, Univ. of California at Berkeley (July 1985).

18. Ronald Fagin, "Normal Forms and Relational Database Operators," *Proc. 1979 ACM SIGMOD International Conference on Management of Data* (May/June 1979).

19. A. van Wijngaarden et al., "Report on the Algorithmic Language ALGOL 68," *Numerische Mathematik* 14, No. 2 (1969).

20. Jacob Stein and David Maier, "Concepts in Object-Oriented Data Management," *Database Programming and Design* 1, No. 4 (April 1988).

21. Andrew Warden, "The Naming of Columns" (in this volume).

APPENDIX A:
USER-DEFINED VS. "EXTENDED" DATA TYPES

In the body of this paper, I have argued strongly that a domain is, precisely, a user-defined data type. However, Codd does not agree with this position. In a recent paper (reference [5]), he says: "Each domain is declared as an extended data type (not as a mere basic data type) . . . The distinction between extended . . . and basic data types is NOT that the first is user-defined and the second is built into the system." He goes on to claim that basic and extended data types may both be either builtin or user-defined (though it is not clear what a "user-defined basic" data type would look like; Codd does not give any instance of such a data type in his paper).

In response to these statements, I have to say that I do not find the distinction between basic and extended data types a particularly useful one (in fact, I do not think it is even meaningful—see further discussion below). By contrast, I do think that the distinction between builtin (i.e., system-defined) and user-defined data types is useful. Of course, I agree that one user A may define a data type D which then becomes a builtin (system-defined) data type from the standpoint of another user B; so the "system-vs. user-defined" distinction does have to be interpreted *relative to a particular user*. Nevertheless, it is still a distinction worth making, because it has operational meaning for the user in question. I do not see how the basic vs. extended distinction does.

Let us examine Codd's position in a little more detail. Later in reference [5], in a section entitled "Extended Data Types: Builtin and User-Defined," he requires the DBMS to support "calendar dates, clock times, and decimal currency as builtin extended data types." Questions:

1. What does the word "extended" add to this requirement? How would matters be different if it was replaced by "basic"?

2. What are the criteria for deciding whether a given data type is basic or extended?

3. Are those criteria subjective or objective?

4. Consider the data types supported in the IBM product DB2. Which of them are basic and which extended? For example, what about CHAR? What about VARCHAR? What about GRAPHIC? What about TIMESTAMP? What about TIME? Note, incidentally, that only one of these (CHAR) is directly representable by the underlying System/

370 machine architecture, and in *none* of the cases does the machine architecture support all of the applicable operators (e.g., substring, concatenate, etc., in the case of CHAR).

In the same paper [5], Codd gives a table that summarizes what he conceives to be the distinctions between basic and extended data types. That table looks more or less as follows:

	basic data type	extended data type
1.	property-oriented name	object-oriented name
2.	a property of an object	an object
3.	not independently declarable	independently declarable
4.	range of values not specifiable	range of values specifiable
5.	applicability of ">," "<" not specifiable	applicability of ">", "<" specifiable
6.	two values with the same basic data type need not have the same extended data type	

I would like to examine the points in this table one by one.

1. *Naming: All* data types have names (e.g., the name of the data type CHAR is "CHAR"). But some of those names are prescribed by the system (for builtin data types) and some are chosen by the user (for user-defined data types). Codd explains the "property-oriented" vs. "object-oriented" distinction as follows: ". . . [unless it is builtin] . . . an extended data type must be declared as an object itself prior to any use being made of it. In contrast, a basic data type is normally a property associated with an object at the time of the object's declaration." But surely an "extended" data type is also "associated with an object" [of that type] "at the time of the object's declaration"? I fail to see any fundamental distinction here, other than the system- vs. user-defined one. See also paragraphs 2 and 3 below.

2. *Property vs. object:* One problem with this particular point is that there is no precise, objective definition of what a property is or what an object is. Suppose I create a user-defined data type called, let us say, POLYGON; and suppose now that I declare a variable of that data type:

        DECLARE P POLYGON ;

It seems to me that POLYGON here is performing *exactly* the same function with respect to P as CHAR is performing with respect to C in the declaration

```
DECLARE C CHAR ;
```

Both surely represent *properties* of the declared variable.

Furthermore, POLYGON and CHAR are both *objects* also, with properties of their own. The difference between them is simply that, in the case of builtin data types such as CHAR, the system specifies the properties of the object; in the case of user-defined data types such as POLYGON, the user specifies those properties.

3. *Declarability:* It is of course true that CHAR is not independently declarable by the user and POLYGON is. But what else is this than just another way of saying that CHAR is builtin and POLYGON is user-defined?

4. *Range of values:* The range of values for a system-defined data type is specified by the system. The range of values for a user-defined data type is specified by the user doing the defining. For the person *using* the data type in question, it comes to the same thing—except that, in both cases (system- and user-defined), that person may be able to specify *additional* range constraints, to be "ANDed" on to the prescribed ones. So I believe, again, that the difference here between "basic" and "extended" is neither more nor less than the difference between system- and user-defined.

5. *Applicability of ">" and "<":* The applicability or otherwise of these operators for a system-defined data type is specified by the system. Their applicability or otherwise for a user-defined data type is specified by the user doing the defining. Once again, the distinction is, precisely, the distinction between system- and user-defined.

6. *Representation:* "Two values with the same *basic* data type need not have the same *extended* data type" (my italics)—in other words, the character string (e.g.) "X4" might simultaneously represent both a valid supplier number and a valid part number (see the discussion of this example in Section 6 in the body of the paper). But I could equally well maintain that two values with the same *internal* data type need not have the same *basic* data type—e.g., the bit string "1111000111110010" might (and in fact does) simultaneously represent both a valid binary integer and a valid character string. It's simply a matter of levels of abstraction.

To conclude, I am not convinced that "basic vs. extended" data types is a useful distinction. I think a more useful one is "system- vs. user-defined." I would revise Codd's table of differences (see earlier) to read as follows:

	system-defined (= builtin)	user-defined
1.	name defined by system	name defined by user
2.	system-defined property type	user-defined property type
3.	declared by system	declared by user
4.	system-defined range of values	user-defined range of values
5.	system-defined operators	user-defined operators
6.	identical representation does not imply identical interpretation	

3

Defining Data Types in a Database Language

ABSTRACT

The question of defining data types in a database language is examined. In order to illustrate the general ideas and make them more concrete, the specific case of adding support for dates and times to the database language SQL is considered in detail.

COMMENTS ON REPUBLICATION

This paper was originally published under the alternative title "A Proposal for Adding Date and Time Support to SQL," and hence could equally well have been included in Part III of the present book instead of Part I. Since the ideas it contains are directly relevant to the discussions in the previous chapter ("What Is a Domain?"), however, I decided that this was the best place for it. But it is worth mentioning that those ideas are also directly

Originally published in *ACM SIGMOD Record* 17, No. 2 (June 1988). Reprinted with permission.

relevant to the discussions in Chapter 15 ("Dates and Times in IBM SQL: Some Technical Criticisms"), which does appear in Part III.

1.   INTRODUCTION

There is a continuing requirement as database languages evolve to extend those languages to incorporate new data types—certainly system-defined (builtin) data types, and eventually user-defined data types also. An examination of existing database products will readily show that this activity has sometimes been carried out in the past in a rather ad hoc manner. The purpose of this paper is to describe a systematic approach to the problem, in the hope that future data type extensions will be defined in a more systematic fashion. Please note, however, that I do not claim that the ideas presented are particularly original—they are basically part of the conventional computer language designer's stock-in-trade—but they do not appear to be common knowledge in the database world, and I am aware of only a few papers that consider the problem from a database perspective [1,2,4].

In order to illustrate the ideas and make them more concrete, I will consider a specific (and nontrivial) example in some detail—namely, the problem of adding support for dates and times to the database language SQL. The paper may thus also be regarded as a concrete change proposal for SQL. (Though I feel bound to add that this choice of example is less than ideal, involving as it does an attempt to extend an already unsystematic language in a systematic manner. It is of course a choice that more or less makes itself, given the widespread acceptance and importance of the SQL language.)

Of course, several commercial products that include SQL date and time support do already exist, and the ANSI and ISO SQL standards committees are also currently at work on the problem. Most of the existing commercial implementations are regrettably ad hoc, however. A detailed tutorial treatment of one particular implementation, that of IBM in its products DB2 and SQL/DS, appears in references [7] (for DB2) and [9] (for SQL/DS); a critical analysis of that implementation can be found in reference [10]. It is perhaps worth mentioning that the process of preparing this paper involved development and investigation of a variety of different attacks on the date/time problem; the approach described herein seems (to my mind) to be more satisfactory than most.

As will be seen, the process of defining a new data type involves a sequence of several interdependent steps. I list those steps here for purposes of reference.

- Deciding required semantics
  - what is required in intuitive terms?
  - basic data elements
  - conversion operations
  - comparison operations
  - computational operations
  - builtin functions
  - assignment operations
- Defining syntactic details
  - literals
  - variables
  - operators and expressions
  - input/output formats
- Deciding implementation details
  - internal representation
  - operator implementation
  - host language interfacing

2. PRELIMINARIES

As the foregoing list of steps indicates, there are at least three sets of issues involved in language design: semantic, syntactic, and implementation issues. It is important to keep these three aspects separate as far as possible. Unfortunately, this goal of separation has not not always been achieved in the past. One problem is that semantic ideas must necessarily be presented in *some* syntactic form, with the result that semantic and syntactic issues, at least, do tend to get confused. Another problem is that designers in the past have all too often been overly concerned with implementation issues, with the result that the design has proceeded from the inside out and internal details have been allowed to dictate external function. In this paper I will attempt to keep separate issues separate as much as I can. My general approach will be to try to get the semantic aspects right first, then worry about the syntactic and implementation aspects later; these latter aspects are important, but they are secondary.

(Of course, I am not so naive as to think that the various issues can always be clearly differentiated. There will certainly be situations in which syntactic or implementation considerations will have some impact on the semantic design. But I still believe that concentrating on semantics first is the right approach.)

Turning now to the example at hand (adding date and time support to SQL): I will assume for the purposes of this paper that we do already have a reasonable idea of the objective we are trying to achieve (i.e., we already have a good intuitive understanding of the desired functionality)—basically, the ability to represent dates and times in the database, the ability to perform sensible arithmetic operations on such dates and times (e.g., to subtract one date from another to yield an interval), the ability to extract the year, month, etc., components of a date separately when necessary, the ability to compare two dates to find the more recent, and so on. The first thing we have to do, then, is decide precisely what the basic data elements are that we need to deal with.

3. BASIC DATA ELEMENTS

In the real world we are accustomed to regarding past, present, and future as forming an infinite linear continuum, the *timeline*. Individual dates and times correspond to individual points on the line. For brevity, let us agree to refer to each point on the line as a date, even though it actually includes a time component. In order to provide a way of uniquely identifying individual dates, we choose some specific point on the line as the *origin;* the origin is actually arbitrary, but convention dictates that we choose some commonly accepted point, such as midnight on the day immediately preceding January 1st, Year One A.D., Greenwich Mean Time (GMT). We can then refer to individual dates in terms of their relative position with respect to that origin.

As already indicated, the real-world timeline is infinitely long; furthermore, an infinite number of distinct dates (time points) exist within any given segment of the line. The computerized version has to be constrained by the limitations of finite digital devices, however. We therefore have to adopt some compromises. Specifically, we have to decide the *granularity* we will use (i.e., the time distance between one point and "the next" on the line); we also have to decide the *range of values* we can represent (i.e., the extreme points on the line). Once again, these decisions are somewhat arbitrary, of course; our later decisions and discussions will not be affected in any fundamental way by our choices at this stage. For purposes of definiteness, therefore, let us agree on the following:

granularity	=	1 second
origin	=	midnight on the day immediately preceding January 1st, 1 A.D., GMT

range of values   =   from midnight, December 31st, 10,000 B.C., to
one second before midnight, December 31st,
9,999 A.D., both GMT

Notes:

1. It is a peculiarity of our calendar that there is no "Year Zero"; December 31st, Year 1 B.C., immediately precedes January 1st, Year 1 A.D.

2. For the purposes of this paper, we ignore the complications caused prior to the 17th century A.D. by the irregularities of the calendar in use at that time (the Julian calendar).

3. The extreme values in the range are basically arbitrary; indeed, there is no particular reason why they even have to lie on exact year boundaries. As already stated, we take the extreme points we do purely for reasons of definiteness.

4. Facilities must be provided by which users who are not interested in precisions down to the second—for example, users who wish to deal only with precisions to the nearest day—can easily ignore the less significant portions of any given date. Facilities must also be provided for the extraction of individual components (in particular, the time components, either individually or en bloc) of a given date.

Next, in order to be able to perform arithmetic on dates, we need the concept of an *interval,* so that we can (for example) add an interval to a date to obtain another date. Now, at first sight it might appear that intervals and dates are fundamentally different kinds of object. However, a date is really nothing more than a special case of an interval, representing as it does a specific interval of time relative to the origin point. What is more, attempting to treat dates and intervals as different kinds of object leads to certain logical inconsistencies. For example, if D is a date and I is an interval, then the expressions

```
D + I
I / 2
```

both seem to make sense (assuming that we agree that normal arithmetic operators can be applied to dates and intervals); the result is a date in the first case and an interval in the second case. Likewise, if D1 and D2 are two dates, the expression

```
D1 - D2
```

also seems to make sense (the result is an interval). On the other hand, the expression

```
D1 + D2
```

does not seem to make much sense and would therefore probably have to be outlawed. It therefore follows that the expression

```
( D1 + D2 ) / 2
```

would have to be outlawed also, even though the overall expression does make sense ("find the date midway between D1 and D2"). So one consequence of treating dates and intervals as distinct objects is that certain apparently meaningful expressions would have to be declared illegal.

A second consequence, and one that makes matters even worse, is that the expression

```
D1 + ( D2 - D1 ) / 2
```

would *not* be outlawed—it is of the form "date + interval"—and yet it is logically equivalent to the previous one.

Here is another example of an inconsistency: If we decide that date subtraction does make sense but date addition does not, then, if D1, D2, D3, and D4 are all dates, the comparison

```
D1 - D2  >  D3 - D4
```

is obviously legal, but the logically equivalent comparison

```
D1 + D4  >  D3 + D2
```

is not.

As a result of considerations such as the foregoing, we will *not* distinguish between dates and intervals internally. Instead, we will simply regard a date—sometimes called a calendar date—as an interval relative to the origin. Of course, we will probably still wish to make certain distinctions *externally* between calendar dates and intervals, for obvious pragmatic reasons. From this point on, therefore, we will regard the interval as the primary (indeed, the only) fundamental data object, but we will use the term "date" (or "calendar date") to refer to an interval that we wish to interpret as a date in the conventional sense. Please note, however, that the distinction is purely one of convention; all dates can be regarded as intervals and all intervals can be regarded as dates. The algorithm for converting from intervals to calendar dates and vice versa is of course well-defined (assuming that all calculations are based on the Gregorian calendar). For example, the interval "10 hours 30 minutes" can be converted to the calendar date "January 1st, Year One A.D., 10:30 a.m.," and vice versa.

There is, of course, one major complicating factor in regard to the concept of an interval (or date), namely as follows: *Different months have different numbers of days.* (Indeed, different *years* have different numbers of days also, owing to the existence of leap years.) This fact can be the source of much complexity and confusion. For example, it is the direct cause of the following anomaly in the IBM support for dates and times [10]:

```
DATE ('1987-3-31')  + 1 MONTH  - 1 MONTH   yields  '1987-3-30'
```

(*not* '1987-3-31'); that is, adding one month to a date and subtracting it again does not necessarily take us back to where we started. And yet:

```
DATE ('1987-3-31')  + 2 MONTHS - 2 MONTHS  yields  '1987-3-31'
```

Many similar anomalies can be identified [10].

For reasons such as the foregoing, we do *not* include a years or months component in an interval. Instead, we define an interval as consisting of just four components: days, hours, minutes, and seconds (in major-to-minor order, of course; remember that we have adopted a one-second granularity). Operations such as adding two intervals or comparing two intervals can then be defined to obey normal mathematical laws, such as the law of associativity (which guarantees among other things that $x + y - y$ is always equal to x). Special operators can be defined to support "calendar-style" arithmetic (e.g., ADD_MONTHS; see later in the paper for details). In informal contexts we may choose to regard an interval as so many years, so many months, so many days, etc.; but we have to understand that such a perception is only approximate and may lead to erroneous conclusions if taken too literally. *Formally,* to repeat, an interval consists of an integral number of days, hours, minutes, and seconds.

Any interval, then, can be logically regarded as a signed concatenation of four numeric components *d, h, m,* and *s,* all with the obvious meanings. For intervals in the conventional sense, the sign has the obvious interpretation; for calendar dates, positive = A.D., negative = B.C. Without loss of generality, we assume that all four components arc always present (some of them might be zero, of course); we also assume that each component is always within its legal range—for example, the hours component is never greater than 23. Legal ranges are defined as follows:

d : $0 - x$ (where x is actually arbitrary, but for the purposes of this paper is the number of days in 9,999 Gregorian years, minus one)
h : $0 - 23$
m : $0 - 59$
s : $0 - 59$

Note: Remember that we are discussing a formal representation here, in which, e.g., the first day of the year is considered to be day zero, not day one. This choice of formal representation does *not* necessarily preclude users from representing intervals (and calendar dates) in a more conventional manner externally (see later). Nor does it mean that users always have to worry about precisions down to the second in every case.

We have now pinned down the basic data objects we will be dealing with. Next we have to decide what kinds of operations we want to be able to perform on those objects. We can divide those operations up into various classes:

- conversions
- comparisons
- computational operations
- builtin functions
- assignment

We consider each class in turn.

4.   CONVERSIONS

The first question to address is: What conversions are needed between the new data type (intervals) and existing types in the language? At least the conversions listed below seem to be desirable. [*Note:* We assume that each is performed by means of an explicit builtin conversion function; for reference, we give the names of those functions in square brackets.]

- The ability to convert a specified interval to some standard external representation of an interval (e.g., a character string of the form *d:h:m:s,* with a leading minus sign if the interval is negative), and vice versa [INTERVAL_TO_CHAR, CHAR_TO_INTERVAL]
- The ability to convert a specified interval, considered as a calendar date, to some standard external representation of such a date (e.g., a character string of the form *y:n:d:h:m:s,* with a BC indication if necessary), and vice versa [DATE_TO_CHAR, CHAR_TO_DATE]
- The ability to convert a specified interval to a number representing the number of specified time units (days, minutes, etc.) in that interval, and vice versa [INTERVAL_TO_NUM, NUM_TO_INTERVAL]
- The ability to convert a specified interval, considered as a calendar date, to an integer (1 to 7, where 1 = Sunday, etc.) representing the corresponding day of the week [DAY_OF_WEEK]
- The ability to convert a specified interval, considered as a calendar date, to an integer (1 to 366) representing the corresponding day of the year [DAY_OF_YEAR]

- The ability to convert a specified interval, considered as a calendar date, to an integer (1 to 52, or maybe 53) representing the corresponding week of the year [WEEK_OF_YEAR]

The following can also be regarded as conversions of a kind:

- The ability to treat a specified interval as a calendar date, to extract any individual component (years, months, etc.) of that date, and convert the result to an integer [YEARS_PART, MONTHS_PART, DAYS_PART, HOURS_PART, MINUTES_PART, SECONDS_PART]
- The ability to extract the time components (hours, minutes, and seconds) of a specified interval en bloc and treat the result as another interval [TIME]
- The ability to extract the days component of a specified interval (ignoring the time components) and treat the result as another interval [TRUNC_TO_DAYS]

Notes:

1. The choice of keywords such as "HOURS_PART" (etc.), rather than the more obvious "HOURS" (etc.), is made deliberately. The keyword "HOURS" might tend to suggest that the given interval is to be converted to the *total number* of hours in that interval. Similarly for "MINUTES," etc., of course.

2. It would obviously be possible to define some implicit conversions (also known as *coercions)* to be applied on, e.g., assignment from an interval to a character string or comparison between an interval and a character string (etc., etc.). Such implicit conversions can be regarded as shorthands for the appropriate explicit conversions; as such, they are merely matters of concrete syntax, not worthy of consideration at this stage. In fact, I think it just confuses the issue to get into such questions before the semantic requirements have been properly pinned down.

3. The problem of conversion also arises in the context of source/sink I/O (how should dates and intervals be presented externally to the user?) and in the context of interfacing the database language to a host language (how do dates and intervals interact with the data types of that host?). Once again, however, these are not truly semantic issues; the first is syntax again and the second is more of an implementation issue. I will address them (briefly) toward the end of the paper.

5. COMPARISONS

There is really not too much to be said under this heading, thanks to our choice of intervals (days, hours, minutes, and seconds) as the basic data object. Essentially, any two intervals can be compared by means of the usual scalar comparison operators =, < >, <, < =, >, and > =; such comparisons are algebraic, with the days component being more significant than the hours component, the hours component more significant than the minutes component, etc. Fancy comparison operators such as IN, BETWEEN, etc., can be defined (if desired) in terms of the basic operators. Likewise, the aggregate operators MAX and MIN applied to intervals can be defined in terms of repeated scalar comparisons; the result in each case is another interval.

6. COMPUTATIONAL OPERATIONS

Let I, I1, and I2 be intervals and let N be a number. Because intervals can be regarded as (mixed-radix) integers, the following operations are clearly well-defined and return another interval as a result in each case:

```
     + I
     - I

I1 + I2
I1 - I2

I  *  N
N  *  I
I  /  N
```

Multiplication and division of an interval by a number are defined in terms of repeated addition and subtraction, respectively; the result is an interval, with rounding (if any) to the nearest second. The aggregate operators COUNT, SUM, and AVG applied to intervals are defined in terms of repeated scalar arithmetic operators; COUNT yields a numeric value (actually an integer), SUM and AVG each yield another interval.

It is also possible to divide one interval by another:

```
I1 / I2
```

Such a division is defined by converting each operand to seconds and performing a numeric division. The result is a number, not another interval.

Finally, in order to support calendar arithmetic, we introduce two special computational functions:

```
ADD_MONTHS ( I1, N )        adds N months to I1

ADD_YEARS  ( I1, N )        add N years to I1
```

ADD_MONTHS operates as follows. Let interval I1, considered as a calendar date, have components

```
Y1    N1    D1    H1    M1    S1
```

(where Y1 is the years component, N1 the months component, etc.; note that N1 is in the range 1 to 12 and D1 is in the range 1 to 31). Then the value of ADD_MONTHS(I1,N) is an interval I2, with components (when considered as a calendar date)

```
Y2    N2    D2    H2    M2    S2
```

defined by the following pseudocode:

```
let N = 12y + n (0 <= n <= 11) ;
S2 := S1 ;
M2 := M1 ;
H2 := H1 ;
D2 := D1 ;
N2 := N1 + n ;
Y2 := Y1 + y ;
if N2 > 12 ;
   then do ;
              N2 := N2 - 12 ;
              Y2 := Y2 + 1 ;
         end ;
if N2 in (April,June,September,November) and D2 = 31
   then D2 := 30 ;
if N2 = February and Y2 is a leap year and D2 in (31,30)
   then D2 := 29 ;
if N2 = February and Y2 is not a leap year and D2 in (31,30,29)
   then D2 := 28 ;
```

We are assuming here that I1 and N are both positive. The extension to deal with negative values of I1 and/or N is tedious but straightforward.

ADD_YEARS is defined analogously (the only "interesting" case is that in which I1 represents February 29th for some leap year and adding N years takes us to a nonleap year).

7. BUILTIN FUNCTIONS

This heading is a catchall for any additional functions that may be needed over and above the conversion and computation functions already covered briefly above. In the case of dates and intervals, at least the following additional functions seem to be required:

- A zero-argument function that returns the absolute date "now," i.e., as of the point of invocation [NOW]

- Functions to convert a GMT date to some local timezone and vice versa. Details of these functions are not given in this paper; for simplicity we assume throughout that all dates are GMT.

8. ASSIGNMENT

The only new form of assignment we need in the database language per se is the assignment of an interval value to an interval variable (i.e., column). In SQL terms, assignment is performed only in the context of INSERT and UPDATE operations.

Notes:

1. The "interval assignment" operation should include the ability to assign to individual components (such as the hours component) of an interval variable. Such functionality can be provided by using the component extraction functions discussed earlier (YEARS_PART, MONTHS_PART, etc.) as "pseudovariables" (to use a PL/I term). For example (using the syntax to be introduced later):

```
UPDATE  LAUNCH_SCHEDULE
SET     HOURS_PART ( LIFTOFF ) = 15
WHERE   ROCKET = 'Saucy Sue' ;
```

   The intent of this example is to set the hours component of the LIFTOFF value within the specified row to 3 p.m.

2. Assignment of an interval value to an interval variable may include truncation or padding to match the precision of the target. See the discussion of variables in Section 10.

9. LITERALS

Having decided the semantics (functionality) we want, we can now turn our attention to syntactic issues. *Note:* My primary objective in this paper with respect to syntax is simply to arrive at a concrete syntax that is capable of expressing all required functionality in an unambiguous fashion. The specific syntax shown could probably do with some refinements in order to improve its usability, but first things first.

First we need a syntax for literals:

```
interval-literal
    ::=      [ + | - ] DAYS      'd[:h[:m[:s]]]'
             [ + | - ] HOURS     'h[:m[:s]]'
             [ + | - ] TIME      'h[:m[:s]]'
             [ + | - ] MINUTES   'm[:s]'
             [ + | - ] SECONDS   's'
                       DATE      'y[:n[:d[:h[:m[:s]]]]]' [ AD | BC ]'
```

Examples:

```
      DAYS     '100'
    - HOURS    '3:10:30'
      TIME     '3:10:30'
```

```
⊢ MINUTES '5'
  SECONDS '1'

  DATE '1941:1:18:9:30:45'
  DATE '1941:1:18:9:30'
  DATE '1941:1:18:9'
  DATE '1941:1:18'
  DATE '1941:1'
  DATE '1941'
  DATE '1941 BC'
```

Syntax rules:

1. The DAYS, HOURS, TIME, MINUTES, SECONDS, and DATE keywords specify the units for the leftmost integer value (y, d, h, m, or s) appearing within the single quotes; DAYS, HOURS, MINUTES, and SECONDS have the obvious meanings, TIME is a synonym for HOURS, and DATE means years. Note that there are no YEARS or MONTHS forms.

2. If neither AD nor BC is specified for a DATE literal, AD is assumed.

3. For DATE literals, the syntactic categories y, n, d, h, m, and s are defined as follows:

   y = unsigned decimal integer of 1–4 digits (1–9999)
   n = unsigned decimal integer of 1–2 digits (1–12)
   d = unsigned decimal integer of 1–2 digits (1–31)
   h = unsigned decimal integer of 1–2 digits (0–23)
   m = unsigned decimal integer of 1–2 digits (0–59)
   s = unsigned decimal integer of 1–2 digits (0–59)

   For other literals, y and n do not appear, and d, h, m, and s are basically as for DATE, except that the legal range for d is 0 − x (where x is the number of days in 9,999 years, minus one).

4. In all cases, omitting a value for h or m or s is equivalent to specifying a value of 0. For a DATE literal, omitting a value for n or d is equivalent to specifying a value of 1. For other literals, omitting a value for d is equivalent to specifying a value of 0.

5. Illegal DATE literals such as DATE '1987:4:31' and DATE '1987:2:29' (etc., etc.) are prohibited, and appropriate syntax rules are required to define the details. I omit those details here.

Discussion:

1. There are no YEARS or MONTHS literals because it seems to be impossible to construct such literals in such a way that they can be simultaneously (a) precisely defined and (b) intuitively useful. For example, what would MONTHS'5' mean? 150 days (five average months of 30

days)? 151 days (the actual number of days in the first five months of the year)? Or 152 days (if it is a leap year)?

2. DATE literals and DAYS, HOURS, etc., literals both correspond to the same data type (the interval), and they can be used interchangeably. The reason for including both is usability.

3. The interval literal DAYS '0:0:0:0' (which can be abbreviated to just DAYS '0') represents the origin point. The DATE equivalent is DATE '1:12:31:23:59:59 BC'.

4. The purpose of the DATE, DAYS, etc., keywords is to make interval literals syntactically distinguishable from all other tokens in the language, including in particular string and numeric literals. As a general principle, I favor a context-free approach to syntax. Not all current systems abide by this principle. The opposite of "context-free" is "context-sensitive"; and the trouble with context-sensitivity is that it can lead to strange and complicated syntax rules. For example, in ORACLE [5], date literals are written in the form

```
'dd-mon-yy'
```

and hence are indistinguishable from string literals. What then are we to make of the following expression?

```
'29-APR-87' - '18-JAN-41'
```

Subtraction of one date from another is legal, but subtraction of one string from another is not. I have no idea what ORACLE will do with this expression, though I do know the following is legal:

```
'29-APR-87' + 5
```

(it evaluates to '4-MAY-87').

5. A small point: Intervening blanks could be permitted within an interval literal if desired without causing any ambiguity, but by analogy with string literals it is probably better to prohibit them. On the other hand, it probably *is* desirable to permit blanks between the keyword (DATE, DAYS, etc.) and the actual value, for reasons of readability.

6. Another small point: The proposals of this paper assume a 24-hour clock; in particular, there are no explicit "a.m." or "p.m." literals. Of course, a.m. and p.m. support could easily be added if desired.

10. VARIABLES

The next thing to do is to define a syntax for the definition of interval variables (i.e., columns, in SQL terms):

```
interval-column-definition
    ::=  column INTERVAL [ precision ] [ NOT NULL [ WITH DEFAULT ] ]

precision
    ::=  ( start [ : end ] )

start
    ::=  DAYS | HOURS | MINUTES | SECONDS

end
    ::=  DAYS | HOURS | MINUTES | SECONDS
```

Examples:

```
    REVIEW_DATE  INTERVAL ( DAYS : DAYS )
    BIRTH_DATE   INTERVAL ( DAYS )
    LIFTOFF      INTERVAL
    WAIT_TIME    INTERVAL ( HOURS : SECONDS )
```

Syntax rules:

1. If "precision" is omitted, a precision of (DAYS : SECONDS) is assumed.

2. If "end" is omitted, it is assumed to be equal to "start".

3. "Start" must be greater than or equal to "end", according to the ordering DAYS > HOURS > MINUTES > SECONDS.

Discussion:

1. The precision specification allows the user to indicate that he or she is interested only in certain components of the general interval. One common special case would be "(HOURS:SECONDS)" (meaning time components only—ignore the days). A special shorthand could be introduced for this case if desired.

2. The WITH DEFAULT specification follows the style of IBM SQL, not ISO/ANSI standard SQL; IBM SQL includes the concept of system-defined default values, which ISO/ANSI SQL does not. On the other hand, the proposed extensions to the ISO/ANSI standard [11] include the concept of user-defined default values, which IBM SQL does not. Either way, default values (whether system or user-defined) are used in lieu of nulls if the user does not supply a value for the column on INSERT—also for values in existing rows for columns added to an existing table via ALTER TABLE (assuming in both cases that nulls are not allowed for the column in question).

   [Just as an aside, it is extremely annoying in SQL that several options, such as "defaults not allowed," can be specified only by the *absence* of some particular syntactic construct. This state of affairs makes it very difficult to talk about such cases. A good rule in designing a language's concrete syntactic form is that *every* option should be explicitly expressible. But I digress. To continue with the main discussion:]

3. The obvious system-defined default value to choose is the origin point (DAYS '0:0:0:0').

4. There would be no real harm in allowing DATE as an alternative spelling for INTERVAL, for usability reasons—except that the DATE version of the "obvious" system-defined default, namely DATE '1:12:31:23:59:59 BC' might seem a trifle *un*obvious to the user.

11.   OPERATORS AND EXPRESSIONS

Every time we add a new kind of data object to an existing language, we need to decide

(a) whether existing operators of the language apply to such objects, and

(b) whether any new operators will be needed for such objects.

Then we need to decide how objects and operators can be combined to form expressions. We also need to decide the data type of the result of any such expression. Finally, it is desirable that all such expressions conform (to the maximum extent possible) to the well-known principle of *orthogonality*. (A language is said to be orthogonal if independent concepts are kept separate and are not mixed together in confusing ways.)

Since the objects we are adding to SQL (namely, intervals) are scalar objects, let us begin with the concept of a scalar expression. A scalar expression is any expression that evaluates to a scalar value. Orthogonality dictates that such expressions should be permitted to appear wherever a scalar literal can appear—which (in the case under discussion) means all of the following contexts:

- Within a SELECT clause (to represent a value to be "selected" or retrieved);

- Within a WHERE or HAVING clause (to represent a comparand in a comparison expression—see later);

- Within a VALUES clause (to represent the value to be assigned to a column in an INSERT operation);

- On the right-hand side of an assignment within a SET clause (to represent the value to be assigned to a column in an UPDATE operation);

and also (arguably)

- Within a GROUP BY or ORDER BY clause.

Note: Clearly, any expression that selects a scalar value from the database should also be regarded as a scalar expression. However, SQL—regrettably—does not currently abide by this principle. In fact, SQL violates orthogonality in numerous additional ways; for example, even a simple scalar expression such as X + 1 is not currently permitted in the VALUES clause [3,6,8]. Details of further violations are beyond the scope of this paper, however.

Here then is an orthogonal syntax (with explanations) for scalar expressions that includes intervals. For brevity, I abbreviate "expression" to "exp" in this syntax.

```
1. scalar-exp
   ::=    interval-exp
        | numeric-exp
        | string-exp
        | comparison-exp
```

Aside: Comparison expressions cannot strictly be regarded as scalar expressions in existing SQL because they are truth-valued and SQL does not currently support a truth-valued data type (which means in turn that such expressions cannot appear "wherever a scalar literal can appear," but only in certain specific contexts—to be precise, in WHERE and HAVING clauses). Support for a truth-valued data type in SQL is desirable. *End of aside.*

```
2. interval-exp
   ::=    interval-literal
        | interval-variable
        | interval-exp { + | - } interval-exp
        | interval-exp { * | / } numeric-exp
        | numeric-exp * interval-exp
        | NOW
        | ADD_MONTHS ( interval-exp, numeric-exp )
        | ADD_YEARS ( interval-exp, numeric-exp )
        | { SUM | AVG } ( [ ALL | DISTINCT ] interval-exp )
        | { MAX | MIN } ( interval-exp )
        | TRUNC_TO_DAYS ( interval-exp )
        | TIME ( interval-exp )
        | CHAR_TO_DATE ( string-exp )
        | CHAR_TO_INTERVAL ( units, string-exp )
        | NUM_TO_INTERVAL ( units, numeric-exp )
        | { + | - } interval-exp
        | ( interval-exp )
```

The only cases requiring further explanation here are those involving the builtin functions NOW, TRUNC_TO_DAYS, TIME, CHAR_TO_DATE, CHAR_TO_INTERVAL, and NUM_TO_INTERVAL.

- The zero-argument function NOW returns the date (including the time) "now," i.e., as of the point of invocation. Multiple references to NOW within the same SQL statement are defined to return identical values.

- The TRUNC_TO_DAYS function returns an interval equal to the days portion (only) of its argument.

- The TIME function returns an interval equal to the hours, minutes, and seconds portions (only) of its argument.

- The CHAR_TO_DATE function takes the value of its argument, which must be a character string representation of a DATE literal (excluding the DATE keyword and enclosing quotes), and returns the corresponding interval.

- The CHAR_TO_INTERVAL function takes the value of its argument, which must be a character string representation of an interval literal (excluding the keyword and enclosing quotes, and not of DATE format), and returns the corresponding interval. The "units" argument effectively supplies the missing keyword (DAYS, HOURS, TIME, MINUTES, or SECONDS: see below).

- The NUM_TO_INTERVAL function returns an interval corresponding to N "units," where N is the value of the second argument and "units" is the value of the first argument (DAYS, HOURS, TIME, MINUTES, or SECONDS: again, see below). The result is rounded (if necessary) to the nearest second.

```
3. units
   ::=  string-exp
```

The string expression must evaluate to one of the strings 'DAYS', 'HOURS', 'MINUTES', 'SECONDS', or 'TIME'. TIME is a synonym for HOURS. In practice the string expression will usually consist of a simple character string literal.

Here are some examples (refer back to the sample column definitions given under Section 10, "Variables," earlier). Note in the first two examples that (a) *some* table has to be named in the FROM clause, (b) the statement unfortunately yields a surprising result if that table happens to be empty, and (c) the DISTINCT specification is highly desirable, though not strictly necessary.

```
SELECT DISTINCT NOW
FROM   EMP ;

SELECT DISTINCT TIME ( NOW )
FROM   EMP ;

UPDATE EMP
SET    REVIEW_DATE = ADD_MONTHS ( REVIEW_DATE, 8 )
WHERE  EMP# = '123456' ;

SELECT MIN ( BIRTH_DATE )
FROM   EMP ;
```

```
SELECT  EMP#, TRUNC_TO_DAYS ( NOW ) - BIRTH_DATE
FROM    EMP
WHERE   BIRTH_DATE =
      ( SELECT MAX ( BIRTH_DATE )
        FROM    EMP ) ;

SELECT  *
FROM    EMP
WHERE   REVIEW_DATE < CHAR_TO_DATE ( :DATE_PARAM ) ;

SELECT  *
FROM    LAUNCH_SCHEDULE
WHERE   TIME ( LIFTOFF ) > TIME '12:30' ;

SELECT  *
FROM    LAUNCH_SCHEDULE
WHERE   TIME ( LIFTOFF ) >
        CHAR_TO_INTERVAL ( 'TIME', :TIME_PARAM ) ;

UPDATE  EMP
SET     REVIEW_DATE  =
        NOW + NUM_TO_INTERVAL ( 'DAYS', :NUM_PARAM )
WHERE   EMP# = '123456' ;
```

4. numeric-exp
```
::=    COUNT ( [ ALL | DISTINCT ] interval-exp )
     | DAY_OF_WEEK ( interval-exp )
     | DAY_OF_YEAR ( interval-exp )
     | WEEK_OF_YEAR ( interval-exp )
     | INTERVAL_TO_NUM ( units, interval-exp )
     | YEARS_PART ( interval-exp )
     | MONTHS_PART ( interval-exp )
     | DAYS_PART ( interval-exp )
     | HOURS_PART ( interval-exp )
     | MINUTES_PART ( interval-exp )
     | SECONDS_PART ( interval-exp )
     | interval-exp / interval-exp
     | ... other formats beyond the scope of this paper
     | ( numeric-exp )
```

- The DAY_OF_WEEK function returns an integer of default precision representing the day of the week (1 = Sunday, etc.) corresponding to the interval argument, considered as a calendar date; the DAY_OF_YEAR and WEEK_OF_YEAR functions are defined analogously.

- The INTERVAL_TO_NUM function returns the float value N (with default precision), where N is the value of the second argument considered as a number of "units" and "units" is the value of the first argument.

- The YEARS_PART function returns a signed integer of default precision representing the years portion (-9999 to $+9999$) of the interval argument, considered as a calendar date; the MONTHS_PART, DAYS_PART, HOURS_PART, MINUTES_PART, and SECONDS_PART functions are defined analogously.

- Dividing one interval by another yields a float value of default precision.

Some examples:

```
SELECT *
FROM    EMP
WHERE   DAY_OF_WEEK ( BIRTH_DATE ) = 7 ;

SELECT INTERVAL_TO_NUM ( 'SECONDS', LIFTOFF - NOW )
FROM    LAUNCH_SCHEDULE
WHERE   ROCKET = 'Saucy Sue' ;

SELECT EMP#, EMPNAME
FROM    EMP
WHERE   MONTHS_PART ( BIRTH_DATE ) = 12 ;

SELECT X.EMP#, Y.EMP#
FROM    EMP X,   EMP Y
WHERE   YEARS_PART ( X.HIRE_DATE ) = YEARS_PART ( Y.HIRE_DATE ) ;
```

```
5. string-exp
   ::=    DATE_TO_CHAR ( interval-exp )
       |  INTERVAL_TO_CHAR ( interval-exp )
       |  ... other formats beyond the scope of this paper
```

The DATE_TO_CHAR function converts the specified interval, considered as a calendar date, to its standard character string representation (i.e., *y:n:d:h:m:s* [BC]). Likewise, the INTERVAL_TO_CHAR function converts the specified interval to its standard character string representation (i.e., [−] *d:h:m:s*). *Note:* Some minor syntactic details need to be pinned down in both cases here regarding leading zeros, blanks, etc.

```
6. comparison-exp
   ::=    interval-comparison
       |  numeric-comparison
       |  string-comparison

7. interval-comparison
   ::=    interval-exp  scalar-comparison-op  interval-exp

8. scalar-comparison-op
   ::=    = | <> | < | <= | > | >=

9. numeric-comparison
   ::=    numeric-exp  scalar-comparison-op  numeric-exp

10. string-comparison
    ::=    string-exp  scalar-comparison-op  string-exp
```

12. INPUT/OUTPUT FORMATS

A comment: The question of input/output formats is primarily a syntactic issue. Some systems seem to get hung up on this secondary question before getting the primary (i.e., semantic) issues properly resolved. This is probably why many existing proposals involve a certain degree of context sensitivity. But I would obviously agree that it is desirable to be able to represent intervals in general, and calendar dates in particular, on external media (e.g., on the terminal screen) in a variety of different formats—for example:

1941:1:18	5 hrs 32 mins 15 secs
1/18/1941	5:32:15
18/1/1941	− 1 hour
1-18-41	1 yr 2 mos 3 days
18.i.1941	− 1 yr 2 mos 3 days
January 18th, 1941	100 years 1 day
18 Jan 1941 AD	96 hours
Saturday, Jan 18th, 1941	100 days
Jan. 18th 41, 9:30 a.m.	0 hrs 10 mins
1/18/41 9:30 am PST	17.5 hours
le 18 janvier, 1941	1.000 ans

(etc., etc., etc.). It would clearly be possible to define some kind of FORMAT option that can be specified at the session level and/or the column definition level and/or the individual statement level. Again, the details are tedious but should be straightforward.

Note: It might prove desirable to support alternative formats for literals also. My only comment in this regard is that, again, any such alternative formats must not violate the context-free requirements discussed earlier in this paper.

13. IMPLEMENTATION ISSUES

Implementation details are really beyond the scope of this paper. However, I offer the following brief comments:

1. *Internal representation:* How are dates and intervals to be represented internally? A string representation may facilitate input/output format conversions; it may also make it easier to extract specific components of the value (e.g., the days or minutes component) and to check for illegal dates. On the other hand, a numeric representation—e.g., integer number of seconds (relative to the origin, in the case of dates), may simplify calendar arithmetic operations. Either way it may prove desir-

able to introduce some form of data compression on the disk, for storage space reasons. Of course, whatever internal representation is chosen should *not* be permitted to affect the language semantics.

2. *Operator implementation:* It would be nice if the new operators (ADD_MONTHS, etc.) could be defined in terms of constructs already existing in the language—in effect, as SQL subroutines. Unfortunately this is not possible, in general; SQL is only a "data sublanguage" and is not computationally complete. Note the implication that adding new *user-defined* data types to SQL is therefore likely to require expertise in some other language in addition to SQL per se and will thus get into the question of interfacing between SQL and that other language.

3. *Host interfacing:* Most host languages do not provide direct support for dates and intervals. The question therefore arises of mapping between dates and intervals in SQL and host data types. The functions CHAR_TO_DATE, DATE_TO_CHAR, CHAR_TO_INTERVAL, INTERVAL_TO_CHAR, NUM_TO_INTERVAL, and INTERVAL _TO_NUM can be used for this purpose (assuming that the host language does at least support character strings and numbers).

14. SUMMARY

In this paper I have considered what is involved in adding a new data type to an existing database language such as SQL. The paper has been primarily concerned with system-defined data types, though most of the ideas are in fact directly relevant to the question of adding support for user-defined data types also. By way of example, I have considered in some depth the case of adding support for dates and times to SQL specifically. To recap, the following steps are involved:

- Deciding required semantics
  - what is required in intuitive terms?
  - basic data elements
  - conversion operations
  - comparison operations
  - computational operations
  - builtin functions
  - assignment operations
- Defining syntactic details
  - literals

- variables
- operators and expressions
- input/output formats
- Deciding implementation details
  - internal representation
  - operator implementation
  - host language interfacing

The paper is intended to serve a dual purpose: first, to assist in the process of formulating proposals for adding new data types to database languages in a systematic manner; second, to assist in the process of critically examining any such proposals. In addition, of course, it can be regarded as the beginnings of a systematic proposal for adding date and time support to the database language SQL.

ACKNOWLEDGMENTS

I am grateful for helpful comments on earlier drafts of this paper to my friends and colleagues Ted Codd, Nat Goodman, Hugh Darwen, Sharon Weinberg, and Colin White.

REFERENCES AND BIBLIOGRAPHY

1. Michael Stonebraker, Brad Rubinstein, and Antonin Guttman, "Application of Abstract Data Types and Abstract Indices to CAD Data Bases," *Proc. ACM SIGMOD Database Week, Engineering Applications Stream,* San Jose, California (May 1983).

2. J. Ong, D. Fogg, and M. Stonebraker, "Implementation of Data Abstraction in the Relational Database System INGRES," *ACM SIGMOD Record* 14, No. 1 (March 1984).

3. C. J. Date, "A Critique of the SQL Database Language," in C. J. Date, *Relational Database: Selected Writings* (Reading, MA: Addison-Wesley, 1986). Republished in revised form in C. J. Date, *A Guide to the SQL Standard,* 2nd edition (Reading, MA: Addison-Wesley, 1989).

4. Michael Stonebraker, "Inclusion of New Types in Relational Data Base Systems," Memorandum No. UCB/ERL M85/67, UC Berkeley, CA 94720 (July 1985).

5. Oracle Corp., ORACLE Terminal Users' Guide (1987).

6. C. J. Date, "What's Wrong with SQL?" (in this volume).

7. C. J. Date and Colin J. White, *A Guide to DB2,* 3rd edition (Reading, MA: Addison-Wesley, 1989).

8. Andrew Warden, "The Naming of Columns" (in this volume).

9. C. J. Date and Colin J. White, *A Guide to SQL/DS* (Reading, MA: Addison-Wesley, 1988).

10. C. J. Date, "Dates and Times in IBM SQL: Some Technical Criticisms" (in this volume).

11. ISO/IEC JTC1/SC21/WG3 / ANSI X3H2, ISO-ANSI (working draft) SQL2. Document ISO/IEC JTC1/SC21/WG3 N449 / ANSI X3H2-88-1 (December 1987).

4

Why Duplicate Rows Are Prohibited

ABSTRACT

We present a series of arguments in support of the relational requirement that tables not contain any duplicate rows (usually referred to herein as just "duplicates").

COMMENTS ON PUBLICATION

Like one or two other papers in this book, the paper that follows does not actually contain very much in the way of new material. Rather, it is intended as a convenient summary of a set of arguments that individually may be quite well known, but (so far as I am aware) collectively do not seem to have been pulled together into a single place before. One word of warning: The subject under discussion—again like one or two others in this book, especially in Part I—is one of those in which the arguments are sometimes a little philosophical in nature, not just technical. (By "technical" here I

Previously unpublished.

am referring specifically to DP technology per se; philosophical arguments can also be regarded as technical, of course, but in a different way.)

See also Chapter 19, "The Keys of the Kingdom," for an alternative presentation of some of the arguments contained herein.

1. WHY DUPLICATES ARE GOOD (?)

The relational model does not allow tables to contain duplicate rows. But why not? People often ask this question, and indeed sometimes criticize the relational model precisely on the grounds that it *does* prohibit duplicate rows—especially since most current relational DBMSs do not in fact enforce the prohibition (a major flaw in those products, incidentally). The following arguments are usually heard in this connexion:

1. Duplicates occur naturally in practice. Consider, e.g., the daily temperature readings at some vacation resort, or the recorded items in someone's phonograph record collection, or the birthdates for the employees in some given department, etc., etc. (these examples are taken from reference [4]).

2. Given that duplicates do occur naturally, it is a burden for the user to have to invent some artificial identifier in order to make them unique.

3. It is costly (and represents unnecessary overhead) for the system to have to prevent duplicates from occurring (in the case of base tables), or to eliminate them if they do occur (in the case of derived tables).

4. Surely duplicates are harmless enough, anyway. What problems can they cause?

These arguments are misleading, however, as we will try to show in the remainder of the paper. In particular, duplicates certainly can cause problems, both for the user and for the system, as we will see.

2. WHY DUPLICATES ARE BAD (I):
THE FUNDAMENTAL ISSUE

In order to see why duplicates are *not* "a good thing," it is helpful to consider the original objectives of the relational model. The relational model was intended to be *simple* but *sound—simple,* so that it would be understandable and usable, but *sound,* so that it would be solid and stable and free from unpleasant surprises (a good long-term foundation for the future, in fact). Mathematical set theory thus seemed a good basis on which to construct the model, because:

(a) First, set theory certainly does possess the desired properties of simplicity and soundness;

(b) Second (as Codd demonstrated in reference [1]), the objects and operators of set theory can be directly applied to the database problem. In particular, it is fruitful to regard a set (or more specifically a relation) as a mathematical abstraction of a database file.

Thus we see that a relation (i.e., table) in the relational model is essentially just a special kind of mathematical set (specifically, a set of *tuples* or rows). And sets in mathematics do not contain duplicate members. Therefore, tables in the relational model do not contain duplicate rows.

In a sense, the paper could stop right here; the original question has been answered, after all. However, the reader might be forgiven for objecting that all we have done is push the problem back one level: *Why* do mathematical sets not permit duplicate members? Let us therefore examine this latter question in turn.

Fundamentally, the answer has to do with *identifiability.* It is a truth universally acknowledged that individual objects must be identifiable (i.e., distinguishable from all other objects)—for if an object is not identifiable, it is impossible even to talk about it, let alone perform any kind of operation upon it or use it for any sensible purpose. In other words, objects must have *identity* (in computer terms, they must be *addressable*).

Now, in a collection of objects in which there are no duplicates (i.e., a mathematical set), objects are obviously identifiable, because they are in fact *self-identifying.* For example, in the set of integers (e.g.)

    3, 6, 8, 11,

there is no ambiguity as to which member of the set is "6" and which is "8" (etc.). However, in the collection (e.g.)

    3, 6, 6, 8, 8, 8, 11,

(which is certainly *not* a mathematical set), we cannot make an analogous statement; both "6" and "8" are now ambiguous.

So what *is* the identification mechanism in a collection that permits duplicates? For example, in the collection shown above, how can we distinguish the two "6"s from one another? Note that there still must be an identification mechanism; if we cannot distinguish the two "6"s from one another somehow, *we cannot even tell that there are two of them.* In other words, we would not even know that there were any duplicates in the first place!

Aside: A common reaction to this argument is "But I really don't need to distinguish among the duplicates—all I want to do is ask how many of them there are (i.e., I just want to be able to count them)." The point I am trying to make is that you do need to distinguish them, even just to count them. This point is crucial, of course, and I really don't know how to make it any more strongly than I already have. *End of aside.*

To repeat, then: The question is, how can we distinguish the two "6"s in the collection shown above? The obvious answer (though not necessarily the only one) is, of course, that we distinguish the two "6"s *by their relative position;* we say something like "this 6 is here and that 6 is over there." In other words, the possibility that duplicates might occur leads us into some kind of *positional addressing.* For example, we might introduce an *ordering* for the collection of objects—say the left-to-right ordering as shown above—and then we can say that the two "6"s occupy the second and third positions respectively with respect to that ordering.*

In a pure set, by contrast, there is no need for any positional concepts—as stated earlier, objects in a set are self-identifying, because they are all distinct. In fact, sets do not have any notion of ordering or position at all; for example, the set {3,6,8,11} and the set {6,3,11,8} are *exactly the same set.* As a result, tables in the relational model do not have any ordering either—that is, there is no top-to-bottom order to the rows in a relational table. The two tables shown in Fig. 1 below are *exactly the same table,* relationally speaking.

Aside: Of course, when we represent a relation as a table on paper, we are forced to show the rows in some top-to-bottom order, but that order is there merely because of limitations of the paper medium. It is not inherent in the notion of a table per se. Nor do any of the relational

S	S#	SNAME	STATUS	CITY		S	S#	SNAME	STATUS	CITY
	--	-----	------	------			--	-----	------	------
	S1	Smith	20	London			S3	Blake	30	Paris
	S2	Jones	10	Paris			S5	Adams	30	Athens
	S3	Blake	30	Paris			S1	Smith	20	London
	S4	Clark	20	London			S4	Clark	20	London
	S5	Adams	30	Athens			S2	Jones	10	Paris

Fig. 1 Relational tables have no row ordering

---

*Strictly speaking, positional addressing does not necessarily imply ordering per se. However, any other version of positional addressing will suffer from problems analogous to those identified in what follows as problems having to do with ordering. Our assumption that ordering is implied is an acceptable simplification for the purposes of this paper.

operators (join, etc.) depend on the rows of their operand(s) being in any particular order. *End of aside.*

Let us now translate the foregoing into database terms. What we are saying is that, if we are going to permit duplicate rows to appear in a table, then we must also have some notion of row position within such a table. As a consequence, we will need an appropriate set of operators to deal with that positional information—for example:

- Find the first row
- Find the last row
- Find the next row
- Find the previous row
- Find the Nth row after the beginning
- Find the Nth row before the end
- Find the Nth row after the current row
- Find the Nth row before the current row
- Retrieve the current row
- Update the current row
- Delete the current row
- Insert a new row before the current row
- Insert a new row after the current row

(etc., etc.). Note in particular that we will need some kind of "current row" concept—and it is well known that such concepts are a notorious source of errors for application programmers and are probably beyond the capability (or inclination) of end-users to deal with at all. None of this complex machinery is needed in a pure relational system.

> *Note:* It is true that a simple form of positional addressing is required, even in a pure relational system, in the interface to host languages such as COBOL and PL/I. But it is the host languages, not the relational DBMS, that give rise to this requirement, owing to the record-at-a-time orientation of those languages. In effect, such languages require *unordered* sets of rows to be converted into *ordered* lists of records, so that operations such as "Find next" can have a meaning. Note, however, that those positional addressing facilities form part of the application programming interface only—they are not exposed to end-users.

Duplicate rows thus inevitably lead to increased complexity in the system—increased complexity for the system, of course, and increased complexity for the user also, because the additional operators must be exposed at the user interface.* What is more, that increased complexity does not bring with it any increased functionality; there is nothing (at least, nothing useful) that can be achieved with such a more complex system that cannot also be achieved with a pure relational system.

> *Caveat:* By the foregoing remarks, I do not mean to imply that the relational approach is a panacea; it is not [4]. There are certainly some problems for which it is awkward at best. However, there is also a very large class of problems for which the relational approach is extremely good. And the fact that there are some problems for which the approach is a little awkward is *not* in itself an argument for complicating the model by (e.g.) allowing duplicate rows. To quote reference [4], the penalty for solving one user's problem in such a manner would be increased complexity for *all* users, which hardly seems reasonable.

It is worth pointing out that it is the fact that no table in a true relational system ever contains any duplicate rows that allows us to assert—without fear of contradiction!—that every table (base table or derived) *always has a primary key* [1,3,7]. This is why we are able to say that primary keys provide the necessary row-level addressing mechanism in the relational model, and therefore in a true relational system also [3].

One final remark: In a sense, it would be possible to stand the entire argument of this section on its head. We have been arguing somewhat as follows:

1. Relations are sets;
2. Sets do not contain duplicates;
3. Therefore relations do not contain duplicates.

In other words, we have presented what might be regarded as a *formal* argument, starting from set theory and winding up with a particular method of representing the real world in a database. We might alternatively have argued in a more *intuitive* manner, starting from the real world and winding up with sets:

1. Entities are distinguishable (uniquely identifiable) in the real world;
2. Therefore entity representatives must be distinguishable (uniquely identifiable) in the database;

---

*This statement is correct in principle. In practice, however, the fact is that most relational products available today (especially those based on SQL) do permit duplicate rows but lack an adequate mechanism for distinguishing between them and an adequate set of operators for dealing with them. (Actually, these lacks are a blessing in disguise, since they effectively serve as an incentive to users not to have duplicate rows in the first place.)

3. So we need a theory of unique objects that can be adapted to our database purposes;

4. Set theory is such a theory.

Thus, the formal argument says "We are dealing with sets, and therefore there are no duplicates"; the intuitive argument says "There are no duplicates, and therefore we are dealing with sets."

3. WHY DUPLICATES ARE BAD (II): THE QUESTION OF MEANING

For the reader who may still remain unconvinced, we now offer some additional arguments. The basic question addressed in this section is "What do duplicates *mean*?" For example, consider the database shown in Fig. 2 (a modified version of the usual suppliers-and-parts database, in which we assume for the sake of the example—though it sticks in the gullet—that duplicate rows are permitted):

```
P    P#   PNAME        SP   S#   P#
--   -----             --   --
     P1   Screw             S1   P1
     P1   Screw             S1   P1
     P1   Screw             S1   P2
     P2   Screw
```

Fig. 2 A sample database containing duplicate rows

First of all, what does it *mean* to have three "(P1,Screw)" rows in table P and not two or four or seventeen? It must mean *something,* for if it means nothing, then why are there any duplicates in the table in the first place? To paraphrase a point first nicely made by Codd in reference [2]: If something is true, saying it twice doesn't make it any *more* true.

For the sake of the ensuing discussion, therefore, we assume that there is some meaning attached to the existence of duplicates, even though that meaning (whatever it is) is hardly very explicit. (We note in passing that duplicates thus contravene another of the objectives of the relational model, namely the objective of *explicitness*—the meaning of the data should be made as explicit as possible.) In other words, given that duplicates do have some meaning, there are presumably going to be business decisions made on the basis of the fact that (e.g.) there are three "(P1,Screw)" rows in table P, and not two or four.

Let us therefore investigate this question of the meaning of duplicates a little more carefully. Consider the following sample query on the parts-and-shipments database of Fig. 2:*

"List part numbers for parts that either are screws or are supplied by supplier S1 (or both)."

We show a number of candidate SQL formulations for this query, together with the output produced in each case. The formulations are numbered for ease of subsequent reference.

```
1.   SELECT  P.P#
     FROM    P
     WHERE   P.PNAME = 'Screw'
     OR      P.P# IN
             ( SELECT SP.P#
               FROM    SP
               WHERE   SP.S# = 'S1') ;        Results:  P1 * 3, P2 * 1

2.   SELECT  SP.P#
     FROM    SP
     WHERE   SP.S# = 'S1'
     OR      SP.P# IN
             ( SELECT P.P#
               FROM    P
               WHERE   P.PNAME = 'Screw') ;   Result:  P1 * 2, P2 * 1

3.   SELECT  P.P#
     FROM    P, SP
     WHERE   ( SP.S# = 'S1' AND
               P.P#  =  SP.P# )
     OR      P.PNAME = 'Screw' ;              Result:  P1 * 9, P2 * 3

4.   SELECT  SP.P#
     FROM    P, SP
     WHERE   ( SP.S# = 'S1' AND
               P.P#  =  SP.P# )
     OR      P.PNAME = 'Screw' ;              Result:  P1 * 8, P2 * 4

5.   SELECT  P.P#
     FROM    P
     WHERE   P.PNAME = 'Screw'
     UNION   ALL
     SELECT  SP.P#
     FROM    SP
     WHERE   SP.S# = 'S1' ;                   Result:  P1 * 5, P2 * 2

6.   SELECT  DISTINCT P.P#
     FROM    P
     WHERE   P.PNAME = 'Screw'
     UNION   ALL
     SELECT  SP.P#
     FROM    SP
     WHERE   SP.S# = 'S1' ;                   Result:  P1 * 3, P2 * 2
```

---

*This example is based (with permission) on one first given in a live presentation by Nat Goodman.

```
 7.    SELECT  P.P#
       FROM    P
       WHERE   P.PNAME = 'Screw'
       UNION   ALL
       SELECT  DISTINCT SP.P#
       FROM    SP
       WHERE   SP.S# = 'S1' ;                 Result:   P1 * 4, P2 * 2

 8.    SELECT  DISTINCT P.P#
       FROM    P
       WHERE   P.PNAME = 'Screw'
       OR      P.P# IN
              ( SELECT SP.P#
                FROM    SP
                WHERE   SP.S# = 'S1') ;        Result:   P1 * 1, P2 * 1

 9.    SELECT  DISTINCT SP.P#
       FROM    SP
       WHERE   SP.S# = 'S1'
       OR      SP.P# IN
              ( SELECT P.P#
                FROM    P
                WHERE   P.PNAME = 'Screw') ;   Result:   P1 * 1, P2 * 1

10.    SELECT  P.P#
       FROM    P
       GROUP   BY P.P#, P.PNAME
       HAVING  P.PNAME = 'Screw'
       OR      P.P# IN
              ( SELECT SP.P#
                FROM    SP
                WHERE   SP.S# = 'S1' ) ;       Result:   P1 * 1, P2 * 1

11.    SELECT  P.P#
       FROM    P, SP
       GROUP   BY P.P#, P.PNAME, SP.S#, SP.P#
       HAVING  ( SP.S# = 'S1' AND
                 P.P#  =  SP.P# )
       OR      P.PNAME = 'Screw' ;             Result:   P1 * 2, P2 * 2

12.    SELECT  P.P#
       FROM    P
       WHERE   P.PNAME = 'Screw'
       UNION
       SELECT  SP.P#
       FROM    SP
       WHERE   SP.S# = 'S1' ;                  Result:   P1 * 1, P2 * 1
```

Points arising:

- Note first that the twelve different formulations produce nine different results! Thus, if the user really cares about duplicates, then he or she needs to be able to specify which of those nine results is required. Needless to say, no language feature exists in SQL today that would permit any such specification. Moreover, it is very hard to imagine what such a feature would look like.

- I make no claim, incidentally, that either the twelve different formulations or the nine different results are the only ones possible (indeed, they are certainly not). However, note that:

- Formulations 1, 3, 8, 10, and 11 all rely on the (reasonable) assumption that every part number appearing in table SP also appears in table P. I will refer to this assumption as "the foreign key assumption" below, although the term is not quite appropriate, because column SP.P# is not a foreign key, because column P.P# is not a primary key (because, remember, values of column P.P# are not unique). *Note:* A more accurate term would be "the inclusion assumption," because the constraint is in fact an *inclusion constraint* [8]. Every foreign key constraint is an inclusion constraint, but the converse is not true. However, I prefer the term "foreign key assumption" for reasons of familiarity, among others.

- Formulations 2, 4, and 9 rely on the (arguably less reasonable) assumption that every part number appearing in table P also appears in table SP. I will refer to this assumption as "the converse assumption" below.

- Since different formulations produce different results (in general), users cannot freely choose the formulation they prefer, but rather have to be aware of the effect of different formulations on the number of duplicates in the result. They might also have to be aware of performance implications (see the next point below).

- Analogous remarks apply to the system itself: Because (again) different formulations can produce different results, the system optimizer's ability to transform one formulation into another is very severely curtailed. In other words, duplicate rows act as a significant *optimization inhibitor.**

  What this means for the user is that either (a) system performance is likely to be worse than it might be (which is bound to upset some users), or (b) the user is going to have to get involved in performance issues (e.g., the user might have to spend time and effort on figuring out the best way to state a given query).

- Since I do not believe in duplicates anyway, I would argue that the only correct result is (P1 * 1, P2 * 1). This is the result produced by formulations 8, 9, 10, and 12. Of those formulations, however, numbers 8 and 10 rely on the foreign key assumption, and number 9 relies on the converse assumption. Thus, I would argue that the only formu-

---

*This state of affairs is particularly frustrating in view of the fact that (in most cases) the user probably does not really care how many duplicates appear in the result. In other words: (a) Different formulations produce different results, as demonstrated above; however, (b) the differences are probably irrelevant from the user's point of view; BUT (c) the optimizer is not aware of this latter fact and is therefore prevented—unnecessarily—from performing the query transformations it would like to perform.

lation that is unequivocally correct is number 12 (although I would agree that it is reasonable in practice to formulate queries that rely on some kind of foreign key assumption, so that numbers 8 and 10 can probably be regarded as acceptable also).

- On the basis of the foregoing example (and others like it), I would conclude that, regardless of whether any foreign key assumption is invoked, users should *always* ensure that query results contain no duplicates—e.g., by specifying DISTINCT at appropriate points in the query [6]—and thus simply forget about the whole problem. (And if this advice is followed, of course, then there can be no good reason for having duplicates in the database in the first place.)

Aside: The alternative in SQL to SELECT DISTINCT is SELECT ALL (and SELECT ALL is unfortunately the default). The foregoing discussion suggests that a more appropriate alternative might have been SELECT *IN*DISTINCT. . . . On a more serious note: The trouble is, of course, that SELECT DISTINCT takes longer to execute than SELECT ALL, in general, even if the DISTINCT is effectively a "no-op." But this problem arises because SQL systems are unable to optimize properly over duplicate removal, owing to their lack of knowledge of primary keys and (especially) of primary key inheritance. (I am grateful to Hugh Darwen for this observation.) See reference [7] for a discussion of the question of primary key inheritance. *End of aside.*

4. WHY DUPLICATES ARE BAD (III): MISCELLANEOUS POINTS

In this section, I simply summarize a few additional points that have not been called out explicitly in the foregoing sections.

- The first point is a very pragmatic one. Suppose we have some table that does permit duplicate rows, and suppose we are doing data entry on that table. Data entry typically involves filling out a form on the terminal screen for each row to be entered into the table; hitting "Enter" (or its equivalent) on the keyboard then causes the row to be inserted into the table. Consider the following sequence of events.

  1. Suppose first that we have filled out the form with the data for some row *r1* and we have hit "Enter" for that row. The row has been inserted.

  2. Suppose now that, by mistake (and before we have made any changes to the form on the screen), we hit "Enter" again (a mistake easily

made, incidentally). A second copy of row *r1*—a duplicate—will be inserted into the table.

3. The table now contains two identical rows, *r1* and *r2* say.* But the second insertion was a mistake. Obviously, we would like to be able to delete one of the two identical rows. But how? If we are limited to accessing rows on the basis of their data content only (which we are), then *there is no way to refer to just one of the two:* Any expression— and hence any WHERE clause—that identifies either one of the two will necessarily identify the other one also. Hence, we can only delete *both* rows and then start again—which is VERY ANNOYING.

4. Note too that a curious side-effect in such a system is that the INSERT and DELETE operations are not quite symmetric; i.e., they are not quite inverses of one another.

Aside: I am of course discounting the possibility of writing an application program to do the deletion. As mentioned earlier in this paper, the application programming interface effectively converts unordered sets into ordered lists, and so would indeed make it possible to distinguish between the duplicates. But if it is necessary to write a program, then (a) the deletion obviously could not be done at all by most users, and (b) in any case, we would now be outside the bounds of the relational system per se. *End of aside.*

▪ Second, I must stress the point that the "no duplicates" rule applies to *all* tables (not just to base tables)—views, snapshots, query results, intermediate results, and any other derived tables that might ever exist in the system. Most of the arguments of this paper carry directly over to derived tables without any significant modification. In addition, if the rule applied to base tables only, then a derived table that did in fact contain duplicates could not be converted into a base table, and an expression that generated such a table could not be used in a completely orthogonal manner (the relational closure property would break down).

▪ The next point is perhaps a little more theoretical in nature (though in fact all theoretical aspects of the relational model do have very direct and significant practical consequences [5]). It has to do with the relational operators such as join. Those operators are (of course) defined to work on *relations*. Now, if a table contains any duplicates, *it is not a relation* (by definition). As a consequence, if the basic data object in

---

*Notice how we have to distinguish between the duplicates in order just to be able to talk about them!

a given DBMS is not a relation but rather a table that can contain duplicate rows (as is unfortunately the case in most DBMSs on the market today), then *join does not work*.

Now, I am obviously not claiming here that "join does not work" in (for example) the IBM product DB2. Rather, what I am claiming is that what the DB2 implementers implemented is not really the genuine relational join. Instead, it is what we might call "join prime"—where "join prime" is similar to the genuine join, except that its operands are not necessarily relations (in general), but rather tables that might contain duplicate rows.* And "join prime" is *more complicated* than the genuine join, but it is *no more powerful;* i.e., there is nothing—at least, nothing useful—that can be achieved with "join prime" that cannot also be achieved with the genuine join. Note too that when I say "more complicated," I mean (among other things) "more expensive to implement"—which in turn means that *everyone pays* (even users who avoid duplicates); the product is harder to build in the first place, harder to maintain, less reliable, and more expensive.

■ The final point is in fact an extension and generalization of the previous one, and is very serious. It runs as follows: *Anyone who proposes a data model or a query language or a DBMS in which duplicates are allowed is morally obliged to produce an appropriate theoretical foundation for that model or language or DBMS.* For how otherwise can we be sure that the proposal is sound? Furthermore, if the proposal is to be seriously considered as an alternative to the relational approach, then that theoretical foundation really needs to be as solid, extensive, general, and complete as existing set theory and existing predicate logic (which together constitute the theoretical foundation for the relational approach).

What is needed, therefore, is a formal theory and logic for collections of not-necessarily-all-distinct objects. Such collections are sometimes referred to in the literature as "bags" or "multisets." So far as I am aware, however, nobody ever has produced a "bag theory" or "bag logic" that can compare in comprehensiveness and general satisfactoriness with conventional set theory and predicate logic. In other words, we are asking our hypothetical advocate of duplicate rows to come up with some fundamental developments in mathematics and logic—probably a pretty tall order.

---

*Of course, I am not suggesting for a moment that the DB2 implementers thought about what they were doing in these terms, but this is conceptually what they did.

5. CONCLUSION

There is a very simple way to sum up the argument of this paper, namely as follows. Objects are distinguishable in the real world (i.e., they have identity); therefore, their representatives in the database must be distinguishable (or have identity) also. The relational model simply requires that object identities be represented by *value,* just like everything else (the advantages of representing all data in one and only one way are well known [5]). It follows a fortiori that tables will never contain any duplicate rows.

By way of conclusion, let me repeat, and respond to, the four alleged arguments in favor of duplicates from Section 1.

1. Duplicates occur naturally in practice.

    I categorically deny the assertion that duplicate *objects* can occur. Of course, two objects that are distinct in themselves can nevertheless have the same value for some property, or even for all properties (excluding the identifier property); for example, two temperature readings might both show the same temperature. Nevertheless, there are still two distinct objects (two readings, in the example), and they need to be distinguished. In the case of the temperature readings, for example, it would be entirely natural, and normal, and useful, to introduce a date or time or timestamp to identify the individual readings [4].

2. Inventing an artificial identifier is a burden for the user.

    In some cases this is true. Suppose I want to keep a name and address list for my friends and acquaintances and business contacts in a relational database. Then (a) on the one hand, there can be no guarantee that (for example) everyone in the list has a unique name—in fact, they do not!—but equally (b) I do not want the bother of having to invent and maintain some kind of artificial "person number" in order to guarantee uniqueness. The solution to such problems, of course, is to have the system provide the necessary function automatically, in the form of *system-generated primary keys.* See reference [7] for further discussion of this possibility.

    (Note, however, that even if the system does not provide such a function, I would still not accept this "burden" argument as a reason for permitting duplicates. The burden is slight, after all, and the advantages of relieving it by permitting duplicates are outweighed a hundredfold by the disadvantages.)

3. Preventing and/or eliminating duplicates is costly.

    Maybe it is—but not so costly as not doing so.

4. Duplicates are harmless.

No, they're not. See Sections 2–4 above.

ACKNOWLEDGMENTS

I am grateful to Nagraj Alur and Nat Goodman of Codd and Date for their comments on an earlier draft of this paper and for several helpful discussions. Thanks also to Charley Bontempo and Hugh Darwen for their comments and suggestions. I am also grateful to Linda Lorence of Codd and Date for checking out some of my SQL examples for me on her XDB system.

REFERENCES AND BIBLIOGRAPHY

1. E. F. Codd, "A Relational Model of Data for Large Shared Data Banks," *Communications of the ACM* 13, No. 6 (June 1970). Republished in *Communications of the ACM* 26, No. 1 (January 1983).

2. E. F. Codd, "Fatal Flaws in SQL," Part 1, *Datamation* (August 15, 1988); Part 2, *Datamation* (September 1, 1988).

3. C. J. Date, "Why Every Relation Should Have Exactly One Primary Key," in C. J. Date, *Relational Database: Selected Writings* (Reading, MA: Addison-Wesley, 1986).

4. C. J. Date, "Some Relational Myths Exploded," in C. J. Date, *Relational Database: Selected Writings* (Reading, MA: Addison-Wesley, 1986).

5. C. J. Date, "Why Relational?" (in this volume).

6. C. J. Date, "SQL Dos and Don'ts" (in this volume).

7. Andrew Warden, "The Keys of the Kingdom" (in this volume).

8. Marco A. Casanova, Ronald Fagin, and Christos H. Papadimitriou, "Inclusion Dependencies and Their Interaction with Functional Dependencies," *Proc. 1st ACM SIGACT-SIGMOD Symposium on Principles of Database Systems* (March 1982).

5

Referential Integrity and Foreign Keys Part I: Basic Concepts

ABSTRACT

This is Part I of a two-part paper on the subject of referential integrity and related matters. Part I discusses the history of the subject and offers a preferred set of basic definitions (with rationale). Part II provides further justification and offers some specific practical recommendations.

COMMENTS ON PUBLICATION

This was initially intended as a private working paper. The original version [28] was prepared as a basis for discussion with (primarily) Dr. Codd, plus anyone else who might be interested. It seemed to me at the time when I prepared the original version (April 1987) that the topic was in urgent need

---

Previously unpublished.

of clarification, and I hoped to persuade Dr. Codd of that fact and of the need to produce a definitive paper on the subject, which (I suggested) could be a joint production between him and myself. Dr. Codd did agree that such a paper was needed, but rejected the idea of joint publication; instead, he wrote a paper of his own [14], which paper, however, I felt still did not fully serve as the much needed definitive statement, even though it did incorporate some of my own comments, suggestions, and examples. I therefore decided to preserve my original working paper as my own attempt at clarifying a confused but very important area. It now seems appropriate to make that paper available (in this revised and expanded form) to a wider audience.

In preparing this expanded version, I found that there was so much that needed saying that it seemed expeditious to split the paper into two parts, one dealing with the basic concepts per se, the other with a variety of implications and ramifications of those concepts. This first part, the "basic concepts" part, consists primarily of a set of introductory examples, together with a survey—with analysis and comments—of the discussions and definitions in several of Dr. Codd's papers, including the one referred to above (the "definitive statement" paper [14]). It also includes my own preferred set of definitions.

It is worth mentioning that the discussions of this paper (both parts, but especially Part II) are directly relevant to the question of database design.

1. INTRODUCTION

The foreign key and referential integrity concepts originated in a series of papers by Codd [9,11,13,14]. The concepts are of paramount importance in the field of database technology. Yet they are surrounded by an extraordinary degree of confusion—confusion in the open literature, confusion in the database community at large, and (especially) confusion in the database marketplace. There are certainly numerous conflicting definitions in various books, papers, trade journals, and elsewhere. Clarification is urgently needed. The present two-part paper represents my own attempt at providing such clarification. Part I surveys the various discussions given in Codd's publications on the subject, analyzing and commenting on those discussions; it then gives my own preferred definitions and approach to the subject. Part II offers additional discussion and explanation, together with some concrete recommendations for using the ideas in practice.

Note: Throughout the paper (both parts), I treat the terms "relation" and "table" as synonymous: likewise for the terms "attribute" and "column" and the terms "tuple," "row," and "record."

2. EXAMPLES

This section presents a number of introductory examples. The examples make use of a "pseudoSQL" syntax based on one first introduced in reference [15] and explained in detail in Section 8 of the present paper; for the purposes of this section, I will simply assume that the syntax is more or less self-explanatory. *Note:* Domain declarations are not shown, for reasons of brevity. Please understand, however, that this fact is not to be construed as meaning that I think that domains are not important (see reference [24]).

```
1. DEPT    ( DEPT#, ... )
           PRIMARY KEY ( DEPT# )

   EMP     ( EMP#, ..., DEPT#, ... )
           PRIMARY KEY ( EMP# )
           FOREIGN KEY ( DEPT# ) REFERENCES DEPT
```

Example 1 is the "simplest possible" example (departments and employees). Here are some sample values:

```
DEPT   DEPT#   ...      EMP   EMP#   ...   DEPT#   ...
       -----                  ----         -----
       D1                     E1           D1
       D2                     E2           D1
       D3                     E3           D2
                              E4           D2
                              E5           null
```

Points arising:

- First, terminology. Here are some rough definitions of the terms "primary key" and "foreign key" (precise definitions can be found in Section 7, later).

  1. *Primary key:* Loosely, a primary key is just a unique identifier. A little more precisely: The *primary key* for a table T1 is a column PK of T1 such that, at any given time, no two rows of T1 have the same value for PK.

  2. *Foreign key:* Loosely, a foreign key is a column in one table whose values are values of the primary key of some other table (or possibly the same table). A little more precisely: A *foreign key* is a column FK of some table T2 such that, at any given time, every nonnull value of FK in T2 is required to be equal to the value of the primary key PK in some row of some table T1. Table T2 here is the *referencing* table, table T1 the *referenced* or *target* table. The two tables are not necessarily distinct.

- More terminology: Since a given foreign key value obviously represents a *reference* to the row containing the matching primary key value (the *referenced row* or *target row*), the problem of ensuring that the database does not contain any invalid foreign key values is known as the *referential integrity* problem. The constraint that values of a given foreign key must match values of the corresponding primary key is known as a *referential constraint*.

■   Referential constraints can be represented diagrammatically as follows:

referencing table ⟶ referenced table

For example:

EMP ⟶ DEPT

The arrow means that there is a foreign key in the table from which the arrow emerges that refers to the primary key of the table to which the arrow points. *Note:* In some circumstances it might prove desirable to label the arrow with the name of the relevant foreign key, but we shall not bother to show such labels in our examples in this paper.

   Aside: Referential arrows such as those in the diagrams above are basically nothing more than an extended form of the conventional functional dependency arrow (see, e.g., reference [10]). They represent many-to-one relationships. *End of aside.*

■   As we shall see later, primary keys in base tables are not permitted to accept nulls. In the example, therefore, neither DEPT.DEPT# nor EMP.EMP# can accept nulls.

■   By contrast, foreign keys (at least, some foreign keys), unlike primary keys, must generally be permitted to accept nulls. In the example, the department number for employee E5 is null (meaning, e.g., that the department for employee E5 is unknown, or perhaps that employee E5 simply does not have a department).

■   Note that, although of course every (nonnull) value of the foreign key EMP.DEPT# is required to appear as a value of the corresponding primary key DEPT.DEPT#, the converse is not a requirement—that is, the primary key corresponding to some given foreign key might contain a value that currently does not appear as a value of that foreign key. In the example, the department number D3 appears in table DEPT but not in table EMP (department D3 currently has no employees).

   From this point on, choosing a set of sample values to illustrate the various points arising will generally be left as an exercise for the reader.

```
2.  COURSE    ( COURSE#, ... )
              PRIMARY KEY ( COURSE# )
```

```
OFFERING ( COURSE#, OFF#, ... )
        PRIMARY KEY ( COURSE#, OFF# )
        FOREIGN KEY ( COURSE# ) REFERENCES COURSE

ENROLLEE ( COURSE#, OFF#, EMP#, ... )
        PRIMARY KEY ( COURSE#, OFF#, EMP# )
        FOREIGN KEY ( COURSE#, OFF# ) REFERENCES OFFERING
```

Example 2—courses, offerings, and "enrollees," where the "enrollee" table represents enrollments of employees (EMP#) in offerings (OFF#) of courses (COURSE#)—illustrates a number of additional points:

- Keys (both primary and foreign) can be composite (i.e., multiple-column). Note that a foreign key will be composite if and only if the primary key it matches is composite also.

- In addition to the foreign keys shown, column ENROLLEE. COURSE# can also be regarded as a foreign key, referencing table COURSE. This point will be discussed further in Part II of this paper (Section 15).

- It is not necessarily the case that every component of a composite key (either primary or foreign) is itself a foreign key. Specifically, columns OFFERING.OFF#, ENROLLEE.OFF#, and ENROLLEE.EMP# in the example are not foreign keys.

- Table OFFERING illustrates the point that the same table can be both a referenced (or target) table and a referencing table: There is a referential constraint *to* table OFFERING from table ENROLLEE, and a referential constraint *from* table OFFERING to table COURSE, as the following diagram indicates:

```
ENROLLEE ──────▶ OFFERING ──────▶ COURSE
```

It is convenient to introduce the term "referential path." Let tables Tn, T(n−1), . . . , T2, T1 be such that there is a referential constraint from table Tn to table T(n−1), a referential constraint from table T(n−1) to table T(n−2), . . . , and a referential constraint from table T2 to table T1:

```
Tn ──────▶ T(n-1) ──────▶ T(n-2) ──────▶ ... ──────▶ T2 ──────▶ T1
```

Then the chain of arrows from Tn to T1 represents a referential path from Tn to T1. More precisely: There is *a referential path from Tn to T1* if and only if (a) Tn references T1 directly, or (b) Tn references some T(n−1) such that there is a referential path from T(n−1) to T1. In the example, there are referential paths from ENROLLEE to OFFERING, from OFFERING to COURSE, and from ENROLLEE to COURSE.

In fact, there are *two distinct* referential paths from ENROLLEE to COURSE—one direct, and one via OFFERING:

ENROLLEE ──→ OFFERING ──→ COURSE

As already stated, this point will be discussed further in Part II of this paper (Section 15).

```
3. S    ( S#, SNAME, STATUS, CITY )
        PRIMARY KEY ( S# )

   P    ( P#, PNAME, COLOR, WEIGHT, CITY )
        PRIMARY KEY ( P# )

   SP   ( S#, P#, QTY )
        PRIMARY KEY ( S#, P# )
        FOREIGN KEY ( S# ) REFERENCES S
        FOREIGN KEY ( P# ) REFERENCES P
```

This is the familiar suppliers-and-parts example, described in detail in reference [15] and elsewhere. It illustrates the point that a single table—table SP in the example—can include multiple distinct foreign keys:

S ◄── SP ──► P

It also so happens in the example that the combination of the two foreign keys serves as the primary key of the containing table (we are assuming that there cannot be multiple shipments—i.e., SP rows—for a given supplier and a given part). However, as we have already seen from the first two examples above, it is not necessarily the case that every component of a composite primary key is a foreign key, nor is it necessarily the case that every foreign key is a component of a composite primary key.

```
4. EMP   ( EMP#, ..., SALARY, ..., MGR_EMP#, ... )
         PRIMARY KEY ( EMP# )
         FOREIGN KEY ( MGR_EMP# ) REFERENCES EMP
```

Here the value of MGR_EMP# (in a given EMP row) represents the employee number of the employee represented by the value of EMP# (in that row). This example illustrates the point that the referenced table and the referencing table are *not necessarily distinct;* i.e., a foreign key can reference the primary key of its own containing table. Such a table is sometimes called a *self-referencing table,* because there is a (very short) referential path from the table to itself.

EMP

Note that it is likely in this example that the foreign key MGR_EMP# would have "nulls allowed," because at least one employee, namely the president of the company, has no manager (unless, of course, the president acts as his or her own manager). Note too that if the president's manager *is* given as null, then that null would conceptually be of the "value does not exist" variety, not the "value unknown" variety.

```
5. DEPT   ( DEPT#, ..., MGR_EMP#, ... )
          PRIMARY KEY ( DEPT# )
          FOREIGN KEY ( MGR_EMP# ) REFERENCES EMP

   EMP    ( EMP#, ..., DEPT#, ... )
          PRIMARY KEY ( EMP# )
          FOREIGN KEY ( DEPT# ) REFERENCES DEPT
```

A self-referencing table such as EMP in Example 4 is actually just a special case of a more general situation, namely a situation in which there is a *cycle* of referential constraints. Such a cycle arises whenever there is a referential path from some table to itself. The present example shows a cycle involving two tables: Table EMP includes a foreign key (DEPT#) referencing table DEPT, and table DEPT includes a foreign key (MGR_EMP#) referencing table EMP. Note, therefore, that there is thus a referential path from each table to itself (via the other table):

$$EMP \quad \overset{\longrightarrow}{\underset{\longleftarrow}{}} \quad DEPT$$

In general, of course, cycles can involve any number of tables (i.e., be of any length N, where N is greater than or equal to one, and N = 1 is the self-referencing case). The general picture of a cycle is thus as follows:

$$Tn \longrightarrow T(n-1) \longrightarrow T(n-2) \longrightarrow \ldots \longrightarrow T2 \longrightarrow T1 \longrightarrow Tn$$

As suggested in the discussion of the self-referencing case (Example 4 above), it is likely that at least one foreign key in a cycle will have "nulls allowed"—likely, but not absolutely necessary, if integrity checking is deferred. See Section 8, later (paragraph 8.5).

```
6. P     ( P#, ... )
         PRIMARY KEY ( P# )

   PP    ( MAJOR_P#, MINOR_P#, QTY, ... )
         PRIMARY KEY ( MAJOR_P#, MINOR_P# )
         FOREIGN KEY ( MAJOR_P# ) REFERENCES P
         FOREIGN KEY ( MINOR_P# ) REFERENCES P
```

This is the well-known "bill-of-materials" example: Table P represents a master list of parts, and table PP shows which parts (MAJOR_P#) contain which other parts (MINOR_P#) as components. It is usual to assume that each part can contain many components and that each part can be a component of many parts, so that there is a many-to-many relationship between parts and parts; hence the need for a separate table (PP) to represent that relationship. The example illustrates the point that a single table can include multiple foreign keys, all of them referencing the same target table.

$$PP \rightrightarrows P$$

In an example like this one, incidentally, there are again multiple referential paths (all of them very short) from the referencing table to the target table. Again, the "multiple referential paths" problem will be discussed in Part II of this paper (Section 15). *Note:* The situation illustrated by this example is sometimes confused (but should not be) with that illustrated by the previous example (the referential cycle example). There is no cycle here.

```
7. EMP     ( EMP#, ..., JOB, ... )
           PRIMARY KEY ( EMP# )

   PGMR    ( EMP#, ..., LANG, ... )
           PRIMARY KEY ( EMP# )
           FOREIGN KEY ( EMP# ) REFERENCES EMP
```

This final example illustrates the point that a foreign key can in fact also be the primary key of its containing table. Table EMP lists all employees, and table PGMR lists just those employees that are programmers. Thus, every employee appearing in PGMR must also appear in EMP (but of course the converse is not true). The primary key of table PGMR is also a foreign key, referring to the primary key of table EMP. Note that the two tables can be regarded as representing, respectively, an entity supertype (employees) and an entity subtype (programmers). In fact, the example is typical of the way entity supertypes and subtypes would be represented in a relational database [22,27].

> *Aside:* Note that there is another integrity constraint that also needs to be maintained in this example—namely, the constraint that a given employee must be represented in table PGMR if and only if the value of EMP.JOB for that employee is "Programmer." This constraint is not a *referential* constraint, however. See reference [26] for a discussion of integrity constraints in general. *End of aside.*

In sum, the foregoing examples illustrate the general point that *absolutely any column* can be a foreign key. Furthermore, of course, any column can *become* a foreign key as the database evolves over time.

Let us now proceed to examine some of Codd's writings on this subject. The titles of the next four sections are taken from Codd's own papers. Quotations in those sections are taken from the corresponding papers (I have numbered the quotations for ease of subsequent reference). *Note:* I hope it goes without saying that the next four sections are not intended as any kind of attack on Codd's ideas; rather, the intent is merely to attempt some clarification of those ideas, where such clarification seems to me to be necessary or desirable.

3. A RELATIONAL MODEL OF DATA FOR LARGE SHARED DATA BANKS [9]

[Quote 3.1] "We shall call a domain (or domain combination) of relation R a *foreign key* if it is not the primary key of R but its elements are values of the primary key of some relation S (the possibility that S and R are identical is not excluded)".*

Comments:

3.1 "Domain" here should really be "attribute"—but the term "attribute" was not used at all in reference [9].

3.2 Note that domain (or rather, attribute) combinations are explicitly permitted in the definition—i.e., foreign keys are explicitly permitted to be composite.

3.3 The possibility that a primary key might additionally be a foreign key should not be excluded (see Example 7 in the previous section).

3.4 Note that the definition requires a *single* corresponding target relation S. I am in sympathy with this requirement (see Sections 4 and 7 below, also Section 20 in Part II of the paper).

3.5 The phrase "its elements" should read "its *nonnull* elements"—but nulls also were not mentioned at all in reference [9].

4. EXTENDING THE DATABASE RELATIONAL MODEL TO CAPTURE MORE MEANING [11]

[Quote 4.1] "For a given database, those domains upon which the simple (i.e., single-attribute) primary keys are defined are called the *primary domains* of that database . . .

"[*Entity integrity*] No primary key value of a base relation is allowed to be null or to have a null component.

"[*Referential integrity*] Suppose an attribute A of a compound (i.e., multiattribute) primary key of a relation R is defined on a primary domain D. Then, at all times, for each value v of A in R there must exist a base

---

*A definition virtually identical to this one (except that it talked in terms of attributes instead of domains—see comment 3.1 below) was included in the second edition of my book *An Introduction to Database Systems: Volume I* (Addison-Wesley, 1977). The first edition, I regret to say, did not discuss foreign keys at all.

relation (say S) with a simple primary key (say B) such that v occurs as a value of B in S."*

Comments:

4.1 The primary keys referred to in the definition of primary domain are presumably intended to be primary keys of *base relations*.

4.2 Note that the term "foreign key" is not mentioned.

4.3 Attribute B should be defined on domain D.

4.4 Foreign keys should not be restricted to being components of compound primary keys. In fact, *any* attribute, simple or compound (i.e., composite), should be allowed to act as a foreign key. See Section 2 above for several examples.

4.5 The phrase "for each value v" should read "for each *nonnull* value v."

4.6 The definition does not actually require foreign keys to be simple (i.e., single-attribute), but I believe that this was Codd's intention (his definition of referential integrity refers only to single-attribute primary keys as targets). However, the justification for this change from the original definition in reference [9] is not clear.

4.7 I do not believe that *every* attribute defined on a primary domain should be regarded as a foreign key. Consider the following example:

```
DOMAINS

    DATE
    EMP#
    etc

RELATIONS

    HOLIDAYS   ( DATE      DOMAIN ( DATE ) ,
               ..................   )
          PRIMARY KEY ( DATE )

    EMPLOYEES ( EMP#       DOMAIN ( EMP# ) ,
              HIREDATE  DOMAIN ( DATE ) ,
              ..................   )
          PRIMARY KEY ( EMP# )
```

DATE here is a primary domain, but HIREDATE is not a foreign key: It is not the case that every nonnull value of HIREDATE appears as a value of

---

*Definitions similar to these (except that they addressed the criticisms in comments 4.2, 4.3, 4.4, and 4.5) were included in the third edition of my book *An Introduction to Database Systems: Volume I* (Addison-Wesley, 1981). The same definitions were repeated, but then considerably revised and elaborated, in my paper "Referential Integrity" (reference [17]), and the proposals of that paper were subsequently incorporated into the fourth edition of the book (reference [15]). In particular, reference [17] was the paper that first introduced the foreign key rules discussed in Section 8 of the present paper.

HOLIDAYS.DATE. Nor does it appear as a value of the primary key of any other relation.

[Codd subsequently agreed to this position, using essentially the same example [14]. See quotes 6.6 and 6.10, later.]

4.8 The definition no longer requires a *single* target relation, but the justification for this change from the original definition is not clear, and neither are the implications of there being more than one such target. Suppose a given foreign key R.A corresponds to multiple target relations S1, S2, . . . , Sn. For a given nonnull value v of R.A, is a corresponding row required to exist in

1. exactly one of S1, S2, . . . , Sn?
2. every one of S1, S2, . . . , Sn?
3. at least one of S1, S2, . . . , Sn?

Whichever of 1., 2., or 3. is the answer, what is the justification? Note too that each of 1., 2., and 3. is likely to lead to some rather complex insert–update–delete rules (see Section 8 of this paper). To pursue the point a little further:

1. Case 1 I can just about see a justification for, though it is tempting to suggest that the database design is not very good. It looks as if there should be a single master relation S, representing an entity supertype (with common descriptive information); S1, S2, . . . , Sn would represent subtypes of that supertype; and the referential constraint should be from relation R to relation S. (There would also be constraints from each of S1, S2, . . . , Sn to S.)
2. Case 2 again looks as if there should be a single master relation S, with a referential constraint from R to S and a one-to-one (primary-key-to-primary-key) constraint from each of S1, S2, . . . , Sn to S. (There would also be primary-key-to-primary-key constraints between every one of S1, S2, . . . , Sn and every other.)
3. I cannot see a good argument for Case 3 at all. In addition, it looks as if it might be difficult to implement efficiently.

In my original paper on referential integrity [17] I did permit all three cases, but I now feel the proposals of that paper were too general and have since publicly retracted (in a revised version of the paper [18]). Note also that Codd himself departs from the "multiple-target" suggestion later in his own paper: In his proposals for the extended version of the relational model called RM/T [11], he requires all foreign keys to refer specifically to what he calls an *E-relation,* of which there is exactly one for each entity type represented in the database.

Aside: The idea of allowing multiple targets for a given foreign key reminds me a little of the idea of allowing multiple primary keys for a given relation, which the relational model expressly prohibits [14,19]. *End of aside.*

I will return to this topic in Part II of this paper (Section 20).

5. REFERENTIAL INTEGRITY
(one section in reference [13])

In this paper, Codd argues that referential integrity should apply to simple foreign keys only. That is, he apparently allows composite foreign keys, but does not require referential integrity to apply to them (contrary to the original definition of foreign key—see comments 3.2 and 4.6, earlier). This position seems to me to introduce unnecessary confusion. What is the point of saying that something is a foreign key if it is not subject to the referential integrity requirement? Let us examine Codd's argument.

He begins by giving a definition of referential integrity which he says corresponds closely to that in his RM/T paper [11]:

[Quote 5.1] "Let D be a domain from which one or more single-attribute primary keys draw their values. Let K be a foreign key which draws its values from domain D. Every unmarked (i.e., nonnull) value which occurs in K must also exist in the database as a value of the primary key of some base relation."

Comments:

5.1 I don't really understand this definition. It is defining referential integrity in terms of foreign keys; but what is a foreign key? I think it has to be defined in terms of referential integrity! In other words, foreign keys are the mechanism in terms of which referential integrity is defined, and by means of which it is enforced. It is true that the original definition of foreign key [9] did not mention referential integrity by name, and likewise the original definition of referential integrity [11] did not mention foreign keys by name either, but each definition certainly involved the other *concept.* Thus, I regard the two concepts as being inextricably interwoven.

5.2 Most of the comments from Section 4 (in fact, all except 4.2, 4.4, and 4.5) still apply to this revised definition.

But to continue:

Codd goes on to give an example of two databases, both involving a relation R3 with a composite primary key (S#,P#) and another relation R4 with a composite attribute (S#,P#):

```
R3   ( S#, P#, ... )
     PRIMARY KEY ( S#, P# )

R4   ( ..., S#, P#, ... )
```

In one of the two databases, X say, values of R4.(S#,P#) are required to match values of the primary key of R3, whereas in the other database Y they are not.

- In database Y, therefore, referential integrity clearly does not apply to attribute R4.(S#,P#), and it seems to me that the attribute should therefore not be regarded as a foreign key. However, Codd does seem to regard it as a foreign key, but one to which referential integrity does not apply (?).

- What about database X? Here Codd argues as follows:
    [Quote 5.2] "There are two ways in which this example . . . could be handled:
    "1. Make the referential integrity rule applicable to all PK-FK pairs of keys, whether simple or compound . . ."
    [i.e., treat attribute R4.(S#,P#) as a foreign key in database X but not in database Y]
    "2. Make the referential integrity rule applicable to simple PK-FK pairs of keys only, and require the [database administrator] to impose a referential constraint on just those compound PK-FK pairs of keys for which the constraint [happens to apply] by specifying a user-defined integrity constraint . . .
    [i.e., treat attribute R4.(S#,P#) as a foreign key in both cases but specify that referential integrity applies only in the case of database X]
    "Method 2 complies with [the definition of referential integrity in the RM/T paper] and with [the earlier] definition of the foreign key concept. In addition, Method 2 is cleaner than Method 1, because it separates the foreign key concept from the more complicated referential integrity concept. Thus Method 2 is adopted."
    [Note, however, that Codd later reversed his position on this point. See quote 6.11, later.]

Comments:
    5.3 "Method 2 complies with [the original, i.e., RM/T, definition] of referential integrity. . . ." Well, maybe it does; but Method 1 complies more closely with the original definition of foreign key. As already indicated, I think the original definition of referential integrity was deficient in a number of respects anyway. In any case, it is surely more important to come up with a set of rules that are both definitive and truly useful rather than just to preserve earlier definitions for their own sake.
    5.4 I do not see why Method 2 is cleaner than Method 1. What *exactly* is the distinction between the foreign key concept and the referential integrity concept? What *use* are foreign keys without referential integrity?

How do you *define* foreign keys without mentioning referential integrity (the concept, at least, if not the term)?

Codd then continues:

[Quote 5.3] "Referential integrity should be implemented as far as possible as a special case of user-defined integrity . . . Further, it should be remembered that referential integrity is a particular application of a subset constraint . . . Subset constraints may, however, apply between other pairs of attributes also (e.g., nonkeys and keys that are nonsimple)."

Comments:

5.5 "Referential integrity should be implemented as far as possible as a special case of user-defined integrity. . . ." I am not quite sure what this statement means. I certainly feel that special treatment is desirable, in both syntax and implementation, for referential constraints. Of course, I agree that referential constraints are "user-defined," in the sense that they do have to be defined, either implicitly or explicitly, by some authorized user (probably by the database administrator).

> [But then surely *all* integrity constraints have to be defined by "some authorized user"; the term "user-defined integrity" does not quite seem to capture the concept that Codd is aiming at in his comment. See reference [26] for further discussion of this point. However, to continue:]

In particular, referential constraints, like all constraints, do require some suitably authorized user to specify the "violation response" (i.e., the action to be taken if the constraint is violated [26]). But in the case of referential constraints specifically, certain extremely common responses (e.g., "cascade delete") can be and have been identified (see Section 8 of the present paper). In the case of referential constraints, therefore, special-casing both the constraints per se and those common responses seems desirable, for reasons of both usability and efficiency. See Part II of this paper (Section 14) for further discussion of this point.

5.6 ". . . referential integrity is a particular application of a subset constraint. . . ." If a subset constraint applies between attributes B and A (meaning that every value of B must be a value of A), then:

(a) If in addition values of A are unique, then I believe A should be the primary key of its containing relation (for otherwise we are back in the "multiple primary key" situation once again [14,19])—in which case the subset constraint is in fact a referential constraint once more;

(b) If on the other hand values of A are not unique, then the situation is quite different (e.g., the insert–update–delete rules are likely to be quite different), and the relevance of the point to a discussion of foreign keys and referential integrity is not clear.

6. DOMAINS, KEYS, AND REFERENTIAL INTEGRITY IN RELATIONAL DATABASES [14]

Note: The "quotes" in this section are not given verbatim but instead have been rephrased slightly for copyright reasons.

[Quote 6.1] "If D is a domain on which some primary key K is defined, it is often useful to refer to D as a *primary domain* . . . If K is composite, then D is a composite primary domain."

Comments:
   6.1 As in Section 4 (see comment 4.1), "primary key" here should read "primary key of a base relation." Note that Codd now permits *composite* primary domains (contrast his definition in reference [11], discussed in Section 4 above). Actually the utility of the primary domain concept is not clear, given the remarks under quote 6.10 below.

   [Quote 6.2] "Note that (a) not every component of a composite primary domain is itself a primary domain; (b) not every component of a composite primary key is itself a primary key."

Comments:
   6.2 I agree that assertion (a) here is true; see Example 2 in Section 2 above (courses, offerings, and enrollees) for an example. I also agree that assertion (b) is true if (as I presume Codd intended) the phrase "itself a primary key" is replaced by "a foreign key" (again, see Example 2 in Section 2).

   [Quote 6.3] "A *foreign key* is a column (possibly composite) of some relation S, whose domain D is that of a primary key in the database, and each of whose unmarked (i.e., nonmissing) values is required at all times to equal the value of the primary key (with domain D) of at least one relation R. R and S are not necessarily distinct."

Comments:
   6.3 Why not replace "whose domain D is that of a primary key in the database" by "defined on some primary domain D"? (Of course, this question assumes that we agree to retain the primary domain concept in the first place—again, see quote 6.10 below.) Also, "the value of the primary key (with domain D) of at least one relation" should be replaced by "the value of the primary key (with domain D) *of some row* of at least one relation." And R, at least, if not S as well, should be a *base* relation.

   [Quote 6.4] "Whether or not a given foreign key is permitted to accept missing values depends on a decision that is normally made by the database administrator. Note, however, that if a composite foreign key includes the primary key of its containing relation as a component, then that component cannot be permitted to accept missing values."

Comments:

6.4 Replace "the primary key" by "a component of the primary key." Also, I tend to believe—contrary to what Codd apparently believes, judging by the passage quoted, though in fact his position on the point is not totally clear from reference [14]—that composite foreign keys should have either "nulls allowed" for all components or "nulls not allowed" for all components; furthermore, if nulls are allowed, I also believe that each individual foreign key *value* should be either entirely null or entirely nonnull. These points are elaborated in Part II of this paper (Section 17).

[Quote 6.5] "A given foreign key can correspond to any number of primary keys (N, say, where N is greater than or equal to one, and one is the normal case). If N > 1, then each individual value of the foreign key is *required* to equal at least one value of the N primary keys in question, but is *permitted* to equal any number of them."

Comments:

6.5 See comment 4.8 earlier, also Part II of this paper (Section 20).

[Quote 6.6] "The DBMS should not be designed to deduce foreign keys from primary keys and their domains, unless it also allows the database administrator to override its deductions where necessary."

Comments:

6.6 I agree, but note that this is a change from Codd's original position as implied by his definition of referential integrity in reference [11] (quote 4.1).

[Quote 6.7] "*Referential integrity:* Let D be a primary domain (possibly composite), and let K be a foreign key defined on D. Every unmarked (i.e., nonmissing) value of K must be equal to some value of the primary key (also defined on D) of some base relation."

Comments:

6.7 Compare the definition of foreign key in this same paper of Codd's (see quote 6.3 above). Again, foreign keys and referential integrity seem to be defined in terms of one another.

[Quote 6.8] "Full support for foreign keys includes full support for referential integrity. However, it is useful to distinguish between the two concepts, because referential integrity is just one of the five forms of integrity in a relational system."

Comments:

6.8 It is possible, and may be useful, to keep the two concepts separate—a foreign key is a kind of object, referential integrity is a kind of integrity—so long as the interdependence of the two is recognized. But I do not feel that the quoted justification for the separation (". . . referential integrity is just one of the five forms of integrity . . .") has much relevance to the point at issue. (Moreover, I do not think the "five forms of integrity" classification scheme is a particularly good one, but further discussion of this particular point would be out of place here. See reference [26].)

[Quote 6.9] "A DBMS could support primary and foreign key declarations but omit support for referential integrity (i.e., it could provide *partial* foreign key support)."

Comments:

6.9 I would not regard such a DBMS as providing any real support for foreign keys at all! After all, such a simple level of "support" could be achieved via the system's ordinary comment mechanism. What would be the point of supporting the declaration of foreign keys but not enforcing the corresponding constraints?

> *Aside:* After the foregoing was first written, a product was in fact announced that did exactly this—i.e., it allowed foreign keys to be declared, but did not enforce the corresponding constraints! The stated intent was to enable users to prepare for some future release of the product in which the constraints *would* be enforced. But I stand by my original contention that such a facility does not constitute true foreign key *support* in any significant sense. *End of aside.*

[Quote 6.10] "A column could be defined on a primary domain and yet be neither a primary key nor a foreign key."

Comments:

6.10 This statement is true. This is why I am not convinced that the primary domain concept is particularly useful (though I have no deep objection to it).

[Quote 6.11; Codd first repeats the example of the two databases X and Y—see Section 5, earlier—and then continues:] "Method 2 is undesirable, in that it treats simple and composite keys differently. The relational model therefore now supports Method 1. This represents a change in my position with respect to one paragraph of reference [11] and one of reference [13]."

Comments:

6.11 See comments 5.3 and 5.4, earlier.

[Quote 6.12] "Primary and foreign keys serve as surrogates for entities in the real world."

Comments:

6.12 I completely agree! This is one reason why I believe that keys, both primary and foreign, should ALWAYS BE TREATED AS IF THEY WERE INDIVISIBLE (except possibly for retrieval purposes), even if they are in fact composite. In particular, this is why I believe that a foreign key value should never be permitted to be partly null and partly nonnull. See Part II of this paper (Section 19) for further discussion.

7. A PROPOSAL

My own preferred definitions are as follows.

- *Primary key*

In order to define the primary key concept precisely, it is first necessary to define a more primitive notion, namely "candidate key." Attribute CK (possibly composite) of relation R is a *candidate key* for R if and only if it satisfies the following two time-independent properties:

1. *Uniqueness:* At any given time, no two rows of R have the same value for CK.
2. *Minimality:* If CK is composite, no component of CK can be eliminated without destroying the uniqueness property.

From the set of candidate keys for a given relation, exactly one is chosen as the *primary* key for that relation; the remainder, if any, are called *alternate* keys [15]. An alternate key is thus a candidate key that is not the primary key.

A couple of asides:

- First, note that in practice it is the *primary* key that is really the important one; candidate keys and alternate keys are merely concepts that necessarily arise during the process of defining the more important concept "primary key." (Though alternate keys can occasionally be significant also. See reference [27] for further discussion of this point.)
- Second, note that the rationale by which the primary key is chosen, in

cases where there is a choice, is outside the scope of the relational model per se. In practice the choice is usually straightforward.

End of asides.

■   *Foreign key*

Attribute FK (possibly composite) of base relation R2 is a *foreign key* if and only if it satisfies the following two time independent properties:

1. Each value of FK is either wholly null or wholly nonnull.
2. There exists a base relation R1 with primary key PK such that each nonnull value of FK is identical to the value of PK in some row of R1.

Relations R1 and R2 are known as the referenced (or target) relation and the referencing relation, respectively. They are not necessarily distinct.

Discussion:

7.1 My definition of primary key is intended to be equivalent to Codd's [14]. The only point that seems to need any elaboration here is the requirement that candidate keys (and hence primary keys) satisfy the *minimality* property. The purpose of that requirement is merely to ensure that, for example, in the case of the suppliers-and-parts database (Example 3 in Section 2), the composite attribute S.(S#,CITY) is not considered as a candidate key (because CITY is irrelevant for unique identification purposes). *Note:* As Codd points out in reference [14], the fact that a given candidate key CK1 satisfies the minimality requirement does not mean that another candidate key CK2 cannot be found that involves fewer components (i.e., simple attributes); it is entirely possible, for example, that CK1 involves three simple attributes and CK2 only two.*

7.2 Attributes R1.PK and R2.FK in the definition of foreign key should be defined on the same domain. (Actually, this point is implied by the definition of domain [14,24]; I deliberately do not call it out explicitly in my definition, however, because a system can provide a useful level of support for foreign keys and referential integrity without necessarily having to support domains as well. I do agree that *full* support for foreign keys would require support for domains as well.)

7.3 As the definitions indicate, both primary and foreign keys are allowed to be composite. (As pointed out in Section 2, a foreign key will be

---

*We remark that one reason for the minimality requirement is the following: If relation R were to include a foreign key for which the corresponding primary key did not satisfy the requirement, then relation R would probably not be in third normal form [10].

composite if and only if its matching primary key is composite. This fact is implied by the fact that the foreign key and its matching primary key must be defined on the same domain—the domain being composite in the case under consideration—but is probably worth spelling out explicitly. See paragraph 7.2 above.) However, I do believe, as suggested earlier in this paper, that composite keys need to be treated with care. Once again, see Part II of this paper for further discussion (Sections 16–19).

7.4 I agree with Codd that nulls should not be allowed for primary keys (at least in base tables). Codd refers to this constraint as "the entity integrity rule" (see Section 4). For completeness, I will state the rule again here:

- The *entity integrity* rule states that no attribute that participates in the primary key of a base relation is allowed to accept nulls.

See Part II of this paper (Section 16) for further discussion.

7.5 In contrast to point 7.4 above, I believe that both types of null (or "mark" [12])—namely, "value unknown" and "property does not apply"—should be legal for foreign keys, in general. In fact, I suspect that the "property does not apply" type is likely to be needed more often than the "value unknown" type in this context.*

7.6 The expression "wholly null or wholly nonnull" in the definition of foreign key is explicitly intended to exclude the possibility that a multiattribute foreign key value might have some components null and others nonnull (because—as I have suggested several times already—I believe this latter possibility leads to undesirable and unnecessary complexity). Once again, see Part II of this paper for further discussion (Section 17).

7.7 I do not find the concept of "primary domains" to be particularly useful (in this context; it might be useful in other contexts, such as the context of database design). I have therefore excluded it from my proposed definitions.

7.8 Note that the foreign key definition is framed explicitly in terms of *base* relations. Extensions to handle derived relations (views, snapshots, etc.) can be added at a later time if desired. *Note:* The question of foreign keys in views in particular is deliberately excluded from this paper. The topic is interesting, and important for view updating purposes [21], but it is not directly relevant to referential integrity per se.

7.9 I deliberately require there to be a single target relation for each foreign key. I feel that this is a justifiable simplification at this stage of development. If someone comes along with a genuine requirement for one

---

*Other types of null might also be required (in this context as well as others). See Chapter 8.

of the three cases discussed under 4.8 earlier, then there are two ways we can go:

1. Extend the definition of foreign key accordingly;
2. Leave the definition of foreign key alone and insist that the situation be treated as an instance of a "general" integrity constraint (i.e., a constraint that is handled by means of a general integrity language such as that described in reference [26], instead of by means of special-case syntax).

Method 2 complies with my preferred definition of foreign key, it is simpler, it has the virtue of encouraging clean database designs, and it does not preclude the implementation of Method 1 at a later time. Method 1 can be implemented subsequently if desired (when all the ramifications are thoroughly understood); note too that if Method 1 does subsequently prove desirable, it will be a compatible extension—existing programs and databases will not be invalidated. I therefore vote for Method 2.*

7.10 Finally, I do not propose a definition for referential integrity that is separate from the concept of foreign key. I do not find such a separation either useful or desirable. However, both terms need to be explained, since both appear in the existing literature. I therefore offer the following definition:

- The *referential integrity rule* states that the database must not contain any unmatched foreign key values (where an unmatched foreign key value is a nonnull foreign key value for which there does not exist a matching value of the primary key in the relevant target relation).

8. FOREIGN KEY RULES

Reference [17] extended the basic idea of referential integrity by introducing a set of *foreign key rules,* which specified what the DBMS should do if a user attempted to perform an update that (if just blindly executed) would violate some referential constraint. The general intent of the rules was to enable the DBMS to maintain the integrity of the data by either (a) rejecting such an attempted update, or (b) accepting it but performing some appropriate compensating update on some other part of the database. The following rules were identified:

---

*This preference is in accordance with "The Principle of Cautious Design," which is introduced and discussed in Part II of this paper (Section 11).

- A nulls rule (ALLOWED or NOT ALLOWED)
- A delete rule (RESTRICTED or CASCADES or NULLIFIES)
- An update rule (RESTRICTED or CASCADES or NULLIFIES)

The following explanation of these rules is based on that given in reference [15], which uses the standard suppliers-and-parts database (Example 3 in Section 2) as a basis for its discussions and explanations.

First, note that the referential integrity rule (see the end of Section 7 above) is framed purely in terms of database *states*. Any state of the database that does not satisfy the rule is by definition incorrect; but how exactly are such incorrect states to be avoided? The rule itself does not say.

One possibility, of course, is that the system could simply reject any operation that, if executed, would result in an illegal state. In many cases, however, a preferable alternative would be for the system to accept the operation but to perform certain additional compensating operations (if necessary) in order to guarantee that the overall result is still a legal state. For example, if the user asks to delete supplier S1 from relation S, it should be possible to get the system to delete the shipments for supplier S1 from relation SP as well, without any further action on the part of the user (assuming that such a "cascade delete" effect is what is wanted).

It follows that, for any given database, it should be possible for the user (in this context, probably the *database designer* [22]) to specify which operations should be rejected and which accepted, and, for those that are accepted, what compensating operations (if any) should be performed by the system. For each foreign key, therefore, the database designer needs to answer three questions, as follows:

1. Can that foreign key accept nulls? For example, does it make sense for a shipment to exist for which the supplier is unknown? The answer in this case is, "Probably not." But in some other case the answer might well be different. For example, it might well be possible in the case of the departments-and-employees database for some employee to be currently assigned to no department at all (see Example 1 in Section 2 of this paper).

2. What should happen on an attempt to delete the target of a foreign key reference?—for example, an attempt to delete a supplier for which there exists at least one matching shipment? For definiteness let us consider this case explicitly. In general there are at least three possibilities:

   - RESTRICTED — The delete operation is "restricted" to the case where there are no such matching shipments (it is rejected otherwise)

- CASCADES — The delete operation "cascades" to delete those matching shipments also

- NULLIFIES — The foreign key is set to null in all such matching shipments and the supplier is then deleted (of course, this case could not apply if the foreign key cannot accept nulls in the first place)

3. What should happen on an attempt to update the primary key of the target of a foreign key reference?—for example, an attempt to update the supplier number for a supplier for which there exists at least one matching shipment? For definiteness, again, let us consider this case explicitly. In general there are at least the same three possibilities as for DELETE:

- RESTRICTED — The update operation is "restricted" to the case where there are no such matching shipments (it is rejected otherwise)

- CASCADES — The update operation "cascades" to update the foreign key in those matching shipments also

- NULLIFIES — The foreign key is set to null in all such matching shipments and the supplier is then updated (of course, this case could not apply if the foreign key cannot accept nulls in the first place)

For each foreign key in the design, therefore, the database designer should specify, not only the attribute or attribute combination constituting that foreign key and the target relation referenced by that foreign key, but also the answers to the foregoing three questions (i.e., the three rules that apply to that foreign key). Hence the following syntax proposal for a FOREIGN KEY clause (part of a base table definition):

```
FOREIGN KEY ( foreign-key ) REFERENCES target
        NULLS [ NOT ] ALLOWED
        DELETE OF target effect
        UPDATE OF target-primary-key effect
```

where "effect" is RESTRICTED or CASCADES or NULLIFIES.

The foregoing was originally written in 1981 or thereabouts. Some additional comments are appropriate at this time:

8.1 First, it is important to understand that, from a logical point of view, database update operations are always atomic (all or nothing), even if "under the covers" they involve multiple row updates on multiple tables because of, e.g., a CASCADES delete rule (or even multiple such rules).

8.2 Note that there is no explicit "insert rule." Instead, INSERTs on the referencing table (also UPDATEs on the foreign key in the referencing table) are governed by the combination of (a) the nulls rule and (b) the basic referential integrity rule itself, i.e., the requirement that there be no nonnull unmatched foreign key values. In other words, taking suppliers-and-parts as a concrete example:

- An attempt to INSERT a shipment (SP) row will succeed only if (a) the supplier number in that row exists as a supplier number in table S (or is null, if nulls are allowed), *and* (b) the part number in that row exists as a part number in table P (or is null, if nulls are allowed).
- An attempt to UPDATE a shipment (SP) row will succeed only if (a) the supplier number in the updated row exists as a supplier number in table S (or is null, if nulls are allowed), *and* (b) the part number in the updated row exists as a part number in table P (or is null, if nulls are allowed).

Note carefully also that the foregoing applies to the *referencing* table, whereas the (explicit) delete and update rules apply to the *referenced* table. Thus, to talk about an "insert rule," as if that rule were somehow similar to the existing delete and update rules, is really a rather confusing thing to do. This fact provides additional justification for not including any explicit "insert rule" in the concrete syntax.

8.3 Let T2 and T1 be, respectively, a referencing table and the corresponding referenced table:

$$T2 \longrightarrow T1$$

Let the delete rule for this referential constraint be CASCADES. Thus, a DELETE on a given row of table T1 will imply a DELETE on certain rows of table T2 (in general). Now suppose that table T2 in turn is referenced by some other table T3:

$$T3 \longrightarrow T2 \longrightarrow T1$$

Then the effect of the implied DELETE on rows of T2 is defined to be exactly as if an attempt had been made to delete those rows directly; i.e., it depends on the delete rule specified for the referential constraint from T3 to T2. If that implied DELETE fails (because of the delete rule from T3 to T2 or for any other reason), then the entire operation fails and the database remains unchanged. And so on, recursively, to any number of levels.

8.4 The remarks of paragraph 8.3 above apply to the CASCADES update rule also, mutatis mutandis, if the foreign key in table T2 is part of (or has any columns in common with) the primary key of that table.

8.5 The fact that referential cycles are possible—i.e., table Tn references table $T(n-1)$, and table $T(n-1)$ in turn references table $T(n-2)$, ...,
and finally table T1 references table Tn again:

$$Tn \longrightarrow T(n-1) \longrightarrow T(n-2) \longrightarrow \cdots \longrightarrow T2 \longrightarrow T1 \longrightarrow Tn$$

—means that either:

(a) At least one foreign key in the cycle must have nulls allowed, or

(b) Some constraint checking cannot be done at the time of the individual
update but must instead be deferred to some later time, e.g., to end-
of-transaction (COMMIT time).

For if neither (a) nor (b) applies, there will be no way to insert the first row
into the database.

For reasons such as this (possibly for other reasons also, beyond the
scope of this paper), integrity constraints—i.e., integrity constraints in general, not just referential constraints—need to be divided into two categories,
immediate and *deferred*.

- ■ "Immediate" means that the constraint is (logically) checked as part of
the processing of every update statement that might violate it. Immediate constraints are required to be satisfied at statement boundaries. The
system is responsible for ensuring that this requirement is met.

- ■ "Deferred" means that such immediate checking is not performed,
but rather that the checking is deferred to some later time (e.g., to
COMMIT time, or perhaps even later).

Now, in the case of integrity constraints in general, additional research
is certainly needed to identify all of the requirements and implications of
deferred checking in full detail. In the case of referential constraints specifically, however, deferred checking simply means that if table T2 contains a
foreign key FK referring to the primary PK of table T1, then a nonnull
value can be introduced into column T2.FK (via an INSERT or UPDATE
on table T2) that does not currently exist as a value in column T1.PK. Of
course, it will still be an error if any such unmatched values still exist in
column T2.FK at the time the checking is performed, whenever that happens to be.

In order to cater for the foregoing, it is necessary to introduce an extension to the FOREIGN KEY clause to allow the checking time to be specified, e.g., as follows:

```
FOREIGN KEY ( foreign-key ) REFERENCES target
                           CHECK checking-time
          NULLS ...
          DELETE ...
          UPDATE ...
```

where "checking-time" is either IMMEDIATE or AT COMMIT. (Other possible "checking-times" might conceivably be introduced at some future point.)

From the rest of this paper (both parts), I will assume that all referential constraint checking is immediate, barring any explicit statement to the contrary—i.e., CHECK IMMEDIATE is the default.

8.6 The nulls rule (nulls allowed or not allowed) will require some refinement if the relational model and/or relational products are ever extended to incorporate multiple distinct kinds of null—for example, if "value unknown" is ever formally distinguished from "property does not apply." Of course, an analogous remark applies to every aspect of the model and/or products that involves nulls—e.g., the entity integrity rule, the outer join operation, etc.

8.7 The SQL standard committees are currently (1988) proposing a set of extensions to the SQL standard somewhat along the lines sketched above [5]. IBM also has recently incorporated some (but not all) of the proposed function into Version 2.1 of DB2 and Version 2.2 of SQL/DS [2,3,7,23]. But the standard and IBM versions both suffer from an unfortunate excess of complexity, owing in part to the fact that they are defined at too low a level of abstraction (essentially row-at-a-time instead of set-at-a-time). See Part II of this paper, Appendixes A and B, for a brief sketch of the two versions.

8.8 Of course, the RESTRICTED–CASCADES–NULLIFIES options for the foreign key delete and update rules do not exhaust the possibilities; they merely represent a set of cases that are very commonly required in practice. (NULLIFIES is perhaps less commonly required than the other two.) In principle, however, there could be an arbitrary number of possible responses to, e.g., an attempt to delete a particular supplier. For example:

- A conversation could be held with the end user
- Information could be written to some archive file
- The shipments for the supplier in question could be transferred to some other supplier

It will never be feasible to provide declarative syntax for all conceivable responses. In general, therefore, "effect" in the syntax above should include the possibility of invoking an installation-defined database procedure. It is unfortunate that this possibility was overlooked in reference [17].

Note: The proposals of reference [5] in fact do include at least one additional explicitly defined "effect," namely PENDANT, which can be informally characterized as "last one out turns off the light"—for example, deleting the last employee in a given department causes the department to be deleted also. However, the PENDANT rule seems to lead to a very great deal of complexity. My own feeling is that the whole area of additional possible "effects" stands in need of further research.

8.9 For reasons beyond the scope of this paper—see reference [32] for further discussion—it might be the case that some tables will not permit direct DELETE operations at all (i.e., DELETE NOT ALLOWED will be specified as part of the definition of the table in question). If T1 is such a table and T2.FK is a foreign key that references it, then any delete rule for that foreign key would be completely irrelevant and should not be specified at all.

8.10 In a similar vein—see Part II of this paper, Section 19, paragraph 19.7, for further discussion—some primary keys will not permit UPDATE operations at all (i.e., UPDATE NOT ALLOWED will be specified as part of the definition of the primary key in question). If T1.PK is such a primary key and T2.FK is a foreign key that references it, then any update rule for that foreign key would be completely irrelevant and should not be specified at all.

9. BENEFITS OF FOREIGN KEY SUPPORT

Let me conclude this first part of the paper by summarizing the benefits that accrue if the system does provide support for foreign keys (including, of course, support for an appropriate set of foreign key rules—cascade delete, etc.). Those benefits include:

- Integrity

  Integrity is the primary reason for providing foreign key support in the first place (of course).

- Productivity

  Foreign key support means that referential integrity requirements are specified declaratively, not procedurally. All of the standard productivity arguments apply.

- Usability

  Lack of support for foreign keys can make the system totally *un*usable for some users and/or in some situations.

- Availability

  Lack of support for foreign keys can mean that, in order to protect the integrity of the database, certain users (especially interactive, ad hoc query users) might have to be prevented from performing certain operations on certain data. In the case of suppliers-and-parts, for example, if the system does not support foreign keys, then it might be necessary to control very carefully who is allowed to delete rows from the suppliers table. In other words, lack of foreign key support can lead to a loss of data availability.

- Statement atomicity

  If the system does not enforce referential integrity, the user (that is, *some* user) has to do it. And user enforcement will frequently mean that what is logically a single, atomic update operation will have to involve several distinct user update operations on the database (consider cascade delete, for example). As a result, there may be no way for the user to guarantee that the overall update is atomic (short of rolling back the entire transaction if an error occurs, which is a trifle heavy-handed, to say the least). Certainly there is no way to provide such a guarantee in standard SQL, for example, nor in the currently proposed extensions to that standard [5]. If, on the other hand, the system does enforce referential integrity, then the system can also provide the necessary atomicity—atomicity, that is, at a finer level of granularity than just the overall transaction level.

- Support for join view updating

  Loosely speaking, a view V that is defined as the (natural) join of two tables T1 and T2 is updatable only if tables T1 and T2 are themselves updatable and the join in question is a primary-to-foreign-key (or primary-to-primary-key) join. (The details are beyond the scope of this paper; see reference [21] for further discussion.) Hence foreign key support is prerequisite to proper support for updates on join views. *Note: Primary* key support is prerequisite to proper support for updates on projection and restriction views. Of course, primary key support is also prerequisite to proper foreign key support.

- Performance

  System support for foreign keys should yield better performance for at least the following two reasons:

  1. The system is doing the work instead of the user. All of the usual optimization arguments apply. In particular, there will be fewer calls from the application program to the system, and hence fewer trips across the interface.

  2. Semantic optimization is possible. For example, given the SQL request

```
SELECT DISTINCT SP.P#
FROM    S, SP
WHERE   S.S# = SP.S# ;
```

(using the suppliers-and-parts database once again), the system can safely transform the request into

```
SELECT DISTINCT SP.P#
FROM    SP ;
```

(thereby eliminating a join entirely). However, the transformation is valid *only* because the join in question is a primary-to-foreign-key join; that is, it is valid *only* because table SP cannot contain any S# values that do not appear in table S. Thus the system can validly make the transformation *only* if it is aware of foreign keys.

This latter example is in fact an illustration of a more general point, namely as follows: *The more knowledge the system has, the more intelligently it can behave*—and "behaving more intelligently" can include giving better performance. (Of course, "knowledge" in this context means "knowledge of the data," and integrity constraints in general can constitute a major part of such knowledge. Thus, the foregoing remarks concerning potential for improved performance apply to integrity constraints in general, not just to referential constraints specifically.)

To be continued . . .

REFERENCES AND BIBLIOGRAPHY

1. Data Base Task Group of CODASYL Programming Language Committee, Final Report (April 1971).

2. IBM Corporation, Programming Announcement IBM DATABASE 2 (DB2) Version 2 (April 19, 1988).

3. IBM Corporation, Programming Announcement Structured Query Language / Data System (SQL/DS) Version 2 Release 2 (June 21, 1988).

4. ISO/TC97/SC21/WG3 / ANSI X3H2, Database Language SQL Addendum-1. Document ISO DBL AMS-10 / ANSI X3H2-87-205 (1987).

5. ISO/IEC JTC1/SC21/WG3 / ANSI X3H2, ISO-ANSI (working draft) Database Language SQL2. Document ISO DBL CPH-2b / ANSI X3H2-88-210 (April 1988).

6. Nagraj Alur, "IBM DATABASE 2 and Referential Integrity," *InfoDB* 3, No. 1 (Spring 1988).

7. Nagraj Alur, "Primary and Foreign Key Support in SQL/DS," *InfoDB* 3, No. 3 (Fall 1988).

8. Nagraj Alur, "A Comparison of IBM and ANSI RI Support," *InfoDB* 3, No. 3 (Fall 1988).

9. E. F. Codd, "A Relational Model of Data for Large Shared Data Banks," *Communications of the ACM* 13, No. 6 (June 1970). Republished in *Communications of the ACM* 26, No. 1 (January 1983).

10. E. F. Codd, "Further Normalization of the Data Base Relational Model," in *Data Base Systems,* Courant Computer Science Symposia Series, Vol. 6 (Englewood Cliffs, Prentice-Hall, 1972).

11. E. F. Codd, "Extending the Database Relational Model to Capture More Meaning," *ACM Transactions on Database Systems* 4, No. 4 (December 1979).

12. E. F. Codd, "Missing Information (Applicable and Inapplicable) in Relational Databases," *ACM SIGMOD Record* 15, No. 4 (December 1986).

13. E. F. Codd, "More Commentary on Missing Information in Relational Databases (Applicable and Inapplicable Information)," *ACM SIGMOD Record* 16, No. 1 (March 1987).

14. E. F. Codd, "Domains, Keys, and Referential Integrity in Relational Databases," *InfoDB* 3, No. 1 (Spring 1988).

15. C. J. Date, *An Introduction to Database Systems: Volume I,* 4th edition (Reading, MA: Addison-Wesley, 1985).

16. C. J. Date, *An Introduction to Database Systems: Volume II* (Reading, MA: Addison-Wesley, 1982).

17. C. J. Date, "Referential Integrity," *Proc. 7th International Conference on Very Large Data Bases* (September 1981).

18. C. J. Date, "Referential Integrity" (revised version), in C. J. Date, *Relational Database: Selected Writings* (Reading, MA: Addison-Wesley, 1986).

19. C. J. Date, "Why Every Relation Should Have Exactly One Primary Key," in C. J. Date, *Relational Database: Selected Writings* (Reading, MA: Addison-Wesley, 1986).

20. C. J. Date, "Some Relational Myths Exploded," in C. J. Date, *Relational Database: Selected Writings* (Reading, MA: Addison-Wesley, 1986).

21. C. J. Date, "Updating Views," in C. J. Date, *Relational Database: Selected Writings* (Reading, MA: Addison-Wesley, 1986).

22. C. J. Date, "A Practical Approach to Database Design," in C. J. Date, *Relational Database: Selected Writings* (Reading, MA: Addison-Wesley, 1986).

23. C. J. Date, "Primary and Foreign Key Support in DB2," *InfoDB* 3, No. 3 (Fall 1988).

24. C. J. Date, "What Is a Domain?" (in this volume).

25. C. J. Date, "Why Duplicate Rows Are Prohibited" (in this volume).

26. C. J. Date, "A Contribution to the Study of Database Integrity" (in this volume).

27. C. J. Date, "A Note on One-to-One Relationships" (in this volume).

28. C. J. Date, "Referential Integrity and Foreign Keys: A Working Paper" (private communication to E. F. Codd, April 1987).

29. C. J. Date and Colin J. White, *A Guide to DB2,* 3rd edition (Reading, MA: Addison-Wesley, 1989).

30. C. J. Date and Colin J. White, *A Guide to SQL/DS* (Reading, MA: Addison-Wesley, 1988).

31. K. P. Eswaran and D. D. Chamberlin, "Functional Specifications of a Subsystem for Data Base Integrity." *Proc. 1st International Conference on Very Large Data Bases* (September 1975).

32. B.-M. Schueler, "Update Reconsidered," in G. M. Nijssen (ed.), *Architecture and Models in Data Base Management Systems* (North-Holland, 1977).

33. Joseph W. Schmitt, "Nametags Reduce Database Integrity Problems" (private communication, November 1988).

34. Theresa Whitener, "Primary Identifiers: The Basics of Database Stability," *Database Programming and Design* 2, No. 1 (January 1989).

APPENDIX A:
SYNTAX SUMMARY

In this appendix we present (for convenience) a brief summary of the syntactic constructs introduced at various points in the body of the paper. Note that the syntax is deliberately a trifle wordy and repetitive; it would require a certain amount of clean up and refinement if it were ever to be considered as a serious candidate for implementation.

```
base-table-definition
    ::=  ... usual table name and column definition details,
         followed by ...
         [ DELETE [ NOT ] ALLOWED ]
         primary-key-definition
         [ alternate-key-definition-commalist ]
         [ foreign-key-definition-commalist ]
```

DELETE NOT ALLOWED means that rows cannot be deleted from the table at all. Any foreign keys that reference a table with DELETE NOT ALLOWED must have the delete rule omitted.

```
primary-key-definition
    ::=       PRIMARY KEY ( primary-key )
                   [ UPDATE [ NOT ] ALLOWED ]
```

UPDATE NOT ALLOWED means that updates are not permitted for this primary key at all. Any foreign keys that reference a primary key with UPDATE NOT ALLOWED must have the update rule omitted.

```
primary-key
    ::=       column-commalist


alternate-key-definition
    ::=       ALTERNATE KEY ( alternate-key )
                   [ NULLS [ NOT ] ALLOWED ]
```

Alternate keys were not discussed in much detail in the body of the paper. However, it is still desirable to be able to specify alternate keys in a table definition. See reference [27] for some specific examples. Note that NULLS ALLOWED is permitted for an alternate key (it is not permitted for a primary key, of course).

```
alternate-key
    ::=       column-commalist
```

```
foreign-key-definition
     ::=       FOREIGN KEY ( foreign-key ) REFERENCES target
                                          [ CHECK checking-time ]
               [ NULLS [ NOT ] ALLOWED ]
               [ DELETE OF target effect ]
               [ UPDATE OF target-primary-key effect ]
```

"OF target" in the delete rule and "OF target-primary-key" in the update rule are included merely for readability. They have no counterpart in the proposed extensions to the SQL standard [5], nor in the IBM products DB2 and SQL/DS [2,3,7,23].

```
checking-time
     ::=       IMMEDIATE
             | AT COMMIT
             | ...
```

The ". . ." stands for some possible additional checking times (further research needed).

```
foreign-key
     ::=       column-commalist
```

```
target
     ::=       table
```

```
effect
     ::=       RESTRICTED
             | CASCADES
             | NULLIFIES
             | procedure
             | ...
```

The ". . ." stands for some possible additional delete or update rules (further research needed).

```
target-primary-key
     ::=       table . column
             | table . ( column-commalist )
```

6

Referential Integrity and Foreign Keys Part II: Further Considerations

ABSTRACT

This is Part II of a two-part paper on the subject of referential integrity and related matters. Part I discussed the history of the subject and offered a preferred set of basic definitions (with rationale). Part II provides further justification and offers some specific practical recommendations. The sections are numbered from 10 to provide continuity with Part I.

COMMENTS ON PUBLICATION

See the previous paper in this collection.

Previously unpublished.

10.   SOME OUTSTANDING QUESTIONS

Most of this part of the paper consists of a set of discussions (in some cases somewhat philosophical in nature) of a number of outstanding questions. The questions are listed below, for convenience.

- Why every table should have exactly one primary key
- Why foreign keys should match primary keys, not alternate keys
- Why foreign keys are not pointers
- Why key declarations should be special-cased
- Why conterminous referential paths should be treated with caution
- Why primary key values in base tables should not be wholly or partly null
- Why composite foreign key values should not be partly null
- Why overlapping keys should be treated with caution
- Why noncomposite keys are a good idea
- Why a single target table is a good idea

The Principle of Cautious Design

As indicated above, several of the discussions that follow have a slightly philosophical flavor. The reason for this state of affairs is very simple:

- In talking about the relational model, we are of course talking about a *formal system*.
- The purpose of that formal system, however, is to be useful as a formal representation of certain aspects of the real world—and the real world is *not* a formal system.
- Thus, the process of mapping between the formal relational model and the informal real world is necessarily not formal either, but only intuitive. (A mapping between two systems can be defined *formally* only if both of those systems are themselves formal in turn.)
- It follows that there must be a certain element of subjectiveness in defining the rules of the formal relational model. Basically, those rules have to be defined in a way that seems—*intuitively*—to be a good fit with the way the world behaves. However, it is of course always possible to argue about matters of intuition. And such arguments are, precisely, philosophical arguments.

To take a concrete example, the relational model insists that a foreign key must always reference a primary key, not an alternate key (see Section

12 below). Now, it is certainly possible to think of situations in which it might seem desirable (at least superficially) to relax this rule; one example of such a situation is discussed in Section 12. However, it is my opinion (and presumably Codd's opinion also) that the *very minor* additional functionality provided by relaxing the rule is outweighed many times over by the additional complexity it causes (complexity, be it noted, not only for the user who wants to "take advantage" of the relaxation of the rule, but rather for *everybody*). Personally, I have never seen a situation in which there was a *genuine* need to have a foreign key reference an alternate key; it has always turned out—in the examples I have seen—that the design of the database was not very good and could be improved to avoid the perceived need.

Given, however, that such matters are (as indicated) somewhat subjective, I would also argue that a good general principle is to stay with the simple version of the rule for as long as possible, waiting until such time as a *genuine* need to relax it comes along (if it ever does). If and when that happens, then that will be the time to relax the rule. Such a general approach will guarantee the maximum simplicity for the maximum time, and will moreover guarantee that extensions to the model are made in an evolutionary, not revolutionary, manner.

The principle just articulated is, I believe, applicable to the design of other formal systems also, not just to the design of the relational model (or extensions thereto). I will refer to it as "The Principle of Cautious Design." The Principle of Cautious Design says, in effect, that when we are faced with a design choice, say between alternative A and alternative B (where A is upward-compatible with B), and the full implications of alternative B are not yet known, then the recommendation is to go with alternative A. If we are forced at some future time to "open up" our design to permit alternative B, then nothing we will have done in the past will be incompatible with that "opening up." If, on the other hand, we go with alternative B initially, and it subsequently becomes apparent that this was a bad decision, *we can never "close our design down" again to return to alternative A*. In other words, we should try to avoid situations in which the model—or the language, or the DBMS, or the database, or whatever it is that we are designing—provides certain options that users have to be explicitly told not to exercise.*

---

*An example is provided by *duplicate rows*. Most SQL-based DBMSs do permit tables to contain duplicate rows. However, users are *strongly* advised not to "take advantage" of this possibility, for reasons documented in reference [25]. It would have been vastly preferable if SQL had not permitted duplicate rows in the first place.

The Principle of Cautious Design is directly relevant to the discussions of Sections 11, 12, 15, 16, 17, 18, 19, and 20 of the present paper.

There is one more general point that is probably worth making before we start getting into details: Several of the issues raised in what follows are somewhat complex in nature, and the reader might be forgiven for concluding that referential integrity is a rather complex topic. However, while I might possibly agree with that conclusion, I would argue very strongly that the complexities in question are *inherent* (for the most part, at any rate). In other words, the complexities are not introduced by the relational model per se or by the relational foreign key and referential integrity concepts; rather, they are complexities that are *intrinsic to the real world*—i.e., they correspond to genuine real-world problems. Indeed, a good case can be made that the foreign key and referential integrity concepts allow us to articulate certain real-world problems in a precise manner, and hence that they allow us to attempt to solve those problems. The discussions in this second part of the paper in Sections 11–20 below are offered in this spirit.

11. WHY EVERY TABLE SHOULD HAVE EXACTLY ONE PRIMARY KEY

I have argued in favor of this position at some length elsewhere [19], and I do not propose to repeat all the details here. The basic argument is essentially as follows:

- Entities are identifiable, by definition (i.e., they have *id*entity);
- The relational model requires entity identifiers (like everything else) to be represented by *value;*
- Primary key values serve, precisely, as those necessary entity identifier representations.

The foregoing argument shows why each table (at least, each *base* table) should certainly have *at least one* unique identifier—i.e., at least one candidate key, in relational terms. (It also shows, by implication, why base tables, at least, do not permit duplicate rows [25].) The next question is, of course, what if some table has *more than one* unique identifier? Here we argue as follows:

- Suppose some given table does have multiple unique identifiers.
- Then not distinguishing one of those identifiers as primary (i.e., treating them all as interchangeable) leads to unnecessary complexity.

To paraphrase an example first given by Codd in reference [14]: A relational system that failed to distinguish one of the identifiers as primary would be something like a memory addressing scheme that failed to provide a single, unique way of addressing individual memory cells. (The point is, of course, that primary keys *are* the [row-level] addressing mechanism in the relational model.)

Now, it is sometimes argued that synonyms (i.e., multiple names for the same thing) are normal and natural in the real world, and hence that having to distinguish one identifier as primary is artificial and unduly restrictive. I would respond to this argument as follows:

- It is certainly true that synonyms can and do exist in the real world, and hence we certainly do need a way of dealing with them in our formal database systems.

- However, it is also true that synonyms can and do cause confusion in the real world. And it is obviously very desirable to try to avoid such confusion, most especially within our (would-be) *disciplined* database systems.

- Inside the database, therefore, "one name for one thing" is a good principle, even if we cannot persuade people to adhere to that principle outside the system. (In fact, using *surrogates*—i.e., primary identifiers with *no inherent meaning*—is frequently an even better principle. See Section 19 for further discussion of this point.)

In general, of course, the database will also need to include special conversion tables, mapping the variety of external synonyms for an object to that object's single internal identifier (in other words, its primary key). And in some cases it *might* be desirable to conceal that internal identifier from users by means of the system's view mechanism—though it is true that this technique might lead to performance and/or updatability problems, given the limitations of most present-day implementations. On the whole, it is probably better to expose the internal identifiers to the user [33].

For further pragmatic arguments in support of the foregoing, see reference [34]. For concrete examples of the kind of complexity that can arise from "multiple primary keys," see reference [19].

Aside: Recently, Codd seems (unfortunately) to have been shifting his position, or at least using a different set of terms, in connexion with the primary key question. Given that certain relational operations can generate tables containing primary key values that are either wholly or partly null, Codd now suggests that the term "primary key" be reserved for tables (perhaps just base tables?) for which it can be guaranteed that the primary key has "nulls not allowed"; for tables (or at least views) for which such a guarantee cannot be made, he suggests that the term "weak identifier" be used instead [14].

This change should be firmly resisted, in my opinion. The term "primary key" has been used with its original meaning in countless places—books, papers, specifications, database designs, manuals, RFPs, etc., not to mention products and presentations and discussions—ever since Codd first introduced it in reference [9]. To change it now can only cause massive confusion. In fact, Codd himself uses it with its original meaning in the very paper in which he introduces the "weak identifier" term, when he says that "each relation [has] *exactly one primary key*" [14]. In this paper, I will continue to use "primary key" in its original sense.* *End of aside.*

12.   WHY FOREIGN KEYS SHOULD MATCH PRIMARY KEYS, NOT ALTERNATE KEYS

As explained in Part I of this paper (Section 7), an alternate key is a candidate key that is not the primary key. For example, the PERSON table might have two candidate keys, SS# (social security number) and LIC# (driver's license number); if we choose SS# as the primary key, then LIC# would be an alternate key. (Actually, as we will see below, it might be the case that *neither* of these candidate keys can serve as the primary key, because they might both have nulls allowed. But let us ignore this point for the moment.)

Now, it is sometimes suggested that foreign keys should be permitted to match, not necessarily the primary key, but rather *any candidate key* in the target table. For example, one table T1 might have a foreign key matching the primary key PERSON.SS#, and another table T2 might have a foreign key matching the alternate key PERSON.LIC#. (In fact, the currently proposed extensions to the SQL standard [4,5] explicitly permit such a possibility. The IBM products DB2 and SQL/DS [2,3]—to their credit—do not.)

The argument against this position is essentially the same as the argument against "multiple primary keys" (see the previous section); indeed, permitting a foreign key to match an alternate key is just one specific aspect of permitting "multiple primary keys." Briefly, allowing "multiple primary keys"—in particular, allowing a foreign key to match an alternate key—does not seem to provide a useful level of additional function, and it cer-

---

*Codd also states in reference [14] that it is "completely unnecessary" for a primary key to be "declared or deduced" for any relation that is not a base relation or a view or a snapshot. (A snapshot is a named derived relation, like a view. Unlike a view, however, a snapshot is "real," not virtual—i.e., it is represented by its own stored data.) I disagree with this position also; there are good reasons why it is highly desirable for the system to be able to deduce the primary key of the result of *any arbitrary relational expression*. See Warden's paper "The Keys of the Kingdom" (later in the present book).

tainly does cause additional complexity (the proposed SQL extensions [4,5] bear eloquent witness to this claim).

In order to amplify the foregoing, let us consider the SS#–LIC# example in a little more detail:

- The argument in favor of allowing one table to have a foreign key matching SS# and another to have a foreign key matching LIC# is basically that the two tables might be part of two different applications, one of which is concerned with taxation and the other with traffic offenses (say).

- But this argument is surely specious. It is true, of course, that the holder of a given social security number and the holder of a given driver's license number might in fact be one and the same entity in the real world. But why should the two applications *care?*—by definition, they are not integrated with one another (if they were, they would surely be using the same foreign key in the first place). In the real world—at least in the USA—the Internal Revenue Service and the Department of Motor Vehicles are not integrated with one another, and a good thing too.

- In fact, the two applications are dealing with two different entity *types,* namely ''persons registered with the social security system'' and ''persons registered as drivers.'' While these two sets are not disjoint in the real world (because the same person can belong to both at the same time), this fact is irrelevant from the point of view of the two applications per se.

  > *Aside:* We remark that the example illustrates the point that it is perfectly possible for the same entity to be of multiple different types simultaneously. Also, of course, it is possible for a given entity to acquire new types or to lose existing types dynamically. *End of aside.*

- Indeed, it is likely that the two applications would not be sharing the same table (PERSON) at all—they would be operating on two different tables, one with primary key SS# and one with primary key LIC#. The fact that a given row in the one table and a given row in the other happened to correspond to the same entity in the real world would be of no concern at all to the two applications.

- Note too that not all holders of a social security number hold a driver's license, and not all holders of a driver's license hold a social security number (in general). Thus, each of the two applications referred to above will be dealing with some entities that the other does not (in general).

> *Aside:* In other words (as suggested above), if SS# and LIC# are
> both included in the PERSON table, then they will typically both
> have to have nulls allowed. It might therefore be necessary to intro-
> duce a surrogate primary key for that table anyway. Again, see
> Section 19 for a discussion of surrogates. *End of aside.*

For further discussion of such problems, the reader is again referred to
reference [19].

13.   WHY FOREIGN KEYS ARE NOT POINTERS

Critics of the relational approach have been known to suggest that foreign
keys are nothing more than pointers in another guise—and pointers, of
course, are explicitly prohibited in the relational model. The following list
of some of the principal distinctions between the two concepts shows why
that suggestion is incorrect.

- Foreign keys are logical, pointers are physical. More precisely: Foreign
  keys are defined at the relational (logical) level, pointers are defined at
  the storage (physical) level. The suggestion that foreign keys are "just
  pointers" thus stems from a basic confusion over *levels of abstraction;*
  foreign keys are a higher-level concept than pointers. (It is certainly
  true that pointers might be used to *implement* foreign keys, but they
  are by no means the only possible implementation.)

- Pointers identify stored records, foreign keys identify entities.

- Foreign keys may have inherent "real-world" meaning, whereas
  pointers certainly do not. Contrast, for example, the foreign key value
  "D4" (i.e., department number D4), which does have meaning outside
  the database system, and a pointer to the stored record for that department, which will probably consist of some obscure disk address.

- Foreign keys do not change their values if the target to which they refer
  moves to another location.

- Foreign keys can be composite, pointers cannot.

- Pointers have physical performance connotations, foreign keys do not.

- Pointers are a special data type, one that is quite different from the
  conventional "real data" data types (numbers, strings, dates, times,
  etc.). As a result, they require special operators of their own—e.g.,
  operators such as CONNECT, DISCONNECT, and RECONNECT
  (these examples are taken from CODASYL [1]). Foreign keys, by contrast, are simply conventional data items, represented by conventional
  data types. They do not require any special operators at all. Functions

equivalent to CONNECT, DISCONNECT, etc., are performed by the conventional data-handling operators (e.g., UPDATE in SQL).

- Pointers *point:* That is, they have directionality, and they have a single, specific target. Foreign key values, by contrast, are *values:* A given foreign key value, e.g., the department number D4, is simultaneously connected—logically speaking—to *all references* to the entity in question, no matter where in the database those references happen to be. In other words, foreign key values (like all values in a relational database) are "multiway associative." For example, the department row for department D4 is logically connected to all employee rows for employees in that department, and each of those employee rows is logically connected to all the others and also to the department row.

     Furthermore, all references to the same entity are represented in a relational database in the same way (i.e., by the same value—see Sections 11 and 12 above), and hence are easily system- and user-recognizable.

- Adding a new foreign key to an existing table and adding a new pointer-based access path to an existing stored file are very different operations—the first might be quite trivial, the second will almost certainly require a physical reorganization.

- Pointers are implementation-dependent: Their properties and behavior depend to some extent on the underlying hardware and/or operating system and/or DBMS. In particular, pointers are *machine-local*. For example, in a distributed system, a pointer cannot point from one machine to another. Foreign keys are not implementation-dependent in any such sense at all.

14. WHY KEY DECLARATIONS SHOULD BE SPECIAL-CASED

A full-function database management system needs to be able to support the declaration and enforcement of integrity rules of arbitrary complexity. Several languages have been proposed for the declaration of such rules; see, for example, reference [26]. (The languages in question are sometimes referred to, though not very aptly, as "assertion/trigger languages" [31], where "assertion" refers to the actual integrity constraint per se and "trigger" refers to the procedure that the system is to execute if the constraint is not satisfied.) And since primary and foreign key constraints are of course just special cases of integrity rules, it follows that primary and foreign key constraints must at least be capable of being expressed in any such general language. Here, for example, is a declaration of the primary key constraint for table S (suppliers), expressed in the hypothetical integrity language described in reference [26]. *Note:* In this formulation, SX and SY are range variables, both of which range over table S.

```
CREATE INTEGRITY RULE S_PK
       ON      INSERT SX.S# ,
               UPDATE SX.S# :
       CHECK FORALL SX
                  ( NOT IS_NULL ( SX.S# ) AND
                    FORALL SY
                        ( IF SX.S# = SY.S#
                             THEN  SAME ( SX, SY ) ) )
       ELSE  REJECT ;
```

However, this formulation is intolerably clumsy. The special-case syntax

```
PRIMARY KEY ( S# )
```

is preferable for several reasons:

- It is better for the user, because it is more user-friendly.

- It is better for the system, because it allows the system to recognize the special case more easily and hence implement it in a special-case (more efficient) way—which is clearly desirable for a constraint that is so fundamental.

- It enables the system to recognize and understand the associated semantics more easily. For example, the system needs to understand the semantics of primary (and foreign) keys in order to be able to handle the problem of view updating correctly, as was mentioned in Part I of this paper (Section 9). Likewise, the optimizer also needs to understand the semantics of primary (and foreign) keys in order to be able to perform certain kinds of optimization, as was also mentioned in Section 9.

The foregoing example was in terms of primary key constraints. Analogous arguments apply, but with even more force, to foreign key constraints also. By way of illustration, here is a "general integrity language" declaration—again based on an example in reference [26]—of the foreign key constraint from SP.S# (in the shipments table SP) to the primary key S.S# in the suppliers table S, with NULLS NOT ALLOWED and RESTRICTED update and delete rules. (The CASCADES and NULLIFIES cases are much worse, by the way!) *Note:* SX and SPX here are range variables, ranging over tables S and SP respectively.

```
CREATE INTEGRITY RULE SP_S_FK
       ON      INSERT SPX.S# ,
               UPDATE SPX.S# ,
               UPDATE SX.S#  ,
               DELETE SX     :
       CHECK FORALL SPX
                  ( NOT IS_NULL ( SPX.S# ) AND
                    EXISTS SX ( SX.S# = SPX.S# ) )
       ELSE  REJECT ;
```

Here is the special-case syntax equivalent:

```
FOREIGN KEY ( S# ) REFERENCES S
                   NULLS NOT ALLOWED
                   DELETE OF S RESTRICTED
                   UPDATE OF S.S# RESTRICTED
```

There is another point to be made under the general heading of special-casing, namely as follows. The foreign key concept is occasionally criticized on the grounds that it is *too rigid;* for example, why does the target row *have* to exist before a referencing row can exist? In the case of suppliers-and-parts, for example, why should it not be possible to insert a shipment row at any time, and have the system automatically create appropriate entries in the suppliers and parts tables if they do not already exist?

I would respond to this criticism by invoking The Principle of Cautious Design once again. Provided the system does support a general integrity language such as the one proposed in reference [26], then *any* integrity rule can always be expressed (albeit in a somewhat clumsy manner in some cases). The question of which specific rules are given special-case treatment thus becomes a judgment call on the part of the DBMS (and language) designer. The objective is to strike a healthy balance between two somewhat conflicting objectives:

(a) On the one hand, it is desirable to special-case those rules that occur frequently in practice, for the reasons sketched earlier in this section;

(b) On the other hand, it is also desirable not to clutter up the interface with an excessive number of special cases, for all the usual reasons (too much to learn, teach, document, remember, implement, etc., etc.).

In the particular case under consideration (the ability to insert a referencing row before the corresponding referenced row), I would argue that the desirability of special-casing is not clear, since it seems to me that the need for such a rule does not arise very often in practice. (By contrast, the desirability of special-casing primary and foreign keys as discussed previously in this paper is surely beyond doubt.) Following The Principle of Cautious Design, therefore, I would argue *against* special-casing such a rule at this time.

15. WHY CONTERMINOUS REFERENTIAL PATHS SHOULD BE TREATED WITH CAUTION

As we saw in Part I of this paper, it can happen that there exist two or more distinct referential paths from some table Tn to some other table T1. Two examples were given in Part I:

(a) The courses–offerings–enrollees example, in which there were two distinct paths from table ENROLLEE to table COURSE:

(b) The bill-of-materials example, in which there were two distinct paths from table PP to table P:

Let us agree to refer to the distinct paths in such examples as "conterminous" paths (since they have the same start and end points). As the title of this section indicates, conterminous paths need to be treated with a certain amount of care, as we now explain.

Note first that the two examples are actually different in kind:

(a) In the first case, the fact that there is a direct path from ENROLLEE to COURSE is really just a logical consequence of the fact that there are paths from ENROLLEE to OFFERING and from OFFERING to COURSE. In other words, if z, y, and x represent an ENROLLEE row, an OFFERING row, and a COURSE row, respectively, and if z references y and y references x, then z necessarily references x directly as well. Hence, if the system enforces the referential constraints from ENROLLEE to OFFERING and from OFFERING to COURSE, it will enforce the direct constraint from ENROLLEE to COURSE automatically.

Since the situation just described is essentially just an extension of the situation that arises in connexion with the familiar concept of transitive functional dependence [10], I will refer to a referential constraint such as the direct constraint from ENROLLEE to COURSE as *transitive* (via OFFERING).

(b) In the second case, the two paths are quite independent of one another. There are no transitive constraints.

Cases (a) and (b) both need careful treatment, though case (a) is more straightforward than case (b). The easiest way of dealing with case (a) is simply not to declare the transitive constraint explicitly at all; as explained above, the constraint will be enforced automatically if the constraints that imply it are enforced. If the transitive constraint is declared, however, then care must be taken to ensure that the delete and update rules for that constraint are defined in a manner that is compatible with the delete and update rules for the constraints that imply it. For example, if the delete rule from ENROLLEE to OFFERING is RESTRICTED, then the delete rule from ENROLLEE to COURSE must be RESTRICTED also, for reasons discussed under case (b) below. So far as the system is concerned, in fact, declaring the transitive constraint has the effect (conceptually) of converting case (a) into case (b), since the system is not aware of the fact that the transitive constraint is in fact transitive.

Let us therefore turn our attention to case (b). Here is a slightly more general example of this case:

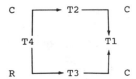

In this example, table T4 references both tables T2 and T3, each of which in turn references table T1. There are two paths from T4 to T1. I will refer to the path via T2 as the upper path and the path via T3 as the lower path.

Let us concentrate for the moment on the question of the delete rules, which we suppose are as indicated in the figure (C = CASCADES, R = RESTRICTED). Suppose for simplicity that each table contains just one column, which is the primary key for each table and also the necessary foreign key for tables T2, T3, and T4; suppose also that each table contains just one row, containing the single value "v" (say) in every case; and suppose finally that we try to delete the single row from table T1. What happens?

- If the system applies the delete rules in the upper path first, the single row in T4 (and the single row in T2) will be deleted, because the rules are both CASCADES. When the system then applies the delete rules in the lower path, an attempt will be made to delete the single row from T3; this attempt will succeed, because there is now no matching row in T4, and hence no row to "restrict" the delete. The net effect is that all four rows will be deleted.

- If, on the other hand, the system applies the delete rules in the lower path first, the net effect is that the database will remain unchanged. For the row in T4 will cause the attempt to delete the row from T3 to fail (because of the RESTRICTED delete rule in the path from T4 to T3), and hence the overall operation will fail.

The foregoing discussion is just by way of illustration, of course; similar problems occur if we change the delete rule from T4 to T2 in the example to NULLIFIES, and similar problems occur also with the update rules (at least in the CASCADES and NULLIFIES cases).

Now, the overall effect of an operation clearly should not depend on the details of how the system chooses to implement that operation; in particular, it should not depend on the sequence in which it chooses to apply the delete or update rules. The unpredictability suggested by the example above simply cannot be tolerated. The following appear to be ways in which such unpredictability might be avoided:

1. We could extend the data definition language to allow the user to specify the order in which the system is to apply the rules.

2. The system could examine all possible execution sequences at run time and fail the overall operation if at least one of those sequences fails.

3. Situations that can potentially lead to such unpredictability could be detected when the database is defined, and disallowed (i.e., the system could reject the definition).

Method 1 suffers from the obvious drawback that it places the burden on the user (and rather a heavy burden at that); in addition, it is likely to be error-prone. Method 2 is likely to have unacceptable performance implications. Method 3 is obviously the most satisfactory. Moreover, it could be argued that a database definition that can lead to unpredictability is logically incorrect—i.e., it cannot correctly represent a real-world situation (unless the "real world" is logically incorrect too, of course!—a state of affairs not unknown in practice)—and hence the system really should reject it. The difficulty is, of course, in deciding exactly which definitions can lead to such unpredictability.

One attempt at identifying such logically incorrect definitions has been made by IBM in its DB2 and SQL/DS products [2,3]. Another has been made by the SQL standards committee [5]. By way of example, we discuss the way DB2 handles the problem.

- First, the only update rule supported is RESTRICTED.

- Second, if table Tn is "delete-connected" to table T1 (see below for an explanation of this term) via two or more distinct referential paths, then every foreign key in table Tn that is involved in any of those paths must have the same delete rule, and furthermore that rule must be either RESTRICTED or CASCADES, not NULLIFIES.

The second of these requirements would prohibit the T1–T2–T3–T4 situation shown above, because T4 is delete-connected to T1 via two distinct paths and the two foreign keys in T4 have different delete rules.

The term "delete-connected" is defined as follows.

- First, an intuitive definition: Table Tn is said to be delete-connected to table T1 if and only if a DELETE on T1 can either *affect* or *be affected by* the content of Tn.

- More formally, table Tn is said to be delete-connected to table T1 if
  and only if (a) Tn references T1 directly, or (b) Tn references some
  table $T(n-1)$ directly and there is a referential path from $T(n-1)$ to
  T1 in which every delete rule is CASCADES:

$$\text{Tn} \xrightarrow{\ *\ } \text{T(n-1)} \xrightarrow{\ c\ } \text{T(n-2)} \xrightarrow{\ c\ } \ \ldots \ \xrightarrow{\ c\ } \text{T2} \xrightarrow{\ c\ } \text{T1}$$

(the "C"'s here represent a CASCADES delete rule, the asterisk stands
for "any" [i.e., "don't care"] delete rule).

Observe that—depending on the content of Tn—an attempt to delete
rows from T1 can

(a) cause rows to be deleted from Tn, if the "*" delete rule is CASCADES;

(b) cause rows to be updated in Tn, if the "*" rule is NULLIFIES;

(c) fail, if the "*" rule is RESTRICTED.

In other words, a DELETE on T1 can indeed either "affect or be affected
by" the content of Tn.

Note: It follows immediately from the definition that every table is
delete-connected to every table it references directly. It follows also, incidentally, that every self-referencing table is delete-connected to itself.

While IBM is to be congratulated on addressing the problem, and it is
probably true that the foregoing rules are sufficient to avoid unpredictability (though I have not seen a proof to that effect), it is certainly not clear
that they are *necessary*. Certainly the justification for the prohibition
against DELETE NULLIFIES, in particular, is very far from obvious.
Moreover, it is certainly also true that the rules are undesirably restrictive
in some situations; consider, e.g., what is involved in the suppliers-and-
parts database in trying to change a given supplier number, say from S1 to
S99 (this problem is discussed in detail in Appendix C to this paper). I agree
with Codd [14] that this whole area is still in need of further research.

16. WHY PRIMARY KEY VALUES IN BASE TABLES SHOULD NOT BE WHOLLY OR PARTLY NULL

This is Codd's "entity integrity rule" [11,14]:

- No component of the primary key of a base table is allowed to accept
  nulls.

I mention the rule here merely for completeness. Arguments in support
of its reasonableness can be found in references [15] and [19]. In essence,
those arguments amount to the following:

- As explained in Section 11 above, primary key values represent entity identifiers;
- "Null" in this context is taken to mean either "not applicable" or "value unknown";
- "Not applicable" clearly makes no sense for an entity identifier;
- Likewise, "value unknown" (either wholly or partly) also makes no sense for an entity identifier. In fact, an entity with unknown *id*entity is a contradiction in terms: If an entity is important enough in the real world to require explicit representation in the database, then that entity must be definitely and unambiguously identifiable—for otherwise it would be impossible even to talk about it in any sensible manner [19]. For this reason, the entity integrity rule is sometimes stated in the form:
  - *In a relational database, we never record information about something we cannot identify.*

Note 1: It is worth stressing the point that the entity integrity rule applies only to *base tables.* Other tables might very well have a primary key for which nulls are allowed. As a trivial example, suppose that nulls are allowed for column P.COLOR in the suppliers-and-parts database, and consider the derived table (perhaps an answer to a query) that is produced by projecting the parts table over the COLOR column. (As mentioned earlier in this paper [end of Section 11], Codd now seems to be referring to primary keys that have nulls allowed as "weak identifiers." We prefer to continue to call them primary keys, for reasons already explained in Section 11.)

Note 2: It is also worth stressing that the entity integrity rule applies only to *primary* keys. *Alternate* keys may or may not have "nulls allowed." For example, employees might have "social security number" as an alternate key; and the rule regarding social security numbers is that you don't have to have one, but if you do, then it must be unique. (We remark in passing that the IBM products DB2 and SQL/DS therefore do not adequately support alternate keys, because the IBM mechanism for enforcing uniqueness is the UNIQUE index, and UNIQUE indexes permit *at most one* null in the indexed column(s)—i.e., they support the constraint "unique, with at most one null," whereas what is required is the constraint "unique unless null.")

17.   WHY COMPOSITE FOREIGN KEY VALUES SHOULD NOT BE PARTLY NULL

As explained in Part I of this paper, foreign keys, unlike primary keys (in base tables), sometimes do have to be allowed to be null. If the foreign key in question is composite, however, it is my position that *every individual value* of that foreign key should either be wholly null (i.e., all components null) or wholly nonnull (i.e., all components nonnull), and not a mixture (i.e., some components null and others nonnull). The basic argument is, again, that foreign key values (like primary key values) are entity identifiers, and a partly null entity identifier does not make much sense.

> *Aside:* A *wholly* null identifier, by contrast, does make sense in this context—it means, e.g., that the corresponding entity is not known, or that no such corresponding entity exists. For example, an EMP row with a null DEPT# may very well be legal—it represents, e.g., an employee for whom the department is not known, or an employee who does not *have* a department. *End of aside.*

Now, it is sometimes argued that a *partially* null foreign key value could also make sense; for example, considering the courses–offerings–enrollees database (Example 2 from Section 2 in Part I of this paper), a (COURSE#,OFF#) foreign key value of <C99,null> in an ENROLLEE row could mean that we know that the employee in question is enrolled in some offering of course C99, but we do not currently know which offering. (For the sake of this discussion, we ignore the point that the foreign key under consideration is actually part of the primary key of the containing table, and hence that nulls would in fact not be allowed at all.) *Note:* Once again, the currently proposed extensions to the SQL standard [4,5] do explicitly permit such a possibility. So too—unfortunately—do the IBM DB2 and SQL/DS products [2,3].

As already stated, it is my feeling that such a possibility does not really provide a useful level of additional function, and it certainly does lead to a very great deal of complexity. In fact, a perceived "need" for partially null foreign key values tends to suggest that the database designer has done a poor design job and has not pinpointed the proper entities. Let me try to explain why I feel this way.

The first point to be made is that, as was already explained in Part I of this paper (Section 2), not all components of a composite foreign key are foreign keys themselves. For example, in the composite foreign key ENROLLEE.(COURSE#,OFF#), COURSE# *is* a foreign key itself, but OFF# is not. We might therefore conceivably agree that a (COURSE#, OFF#) value of <C99,null> is valid, provided that course C99 does exist— but what about a value of <null,O99>? In other words, what kind of constraint applies to OFF# values? It is certainly not a referential constraint.

Next, consider the following example (in which LOC stands for "location"):

```
DEPT   ( DEPT#, LOC, ... )
       PRIMARY KEY ( DEPT#, LOC )
```

```
EMP    ( EMP#, ..., DEPT#, LOC, ... )
       PRIMARY KEY ( EMP# )
       FOREIGN KEY ( DEPT#, LOC ) REFERENCES DEPT
```

Suppose that columns EMP.DEPT# and EMP.LOC both have "nulls allowed," and suppose the two tables contain the following rows (irrelevant columns omitted):

```
DEPT   DEPT#   LOC          EMP    EMP#    DEPT#    LOC
       -----   ---                 ----    -----    ----
       D1      NYC                 E1      D1       null
                                   E2      null     NYC
```

Let us examine the question "Can the existing DEPT row be updated to <D2,SFO>?" Assume first that the relevant update rule (for the foreign key EMP.DEPT#) is RESTRICTED.

(a) Suppose the answer is yes. Then it follows that the two existing EMP rows cannot be considered to match the existing DEPT row (for otherwise the update would certainly not be permitted). After the update, *no component of the foreign key values in those EMP rows matches anything at all.* Thus, we are forced to the conclusion that a partly null foreign key value *must always be legal,* regardless of the values of the nonnull components. Furthermore, after the update:

- There is no possible UPDATE (other than a no-operation) that can legally be applied to LOC in the E1 row, except for an UPDATE that sets LOC to SFO *and simultaneously sets DEPT# to D2.*

- There is no possible UPDATE (other than a no-operation) that can legally be applied to DEPT# in the E2 row, except for an UPDATE that sets DEPT# to D2 *and simultaneously sets LOC to SFO.*

In other words, columns EMP.DEPT# and EMP.LOC are not truly independent of one another. So what does a partly null foreign key value *mean* in this case? E.g., what does it *mean* to say that the location for employee E2 is New York, if there is no department in New York?

(b) Suppose by contrast that the answer is no. Then it must be the case that the two EMP rows *are* considered to match the existing DEPT row. In that case, if the DEPT table additionally includes a row <D2,NYC>, the EMP row for E2 must be considered as matching that DEPT row as well—i.e., it must be considered as matching *both* the D1 and D2 DEPT rows. But for a given EMP row there is supposed to be exactly one corresponding DEPT row. Is this not a contradiction?

Note: Case (a) above corresponds to the way in which the proposed SQL standard actually works [4,5]; likewise for DB2 and SQL/DS [2,3]. Now suppose by contrast that the relevant update rule is CASCADES.

In this case, updating the DEPT row to <D2,SFO> will always succeed. But does that update cascade to update anything in table EMP?

(a) If the answer is no, then it must be the case that the two existing EMP rows are not considered to match the existing DEPT row. This possibility was examined under the discussion of RESTRICTED above (paragraph (a)).

(b) If the answer is yes, then it must be the case that the two EMP rows *are* considered to match the existing DEPT row. This possibility was examined under the discussion of RESTRICTED above (paragraph (b)). However, there is now a subsidiary question: What is the *effect* of the cascade? Specifically, is the EMP row <E1,D1,null> updated to <E1,D2,null> or to <E1,D2,SFO>? Whichever it is, *why*? (Similarly for the EMP row <E2,null,NYC>, of course.)

Consideration of the case of the NULLIFIES update rule is left to the reader. Consideration of the effect of attempting to delete the existing DEPT row under the various possible delete rules is also left to the reader— except that it is worth mentioning that the possibilities quickly become very complex indeed (in the general case) if distinct foreign keys are allowed to overlap (see Section 18 below).

The foregoing gives some idea of the kind of complexity that can arise from the possibility that foreign key values might be partly but not wholly null. (Please note that I certainly do not claim that the discussion above has covered all possible problems.) My recommendation, that foreign key values not be allowed to be partly null, enables such complexities to be avoided, while (in my opinion) representing no significant loss of function.

Of course, I have not yet answered the question "What if there is (apparently) a genuine business requirement to have a partly null foreign key value?" For example, what if there is (apparently) a genuine requirement to be able to record the fact that some employee is enrolled in some offering of course C99, but we do not currently know which offering? The following design for the courses–offerings–enrollees database represents one possible approach to this problem, an approach that does not flout the principle that foreign key values should not be partly null:

```
COURSE     ( COURSE#, ... )
           PRIMARY KEY ( COURSE# )

OFFERING ( X#, COURSE#, OFF#, ... )
           PRIMARY KEY ( X# )
           ALTERNATE KEY ( COURSE#, OFF# )
           FOREIGN KEY ( COURSE# ) REFERENCES COURSE

ENROLLEE ( X#, EMP#, ... )
           PRIMARY KEY ( X#, EMP# )
           FOREIGN KEY ( X# ) REFERENCES OFFERING
```

Here X# is a single-column surrogate identifier for OFFERING (see Section 19 below for further discussion of surrogates), and the combination (COURSE#,OFF#) is now an alternate key for that table. (Note that, as explained earlier in Section 16, there is no prohibition against *alternate* key values being [either wholly or partly] null.) The composite foreign key (COURSE#,OFF#) in the ENROLLEE table has been replaced by the *non-*composite foreign key X#. In the following set of sample values, employee E1 is shown as being enrolled in offering O1 of course C1 and an unknown offering of course C99:

```
COURSE      COURSE#    ...
            -------
            C1
            C99

OFFERING    X#    COURSE#    OFF#    ...
            --    -------    ----
            X1    C1         O1
            X2    C99        null

ENROLLEE    X#    EMP#    ...
            --    ----
            X1    E1
            X2    E1
```

18. WHY OVERLAPPING KEYS SHOULD BE TREATED WITH CAUTION

As has been made abundantly clear at numerous points in this paper, the relational model does permit keys (both primary and foreign) to be composite, and indeed several composite keys were shown—for tutorial reasons—in the examples in Part I of this paper (Section 2). However, there are a number of arguments to suggest that it is a good idea to be very sparing in the use of composite keys (see Section 19 below). If, despite those arguments, composite keys are still used, then it is my belief that such keys should be treated for the most part as *indivisible entity identifiers* (except possibly for retrieval purposes); in other words, they should be treated for the most part as if they were in fact *not* composite.

Now, the reader will probably have realized already that the recommendation of the previous section (namely, that composite foreign key values not be allowed to be partly null) is actually a consequence of this overall recommendation. Another consequence is that *composite keys should not overlap* (if possible). At least, it is certainly the case that keys that do overlap need to be treated with considerable circumspection—so much so, in fact, that it is my feeling that it is generally better to avoid such overlapping altogether (again if possible).

Let me begin my discussion of this issue by first making my "nonoverlapping" recommendation more precise:

(a) Let FK1 and FK2 be two foreign keys in the same table T. Then there should not exist three distinct columns C1, C, and C2 in table T such that C1 appears in FK1 and not in FK2, C2 appears in FK2 and not in FK1, and C appears in both FK1 and FK2:

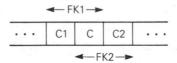

(b) Let PK and FK be primary key and a foreign key, respectively, in the same table T. Then there should not exist three distinct columns P, C, and F in table T such that P appears in PK and not in FK, F appears in FK and not in PK, and C appears in both PK and FK:

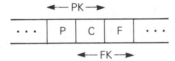

In other words, it is acceptable to have one key that is totally included within another or coextensive with another (see Part I of this paper for several examples), but it is not a good idea to have two keys such that each has some column in common with the other *and* some column not so in common.

Why is such nonoverlapping desirable? The fundamental reason is that overlapping obviously implies a certain loss of independence—for example, changing a value of one of the overlapping keys will necessarily cause a change in the other key(s) also. In other words, overlapping gives rise to *side effects* (and it is all too well known that side effects can lead to a great deal of unnecessary complexity). Consider the following example:

```
DEPT   ( DEPT#, LOC, ... )
       PRIMARY KEY ( DEPT#, LOC )

PROJ   ( LOC, PROJ#, ... )
       PRIMARY KEY ( LOC, PROJ# )

EMP    ( EMP#, ..., DEPT#, LOC, PROJ#, ... )
       PRIMARY KEY ( EMP# )
       FOREIGN KEY ( DEPT#, LOC ) REFERENCES DEPT
       FOREIGN KEY ( LOC, PROJ# ) REFERENCES PROJ
```

The PROJ table here represents project information, and the (LOC,PROJ#) foreign key means that the indicated employee works on the indicated project at the indicated location. The (DEPT#,LOC) foreign key means that the indicated employee works for the indicated department at the indicated location.

The first point, of course, is that for the design shown for table EMP to be even feasible, there must be another constraint in effect, namely as follows:

- If employee e works for department d at location l1 and also works on project j at location l2, then l1 and l2 must be the same location.

Even if this constraint does indeed apply today, of course, there is no guarantee that it will *always* apply. Thus, the design shown above for table EMP is not a very good one, because it assumes that this constraint will never change. Surely it would be better to include two distinct columns, DEPT_LOC and PROJ_LOC say, in the EMP table; then, if it is in fact true today that the DEPT_LOC and PROJ_LOC values must be equal (for any given employee), that constraint can be separately stated and separately maintained—and subsequently changed, if need be.

Next, suppose that (despite the argument just given) we do in fact stay with the overlapping key design, and suppose the tables contain the following rows (irrelevant columns omitted once again):

DEPT	DEPT#	LOC
	D1	NYC

EMP	EMP#	DEPT#	LOC	PROJ#
	E1	D1	NYC	J1

PROJ	LOC	PROJ#
	NYC	J1

Then:

- If the recommendation of the previous section (no partly null foreign key values) is accepted, then either both foreign keys—i.e., EMP.(DEPT#,LOC) and EMP.(LOC,PROJ#)—must have "nulls allowed" or both must have "nulls not allowed"; it is not possible to have nulls allowed for one and not the other. Hence, as suggested earlier, there is a certain lack of independence between the two foreign keys.

- Second, suppose (again) that the "no partly null foreign key values" recommendation is accepted, and suppose that nulls are in fact allowed for the two foreign keys. Consider the effect of a NULLIFIES delete rule for the foreign key EMP.(DEPT#,LOC). A DELETE for the DEPT row <D1,NYC> will accordingly set DEPT# and LOC in the

EMP row for E1 to null. *The DELETE should therefore set PROJ# to null in that row as well*—because PROJ# cannot be nonnull if LOC is null. In other words, the DELETE should produce a side-effect, and that side-effect is clearly necessary as we have just seen—yet it is also undesirable, because it means that project information is lost for certain employees. (As suggested earlier, side-effects are usually undesirable.)

- Detailed consideration of the update rules and the other delete rules is left as an exercise for the reader. Note, however, that if we agree that every LOC value appearing in EMP must appear in both DEPT and PROJ, then it is likely that we have an additional integrity constraint to maintain, namely that every LOC value in DEPT must also appear in PROJ, and vice versa. (For there would be little point in having a LOC value in one and not in the other, because no EMP could have that LOC value.) Is it really likely that DEPT.LOC and PROJ.LOC are so totally interdependent in this manner? It begins to look once again as if the database design is bad—bad in the sense that it cannot be an accurate model of reality.

We turn now to a second, more complicated, example. The point of this example is to show that overlapping keys may sometimes be desirable, but that (as claimed at the beginning of this section) they certainly do need careful treatment. The database concerns suppliers (S), parts (P), and projects (J):

```
S    ( S#, ... )
     PRIMARY KEY ( S# )

P    ( P#, ... )
     PRIMARY KEY ( P# )

J    ( J#, ... )
     PRIMARY KEY ( J# )
```

The following table (SP) indicates which suppliers are *allowed* to supply which parts:

```
SP   ( S#, P# )
     PRIMARY KEY ( S#, P# )
     FOREIGN KEY ( S# ) REFERENCES S
     FOREIGN KEY ( P# ) REFERENCES P
```

Likewise, tables PJ and JS indicate, respectively, which parts are allowed to be supplied to which projects and which projects are allowed to be supplied by which suppliers:

```
PJ   ( P#, J# )
     PRIMARY KEY ( P#, J# )
     FOREIGN KEY ( P# ) REFERENCES P
     FOREIGN KEY ( J# ) REFERENCES J
```

```
JS  ( J#, S# )
    PRIMARY KEY ( J#, S# )
    FOREIGN KEY ( J# ) REFERENCES J
    FOREIGN KEY ( S# ) REFERENCES S
```

Finally, table SPJ indicates which suppliers *actually* supply which parts to which projects:

```
SPJ ( S#, P#, J# )
    PRIMARY KEY ( S#, P#, J# )
    FOREIGN KEY ( S#, P# ) REFERENCES SP
    FOREIGN KEY ( P#, J# ) REFERENCES PJ
    FOREIGN KEY ( J#, S# ) REFERENCES JS
```

Table SPJ obviously has three foreign keys, each one of which overlaps the other two. For example, the combination SPJ.(S#,P#) is a foreign key that references table SP (because a particular value for (S#,P#) can appear in table SPJ only if the indicated supplier *can* supply the indicated part— i.e., only if the (S#,P#) value in question appears in table SP).

Points arising:

- Every foreign key in this database obviously has NULLS NOT ALLOWED (because every foreign key is in fact a component of the primary key of its containing table).

- Columns S#, P#, and J# in table SPJ can also be regarded as foreign keys, referencing tables S, P, and J, respectively. However, there is no need to declare those foreign keys explicitly, since the corresponding referential constraints are *transitive*. Refer back to Section 15 for a discussion of transitive constraints.

- Note that there are several conterminous referential paths (quite apart from those arising from the transitive constraints just mentioned). For example, there are two paths from SPJ to S, one via SP and one via JS. The complete "referential graph" (to coin a term) looks something like this:

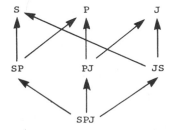

The discussions of Section 15 regarding conterminous paths are therefore relevant to this example.

- Note also that we have some additional (nonreferential) integrity constraints to maintain, over and above the foreign key constraints. For example, every S# value appearing in table S must also appear in table SP (because it makes no sense to have a supplier who is not allowed to supply any parts). This is not a referential constraint, because it is not the case that for every S# value in table S there must be *exactly one* corresponding row in table SP. We can express it as follows, using the hypothetical integrity language of reference [26] once again:

```
CREATE INTEGRITY RULE S_SP
       AT COMMIT :
       CHECK FORALL S ( EXISTS SP ( SP.S# = S.S# ) ) ;
```

Note that the checking must be done "AT COMMIT" (i.e., it must be deferred), for otherwise there would be no way to insert a new supplier into table S, nor to delete the last SP row for a given supplier (etc., etc.).

Analogous deferred constraints P_SP, P_PJ, J_PJ, J_JS, and S_JS must also be defined and maintained, of course:

```
CREATE INTEGRITY RULE P_SP
       AT COMMIT :
       CHECK FORALL P ( EXISTS SP ( SP.P# = P.P# ) ) ;

CREATE INTEGRITY RULE P_PJ
       AT COMMIT :
       CHECK FORALL P ( EXISTS PJ ( PJ.P# = P.P# ) ) ;

CREATE INTEGRITY RULE J_PJ
       AT COMMIT :
       CHECK FORALL J ( EXISTS PJ ( PJ.J# = J.J# ) ) ;

CREATE INTEGRITY RULE J_JS
       AT COMMIT :
       CHECK FORALL J ( EXISTS JS ( JS.J# = J.J# ) ) ;

CREATE INTEGRITY RULE S_JS
       AT COMMIT :
       CHECK FORALL S ( EXISTS JS ( JS.S# = S.S# ) ) ;
```

- Now consider the foreign key SP.S# (representing the referential constraint from table SP to table S). What is the delete rule? It obviously cannot be NULLIFIES. Can it be CASCADES? If it is, symmetry dictates that the delete rule for the foreign keys SP.P#, PJ.P#, PJ.J#, JS.J#, and JS.S# must all be CASCADES also. Similarly for RESTRICTED, mutatis mutandis. Analogous remarks apply to the update rules for these foreign keys also.

- What about the foreign key SPJ.(S#,P#)? What is the delete rule here? Again NULLIFIES is clearly not possible, but RESTRICTED and CASCADES both seem to be acceptable. Again symmetry suggests that whatever the answer is, it should be the same for foreign keys SPJ.(P#,J#) and SPJ.(J#,S#) also. Similar remarks apply to the update rule—except that, once again, an update rule of CASCADES will cause possibly undesirable side effects.

To conclude the discussion of this example, I sketch below an alternative design that avoids the overlapping keys. (Tables S, P, and J are the same as before and are not explicitly shown.)

```
SP   ( SP#, S#, P# )
     PRIMARY KEY ( SP# )
     ALTERNATE KEY ( S#, P# )
     FOREIGN KEY ( S# ) REFERENCES S
     FOREIGN KEY ( P# ) REFERENCES P

PJ   ( PJ#, P#, J# )
     PRIMARY KEY ( PJ# )
     ALTERNATE KEY ( P#, J# )
     FOREIGN KEY ( P# ) REFERENCES P
     FOREIGN KEY ( J# ) REFERENCES J

JS   ( JS#, J#, S# )
     PRIMARY KEY ( JS# )
     ALTERNATE KEY ( J#, S# )
     FOREIGN KEY ( J# ) REFERENCES J
     FOREIGN KEY ( S# ) REFERENCES S

SPJ  ( SPJ#, SP#, PJ#, JS# )
     PRIMARY KEY ( SPJ# )
     ALTERNATE KEY ( SP#, PJ#, JS# )
     FOREIGN KEY ( SP# ) REFERENCES SP
     FOREIGN KEY ( PJ# ) REFERENCES PJ
     FOREIGN KEY ( JS# ) REFERENCES JS
```

The primary keys SP#, PJ#, JS#, and SPJ# are single-column surrogate identifiers (once again, refer to Section 19 for further discussion of surrogates). The constraints S_SP, P_SP, P_PJ, J_PJ, J_JS, and S_JS remain as before and are not shown.

The preceding discussions give some idea of the kind of complexity that can arise from overlapping keys. Again, of course, I make no claim that I have covered all possible problems. The recommendation that keys not be allowed to overlap enables such problems to be avoided.

Note: There is one further point—perhaps a trifle obscure—that ought to be mentioned under the heading of overlapping keys, namely as follows. As stated near the beginning of this section, it *is* generally acceptable to have two keys that "overlap" in the sense that one key is totally included in the other. However, if the two keys in question are both foreign keys, there is still some need for caution. Consider the following example (which is deliberately a trifle abstract; however, the table and column names have been chosen to be reminiscent of the courses–offerings–enrollees example). Irrelevant specifications are omitted.

```
C    ( C# )
     PRIMARY KEY ( C# )

O    ( C#, O# )
     PRIMARY KEY ( C#, O# )

E    ( C#, O#, E# )
     FOREIGN KEY ( C# )       REFERENCES C
     FOREIGN KEY ( C#, O# ) REFERENCES O
```

In table E, foreign key C# is totally included in foreign key (C#,O#). There are two cases to consider:

(a) Column C# in table O is also a foreign key, referring to table C.

(b) Column C# in table O is not a foreign key referring to table C.

Case (a) is essentially the courses–offerings–enrollees example of Section 2, and is perfectly acceptable (subject to the discussions of Sections 15 and 17 above). Case (b), however, is rather strange. Case (b) apparently permits a row <c,o> to appear in table O without a corresponding row <c> in table C.

Note carefully, however, that the row <c,o> *cannot in turn have a corresponding row* <c,o,e> *in table E.* For if such a row <c,o,e> did appear in table E, then row <c> would have to appear in table C, because E.C# is a foreign key referring to table C. Hence the row <c,o> in table O has no logical connexion with *either* of the other two tables. Such a combination of circumstances *might* occur in practice, but it does not seem very likely. Thus, I do not say that such a case is impossible, but I do feel it should at least give the database designer cause to reflect awhile.

19.   WHY NONCOMPOSITE KEYS ARE A GOOD IDEA

As suggested in Sections 17 and 18, I tend to feel that composite keys (primary and foreign) are generally to be avoided—even though several examples of such keys were in fact shown in Section 2, for tutorial reasons. Thus, every time a composite key arises during the database design process, it is a good idea to consider very carefully whether it might not be better to introduce a new, noncomposite column to act as the key instead. In the case of shipments, for example (table SP), it might be worth introducing a new SHIP# column (''shipment number'') as the primary key. (The composite column SP.(S#,P#) would then be an alternate key.) In this section I present some of the arguments in favor of such an approach. *Note:* Some of the following arguments have been presented before in reference [22].

19.1 The first and most obvious point is that all of the problems discussed in Sections 17 and 18 simply do not arise if keys are always noncomposite. In fact, an argument can be made that those problems (like so many others) all stem from *a confusion over levels of abstraction.* From an abstract point of view, foreign keys are nothing more than references from one entity to another; the possibility of such references overlapping and the possibility of such references being partly null simply do not arise. It is only because (a) foreign keys happen to be represented by columns, and (b) those columns happen to be allowed to be composite, that such questions even occur in the first place. In other words, the complications of Sections 17 and 18 arise only because of a confusion between an abstract concept, on the one hand, and the concrete realization of that concept in the relational model, on the other.

19.2 Composite keys can be clumsy, in the sense that they can lead to very cumbersome WHERE clauses (e.g., in joins). For example:

```
SELECT *
FROM    OFFERING, ENROLLEE
WHERE   OFFERING.COURSE# = ENROLLEE.COURSE#
AND     OFFERING.OFF#    = ENROLLEE.OFF# ;
```

Such clumsy formulations do not represent any kind of fundamental problem, of course, but they can be awkward and tedious for the user. It would be nice if the system allowed composite columns to be given noncomposite names [24], so that the above join could be simplified to (e.g.)

```
SELECT *
FROM    OFFERING, ENROLLEE
WHERE   OFFERING.X# = ENROLLEE.X# ;
```

where X# stands for the combination of COURSE# and OFF#. Unfortunately, few systems today provide any support for such composite column naming. Instead, therefore, it might be desirable to introduce X# as a noncomposite primary key for OFFERING and as a corresponding noncomposite foreign key in ENROLLEE, as in the example at the end of Section 17:

```
OFFERING ( X#, COURSE#, OFF#, ... )
         PRIMARY KEY ( X# )
         ALTERNATE KEY ( COURSE#, OFF# )

ENROLLEE ( X#, EMP#, ... )
         .....
         FOREIGN KEY ( X# ) REFERENCES OFFERING
```

As in the example at the end of Section 17, the combination (COURSE#,OFF#) now serves as an alternate key for OFFERING and has been removed entirely from ENROLLEE. One consequence of this revised design—not the only one, of course—is that it simplifies the formulation of the join.

19.3 Another problem with composite keys is that they can lead to re-dundancy—redundancy, that is, at the *logical level*. (They may or may not lead to redundancy at the physical level.) For example, if offering 3 of course 86 has 20 students enrolled, then the fact that course 86 *has* an offer-ing 3 appears 21 times in the composite-key design—once in an OFFERING row and 20 times in an ENROLLEE row. Again, therefore, it might be better to introduce a new, noncomposite key X# (say) for the OFFERING table and then to use X# in the ENROLLEE table, as suggested in para-graph 19.2 above. This revised design has the effect of eliminating the re-dundancy. (Though in fairness it must be pointed out that—*provided* the system enforces referential integrity—redundancy of the kind described is probably not a problem at the logical level. As already suggested, it may or may not be a problem at the physical level.)

19.4 If we assume that there is a one-to-one correspondence between (base table) rows and stored records, as is in fact the case in most relational systems at the time of writing, then:

- Introducing the noncomposite key X# as above will probably have the additional advantage that it will reduce disk space requirements.

- On the other hand, there is a disadvantage also—namely, more joins will now be needed. For example, the query "List course numbers for courses attended by employee E5" will now require a join, whereas previously it did not. It is true that a view could be defined to conceal the join from the user, but of course the join would still be there; furthermore, most systems today would probably not allow that view to be updated. Also, of course, the join will probably represent a performance penalty (under my stated assumption that there is a one-to-one correspondence between rows and stored records).

- A related point (again under my stated assumption) is as follows: With the original (composite-key) design, it would be possible to in-dex the ENROLLEE table on COURSE#, and hence to get good per-formance for a query such as "List employees who have attended course C5." With the revised design, such an index would not be possible (in most systems today).

19.5 Another argument against composite primary keys is that the col-umn combination in question might lose its uniqueness property. Consider the suppliers-and-parts database, for example, in which we have been as-suming that, at any given time, there cannot be more than one shipment for a given supplier and a given part. Under that assumption, the composite column SP.(S#,P#) of the shipments table does possess the uniqueness prop-erty and so can be used as the primary key. But suppose now that the business rules are changed, so that (e.g.) there now *can* be more than one shipment for a given supplier and a given part, but not on any given date. Now the previous assumption is no longer valid, and the combination (S#,P#) can no longer serve as the primary key (we need to introduce a new SHIPDATE column, and specify the combination (S#,P#,SHIPDATE) as the primary key). Such a change is likely to be extremely disruptive for existing users and existing applications. But if we had already introduced a noncomposite key—SHIP#, say—in our original design, it is at least possible that there would be less disruption.

19.6 Analogously, the column combination that was previously being used as the primary key might lose its "nulls not allowed" status. Arguments very similar to those of the previous paragraph apply in this case also.

19.7 Introduced keys such as X# and SHIP# in the examples above do not have to have any intrinsic meaning. For example, the program that creates OFFERINGs can simply maintain a counter in the database, increasing that counter by one each time a new OFFERING is created in order to generate a new X# value. One consequence of this lack of intrinsic meaning is that *there would never be any need to update column OFFERING.X# at all,* which in turn means that any update rule for the foreign key ENROLLEE.X# would be completely irrelevant and need not be specified at all (see Part I of this paper, Section 8, paragraph 8.10).

19.8 Columns such as X# and SHIP# whose sole function is to represent the existence of an entity are sometimes referred to as *surrogates* [11]. In addition to all of the advantages listed above, surrogates offer another very important benefit, which is precisely that (as already stated) *they have no intrinsic meaning;* their *only* function is to stand for the entity they represent. It is an unfortunate fact that database designers love to encode all kinds of meaning into primary keys, and that such encoding can lead to horrendous problems of a very practical nature [22,34]. Surrogates avoid such problems. Thus, I tend to feel that there are strong arguments in favor of the use of surrogates, even if the entities in question already have noncomposite keys anyway.

> *Aside:* In fact, a good case could be made that familiar real-world identifiers such as "employee number," "social security number," "part number," "driver's license number," etc., etc., are all in fact nothing but surrogates in the above sense. The notorious identifiers 1040, 1099, etc., provide an example that is all too familiar (at least in the United States). *End of aside.*

19.9 Another argument in favor of surrogates is provided by the example discussed briefly in Section 12 concerning social security numbers (SS#)

and driver's license numbers (LIC#). Suppose first that we have two distinct "person" tables (used in two distinct applications), one with primary key SS# and the other with primary key LIC#. Suppose now that it is required to coalesce these previously separate tables in some manner, perhaps by replacing them by their outer union [11]. Since some persons have a social security number but no driver's license and some the opposite, neither of SS# and LIC# can serve as the primary key for the resulting table. Hence the coalescing is bound to be disruptive for *both* of the existing applications. By contrast, if the two original tables had had surrogate primary keys, then the coalesced table could retain the same primary key, and it is at least possible that the existing applications could continue to work unchanged.

See reference [22] for further discussion of surrogates.

20. WHY A SINGLE TARGET TABLE IS A GOOD IDEA

In his RM/T paper [11], Codd tacitly opened the door to the possibility of multiple target tables per foreign key (see the discussion in Section 4 in Part I of this paper). I elaborated on this idea in reference [17], proposing a possible concrete syntax somewhat along the following lines:

```
FOREIGN KEY ( foreign-key )
            REFERENCES   quantifier  ( target-commalist )
```

where "quantifier" is EXACTLY ONE OF, AT LEAST ONE OF, or ALL OF, and the quantifier and the parentheses surrounding "target-comma-list" can be omitted if the list in fact contains only one table. For the semantics of the various quantifiers, see Section 4 in Part I of this paper (paragraph 4.8).

Here are some examples. Consider the suppliers table from the suppliers-and-parts database:

```
S ( S#, SNAME, STATUS, CITY )
```

Suppose we have sample values as follows:

```
S    S#    SNAME    STATUS    CITY
     --    -----    ------    ----
     S1    Smith        20    London
     S2    Jones        10    Paris
     S3    Blake        30    Paris
     S4    Clark        20    London
     S5    Adams        30    Athens
```

Suppose first that this table is split "horizontally" into tables LS, PS, AS (i.e., London suppliers, Paris suppliers, Athens suppliers):

```
LS ( S#, SNAME, STATUS )
PS ( S#, SNAME, STATUS )
AS ( S#, SNAME, STATUS )
```

(the CITY column can now obviously be dropped). Then in table SP we have a referential constraint involving the quantifier EXACTLY ONE OF:

```
FOREIGN KEY ( SP.S# ) REFERENCES EXACTLY ONE OF ( LS, PS, AS )
```

Second, suppose the suppliers table S is split "vertically" into tables

```
SN ( S#, SNAME )
ST ( S#, STATUS )
SC ( S#, CITY )
```

Now we have a referential constraint involving ALL OF:

```
FOREIGN KEY ( SP.S# ) REFERENCES ALL OF ( SN, ST, SC )
```

However, as indicated in Section 4 in Part I of this paper, I now feel that the foregoing was too general, and have since publicly retracted (in a revised version of the original paper [18]). Let me explain why I now feel this way.

1. Consider the first example above once again (the "horizontal split" example). In that example, London, Paris, and Athens suppliers can all be regarded as *subtypes* of the general type "supplier" (each subtype having both a set of common properties that apply to all suppliers, together with a set of properties of its own that do not apply to the other subtypes). Surely, therefore, there should be a single "master" (or supertype) suppliers table S, containing the common properties, and tables LS, PS, and AS should contain the special properties that apply to London, Paris, and Athens suppliers, respectively. The foreign key SP.S# would then reference that supertype table:

```
FOREIGN KEY ( SP.S# ) REFERENCES S
```

We would also have:

```
FOREIGN KEY ( LS.S# ) REFERENCES S
FOREIGN KEY ( PS.S# ) REFERENCES S
FOREIGN KEY ( AS.S# ) REFERENCES S
```

This seems to me to be a much cleaner design. Note in particular what would happen to the referential constraint for the foreign key SP.S# with this design (vs. what would have happened with the previous version) if new supplier cities become legal (Rome, Oslo, Madrid, etc.).

2. As for the second example (the "vertical split" example), note first that we also have the constraints:

```
FOREIGN KEY ( SN.S# ) REFERENCES ST
FOREIGN KEY ( ST.S# ) REFERENCES SN
FOREIGN KEY ( SN.S# ) REFERENCES SC
FOREIGN KEY ( SC.S# ) REFERENCES SN
FOREIGN KEY ( ST.S# ) REFERENCES SC
FOREIGN KEY ( SC.S# ) REFERENCES ST
```

What are the delete rules here? The update rules? Which table is in charge? Surely (again) there should be a "master" suppliers table S—even if that table contains nothing except the master list of all supplier numbers. Again, then, we would have:

```
FOREIGN KEY ( SP.S# ) REFERENCES S
```

We would also have:

```
FOREIGN KEY ( SN.S# ) REFERENCES S
FOREIGN KEY ( ST.S# ) REFERENCES S
FOREIGN KEY ( SC.S# ) REFERENCES S
```

Once again, a much cleaner design!

> *Aside:* The idea of replacing a table by a set of primary-key-preserving projections, as in the example above, is discussed in some detail in reference [27]. *End of aside.*

3. As for the quantifier AT LEAST ONE OF, it is hard to find a sensible example—and it seems likely that it would be difficult to implement efficiently.

So my overall feeling is that permitting multiple target tables for a given foreign key is not a particularly good idea. Of course, if we agree to stay with a single target table for now, there is always the possibility of extending to multiple targets at some future time—whereas, of course, the same argument does not apply in the opposite direction; that is, once we are committed to the idea of multiple targets, we will never be able to fall back to the single-target position. (As explained in Section 10, I strongly believe in being conservative with regard to language extensions—The Principle of Cautious Design once again.)

In closing this section, I should mention that Codd does not agree with the foregoing; that is, he believes that it is necessary to permit multiple target tables for a given foreign key [14]—even though he does explicitly require the single-target discipline in his extended relational model RM/T [11], as mentioned in Part I of this paper (end of Section 4).

21. SOME OPERATIONAL CONSIDERATIONS

In this section I very briefly consider a few operational aspects of the referential integrity concept.

- It must be possible to create and destroy referential constraints dynamically. If an attempt is made to create a new constraint over existing (nonempty) tables, the system must check that the constraint is satisfied by existing data values before accepting that new constraint and recording it in the system catalog. That check can be done either at the time the constraint is defined (this is the SQL/DS approach [3]) or at some later time (this is the DB2 approach [2]); if it is done at a later time, the constraint must remain in a "not yet effective" state until that time.

■ Referential integrity clearly has some implications for point-in-time recovery operations. Basically, point-in-time recovery must recover logically related data as a unit (for otherwise the restored data will not be consistent). We therefore introduce the notion of a *referential structure* (this term is taken from reference [23]). Informally, a referential structure is just a set of tables that are interconnected via referential constraints. More precisely, a referential structure consists of a set of tables such that:

(a) Every table in the set either references or is referenced by some table in the set (possibly the same table, in the case of a self-referencing table);

(b) No table not in the set either references or is referenced by any table in the set;

(c) No proper subset of the tables in the set satisfies conditions (a) and (b). (Condition (c) is necessary in order to prevent, e.g., the collection of tables T2, T1, U2, U1, with the only foreign key references being from T2 to T1 and from U2 to U1, from being considered as a referential structure.)

   Then point-in-time recovery needs to operate in terms of such referential structures. In particular, utilities are needed to dump and restore such structures as a unit.

■ Let T1 be a base table. Creating another base table T2 that includes a foreign key referencing table T1 can have the effect of constraining the operations that can legally be performed on table T1. For example, a previously acceptable DELETE against T1 might now fail (if the delete rule for the foreign key in T2 is RESTRICTED). In order to prevent certain unpleasant surprises, therefore, it seems desirable to require the creator of the foreign key in table T2 to hold some suitable authorization before he or she is allowed to create that foreign key. In SQL/DS, for example [3,7], the owner of table T1 would have to grant the creator of table T2 the REFERENCES privilege on table T1. (By contrast, a user in SQL/DS who deletes a row in table T1 and thereby deletes or updates one or more rows in table T2—by virtue of a CASCADES or NULLIFIES delete rule—does not require any particular authorization at all on table T2.)

■ Finally, let us consider the question of locking. In implementing update operations against tables that are part of some referential structure, the system must follow an appropriate set of locking protocols to guarantee that it is not possible, for example, for user B to insert a shipment (SP row) that references a supplier (S row) that user A is currently halfway through deleting. The details are beyond the scope of this paper; however, some idea of what is involved can be found in a paper by Alur (reference [6]). The interested reader is referred to that paper for further discussion.

22. CONCLUSION

In this paper, I have surveyed the question of referential integrity and related matters in considerable detail. I have tried to be reasonably comprehensive, but I make no claim that the treatment is in any way exhaustive. Certainly there are some unsolved research problems, as I have indicated at one or two points in the body of the paper. I will close by mentioning another such problem (a challenge for the reader): What are the implications for referential integrity of distributed database technology? This is a problem that is likely to acquire considerable practical significance over the next few years.

ACKNOWLEDGMENTS

I am grateful, first and foremost, to Ted Codd for inventing the basic ideas on which this paper is based—namely, the primary and foreign key concepts, which have contributed immeasurably to our overall understanding of data and database systems and have provided the foundation for a wealth of interesting and important developments in the database field. My critical remarks in Sections 3–6 of Part I of this paper are intended merely to clarify those concepts, not to suggest in any way that there is anything fundamentally wrong with them. I am also grateful to numerous friends and colleagues, especially Nagraj Alur, Charley Bontempo, Hugh Darwen, Nat Goodman, Sharon Weinberg, and Colin White, for many helpful discussions. Needless to say, however, the opinions expressed in the paper are my own, and all errors, whether of omission or commission, are my own also.

REFERENCES AND BIBLIOGRAPHY

1. Data Base Task Group of CODASYL Programming Language Committee, Final Report (April 1971).

2. IBM Corporation, Programming Announcement IBM DATABASE 2 (DB2) Version 2 (April 19, 1988).

3. IBM Corporation, Programming Announcement Structured Query Language/ Data System (SQL/DS) Version 2 Release 2 (June 21, 1988).

4. ISO/TC97/SC21/WG3 / ANSI X3H2, Database Language SQL Addendum-1. Document ISO DBL AMS-10 / ANSI X3H2-87-205 (1987).

5. ISO/IEC JTC1/SC21/WG3 / ANSI X3H2, ISO-ANSI (working draft) Database Language SQL2. Document ISO DBL CPH-2b / ANSI X3H2-88-210 (April 1988).

6. Nagraj Alur, "IBM DATABASE 2 and Referential Integrity," *InfoDB* 3, No. 1 (Spring 1988).

7. Nagraj Alur, "Primary and Foreign Key Support in SQL/DS," *InfoDB* 3, No. 3 (Fall 1988).

8. Nagraj Alur, "A Comparison of IBM and ANSI RI Support," *InfoDB* 3, No. 3 (Fall 1988).

9. E. F. Codd, "A Relational Model of Data for Large Shared Data Banks," *Communications of the ACM* 13, No. 6 (June 1970). Republished in *Communications of the ACM* 26, No. 1 (January 1983).

10. E. F. Codd, "Further Normalization of the Data Base Relational Model," in *Data Base Systems,* Courant Computer Science Symposia Series, Vol. 6 (Englewood Cliffs, NJ: Prentice-Hall, 1972).

11. E. F. Codd, "Extending the Database Relational Model to Capture More Meaning," *ACM Transactions on Database Systems* 4, No. 4 (December 1979).

12. E. F. Codd, "Missing Information (Applicable and Inapplicable) in Relational Databases," *ACM SIGMOD Record* 15, No. 4 (December 1986).

13. E. F. Codd, "More Commentary on Missing Information in Relational Databases (Applicable and Inapplicable Information)," *ACM SIGMOD Record* 16, No. 1 (March 1987).

14. E. F. Codd, "Domains, Keys, and Referential Integrity in Relational Databases," *InfoDB* 3, No. 1 (Spring 1988).

15. C. J. Date, *An Introduction to Database Systems: Volume I,* 4th edition (Reading, MA: Addison-Wesley, 1985).

16. C. J. Date, *An Introduction to Database Systems: Volume II* (Reading, MA: Addison-Wesley, 1982).

17. C. J. Date, "Referential Integrity." *Proc. 7th International Conference on Very Large Data Bases* (September 1981).

18. C. J. Date, "Referential Integrity" (revised version), in C. J. Date, *Relational Database: Selected Writings* (Reading, MA: Addison-Wesley, 1986).

19. C. J. Date, "Why Every Relation Should Have Exactly One Primary Key," in C. J. Date, *Relational Database: Selected Writings* (Reading, MA: Addison-Wesley, 1986).

20. C. J. Date, "Some Relational Myths Exploded," in C. J. Date, *Relational Database: Selected Writings* (Reading, MA: Addison-Wesley, 1986).

21. C. J. Date, "Updating Views," in C. J. Date, *Relational Database: Selected Writings* (Reading, MA: Addison-Wesley, 1986).

22. C. J. Date, "A Practical Approach to Database Design," in C. J. Date, *Relational Database: Selected Writings* (Reading, MA: Addison-Wesley, 1986).

23. C. J. Date, "Primary and Foreign Key Support in DB2," *InfoDB* 3, No. 3 (Fall 1988).

24. C. J. Date, "What Is a Domain?" (in this volume).

25. C. J. Date, "Why Duplicate Rows Are Prohibited" (in this volume).

26. C. J. Date, "A Contribution to the Study of Database Integrity" (in this volume).

27. C. J. Date, "A Note on One-to-One Relationships" (in this volume).

28. C. J. Date, "Referential Integrity and Foreign Keys: A Working Paper" (private communication to E. F. Codd, April 1987).

29. C. J. Date and Colin J. White, *A Guide to DB2*, 3rd edition (Reading, MA: Addison-Wesley, 1989).

30. C. J. Date and Colin J. White, *A Guide to SQL/DS* (Reading, MA: Addison-Wesley, 1988).

31. K. P. Eswaran and D. D. Chamberlin, "Functional Specifications of a Subsystem for Data Base Integrity." *Proc. 1st International Conference on Very Large Data Bases* (September 1975).

32. B.-M. Schueler, "Update Reconsidered," in G. M. Nijssen (ed.), *Architecture and Models in Data Base Management Systems.* North-Holland (1977).

33. Joseph W. Schmitt, "Nametags Reduce Database Integrity Problems" (private communication, November 1988).

34. Theresa Whitener, "Primary Identifiers: The Basics of Database Stability," *Database Programming and Design* 2, No. 1 (January 1989).

APPENDIX A:
REFERENTIAL INTEGRITY IN THE SQL STANDARD

At the time of writing (late 1988), the existing SQL standard is on the point of being extended to incorporate some minimal support for referential integrity. The salient features of that support are summarized in this appendix.

Primary and Foreign Key Specifications

1. Any base table can optionally have zero or more candidate keys. If a given table has at least one candidate key, then at most one of those candidate keys can optionally be specified as the primary key. Candidate keys are defined by means of a UNIQUE specification; the primary key is defined by means of a PRIMARY KEY specification. (UNIQUE and PRIMARY KEY specifications are part of CREATE TABLE; PRIMARY KEY implies UNIQUE. Every column involved in a candidate key must be explicitly defined to be NOT NULL.)

2. Any base table can have any number of foreign keys, defined via a FOREIGN KEY specification in CREATE TABLE. The only delete rule supported (implicitly) is RESTRICTED; likewise, the only update rule supported (implicitly) is also RESTRICTED. Foreign keys are allowed to reference any candidate key.

3. To define a foreign key that references a given candidate key (*not* a given table, notice), the user needs the REFERENCES privilege on that candidate key.

4. Composite foreign key values are allowed to be partly null; a composite foreign key value that is partly null is always legal, regardless of the values of its nonnull components. Composite keys (primary and/or foreign) are allowed to overlap.

5. All constraint checking is immediate.

Some Comments

The proposed support for referential integrity in the standard is (paradoxically) too complex and yet at the same time inadequate. Of course, it is true that the proposals do allow integrity to be maintained, and they can be used in a sensible manner (with a certain amount of discipline). But:

- Primary keys should be mandatory, not optional.
- Alternate keys should not be required to be NOT NULL.
- Foreign keys should reference primary keys, not candidate keys.
- Composite foreign key values should not be allowed to be partly null.
- Composite keys should not be allowed to overlap.
- The only delete rule supported is RESTRICTED; support for other rules—especially CASCADES—is highly desirable. Similarly for the update rule.
- Cycles are apparently not supported—except possibly cycles of length one (i.e., self-referencing tables).
- Support for deferred checking is desirable.

APPENDIX B:
REFERENTIAL INTEGRITY IN DB2 AND SQL/DS

Perhaps the most sophisticated commercial implementations of referential integrity (at the time of writing—late 1988) are to be found in the IBM products DB2 and SQL/DS. For that reason, it seems appropriate to devote this appendix to a brief examination of those implementations. *Note:* Most of what follows is based on material first published in references [7,23,29,30]. See those references for more detail. For consistency with the body of the paper, I use the terms RESTRICTED, CASCADES, and NULLIFIES instead of the DB2 and SQL/DS equivalents RESTRICT, CASCADE, and SET NULL. Also, for ease of presentation, I will describe the DB2 implementation first, then summarize the SQL/DS differences in a separate subsection.

DB2 Primary and Foreign Key Specifications

1. Any base table can have at most one primary key, defined via a PRIMARY KEY specification in CREATE TABLE or ALTER TABLE; every column involved must be defined to be NOT NULL. A UNIQUE index (the "primary index") must be created on the primary key before the table can be used.

2. Any base table can have any number of foreign keys, defined via a FOREIGN KEY specification in CREATE TABLE or ALTER TABLE. All three delete rules are supported (RESTRICTED, CASCADES, NULLIFIES); the only update rule supported (and that only implicitly) is RESTRICTED.

3. To define a foreign key that references a given base table, the user needs the ALTER privilege on that table.

4. Composite foreign key values are allowed to be partly null; a composite foreign key value that is partly null is always legal, regardless of the values of its nonnull components. Composite keys (primary and/or foreign) are allowed to overlap.

5. All constraint checking is immediate, except that it is possible to load data via the LOAD utility with checking disabled (see the subsection on "DB2 utilities" below).

172

A Note on Terminology

The terminology used by IBM in connexion with referential integrity is a trifle unfortunate (to say the least). We can summarize that terminology as follows:

- The IBM term for a referenced (or target) table is *parent* table.
- The IBM term for a referencing table is *dependent* table (*not* child, note).
- A table that is not a dependent table *and not a parent table* is said to be an *independent* table.
- A dependent of a dependent table is said to be a *descendant* table.

Note that "independent" does not mean "not dependent," and note also that a dependent is not a descendant! There are rich possibilities for confusion here.

There is another remark that must be made while we are on the general subject of terminology and notation: Perversely, IBM documentation shows referential arrows *going the other way* (i.e., from the referenced table ["parent"] to the referencing table ["dependent"], or equivalently from the primary key to the foreign key, instead of the other way around)—for example:

    DEPT ——→ EMP

instead of

    EMP ——→ DEPT

(the latter figure illustrates the convention adopted in the present paper). Our convention accords better with intuition and is consistent with relational and mathematical literature (as pointed out in Part I of this paper, Section 2, referential arrows are basically just an extended form of the conventional functional dependency arrow). Again it must be said that the IBM convention is likely to cause a great deal of unnecessary confusion.

DB2 Implementation Restrictions

Referential integrity support was introduced into DB2 with Version 2 Release 1. The initial support suffers from a number of implementation restrictions, the most important of which are summarized below. Of course, it might be possible to relax some of these restrictions at some future time. The basic problem in most cases is that, for performance reasons, DB2 applies the primary and foreign key integrity checks to each individual row *as it updates that row,* whereas in some cases it would be more correct to defer the checking either to the end of the overall statement or (in some cases) to COMMIT time, i.e., to the end of the *transaction.* But DB2 does not support any deferred checking (except via the LOAD utility—see later).

■   As a trivial example, suppose we had a table T with two rows, with primary key values 1 and 2, respectively. Consider the request "double every primary key value in T." The correct result is that the rows should now have primary key values 2 and 4, respectively. However, DB2 will reject the request entirely, on the grounds that if it updated the row with primary key value 1 first (to yield 2) it would run into a primary key uniqueness violation.*

As a consequence of such row-level checking, *different row-level processing sequences might yield different results* (in general); in other words, the result of a given set-level operation might be unpredictable. Most of the restrictions listed below represent attempts to outlaw situations in which such unpredictability might otherwise occur.

The restrictions follow. *Note:* Number 6 was discussed in some detail in the body of the paper (Section 15). See that section also for an explanation of the term "delete-connected."

1. If (a) the user issues a DELETE on table T1, and (b) table Tn is delete-connected to table T1, and (c) the DELETE includes a subquery, then the FROM clause in that subquery must not refer to table Tn unless the last delete rule in the path—i.e., the delete rule from Tn to T(n − 1)—is RESTRICTED. For example, if the referential constraint from shipments (table SP) to suppliers (table S) has a delete rule of CASCADES, then the following attempt to delete all suppliers who currently supply no parts (unfortunately, and perhaps rather surprisingly) will fail:

```
DELETE
FROM    S
WHERE   NOT EXISTS
      ( SELECT *
        FROM    SP
        WHERE   SP.S# = S.S# ) ;
```

Instead, the user should first compile a list of relevant supplier numbers, and then delete all suppliers whose number is given in that list as a separate operation.

---

*Interestingly, the same problem exists in DB2 with any column on which a UNIQUE index is defined. However, the implementation restriction applies only to primary keys specifically (i.e., the result in other cases is genuinely unpredictable).

2. Any UPDATE statement that updates a primary key value must be "single-row" (i.e., there must be at most one row at execution time that satisfies the WHERE clause). Thus, for example, the following UPDATE is valid (because S# is the primary key for table S):

```
UPDATE S
SET    S# = 'S10'
WHERE  S# = 'S5' ;
```

whereas the following may or may not be valid, depending on the values in the database:

```
UPDATE S
SET    S# = 'S10'
WHERE  CITY = 'Athens' ;
```

3. UPDATE CURRENT (i.e., UPDATE via a cursor) is not allowed to assign a value to a primary key.

4. In a self-referencing table:

- The delete rule must be CASCADES.
- DELETE CURRENT (i.e., DELETE via a cursor) is not allowed.
- INSERT . . . SELECT is allowed only if it inserts at most one row, i.e., the SELECT selects at most one row.

5. In a cycle of length N, where N is greater than one, no table is allowed to be delete-connected to itself.

6. If table Tn is delete-connected to table T1 via two or more distinct referential paths, then every foreign key in table Tn that is involved in any of those paths must have the same delete rule, and furthermore that rule must not be NULLIFIES.

DB2 Utilities

The following DB2 utilities are affected by referential integrity: CHECK, COPY, LOAD, QUIESCE (new), RECOVER, REORG, REPAIR, and REPORT (new). The effects are summarized below.

First, as explained in Section 21, it is clear that point-in-time recovery (that is, *media* recovery) logically needs to operate in terms of "referential structures." However, media recovery in DB2 operates in terms of physical storage units (e.g., "tablespaces"), not logical units such as tables or referential structures. DB2 therefore defines another construct, the *tablespace set,* which is the set of all tablespaces that contain any table(s) of a given referential structure; and it is the tablespace set, not the referential structure, that acts as the unit of integrity so far as recovery is concerned.

Now let T be a tablespace. Certain operations will cause T to be placed in the "check pending" state. "Check pending" means that T either actually or potentially contains one or more (nonnull) foreign key values for which no target primary key value exists. The operations that set "check pending" are as follows:

- Actual detection of such a foreign key value (via the CHECK utility—see below);

- Definition of a new foreign key for an existing nonempty table in T (via ALTER TABLE);

- Data load or recovery operations (via the LOAD or RECOVER utilities—see below), either on some referencing table in T or on some target table that is referenced by some table in T, if such operations might possibly violate some referential constraint.

While T is in the "check pending" state, data manipulation operations (SELECT, UPDATE, etc.) and COPY, REORG, and QUIESCE utility operations will not be accepted on T. Data definition operations will be accepted, however. The "check pending" condition can be reset either by the CHECK utility or by the REPAIR utility (see below).

Next, the LOAD, RECOVER, CHECK, and REPAIR utilities have all been extended, as follows:

- LOAD on a table that contains a foreign key can be run with referential constraint checking enabled or disabled. If checking is enabled, input rows that violate the constraint will not be loaded (however, they can optionally be placed in a separate rejects file). If checking is disabled, a "check pending" condition will be set on the applicable tablespace.

- RECOVER can be used to recover an entire tablespace set as a unit. RECOVER will set "check pending" on the applicable tablespace(s) unless (a) the entire tablespace set is recovered as a unit *and* (b) recovery is to a "point of consistency" (established via QUIESCE—see below).

- CHECK is extended to perform referential integrity checking. Referencing rows that violate a referential constraint can optionally be copied to an exception table, and optionally deleted as well. If they are deleted, or if no such rows are found, any "check pending" condition will be reset.

- REPAIR is extended to allow the user to force a "check pending" condition to be reset.

Finally, two new utilities, QUIESCE and REPORT, are provided:

- QUIESCE is used to quiesce operations (temporarily) on a specified collection of tablespaces. The quiesced state corresponds to a single point in the log, so that the collection of tablespaces can subsequently be recovered as a unit. For example, QUIESCE can be useful in connexion with dumping (and subsequently restoring) an entire disk volume as a unit. In particular, QUIESCE can be used to establish a point of consistency for a tablespace set, thus ensuring that subsequent recovery to that point will restore the data to a consistent state (see the discussion of RECOVER, above).

- The REPORT utility can be used to determine the collection of tablespaces that constitute a tablespace set, and hence the tablespaces that need to be quiesced as a unit.

DB2 Implementation Considerations

1. All integrity checking is performed by the DB2 Data Manager, not by generated code in the application plan(s).

2. The action of adding a primary or foreign key definition to an existing table (via ALTER TABLE) can have the effect of invalidating certain existing application plans. To be specific:

- Adding a primary key definition to base table T will invalidate all plans that operate on T.
- Adding a foreign key definition to base table T2 that references base table T1:
  - If T2 and T1 are the same table, will invalidate all plans that operate on that table;
  - If the delete rule in the new foreign key definition is CASCADES or NULLIFIES, will invalidate all plans that operate on any table to which T2 is now delete-connected (including in particular all plans that operate on T1).

The purpose of the foregoing invalidations is to enable the DB2 Bind component to catch violations of certain of the implementation restrictions described earlier in this appendix—for example, the restriction that DELETE CURRENT is not allowed against a self-referencing table. (As usual, invalidated plans will automatically be rebound the next time they are invoked.) Note that the foregoing could cause migration problems in some circumstances—that is, a plan that worked perfectly (and did not cause any referential integrity violations) under DB2 Version 1 might fail to rebind under DB2 Version 2. A source code change will be required in such a situation.

3. There are no new catalog tables; however, there are several new columns in existing tables, and several possible new entries in existing columns. For example, the SYSINDEXES catalog table has a new possible

UNIQUERULE entry (P, meaning primary index; the other possible entries are U, meaning other unique index, and D [= duplicates allowed], meaning nonunique index). Further details are beyond the scope of this appendix.

SQL/DS Differences

Note: The following list is not intended to be exhaustive. See reference [8] for more details.

1. It is not necessary to create a UNIQUE index on the primary key in SQL/DS; SQL/DS will create such an index automatically.

2. If table T2 references table T1 and the delete rule is CASCADES, then no table T3 can reference table T2 in turn (i.e., table T2 cannot be a target table). This is a major restriction in SQL/DS—but it does have the effect of simplifying several aspects of the product; in particular, the DB2 concept of "delete-connected" (see Section 15 in the body of the paper) becomes totally irrelevant. The DB2 restrictions regarding delete-connected tables are therefore irrelevant also—except that the following restrictions (simplified forms of two of DB2's "delete-connected" restrictions) do still apply:

- If table T2 references table T1, then a DELETE on table T1 must not include a subquery in which table T2 is named in the FROM clause unless the delete rule from T2 to T1 is RESTRICTED.

- If table T2 has two or more foreign keys that reference the same table T1, then the delete rules for those foreign keys must all be the same, and furthermore they must not be NULLIFIES.

3. Self-referencing tables are not supported. The DB2 restrictions on self-referencing tables therefore do not apply.

4. To define a foreign key that references table T, the user needs the REFERENCES privilege on T. (The REFERENCES privilege was first defined as part of the proposed extensions to the SQL standard [4].) DB2 does not support the REFERENCES privilege but uses the existing ALTER privilege for the same purpose.

5. Individual primary and foreign key constraints can be dynamically deactivated and subsequently reactivated (via ALTER TABLE). While a constraint is active, all checking is immediate. While a constraint is inactive, only the owner of the table (or the database administrator) can access the affected table(s). Reactivating an inactive constraint causes all applicable checks to be performed; if any of those checks fails, the reactivation fails also.

6. SQL/DS does not support the "check pending" condition. SQL/DS utilities are not affected by referential integrity. (SQL/DS does not support point-in-time recovery.)

7. Integrity checking is performed by the RDS component, not by the Data Base Storage System (the SQL/DS analog of the DB2 Data Manager). As a consequence, there are far more situations in which "application plans" (access modules in SQL/DS) are invalidated. The details are beyond the scope of this appendix.

Some Comments

Overall, the IBM support for primary and foreign keys in DB2 and SQL/DS is quite impressive. The single most significant point is, of course, that referential constraints can now be specified declaratively, and hence that referential integrity can be guaranteed, without involving any user-written procedural code. All the standard benefits apply as described in Section 9 of this paper (excluding the last two points listed in that section). At a more detailed level, the majority of functions that are most frequently needed in practice—e.g., cascade delete—are at least optionally supported, and those functions can be used (with a little discipline) in a fairly straightforward manner.

However, the support is not 100 percent perfect. Several complications are caused by the fact that the support is being added after the event (i.e., it ought to have been included in the products at the time of the very first release). For example, primary key information is not returned by DESCRIBE, though it really ought to be, and the catalog structure is not as straightforward as it might have been. Some detailed criticisms follow.

- The IBM terminology is very bad; so too is the IBM convention regarding arrow direction!
- Primary keys should be mandatory, not optional.
- If the primary key is composite, then the order in which columns are specified unfortunately has performance implications (because it affects the structure of the primary key index).
- Alternate keys should be supported.
- Composite foreign key values should not be allowed to be partly null.
- Composite keys should not be allowed to overlap.
- The delete rules RESTRICTED, CASCADES, and NULLIFIES, though certainly the most commonly required in practice, do not cover all possibilities.

- The only update rule supported is RESTRICTED. Support for other rules—especially CASCADES—is desirable. As an interesting exercise, the reader might like to consider what is involved in trying to change a given supplier number, say from S1 to S99. (This example was touched on briefly in Section 15. See Appendix C immediately following for further discussion.)

- The fact that integrity checking is done row by row leads to a number of restrictions, not all of which are immediately obvious. The consequences of those restrictions are not immediately obvious either. The ability to specify that certain checks are to be deferred until end-of-transaction is needed, especially for cycles. Whether the SQL/DS "deactivate/reactivate" mechanism is a satisfactory (or adequate) solution to this latter problem is not clear; probably it is not [26].

- The special restrictions that apply to SQL/DS and not to DB2 (only single-level cascade delete, no self-referencing tables) seem rather severe.

- SQL/DS's REFERENCES privilege is more satisfactory than DB2's special use of the ALTER privilege.

- It is unfortunate that the support is different in the two products, both at the internal level and—more seriously—at the external level (i.e., the data definition facilities are not 100 percent compatible across the two systems).

APPENDIX C:
WHY "UPDATE CASCADES" IS DESIRABLE

In this appendix we present an example to show why support for the CASCADES update rule is desirable. The example is based on one first presented in reference [30], and makes use of the usual suppliers-and-parts database (see Part I of this paper, Section 2, Example 3). Suppose it is required to change the supplier number of supplier Sx to Sy (where Sx and Sy are given). We assume that the implementation restrictions of DB2 (as described in Appendix B immediately preceding) are in effect.

Note first that a simple UPDATE statement along the following lines—

```
UPDATE  S
SET     S# = Sy
WHERE   S# = Sx ;
```

—will not work, because supplier Sx will have some matching shipments (in general), and hence the RESTRICTED update rule will come into play. (Of course, it would work with a CASCADES update rule, which is the whole point of this appendix.)

Second, note that the following sequence of operations also will not work:

```
UPDATE  SP
SET     S# = Sy
WHERE   S# = Sx ;

UPDATE  S
SET     S# = Sy
WHERE   S# = Sx ;
```

The attempt to UPDATE the shipment (SP) records for supplier Sx will fail for at least two reasons: First, it would violate the foreign key constraint; second, UPDATEs to a primary key column in DB2 must be "single-row"—i.e., there must be at most one row at run time that satisfies the WHERE clause (note that SP.S# is a component of the primary key of SP, as well as being a foreign key). Interchanging the two UPDATEs makes no difference, of course.

It follows that it is probably necessary to write a program to handle the problem. An example of such a program follows (written in PL/I with embedded SQL). We make the assumption in that program that any attempt to introduce a new shipment for supplier Sx (via an INSERT or UPDATE on table SP) will request at least a shared lock (S lock) on the supplier record for Sx in table S. *Note:* For typographical reasons, we use the symbol "< >" to represent "not equals." This is legal syntax in SQL but not in PL/I.

```
UPDS#: PROC OPTIONS (MAIN) ;              /* change S# "Sx" to "Sy" */

        DCL SX              CHAR(5) ;
        DCL SY              CHAR(5) ;
        DCL SNAME           CHAR(20) ;
        DCL STATUS          FIXED BINARY(15) ;
        DCL CITY            CHAR(15) ;
        DCL P#              CHAR(6) ;
        DCL MORE_SHIPMENTS BIT(1) ;

        EXEC SQL INCLUDE SQLCA ;

        EXEC SQL DECLARE Y CURSOR FOR
                 SELECT S.SNAME, S.STATUS, S.CITY
                 FROM   S
                 WHERE  S.S# = :SX
                 FOR UPDATE OF SNAME ;

        EXEC SQL DECLARE Z CURSOR FOR
                 SELECT SP.P#
                 FROM   SP
                 WHERE  SP.S# = :SX ;

        EXEC SQL WHENEVER NOT FOUND CONTINUE ;
        EXEC SQL WHENEVER SQLERROR CONTINUE ;
        EXEC SQL WHENEVER SQLWARNING CONTINUE ;

        ON CONDITION ( DBEXCEPTION )
        BEGIN ;
           PUT SKIP LIST ( SQLCA ) ;
           EXEC SQL ROLLBACK WORK ;
           GO TO QUIT ;
        END ;
     GET LIST ( SX, SY ) ;
     EXEC SQL OPEN Y ;
     IF SQLCODE <> 0
     THEN SIGNAL CONDITION ( DBEXCEPTION ) ;

     /* fetch column values for supplier Sx */
     EXEC SQL FETCH Y INTO :SNAME. :STATUS, :CITY ;
     IF SQLCODE <> 0
     THEN SIGNAL CONDITION ( DBEXCEPTION ) ;

     /* make sure supplier Sx stays locked exclusive (X-locked), */
     /* thus preventing concurrent creation of new shipments for */
     /* supplier Sx and concurrent UPDATE/DELETE on supplier Sx  */
     EXEC SQL UPDATE S
              SET    SNAME = :SNAME        /* effectively a no-op */
              WHERE  CURRENT OF Y ;
     IF SQLCODE <> 0
     THEN SIGNAL CONDITION ( DBEXCEPTION ) ;

     /* insert new supplier Sy record */
     EXEC SQL INSERT
              INTO   S ( S#, SNAME, STATUS, CITY )
              VALUES ( :SY, :SNAME, :STATUS, :CITY ) ;
```

```
   IF SQLCODE <> 0
   THEN SIGNAL CONDITION ( DBEXCEPTION ) ;

   /* prepare to loop through shipments for Sx */
   EXEC SQL OPEN Z ;
   IF SQLCODE <> 0
   THEN SIGNAL CONDITION ( DBEXCEPTION ) ;
   MORE_SHIPMENTS = '1'B ;

   /* loop through shipments for Sx */
   DO WHILE ( MORE_SHIPMENTS ) ;
      EXEC SQL FETCH Z INTO :P# ;
      SELECT ;                    /* a PL/I SELECT, not a SQL SELECT */
         WHEN ( SQLCODE = 100 )
            MORE_SHIPMENTS = '0'B ;
         WHEN ( SQLCODE <> 100 & SQLCODE <> 0 )
            SIGNAL CONDITION ( DBEXCEPTION ) ;
         WHEN ( SQLCODE = 0 )
            DO ;
               /* update current shipment -- */
               /* but not via cursor Z  !!!  */
               EXEC SQL UPDATE SP
                        SET    S# = :SY
                        WHERE  S# = :SX
                        AND    P# = :P# ;
               IF SQLCODE <> 0
               THEN SIGNAL CONDITION ( DBEXCEPTION ) ;
            END ;
      END ;    /* PL/I SELECT */
   END ;   /* DO WHILE */
   EXEC SQL CLOSE Z ;
   /* delete supplier Sx */
   EXEC SQL DELETE
            FROM   S
            WHERE  CURRENT OF Y ;
   IF SQLCODE <> 0
   THEN SIGNAL CONDITION ( DBEXCEPTION ) ;
   EXEC SQL CLOSE Y ;
   EXEC SQL COMMIT WORK ;
QUIT:
   RETURN ;
END ;   /* UPDS# */
```

We remark that this example provides additional evidence in support of the claim in Section 19 that it is often a good idea to avoid composite keys. If table SP had a noncomposite primary key SHIP# (say), the entire loop over shipments—

```
DO WHILE ( MORE_SHIPMENTS ) ;
   .....
END ;   /* DO WHILE */
```

(18 lines of code, not counting comments)—could be replaced by the single statement

```
EXEC SQL UPDATE SP
         SET    S# = :SY
         WHERE  S# = :SX ;
```

One final point: The original problem of changing supplier number Sx to Sy might be solved (albeit in a rather heavy-handed manner) in SQL/DS—but not in DB2—by making use of SQL/DS's facility for dynamically deactivating and reactivating constraints. Such a solution might look somewhat as follows. (Note that the operation of deactivating a particular primary key automatically has the effect of deactivating any foreign keys that refer to that primary key. It also has the effect of dropping the primary key index.)

```
ALTER TABLE S DEACTIVATE PRIMARY KEY ;
ALTER TABLE SP DEACTIVATE PRIMARY KEY ;

UPDATE S
SET    S# = Sy
WHERE  S# = Sx ;

UPDATE SP
SET    S# = Sy
WHERE  S# = Sx ;

ALTER TABLE SP ACTIVATE PRIMARY KEY ;
ALTER TABLE S ACTIVATE PRIMARY KEY ;

COMMIT WORK ;
```

Note: Instead of deactivating (and subsequently reactivating) the primary key constraint for table S, we could alternatively have deactivated (and subsequently reactivated) the foreign key constraint from table SP to table S. This latter approach might conceivably be more efficient in practice.

7

A Contribution to the Study of Database Integrity

ABSTRACT

Database integrity is a significant problem. It is also, unfortunately, one that is still far from being completely solved. This paper attempts to impose some structure on the problem by (a) proposing a classification scheme for integrity rules, (b) using that scheme to clarify the principal underlying concepts of data integrity, (c) sketching an approach to a concrete language for formulating integrity rules, and (d) pinpointing some specific areas for further research. The paper is written in tutorial style and contains numerous worked examples.

COMMENTS ON PUBLICATION

In some respects, database integrity is an idea whose time has come. The desirability of being able to state integrity rules declaratively and have them

---

Previously unpublished.

enforced by the system has been recognized for many years; early proposals along such lines were included in the first edition of my book *An Introduction to Database Systems* [4], in a well-known paper by Eswaran and Chamberlin [13], and in many other places, and of course several early DBMSs did include some integrity facilities (albeit fairly limited in scope in most cases). When relational products at last began to come to market in the early 1980s, the potential for good integrity support was there, but the initial emphasis (perhaps understandably) in those products was primarily on performance and other physical matters, not on logical issues such as integrity. More recently, however, the true significance of logical issues in general, and integrity support in particular, has begun to receive increasing recognition and attention—witness the recent addition of referential integrity facilities to the IBM products DB2 and SQL/DS [11,12].

Despite this increased recognition, however, support for integrity in commercially available products is still a long way from perfect. Some products do support important special cases but not the general case.* Others support the general case (or at least, an approximation to the general case) but not the important special cases. Some do support deferred checking, but only in an ad hoc manner. No product supports transition rules (so far as I am aware). No product supports domains properly (again, so far as I am aware). And every system I know suffers from implementation restrictions, usually (again) of a somewhat ad hoc nature. From all of this, I conclude that the integrity issue is still not particularly well understood; in fact, I believe that parts of it must still be considered as lying in the realms of research.

The purpose of the present paper is thus to try to lay out a framework by which the nature of the integrity problem can (I hope) be better understood, and hence to suggest some directions for future investigation. As indicated in the Abstract, that framework consists essentially of *an integrity rule classification scheme,* which is accordingly the major topic of the paper. Along the way, however, I do use a hypothetical integrity language to illustrate the ideas (not too different from the language described in references [5] and [6]), and that language could in fact be used as the basis for constructing a real implementation. But the language is still in a somewhat fluid state, and is certainly not fully defined in the present paper. *Note:* In this paper (unlike most of the others in the book), I decided not to use SQL (or ''pseudoSQL'') as the basis for examples, because SQL suffers from too many problems in this area. In particular, it does not support the universal quantifier FORALL (a major omission).

---

*The present paper is concerned primarily with the general case, not just with special cases such as referential integrity that are adequately dealt with elsewhere [9].

The paper certainly does not claim to solve all (or even any) of the myriad unsolved problems having to do with integrity; it is only a working paper. But it still seemed to me desirable to publish it at this time for what it is, namely (as explained above) an attempt to structure the overall problem. The paper includes a certain amount of material that has been plagiarized from my earlier writings on the subject (particularly in the introductory sections), in order to keep it reasonably self-contained. However, I suppose I should say that it is meant to supersede those earlier writings, or at least portions of them. Specifically, it is intended to replace Sections 19.5 and 19.6 of reference [5] and Sections 2.2, 2.3, and 2.4 of reference [6].

1. THE BASIC IDEA

The term "integrity" is used in database contexts to refer to the accuracy, validity, or correctness of the data in the database. Maintaining integrity is of paramount importance, for obvious reasons; and it is desirable, again for obvious reasons, that the task of maintaining integrity be handled by the system rather than by the user, at least so far as possible.

In order that it may carry out this task, the system needs to be aware of any *integrity constraints* or *rules* that apply to the data. It then needs to monitor update operations to ensure that they do not violate any of those constraints or rules. As a simple example, the suppliers-and-parts database [5] will probably be subject to the rule that part weights must be greater than zero. INSERT and UPDATE statements (in SQL terms) will therefore need to be monitored to ensure that they do not introduce a part weight that fails to conform to this simple rule.

The general idea, then, is that integrity rules should be specified as part of the database definition;* they will then be stored in the system catalog, and used by the system to control updates to the database. It is important to appreciate the fact that the number of rules that apply to any given database is likely to be quite large. For example, the list of rules for the suppliers-and-parts database might easily include all of the following:

1. Supplier numbers must be of the form "S9999" (where "9999" stands for up to four decimal digits);
2. No two suppliers have the same supplier number (at any given time);
3. No two suppliers have the same supplier name (at any given time);
4. Supplier status values must be in the range 1 to 100;

---

*Indeed, they should be specified during the process of database *design;* they are just as much part of the design as the underlying data structures are.

5. A supplier's status must never decrease;

6. Supplier cities must be drawn from a specified list;

7. If the supplier city is London, then the status must be 20;

8. Part numbers must be of the form "P99999" (where "99999" stands for up to five decimal digits);

9. No two parts have the same part number (at any given time);

10. Part colors must be drawn from a specified list;

11. Part weights must be greater than zero;

12. Part cities must be drawn from a specified list (the same list as for suppliers);

13. All red parts must be stored in London;

14. No two shipments have the same supplier number and the same part number (at any given time);

15. Every shipment must be for a known supplier and a known part;

16. Shipment quantities must be greater than zero and must be a multiple of 100;

17. Part P2 cannot be shipped in quantities greater than 1000;

18. Suppliers with status less than 20 must not supply any part in a quantity greater than 500;

19. The total shipment quantity for part P3 (from all suppliers) must not exceed 2000;

20. The total shipment quantity for any individual part (from all suppliers) must not exceed 3000;

and many others.* In fact, it has been suggested that the specification of integrity constraints could easily account for as much as 90 percent of a typical database definition. A system that supported such specifications would thus relieve application programmers of a considerable burden, and hence enable those programmers to become considerably more productive. Integrity support is an important area for development.

2. INTEGRITY VS. RECOVERY VS. CONCURRENCY VS. SECURITY

Before we go any further, there are a few basic matters that need to be cleared up. First, integrity is sometimes confused with either *recovery* or

---

*Most constraints in this list will be used as the basis for examples in the hypothetical integrity language discussed later in the paper.

concurrency, though it really ought not to be. The fact is, most database products today are quite strong on support for recovery and concurrency, but not many provide much in the way of support for integrity (though some do, and others are beginning to). The differences among the three concepts can be summarized as follows:

- To say that the database is in a state of integrity means, precisely, that the database state is *correct,* in the sense that the values in the database do not violate any of the known integrity constraints. In other words, we regard the database state as correct if and only if it satisfies the logical "AND" of all known constraints. Clearly, however, a system that does not support much in the way of integrity constraint definition (or enforcement) will have only a very weak sense of what it means for a database state to be correct.

- The term *recovery* refers to the process of restoring the database to some previous state after some error (e.g., a hardware or software failure) has destroyed the current state, or at least rendered the current state suspect. But—of course—that restored state will only be "correct" in the system's own, probably rather weak, sense of that term, as explained in the previous paragraph.

- The term *concurrency* refers to the ability to have multiple transactions executing in parallel. Now, it is well known that concurrency, if not properly controlled, can lead to errors; that is, two concurrent transactions, each correct in itself, might interfere with one another in such a manner as to produce an overall result that is incorrect. Systems that provide proper concurrency control, however, guarantee that such interference cannot occur. Note, however, that such systems typically do not concern themselves with the question as to whether individual transactions are correct in themselves; they merely guarantee that errors are not *introduced* by executing such transactions in parallel.

  Aside: We say that a transaction is "correct in itself" if its effect when executed in isolation is to transform a correct state of the database into another correct state. Once again, therefore, we are immediately led back to the system's own definition of what it means for a database state to be correct. *End of aside.*

The concept of integrity is also sometimes confused with the concept of *security.* Certainly the terms are frequently heard together in database contexts, though the concepts are actually quite distinct. Briefly, *security* refers to the protection of data against unauthorized disclosure, alteration, or destruction; *integrity* (once again) refers to the accuracy of the data. In other words:

- Security involves ensuring that users are *allowed* to do the things they are trying to do.

- Integrity involves ensuring that the things they are trying to do are *correct*.

To put it rather glibly: Security means protecting the database against *unauthorized* users; integrity means protecting it against *authorized* users.

One final point: Note that integrity is a property of the *data,* not of individual users (indeed, integrity would be an issue even in a single-user system). In other words, integrity applies to the *base tables* (principally, at any rate, though it is conceivable that there might be some additional constraints that apply to views defined on top of those base tables; see, e.g., the discussion of the CHECK option on CREATE VIEW in DB2 in reference [11]).

3. INTEGRITY RULES

There have been numerous proposals for languages in which to formulate integrity rules, and this paper sketches yet another. However, this new proposal is not too far removed from those previously discussed in references [5] and [6]. Indeed, the major purpose of the present paper is not so much to propose a specific language per se, but rather to clarify the concepts and principles that must underlie any such language. In order to attempt such a clarification, however, it is obviously helpful to have some language to hand to serve as a basis for illustrations and examples. The language of this paper has been specifically designed for such a purpose (though it could serve as a basis for a concrete implementation also, with some refinement).

Here is an example of a simple integrity rule in the proposed language (together with the definition of a range variable PX that is used in that rule):

```
RANGE OF PX IS TABLE P ;

CREATE INTEGRITY RULE R11
        ON      INSERT PX.WEIGHT ,
                UPDATE PX.WEIGHT :
        CHECK   FORALL PX ( PX.WEIGHT > 0 )
        ELSE    REJECT ;
```

("part weights must be greater than zero"). The example will probably appear a trifle longwinded at first sight! It has deliberately been spelled out in detail, however, in order to illustrate the point that, at least in the abstract, integrity rules have *four components,* as follows:

- A *name* ("R11" in the example; note that most of our examples are keyed to the sample list of constraints in Section 1). The rule will be registered in the system catalog under the specified name. That name will also appear in any diagnostics produced by the system in response to a violation of the rule (see the discussion of REJECT below).

- One or more *checking times* ("ON INSERT PX.WEIGHT, UPDATE PX.WEIGHT:" in the example).* The checking times specify when the CHECK clause is to be executed—at least conceptually. We say "conceptually," because various optimizations (beyond the scope of the present discussion) might be possible in practical situations; in some
- cases, it might even be possible to enforce some constraints at compile time.

   Note: It is quite definitely *not* our intention that the user should always have to specify checking times explicitly in the concrete syntax. Quite apart from considerations of convenience, usability, etc., there would always be the problem that the user might make a mistake. Checking times must be included in the *abstract* syntax, of course, but ideally the system should be able to infer the appropriate specifications for itself (we will briefly discuss what might be involved in making such inferences in Section 13). As we will see in Sections 9 and 10, however, there will be some situations in which the user *has* to specify the checking time(s) explicitly. But we will omit such explicit specifications from our examples until further notice (i.e., whenever the checking times are "obvious").

- A *constraint* (specified via the CHECK clause). The constraint consists of an arbitrary "well-formed formula" (abbreviated wff, pronounced "weff") of the relational calculus.† In other words, it is an expression that must evaluate to *true* for the integrity rule to be satisfied. In the example, the expression is

```
FORALL PX ( PX.WEIGHT > 0 )
```

("for all parts PX, the weight component of part PX must be greater than zero"). PX is defined by the preceding RANGE statement to be a range variable that ranges over table P.‡

---

*Observe that we find it convenient (for reasons of explicitness) to talk in terms of inserting into individual columns, not just into whole rows. A checking time specification of the form "INSERT row" will have the same semantic effect, however.

†It was always one of the purposes of the relational calculus (or, equivalently, the relational algebra) to serve as a basis for formulating integrity constraints [7]. In this paper, however, we are assuming a version of the calculus that has been augmented to include certain scalar computational operators such as " + " and " − " and certain aggregate functions such as SUM and AVG. The syntax we use for that augmented calculus is intended to be self-explanatory.

‡Although it is really beyond the scope of the present paper, we should mention that it is our intention that the RANGE statement be able to define the range of a given variable to be *any* *relational expression* (including, in particular, a union), not just a named table [5].

Note 1: Although the CHECK clause specifies that the constraint must be satisfied "for all" parts PX, it is obviously sufficient for implementation purposes to check just a single row—namely, the row being inserted or updated, as indicated by the specification of the checking time ("ON INSERT PX.WEIGHT . . .").

Note 2: Technically, the checking time specification ("ON INSERT PX.WEIGHT . . .") should appear within the scope of the quantifier "FORALL PX," in order to bound the appearance in that specification of the variable PX. But the overall rule reads better (in English, at any rate) the way we have shown it. From a logical point of view, however, integrity rules in our language are to be interpreted as if the scope of all quantifiers were suitably extended to include (appropriate portions of) the applicable checking time specification.

Note 3: We also introduce a syntax rule (to save ourselves some syntax problems later) to the effect that if a variable is bound by *no* explicit quantifier at all, then it is implicitly considered to be bound by a universal quantifier whose scope is the entire integrity rule. This syntax rule will not be invoked until Section 7, however.

Note 4: From this point on, we will draw a distinction between an integrity *rule* and an integrity *constraint*—an integrity rule is the complete 4-part construct (the overall topic of the present section), an integrity constraint is just one component (the most important component, of course) of such an integrity rule.

- A *violation response* (specified via the ELSE clause). The violation response consists of a procedure to be executed if the constraint in the CHECK clause does not evaluate to *true*. *Note:* We are assuming two-valued logic here, of course (and we will continue to make the same assumption throughout the rest of this paper). If the system supports three-valued logic instead [1,2,10], then we will need two different ELSE clauses, one for the case where the constraint evaluates to *false* and one for the case where it evaluates to *unk* (meaning the *unknown* truth value [10]).

    The violation response in the example has been specified as simply REJECT. We take REJECT to mean "reject the update operation that caused the constraint violation (backing out its effects on the database, if any), with a suitable diagnostic that includes at least the integrity rule name." We also take REJECT to be the default if no explicit ELSE clause is specified (and we will usually omit the ELSE clause in our examples from this point on).

    Note: After the procedure in the ELSE clause has been executed, the constraint in the CHECK clause will need to be checked again (at least in principle), because there is always the possibility that the violation response might leave the constraint still unsatisfied, which obviously cannot be allowed. Of course, that repeat checking will not be necessary if the ELSE procedure includes a REJECT (and does not itself perform any updates that might violate the constraint). If the ELSE procedure does leave the constraint unsatisfied, there is the potential for an infinite loop.

Some Simplifications

As stated at the beginning of this section, it is not our purpose in this paper to get deeply involved in issues of concrete syntax per se. However, there are some very obvious simplifications that can be made to the syntax as we have presented it so far that are probably worth mentioning in passing.

- First, we can play the usual syntactic games by which the name of a given table can also be used without explicit definition to refer to an implicit range variable that ranges over that given table.
- Second, the wff in the CHECK clause will almost always start with a universal quantifier ("FORALL range-variable")—and in the cases where it does not, one can be assumed without changing the meaning. Consequently, that quantifier (and its associated scoping parentheses) could be omitted from the concrete syntax.
- Third, the checking time and violation response specifications can both very often be omitted, as already explained above.

Applying all of these simplifications, we obtain the following reduced form of our original example:

```
CREATE INTEGRITY RULE R11
       CHECK  P.WEIGHT > 0 ;
```

The general syntax is thus:

```
CREATE INTEGRITY RULE rule
    [ checking-time-specification : ]
       CHECK  wff
    { ;  |  ELSE  procedure }
```

As already mentioned, we will frequently omit the "checking-time-specification" and the ELSE clause in our examples, but we will usually *not* omit the leading universal quantifier, and we will usually use explicit range variables.

4.   A CLASSIFICATION SCHEME FOR INTEGRITY RULES

Our principal objective in this paper (to repeat from Section 3) is to try to clarify the major concepts of database integrity. The following classification scheme is intended to help in achieving this objective. (We summarize the scheme in the present section, then go on to elaborate on it in the sections that follow.) Briefly, we can divide the universe of discourse—i.e., the set of all possible integrity rules—into several different but overlapping classes according to several different (and more or less independent) criteria, as follows:

- First, they can be classified according to the form of the constraint in the CHECK clause, into *domain* vs. *table* rules. Moreover, table rules can be further divided into *single-row* vs. *multi-row* rules, and multi-row rules in turn have a subclass of rules that involve *aggregate functions* such as SUM and AVG. See Sections 5–8 below.

- Second, they can be classified according to whether they apply to database states per se (*state* rules) or to transitions between states (*transition* rules). See Section 9.

- Third, they can be classified according to whether the constraint is to be checked at the time of the update (*immediate* rules) or at some later time (*deferred* rules). See Section 10.

Not all combinations of the foregoing make sense, however, as we will see in the sections that follow.

5.   DOMAIN RULES

A domain rule is neither more nor less than a specification of the set of values in the relevant domain; hence the definition of such a rule is, precisely, the definition of the domain (as a consequence, domain rules are usually much simpler than table rules). Here is an example (based on one given in reference [8]); note the necessary range variable definition once again.*

```
RANGE OF CX IS DOMAIN COLOR ;

CREATE DOMAIN COLOR CHAR(6)
        CHECK   FORALL CX
              ( CX IN ('Red','Yellow','Blue','Green') ) ;
```

---

*Observe that our version of the relational calculus includes both domain and tuple variables.

Points arising:

- The name of the rule is just the name of the domain.

- The checking time for a domain rule is *always* "ON INSERT or UPDATE on any column defined on the domain." As a consequence, there is never any need to specify the checking time explicitly, and in fact we do not provide any mechanism for doing so in our syntax. *Note:* In order for the system to be able to enforce such a rule, of course, it must provide a means by which the user can specify the relevant domain for each column in each named table [8].

  Domain rules are always *immediate, state* rules; the deferred checking and transition constraint concepts make no sense for domains (see the further discussion of these concepts in Sections 9 and 10).

- The formula representing the constraint in the CHECK clause *must* be universally quantified, and it *must* contain exactly one range variable (namely, the variable that is bound to the universal quantifier), which *must* range over the domain in question. By means of syntactic simplifications analogous to those discussed at the end of Section 3, therefore, we could simplify the CHECK clause in the example to just

  ```
  CHECK COLOR IN ('Red','Yellow','Blue','Green')
  ```

  As stated earlier, we are not so much concerned in this paper with matters of concrete syntax as we are with the underlying concepts, but the foregoing simplifications are so obvious that we will use them in all of our subsequent examples of domain rules.

  Note: Logically speaking, the underlying data type of the domain (CHAR(6) in the example above) is also part of the constraint, of course. Thus, the following is also a valid example (a particularly simple example) of a domain rule:

  ```
  CREATE DOMAIN QTY INTEGER ;
  ```

- The violation response (not specified explicitly in the COLOR or QTY examples above) is just REJECT.

As explained in reference [8], there are in fact several ways in which the user might specify the set of values appearing in a given domain:

1. By specifying the underlying data type (as in the QTY example)
2. By actually enumerating the values (as in the COLOR example)
3. By specifying one or more value ranges
4. By specifying a template or pattern

5. By means of an arbitrary wff in which there is just one variable (in practice usually represented by the name of the domain itself), which ranges over the domain in question

6. By means of a checking procedure (i.e., an exit routine) that is to be invoked every time a value is introduced into a column defined on the domain

Of the foregoing, however, numbers 2, 3, and 4 are really just special cases of number 5. Number 6 is an "escape" and should only be used as a last resort. We give examples of numbers 2, 3, and 4 (numbered appropriately), with an equivalent "number 5" form in each case:

2.
```
CREATE DOMAIN COLOR CHAR(6)
       CHECK  COLOR IN ('Red','Yellow','Blue','Green') ;
```

Equivalent form:

```
CREATE DOMAIN COLOR CHAR(6)
       CHECK  COLOR = 'Red'
       OR     COLOR = 'Yellow'
       OR     COLOR = 'Blue'
       OR     COLOR = 'Green' ;
```

3.
```
CREATE DOMAIN STATUS SMALLINT
       CHECK  STATUS BETWEEN 1 AND 100 ;
```

Equivalent form:

```
CREATE DOMAIN STATUS SMALLINT
       CHECK  STATUS >=   1
       AND    STATUS <= 100 ;
```

4.
```
CREATE DOMAIN S# CHAR(5)
       CHECK  S# IS PICTURE 'S9999' ;
```

Equivalent form:

```
CREATE DOMAIN S# CHAR(5)
       CHECK  SUBSTR ( S#, 1, 1 ) = 'S'
       AND    IS_INTEGER ( SUBSTR ( S#, 2, 4 ) ) ;
```

The function IS_INTEGER in this example is intended to test a character string value to see if it represents a legal (unsigned) decimal integer.

We close this section with an example to illustrate the point that integrity rules, even domain rules, can be arbitrarily complex. Suppose we have a composite domain DATE, defined over the simple domains MONTH, DAY, YEAR, with underlying data types CHAR(2), CHAR(2), and CHAR(4), respectively (see reference [8] for a discussion of composite domains). Then the following domain rules (i.e., domain definitions) together serve to constrain DATE values to legal A.D. dates. *Note:* We assume the existence of two functions, IS_INTEGER (as defined above) and NUM (which converts a character string value that represents an unsigned decimal integer to the corresponding numeric form). We also ignore the complexities caused by the irregularities in the Julian calendar prior to the 17th century A.D.

```
CREATE DOMAIN MONTH CHAR(2)
       CHECK  IS_INTEGER ( MONTH )
              AND NUM ( MONTH ) >=  1
              AND NUM ( MONTH ) <= 12 ;

CREATE DOMAIN DAY   CHAR(2)
       CHECK  IS_INTEGER ( DAY )
              AND NUM ( DAY ) >=  1
              AND NUM ( DAY ) <= 31 ;

CREATE DOMAIN YEAR  CHAR(2)
       CHECK  IS_INTEGER ( YEAR )
              AND NUM ( YEAR ) >=  0
              AND NUM ( YEAR ) <= 99 ;        /* superfluous */

CREATE DOMAIN DATE ( MM   DOMAIN ( MONTH ),
                     DD   DOMAIN ( DAY ),
                     YYYY DOMAIN ( YEAR ) )
       CHECK  IF NUM ( MM ) IN (4,6,9,11)
                 THEN NUM ( DD ) < 31
       AND    IF NUM ( MM ) = 2
                 THEN NUM ( DD ) < 30
       AND    IF NUM ( MM ) = 2 AND
                 MOD ( NUM ( YYYY ), 4 ) = 0 AND
                 MOD ( NUM ( YYYY ), 100 ) <> 0
                 THEN NUM ( DD ) < 29 ;
```

6. SINGLE-ROW RULES

From a formal point of view, the difference between domain rules and table rules is that table rules involve variables that range over tables, not domains. As indicated in Section 4, table rules can be further subdivided into single- and multi-row rules (also known as single- and multi-variable rules, where "variable" stands for a range variable of the tuple relational calculus). That further subdivision is primarily a pragmatic one, however; single-row rules are syntactically easier to specify, and are likely to be easier and more efficient to enforce, than multi-row rules (in general). We discuss single-row rules in the present section and multi-row rules in Sections 7 and 8.

A single-row rule is a rule that applies to the values within a single row of a single table, such that the constraint can be tested (to yield *true* or *false*) for a given row by examining *just that row in isolation*.* Here is an example:

---

*In other words, the expression contained within the scoping parentheses following the universal quantifier is a *restriction predicate* (more correctly, restriction *condition*).

```
CREATE INTEGRITY RULE R7
       CHECK FORALL SX
             ( IF SX.CITY = 'London' THEN SX.STATUS = 20 ) ;
```

SX here is a variable that is defined to range over table S:

```
RANGE OF SX IS TABLE S ;
```

Note: From this point on we will not normally bother to show the necessary range variable definitions, but instead will adopt a convention by which SX, SY, . . . , PX, PY, . . . , SPX, SPY, . . . , are range variables that range over tables S, P, and SP, respectively.

Points arising:

- The name of the rule is the specified name ("R7" in the example).

- Single-row rules can be state rules or transition rules, but they must always be immediate (a deferred single-row rule makes no sense). For a single-row *state* rule, the checking time is always "ON INSERT or UPDATE on any column involved in the rule," and there is never any need to specify it explicitly—though there is nothing wrong in doing so:

```
CREATE INTEGRITY RULE R7
       ON    INSERT ( SX.CITY, SX.STATUS ) ,
             UPDATE ( SX.CITY, SX.STATUS ) :
       CHECK FORALL SX
             ( IF SX.CITY = 'London' THEN SX.STATUS = 20 ) ;
```

  The checking time for single-row *transition* rules is discussed in Section 9.

- The formula representing the constraint *must* be universally quantified, and it *must* contain exactly one variable (namely, the variable that is bound to the universal quantifier), which *must* range over the table in question. In other words, a single-row table constraint is syntactically very similar to a domain constraint, except that the single variable ranges over the table in question instead of a domain.

- The violation response (not specified explicitly in the example) is just REJECT, by default.

Note: In principle, single-row rules could be specified as part of the relevant table definition (since they obviously apply just to that specific table); however, such an approach does smack faintly of "bundling," which is generally something to be avoided. In this paper, we will generally keep all integrity specifications in separate statements, and we will regard any "bundled" forms merely as a shorthand.

Two more examples of single-row rules:

```
CREATE INTEGRITY RULE R13
      CHECK FORALL PX
           ( IF PX.COLOR = 'Red' THEN PX.CITY = 'London') ;

CREATE INTEGRITY RULE R17
      CHECK FORALL SPX
           ( IF SPX.P# = 'P2' THEN SPX.QTY <= 2000 ) ;
```

A very common special case of a single-row rule is the so-called single-*column* rule. In other words, it is very common to find that the constraint in a single-row rule refers to just one column of the relevant table. Here is an example:

```
CREATE INTEGRITY RULE RRA
      CHECK FORALL SPX ( SPX.QTY > 0 ) ;
```

And here is another ("shipment quantities must be a multiple of 100"):

```
CREATE INTEGRITY RULE RRB
      CHECK FORALL SPX ( MOD ( SPX.QTY, 100 ) = 0 ) ;
```

Of course, these two examples can be combined. The result is still a single-column rule:

```
CREATE INTEGRITY RULE R16
      CHECK FORALL SPX
           ( SPX.QTY > 0 AND MOD ( SPX.QTY, 100 ) = 0 ) ;
```

The foregoing example illustrates the general point, already alluded to earlier in this paper, that distinct constraints (i.e., constraints specified in distinct integrity rules) are logically "ANDed" together. The only way to obtain an "OR" between two constraints is to include the two constraints with an explicit OR connective within the same integrity rule.

The checking time for a single-column rule, of course, is "ON INSERT or UPDATE on the relevant column." *Note:* In principle, single-column rules could be specified as part of the relevant column definition, but once again such an approach smacks faintly of bundling. In fact, however, there are several common special cases of single-column rules that many systems do support today and that typically *are* bundled with the relevant column definition. For example:

- Range checks (at the column level, not the domain level)
- Enumerated values (ditto)
- Template or pattern checks (ditto)
- "Nulls [not] allowed" (ditto)

In connexion with the last of these, note that the application of Codd's entity integrity rule ("primary keys in base tables must not allow nulls" [9]) to any given base table results in a special case of a single-row rule. (It will be a single-*column* rule only if the relevant primary key is single-column, of course.) We will have a little more to say regarding the entity integrity rule in Section 13 at the end of the paper.

7.   MULTI-ROW RULES

A multi-row rule, also known as a multi-variable rule, is a rule that applies to a combination of multiple rows (from one table or several tables). Here is an example ("suppliers with status less than 20 must not supply any part in a quantity greater than 500"):

```
CREATE INTEGRITY RULE R20
       CHECK FORALL SX
          ( IF SX.STATUS < 20
                THEN NOT EXISTS SPX
                     ( SPX.S# = SX.S# AND SPX.QTY > 500 ) ) ;
```

Points arising:

- The name of the rule is the specified name ("R20" in the example).
- Any combination of state vs. transition and immediate vs. deferred checking can apply to a multi-row rule, in general. The example above is an immediate state rule. The checking time in this example (not shown explicitly above) is slightly complicated:

```
ON INSERT ( SX.S#,   SX.STATUS ) ,
   UPDATE ( SX.S#,   SX.STATUS ) ,
   INSERT ( SPX.S#, SPX.QTY   ) ,
   UPDATE ( SPX.S#, SPX.QTY   ) :
```

  However, it still seems feasible to require the system to deduce the checking time for itself, i.e., to omit the specification from the concrete syntax (see Section 13). *Note:* In the foregoing checking time specification, "SX" is bound by the quantifier "FORALL SX," "SPX" is bound by the (negated) quantifier "NOT EXISTS SPX."
- The constraint is an arbitrary wff involving two or more distinct variables ranging over two or more tables. The tables in question are *not* necessarily all distinct.
- The violation response in the example is REJECT (by default once again).

Multi-row rules cannot sensibly be specified as part of a table definition, in general, because they involve multiple distinct tables (again in general). However, there are several important exceptions to this general statement—for example, primary key uniqueness specifications, foreign key specifications, and possibly others besides (see Section 12).

Here are some more examples of multi-variable rules:

(a) CREATE INTEGRITY RULE RRC
        CHECK FORALL PX
                (EXISTS SPX
                    (SPX.P# = PX.P#)) ;

Meaning: "Every part participates in at least one shipment." This would presumably have to be a deferred rule, because otherwise there would be no way to insert a new part. We will discuss this example further in Section 10.

(b) CREATE INTEGRITY RULE R2
        CHECK FORALL SX
                (FORALL SY
                    (IF SX.S# = SY.S#
                        THEN SAME (SX, SY))) ;

Meaning: "Supplier numbers are unique" (we assume the existence of a function SAME, which returns the value *true* if and only if its two range variable arguments designate the same object). In other words, this integrity rule specifies the uniqueness requirement for the primary key (S.S#) in table S, which shows that *primary key uniqueness* is a multi-row rule.* We will discuss this example further in Section 12.

(c) CREATE INTEGRITY RULE R3
        CHECK FORALL SX
                (FORALL SY
                    (IF SX.SNAME = SY.SNAME
                        THEN SX.S# = SY.S#)) ;

Meaning: "Supplier names are unique"; in other words, S.SNAME is an alternate key for table S. The formulation above relies on the fact that S.S# is the primary key for table S.

(d) CREATE INTEGRITY RULE RRD
        CHECK FORALL SX
                (FORALL SY
                    (IF SX.CITY = SY.CITY
                        THEN SX.STATUS = SY.STATUS)) ;

Meaning: "Whenever two suppliers have the same city, they also have the same status" (note that this constraint does *not* apply to the usual suppliers-and-parts database). This example specifies a *functional dependence* from column S.CITY to S.STATUS, which shows that functional dependence is a multi-row rule (so also are multivalued dependence and the general join dependence [14]). We will discuss this example further in Section 12 also.

(e) CREATE INTEGRITY RULE RRE
        CHECK NOT EXISTS PX
            OR EXISTS PX (PX.COLOR = 'Red') ;

---

*Primary key uniqueness could also be specified as a transition rule. See Section 9 later.

202

I / Relational Database Management

Meaning: "There must be at least one red part" (loosely speaking; the first part of the constraint—"NOT EXISTS PX"—is needed to handle the initial condition, in which table P is empty). *Note:* The CHECK clause in this example could alternatively (and equivalently) be stated as follows:

```
CHECK IF   EXISTS PX
     THEN EXISTS PX ( PX.COLOR = 'Red') ;
```

Exercise: What is the checking time for this example?

(f) `CREATE INTEGRITY RULE R15`
```
        CHECK FORALL SPX
                   ( EXISTS SX ( SX.S# = SPX.S# ) ) ;
```

Meaning: "Every shipment is for a known supplier." In other words, this rule specifies the requirement that column SP.S# is a foreign key matching the primary key (S.S#) of table S, which shows that *foreign-to-primary-key matching* is a multi-row rule (of course). The rule as shown will have the effect of:

- Preventing an INSERT or UPDATE on table SP that introduces a supplier number value into that table that does not exist in table S. *Note:* For simplicity, we assume that column SP.S# is defined to have "nulls not allowed."

- Preventing a DELETE or UPDATE on table S that removes a supplier number value from that table that does exist in table SP.

The rule thus effectively defines, not only the basic foreign key constraint from SP.S# to S.S#, but also RESTRICTED delete and update rules for that foreign key [9]. Suppose, by contrast, that we wished to define a delete rule of CASCADES. First attempt:

```
CREATE INTEGRITY RULE R15D
       ON     DELETE SX :
       CHECK FORALL SX
                  ( NOT EXISTS SPX ( SPX.S# = SX.S# ) )
       ELSE   DELETE SPX WHERE SPX.S# = SX.S# ;
```

Observe first that we *must* now specify a checking time ("ON DELETE SX"), because the violation response is to be invoked *only* if the original update that caused the violation was in fact a DELETE. However, note that the CHECK clause is now logically redundant; it says that there must not be any shipments for supplier SX (the target of the DELETE)—but if there are, then the ELSE clause will delete them anyway. Hence our next attempt:

```
CREATE INTEGRITY RULE R15D
       ON DELETE SX :
          DELETE SPX WHERE SPX.S# = SX.S# ;
```

(we have removed the CHECK clause and the EI.SE keyword; the variable SX is no longer explicitly quantified, but it is still *im*plicitly—and universally—quantified, thanks to the syntax rule introduced to this effect in Section 3). *Note:* Of course, the "DELETE SPX . . ." should still succeed, even if supplier SX in fact does not have any shipments; a set containing no members is still a set.

Now, however, what we are left with is not really an integrity rule at all, in the sense that it specifies a constraint to be checked; rather, it is an instance of what is usually called a *triggered procedure*. A triggered procedure is a procedure that is invoked when some specified event occurs (the *triggering event*). In the example, the triggering event is a DELETE of a specific supplier, and the triggered procedure is the DELETE of all shipments for that supplier. Hence our final version is as follows (note that we have changed the keyword ON to BEFORE, for reasons to be discussed below):

```
CREATE TRIGGERED PROCEDURE T15D
     BEFORE DELETE SX :
          DELETE SPX WHERE SPX.S# = SX.S# ;
```

Triggered procedures form a separate (and large) topic in their own right, and we will not discuss them in detail in the present paper. We will, however, give a triggered procedure corresponding to the CASCADES update rule for suppliers and shipments:

```
CREATE TRIGGERED PROCEDURE T15U
     BEFORE UPDATE SX.S# FROM S#_PARAM :
          UPDATE SPX
          SET    SPX.S# = S#_PARAM
          WHERE  SPX.S# = SX.S# ;
```

S#_PARAM here is a formal parameter, to be replaced by an actual parameter when an actual UPDATE is applied to column S# in table S.

Note: The foregoing example does raise one further interesting point, which we illustrate as follows:

- Consider an attempt to update the supplier number for supplier S1 (say) to "S99". The procedure defined above (T15U) will be invoked to update the supplier numbers accordingly in all shipments for S1 (a multirow update, in general). However, this latter update will violate the referential constraint from SP.S# to S.S#, defined earlier as integrity rule R15. (Of course, it makes no difference if the supplier row is updated first—rule R15 will still be violated.)

We conclude that, logically speaking, triggered procedures need to be executed (a) as an integral part of the statement that causes them to be invoked and (b) prior to the checking of any relevant integrity constraints (hence our replacement of ON by BEFORE). This whole area is a subject in need of further research.

8. AGGREGATE FUNCTION RULES

Constraints—that is, well-formed formulas of the relational calculus (or, at least, our version of that calculus)—can involve aggregate functions such as COUNT, SUM, and AVG. If they do, however, there are one or two special considerations that apply. Here is an example:

```
CREATE INTEGRITY RULE R18
        CHECK SUM ( ALL SPX.QTY WHERE SPX.P# = 'P3') <= 2000 ;
```

("total shipment quantity for part P3 must not exceed 2000"). Points arising:

- Aggregate functions such as SUM must be regarded as implicitly quantifying each otherwise unquantified variable in their argument, in order to abide by the requirement that all variables in a wff be quantified (for otherwise the formula is not well-formed). In other words, SUM, AVG, etc., must be regarded (among other things) as new kinds of quantifiers.

- The ALL in "ALL SPX.QTY" is intended to mean "do not eliminate duplicate QTY values before computing the sum." I freely confess that this is a syntactic trick, and a little ad hoc; more language design work is needed here.

- The checking time is

```
ON   INSERT ( SPX.P# ) ,
     UPDATE ( SPX.P#, SPX.QTY ) :
```

- The "sum of an empty set" specter rears its ugly head in this example, of course; what if there are no shipments at all for part P3? Detailed discussion of this problem would be out of place in the present paper; we refer the interested reader to reference [10]. For present purposes, we can (and probably should) define the problem away by revising the CHECK clause as follows:

```
CHECK IF   EXISTS SPX (SPX.P# = 'P3')
      THEN SUM ( ALL SPX.QTY WHERE SPX.P# = 'P3') <= 2000 ;
```

Another example:

```
CREATE INTEGRITY RULE R19
        CHECK FORALL SPX
             ( SUM ( ALL SPY.QTY WHERE SPY.P# = SPX.P# ) <= 3000 ) ;
```

("total shipment quantity for any part must not exceed 3000"). Note that there is another way in which this rule might be formulated:

```
CREATE INTEGRITY RULE R19
       CHECK FORALL PX
          ( IF EXISTS SPY ( SPY.P# = PX.P# ) THEN
              SUM ( ALL SPY.QTY WHERE SPY.P# = PX.P# ) <= 3000 ) ) ;
```

(quantifying over all parts that exist rather than all parts that are supplied; note the need to guard against the possibility of an empty set once again). However, the two formulations are semantically equivalent *only* because it is guaranteed that every part number in table SP also appears in table P. Note also that variable SPY is implicitly quantified in both versions. *Exercise:* What are the checking times for the two formulations?

All combinations of state vs. transition and immediate vs. deferred checking are possible for aggregate function rules (as indeed they are for multi-row rules in general).

9.   STATE VS. TRANSITION RULES

Preliminary remark: This section must be regarded as even more tentative in nature than the sections that have preceded it—not on account of any lack of desirability of the function, but because there are some significant definitional issues to be resolved. The basic problem is that we need a clean and logically simple way of referring to both the "old" and "new" states of a variable simultaneously—where by "variable" I mean an individual scalar variable, or an entire database, or anything in between.

As explained in Section 4, a *state* integrity rule is one that applies to individual states of the database. Most integrity rules are probably state rules in practice. A *transition* rule, by contrast, applies to transitions from one state to another. In a database concerning people, for example, there may be a series of transition rules having to do with valid changes of marital status. For instance, the following transitions are all valid—

- Never-married to married
- Married to widowed
- Married to divorced
- Widowed to married

(etc., etc.), whereas the following are not—

- Never-married to widowed
- Never-married to divorced

- Widowed to divorced
- Divorced to widowed

(etc., etc.).*

Reverting to our suppliers-and-parts example, there is just one transition rule in the list of constraints in Section 1: "A supplier's status must never decrease." In our syntax, this becomes:

```
CREATE  INTEGRITY  RULE  R5
        BEFORE  UPDATE  SX.STATUS  FROM  STATUS_PARAM :
        CHECK   STATUS_PARAM >= SX.STATUS ;
```

Notice that the checking time needs to be stated explicitly in order to provide a mechanism for introducing the formal parameter STATUS_PARAM. Once again we have replaced the keyword ON by BEFORE, in order to stress the point that the CHECK clause needs to be executed *before* the update is done, logically speaking.†

Primary key uniqueness can also be specified by means of a transition rule:

```
CREATE  INTEGRITY  RULE  R2
        BEFORE  INSERT  SX.S# FROM S#_PARAM ,
                UPDATE  SX.S# FROM S#_PARAM :
        CHECK   NOT EXISTS ( SY WHERE SY.S# = S#_PARAM ) ;
```

(some language definition tricks are needed here to explain what "SX" means in the phrase "BEFORE INSERT SX.S# FROM S#_PARAM," but such matters—again—are beyond the scope of the present paper).

Unsolved problem: The mechanism sketched above (using the BEFORE clause to introduce formal parameters) does not seem to be adequate to deal with aggregate function transition rules. Consider, e.g., the constraint: "The average quantity of any individual part, taken over all suppliers, can only increase." (The problem is that we need to be able to include formal parameters in the argument to the aggregate function.) Further research is needed.

10.   IMMEDIATE VS. DEFERRED RULES

An *immediate* integrity rule is a rule that is (logically) checked as part of the processing of every update statement that could potentially violate it. Immediate integrity rules are required to be satisfied at statement boundaries. A *de-*

---

*Actually, if the legal transitions are all precisely known and constitute a fairly small set, the transition rule can probably be formulated just as easily as a state rule.

†Of course, there is no way to stop the user from mixing state and transition constraints within the same rule (nor is there any particular reason to, except perhaps for clarity and ease of understanding).

ferred rule, by contrast, is not checked during update processing per se, but rather at some later time, typically at COMMIT. The need for deferred rules arises from the possibility that two or more values in the database may be required to be "in synch" in some respect, and it is not feasible to update them both within a single operation.

By way of example, consider the following (a revised form of Example (a) from Section 7): "Every part participates in at least one shipment." In our integrity language:

```
CREATE INTEGRITY RULE RRC
       AT COMMIT :
       CHECK FORALL PX
               ( EXISTS SPX
                       ( SPX.P# = PX.P# ) ) ;
```

Consider what happens if a new part is inserted into table P. Clearly, that new part will not yet be involved in any shipments; instead, at least one INSERT (or UPDATE) will have to be performed on table SP in order to introduce such a shipment. (I ignore the possibility that the original INSERT might have invoked a triggered procedure to perform that INSERT or UPDATE.) The integrity constraint thus has to be checked "AT COMMIT," not at the time of the original INSERT;* if the check fails, then the violation response should probably be to cancel (i.e., ROLLBACK) the entire transaction.

Note: There is at least one system, namely SQL/DS [12], that allows certain checks to be deferred to some arbitrary later time (i.e., possibly past COMMIT, possibly a *long* time [days or weeks] past COMMIT). The SQL/DS mechanism involves dynamic DEACTIVATE and ACTIVATE operations, which can be used to deactivate and subsequently reactivate primary and foreign key constraints. However, the result of deactivating a given constraint is effectively to take the relevant tables "out of commission" for an arbitrarily long period of time; they are no longer available, not even for retrieval, except to the user who owns them, and they remain in this state until the constraint is successfully reactivated again. In my opinion, this approach gives too much freedom—and too much responsibility—to the user. It may indeed be the case that other deferred checking times are needed in addition to COMMIT, but once again I feel that this is an area in which additional research is needed.

---

*In principle, the user could issue some kind of "EXECUTE INTEGRITY CHECK" statement when he or she believes that the database is back in a correct state—i.e., it might not be absolutely necessary to wait until COMMIT. Such an approach was proposed in reference [13]. However, (a) relying on the user to do the right thing is not a good system design principle, and (b) precisely because of point (a), the system must at least be prepared to perform the check at COMMIT anyway, in case the user has forgotten.

11.   COMBINATIONS OF THE FOREGOING

We summarize in this section the various combinations of integrity rule classifications that make sense (refer to the table below). *Exercise:* Convince yourself that the "N" cases do not make sense. Give examples for each of the "Y" cases.

	immediate state	immediate transition	deferred state	deferred transition
domain	Y	N	N	N
single-row	Y	Y	N	N
multi-row	Y	Y	Y	Y
aggregate	Y	Y	Y	Y

12.   SPECIAL CASES

The integrity language discussed in the preceding sections is intended to permit the specification of general integrity constraints of arbitrary complexity. However, I have argued elsewhere (see, e.g., reference [9]) that special-casing is highly desirable for certain commonly occurring cases. I will not repeat all the arguments here, but merely mention some of those common cases, with examples. First, consider the following (a revised version of Example (b) from Section 7):

```
CREATE INTEGRITY RULE R2
       CHECK FORALL SX
                   ( NOT IS_NULL ( SX.S# ) AND
                     FORALL SY
                          ( IF SX.S# = SY.S#
                               THEN  SAME ( SX, SY ) ) ) ;
```

The following is obviously preferable:

```
PRIMARY KEY ( S# )
```

This specification is intended to be included as part of the definition of table S.

However, I must make it clear that this special-case syntax for a primary key specification (like all of the other special cases discussed below) should be regarded from a logical point of view as merely a shorthand for its "general integrity language" equivalent.

I would also argue—quite strongly, in fact—in favor of special-case ALTERNATE KEY and FOREIGN KEY specifications (especially if the delete and update rules are to be anything other than RESTRICTED, in the case of foreign keys).

Here is another example from Section 7 (Example (d))—a general integrity language specification of a functional dependence from S.CITY to S.STATUS in table S:

```
CREATE INTEGRITY RULE RRD
       CHECK FORALL SX
               ( FORALL SY
                       ( IF SX.CITY = SY.CITY
                         THEN SX.STATUS = SY.STATUS ) ) ;
```

The following syntax [14] *might* be preferable:

```
S.CITY ---> S.STATUS
```

(again, included as part of the definition of table S). On the other hand, I would argue that functional dependence constraints are usually better handled by appropriate normalization of the tables concerned (see Section 13 below); providing special-case syntax support just encourages people to produce sloppy database designs.

Special-casing might also be desirable (though it is really not a major concern) for certain single-column constraints—in particular, the ones mentioned at the end of Section 6 (range checks, enumerated values, template checks, and "nulls [not] allowed").

13. MISCELLANEOUS CONSIDERATIONS

I close this paper with a number of miscellaneous remarks on the overall integrity problem.

- First, of course, we obviously need the ability to CREATE and DROP integrity rules dynamically. If the user attempts to create a new rule, the system should first check to see that the rule is satisfied by the existing data in the database;* if it is not, the rule must be rejected, otherwise it must be accepted and enforced from this point on (until such time as it is dropped).

- Integrity enforcement raises some difficult questions of optimization.
  - First, *immediate* rules are required to be satisfied at statement boundaries. For domain rules and single-row rules, the implementation problem seems straightforward, but for multi-row rules there are some difficulties; the implementation might be tempted (for perform-

---

*This remark applies to state rules only. New transition rules can be accepted at any time.

ance reasons) to perform its checking not after the update statement is complete, but during the statement instead, with potentially anomalous effects (see references [3,11,12] for a discussion of some specific cases). The system needs to guard against such anomalies somehow. Furthermore, it might not be sufficient to examine just the portion of the database that is actually being updated; consider, e.g., the rule "Athens suppliers must not supply any green parts." Inserting (and possibly updating) a shipment will require a check of the corresponding supplier and part rows, even though they are not being changed.

- As for *deferred* rules, there are likely to be additional problems in deciding which portions of the database need to be checked. It is true that the implementation needs to keep a record (namely, in the log) of the portions that have changed, in case it has to cancel the transaction and undo its updates. But in some cases (again) it may additionally have to examine portions that have not changed. Deferred checking is likely to be expensive whatever the system does, and should probably be avoided wherever possible.

■ I have suggested several times in this paper that (for immediate state rules) the system should be able to deduce the checking times for itself. In the case of domain rules, this process is straightforward: The checking time is "ON INSERT or UPDATE on any column defined on the domain," as explained in Section 5. What about table rules? Here, I offer the following conjecture (but it is only a conjecture at this time). Remember that the constraint is a wff of the relational calculus; in other words, every variable mentioned in the constraint must be quantified (though the quantifier might sometimes be implicit). *Conjecture:*

- Assume without loss of generality that the constraint is in a form (e.g., prenex normal form) in which there are no negated quantifiers. (If it is not in such a form already, then convert it to such a form by applying the well-known wff transformation rules.) Let the negation-free form be Q.

- If variable TX is universally quantified in Q, then include "INSERT TX" in the checking times.

- If variable TX is existentially quantified in Q, then include "DELETE TX" in the checking times.

- If column TX.C is mentioned in Q, then include "UPDATE TX.C" in the checking times.

- If column TX.C is the subject of an aggregate function (such as SUM) in Q, then include "INSERT TX," "DELETE TX," and "UPDATE TX.C" in the checking times.

- If the set of checking times derived by the application of the forcgo-
  ing rules includes any of the following pairs
  (a) INSERT TX   and INSERT TY
  (b) DELETE TX   and DELETE TY
  (c) UPDATE TX.C and UPDATE TY.C
  (where TX and TY range over the same table and are both universally
  quantified or both existentially quantified), then the checking time
  involving (arbitrarily) TY can be eliminated. This rule is to be applied
  repeatedly until no such pairs remain.

- The possibility of having the system deduce checking times for itself
  raises numerous further optimization-type questions. For example, consider integrity rule R18 from Section 8: "The total shipment quantity
  for part P3 must not exceed 2000." In general, inserting and deleting a
  shipment for part P3 will both have the effect of changing the corresponding total quantity. Thus, the system will have to check rule
  R18 after such INSERTs or DELETEs, in general. But if integrity rule
  R16 is also enforced ("Shipment quantities must be greater than zero
  . . ."), then *deleting* a shipment for part P3 cannot possibly increase
  the corresponding total quantity, and there is no logical necessity for
  rule R18 to be checked on such an operation. Can the system determine
  this fact for itself?

- Following on from the previous point: How much analysis by the system of the rules as specified by the user is necessary, or possible, or
  desirable? We cannot necessarily require users to specify the rules in
  the simplest possible form, nor even consistently. Can the system detect
  inconsistencies? Can the system take the logical "AND" of the rules as
  specified and combine them and simplify them and partition them on
  the basis of the tables to which they apply? Etc., etc., etc.

- Another related point: In DBMSs today, which typically provide little
  or nothing in the way of declarative integrity support, integrity rules
  are generally enforced by user-written application programs. Such programs are typically written by a small team of DP specialists and very
  carefully tested to ensure that they do in fact enforce exactly the required constraints. (As an aside, note that this observation implies that
  the people responsible for performing the testing must in fact have
  some kind of declarative specification of the integrity rules concerned.
  The trouble is, they may not have a very precise or systematic language
  in which to formulate those rules, and whatever language they do have
  is certainly not executable.) When integrity rules can be specified declaratively in the manner suggested in this paper instead of procedur-

ally, what kind of testing will be required then? In other words, how should declarative integrity rules be debugged?

- I have assumed throughout this paper that all integrity checking is performed by the base DBMS per se, not by a frontend component such as a data entry subsystem. That assumption is consistent with the claim at the end of Section 2 that integrity is a property of the data, of course. However, one implication of that assumption is that it might be difficult to produce good "user-friendly" diagnostics in any such frontend component. Certainly the DBMS needs to provide as much information as possible in the event of a failure in order to permit any such frontend to do a good job in this area. Consider, for example, the case of a data entry clerk entering a row that includes five foreign key values. It would be desirable for the DBMS to check all five before returning control to the user, instead of giving up as soon as it finds that one is wrong. For otherwise the clerk might have to resubmit the "same" row as many as five times (in the extreme case), which would be quite annoying.

- It is frequently (perhaps always) the case that *some integrity constraints imply others.* As a trivial example, the constraint that part weights are greater than zero certainly implies the constraint that they are greater than −1. Now, if constraint A implies constraint B, then *enforcing A will enforce B automatically* (it will not even be necessary to declare B explicitly, except perhaps in the form of a comment). Given that it is desirable that all applicable constraints be enforced, it seems useful to look for ways to minimize the number of constraints that need to be explicitly declared—i.e., to look for a small set of constraints with the property that those constraints imply *all* applicable constraints for the database under consideration.

    The normalization discipline [14] is relevant in this connexion. Minimizing the number of constraints that need to be explicitly declared is, precisely, one of the objectives of the normalization process. In fact, if all relations are in the "ultimate" (i.e., fifth) normal form, then the system need only enforce candidate key uniqueness constraints, and all functional, multivalued, and join dependences will be enforced automatically [14]. This is one reason why the normalization discipline is important—it allows certain common and important constraints to be enforced very simply, with very little necessary in the way of explicit constraint declaration.

- In a recent paper [3], Codd referred in passing to a proposed classification scheme of his own for integrity rules. It is interesting to compare his proposal with the one sketched in the present paper. First, he classifies rules into "C-timed" and "T-timed" (where C means command and T means transaction); C- and T-timed rules correspond to our immediate and deferred rules, respectively. Second, he suggests that there are "five forms of integrity," namely:

D — domain
C — column
E — entity
R — referential
U — user-defined

Comments:

- Type D here is presumably the same as our domain rules, discussed in Section 5 (though Codd does not explicitly say that T-timed domain rules make no sense).

- Type C corresponds to our single-column rules, discussed in Section 6 (as a special case of single-row rules; it is not clear exactly why Codd calls out single-column rules but not single-row rules as a category of their own, though I would agree that single-column rules do occur very frequently in practice). As with type D rules, it is not clear whether Codd permits type C rules to be T-timed.

- Types E and R are different in kind from the previous two types. They are really *metarules,* i.e., rules about rules. The entity integrity rule, for example, effectively says that there must be a specific integrity rule for each base table to the effect that the primary key of that base table must not permit nulls. Each such specific rule can be regarded in a sense as a specific *instance* of the generic entity integrity rule. Analogous remarks apply to the referential integrity rule also [9].

- As for the final category, type U: I find this category to be neither very well named, nor a sufficiently fine classification to be useful, for the following reasons.

(a) First, I do not think "user-defined" is a very good name, because in fact *all* integrity rules must be user-defined in the final analysis. Even the entity and referential integrity rules must be user-defined *in every specific instance* (by means of appropriate primary and foreign key specifications). Domain and column rules are certainly user-defined.

(b) Second, type U presumably has to include all single-row rules (excluding those that are in fact single-*column*), all multi-row rules, all aggregate function rules, and all transition rules. Even accepting that it makes sense to separate out types D and E and R (which it might) and C (which I am not so sure about), it seems to me that a finer classification of the remaining cases is desirable for conceptual reasons, at least, if not for any other.

Perhaps *database-specific* would be a better term than "user-defined." Then we could usefully distinguish between the general metarules (types E and R), on the one hand, and rules that apply to specific databases—including, in particular, database specific instances of the metarules—on the other hand. (As a matter of fact, domain rules (type D) also exist in both a metarule version—"Every column must contain only values from the corresponding domain"—and in database-specific versions.) But I would still argue that the "database-specific" category could do with some refinement. Indeed, that is exactly what this paper has been all about.

ACKNOWLEDGMENTS

I am grateful to Nat Goodman of Codd and Date and Adrian Walker of IBM Research for helping me to understand the relational calculus a little better, and to Nat again for his helpful review of an earlier draft of this paper.

REFERENCES AND BIBLIOGRAPHY

1. E. F. Codd, "Missing Information (Applicable and Inapplicable) in Relational Databases," *ACM SIGMOD Record* 15, No. 4 (December 1986).

2. E. F. Codd, "More Commentary on Missing Information in Relational Databases (Applicable and Inapplicable Information)," *ACM SIGMOD Record* 16, No. 1 (March 1987).

3. E. F. Codd, "Domains, Keys, and Referential Integrity in Relational Databases," *InfoDB* 3, No. 1 (Spring 1988).

4. C. J. Date, *An Introduction to Database Systems: Volume I,* 1st edition. (Reading, MA: Addison-Wesley, 1975).

5. C. J. Date, *An Introduction to Database Systems: Volume I,* 4th edition. (Reading, MA: Addison-Wesley, 1986).

6. C. J. Date, *An Introduction to Database Systems: Volume II* (Reading, MA: Addison-Wesley, 1982).

7. C. J. Date, "Some Relational Myths Exploded," in C. J. Date, *Relational Database: Selected Writings* (Reading, MA: Addison-Wesley, 1986).

8. C. J. Date, "What Is a Domain?" (in this volume).

9. C. J. Date, "Referential Integrity and Foreign Keys. Part I: Basic Concepts; Part II: Further Considerations" (in this volume).

10. C. J. Date, "NOT Is Not "Not"! (Notes on Three-Valued Logic and Related Matters" (in this volume).

11. C. J. Date and Colin J. White, *A Guide to DB2,* 3rd edition (Reading, MA: Addison-Wesley, 1989).

12. C. J. Date and Colin J. White, *A Guide to SQL/DS* (Reading, MA: Addison-Wesley, 1988).

13. K. P. Eswaran and D. D. Chamberlin, "Functional Specifications of a Subsystem for Data Base Integrity," *Proc. 1st International Conference on Very Large Data Bases* (September 1975).

14. Ronald Fagin, "Normal Forms and Relational Database Operators," *Proc. 1979 ACM SIGMOD Conference on Management of Data* (May/June 1979).

8

NOT Is Not "Not"!
(Notes on Three-Valued
Logic and
Related Matters)

ABSTRACT

Codd's proposed approach to missing information (based on three-valued logic) is described and illustrated. Some pertinent questions are raised.

COMMENTS ON PUBLICATION

I am a little embarrassed to be dredging up the somewhat hackneyed topic of nulls and missing information yet again; there are already numerous papers on the subject available in the open literature, including, of course, one by myself [5]. However, that previous paper of mine had a heavy emphasis on nulls as implemented in SQL, whereas the present paper, by contrast, is much more concerned with the underlying ideas.

Previously unpublished.

In writing the paper, I had two principal objectives in mind:

- First, I am frankly still not convinced as to the suitability of three-valued logic as a basis for dealing with the missing information problem. I did previously convey some of my concerns in this regard to Dr. Codd [10], but it now seems appropriate to air those concerns in front of a wider audience. Now, it may very well be the case (probably it *is* the case) that I simply do not adequately understand the three-valued logic proposal; if this is so, however, I know that I am not alone, so the paper can be seen as a request for clarification (and for reassurance that we are not marching off down the wrong path).

- Second, given that database management systems probably will be extended eventually to incorporate some kind of support for the three-valued logic approach, it seemed a good idea to try to explain in semi-formal, semi-tutorial style (with nontrivial examples) what such an approach is all about and what problems it is trying to solve.

I should also mention that this book includes another paper (by Andrew Warden) on this same general subject [12]. I hope that readers will find that the two papers complement each other reasonably well. In fact, readers would probably be advised to read Warden's paper *before* tackling the following (at least some of the more detailed parts).

1. INTRODUCTION

I have stated elsewhere [5] that I regard the missing information problem as an important one, one for which a systematic solution is highly desirable. I have also indicated that SQL-style nulls are *not* a satisfactory solution to the problem—so much so, in fact, that my general recommendation would be to avoid them altogether [9]. It is true that SQL style nulls do possess a superficial attractiveness, but I firmly believe they cause far more problems than they solve, as references [5] and [8] amply demonstrate. The present paper is not primarily concerned with SQL per se, however (though it does point out a few specific SQL anomalies), but rather with the more fundamental question of whether it is possible to find *any* fully satisfactory method of dealing with the missing information problem.

The best-known proposal for a systematic approach to the problem is probably Codd's, introduced in reference [1] under the heading "Extensions of the [Relational] Algebra for Null Values," and further elaborated in references [2] and [3]. In fact, Codd himself now regards those extensions as part of the underlying relational model [4]. Codd's ideas are undoubtedly more systematic and more carefully thought through than the SQL facilities referred to above, and for that reason are certainly more attractive as a basis for an approach to the overall problem. Even so, however, I have some reservations; it seems to me that there are some serious questions— both logical and psychological questions—that need to be answered (and answered satisfactorily) before we commit ourselves too heavily to Codd's approach. Some of those questions are raised in the present paper.

The plan of the paper is as follows. Following this introductory section, Section 2 discusses various different kinds of missing information—value unknown, value not applicable, and so on. The rest of the paper then homes in on the "value unknown" case specifically. Section 3 consists of a careful and fairly rigorous development of Codd's three-valued logic proposal for dealing with that case, and Section 4 presents some important logical consequences of that proposal. Section 5 then discusses some examples in considerable detail; in particular, it uses those examples to highlight the (arguably) counterintuitive behavior of three-valued logic in certain situations. Section 6 then raises some important questions; Section 7 addresses a few miscellaneous issues, and Section 8 presents a conclusion.

2. TYPES OF NULL

Following normal convention, I will use the term "null" as a convenient shorthand to mean that some item of information is missing. For example, the statement that "Joe's salary is null" is intended to mean that there is a position in the database for recording Joe's salary, but no value is recorded at that position at the present time. Note immediately, therefore, that *null is not a value;* rather, it is a representation of the fact that there *is* no value. (We will examine the question of *why* there is no value in just a moment.)

Because null is not a value, the term "null value" is deprecated.* Indeed, in reference [2], Codd suggests that we should talk in terms of "marks," not nulls, in order (among other things) to avoid any hint that missing information could be regarded as a value. Thus, for example, the fact that Joe's salary is missing would be expressed as "Joe's salary is marked"—meaning that the position that would normally hold Joe's salary in the database is marked somehow to show that the information is missing. (As an aside, note that the IBM product DB2 represents nulls in precisely this manner, i.e., by marking the stored value appropriately on the disk.) I tend to agree with Codd that some systematic kind of "mark" terminology is preferable to the more usual "nulls" terminology, but in this paper I will mostly talk in terms of nulls, for reasons of familiarity.

There are, of course, many reasons why a given piece of information

---

*Some of the problems with SQL-style nulls arise precisely because in some contexts (though not in all) SQL does treat null as a value [5,8,12].

might be missing—i.e., many possible interpretations of the statement "v is null" (for some v). In other words, there are many distinct types of null. Some of those types are identified below.

1. *Value not applicable.* Suppose the database includes an employees table EMP, with columns EMP#, DEPT#, SALARY, and COMMISSION; suppose the property COMMISSION applies only to employees in the sales department; and suppose finally that employee Joe is not in that department. Then the statement "Joe's commission is null" means that Joe does not have a commission, because the property of having a commission does not apply to him. In reference [2], Codd calls this type of null an "I-mark" ("I" for inapplicable).

2. *Value unknown.* By contrast to the previous example, the statement "Joe's salary is null" presumably means that Joe does have a salary (because all employees have a salary), but we don't know what it is. Codd calls this type of null an "A-mark" ("A" for applicable—the property of having a salary does apply to Joe, even though the specific value is unknown).

3. *Value does not exist.* Consider the property "social security number." This property does apply to employees in general (in fact, to United States residents in general), but not everyone actually has a social security number. Thus, the statement "Joe's social security number is null" could mean that *no social security number exists* for Joe. Note the difference between this case and Case 1—"value not applicable"—above. In the example, the property of having a social security number is certainly *applicable* to Joe (because it is applicable to everyone), it is just that Joe does not actually happen to have such a number at this time.

4. *Value undefined.* Certain items are explicitly undefined—for example, the result of dividing any number by zero, or the maximum number in a set of numbers if that set happens to be empty. Thus, for example, in a table T with columns A, B, C, and D, where A stands for "person," B for "total payment made," C for "number of payments made," and D for "average payment made," column D will be *undefined* (another type of null) for anyone who has made no payments at all.*

---

*More problems arise in SQL because SQL takes the AVG (also the MAX and the MIN and the SUM) of an empty set to be *unknown,* not *undefined* [8]. A more appropriate approach, if the system does not support *undefined* (as SQL does not), would be to allow an optional second argument to be specified for such functions, representing the value to be returned if the first argument evaluates to the empty set. It would then be an error if that second argument were omitted and the first argument did indeed evaluate to "empty."

Incidentally, I believe in the specific case of SUM that the result should be zero anyway, not undefined (SQL is doubly wrong in this particular instance). In the example above, column B ("total payment") should clearly be zero for anyone who has made no payments at all.

5. *Value not valid.* During data entry, it might be discovered that some value is invalid—e.g., employee age = 80, when employees are required to retire at 65. There might be good reasons for entering the employee into the database anyway, but marking the employee's age as "invalid" (rather than "unknown")—if for no other reason than to permit subsequent analysis in order to discover, precisely, which values in the original data were in fact invalid.

6. *Value not supplied.* "Refused to answer" (or "no comment") is a perfectly legitimate response to some questions in census-taking operations and the like. Once again, there might be very good operational reasons for distinguishing such cases appropriately in the database, instead of just marking them as "unknown."

7. *Value is the empty set.* Consider the *left outer natural join* [6] of departments and employees over department number. Assume that department *D* has no employees at the present time. In the result table, therefore, there will be exactly one row for department *D,* with a null in the employee number position. That null means that *the set of employees in department D is the empty set.**

And there are certainly other possibilities also (for example, see reference [12] for an interesting discussion of the nulls that are generated by outer union, which appear to be different from all of the cases discussed above). The point is, however, that each one has its own special properties and its own special behavior; thus, representing and manipulating them all in the same way is clearly not the right thing to do.

> *Aside:* This latter remark raises another point. In a system that supports—or tries to support—just one type of null, say "value unknown," in a systematic manner, there is a strong likelihood that users will be tempted to use that null for purposes for which it is not appropriate. In other words, the fact that "null support" is provided is likely to lull users into a false sense of security ("Missing information?— Don't worry, the system can handle it"). Indeed, many examples of such misuse are to be found in SQL systems today.
>
> As a concrete example of such a misuse, it is quite likely in such a system that employee Joe's commission (see item 1 above) would erroneously be represented by means of a "value unknown" null (it should of course be a "value does not apply" null). One consequence of this

---

*If R is the result table in question, the "obvious" query to determine the number of employees in each department (e.g., "SELECT DEPT#, COUNT (*) FROM R GROUP BY DEPT#;" in SQL) will return one, not zero, for department *D*. This result is at best counterintuitive, at worst plain wrong.

mistake is that, in attempting to compute Joe's total compensation (i.e., salary plus commission), the system will produce the result "unknown" (see Section 3, later), whereas of course it should produce just the salary value.*

Furthermore, it must be pointed out that the foregoing argument will continue to apply so long as the system supports fewer types of null than are logically necessary. In other words, simply adding support for a "value does not apply" null might solve the specific problem mentioned in the previous paragraph, but it will not solve the general problem. In a sense, therefore, it can be argued that a system that does provide some support for nulls, but not at the 100 percent level (whatever the "100 percent level" might be), is just as open to misuse—perhaps even more so, perhaps even *dangerously* more so—than a system that makes no pretense of providing any such support at all.

End of aside.

Now, in Codd's approach, the introduction of a single kind of null (the A-mark) requires an extension of the traditional two-valued logic to a logic of three values (see Section 3 below), and the introduction of a second kind (the I-mark) requires a further extension to a logic of four values. To deal with the seven (or eight) kinds of null identified above would thus presumably need a logic of nine (or ten) values; more generally, N kinds of null would apparently require an $(N+2)$-valued logic. This fact alone should at least give us pause, I believe. But matters are worse than that. It seems to me that, in principle at any rate, there must be an *infinite number* of different kinds of null. Consider the following argument:

- Suppose again that the database includes an EMP table, with columns EMP#, DEPT#, SALARY, and COMMISSION, where COMMISSION applies only to employees in the sales department.

- Suppose also that employee Joe's department is "A-marked," meaning that Joe does have a department but we don't know what it is.

- So what do we do about employee Joe's commission? It surely must be null—the information is surely missing—*but we don't know whether that null is an A-mark or an I-mark*. If Joe is in the sales department it should be an A-mark, otherwise it should be an I-mark.

---

*I find myself in diagreement with Codd here. In reference [2], Codd states that adding a "value does not apply" null (I-mark) to a genuine value should yield "value does not apply." But (to pursue the "salary plus commission" example a little further) the total compensation for an employee for whom the commission property is inapplicable should clearly be just that employee's salary; in other words, "v + i" (where "v" is a genuine value and "i" represents an I-mark) should surely yield v, not i.

- So we apparently need a new kind of null or mark, meaning "not known whether mark is type A or type I." Call this new kind of null "null-3" (A- and I-marks being null-1 and null-2, respectively).

- Now we need a new kind of null to represent "not known whether mark is null-1 or null-2 or null-3." Call this one "null-4."

- Now we need a new kind of null to represent "not known whether mark is null-1 or null-2 or null-3 or null-4." Call this one "null-5."

- Etc., etc., ad infinitum.

Despite all of the foregoing, however, I will concentrate in the remainder of this paper (as Codd did in reference [1]) on just one case, namely the "value unknown" case. (If we cannot adequately handle the case of just one kind of null, there seems little point on going on to try to deal with multiple different kinds.) For explicitness, I will henceforth frequently refer to the "value unknown" null (the A-mark) as UNK.

3.   THE THREE-VALUED LOGIC APPROACH

In this section, I present an extended and systematic description of an approach to dealing with UNK-type nulls based on three-valued logic. The approach is intended to be essentially the same as that proposed by Codd in references [1,2,3], except that I have spelled out a few details that were not explicitly discussed in those references. The description is intended to be reasonably rigorous, though not absolutely so. *Note:* Portions of this material are repeated from reference [5].

3.1 *Scalar computational expressions.* Let *alpha* stand for any (binary) scalar computational operator, such as $+$, $-$, etc., and let x and y be scalar values such that the expression "x *alpha* y" is a semantically valid expression. What is the result of evaluating this expression if x or y or both happen to be UNK? Since by definition UNK represents an unknown value, we define the result in every case to be UNK also, rather than some definite known value. Unary $+$ and $-$ are treated analogously—i.e., if x is UNK, then "$+x$" and "$-x$" are both UNK also.

Points arising:

1. An anomaly arising from the foregoing definition is that the expression "x $-$ x" evaluates to UNK, not zero, if x happens to be UNK. The implications of this anomaly are not clear.

3.2 *Scalar comparisons.* Let *theta* stand for any of the scalar comparison operators $=$, $<>$, $<$, $<=$, $>$, and $>=$, and let x and y be scalar values such that the expression "x *theta* y" is a semantically valid expression.

What is the result of evaluating this expression if x or y or both happen to be UNK? Since by definition UNK represents an unknown value, we define the result in every case to be *unknown* also, rather than *true* or *false*. In other words (as indicated in Section 2), we adopt a three-valued logic in place of the more usual two-valued logic. The three truth values are *true, false,* and *unknown* (which we abbreviate to *unk*). Note that *unk* might reasonably be interpreted as "maybe."

Points arising:

1. An anomaly arising from the foregoing definition is that the logical expression "x = x" evaluates to *unknown,* not *true,* if x happens to be UNK. The implications of this anomaly are not clear.

2. Note that *unk* is not the same as UNK!—i.e., the *unknown* truth-value is not the same as "truth-value unknown." Let v be a logical variable, i.e., a variable of data type "truth value." If the value of v happens to be *unk,* then the value of v is known to be *unk,* which is not the same as *not being known.* If, on the other hand, v is UNK (i.e., the value of v is not known), then it is not known whether the value of v is *true* or *false* or *unk.*

    To state the foregoing in a different way: If v is *unk,* then "v = v" yields *true;* if v is UNK, then "v = v" yields *unk.*

    Incidentally, in reference [1], Codd says (paraphrasing slightly): "We use the same symbol . . . to denote [both null and] the *unknown* truth-value, because truth-values can be stored in databases and we want the treatment of all unknown or null values to be uniform." This remark seems to suggest that Codd believes that *unk* is the same as UNK (to use my terms). In a later paper (reference [2]), however, he says (again paraphrasing): "The *unknown* truth-value can be thought of as a value-oriented counterpart for the A-mark [i.e., UNK] when focusing on the domain of truth values." This remark suggests that they are *not* the same, but that there might be certain parallels between them (?).

3.3 *Duplicate scalars.* As pointed out in subsection 3.2 above, it is a consequence of the foregoing that the logical expression "x = y" evaluates to *unk* if x is null or y is null *or both;* i.e., the value of the logical expression "UNK = UNK" is *unk,* not *true.* According to Codd, however, two UNKs still need to be considered as duplicates of one another for purposes of duplicate elimination (e.g., when taking a projection). Codd defines away this apparent contradiction as follows:

> ". . . identification for duplicate removal is . . . at a lower level of detail than equality testing in the evaluation of retrieval conditions. Hence, it is possible to adopt a different rule" [1].

If this position is accepted, we can define the notion of duplicate scalars as follows: Two scalar values x and y are *duplicates* of one another if and only if (a) they are both nonnull and "x = y" is *true,* or (b) they are both null. More precisely, we define an operator DUP_OF, as follows: The expression "x DUP_OF y" (where x and y are compatible, in the sense that the expression "x = y" is a semantically valid expression) is defined to evaluate to *true* if x and y are duplicates of one another, *false* otherwise. Note, therefore, that testing two scalars to see if they are duplicates always returns *true* or *false,* never *unk.* (Testing them for *equality,* by contrast, can return *true* or *false* or *unk.*)

3.4 *Testing for null.* We introduce a primitive function IS_UNK for testing whether a given scalar value is UNK. IS_UNK is defined to take an arbitrary scalar expression as its argument and to return *true* if that argument evaluates to UNK, *false* otherwise. Thus, e.g., the expression

```
IS_UNK ( EMP.JOB )
```

will return *true* if EMP.JOB is UNK, *false* otherwise.

3.5 *Logical operators NOT, AND, OR.* We define the logical operators NOT, AND, and OR by means of the following truth tables (for convenience, *true, false,* and *unk* are abbreviated to just t, f, u in these tables):

```
NOT|          AND| t u f        OR | t u f
---+---       ---+------        ---+------
 t | f         t | t u f         t | t t t
 u | u         u | u u f         u | t u u
 f | t         f | f f f         f | t u f
```

Points arising:

1. Let v be a logical variable, i.e., a variable of data type "truth value." Note that the two statements
   (a) "v is not *true*"

   and
   (b) "v is NOT *true*"

   are not equivalent! (Hence my title for this paper.) Statement (a) means that v is either *false* or *unk.* Statement (b) means that v is *false* (see the truth table for NOT). There are clearly rich possibilities for confusion in this field.

2. As pointed out in subsection 3.2 above, "*unk* is not UNK." Suppose the logical variable v happens to be UNK. What is the result of applying one of the logical operators NOT or AND or OR to v? We might agree that "*true* OR UNK" yields *true* and "*false* AND UNK" yields *false,* but it seems to me that all other cases can only yield UNK; for example, "NOT UNK" must surely evaluate to UNK. So are we really dealing

with *four* possible truth-values? In other words, are we already in the realm of *four*-valued logic? (Is this problem just the problem of an infinite number of different types of null rearing its head again in a different guise?)

3.6 *MAYBE operator.* We also need a new logical operator MAYBE. MAYBE applied to a given logical expression p is defined to return the value *true* if p evaluates to *unk,* the value *false* otherwise (i.e., if p evaluates to *true* or *false*). Thus, MAYBE is defined by the following truth table:

```
MAYBE|
-----+---
  t  | f
  u  | t
  f  | f
```

Points arising:

1. Note that MAYBE is a unary operator, like NOT. In other words, just as we might write (e.g.)

   ```
   NOT ( EMP.JOB = 'Programmer' )
   ```

   so we might write (e.g.)

   ```
   MAYBE ( EMP.JOB = 'Programmer' )
   ```

   The first of these two expressions will return *true* if the variable EMP.JOB does have the value "Programmer," the second will return *true* if it *might* have that value (in other words, if it is UNK; see point 2 below).

   Note: We are departing slightly from Codd's proposal here; Codd does not introduce a MAYBE logical operator per se, but instead talks in terms of a MAYBE option or qualifier on queries. He also discusses MAYBE versions of certain of the relational algebra operators (see subsection 3.12 below).

2. It is sometimes claimed that the IS NULL predicate in SQL provides the functionality of the MAYBE operator. This claim is "almost" true, in the sense that if we are given a logical expression involving MAYBE, it is usually possible to construct an expression that is equivalent to that given expression using IS NULL instead. (Only "almost" true, because the argument to IS NULL in SQL cannot be any arbitrary scalar expression—it must be a simple reference to a named column. By contrast, the IS_UNK function introduced in subsection 3.4 above does permit its argument to be any arbitrary scalar expression.) However, using IS NULL instead of MAYBE typically requires an unreasonable amount of work on the part of the user and is somewhat error-prone besides. Consider the following sample query:

Find employee numbers for employees who *may be* programmers born prior to January 18th, 1941, with a salary less than $50,000.*

In a hypothetical version of SQL that supports the MAYBE operator, this query could be expressed very succinctly as follows:

```
SELECT EMP.EMP#
FROM    EMP
WHERE   MAYBE ( EMP.JOB = 'Programmer' AND
                EMP.DOB < DATE ('1941-1-18') AND
                EMP.SALARY < 50000.00 ) ;
```

However, in conventional SQL it would look like this:

```
SELECT EMP.EMP#
FROM    EMP
WHERE        ( EMP.JOB IS NULL AND
               EMP.DOB < DATE ('1941-1-18') AND
               EMP.SALARY < 50000.00 )

OR           ( EMP.JOB = 'Programmer' AND
               EMP.DOB IS NULL AND
               EMP.SALARY < 50000.00 )

OR           ( EMP.JOB = 'Programmer' AND
               EMP.DOB < DATE ('1941-1-18') AND
               EMP.SALARY IS NULL )

OR           ( EMP.JOB IS NULL AND
               EMP.DOB IS NULL AND
               EMP.SALARY < 50000.00 )

OR           ( EMP.JOB IS NULL AND
               EMP.DOB < DATE ('1941-1-18') AND
               EMP.SALARY IS NULL )

OR           ( EMP.JOB = 'Programmer' AND
               EMP.DOB IS NULL AND
               EMP.SALARY IS NULL )

OR           ( EMP.JOB IS NULL AND
               EMP.DOB IS NULL AND
               EMP.SALARY IS NULL ) ;
```

3. In practice we would probably want a TRUE_OR_MAYBE logical operator instead of (or as well as) the MAYBE operator. TRUE_OR_MAYBE would yield *true* if its operand evaluated either to *true* or to *unk*. The reason why such an operator would be useful is that it seems likely, or at least plausible, that users would more often need both the true and the maybe cases, not just the maybe cases alone; e.g., consider the query "List all people who either definitely have been or might have

---

*Note that the English statement is ambiguous! Furthermore, it is difficult to make it precise without some kind of MAYBE operator. A precise statement would be something like the following: "Find employee numbers for employees for whom it *may be the case that* all three of the following are true: (a) They are programmers; (b) they were born prior to January 18th, 1941; (c) they have a salary less than $50,000."

been in contact with employee Joe" (who has just been diagnosed as suffering from measles).

4. The previous point notwithstanding, I would still argue that our IS_UNK function (see subsection 3.4 above) is desirable. It is true that the expression

```
IS_UNK ( EMP.JOB )
```

will return *true* if and only if the expression

```
MAYBE ( EMP.JOB = 'Programmer' )
```

also returns *true,* and *false* if and only if that expression also returns *false* (neither of them will ever return *unk*). Hence, we could logically replace the first expression by the second. But to do so does smack a little of trickery; note that it makes *absolutely no difference* to the value of the second expression if we replace "Programmer" by "Engineer," or "Salesperson," or "King Arthur," or indeed anything at all (except UNK).

3.7 *Rows and tables.* We assume that readers of this paper are fully familiar with the relational concepts of *row* and *table*. Basically, of course, a *row* is an ordered collection of scalars, and a *table* is an unordered set of rows. Points arising:

1. As these simple "definitions" suggest, we are ignoring the question of column names within tables; thus, we are assuming rather that columns can be identified by their ordinal position. This assumption is made purely to simplify the exposition.

2. By virtue of the previous point, we can (unambiguously) use the notation "r[i]" to refer to the ith component of row r.

3. Note that a row in which one or more components (possibly all components) are UNK is still a well-formed row. *Note very carefully also* that such a row is not itself an "UNK row" or "null row," however. We do not use the concept of a null row per se at all, in fact.

4. No two rows in a table can be duplicates of one another (see subsection 3.8 below). In particular, a table can contain at most one "all-UNK row," i.e., a row in which all the components are UNK.* The operators of the relational algebra are carefully defined to ensure that these properties are preserved (see subsection 3.11 below).

---

*Of course, a *base* table cannot contain such a row at all, by virtue of the entity integrity rule [1].

3.8 *Duplicate rows.* We remind the reader that (as mentioned in subsection 3.3 above) two UNKs are considered as duplicates of one another for purposes of duplicate elimination, even though the expression "UNK = UNK" does not evaluate to *true.* We extend this idea to rows also, as follows. Let x and y be two union-compatible rows [1], and let corresponding scalar components of x and y be (x1,y1), (x2,y2), . . . , (xn,yn). Then x and y are duplicates of one another if and only if, for all i (i = 1,2, . . . ,n), xi and yi are duplicates of one another—meaning that *either* xi = yi *or* xi and yi are both UNK.

We now extend the operator DUP_OF, introduced in subsection 3.3 for scalars, to deal with rows also. The expression "x DUP_OF y" (where x and y are union compatible rows) is defined to evaluate to *true* if x and y are duplicates of one another, *false* otherwise. Note, therefore, that testing two rows to see if they are duplicates always returns *true* or *false,* never *unk.* (Testing them for *equality,* by contrast, can return *true* or *false* or *unk.*)

3.9 *The IN operator.* We define what it means for a given row to be "in" a given table. Our definition is deliberately framed in such a manner as to simplify certain subsequent definitions (in particular, the definition of projection) in subsection 3.11; it is *not* an accurate representation of the set membership operator "belongs to," because it returns *true* in certain cases where "belongs to" would more correctly return *unk.* (Our reason for not wanting to define "belongs to" properly is that it turns out to be extremely tricky—perhaps impossible?—to define projection precisely in terms of "belongs to." The interested reader might like to try it as an exercise.)

Let r be a row and T be a table containing rows t1, t2, . . . ,tm; also, let r and T be union-compatible. Then we define the logical expression

    r IN T

to be equivalent to the logical expression

    (r DUP_OF t1) OR (r DUP_OF t2) OR ... OR (r DUP_OF tm)

Note that the expression "r IN T" always returns *true* or *false,* never *unk.*

Examples: Let a, b, c, d, e be union-compatible rows, with scalar components as follows:

```
a :     (   1,   2,   3   )
b :     (   1,   2,   4   )
c :     (   1,   2, UNK   )
d :     (   1,   5, UNK   )
e :     ( UNK, UNK, UNK   )
```

Also, let T be a union-compatible table containing the following rows:

```
(   1,    2,    3   )
(   1,    2,   UNK  )
(  UNK,  UNK,  UNK  )
```

Then the expressions "a IN T," "c IN T," and "e IN T" evaluate to *true,* and the expressions "b IN T" and "d IN T" evaluate to *false.* (By contrast, if we replaced each "IN" by "belongs to," the expressions for b, c, d, and e would each evaluate to *unk.*)

3.10 *Quantifiers.* Next, we define the quantifiers EXISTS and FORALL as iterated OR and AND, respectively. In other words, if T is a table with rows t1, t2, . . . , tm, and t is a variable that ranges over that table (and p is a logical expression involving t), then the logical expression

```
EXISTS t ( p ( t ) )
```

is defined to be equivalent to the logical expression

```
( p ( t1 ) )  OR  ( p ( t2 ) )  OR  ...  OR  ( p ( tm ) )
```

Likewise, the logical expression

```
FORALL t ( p ( t ) )
```

is defined to be equivalent to the logical expression

```
( p ( t1 ) )  AND  ( p ( t2 ) )  AND  ...  AND  ( p ( tm ) )
```

Examples: Let table T be as in the examples in subsection 3.9 above. Then the following expressions have the indicated values:

```
EXISTS t ( t[3] > 1 )             --    true
EXISTS t ( t[2] > 2 )             --    unk
EXISTS t ( MAYBE ( t[1] > 3 ) )   --    true
EXISTS t ( IS_UNK ( t[3] ) )      --    true

FORALL t ( t[1] > 1 )             --    false
FORALL t ( t[2] > 1 )             --    unk
FORALL t ( MAYBE ( t[3] > 1 ) )   --    false
```

3.11 *Relational algebra.* We consider the effect of the foregoing definitions on the restrict, project, product, union, intersection, and difference operators of the relational algebra. (We leave join and divide as exercises for the reader. Note, however, that another curious consequence of the distinction between "DUP_OF" and "="—see subsections 3.3 and 3.8 above—is that intersection is no longer a special case of natural join. Yet another is that the natural join of a table with itself over all columns is no longer guaranteed to return the original table. The consequences of these anomalies are not clear.)

- *Restrict:* Restrict is unaffected. Remember, however, that the operation returns only those rows for which the defining expression evaluates to *true,* i.e., not to *false* and not to *unk.*
- *Project:* The projection of table T on its ith column, written T[i], is obtained by eliminating all other columns and then eliminating redundant duplicates from what remains:

```
T[i]  =  { r[i] : r IN T }
```

The extension needed to the definition in order to handle projection over multiple columns is tedious but essentially straightforward.
- *Product:* Product is unaffected.
- *Union:* The union of two union-compatible tables T1 and T2 is the set of rows r such that r is a duplicate of some row of T1 or of some row of T2 (or both):

```
T1  UNION  T2  =  { r : ( r IN T1 ) OR ( r IN T2 ) }
```

- *Intersection:* The intersection of two union-compatible tables T1 and T2 is the set of rows r such that r is a duplicate of some row of T1 and of some row of T2:

```
T1  INTERSECT  T2  =  { r : ( r IN T1 ) AND ( r IN T2 ) }
```

- *Difference:* The difference between two union-compatible tables T1 and T2 (in that order) is the set of rows r such that r is a duplicate of some row in T1 and not of any row in T2:

```
T1  MINUS  T2  =  { r : ( r IN T1 ) AND NOT ( r IN T2 ) }
```

3.12 *MAYBE operations.* In his development [1,2], Codd also defines "maybe" versions of the restrict, join, and divide operators. For reasons of simplicity, we are ignoring join and divide in the present discussion, as explained in the previous subsection. "Maybe-restrict" (Codd calls the operation "maybe theta-select") differs from the normal—i.e., "true"—restrict operator in that it returns those rows for which the defining expression evaluates to *unk* instead of *true.* In other words, the expression

```
MAYBE_RESTRICT table WHERE      ( logical-expression )
```

can be defined (in our terms) to be equivalent to the expression

```
TRUE_RESTRICT  table WHERE MAYBE ( logical-expression )
```

4. SOME IMPORTANT TAUTOLOGIES

A *tautology* in logic is a statement or expression that is true regardless of the values of any variables involved. Such expressions are important in the transformation of queries (either by the user or by the system) into simpler forms. In this section, we briefly discuss a few important tautologies.

First, let x be a logical (i.e., truth-valued) variable. In conventional two-valued logic, the following expressions are tautologies:

```
1.   x   OR   NOT ( x )   =   true

2.   x   AND  NOT ( x )   =   false
```

More generally, if p is a logical expression, i.e., an expression that evaluates to *true* or *false,* then the following are tautologies in two-valued logic:

```
3.   p   OR   NOT ( p )   =   true

4.   p   AND  NOT ( p )   =   false
```

Note carefully, however, that these are *not* tautologies in three-valued logic: If x is *unk* (in nos. 1 and 2) or p is *unk* (in nos. 3 and 4), then the left-hand side evaluates to *unk* in each case. No. 3 in particular accounts for a well-known counterintuitive property of three-valued logic, namely that illustrated by the following example: If we issue the query "Find all suppliers in London," followed by the query "Find all suppliers not in London," and take the union of the two results, we do *not* necessarily get all suppliers. Instead, we need to include "All suppliers who *may be* in London."

As this example suggests, an expression that *is* a tautology in three-valued logic—a counterpart to no. 3 above—is:

```
5.   p   OR   NOT ( p )   OR   MAYBE ( p )           =   true
```

(informally, "p must be *true* or *false* or *unk*"). The following expression, however, which might be proposed as the "obvious" counterpart to no. 4 above, is not a tautology at all:

```
6.   p   AND  NOT ( p )   AND   MAYBE ( p )          =   false
```

Reason: If p is *unk,* the left-hand side is "*unk* AND *unk* AND *true*," which evaluates to *unk,* not *false.* The correct counterpart to no. 4 above is:

```
7.   p   AND  NOT ( p )   AND   NOT ( MAYBE ( p ) )  =   false
```

The following tautologies, however (usually known as De Morgan's Laws), hold in both two- and three-valued logic:

```
8.   NOT ( p AND q )   =   ( NOT ( p ) )   OR    ( NOT ( q ) )

9.   NOT ( p OR  q )   =   ( NOT ( p ) )   AND   ( NOT ( q ) )
```

We prove the three-valued logic version of no. 8 by means of the following truth table. The proof of no. 9 is left as an exercise.

```
p   q   p AND q   lhs  |  NOT p   NOT q   rhs
----------------------+---------------------
t   t     t        f   |    f       f       f
t   u     u        u   |    f       u       u
t   f     f        t   |    f       t       t
u   t     u        u   |    u       f       u
u   u     u        u   |    u       u       u
u   f     f        t   |    u       t       t
f   t     f        t   |    t       f       t
f   u     f        t   |    t       u       t
f   f     f        t   |    t       t       t
```

The columns headed "lhs" and "rhs" denote the values of the expressions on the left- and right-hand side, respectively, of the equals sign. Since these two columns are identical, the tautology is proved.

The following expressions are also tautologies in both two- and three-valued logic. Again the proofs are left as an exercise for the reader. *Note:* The expression "p(x)" stands for an expression in which there is at most one free variable, namely x.

```
10.   FORALL x ( p ( x ) )  =  NOT ( EXISTS x ( NOT ( p ( x ) ) ) )

11.   EXISTS x ( p ( x ) )  =  NOT ( FORALL x ( NOT ( p ( x ) ) ) )
```

5. EXAMPLES

Intuition is frequently very misleading in dealing with problems involving three-valued logic. The present section discusses some examples that demonstrate the truth of this claim. As a basis for those examples, we take a slight variation on the usual suppliers-and-parts database:

```
S    ( S#, SNAME, STATUS, CITY )
     PRIMARY KEY ( S# )

P    ( P#, PNAME, COLOR, WEIGHT, CITY )
     PRIMARY KEY ( P# )

SP   ( SHIP#, S#, P#, QTY )
     PRIMARY KEY ( SHIP# )
     ALTERNATE KEY ( S#, P# )
     FOREIGN KEY ( S# ) REFERENCES S
                   NULLS ALLOWED
     FOREIGN KEY ( P# ) REFERENCES P
                   NULLS ALLOWED
```

The only difference between this version of the database and the more familiar version is that table SP includes an additional column, SHIP# ("shipment number"), which serves as the primary key for that table, and columns SP.S# and SP.P# do NOT have "nulls not allowed."

Suppose these tables contain the following data at the present time:

```
S   S#   SNAME   STATUS   CITY          SP   SHIP#   S#   P#    QTY
    --   -----   ------   ------             -----   --   --    ---
    S1   Smith      20    London             SHIP1   S1   P1    300
    S2   Jones      10    Paris              SHIP2   S2   P2    200
    S3   Blake      30    Paris              SHIP3   S3   UNK   400
    S4   Clark      20    UNK

P   P#   PNAME   COLOR   WEIGHT   CITY
    --   -----   -----   ------   ------
    P1   Nut     Red         12   London
    P2   Bolt    Green       17   Paris
```

The first difficulty is illustrated by the following simple problem (repeated from Section 4): Given the sample data values shown, the query "Find all suppliers in London" together with the query "Find all suppliers not in London" will not between them produce all suppliers (to be specific, the first query will return supplier S1 and the second will return suppliers S2 and S3; supplier S4 will not appear in either result).

The point, of course, is that while the two states "location is London" and "location is not London" are mutually exclusive and exhaust the full range of possibilities in the real world, the database does *not* contain the real world—it only contains *knowledge about* the real world. And there are three states, not two, of knowledge about the real world in this example—namely, "location is known to be London," "location is known not to be London," and "location is not known." Furthermore, of course (as reference [8] puts it), we obviously cannot ask the system questions about the real world per se, only about its knowledge of the real world as represented by the values in the database. The (alleged) counterintuitive nature of this first example thus derives from a simple confusion over levels: The user is thinking at the real-world level, but the system is thinking at the level of its knowledge concerning that real world.

If the foregoing were the only kind of difficulty arising in connexion with three-valued logic and intuition, I do not think there would be much of a problem—it would just be a question of simple education. Unfortunately, however, matters do not stop there. First, consider the following example*—let us refer to it as "Query 1":

```
S.SNAME WHERE EXISTS SP ( SP.S# = S.S# AND SP.P# = 'P2' )
```

What is the real-world interpretation of this query?—i.e., what does the query "mean"? An intuitive answer to this question is surely that it means "Find names of suppliers who supply part P2." But, of course, this interpretation is not strictly correct. What the query really means is "Find

---

*We deliberately express the queries of this section in relational calculus rather than SQL, because SQL suffers from some significant bugs in this area [8].

names of suppliers who are *known to the system* to supply part P2."
(Again, we can only ask queries regarding the system's *knowledge,* not
about the real world per se.)

Let us consider how the query is evaluated. (The following explanation
will be familiar to most readers, but it is necessary to go through it in detail
in order to set the scene for subsequent examples.)

1. The variable S (which is a range variable that ranges over table S) takes
   on one of its permitted values. For simplicity, let us assume that variable S iterates over the rows of table S in the top-to-bottom order
   shown, so that the first value taken is the row for supplier S1. The
   expression in the WHERE clause thus becomes

   ```
   EXISTS SP ( SP.S# = 'S1' AND SP.P# = 'P2' )
   ```

   which evaluates to *false* (there is no SP row for S1 and P2), so the
   SNAME for supplier S1 does not appear in the result.

2. For the next supplier row (for supplier S2), the expression becomes

   ```
   EXISTS SP ( SP.S# = 'S2' AND SP.P# = 'P2' )
   ```

   which evaluates to *true* (there is an SP row for S2 and P2), and so the
   SNAME for supplier S2 ("Jones") does appear in the result.

3. For the next supplier row (for supplier S3), the expression becomes

   ```
   EXISTS SP ( SP.S# = 'S3' AND SP.P# = 'P2' )
   ```

   which evaluates to *unk* (there is no SP row for S3 and P2, but there is
   an SP row for S3 in which the P# value is UNK). However, the overall
   query returns values only where the expression in the WHERE clause
   evaluates to *true,* not to *false* or *unk,* and so the SNAME for supplier
   S3 does not appear in the result.

4. For the last supplier row (for supplier S4), the expression becomes

   ```
   EXISTS SP ( SP.S# = 'S4' AND SP.P# = 'P2' )
   ```

   which evaluates to *false* (there are no SP rows for S4 at all), so the
   SNAME for supplier S4 does not appear in the result.

Hence the final result is a set containing just the one supplier name
"Jones."

In the light of the foregoing explanation, what can we say about the
following example ("Query 2")? In other words, what does *this* query
mean?*

---

*It is germane to the thesis of this section to mention that Ted Codd, Nat Goodman, and I
all got the wrong answer to this question when we first discussed it.

```
S.SNAME WHERE NOT ( EXISTS SP ( SP.S# = S.S# AND SP.P# = 'P2' ) )
```

Possible interpretations include at least the following:

(a) Find names of suppliers who do not supply part P2

(b) Find names of suppliers who are not known to supply part P2 (i.e., they *might* supply part P2, but the system does not know whether they do or not)

(c) Find names of suppliers who are known not to supply part P2 (i.e., they are *definitely* known not to supply part P2)

(d) Find names of suppliers who are either known not or not known to supply part P2 (this is the union of (b) and (c))

I suggest you try to decide which of these interpretations (if any) you think is correct before continuing. (If you're having difficulties over the "not known" vs. "known not" distinction, you might like to meditate on the difference between the following two statements: (a) "I know you don't have measles," (b) "I don't know if you do have measles.")

Discussion: Interpretation (a) is clearly not correct—even though it would be the one normally given, because it is "obviously" and "intuitively" right!—because (once again) it talks in terms of the real world instead of what the system knows about the real world. Interpretations (b), (c), and (d), by contrast, do talk only in terms of what the system knows. How do these three interpretations differ? In order to answer this question, let us first consider what knowledge the system has (in terms of the sample values shown above):

- Supplier S1 is definitely *known not* to supply part P2
- Supplier S2 is definitely *known* to supply part P2
- Supplier S3 is *not known* to supply part P2 (but not known not to, either)
- Supplier S4 (like supplier S1) is *known not* to supply part P2

If interpretation (b) is the correct one for Query 2, therefore, the query should return "Blake"; if interpretation (c) is correct, it should return "Smith" and "Clark"; if interpretation (d) is correct, it should return "Smith," "Blake," and "Clark." So let us consider exactly how the query is evaluated:

1. For the first supplier (supplier S1), the expression in the WHERE clause becomes

```
NOT ( EXISTS SP ( SP.S# = 'S1' AND SP.P# = 'P2' ) )
```

which evaluates to "NOT *false*" (i.e., *true*)—since there is no SP row for S1 and P2—and so the SNAME for supplier S1 ("Smith") does appear in the result.

2. For supplier S2, the expression becomes

```
NOT ( EXISTS SP ( SP.S# = 'S2' AND SP.P# = 'P2' ) )
```

which evaluates to "NOT *true*" (i.e., *false*)—since there is an SP row for S2 and P2—and so the SNAME for supplier S2 does not appear in the result.

3. For supplier S3, the expression becomes

```
NOT ( EXISTS SP ( SP.S# = 'S3' AND SP.P# = 'P2' ) )
```

which evaluates to "NOT *unk*" (i.e., *unk*), since there is no SP row for S3 and P2, but there is an SP row for S3 in which the P# value is UNK. However, the overall query returns values only where the expression in the WHERE clause evaluates to *true,* not to *false* and not to *unk,* and so the SNAME for supplier S3 does not appear in the result.

4. For supplier S4, expression becomes

```
NOT ( EXISTS SP ( SP.S# = 'S4' AND SP.P# = 'P2' ) )
```

which evaluates to "NOT *false*" (i.e., *true*), since there are no SP rows for S4 at all, and so the SNAME for supplier S4 ("Clark") does appear in the result.

Hence the final result is the set ("Smith," "Clark"). We conclude that interpretations (b) and (d) are definitely incorrect; the right interpretation is (c). (Are you sure?)

To follow on from this example: Given that the right interpretation for Query 2 is interpretation (c), how can we formulate a query for interpretation (b)? Interpretation (b), to repeat, is:

(b) Find names of suppliers who are not known to supply part P2 (i.e., they *might* supply part P2, but the system does not know whether they do or not)

Note first that (as the parenthetical remark suggests) the English statement of the problem can be reduced to the following simpler form:

(b) Find names of suppliers who *might* supply part P2

(where "might" means "might, according to the system's knowledge"). In other words, we want to exclude any suppliers who (according to the system) either definitely do supply part P2 or definitely do not. First attempt ("Query 3"):

```
S.SNAME WHERE EXISTS SP ( MAYBE ( SP.S# = S.S# AND SP.P# = 'P2' ) )
```

("supplier names where there exists a shipment saying the supplier might supply part P2"). However, this formulation is not correct (though it does happen to produce the right answer with our sample data). In order to see that this is so, suppose that table SP includes another row in addition to those shown above, namely the row (SHIP4,S3,P2,500), and consider what happens when the variable S takes as its value the supplier row for supplier S3:

- The expression in the WHERE clause becomes

```
EXISTS SP ( MAYBE ( SP.S# = 'S3' AND SP.P# = 'P2' ) )
```

  which evaluates to *true,* since there does exist an SP row—namely, the row (SHIP3,S3,UNK,400)—for which the expression

```
( SP.S# = 'S3' AND SP.P# = 'P2' )
```

  evaluates to *unk.* Thus the SNAME for supplier S3 ("Blake") appears in the final result. But it should not, because there is *also* an SP row—namely, the row (SHIP4,S3,P2,500)—saying that supplier S3 *definitely does* supply part P2. Error!

The correct interpretation of Query 3 is "Find names of suppliers who may or may not be *known* to supply part P2, but are definitely known to be *possible* suppliers of part P2" (!).

Here then is our next attempt ("Query 4") at interpretation (b):

```
S.SNAME WHERE MAYBE ( EXISTS SP ( SP.S# = S.S# AND SP.P# = 'P2' ) )
```

("supplier names where there might exist a shipment saying the supplier supplies part P2"). This formulation is correct. *Exercise:* Convince yourself that this is so.

It follows from all of the above that a correct formulation for interpretation (d) is:

```
S.SNAME WHERE NOT    ( EXISTS SP ( SP.S# = S.S# AND SP.P# = 'P2' ) )
       OR    MAYBE ( EXISTS SP ( SP.S# = S.S# AND SP.P# = 'P2' ) )
```

("supplier names where either there does not exist a shipment, or there might exist a shipment, saying the supplier supplies part P2"). *Exercise:* Again, convince yourself that this formulation is correct.

One final point regarding the foregoing example: If table SP includes a row in which the supplier number is UNK and the part number is P2, then Query 3 will produce an answer containing the SNAME of every supplier! This makes sense (?), because if table SP includes such a row, it means that any supplier *might* supply part P2 (regardless of whether there exists another SP row saying that they actually do).

6. SOME QUESTIONS

In this section I raise a couple of questions that I believe need to be answered before we can commit ourselves wholeheartedly to the three-valued logic approach.

The first question (a very fundamental one) is as follows: "Is three-valued logic as presented in this paper a sound and complete logic for dealing with databases that contain UNKs?" [11]. In other words:

(a) [*Soundness*] Is it possible to derive a contradiction using that logic? If so, the logic is not sound.

(b) [*Completeness*] Does there exist an expression that is in fact *true* but cannot be shown to be *true* using that logic? If so, the logic is not complete.

I assume these questions probably can be answered satisfactorily, but until they have been I feel that the logical defensibility of the approach has not been shown, and hence that we should tread very warily in trying to incorporate it into our formal database theories and systems.

Next, assuming that the foregoing questions *can* be answered satisfactorily, is there anything that can be done about the mismatch between three-valued logic and ordinary intuition? If the answer has to be "It's an education problem," then I have to respond that it doesn't seem to me to be a particularly *easy* education problem. The big advantage of the traditional approach to missing information, namely the "default values" approach [5] (which incidentally is the approach adopted in the real world), is precisely that it is intuitively understandable and is *not* a big education problem. It is also easier to implement (which suggests the pragmatic point that the implementation is less likely to contain errors).

7. MISCELLANEOUS ISSUES

Reference [5] discusses numerous detail-level problems having to do with UNK-type nulls (and SQL-style nulls in particular). In what follows, we briefly consider a few additional issues that were not included in that earlier paper.

▪ The entity integrity rule [1] states that primary keys in base tables are not permitted to contain nulls. One argument that is sometimes quoted in support of this requirement (I have used it myself) is that if, for example, one or more rows in the EMP table had an EMP# of UNK, we would not know how many employees there were (some of the UNKs might stand for EMP# values that already existed elsewhere in the table). However, the same argument effectively applies to *every single column*. E.g., if some EMP rows have a DEPT# of UNK and we take a projection over the DEPT# column, we don't know how many departments there are in the result (and hence in the original EMP table). The only difference between the two arguments is that the EMP# column corresponds to *entities* and the DEPT# column to *properties,* but this is only an informal distinction. Thus, it appears that UNKs should not be allowed to appear in any column at all (at least in base tables)—?

- Following on from the previous point: The relational model does permit *derived* tables (e.g., query results) to have a primary key that contains nulls.* An obvious example arises in connexion with the projection operation: Consider what happens if we take a projection of table P, the parts table, over the COLOR column, if some parts happen to have an unknown color. However, such a table cannot be "promoted" to base table status, because of the entity integrity rule. While this state of affairs does not actually violate any relational rules, it does seem a little distasteful, and it would be nice if the difficulty could be defined away.

   Aside: It is sometimes suggested that the foregoing *does* violate a relational rule, namely the rule of closure (which states that the result of every relational operation is another relation). This suggestion is incorrect, however: The result of every such operation is still a relation, even if it cannot be a base relation. *End of aside.*

- By contrast with primary keys (in base tables), alternate keys *are* permitted to contain nulls.† But what does this statement mean? The only reasonable interpretation seems to be that *any number* of nulls can appear (if only one null is permitted, then introducing a second null has to fail, which implies that two nulls must be considered to be equal). In other words, for any given row in the table, either the alternate key is null or it has a nonnull value. Since alternate key values are supposed

---

*In recent publications and presentations Codd has been referring to such a key as a "weak identifier," but it seems better to preserve the familiar "primary key" terminology. See reference [7] for further discussion of this point.

†An alternate key is a candidate key that is not the primary key.

to be unique, however, it must be the case that each null stands for a value that is distinct from all the others and distinct from all existing nonnull values (think of the social security number example from Section 2 once again). In other words, these nulls are not really UNK-type nulls, and representing them as UNKs is logically incorrect and is likely to lead to errors. Do we conclude from this fact that the relational model should include another general integrity rule, to the effect that alternate keys must not permit UNK-type nulls?

- Certain relational operators—in particular, the outer join operator [6]—actually generate nulls in their result. The question arises: "What *type* of null should they generate?" To say that they should always generate the same type seems far too simplistic. In the case of outer join, for example, "value unknown," "value not applicable," and "value does not exist" (and probably other types also) can all make sense in certain circumstances. Codd suggests [2] that UNK-type nulls be generated by default but that the user should have the option of specifying other types of null if desired. This is an issue that I feel requires more research.

8. CONCLUSION

In this paper, I have tried to present a careful and yet not too formal treatment of the three-valued logic approach to missing information, on the assumption that users are probably going to have to grapple with these ideas at some time in the near future. However, as I have indicated at various points in the paper, I do have some reservations regarding the overall approach. The following items seem to me to merit careful study:

1. The soundness and completeness questions from Section 6
2. The psychological questions (i.e., the problems of intuition) sketched in Section 5
3. The suitability of the approach for extension to deal with other types of null (see Section 2)
4. The question of how many different types of null exist, or at least how many are needed in practice (again, see Section 2)
5. What it means to deal with logical variables that happen to be UNK rather than *unk* (see Section 3)
6. The justification for the distinction between duplicate elimination and testing for equality (Section 3 again)
7. The justification for the fact that "x − x" does not yield zero, and "x = x" does not yield *true,* if x happens to be UNK (Section 3 yet again)

8. The assertion in reference [5] that a "fundamental theorem of normalization" breaks down. (The theorem in question states that if relation R(A,B,C) satisfies the functional dependence R.A → R.B, then R is equal to the join of its projections R1(A,B) and R2(A,C). It is easy to show that this theorem is no longer valid if R.A has "nulls allowed" [5].) Codd states in reference [2] that he does not agree with this assertion, but his arguments are not very convincing.

One further point: The question of whether a set can contain a null was deliberately never addressed in the body of this paper, though it was discussed briefly in my earlier paper on nulls (reference [5]). (The only sets we have been discussing have been *tables,* i.e., sets of rows, and we have not even considered any such thing as a "null row." A table can certainly contain a row in which every component is null, but—as pointed out in Section 3—such a row is still a well-formed row; it is *not* the same thing as a "null row.") In reference [1], however, Codd does seem to permit a set to contain a null, because he considers the truth-value of the logical expression "{null} subset of X," where X is a nonempty set. If it *is* possible for a set to contain a null, however, then numerous further issues arise:

- The expression "UNK belongs to X" will return *unk* for any set X, regardless of whether X does actually contain an UNK. We therefore need a new primitive function to test whether a given set does in fact contain an UNK.

- The expression "v belongs to X" will return *unk* or *true* (never *false*) for any v if set X in fact does contain an UNK. We therefore need a new primitive function to test whether a given set that does contain an UNK does *not* contain some specified nonUNK value.

- As a consequence of the previous point, if a *domain* contains an UNK, domain integrity checks will never fail. I conclude from this fact that domains should not include UNKs!

- As a consequence of the previous point, a relation that contains an UNK (more precisely, a relation that includes a tuple that contains an UNK) will not be a subset of the Cartesian product of its underlying domains, counter to Codd's original definition of relation.*

---

*An advocate of UNKs might claim that this assertion is false and is due to a "value-oriented misinterpretation" [2]. If the EMP relation includes a row saying that "Joe's salary is UNK," then that UNK is merely a placeholder, not a value; presumably there does exist some value, v say, that actually is Joe's salary, and when we replace the UNK by that value v (and replace all other UNKs in the EMP relation in a similar fashion), then what results is indeed a subset of the Cartesian product of the domains. But this counterargument, even if we accept it in the case of UNK-type nulls, does not seem to be valid for other kinds of null (consider, e.g., the "value is the empty set" null).

- If a set can contain an UNK, the expression "X subset of X" will return *unk,* not *true,* if X in fact contains an UNK. (This anomaly is reminiscent of the anomaly that the scalar comparison "x = x" also returns *unk,* not *true,* if x is UNK.) We therefore need a new operator—an extension of the DUP_OF operator discussed earlier in this paper—to test whether two sets are in fact duplicates of one another (with an appropriately extended interpretation of the term "duplicate," of course).

- What is the cardinality of a set that contains an UNK? Is it UNK also? (Note that the cardinality of such a set is not *totally* unknown, however; consider, e.g., the set {1,2,UNK}, for which the cardinality is unknown but must be either two or three. Such considerations lead us into another problem, known as "distinguished nulls" [5].)

- If a set does contain an UNK, is the set itself in fact UNK also (given that a set is known if and only if its members are known)? And if so, does it mean that the set contains itself as a member? If so, . . . ?

And doubtless other questions also.

ACKNOWLEDGMENTS

This paper owes a very heavy debt to Nat Goodman. Section 4 in particular is based almost entirely on work done by him [11], and I am grateful to him for giving me permission to incorporate it into the paper in this way. Also, it was Nat who made me realize that there was no need to deal with the question of whether a set can contain an UNK (because we are concerned specifically with tables, not general sets), and it was Nat who, through his comments on an earlier note of mine [10], made me understand the precise nature of some of the intuitive difficulties discussed in Section 5 of this paper.

I am also grateful to Charley Bontempo and Hugh Darwen for numerous discussions and for their helpful reviews of an earlier draft of this paper.

REFERENCES AND BIBLIOGRAPHY

1. E. F. Codd, "Extending the Database Relational Model to Capture More Meaning," *ACM Transactions on Database Systems* 4, No. 4 (December 1979).

2. E. F. Codd, "Missing Information (Applicable and Inapplicable) in Relational Databases," *ACM SIGMOD Record* 15, No. 4 (December 1986).

3. E. F. Codd, "More Commentary on Missing Information in Relational Databases (Applicable and Inapplicable Information)," *ACM SIGMOD Record* 16, No. 1 (March 1987).

4. E. F. Codd, "Is Your DBMS Really Relational?" *Computerworld* (October 14, 1985); "Does Your DBMS Run by the Rules?" *Computerworld* (October 21, 1985).

5. C. J. Date, "Null Values in Database Management," in C. J. Date, *Relational Database: Selected Writings* (Reading, MA: Addison-Wesley, 1986).

6. C. J. Date, "The Outer Join," in C. J. Date, *Relational Database: Selected Writings* (Reading, MA: Addison-Wesley, 1986).

7. C. J. Date, "Referential Integrity and Foreign Keys. Part I: Basic Concepts; Part II: Further Considerations" (in this volume).

8. C. J. Date, "EXISTS Is Not "Exists"! (Some Logical Flaws in SQL)" (in this volume).

9. C. J. Date, "SQL Dos and Don'ts" (in this volume).

10. C. J. Date, "Three-Valued Logic" (private communication to E. F. Codd, March 31, 1988).

11. Nathan Goodman, "Some Basic Mathematics of Three-Valued Logic" (private communication, April 19, 1988).

12. Andrew Warden, "Into the Unknown" (in this volume).

APPENDIX A:
THE DEFAULT VALUE APPROACH

In my previous paper on the problem of missing information [5], I proposed an approach based on the systematic use of *default values*. The following summary of that proposal (numerous details omitted) is based on the one given in reference [5]. *Note:* The original proposal treated only one kind of missing information, namely "value unknown," but it could obviously be extended to deal with other kinds also. If it were so extended, however, it would be desirable to replace keywords such as DEFAULT—see below—by some more explicit term such as UNKNOWN. We could then introduce additional keywords such as INAPPLICABLE, UNDEFINED, etc., to deal with other types of missing information. The following summary stays with the single DEFAULT of the original proposal, however.

> *Note:* At the time of writing (early 1989), the SQL standard is on the point of being extended to provide some limited support for user-defined default values. The proposed standard support resembles that sketched in paragraphs 1 and 2 below (only).

1. Associated with the declaration of each column of each named table is either a DEFAULT clause designating the default value for that column, or else the specification NODEFAULT, meaning that the column in question does not have a default value. For example:

```
CREATE TABLE S /* suppliers */
      ( S#      ... NODEFAULT ,
        SNAME   ... DEFAULT ( '    ' ) ,
        STATUS  ... DEFAULT ( -1 ) ,
        CITY    ... DEFAULT ( '???' ) ,
        PRIMARY KEY ( S# ) ) ;
```

NODEFAULT is assumed (and cannot be overridden) for all columns that participate in a base table primary key. For other columns, if no DEFAULT clause is stated explicitly, then it might be possible for the system to assume a "default default"—e.g., blanks for character string columns, zero for numeric columns.

2. When a new row is inserted into a base table:

(a) The user must supply a value for every column that does not have a default value;

(b) For other columns, the system will supply the applicable default value if the user does not provide a value.

3. When a new column is added to a base table:

(a) That new column must have an (explicit or implicit) DEFAULT specification (i.e., NODEFAULT cannot be specified);

(b) The value of the new column is automatically set to the applicable default value in all existing rows in the table.

4. The builtin function DEFAULT (R.C), where R is a range variable ranging over some base table and C is a column of that table, returns the default value applicable to R.C. It is an error if no such default value exists.

5. The entity and referential integrity rules of the relational model are revised to refer to default values instead of nulls.

6. In applying an aggregate function such as AVG to a particular column, the user must explicitly exclude default values, if that is what is desired. For example:

```
SELECT  AVG (SP.QTY)
FROM    SP
WHERE   SP.QTY <> DEFAULT (SP.QTY) ;
```

7. The builtin function IS_DEFAULT (R.C.) returns *true* if its argument R.C evaluates to the applicable default value, *false* otherwise. The foregoing SELECT statement could thus alternatively have been formulated:

```
SELECT  AVG (SP.QTY)
FROM    SP
WHERE   NOT ( IS_DEFAULT (SP.QTY) ) ;
```

8. Aggregate functions such as AVG are extended to include an optional second argument, defining the value to be returned if the first argument evaluates to the empty set. It is an error if the first argument does evaluate to the empty set and the second argument is omitted.

9. For some columns it might be the case that every legal bit configuration is in fact a permissible (nondefault) value of the column in question. Such cases must be handled by explicit, separate, user-controlled indicator columns (as with the host side of the interface in embedded SQL today)—though it would be desirable to be able to tell the system that those separate columns *are* indicator columns, and to define the indicator values in a declarative manner so that the system understands them.

The advantages of the foregoing scheme (compared to the three-valued logic approach described in the body of this paper) include the following:

- It is intuitively easier to understand.

- It is also easier to implement.

- In fact, it directly reflects the way we handle missing information in the real world.

- There are arguably fewer traps for the unwary.

- As already mentioned, it is extendable to other kinds of missing information without the need to resort to four- or five- or . . . n-valued logic (for arbitrary n).

In reference [2], however, Codd argues strongly against the default value approach, on the grounds that it is unsystematic, misrepresents the semantics, and is a significant burden on DBAs and users (inasmuch as they have to choose and understand and manipulate the default values, possibly many different default values). My response to these arguments is as follows:

- I would agree that default values represent a significant burden on DBAs and users—but so too does three-valued logic, in my opinion (not to mention four- and five- . . . and n-valued logic), as the discussions of the present paper have surely demonstrated. The fact is, the missing information problem is a very complex problem, more complicated than I think anyone yet fully understands. A "solution" to that problem that is oversimplified is at least as dangerous as one that is inherently somewhat complex.

- Regarding the "unsystematic" claim: DBAs and users (and DBMSs, I might add) are always going to be able to use system facilities in an unsystematic manner, no matter how carefully defined those facilities might be. The default value approach is not totally unsystematic. At least the default values are explicitly made known to the system, and appropriate functions are provided to avoid the need for hardcoding those values into programs (in fact, users should normally not even know what the specific default values are). Systematic means of dealing with empty sets are also part of the proposal.

- As for the suggestion that default values "misrepresent the semantics": Exactly the same is true of the three-valued logic scheme, if it becomes necessary to deal with more than one kind of missing information. To repeat an argument from Section 2 in the body of this paper: It is at least as dangerous (to my way of thinking) to represent, say, "not applicable" as "value unknown" as it is to represent, say, "value unknown" as " -1 "—possibly even more dangerous, in fact, because in the first case the user might be lulled into a false sense of security. Indeed, we can see exactly this kind of mistake in *the design of the SQL language itself* (in other words, system designers and implementers can make just the same kinds of mistakes as users). For example (as pointed out earlier in this paper), the fact that SQL regards the MAX of an empty set to be null (meaning "value unknown") is just plain wrong, in my opinion.

In conclusion, therefore, I freely admit that the default value scheme is not a particularly elegant approach to the problem, but I am far from being convinced that three-valued logic is any better, and indeed I believe there are reasons to think it may be worse. In other words, I believe the whole area of missing information stands in need of considerable further research.

9

Further Relational Myths

ABSTRACT

The theoretical basis on which relational systems are founded is of course
the relational model. By contrast, the basis on which much criticism of
those systems is founded might more accurately be characterized as the relational *muddle* (I am indebted to Ted Codd and Sharon Weinberg for this
felicitous phrase). The purpose of this paper is to try to do a little bit toward
straightening out that muddle.

COMMENTS ON REPUBLICATION

The original papers on which the present paper is based [6,7] consisted primarily of an extensive and annotated series of quotes on the general subject
of relational technology. The quotes (which included attributions, by the
way) were taken from the trade press and elsewhere; my purpose in repro-
ducing them was to illustrate the truly abysmal level of understanding of
the field that seemed to pervade the DP community at the time, and (by

This paper is based on material from two separate papers, "Relational Database: Further
Misconceptions Number One" (originally published in *InfoDB* 1, No. 1, Spring 1986) and
"Relational Database: Further Misconceptions Number Two" (originally published in *InfoDB*
1, No. 2, Summer 1986). Reprinted with permission.

publishing suitable rejoinders) to try to do something about raising that level. The paper that follows does not include all the original quotes per se—it just gives a few representative ones—but it does discuss some of the major themes that appeared repeatedly in the originals, and (of course) it summarizes my responses to those themes. I refer to those major themes as "further relational myths," for reasons explained in the paper.

1. INTRODUCTION

Some readers may be familiar with an earlier paper of mine [5] entitled "Some Relational Myths Exploded" (subtitle "An Examination of Some Popular Misconceptions Concerning Relational Database Management Systems"). In that paper (which for brevity I will refer to herein as "the myths paper"), I discussed 26 popular misconceptions or "myths" regarding various aspects of relational technology. This new paper can be regarded as a continuation of that earlier paper. To repeat the abstract from that paper:

> "Relational database management is one of the key technologies for the 1980s,* yet the field of relational technology still suffers from a great deal of misunderstanding and misrepresentation. Misconceptions abound. The purpose of this paper is to correct some of those misconceptions."

The situation today is a little better, but not much. Relational systems still receive far more than their fair share of misrepresentation and uninformed criticism. Thus, the raison d'être for this paper is simple: As already stated, misconceptions regarding the true nature of relational systems continue to be widespread; and it seems desirable to try to document and respond to as many of those misconceptions as possible, in the hope that eventually the true state of affairs will become generally understood.

For convenience I will begin by restating the original myths (see Box 1). I will refer to those myths in the present paper by their number—"Myth 1," "Myth 2," etc.

Various statements in the trade press and elsewhere over the last couple of years have made me realize that there were some major misconceptions that I missed in the original paper, however. The purpose of the present paper, therefore, is to document and respond to a few additional myths. I will first state those additional myths (see Box 2), then go on to address

---

*And beyond! I don't know why I was so cautious in my original claim. The fact is, there is still nothing on the horizon to replace relational technology, and in my opinion there is never likely to be. See Section 8 of this paper for further discussion.

1. A relational database is a database in which the data is physically stored as tables.
2. A relation is just a flat file.
3. The relational model is just flat files.
4. "Join" is just the relational version of the parent-child links found in hierarchic and network systems.
5. Relational systems must necessarily perform poorly.
6. The data must be hierarchically clustered for good performance.
7. Hierarchic clustering requires pointers.
8. The relational model presupposes (or requires) content-addressable memory.
9. Relational databases use more storage than other kinds of database.
10. The relational approach is intended purely for query, not for production systems.
11. Automatic navigation does not apply to application programs, because such programs are forced to operate one record at a time.
12. Control is not possible in a relational system.
13. Relational systems provide no data integrity.
14. A relational system that included all necessary integrity controls would be indistinguishable from a hierarchic or network system.
15. Data has a naturally hierarchic structure.
16. Relational systems do not conform to the official database standard.
17. Hierarchic and network structures are more powerful than relational structures.
18. Relational databases involve a lot of redundancy.
19. The relational model is "just theory."
20. Relational databases require "third normal form."
21. The primary key concept is unnecessary.

Box 1   The original 26 myths (part 1 of 2)

22. The relational model is only suitable for simple data (i.e., numbers and character strings).
23. SQL (or QUEL or . . .) is a panacea.
24. Database design is unnecessary in a relational system.
25. Third normal form is a panacea.
26. The relational approach is a panacea.

Box 1 The original 26 myths (part 2 of 2)

27. Updating must be done one record at a time.
28. Relational systems cannot handle the bill-of-materials problem.
29. Relational systems require the physical construction of numerous intermediate result tables.
30. Foreign keys undermine data independence.
31. Relational systems do not support the data dictionary concept.
32. Top-down ("entity/relationship") design and normalization are alternative and competing methodologies. Top-down design does not apply to relational databases.
33. The relational approach is just another technological fad. The relational model does not really differ in kind from the hierarchic and network "models."
34. "There's no such thing as a relational database."

Box 2 Some further myths

them one by one. I have numbered them from 27 for consistency with the original list.

2. *Myth 27:* **UPDATING MUST BE RECORD-AT-A-TIME**

Statements to the effect that updating must be done one record at a time are encountered very frequently—the implication being that, because relational languages are set-at-a-time, relational DBMSs are not appropriate for updating operations (nor, by extension, for transaction processing, production work, etc., etc.). For example:

- "Relational commands deal with whole groups of records, while updating is done one record at a time. Hence, database maintenance is inherently procedural, not relational. Consequently, real languages will incorporate procedural (record-at-a-time) read and write commands for updating the database. They must. To be more useful, languages must be less relational." [11]

- "Database maintenance is typically record-at-a-time, while relational operators are set-oriented."

- "Since the nature of many TP applications is record-oriented rather than set-oriented, traditional systems may be more suited here."

Even if it were true that updating is always record-at-a-time (which I do not fully accept), I fail to see how it follows that relational operators are not suitable for database maintenance. Consider the following points:

- First, relational operators access data *associatively* (associatively at the logical level, that is). In general, therefore, it is true to say they are set-level. However, a set containing just one record (or even zero records, come to that) is still a set. In particular, if the associative access is based on the primary key (a very common special case, of course, and one that is typical of much transaction processing), then the set does contain just one record, and the operator thus effectively becomes record-level. Record-at-a-time is (obviously) just a special case of set-at-a-time.

- Second, relational *programming* languages do provide record-at-a-time operators anyway. For example, embedded SQL provides record-at-a-time access through its cursor operations OPEN, FETCH, UPDATE CURRENT, etc. Hence relational *programs* can still perform "traditional" record-level updating if desired. Note carefully, however, that all the usual relational advantages—associative access, optimization, automatic navigation, maintainability, ease of prototyping, etc., etc. [9]—still apply; the availability of such record-level functions in no way undermines those advantages. See Myth 11 in the original myths paper for further discussion of this latter point, also Myth 10 for a general discussion of the whole question of the suitability of the relational approach for database maintenance operations.

3. *Myth 28:* **RELATIONAL SYSTEMS CANNOT HANDLE BILL-OF-MATERIALS**

There is a widely held, but erroneous, belief that relational DBMSs cannot handle the bill-of-materials problem. The error presumably stems from a misunderstanding of one particular aspect of the relational model—namely, the fact that it is not possible using the operators of the traditional relational algebra to write a "one-liner" (single-expression) query to perform a parts explosion (see further discussion below). Here is a typical quote:

- "Relational products . . . have difficulty handling certain complex data structures, notably recursive relationships in which a file is related or cross-referenced to itself. For example, . . . parts related to parts form a bill of materials. Representing bills of materials normally involves two logical data tables, a master parts table and a product structure table. Each record in the product structure table is logically related to two records, one assembly part and one component part, in the parts table."

This quote concentrates on the *data representation* portion of the problem, of course. The curious thing is that the passage quoted starts by claiming that relational products "have difficulty" with (that portion of) the problem, and then goes on to show exactly how they *solve* it! The bill-of-materials structure is typically represented as follows in a relational system:

```
P     ( P#, ... )
      PRIMARY KEY ( P# )

PP    ( MAJOR_P#, MINOR_P#, QTY, ... )
      PRIMARY KEY ( MAJOR_P#, MINOR_P# )
      FOREIGN KEY ( MAJOR_P# ) REFERENCES P ...
      FOREIGN KEY ( MINOR_P# ) REFERENCES P ...
```

Table P here represents the master parts list, table PP shows which parts contain which other parts as components *and* which parts are components of which other parts (MAJOR_P# represents the assembly and MINOR_P# the component; note that a single table suffices to represent both "directions" of the relationship). Thus, the data representation part of the problem is simple, in fact almost trivial, in a relational system; indeed, I would argue that it is simpler than in a CODASYL system (and *much* simpler than in IMS, with its "virtually paired logical child segments" and the like; this fact is slightly ironic, given that IMS was originally intended to be, precisely, a generalized solution to the bill-of-materials problem).

However, it is true (as indicated at the start of this section) that certain bill-of-materials *processing* problems (such as parts explosion) cannot be done *via a single expression of the relational algebra;** but of course they

---

*This is not the place to go into details on *why* parts explosion is beyond the capabilities of classical relational algebra (see reference [4] for a detailed discussion). Fundamentally, however, the problem is that we need to join table PP to itself n times, where the value of n is not known ahead of time (in general), and hence we physically cannot write the n joins that are needed.

can be done via a program, just as they can be (and are) in nonrelational systems. (In other words, nonrelational systems also cannot perform parts explosions by means of one-liner queries.) Relational systems are thus no *less* functional than hierarchic and network systems in this area. Furthermore, the relational program is typically easier to write, and easier to maintain, and in some cases even performs better, than its nonrelational counterpart.

Of course, we can be sure that the relational algebra will be extended at some future time to include some new operators to help with the bill-of-materials problem (and others like it). When that happens, it presumably *will* be possible to write parts explosion "one-liners"—in relational systems but not in nonrelational ones. Indeed, there are already some relational products on the market today that do provide extensions of their own to address this problem, though I have to admit that I have some reservations (beyond the scope of the present paper) about those product-specific extensions that I have seen to date.

4. *Myth 29:* **BUILDING INTERMEDIATE RESULT TABLES**

The operators of the relational algebra form a *closed system,* in the sense that the result of any given operation is another relation. And because the output from an operation is thus the same kind of object as the input—i.e., both are relations—so the output from one operation can become the input to another, which means that we can write *nested relational expressions.* This closure property is an absolutely fundamental feature of the relational approach, for more reasons than we have room to discuss here (just by way of example, however, let me mention the crucial role played by closure in relational view processing and in query optimization).

But *of course* relational closure does not necessarily mean that the system actually has to materialize (i.e., physically build) all of those intermediate result tables. When we say that the output from one operation is a table which is then fed as input to the next operation, we are *of course* talking from a logical perspective only. Indeed, the relational optimizer tries extremely hard *not* to have to materialize intermediate results in their entirety. This point does not seem to be universally understood, however:

- "Operations exist to create temporary tables that result from pursuing relationships between records. However, with current technology, these operations can be costly . . ."

It goes without saying that these operations would indeed be costly if they were physically executed. For example, to find the suppliers who supply part P2, it would be *possible* to go through the following steps:

- First, build the Cartesian product of the suppliers table S and the shipments table SP. If there are 100 suppliers and 10,000 shipments, the Cartesian product will contain 1,000,000 rows.

- Next, build another table from that Cartesian product by eliminating all rows in which the supplier number of the S portion is not equal to the supplier number of the SP portion. The resulting table is the equijoin of S and SP over supplier numbers; it will contain about 10,000 rows (assuming even data distributions).

- Next, build another table from that equijoin by eliminating all rows in which the part number is not equal to P2. The resulting table is the restriction of the equijoin to just the rows for part P2; it will contain about 100 rows (assuming even data distributions again).

- Finally, build another table from that restriction by eliminating the columns in the SP portion. The resulting table (which will still contain 100 rows) is the desired overall result.

However, any reasonable relational system is much more likely to execute the query by going directly to the shipments for part P2 via an index and then, for each supplier number in those shipments in turn, looking up the relevant supplier record via another index. I leave it as an exercise for the reader to estimate the number of I/O operations required for each of the two approaches; suffice it to say that the second will outperform the first by several orders of magnitude, in general [4].

5.   *Myth 30:*   **FOREIGN KEYS UNDERMINE DATA INDEPENDENCE**

In the myths paper, I wrote ". . . lack of support for foreign keys [is] the biggest single deficiency in relational systems today." This deficiency is at last beginning to be remedied; several relational products are now beginning to provide a certain degree of foreign key support. And, of course, foreign keys have been of major importance in database design ever since Codd first introduced them [1]. It is thus somewhat surprising to encounter statements like the following [11]:

- "Relational concepts do not recognize referential integrity . . . predefined mandatory joins will make real languages less relational but more reliable."

- "Relational does not mean that interrecord relationships [i.e., CODASYL-style links] can be designed into the database. On the contrary, it means they need not be."

and especially this one (from the abstract to a paper [13] advocating a particular approach to database design):

- "The limited adaptability of database designs incorporating foreign keys is demonstrated . . . and a design practice advocated that avoids foreign keys . . ."

This last one in particular is *very* misleading; it clearly suggests that there is something better than foreign keys, whereas the design practice advocated in the paper in no way avoids them—in fact, it actually introduces additional ones! The paper is really about treating many-to-one relationships as if they were (or at least might become) many-to-many relationships, which may or may not be a good idea, depending on circumstances [8].

Incidentally, the paper does not mention the point that if CODASYL-style links were used in place of foreign keys, all of the problems it claims arise with foreign keys would be replaced by significantly worse ones. (It also says virtually nothing about the fact that its proposals would lead to many additional joins—specifically, many additional *outer* joins—nor does it mention the fact that in most current systems most user views would not be updatable.)

6.   *Myth 31:* **RELATIONAL SYSTEMS HAVE NO DICTIONARY**

- "In the long run, the distinction between the data dictionary and the database will disappear. . . . There is no such thing as metadata!" [2]

Now this quote I agree with (despite the fact that it comes from a paper whose overall thesis is that "relational is just a fad"—see Myth 33 below). The point is, however, that the idea that metadata is data has been very well understood (indeed, it has been taken as obvious) by relational advocates ever since the earliest days!—see, e.g., reference [10]. Relational systems do already go a long way toward eliminating the distinction between data and metadata. By contrast, it is hard to imagine how such a distinction could possibly be eliminated in a hierarchic or network system. Certainly it is unlikely that metadata structured as, e.g., a CODASYL-style network would be easily understood by anyone other than a skilled DP person.

Here by contrast is a quote I do *not* agree with, at least not in toto:

- "Relational [DBMS] developers are aware of the need [for a data dictionary] but the systems have grown up without them. They are going to have to go some way to come up with something as good as one on a product designed around one. You need a dictionary that is active, i.e., up to date with what is happening on the system. Anything grafted on afterwards is not going to do this because it tends to relate to the data and not the application programs.''

I suppose I have to admit that these remarks do contain an element of truth: There are certainly some relational products that do not include a full dictionary, only a system catalog that contains descriptors for the objects the DBMS itself cares about (tables, columns, indexes, etc.) but nothing else. However, such catalogs can (and should, and presumably will) be extended to become a full dictionary some day. Moreover, the potential for integration between the data and the ''dictionary'' (even if it is just a system catalog in the foregoing sense) is much greater in a relational system than it is in a nonrelational one, because of the uniformity of data and metadata representation.

7. *Myth 32:* **TOP-DOWN DESIGN VS. NORMALIZATION**

Another claim frequently heard is that relational databases must be ''fully normalized'' (in the sense that all tables must be in [at least] third normal form), or that they *must* be designed using the normalization procedure (as opposed to some top-down design methodology), or that designing a relational database is harder than designing some other kind, or any combination of all of these. For example:

- ''The way you maintain data . . . is different from the way you turn it into information. The former lends itself to entity-relationship design, procedural languages, and pointer-chain connected records. The latter is best served by normalization, relational languages, and transparent select/project/join operators.'' [11]
- ''Using normalization theory to develop third normal form is not easy and may not even be an adequate design methodology for many real-world shops. Entity/relationship modeling is being developed as a synthesis which may be better.''
- ''The [relational] model is seriously biased toward retrieval . . . and doesn't offer the designer assistance in creating [databases] well suited for update and maintenance.''

Some comments:

- First, the suggestion that top-down (''entity/relationship'') design is somehow incompatible with the principles of normalization and is not applicable to relational systems is quite definitely *false*. ''Entity/relationship modeling'' and normalization theory are *not* alternatives; both are necessary in practice, and useful in practice. Reference [8] describes a database design methodology that incorporates the principles of both.

- Second, I would claim that third normal form *is* easy—it is really just formalized common sense. At least, it is easy *provided* the designer understands what the data *means;* and needless to say, the designer *must* have that understanding in order to do the design at all, regardless of whether the system under consideration is relational or something else. Indeed, the question of whether third normal form is easy or not is largely independent of the question of whether relational systems are good or not; the theory of normalization can and should be applied to hierarchic and network designs also (though hierarchic and network designs do also involve the designer in various additional decisions for which the concepts of normalization are not particularly helpful).

- Third, regarding the "bias toward retrieval," I would argue that the theory of further normalization not only does "offer assistance in creating databases well suited for update," it is positively biased in favor of such designs. See Myth 25 in the original myths paper.

- Last, normalization (in the sense of *further* normalization) is not actually required in any given relational database; the only hard requirement is that tables be in at least *first* normal form, which simply means *no repeating groups.* See the original myths paper again, Myths 20 and 25.

Here is another quote on this general topic:

- "Designing a relational database . . . is a lot easier than a DBDGEN in IMS or writing [the] schema and subschema in a CODASYL [system]—but it is comparable [to] or more difficult than designing an inverted [database]."

There are several claims mixed together here:

- Designing a relational database is a lot easier than designing an IMS or CODASYL database: Agreed.

- *Defining* a relational database is a lot easier than *defining* an IMS or CODASYL database: Agreed.

- Designing a relational database is "comparable [to] or more difficult than" designing an inverted database: I fail to see how this statement can possibly be true. "Comparable," maybe, but how can it possibly be "more difficult?"—given that the data structure is essentially the same in both cases? (Well, it would be more accurate to say that the relational structure is a more disciplined version of the inverted structure, but to a first approximation they are the same.)

8. *Myth 33:* **THE RELATIONAL APPROACH IS JUST A FAD**

It seems to be very hard for some people to grasp the fact that *relational really is different*. Unlike previous approaches to the database problem, relational is not ad hoc, but is grounded in solid theory [9]. As a consequence, it is going to be with us for a very long time. And yet many people continue to regard it as just another technological fad, soon to be replaced by yet another "new, improved" approach. Statements arguing this position generally fall into three broad (and somewhat contradictory) categories:

1. The relational model is not really different in kind from the hierarchic and network "models."
2. The term *relational* doesn't really have any meaning. The relational vs. nonrelational argument is a religious argument.
3. The relational approach is inadequate and will soon be superseded.

Let me address each of these points in turn.

Relations vs. Hierarchies and Networks

The point should be made very firmly that hierarchic and network systems (unlike relational systems) were not developed on the basis of any predefined abstract data model. Rather, the hierarchic and network "models" were defined after the event by a process of *induction*—i.e., guesswork—from existing hierarchic and network implementations. The relational model was the *first* example of a data model that was defined prior to any implementation (indeed, it was the first example of a data model, period). At the time of writing, the relational model is still the only one ever to have been fully formally defined, so far as I am aware—though some informal attempts at defining other "models" can be found in reference [4]. For this reason, whenever the word "model" appears in a hierarchic or network context, I always place it in quotes, at least mentally.

Here is a specific quote on this topic:

▪ "Because storage and retrieval methods can be matched to the application, the CODASYL model will typically handle a higher transaction rate (and have better performance on update) than [the] relational model."

The author of this quote has unwittingly put his finger on one of the major problems with the hierarchic and network "models": "Storage and retrieval methods" in those "models" have a very definite effect on the logical structure of the database as perceived by the user. And if the logical structure of the database is tailored to database application A, then it may (and very likely will) be highly unsuitable for some other database application B.

Some more quotes (from reference [2]):

- "Textbooks on data management usually list three major architectures or models for database management systems: hierarchical, network, and relational. The utility of this taxonomy will rapidly diminish in the next few years as systems evolve toward the three-schema architecture. . . . We expect the current relational craze to give way to more robust systems that employ the ANSI three-schema architecture. . . ."

First, the suggestion that systems are "evolving toward" a three-schema architecture is misleading. The fact is, the ANSI three-schema architecture [12] (which was defined in the early 1970s) was really an abstraction of the way database systems *already worked;* that is, DBMSs even at that time already did (and of course still do) support all three levels (internal, external, and conceptual)—though admittedly the three levels were not and still are not always as carefully distinguished as they ought to be. Evidence in support of this claim can be found in the first (1975) edition of my book *An Introduction to Database Systems* [3].

Second, I agree that "the utility of the [relational-hierarchic-network] taxonomy will rapidly diminish in the next few years," but not for the reasons the paper suggests. Rather, it will diminish because, increasingly, most DBMSs will be relational; the need for nonrelational systems will gradually fade away, and the older systems will slowly wither and die.

The paper continues:

- "Relational systems per se will not displace the existing set of products. . . ."

Yes, they will—not overnight, of course, but the change will probably happen more quickly than many people think. (It cannot happen overnight because the migration to relational systems is likely to be painful, and expensive, and therefore user-paced and slow. But eventually the payoff for such migration will clearly outweigh the cost, and I believe that users *will* eventually make the move. They will have to, to compete.)*

One further quote from the same source:

---

*Incidentally, I also believe that migration *from* a relational system to some as yet unimagined future nonrelational system—if such migration should ever prove necessary, which I am very much inclined to doubt—will prove much easier than the original migration *to* that relational system. The reason for this state of affairs is, of course, that relational systems are much more disciplined than older, prerelational systems.

- "We doubt that a pure relational system will achieve a high market penetration."

No comment seems necessary.

"Relational Has No Meaning"

A typical quote:

- "Relational is a nebulous term . . . It seems that the definition . . . is in the mouth of the definer."

"Relational" was *not* originally a nebulous term. To quote from this paper's predecessor [5], one of the objectives of the relational model was precisely to introduce some sorely needed clarity of thinking into the database field; precise definition of terms is obviously prerequisite to such clear thinking, and terms such as "relational" were given the necessary precise definitions in numerous technical papers. It is however (regrettably) true that "relational" and terms like it have *become* somewhat nebulous of late, thanks partly to the activities of certain self-proclaimed DBMS "experts" who do not understand the technology, and partly to extravagant and misleading advertising claims made by the vendors of certain would-be relational products. Replacing precision by fuzziness does not help communication, nor indeed the industry as a whole. We should be doing everything in our power to preserve precision, not bemoaning the fact that it does not exist.

Here is another typical quote:

- "The reason the relational debate continues is that it is religious in nature; it's theological."

To claim that a debate is "religious" or "theological" seems to me to suggest that there is nothing scientific about it. In the case at hand, it suggests that there is no solid scientific basis to the relational advocates' position. Such a suggestion is transparently false at best, and gratuitously disparaging into the bargain.

"Relational Will Soon Be Superseded"

Another common claim! The argument goes basically something like this: "Yesterday we had hierarchies and networks; today we have relations; tomorrow we will have the entity/relationship model [or binary relations, or a functional model, or a three-schema architecture, or universal relation systems, or object-oriented databases, or semantic models, or . . .]." For example:

- "We expect the current relational craze to give way to more robust systems that employ the ANSI three-schema architecture" (repeated from the earlier subsection on relations vs. hierarchies and networks)

- "Many people share my view that [the entity/relationship model] will be the next wave in the DBMS field after the current relational wave is over."

A comment on the second of these quotes: The entity/relationship model is *not* an alternative to the relational model. (Actually it is not even clear that it is truly a data model at all, since it does not seem to include any well-defined set of operators. But I will not pursue that point in detail here.) Rather, the entity/relationship "model" is best thought of as a *very thin layer on top of the relational model*. The fundamental data object is still the relation. The operators (inasmuch as they are defined at all) are still the operators of the relational algebra. Where the two approaches differ from each other slightly is in the area of data integrity: The entity/relationship approach includes a set of *built-in* integrity rules, corresponding to some—but apparently not all—of the relational foreign key rules discussed in reference [4] and elsewhere.

Thus, there is no question of the relational model ever being replaced by the entity/relationship model. It is true that systems will evolve to provide ever higher-level interfaces, and it may be true that some of the entity/relationship ideas (or the object-oriented ideas, or the semantic modeling ideas, or . . .) may be helpful in that evolution; but I believe that the evolution will proceed by building *upwards* and *outwards* from a solid relational base. In my opinion, it is extremely unlikely that the relational *model* per se will ever be replaced by any new *model*. The foundation is *solid* and will endure [9].

The following represents an attack of a different kind:

- "[The relational model] has proved to be a poor model for the internal schema . . . because of performance problems (at least with standard hardware organizations)." [2]

The fallacy here is (I hope) obvious: The relational model was *never intended* as a candidate for the internal level of the system ("at least with standard hardware organizations"). It was intended as a candidate for the conceptual and external levels *only*. To suggest otherwise betrays a serious lack of understanding of the technology. Indeed, I know of no system that ever has attempted to use the relational model as a basis for the internal level.

And one more quote (from the same source):

- "[The relational model] is . . . not a good model for the conceptual schema because it cannot express enough of the semantics of most data problems, nor does it provide the required level of integrity checking."

I assume that the suggestion here is that what we need for the conceptual schema is something higher-level than the relational model (i.e., it is not claimed that the hierarchic or network "models" are more suitable for the task). I would not seriously disagree with this position. However, I do believe any such higher model will consist of an extended form of the relational model, not some totally different formalism. I think it is the only contender.

9. *Myth 34:* THERE'S NO SUCH THING AS A RELATIONAL DATABASE

I have saved this one until last, but in fact it is representative of a fundamental misunderstanding that runs through many of the myths previously discussed (both in this paper and in its predecessor). The misunderstanding appears in perhaps its purest form in the following quote [11]:

- "COBOL can no more access a relational database than a circle can have corners. It's simply a contradiction in terms . . . There's no such thing as a relational database. When you get right down to it, "relational database" is as meaningless as "plaid music" or "scratchy color." The adjective describes languages or processes, not data. The database itself, the pool of shared business data, can be neither procedural nor relational [sic]."

See the myths paper, Myth 1! What we have here is a *total failure to abstract*. Of *course* there is such a thing as a relational database; it is a database that is perceived by the user as a collection of relations—in other words, a database that *at a certain level of abstraction* consists of relations. To suggest that there's no such thing as a relational database, just because what is fundamentally stored on the disk is not relations but merely bits and bytes, is like suggesting that there's no such thing as human thought, because what is fundamentally going on inside the brain is merely neurons firing. It's all a question of the level of abstraction at which the construct in question is viewed. "When you get right down to it," COBOL is an abstraction also, and so too are bits and bytes, and so too are magnetized spots on the disk, . . . , and so on ad infinitum.

10. CONCLUSION

This concludes this survey of further relational misconceptions—for the time being. It is my intention to publish papers in this series as and when necessary (i.e., as and when further inaccuracies regarding relational systems find their way into print). Those papers will continue to appear until such time as the need for them has dwindled into obscurity. I hope that time will be soon.

ACKNOWLEDGMENTS

I am grateful to Ted Codd, Sharon Weinberg, and Colin White for their comments on the original papers [6,7] on which the present paper is based.

REFERENCES AND BIBLIOGRAPHY

1. E. F. Codd, "A Relational Model of Data for Large Shared Data Banks," *Communications of the ACM* 13, No. 6 (June 1970). Republished in *Communications of the ACM* 26, No. 1 (January 1983).

2. Robert M. Curtice and William Casey, "Database: What's in Store?" *Datamation* 31, No. 23 (December 1, 1985).

3. C. J. Date, *An Introduction to Database Systems,* 1st edition (Reading, MA: Addison-Wesley, 1975).

4. C. J. Date, *An Introduction to Database Systems: Volume I,* 4th edition (Reading, MA: Addison-Wesley, 1985).

5. C. J. Date, "Some Relational Myths Exploded," in C. J. Date, *Relational Database: Selected Writings* (Reading, MA: Addison-Wesley, 1986).

6. C. J. Date, "Relational Database: Further Misconceptions Number One," *InfoDB* 1, No. 1 (Spring 1986).

7. C. J. Date, "Relational Database: Further Misconceptions Number Two," *InfoDB* 1, No. 2 (Summer 1986).

8. C. J. Date, "A Practical Approach to Database Design," in C. J. Date, *Relational Database: Selected Writings* (Reading, MA: Addison-Wesley, 1986).

9. C. J. Date, "Why Relational?" (in this volume).

10. Michael Stonebraker, Peter Kreps, Eugene Wong, and Gerald Held, "The Design and Implementation of INGRES," in Michael Stonebraker (ed.), *The INGRES Papers* (Reading, MA: Addison-Wesley, 1986).

11. Frank Sweet, "What, If Anything, Is a Relational Database?" *Datamation* 30, No. 14 (July 15, 1984).

12. D. C. Tsichritzis and A. Klug (eds.), "The ANSI/X3/SPARC DBMS Framework: Report of the Study Group on Data Base Management Systems," *Information Systems* 3 (1978).

13. Richard B. Willmot, "Foreign Keys Decrease Adaptability of Database Designs," *Communications of the ACM* 27, No. 12 (December 1984).

10

What Is a
Distributed Database
System?

ABSTRACT

There is a considerable amount of confusion in the marketplace and elsewhere as to what it means for a database system to be distributed. This
paper attempts to clarify the situation by proposing a set of criteria that a
"full function" distributed system might reasonably be required to meet.

COMMENTS ON REPUBLICATION

The idea for this paper originated in early 1986 with Pete Tierney (at that
time with Relational Technology Inc., currently with Oracle Corporation).

Originally published in two parts in *InfoDB* 2, No. 2 (Summer 1987) and No. 3 (Fall 1987).
A shorter version of the paper appeared earlier under the title "Rules for Distributed Database
Systems" in *Computerworld* (June 8, 1987). Reprinted by permission.

It was clear at that time that distributed database technology was destined to become a hot topic over the next few years. It was also clear that there was already a great deal of confusion surrounding the subject. Pete therefore suggested that I try to produce a more or less succinct summary of what the technology was all about, in an attempt to clear the air somewhat. This paper was the result.

A couple of additional comments are in order at this time:

- First, the version of the paper that follows has been brought up to date in certain minor respects, but essentially remains as it was when originally published. The reason for including it in this part of the book is that—as the paper itself makes clear—it is relational technology that makes distributed database systems possible

- Second, an earlier book of mine [3] also contains a fairly long chapter on distributed systems, and it is probably worth summarizing the principal differences between that chapter and the paper included here (the earlier chapter is not made obsolete by the present paper, although there is of course a certain amount of overlap between the two). Basically, that earlier chapter is somewhat more technical: It describes proposed solutions to some of the problems of distributed database in more detail than the present paper does—for example, schemes for distributed catalog management, object naming, recovery control, and concurrency control are all considered in some depth, and an extensive annotated bibliography is also included. The present paper, by contrast, is concerned more with what the *functionality* of distributed systems ought to be from the user's point of view (though it does also delve a little way into methods for implementing that functionality in certain areas).

1.   BACKGROUND

Distributed database research has been under way in universities, industrial research laboratories, and similar establishments for many years. Now, at last, the fruits of that research are beginning to reach the marketplace; several DBMS vendors have recently announced and/or promised distributed database products, among them Relational Technology Inc. with a distributed version of INGRES called INGRES/STAR (announced June 1986), and Oracle Corp. with a distributed version of ORACLE called SQL*STAR (announced September 1986). Other products will probably also have been announced by the time this paper appears in print. These first products are certain to be the precursors of many more; IBM, for example, is known to be working on a distributed version of DB2* based on its research prototype R* (pronounced "R star"), a distributed version of the earlier IBM prototype System R [9]. Over the next few years, we can expect to see a flood of announcements in this area.

Distributed database is important. In some respects, in fact, it can be regarded as the most significant new development in the commercial database world since the first genuine relational products finally reached the market place in the late '70s and early '80s. And just as the emergence of those products was accompanied by a considerable amount of confusion— some of which seemed to be deliberately fostered, incidentally—as to exactly what the term "relational" really meant, so it is likely that a similar situation will develop with respect to the term "distributed" unless we take care to avoid it. This paper is an attempt to forestall such a situation.

The purpose of the paper is thus to try and explain what it means for a database system to be distributed. It does this by stating and explaining a set of *objectives* for such a system. There is of course no suggestion that the objectives as stated are currently satisfied by any existing product (which is why I use the term "objectives" instead of "requirements"); rather, they are intended to constitute a list of features that might reasonably be required of distributed systems as those systems evolve over the next several years.

Before going any further, I must make a number of preliminary remarks:

1. First, I make no claim that the features identified are new in any sense. So far as I am aware, however, they have not been gathered together before into a convenient single list; at least, no such list has been widely available or easily accessible to the general reader. I hope that his paper will serve to remedy that state of affairs.

2. There is probably no such thing as the "ultimate" distributed system; different problems require different solutions, and different users will attach different degrees of importance to different features in the list. For example, the requirement that individual sites enjoy local autonomy (the first item on the list) might be unimportant or even quite inap-

---

*In October 1988, after this paper was first written, IBM announced its first distributed release of DB2 (namely, DB2 Version 2 Release 2, due to be available in the 3rd quarter of 1989). For information regarding the distributed capabilities of DB2 (also INGRES/STAR, SQL*STAR, and other announced products), the reader is referred to the appropriate vendor manuals. In the case of DB2 and INGRES specifically, descriptions can also be found in references [8] and [7], respectively.

propriate in certain contexts. The paper therefore makes no attempt to quantify the importance of individual features.

3. It is important to distinguish true, generalized, distributed database systems from systems that merely provide remote database access (sometimes called distributed processing or networking systems). In a networking system, the user might be able to operate on data at a remote site, or even on data at multiple remote sites simultaneously, but "the seams show"; the user is definitely aware (to a greater or lesser extent) that the data is distributed, and has to behave accordingly. In a true distributed database system, by contrast, the seams are hidden. (Most of the rest of this paper is concerned with what it means in this context to say that the seams are hidden.) Networking products of various kinds, including in particular several micro-to-mainframe link products, have been around for some time, but true general-purpose distributed database products are new. From this point on, I will use the term "distributed system" to refer specifically to a true, generalized distributed database system, as opposed to a simple networking system. Of course, every true distributed system will be built on top of some networking system; INGRES/STAR, for example, is built on top of INGRES/NET. (Networking systems in turn will be built on top of some commercially available network architecture such as SNA or DECNET; INGRES/NET, for example, currently runs on DECNET and TCP/IP.)

4. In the interest of brevity, this paper makes no attempt to explain the details of distributed systems in great technical depth. However, it is worth mentioning that it is relational technology that makes such systems feasible in the first place; in other words, for a distributed system to be successful, *it must be relational.* Older-style technologies are simply not adequate to the task. For further discussion of this important point, see references [2,3].

5. For the same reason, the paper makes no attempt to explain why distributed systems are desirable. However, it does explain (where appropriate) why individual features in the list of objectives are desirable.

2. A FUNDAMENTAL PRINCIPLE

It is convenient to begin with a couple of working definitions (necessarily incomplete and somewhat imprecise at this point):

- A distributed database system consists of a collection of *sites* (also called *nodes*), connected together via some kind of communications network, in which

(a) each site is a database system site in its own right, but

(b) the sites have agreed to work together (if necessary), so that a user at any site can access data anywhere in the network exactly as if the data were all stored at the user's own site (subject of course to any applicable authorization constraints).

- A distributed database is a *virtual* database whose component parts are physically stored in a number of distinct "real" databases at a number of distinct sites. The distributed database definition (sometimes called *the global schema*) is the union of the various component database definitions (*local schemas*).

Refer to Fig. 1 (overleaf) for an example.

Note that, as stated, *each site is a database system site in its own right.* In other words, each site has its own local "real" databases, its own local users, its own local DBMS and transaction management software (including its own local locking, logging, recovery, and terminal I/O components), and its own communications software. The distributed database system can thus be regarded as a kind of *partnership* among individual local DBMSs at the individual local sites. A new software component at each site (logically an extension of the local DBMS) provides the necessary partnership functions; and it is the combination of this new component together with the existing DBMS that constitutes what is usually called the "distributed database management system" (DDBMS).

Incidentally, it is common to assume that the component sites are physically dispersed—possibly in fact geographically dispersed also, as the example in Fig. 1 suggests—although actually it is sufficient that they be dispersed logically. Two "sites" might even coexist on the same physical machine (especially during the initial system installation and testing period). Indeed, the emphasis in distributed systems has been shifting over the past few years: Whereas most of the original research tended to assume geographic distribution, most of the initial commercial installations have involved *local* distribution instead, with (e.g.) several "sites" all in the same building and connected together by means of a local area network. From a technical point of view, however, it makes little difference (basically, the same technical problems still have to be solved), and so we can reasonably regard Fig. 1 as representing a typical system for the purposes of this paper.

Note too that it is usual to assume that the system is *homogeneous,* in the sense that each site is running a copy of the same DBMS (the *strict homogeneity* assumption). Later in this paper I will explore the possibility of relaxing this assumption (see Section 14 on "DBMS Independence" toward the end of the paper).

New York

London

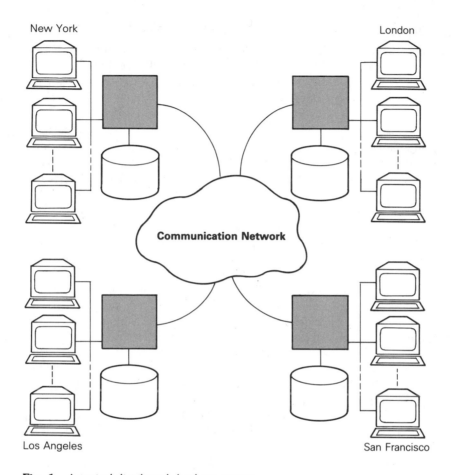

Communication Network

Los Angeles

San Francisco

Fig. 1   A typical distributed database system

Now it is possible to state what I will call *the fundamental principle of distributed database:*

> ## TO THE USER, A DISTRIBUTED SYSTEM SHOULD LOOK EXACTLY LIKE A NONDISTRIBUTED SYSTEM

In other words, users in a distributed system should behave exactly as if the system were *not* distributed. All of the problems of distributed systems are internal or implementation-level problems, not external or user-level problems.

Note: The term "user" is taken throughout this paper to mean either an end-user or an application programmer who is performing *data manipulation* operations. Data definition operations will probably require some extension in a distributed system—for example, so that when a relation is created at site X, the creator can specify that it is to be stored at site Y. (Even if such extensions are necessary, of course, distributed data definition and other operations should still be identical to their nondistributed counterparts to the maximum extent possible.)

The fundamental principle identified above might be referred to as "Rule Zero" for distributed systems. Rule Zero leads to a number of subsidiary objectives or rules—actually twelve of them—which are the subject of the remainder of this paper. Box 1 lists those twelve rules.

---

1. Local autonomy
2. No reliance on a central site
3. Continuous operation
4. Location independence
5. Fragmentation independence
6. Replication independence
7. Distributed query processing
8. Distributed transaction management
9. Hardware independence
10. Operating system independence
11. Network independence
12. DBMS independence

Box 1 The twelve rules for distributed systems

We now proceed to discuss the twelve rules in detail. Please note that (as already stated) there is no claim that the rules are all equally important; nor are they all independent of one another; nor are they discussed in any particular priority order. The only suggestion is that a system that did genuinely support all twelve of the rules might legitimately lay some claim to being a "full function" distributed system.

3. *Rule 1:* **LOCAL AUTONOMY**

The sites in a distributed system should be *autonomous*. Autonomy means a number of things:

1. Local data is locally owned and managed, with local accountability. All data "really" belongs to some local database, even if it is accessible from some remote site. Such matters as security, integrity, and storage representation of local data remain under the control of the local site.

    Aside: A couple of brief comments are in order here:

    - With regard to security, note that an additional level of control, over and above the usual local controls, is desirable in a distributed environment. From a security standpoint, the communication network itself is probably the most vulnerable part of the system. It is therefore desirable that the distributed system provide some kind of encryption/decryption facility, so that data can be transmitted between sites in encrypted form. (Of course, this facility might be provided by the network software or even by the underlying hardware—it does not have to be provided by the distributed DBMS per se. It is not really a database function as such. We will ignore it from this point on.)

    - With regard to integrity, note that some integrity constraints might span multiple sites. In such a case, of course, integrity will obviously no longer be a purely local matter. See the discussion of Rule 7, later (Section 9).

    End of aside.

    To return to the discussion of autonomy per se:

2. Local operations remain purely local. That is, users performing operations involving only local data should not be penalized in any way by the fact that their site is participating in a distributed system. In particular, applications that ran successfully at some site before that site became part of the distributed system should continue to do so afterwards. (Furthermore, they should continue to run successfully even if some of their data is now moved to other sites around the network; see Rules 4, 5, 6, and 8 below.)

3. All operations at a given site are controlled by that site; no site X should depend on some other site Y for its successful functioning. For otherwise some site X might be unable to run, even if there is nothing wrong with that site per se, because some other site Y is down—obviously an undesirable state of affairs.

Actually, as will be seen later, the autonomy objective is not wholly achievable; there are a number of situations in which a given site X *must* relinquish a certain degree of control to some other site Y. The autonomy objective would thus more accurately be stated: Sites should be autonomous *to the maximum extent possible.* For purposes of reference, Box 2 below summarizes the situations in which there must necessarily be some slight loss of autonomy. Each of those situations is amplified and explained later in the paper.

- Individual fragments of a fragmented relation cannot normally be accessed directly, not even from the site at which they are stored (see Rule 5).
- Individual copies of a replicated relation or fragment cannot normally be accessed directly, not even from the site at which they are stored (see Rule 6).
- Let P be the "primary copy" of some replicated relation or fragment R, and let P be stored at site X. Then every site that performs an update on R is dependent on site X, even if another copy of R is in fact stored at the site in question (see Rule 6).
- A relation that participates in a multiple-site integrity constraint cannot be accessed for update purposes within the local context of the site at which it is stored, but only within the context of the distributed database in which the constraint is defined (see Rule 7).
- A site that is acting as a participant in a two-phase commit process must abide by the decision (i.e., commit or rollback) of the corresponding coordinator site (see Rule 8).

Box 2   Situations involving some loss of autonomy

4.   *Rule 2:*   **NO RELIANCE ON A CENTRAL SITE**

Local autonomy implies that all sites must be treated as equals; there must not be any reliance on a central "master" site for some central service, such as centralized query processing or centralized transaction management, such that the entire system is dependent on that central site. This second objective is thus in fact a corollary of the first (if the first is achieved, the second follows a fortiori). But "no reliance on a central site" is desirable in its own right, even if full local autonomy is not achieved. It is therefore worth spelling it out as a separate objective.

Reliance on a central site would be undesirable for at least the following two reasons:

- First, that central site might be a bottleneck;
- Second (and more important), the system would be *vulnerable*—if the central site went down, the whole system would be down.

In a distributed system, therefore, the following functions (among others) must all be distributed:

- Dictionary management
- Query processing
- Concurrency control
- Recovery control

These points are elaborated in the discussion of Rules 3–8 below (Sections 5–10).

5. *Rule 3:* **CONTINUOUS OPERATION**

In a distributed system, just as in a nondistributed one, there should ideally never be any need for a planned system shutdown. Unfortunately, however, there are a few situations in which some kind of shutdown, and hence some disruption of service, seems unavoidable in a distributed environment. The objective should thus be to keep such disruptions to a minimum. To be specific:

- Incorporating a new site X into an existing distributed system D will presumably involve the installation of a new release of the DBMS (i.e., a release of the "distributed" version of the DBMS) at site X. User service at site X will thus inevitably be interrupted. However, it should not be necessary to interrupt service at any other site Y that already participates in D. It should certainly not be necessary to bring the entire system to a halt.

- Incorporating a new site X into an existing distributed system D should not require any changes to existing user programs or terminal activities, either at site X or at any site Y already participating in D. It should also not require any redefinition or unloading/reloading of existing databases at site X or at any other site Y.

- Removing an existing site X from the distributed system should also not cause any unnecessary interruptions in service; that is, it should not be necessary to bring the entire system to a halt, nor should user programs and terminal activities that do not use any of the data at site X be logically impaired in any way.

- Within the distributed system, it should be possible to create and destroy fragments (see Rule 5) and replicas of fragments (see Rule 6) dynamically, without stopping any component site or any component database.

- It should be possible to upgrade the DBMS at any given component site to a newer release without taking the entire system down. Note therefore that the strict homogeneity assumption (see earlier) is not so strict that it requires *the same release* of the same DBMS to be running at every site. Such a requirement would be intolerable in practice; it would simply not be feasible to upgrade every site in the network simultaneously every time a new release of the DBMS became available.

6. *Rule 4:* **LOCATION INDEPENDENCE**

The basic idea of location independence (also known as location transparency) is simple: Users should not have to know where data is physically stored, but rather should be able to behave—at least from a logical standpoint—as if the data was all stored at their own local site. Location independence is desirable because it simplifies user programs and terminal activities. In particular, it allows data to migrate from site to site without invalidating any of those programs or activities. Such migratability is desirable in turn because it allows data to be moved around the network in response to changing performance requirements.

It is worth mentioning that (as might be expected) it is easier to provide location independence for simple retrieval operations than it is for update operations. For example, the first releases of INGRES/STAR and SQL*STAR both provide full location independence for retrieval but only limited location independence for update* (because neither yet allows a single transaction to perform updates on more than one component real database; see Rule 8). In the case of SQL*STAR, in fact, a transaction is not currently allowed to perform any updates at all except at the transaction's own site (i.e., the site at which the entire transaction is executed).

Location independence requires a distributed data naming scheme and corresponding support from the dictionary subsystem. The data naming scheme must be such that users can refer to data by a local name exactly as

---

*The first distributed release of DB2 [8] does not even provide full location independence for retrieval, because a single query (SQL statement) is not permitted to span sites.

if the data were at the user's own local site; from that local name, the dictionary subsystem must be able to locate the actual data. Note therefore that the dictionary in a distributed system must necessarily differ in some respects from its nondistributed counterpart, because (at the very least) it must now additionally specify the component site and database at which each relation resides.

By way of example, here (in outline) is how location independence is supported in INGRES/STAR. (Of course, there is no suggestion that this is the only way to do it. The technique used in R* is quite different, for example. The reader is referred to references [3,9] for details of the R* approach.)

- First, the user in INGRES is always operating within the context of a single database—but with INGRES/STAR that database can be virtual (i.e., distributed) and can span multiple real local databases, as the following paragraphs explain.

- For simplicity, assume that each site in the network involves just one local database. Then the local dictionary at each site will contain entries for the relations that are stored in the database at that site.

- A database administrator at some site X in the network can now create a new distributed database Dx, say, by specifying the (already existing) relations—base relations and/or views—that are to be accessible via Dx. For each relation R to be included in Dx, the DBA specifies:

  - the name, Rx say, by which R is to be known within Dx

  - the site Y that contains R

- A set of dictionary entries are made at site X for the distributed database Dx. In particular, an entry is made for Rx that points to the entry for relation R in the dictionary at site Y.

- Users at site X can now operate on the distributed database Dx exactly as if it were a local database stored at X. In particular, they can operate on relation R in the context of Dx (using the name Rx) exactly as if R were stored at X.

- The database administrator at site X for distributed database Dx can make Dx accessible to some other site Z in the network by causing a dictionary entry for Dx to be made at site Z that points to the dictionary entries for Dx at site X. Now users at site Z can behave exactly as if Dx were a local database stored at Z.

- Any number of distributed databases can be defined, and distinct distributed databases can overlap.

So much for data naming. It is also necessary to say something regarding user naming. How can users be uniquely identified in a distributed environment? Once again this is a problem with several possible solutions, each with its own advantages and disadvantages. One possible scheme is described below.

- First, let us assume that in order for a given user U to be able to operate at multiple sites—either in a true distributed system or in a simple networking system—user U has to have a valid logon ID at each one of those sites.

- Establishing a logon ID at a site is a standard function in any DBMS and will probably not be done any differently if the system is distributed. However, if a user U operating at site X under the logon ID Ux wishes to access data at some remote site Y, the distributed system does need to know the remote logon ID Uy corresponding to U at Y. One way of providing this information (again, not necessarily the only way) is described in the next few paragraphs.

- The dictionary at each site maintains a *user profile* for each valid logon ID at that site, giving among other things a list of the databases (distributed or otherwise) accessible from that site by that logon ID, and giving also the access privileges that apply to each of those databases for that logon ID.

- When a new site is added to the network, users at that site must somehow acquire logon IDs at other sites in the network. Likewise, existing users in the network must somehow acquire logon IDs at the new site. (As mentioned above, this process is basically standard.) A system utility function must then be executed to establish the necessary correspondences between those new logon IDs and existing ones. For example, if user U, with existing logon ID Ux at site X, now acquires a new logon ID Uy at site Y, then the dictionary at site X needs to be updated to show that "Uy at Y" corresponds to "Ux."

  Aside: Note that multiple distinct users (possibly at multiple distinct sites, certainly with distinct local logon IDs) might all share the same logon ID at some remote site. This facility could prove useful if multiple end-users are all sharing the same distributed application—for example, in a distributed order-entry system. *End of aside.*

- Appropriate access privileges must now be granted at each component site to the new logon IDs at that site. Note that (under the scheme described) the operation of granting such privileges will be a purely local operation, as required by the local autonomy rule.

Of course, the process of acquiring new logon IDs and granting privileges (last two bullet items above) does not have to be completed in its entirety as part of the process of adding a new site but can be performed at any subsequent time.

7. *Rule 5:* **FRAGMENTATION INDEPENDENCE**

A distributed system supports *data fragmentation* if a given relation can be divided up into pieces or "fragments" for physical storage purposes. Fragmentation is desirable for performance reasons: Data can be stored at the location where it is most frequently used, so that most operations are purely local and network traffic is reduced. For example, the employee relation EMP might be fragmented such that records for New York employees are stored at the New York site, while records for London employees are stored at the London site. See Fig. 2.

There are basically two kinds of fragmentation, horizontal and vertical, corresponding to the relational operations of restriction and projection respectively. More generally, a fragment can be *any arbitrary subrelation* that

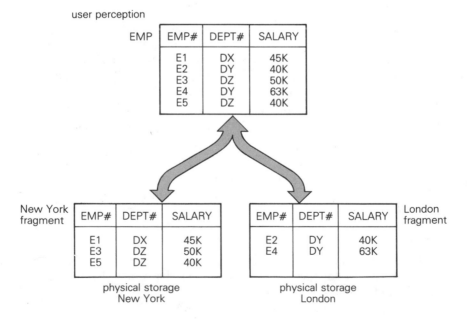

Fig. 2 An example of fragmentation

is derivable from the original relation via restriction and projection operations—except that:

(a) In the case of restriction, the fragmentation need only be a simple parti-
tioning; i.e., each record need belong to only one fragment. There is
no need to allow the fragments to overlap. (If overlap is desirable for
some reason, it can be achieved via the system's data replication support, discussed under Rule 6 in Section 8.)

(b) In the case of projection, the projections must be "nonloss," meaning
that it must be possible to reconstruct the original relation from the
fragments. For example, suppose the original relation is:

```
EMP ( EMP#, DEPT#, SALARY )
```

(where EMP# is the primary key). Then the following vertical fragmentation is nonloss—

```
ED   ( EMP#, DEPT# )
ES   ( EMP#, SALARY )
```

—whereas the following is not:

```
ED   ( EMP#, DEPT# )
DS   ( DEPT#, SALARY )
```

It is important to understand that *fragmentation must be defined within
the context of a distributed database;* that is, the data definition operations
that define the fragmentation will form part of the definition of the distributed database, not of any component local database. At the same time, of
course, the individual fragments themselves will be stored in those component local databases, and the dictionary entries for those local databases
must therefore reflect this fact. Thus, the global operation of defining the
fragmentation must trigger a set of corresponding local update operations
to the individual local dictionaries.

Reconstructing the original relation from the fragments is done via suitable join and union operations (join for vertical fragments, union for horizontal ones). In the case of union, note that if (as suggested above) the
horizontal fragments are disjoint, the union will never require any duplicate
elimination; i.e., the union operation in question will be a "disjoint union."
Note also, incidentally, that ease of fragmentation and ease of reconstruc-
tion are two of the many reasons why distributed systems are relational; the
relational model provides exactly the operations that are needed for these
tasks.

Now we come to the main point: A system that supports data fragmentation should also support *fragmentation independence* (also known as
fragmentation transparency)—i.e., users should be able to behave (at least

from a logical standpoint) as if the data were in fact not fragmented at all. Fragmentation independence (like location independence) is desirable because it simplifies user programs and terminal activities. In particular, it allows the data to be refragmented (and fragments to be redistributed) at any time in response to changing performance requirements, without invalidating any of those user programs or activities.

Fragmentation independence thus implies that users should normally be presented with a view of the data in which the fragments are logically combined together by means of suitable joins and unions. (It then becomes a task for the system optimizer to determine which fragments physically need to be accessed in order to satisfy any given user request. See Section 9 later.) In fact, users should not be allowed to access individual fragments directly—i.e., by name—at all, except under very special circumstances (e.g., in troubleshooting); normally, all access should be via the recombined view. Direct access to fragments would obviously compromise fragmentation independence.

Note: The "view" mentioned in the previous paragraph is not exactly a view in the usual relational sense, but the concept is essentially the same. Note the implication that the system must be able to support updates against certain join and (disjoint) union views (which in turn implies that the system must support primary and foreign keys properly [5]).

8. *Rule 6:* **REPLICATION INDEPENDENCE**

A distributed system supports *data replication* if a given relation (more generally, a given *fragment* of a relation) can be represented at the physical level by many distinct stored copies or replicas, at many distinct sites. See Fig. 3.

Replication is desirable for at least two reasons:

- *Performance:* Applications can operate on local copies instead of having to communicate with remote sites.

- *Availability:* A given replicated object remains available for processing so long as at least one copy remains available (at least for retrieval purposes—see below).

Note that the operation of defining replicas (like that of defining fragments) is by definition not a purely local operation; it must be performed within the context of a distributed database. Again, however, it will trigger a corresponding set of local update operations to the local dictionaries at all affected sites.

The major *dis*advantage of replication is of course that when a given replicated object (say, a record within a replicated relation) is updated, *all* user perception

	EMP#	DEPT#	SALARY
EMP	E1	DX	45K
	E2	DY	40K
	E3	DZ	50K
	E4	DY	63K
	E5	DZ	40K

New York fragment

EMP#	DEPT#	SALARY
E1	DX	45K
E3	DZ	50K
E5	DZ	40K

London fragment

EMP#	DEPT#	SALARY
E2	DY	40K
E4	DY	63K

replica of London fragment

EMP#	DEPT#	SALARY
E2	DY	40K
E4	DY	63K

replica of New York fragment

EMP#	DEPT#	SALARY
E1	DX	45K
E3	DZ	50K
E5	DZ	40K

physical storage
New York

physical storage
London

Fig. 3　An example of replication

copies of that object must be updated—the *update propagation* problem. A common scheme for dealing with this problem (though certainly not the only one possible) is the so-called "primary copy" scheme, which works as follows:

- One copy of each replicated object is designated as the primary copy; the remainder are all secondary copies.

- Primary copies of different objects are at different sites (so this is a distributed scheme—by Rule 2, there must be no reliance on a central "primary copy" site).

- Update operations are deemed to be complete as soon as the primary copy has been updated. The site holding that copy is then responsible for propagating the update to the secondary copies at some subsequent time.

Of course, this scheme leads to several further problems of its own, most of them beyond the scope of this short paper. Note too that it does represent a violation of the local autonomy objective, because a transaction might now fail because a remote copy of some object is unavailable, even if a local copy is available.

Replication, like fragmentation, should be "transparent to the user." In other words, a system that supports data replication should also support *replication independence* (also known as replication transparency)—i.e., users should be able to behave (at least from a logical standpoint) as if the data were in fact not replicated at all. Replication independence (like location independence and fragmentation independence) is desirable because it simplifies user programs and terminal activities. In particular, it allows replicas to be created and destroyed dynamically at any time in response to changing requirements, without invalidating any of those user programs or activities.

Replication independence implies that users should not normally be allowed to access individual replicas directly, just as fragmentation independence implies that they should not normally be allowed to access individual fragments directly.

I conclude this section with a brief mention of *snapshots*. It is clear from the short discussion of update propagation above that there are some serious implementation difficulties in providing full support for data replication. Snapshots represent a simpler (and arguably preferable) approach to the problem: They provide some of the benefits of replication while at the same time avoiding some of the difficulties. (They also provide a number of additional benefits—benefits that are, however, nothing to do with distributed database per se and hence are beyond the scope of this paper.)

A snapshot is a named derived relation, like a view. Unlike a view, however, a snapshot is "real," not virtual—i.e., it is represented by its own stored data. Here is an example:

```
CREATE SNAPSHOT ED
     AS SELECT    EMP#, DEPT#
        FROM      EMP
        REFRESH   EVERY DAY ;
```

Creating a snapshot is much like executing a query, except that the result of that query is stored in the database under the specified name (ED in the example). The definition of the snapshot and the time of its creation are entered into the dictionary. Periodically (EVERY DAY in the example) the snapshot is "refreshed"—i.e., its current value is discarded, the query is reexecuted, and the result of that execution becomes the new value.

Note: The foregoing paragraph describes the refresh process from a logical point of view. In practice, the process does not have to be total, in the sense that the entire snapshot has to be physically rebuilt every time; an "incremental refresh" might be possible, in which only those portions of the snapshot that are no longer valid are physically recreated. Incremental refresh has obvious performance advantages. But now we are straying too far from the main theme of the paper. To resume:

The idea of snapshots is thus not to support replication as such, but rather to have a single "master" copy of each relation (or fragment), together with an arbitrary number of snapshots defined over those master copies. Update operations *must* be directed to the master copy; however, read operations can be directed either to the master copy or to a snapshot (normally the latter). Snapshots are thus not totally "transparent to the user." They might be regarded as a partial implementation of data replication, with partial replication independence.

Note, incidentally, that snapshots *can* be replicated (because they are read-only—except for the periodic refreshing—and are thus not subject to the implementation difficulties referred to earlier). In fact, there could be a replica at every site, which would mean that (almost) all retrievals become purely local operations. Note too that (again because they are basically read-only) snapshots can be fully indexed, without the update performance penalty that full indexing usually entails.

A snapshot scheme along the foregoing lines has been implemented in the R* prototype [9].

9. *Rule 7:* **DISTRIBUTED QUERY PROCESSING**

Note: It is common in relational contexts to refer to every single-statement manipulative operation as a "query," regardless of whether it is in fact a retrieval operation or an update, and regardless of whether it is submitted interactively from a terminal or is embedded in an application program. For convenience, I adopt the same convention in this section.

Because queries in a relational system are expressed at a very high semantic level, there will normally be many possible strategies for executing them. Different strategies will of course have different performance characteristics. *It is crucially important to choose a good strategy.* This is why the optimizer is such a critical component in relational systems: It is the optimizer that is responsible for the choice of strategy. Performance in such a system is thus crucially dependent on the quality of the system optimizer. (By contrast, performance in a nonrelational system is crucially dependent on the quality of the application programmer; and if the application programmer chooses a bad strategy, there is no way the system can convert it into a good one—which is a major disadvantage of nonrelational systems.)

Everything in the preceding paragraph applies with special force to distributed systems, where the difference in performance between a good strategy and a bad one might easily be many orders of magnitude. Query execution in a distributed system will itself be a distributed process; that is, it will involve both

(a) local CPU and I/O activity at several distinct sites (in general),

together with

(b) some amount of data communication among those sites.

This latter component (amount of communication) is a *major* perform-ance factor—indeed, it is quite possible that it will dominate all others, at least in a slow, long-haul network (e.g., telephone lines). A major objective for the optimizer is thus to minimize this factor. Again, it is crucially impor-tant that the optimizer do a good job. A compelling illustration of this point can be found in reference [3], where six different strategies for executing a given query are analyzed and the response time is shown to vary from a minimum of one second to a maximum of two and a third *days* . . . !

It follows from the above that the query optimization process should itself be distributed (just like the query execution process); i.e., it should involve both an overall or global optimization step, as just discussed, to-gether with separate local optimization steps at each site in addition. For example, suppose a query Q is submitted at site X, and suppose that Q involves (among other things) a join of a relation Ry of a hundred records at site Y with a relation Rz of a million records at site Z. The optimizer at site X will choose the overall (global) strategy for executing Q; and it is clearly preferable that it decide to move Ry to Z and not Rz to Y (and certainly not Ry and Rz both to X). Then, once it has decided to move Ry to Z, the strategy for performing the actual join at site Z should be decided by the local optimizer at Z. For example, it might be possible to use access paths at Z that were unknown to the optimizer at X at the time when that latter optimizer chose the global strategy for Q. (This latter factor is espe-cially relevant in a compiling system. See paragraph 1 below.)

Thus, to repeat: It is important that optimization in a distributed sys-tem be performed from a global perspective. Another way of saying the same thing is that the performance of a given query should generally be independent of the site at which the query is submitted (I am indebted to Michael Stonebraker for this observation). A system that simply moves all required data to the query submission site and then completes processing at that site will *not* satisfy the distributed optimization objective.

To conclude, a few additional points regarding query processing in a distributed system:

1. Given that the optimization process itself can involve a certain amount of intersite communication (and can thus itself be somewhat expensive),

the idea of compiling queries ahead of time (instead of interpreting them at execution time) is even more attractive—at least for repetitive transactions—in the distributed environment than it was in the nondistributed case. *Note:* The strategy of query compilation was introduced in the original (nondistributed) IBM research prototype System R and has been extended in the distributed R* prototype.*

2. It should be possible to define views within a distributed database that span multiple sites, just as it is possible to issue queries within such a database that span multiple sites. A view is really nothing more than a predefined ("canned") query.

3. Likewise, it should be possible to define integrity constraints within a distributed database that (again) span multiple sites. (In fact, fragmentation support and replication support in effect imply that certain kinds of multiple-site integrity constraints *must* be supported, albeit in an under-the-covers kind of sense.) Again, an integrity constraint can be regarded as a special kind of query: Given an integrity constraint C, there is always a corresponding query of the form "Retrieve all records where C is false" whose result should be an empty set.

   Note that data that is subject to a multiple-site integrity constraint should be accessible (at least for update) only within the context of the distributed database within which the constraint is defined. Specifically, it should not be accessible (for update) purely within the local context of the site at which it is stored.

Of course, location, fragmentation, and replication independence together mean that multiple-site views and integrity constraints look exactly like single-site views and constraints to the user.

10. *Rule 8:* DISTRIBUTED TRANSACTION MANAGEMENT

There are two major aspects to transaction management, recovery control and concurrency control, each of which requires extended treatment in the distributed environment. Before getting into details, let me review a couple of basic concepts. First, a transaction is *an atomic unit of work.* "Atomic" means that the transaction is an all-or-nothing proposition; specifically, if the transaction logic requires several updates to the database, then either all of those updates are done or none of them is done.

---

*Interestingly enough, the first distributed release of DB2, although it does compile operations on remote data, does not do so until execution time. (By contrast, operations on local data are compiled ahead of time, as in earlier DB2 releases.) Note also that—as mentioned in an earlier footnote—individual queries always refer just to a single site in that first release.

It follows that, if a transaction performs some updates and then fails, for whatever reason, then those updates must be undone ("rolled back"). If, on the other hand, the transaction reaches a successful conclusion, its updates must *not* be rolled back but must be made permanent ("committed"). Rolling back uncommitted updates constitutes recovery of a previous (and presumably correct) state of the database; hence the term "recovery control."

In a distributed system, a single transaction can involve the execution of code at multiple sites and can thus involve updates at multiple sites. Each transaction is therefore said to consist of multiple "agents," where an *agent* is the process performed on behalf of a given transaction at a given site. (For simplicity, I assume that there is at most one agent for a given transaction at a given site. This simplifying assumption does not materially affect the discussion in any way.) In order to ensure that a given transaction still remains atomic in the distributed environment, therefore, the system must ensure that the set of agents for that transaction either all commit in unison or all roll back in unison. This effect can be achieved by means of a protocol called *two-phase commit* (or some variant thereof).

This is not the place to describe the two-phase commit protocol in detail. Suffice it to say that, for a given distributed transaction, one of the sites involved (typically—though not necessarily—the site at which the transaction was initially submitted) must serve as the *coordinator* in that protocol and the others must all serve as *participants*. Since different transactions will be submitted at different sites, distributed transaction management requires that every site must be prepared to serve both as the coordinator for some transactions and as a participant for other transactions (in general). Certainly there must be no central site that serves as the coordinator for all transactions, by virtue of Rule 2 once again. (On the other hand, note that the two-phase commit protocol does violate local autonomy to some extent, inasmuch as a participant site *must* do what it is told—i.e., commit or rollback—by the coordinator site.)

Turning now to concurrency control: Concurrency control in a distributed system will almost certainly be based on locking, just as it is in nondistributed systems. (Other approaches to concurrency control have been investigated in the research world, but in practice locking still seems to be the technique of choice.) Local autonomy says that each site must be responsible for lock management for its own local data; i.e., each site will have its own lock manager. As a result, *global deadlock* is possible. A global deadlock is a deadlock involving two or more sites. For example (refer to Fig. 4):

1. The agent of transaction T2 at site X is waiting for the agent of transaction T1 at site X to release a lock;

SITE X

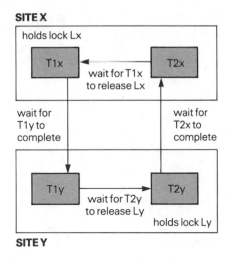

SITE Y

Fig. 4 An example of global deadlock

2. The agent of transaction T1 at site X is waiting for the agent of transaction T1 at site Y to complete;

3. The agent of transaction T1 at site Y is waiting for the agent of transaction T2 at site Y to release a lock;

4. The agent of transaction T2 at site Y is waiting for the agent of transaction T2 at site X to complete. Deadlock!

The problem with a deadlock such as this one is that *neither site can detect it using only information that is internal to that site.* In other words, there are no cycles in the local graphs of "who is waiting for whom," but a cycle will appear if those two local graphs are joined together into a global graph. Hence:

- If the system is to detect such deadlocks, it is necessary for sites to send their graphs to other sites from time to time. Furthermore, there should not be any master "deadlock detector" site to which all sites send their graphs (Rule 2 again); rather, the system should provide some kind of distributed deadlock detection mechanism. A good example of such a mechanism has been implemented in the R* prototype already mentioned several times in this paper [9].

- Alternatively, given that global deadlock detection is liable to be expensive (because of the additional message traffic it entails), it might be preferable to use some kind of timeout mechanism instead. That is, the system might simply assume that any agent that has remained in a wait state for an excessive period of time is deadlocked. Of course, the disadvantage of this scheme is that some transactions might be failed by the system "unnecessarily"—i.e., when they are not actually deadlocked but merely unduly delayed.

Aside: The timeout approach might be needed anyway if the system is trying to provide DBMS independence (see Rule 12), since some component DBMSs do not provide deadlock detection services. This is why INGRES/STAR (for example) uses the timeout approach. *End of aside.*

11.   *Rule 9:*   **HARDWARE INDEPENDENCE**

There is actually not a great deal to be said on this topic—the heading says it all. Real-world computer installations typically involve a multiplicity of different machines—IBM machines, DEC machines, HP machines, UNISYS machines, PCs of various kinds, etc., etc.—and there is a real need to be able to integrate the data on all of those systems and present the user with a "single-system image." Thus, it is desirable to be able to run the same DBMS on different hardware systems, and furthermore to have those different hardware systems all participate as equal partners (where appropriate) in a distributed system. Note carefully that I have still not relaxed the strict homogeneity assumption; I am still assuming that *the same DBMS* is running on all those different hardware systems.

12.   *Rule 10:*   **OPERATING SYSTEM INDEPENDENCE**

This objective is partly a corollary of the previous one. Like the previous one, it really does not need very much discussion. It is obviously desirable, not only to be able to run the same DBMS on different hardware systems, but also to be able to run it on different operating systems—even different operating systems on the same hardware—and have (e.g.) an MVS version and a UNIX version and a PC/DOS version all participate in the same distributed system. From a commercial point of view, the most important operating system environments, and hence the ones that (at a minimum) the DBMS should support, are probably MVS/XA, MVS/ESA, VM/CMS, VAX/VMS, UNIX (various flavors), OS/2, and PC/DOS.

13.   *Rule 11:*   **NETWORK INDEPENDENCE**

Once again there is not very much to say . . . If the system is to be able to support multiple disparate sites, with disparate hardware and disparate operating systems, it is obviously desirable to be able to support a variety of disparate communication networks also. From the point of view of the distributed DBMS, the network is merely the provider of a reliable message transmission service. By "reliable" here I mean that, if the network accepts a message from site X for delivery to site Y, then it will eventually deliver that message to site Y; moreover, messages will not be garbled, will not be delivered more than once, and will be delivered in the order sent. The network should also be responsible for site authentication (in other words, it should guarantee that a message that purports to come from a given site X does in fact come from that site X).

Note that the network does *not* define detailed message layouts. Rather, such layouts are the subject of separate agreements between the programs that make use of the network (i.e., they are defined by the distributed DBMS, since in the case in which we are interested it is the distributed DBMS that is the network user).

Ideally the system should support both local area networks (e.g., Ethernet) and long-haul networks (e.g., telephone lines). It should also support a variety of different network architectures (e.g., SNA, DECNET, TCP/IP, OSI, etc.).

14.   *Rule 12:*   **DBMS INDEPENDENCE**

Under this heading I consider what is involved in relaxing the strict homogeneity assumption. That assumption is arguably a little too strong. All that is really needed is that the DBMSs at different sites *all support the same interface;* they do not necessarily all have to be copies of the same system. For example, if INGRES and ORACLE both supported the official SQL standard, then it *might* be possible to get them to talk to each other in the context of a distributed system. In other words, it might be possible for the distributed system to be *hetero*geneous, at least to some degree.

Support for heterogeneity would definitely be desirable. The fact is, again, that real-world computer installations typically run not only multiple different machines and multiple different operating systems, they very often run different DBMSs as well; and it would be nice if those different DBMSs could all participate somehow in a distributed system. In other words, the ideal distributed system should provide *DBMS independence.*

To make the discussion a little more concrete, let us first consider the case of INGRES and ORACLE specifically (however, the concepts are generally applicable, of course). Note that INGRES and ORACLE do both support SQL—or, at least, dialects thereof—which should simplify matters somewhat. Suppose, therefore, that there are two sites X and Y running INGRES and ORACLE respectively, and suppose some user U at site X wishes to see a single distributed database that includes data from the INGRES database at site X and data from the ORACLE database at site

Y. (For simplicity, I assume there is only one local database at each site.) By definition, user U is an INGRES user, and the distributed database must be an INGRES database so far as that user is concerned. Thus the onus is on INGRES, not ORACLE, to provide the necessary additional support. What must that support consist of?

In principle it is quite straightforward: INGRES must provide an application program (usually referred to as a "gateway") that runs on top of ORACLE and has the effect of "making ORACLE look like INGRES" (see Fig. 5).

The functions of the gateway must thus include all of the following. Observe that many of these functions present implementation problems of a very nontrivial nature.

- Implementing protocols for the exchange of information between INGRES and ORACLE—which involves (among other things) understanding the message format in which SQL source statements are sent from INGRES, and mapping ORACLE results (data values, return codes, etc.) into the message format that INGRES expects.

- Mapping the ORACLE dictionary to INGRES format, so that the INGRES site, and users at the INGRES site, can find out what the ORACLE database contains.

- Accepting INGRES/SQL requests, converting them to ORACLE/SQL, executing them, converting the results (including ORACLE return codes and other feedback information) to INGRES form, and returning them to INGRES. Note that this problem includes as a subproblem

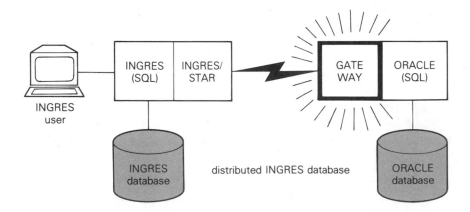

Fig. 5   A hypothetical INGRES-provided gateway to ORACLE

the problem of mapping between ORACLE and INGRES data types (and this problem in turn might include as a further subproblem the problem of mapping between data types on different machines).

Note too that the foregoing amounts to saying that the gateway is providing a "relational server" function against ORACLE (analogous to the function provided by the SQL*PLUS—previously UFI—component of the existing ORACLE product). In other words, the gateway must be able to execute arbitrary (unplanned) SQL operations against the ORACLE database. As a result, it will have to rely heavily on the so-called "dynamic SQL" facility (or a CALL interface) at the ORACLE site. Note also, therefore, that any such facility or interface must be fully documented!

- Serving as a participant in (the INGRES variant of) the two-phase commit protocol (if INGRES transactions are to be allowed to perform updates on the ORACLE database; note, however, that at the time of writing neither INGRES nor ORACLE yet supports two-phase commit). Whether the gateway will actually be able to perform this function will presumably depend on the facilities provided by the transaction manager at the ORACLE site. It is worth pointing out that transaction managers normally do *not* provide what is necessary in this respect—namely, the ability for an application program to instruct the transaction manager to "prepare to commit" (as opposed to instructing it to commit unconditionally).

- Ensuring that data at the ORACLE site that INGRES requires to be locked is in fact locked as and when INGRES needs it to be. Again, whether the gateway will actually be able to perform this function will presumably depend on whether the locking architecture of ORACLE matches that of INGRES or not.

In addition to the foregoing, of course, each INGRES user at site X who wishes to access ORACLE data at site Y needs to have a logon ID at site Y, together with all necessary access privileges at that site. Also, of course, that logon ID at site Y must somehow be made known to INGRES at site X.

Note finally that I have described only what might be termed "the one-way case," in which users at site X can access data at site Y but not the other way around. In the example, INGRES users can access ORACLE data, but not vice versa. If the mapping is to be two-way—if in addition ORACLE users at site Y are to be able to access INGRES data at site X—then ORACLE must provide a gateway at site X that "makes INGRES look like ORACLE." All of the points discussed above apply here also, mutatis mutandis.

Let me stay one moment longer with the one-way case, in which INGRES users can access ORACLE but not vice versa. The INGRES gateway at the ORACLE site means that the ORACLE site can logically function as an INGRES site *but not as an INGRES/STAR site;* that is, ORACLE plus the gateway is logically equivalent to INGRES, not to INGRES/STAR. Thus, users at the INGRES site are operating in a distributed environment, *but users at the ORACLE site are not.* ORACLE is not an equal partner DBMS in the INGRES/STAR system. By the same token, of course, if ORACLE were to provide a gateway to INGRES, then the INGRES site would function as an ORACLE site but not as a SQL*STAR site; INGRES would not be an equal partner DBMS in the SQL*STAR system. Note, however, that each of the two sites does still have local autonomy, despite this lack of equality between them.

To conclude the discussion of the INGRES/ORACLE example, I should mention that there are severe problems of communication between two systems even when they are both SQL-based (as INGRES and ORACLE are). For a discussion of some of those problems, the reader is referred to reference [6].

So far I have discussed DBMS independence in the context of relational systems only. What about the possibility of including a nonrelational site in an otherwise relational distributed system? For example, would it be possible to provide access to an IMS site from within an INGRES/STAR or SQL*STAR system? Again, such a feature would be very desirable in practice, given the enormous quantity of data that currently resides in IMS and other nonrelational systems. But can it be done?

If the question means "Can it be done at the 100 percent level?"—meaning "Can all nonrelational data be made accessible from a relational interface, and can all relational operations be performed on that data?"—then the answer is definitely NO. I have explained why this is so elsewhere [4], and I will not repeat the arguments here. But if the question means "Can some useful level of functionality be provided?", then the answer might possibly be YES. For definiteness, let us consider the specific case of trying to incorporate an IMS site into an INGRES/STAR system (though once again the points discussed are intended to be of general applicability). Some relevant considerations follow:

- The more disciplined the IMS database is—in particular, if it was designed in accordance with relational principles, so that (e.g.) every segment has a unique sequence field, there are no anonymous fields, etc., etc.—the more feasible the proposition becomes. Note, however, that any such discipline merely makes the problem a little more tractable; it certainly does not make it *easy.*

- It is unlikely that the process of mapping the IMS database description to the INGRES dictionary will be completely automatic (IMS databases are rarely sufficiently disciplined or "clean" for an automatic mapping to be possible). Instead, a significant manual effort on the part of the IMS database administrator will probably be necessary.

- A gateway must be provided at the IMS site. However, that gateway cannot really "make IMS look like INGRES"; building such a gateway would be tantamount to implementing an entire relational DBMS on top of IMS, an enormous undertaking. (What is more, that relational DBMS would be one for which the databases have already been constructed, in a less than perfect form.) Probably the gateway will merely provide some kind of "data extract" mechanism. For example, if it is necessary to perform a join involving data from the IMS site, the gateway will probably extract the entire set of records to be joined and ship them to the INGRES site. The join itself will then be performed at that INGRES site.

- The foregoing "data extract" mode of operation might possibly be unnecessary for very simple relational requests (e.g., simple restrictions), where there is some reasonably direct analog of the request within the IMS repertoire of operations (namely, the DL/I language). Note, however, that where it is necessary, the INGRES site must in fact know that the IMS site *is* an IMS site. It is not like the ORACLE case discussed earlier, where the INGRES site might conceivably be unaware that the ORACLE site is in fact an ORACLE site, not an INGRES site.

- Because of the data extract approach, access to the IMS site is likely to be read-only. (Even with read-only access, the difficulties are still considerable. Again, see reference [4] for further discussion.)

15. SUMMARY AND CONCLUSIONS

In this paper I have tried to identify and describe a set of twelve rules or objectives for a "full function" distributed system. The rules all stem from "Rule Zero," which is as follows:

0. To the user, a distributed system should look exactly like a nondistributed system.

For convenience the twelve rules are summarized below:

1. Local autonomy
   - local security constraints
     —site-to-site message encryption also

- local integrity constraints
    —distributed constraints also
- local control of physical storage

2. No reliance on a central site
    - for dictionary management
    - for query processing
    - for concurrency control
    - for recovery control
    - for any other purpose

3. Continuous operation
    - adding/removing sites
    - creating/destroying fragments
    - creating/destroying replicas
    - upgrading to a new DBMS release

4. Location independence
    - for retrieval
    - for update
    - distributed data naming (transparent)
    - distributed user naming (transparent)

5. Fragmentation independence
    - horizontal fragmentation (partitioning)
    - vertical fragmentation (nonloss)

6. Replication independence
    - update propagation

7. Distributed query processing
    - distributed optimization
    - distributed execution
    - distributed views
    - distributed integrity constraints

8. Distributed transaction management
    - two-phase commit
        —any site can be coordinator or participant
    - distributed locking
        —distributed deadlock prevention/detection

9. Hardware independence
10. Operating system independence
11. Network independence
12. DBMS independence
    - for retrieval
    - for update
    - relational DBMSs
    - nonrelational DBMSs

I would like to remind the reader, however, that the rules are not necessarily intended to carry equal weight; in fact, as I explained in Section 1, some of the rules will certainly be completely irrelevant in certain contexts. Thus, while I do believe the rules can be useful as a basis for investigating and characterizing the capabilities of a given distributed system, I do NOT propose them as the basis for a "checklist" approach to system selection, and I do NOT want to be accused of suggesting that some hypothetical "System X" is (say) "7/12 of a good distributed system." Checklists can be useful, but they are only a starting point for a more thorough analysis and evaluation.

Note, incidentally, that the complete set of rules (or possibly some subset of them that includes at least Rules 4, 5, 6, and 8), taken together, seem to be equivalent to Codd's "distribution independence" rule for relational DBMSs (see reference [1]). For reference, I repeat that rule here:

- "A relational DBMS has distribution independence . . . [i.e.,] the DBMS has a data sublanguage that enables application programs and terminal activities to remain logically unimpaired:
    - when data distribution is first introduced (if the originally installed DBMS manages nondistributed data only);
    - when data is redistributed (if the DBMS manages distributed data)."

Note finally that Rules 4–6 and 9–12 can all be regarded as extensions of the familiar notion of data independence, as that concept applies to the distributed environment. As such, they all translate into *protection for the application investment*.

ACKNOWLEDGMENTS

I am grateful to several friends and colleagues for discussions and helpful comments on earlier drafts of this paper—most especially Rob McCord, Mike Stonebraker, Sharon Weinberg, Colin White, and Bob Yost. Needless to say, all remaining errors, whether of commission or omission, are my own responsibility.

REFERENCES AND BIBLIOGRAPHY

1. E. F. Codd, "Is Your DBMS Really Relational?" *Computerworld* (October 14, 1985); "Does Your DBMS Run by the Rules?" *Computerworld* (October 21, 1985).

2. E. F. Codd, "Why Distributed Systems Are Relational" (in preparation).

3. C. J. Date, *An Introduction to Database Systems: Volume II* (Reading, MA: Addison-Wesley, 1982).

4. C. J. Date, "Why Is It So Difficult to Provide a Relational Interface to IMS?" in C. J. Date, *Relational Database: Selected Writings* (Reading, MA: Addison-Wesley, 1986).

5. C. J. Date, "Updating Views," in C. J. Date, *Relational Database: Selected Writings* (Reading, MA: Addison-Wesley, 1986).

6. C. J. Date, "What's Wrong with SQL?" (in this volume).

7. C. J. Date, *A Guide to INGRES* (Reading, MA: Addison-Wesley, 1987).

8. C. J. Date and Colin J. White, *A Guide to DB2,* 3rd edition (Reading, MA: Addison-Wesley, 1989).

9. R. Williams et al., "R*: An Overview of the Architecture," in P. Scheuermann (ed.), *Improving Database Usability and Responsiveness* (New York: Academic Press, 1982); also available from the IBM Almaden Research Center, San Jose, Calif., as IBM Research Report RJ3325.

PART II

RELATIONAL VS. NONRELATIONAL SYSTEMS

11

Support for the Conceptual Schema: The Relational and Network Approaches

ABSTRACT

We present a detailed analysis and comparison of the relative merits of relations and networks as a basis for the conceptual level of the system.

COMMENTS ON REPUBLICATION

When I upgraded the third edition of my book *An Introduction to Database Systems* to the fourth edition (and labeled it *Volume I*, owing to the fact that *Volume II* had appeared in the interim), I dropped the following chapter, because it seemed to me that most of the material it contained was

---

Originally published (in somewhat different form) as Chapter 28 of my book *An Introduction to Database Systems,* 3rd edition (Reading, MA: Addison-Wesley, 1981). Reprinted by permission.

adequately covered elsewhere. I subsequently realized that I was at least partly wrong in that assumption, and that I had been a little hasty in dropping the chapter at that time. By now, of course, the material has largely been overtaken by events—no competent database professional today would seriously consider the CODASYL-style network approach as a candidate for the conceptual level of the system—but for students, at least, it is still convenient to have the reasons for this state of affairs all pulled together into a single place. Furthermore, I began to receive requests from both students and teachers to republish the material somehow, perhaps as a standalone paper. I therefore decided to incorporate it into the present book.

There is some overlap (I hope not too much) between this paper and references [8], [10], and [11], which appear in Part II of this book's predecessor, *Relational Database: Selected Writings* (Addison-Wesley, 1986).

1.   INTRODUCTION

This paper is concerned with the relative merits of the relational and network approaches as a basis for defining what is usually called the *conceptual schema* [24,25]. (It does not deal explicitly with hierarchies, because in this context hierarchies can be seen as merely a restricted form of network [11].) We concentrate on relations and networks because they are clearly in direct competition as candidates for this role.* However, we do not mean to suggest that they are the *only* candidates. Indeed, there is widespread agreement that neither approach is adequate in itself for the task, but rather that some extended formalism such as Codd's RM/T [7] is needed. Notwithstanding this fact, it is still useful to examine the two approaches in some depth, because most such extended formalisms have their basis in one or other of the two.

Although our discussion is couched for the most part in terms of the conceptual level, many of the points made are directly relevant at the external (user) level also.

2.   THE CONCEPTUAL SCHEMA

The conceptual schema is intended to serve as a solid and enduring foundation for the overall operation of the enterprise. It consists of an abstract description of the various types of entity that need to be processed in any way by the enterprise in question. By "solid and enduring," we mean that

---

*No longer true (1989)!

the schema should be *stable.* It should certainly not be dependent on the quirks of any individual DBMS (it might even have to survive the replacement of one underlying DBMS by another). More precisely, a given entry in the schema, say the description of a particular type of entity, *should never have to change*—unless, of course, a change occurs in the portion of the real world that the entry in question describes. If the conceptual schema is not stable in this sense, then applications and external schemas are likely to be unstable too, leading to user confusion, an increased need for reprogramming, and an increased chance of error.

To repeat: The conceptual schema should not have to change unless some adjustment in the real world requires some definition to be adjusted too, so that it can continue to reflect reality. Of course, one type of adjustment that is frequently necessary is the *expansion* of the conceptual schema to reflect a larger portion of reality; in other words, the schema must be able to *grow.* Such growth does not conflict with the basic objective of stability, however; it should be possible for the schema to grow in a nondisruptive fashion. As an example of a change in the real world that would require alteration to, rather than merely expansion of, the conceptual schema, consider the following change in the rule associating employees and departments: Under the old rule, each employee had to belong to exactly one department; under the new rule, an employee can belong to any number of departments simultaneously.

Designing the conceptual schema is without any doubt the most important single step in the installation of a database system. Ideally it should be the *first* such step (though it might be possible to perform the design in a piecemeal manner in some situations). In any case, it should certainly not be unduly influenced by considerations of how the data is to be physically stored and accessed, on the one hand, or how it is going to be used in specific applications, on the other. In other words, the design of the conceptual schema should be undertaken quite independently of the design of the associated internal and external schemas—for if it is not, there is a danger that the design will not be stable but will continually be undergoing revisions, with consequent impacts on other components of the system. Alternatively, if such revisions are not made, the installation will find itself locked into a conceptual schema that becomes increasingly unsuitable as more and more applications are brought into the system.

Given the DBMSs of today, however, the notion of designing the conceptual schema independently of the internal and external schemas is something of an ideal. Most systems currently available severely constrain the set of possibilities available to the designer at the conceptual level. Indeed, it is probably true to say that most existing installations do not really have an explicit conceptual schema at all; today's designers typically provide just an internal schema and a set of external schemas, and the "conceptual schema" is then effectively nothing more than the union of all the external schemas. (Moreover, the degree of variation possible between the external and internal levels is usually quite limited.) But the fact that this is the way that design has traditionally been done does not mean it is the right way. Experience has shown that the problems mentioned above (instability, unsuitability for new applications, etc.) do tend to arise after installations have been running for a while [17].

We would like to suggest, therefore, that it is still important to construct a conceptual schema, at a suitable level of abstraction, even if the DBMS available is such that this schema will exist only in manuscript or typescript form. If the system does not support a true conceptual level, the schema designer—presumably the DBA—will then have to perform a manual mapping of the conceptual design into a form that the system does support. If the system does support the design directly, of course, so much the better. Either way, the installation will find itself immeasurably better off for having a self-contained, succinct description of its operational data, expressed ideally in terms that—albeit precise—are human-oriented rather than machine-oriented. (It is becoming increasingly recognized that the biggest obstacle of all to progress in the use of computers is the difficulty of *communication* among all the many people involved—end-users, enterprise management, programming specialists, the database administrator, and so on [1]. The role of the conceptual schema in helping to overcome such problems is obvious.)

We also venture to hope that DBMSs of the future will cater for conceptual schemas of an adequate level of abstraction, thus more directly supporting the independent design technique advocated above. At the same time, of course, the system should be able to support a wide variety of external schemas, and should do so, moreover, with an efficiency at least comparable to that of today's systems. For the remainder of this paper we shall assume that such a system can and eventually will exist.

As indicated at the beginning of this section, the conceptual schema should not be dependent on the peculiarities of any specific system. However, it must be based on *some* view of data, such as relations or networks. In the next section we describe some properties that the conceptual view of data should possess; then, in Sections 4 and 5, we examine relations and networks in turn to see to what extent they possess these desirable properties.

3.   SOME CRITERIA FOR THE CONCEPTUAL SCHEMA

The two most important properties that the conceptual view of data should possess are the following.

1. It should be as simple as is practically possible.
2. It should have a sound theoretical base.

We consider each of these in turn.

Simplicity

When we say that the conceptual view should be simple, we really mean that it should be easy to understand and manipulate. We do not necessarily mean that it should be *minimal* in any sense. An analogy from arithmetic may help to clarify this distinction. When we represent a number in the familiar positional notation, we generally use decimal as the base, not binary, even though binary is logically sufficient. Binary is minimal, but decimal is simpler (easier to understand and manipulate) from the user's point of view.

The requirement that the view be easy to understand should not require any justification. Comprehensibility is obviously crucial if the communication problem mentioned in Section 2 is to be addressed. Of course, there are many aspects to comprehensibility; we list some of them below.

- The number of basic constructs should be small.

  The conceptual schema will be built out of a set of basic building blocks. It is obviously desirable that the number of distinct building blocks be kept to a manageable and convenient size. (As already indicated, however, we certainly do not want to sacrifice *conciseness* in the interests of this objective. The key word here is "convenient.")

- Distinct concepts should be cleanly separated.

  An individual construct (building block) should not "bundle together" two or more distinct concepts; for if it does, it becomes difficult to tell exactly what purpose that construct is serving in a given situation (and it may be used for a purpose for which it was not intended).

- Symmetry should be preserved.

  It should not be necessary to represent a naturally symmetric structure in an asymmetric manner. To quote Polya (writing in a different context): "Try to treat symmetrically what is symmetrical, and do not destroy wantonly any natural symmetry" [21].

- Redundancy should be carefully controlled.

  Redundancy in the sense of the same fact appearing in two places should probably not be allowed at all. By "fact" here, we mean the association between a given entity and some property of that entity—e.g., the association between an item and its price. However, there are other types of redundancy that cannot be eliminated, in general [4]. In such cases the conceptual schema should include a statement of exactly what the redundancy is. (We note in passing that we do not seem to have a good definition of the term "redundancy"; we have only a somewhat vague idea that it is bad in some situations and good in others.)

Likewise, the requirement that the conceptual view be easy to manipulate should also require little justification. Although users will not actually operate directly at the conceptual level, they must understand what operations are possible at that level, since those operations will be used to model the transactions of the enterprise. In an implementation in which the user's view is the same as or close to the conceptual view, of course, it becomes even more imperative that the operations be easy to understand. To paraphrase reference [8]: "The reader is cautioned to avoid comparing different approaches solely on the basis of differences in the data structures they support. An adequate appreciation of the differences must entail consideration of the operators also."

We list some aspects that will help to make the data easy to manipulate.

- The number of operators should be small.

  No additional comment seems necessary.

- Very high-level (i.e., powerful) operators should be available.

  It goes without saying that the operators must be precisely defined. However, it is also desirable that operators exist at a level close to the imprecise, but very high-level, "operators" used in natural language (consider, for example, the transaction "Increase all programmers' salaries by 10 percent"). Ideally, each transaction would be expressible at the conceptual level in one and only one way. The burden of irrelevant decisions (concerning access strategies, for example) should be removed from the user.

- Symmetry should be preserved.

  Transactions that have a naturally symmetric formulation should be expressible symmetrically in the manipulative language. For example, the queries "List all employees working for department D3" and "List all employees earning a salary of $30,000" should have similar representations.

Theoretical Base

Given the importance of the conceptual level, it is absolutely essential that it be founded on a solid base of theory [24]. Its behavior must be totally predictable and, to the greatest extent possible, should accord with users' intuitive expectations. Surprises, especially unpleasant ones, simply cannot be tolerated. Whatever formal system we choose as a basis for the conceptual level, we *must* be fully aware of exactly what is and is not possible in that system. Specifically, we should be familiar with all potential pitfalls and problem areas, and we should be certain that ambiguity and paradox cannot occur. In short, we should know exactly what we are doing.

4.　THE RELATIONAL APPROACH

[*Note: This section is essentially an early, and very much abridged, version of the paper "Why Relational?", which appears as Chapter 1 of the present book. I repeat the material here merely for convenience; the reader may wish to skip it, or refer to that other chapter for an extended discussion.*]

　　Let us now see how the relational approach measures up to the requirements of the previous section.

- First, there can be little doubt that relations are easy to understand. The number of basic data constructs is *one,* namely the relation (or table) itself; all information in the database is represented using just this one construct, and moreover this one construct is both simple and highly familiar—people have been using tables for centuries. (Note that the schema itself, and all other information in the dictionary, can also be represented in relational form, of course.)

- As for keeping distinct concepts separate, there seem to be few, if any, instances of bundling in the relational approach.* Indeed, it is significant that most of the research since 1970 into such areas as concurrency, locking, security, integrity, view definition, and so on, has taken the relational approach as its starting point precisely *because* it provides a clean conceptual base.

- As for symmetry and nonredundancy, the relational approach again seems to meet the requirements. In the case of nonredundancy, the normalization discipline [13] will guarantee that the same "fact" will not appear in two places.

- Relations are also easy to manipulate; numerous examples can be cited (from the present book and elsewhere) in support of this statement.

- Moreover, the foregoing statement is true at both the record-at-a-time and set-at-a-time levels; in other words, very high level operators are

---

*Some writers would argue that *n*-ary relations do bundle together several distinct *facts,* and that the purposes of the conceptual level would be better served by an equivalent collection of binary relations. There is some merit in this position. However, we consider the distinction between the *n*-ary and binary relational views as being far less significant than that between relational views of any kind and the CODASYL-like network view.

available, as well as the more familiar low-level operators. (The very high-level operators are of course those of the relational algebra and equivalent languages.)

- The number of distinct operators in any given language is small because there is only one type of data construct to deal with; essentially we need just one operator for each of the four basic functions retrieve, insert, update, delete. If we also consider—as we must—the operators we need for authorization and integrity purposes, we again find that a single set of operators is all that is necessary, and for the same reason.

- Last, relational languages generally provide what Codd [4] calls "symmetric exploitation"—i.e., the ability to access a relation by specifying known values for any combination of its attributes, seeking the (unknown) values for its other attributes. Symmetric exploitation is possible because all information is represented in the same uniform way.

As for the question of an underlying theory, the relational approach is not only soundly based on certain aspects of mathematical set theory, it also possesses a considerable body of theory in its own right aimed specifically at its application to database problems. The well-known theory of normalization [13] (already mentioned above) provides a rigorous set of guidelines for the design of a relational schema. The theory of relational completeness [5] provides a valuable tool for measuring the expressive power of a language and for comparing different candidate languages (indeed, now that the concept has been defined, it is incumbent on the designer of any such language either to make that language complete in this sense or else to justify each and every departure from such an objective). Under the heading of theory we should also mention the relational *closure* property: The result of any operation of the relational algebra, or equivalent language, is itself a relation, which allows us to write nested relational expressions.* The closure property is particularly important in the provision of support for the nonprogramming user [8].

5. THE NETWORK APPROACH

Before discussing networks in any detail, we first introduce the important notion of *essentiality* [8]. We say that the declaration D of some data construct in a schema S is *essential* if there exists an instantaneous database B conforming to S such that removal from B of the construct defined by D

---

*Incidentally, binary relations do not possess this same closure property. For example, a join of two binary relations is not a binary relation.

would cause a loss of information from B. (By saying that a loss of information would occur, we mean, precisely, that some relation would no longer be derivable.)

We present some examples to illustrate this idea, using a simplified form of the declarative syntax of UDL [11]. *Note:* The UDL *baseset* construct corresponds to the "base table" construct of SQL; the UDL *fanset* construct corresponds to the "owner-member set" construct of CODASYL, or the "parent-child" construct of IMS. We prefer the "fanset" term to the CODASYL term "set" for numerous reasons, the most important one being that the CODASYL construct is *not* a set in the mathematical sense.

1. Schema S1:

    ```
    BASESET COURSE   ( COURSE#, TITLE )
    BASESET OFFERING ( COURSE#, OFF#, DATE, LOCATION )
    ```

    Both declarations are essential in S1. (Also, both basesets are relations.)

2. Schema S2:

    ```
    BASESET COURSE   ( COURSE#, TITLE )
    BASESET OFFERING ( OFF#, DATE, LOCATION )
    FANSET  OFFERING UNDER COURSE
    ```

    All three declarations are essential in S2. (The first baseset is a relation, the second is not.)

3. Schema S3:

    ```
    BASESET COURSE   ( COURSE#, TITLE )
    BASESET OFFERING ( COURSE#, OFF#, DATE, LOCATION )
    FANSET  OFFERING UNDER COURSE
            WHERE    OFFERING.COURSE# = COURSE.COURSE#
    ```

    The two baseset declarations are essential in S3, the fanset declaration is not; there is no information that can be derived from this database that cannot also be derived from the two basesets alone. (Again, the two basesets are relations.)

Given this notion of essentiality, we can now state *an absolutely crucial distinction* between the relational and network approaches [8]. In a relational schema, the entire information content of the database is represented by means of a single data construct, the *n*-ary relation. In a network schema, by contrast, *there must exist at least one fanset bearing information essentially;* for if there did not, the schema would degenerate into a relational schema with certain access paths explicitly exposed. In other words, there are at least two essential data constructs in the network approach, the baseset and the fanset.*

> *Note added* (1989): The original paper did not really make the point clear, but the fact is that it is the essential fansets that give rise to most (not all) of the complexity of network systems. See reference [11] for evidence in support of this claim.

Now we can consider how the network approach measures up to the criteria specified earlier for the conceptual level of the system. The first criterion was ease of understanding. A comparison of Fig. 1 (a relational version of a simple bill-of-materials structure) and Fig. 2 (a network version of the same data) suggests that, at the data instance level at least, networks are somewhat less easy to understand than relations. (A comparison of the corresponding definitions suggests that the same is true at the schema level also. We omit the details here; see, e.g., reference [11] for some specific comparisons.) One reason for the increase in complexity is the increase in the number of basic constructs the user has to understand and deal with.

A more severe criticism of networks is that the fanset construct bundles together at least three distinct concepts:

1. It *carries information* (either essentially or inessentially), namely the association between the two record types involved.

2. It provides an *access path* (actually several such paths: parent to first and last child, child to next and previous child, child to parent).

3. It represents.certain *integrity constraints* (primarily the constraint that each child has one parent, though the CODASYL concept of "membership class" [9] provides for a number of variations on this basic theme).

COMPONENT	MAJOR_P#	MINOR_P#	QUANTITY
	P1	P2	2
	P1	P4	4
	P5	P3	1
	P3	P6	3
	P6	P1	9
	P5	P6	8
	P2	P4	3

Fig. 1   A bill-of-materials structure (relational view)

---

*In CODASYL in particular, there are actually *six* data constructs, any or all of which can be used to bear information essentially: record type (corresponds to baseset), owner-member set (corresponds to fanset), ownerless (or "singular") set, ordering, repeating group, and area or realm.

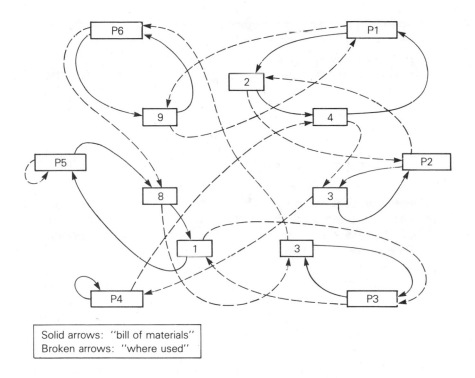

Solid arrows: "bill of materials"
Broken arrows: "where used"

Fig. 2   A bill-of-materials structure (network view)

In addition, fansets can be used to establish a scope for authorization purposes; also, the ordering of children within a given fan can be used to carry information (again, either essentially or inessentially).

A result of all this bundling is that, for example, a program might come to rely on an access path that is really a side effect of the way the designer chose to represent a certain integrity constraint. If that integrity constraint changes, the schema has to be restructured, with a strong likelihood of consequent impact on the corresponding program—even if that program was completely uninterested in the integrity constraint per se. As an example, consider the effect on a program that lists employee numbers by department (a) using a relation ED (EMP#,DEPT#), and (b) using a fanset DEPTEMP (parent DEPT, child EMP), if the department-to-employee correspondence changes from one-to-many to many-to-many.

- In the relational case, the worst that can occur is a trivial change to the external/conceptual mapping—ED might have to be derived as a projection of a department/employee "linking" relation instead of as a projection of the employee relation.

- In the network case, the changes required at the conceptual level are rather more extensive, and either the program or the external/conceptual mapping will require significantly more rewriting. (If the rewriting is contained within the mapping, incidentally, we will then have the situation that the program is using an access path, namely DEPTEMP, that is no longer directly supported. See item 2 below.)

Let us examine each of the three bundled concepts in a little more detail.

1. Fansets represent certain associations between entities. However, not all such associations will be represented as fansets, in general; in all likelihood, not even all one-to-many associations will be so represented. As an example of one that is not, consider the association between cities and suppliers in the usual suppliers-and-parts database. Of course, there is no record type corresponding to cities; but if one were added, would a fanset also be added with cities as parents and suppliers as children? If the answer is yes, the fanset will be inessential, unless the city field is removed from the supplier record type. That removal is unlikely, for the following reasons among others:

(a) Suppliers would have to be MANUAL members of the fanset (to allow for the fact that the supplier records exist *before* the city records are created); therefore,

(b) A new program will be needed to connect suppliers to cities; and

(c) This program will need to obtain the city value for a given supplier from *somewhere*—presumably from the city field.

Furthermore, if the city field *is* removed, then certain existing programs that previously executed successfully will now fail.

We conclude that the addition of essential fansets with existing records as members is a nontrivial operation, which raises questions about the usefulness of the construct in the first place.

2. Fansets represent certain access paths. However, not all such paths are represented by fansets; for example, the system may provide various forms of indexing under the covers [3]. User programs are not dependent on the existence or otherwise of such "invisible" access paths, but they very definitely are dependent on the existence of the visible paths that are represented by fansets. (This observation suggests that fansets cannot be regarded as purely logical constructs—they must be supported fairly directly at the physical level, for otherwise there is little

justification for representing just these particular inter-entity associations in this rather privileged manner.* See item 1 above.) The question arises: Why is this particular form of access path made visible, when others are not?

3. Fansets represent certain integrity constraints. However, not all such constraints are represented by fansets; indeed, most constraints are specified quite separately from the data structure. An example of the problems caused by bundling such constraints with the data structure has already been given. The question arises: Why are these particular constraints given this special treatment?

A more general question arising from the three items above is the following: How does the schema designer decide which associations/paths/constraints to express as fansets and which to represent in some other way?

Returning to our "ease of understanding" criteria, the last two in the list were *symmetry* and *nonredundancy*.

- First, a network schema involving essential fansets has less symmetry of representation than an equivalent relational schema, since some information is represented as records and some as links between records; it follows that such a network cannot totally support "symmetric exploitation."

- Second, a network schema can certainly be just as nonredundant as an equivalent relational schema (but no more so, of course), but only if it does not involve any inessential fansets; an inessential fanset does contain some redundancy, in that the association between parent and child is represented both by field values and by links.

We turn now to *ease of manipulation*.

- Observe first that each information-bearing construct needs its own set of operators to manipulate it. Thus, even if we restrict our attention to just record types and fansets, we see that networks necessarily require more operators than relations. (The truth of this statement is amply demonstrated by the language UDL [11].) For example, in CODASYL we have STORE to create a record and CONNECT to create a link, ERASE to destroy a record and DISCONNECT to destroy a link, and so on.

---

*Fansets are actually a very general and widely applicable construct, considered purely as an access mechanism and not as a logical structure. They are thus a strong candidate for implementation at the *internal* or storage structure level, as opposed to the conceptual level. It is likely, however, that "internal" fansets would not use FIXED, MANDATORY, or AUTOMATIC membership class—everything would be MANUAL and OPTIONAL. The work of Kay [14] supports these remarks.

Aside: Actually, CODASYL does not provide individual operators for each of the four basic functions (retrieve, insert, update, delete) for each information-bearing construct. However, the omissions do not mean that the missing functions are not needed—it simply means that users have to program such functions for themselves. For example, there is no direct way (i.e., no single CODASYL operation) to modify information that is represented by position within a repeating group. Consider, e.g., what the user must do to move the fifth item in a repeating group into the third position. *End of aside.*

Note also the foregoing remarks are applicable *regardless of operator level.* In other words, it is certainly possible to define very high-level (set-at-a-time) operators for networks—see reference [11] for some examples—but those operators will necessarily be more complex than their relational counterparts, and there will necessarily be more of them.

We also need more authorization and integrity operators. Moreover, authorization and integrity controls can be quite complicated to apply. Suppose, for example, that in the department-employee fanset, employees are ordered within department by ascending value of the salary field, and suppose we have a user who needs to see employees by department—perhaps as an access path—but who is not allowed any access to salary information. It is not sufficient simply to omit the salary field from the user's view; the user can still discover (e.g.) that Smith earns more than Jones by observing that Smith follows Jones in the sequence. (Inessential information-carriers do still carry information, and corresponding controls are still necessary.)

Last, we consider the question of a supporting theory. This writer knows of no theory to assist with the design of a network schema that is as complete as the normalization theory is for relations. It is true that normalization theory can be applied to the *records* of the network, but only *after* the decision has been made as to which information is to be represented by records and which by other means—and of course this first decision is critical. The consequences of a wrong choice are likely to be instability in the schema.

- By way of example, consider a network schema representing a subway network, in which each subway line is represented by a "singular (ownerless) set," and the order of the stations on the line is represented by the order of the records in the set (a realistic example of essential ordering, by the way).

- Suppose that at some subsequent time it is required to extend this schema to incorporate the distance between adjacent stations. That distance is a property, not of a station per se, but rather of a pair of adjacent stations; however, adjacency is represented by ordering, not by records, which makes it difficult to find an appropriate point in the schema at which to introduce a distance field.

- If we introduce a new "pair-of-adjacent-stations" record type, we can obviously use it to hold the distance field; however, the existing schema then becomes totally redundant. (The new record type would have to include a field identifying the relevant subway line.)

- Alternatively, if we place the distance field in the existing station record type (more precisely, if we incorporate a "distance to next station" field into the station record type, thus relying once again on the ordering), we introduce an unpleasant asymmetry into the schema. For example, the algorithm for computing the distance between two stations X and Y on a given line will vary significantly depending on whether X precedes or follows Y on the line.

- Placing the distance field in the station record type introduces another problem also: Some stations (namely, interchanges) are on more than one line, and so have more than one "next station." Repeating groups?

The problems sketched above are entirely due to the use of ordering as an essential construct.

Another important theoretical question is the following: Is it possible to support a relational external schema on a conceptual schema that involves essential fansets? It is generally accepted that nonprogramming users, at least, will require a relational view of the database. Again, this writer knows of no completely general method of supporting such a view if the conceptual schema involves essential fansets. It is not hard to construct examples that suggest that such a general mapping would be rather complex.

- The basic problem is that information represented by the essential fanset will be represented by a foreign key in the relational view. Difficulties will arise if the relational user updates this foreign key, especially if the new value does not match any existing parent record, which must sometimes be allowed. (How can an essential fanset deal with a deferred foreign key check?)

It is worth pointing out also that the closure properties of relations do not apply to essential fansets. For example, a "union" of two fans of a given fanset that retains all linkage information is not itself another fan (neither of the given fanset nor of any other).

Some Questions

We can conclude our discussion of the suitability of networks for the conceptual level by turning the problem around and asking (but not answering) a number of questions.* Suppose that we start with relations as the sole data construct available at the conceptual level. What is the effect of introducing new constructs (e.g., fansets) that bear information essentially?

- So far as the *system* is concerned, do not more operators become necessary? Do not concurrency, authorization, and similar controls become more complex? Hence, does not the implementation become more complex and less reliable?

- So far as the *user* is concerned, is there not an increased burden in choosing which operators to use? Is there not an increased variety of possible errors to cope with, and a corresponding variety of possible remedial actions to consider?

- So far as the *database administrator* is concerned, are there not too many structural choices available? *Are there dependable guidelines for making these choices?* (This is one of the most critical questions of all.) Are not the mappings to the internal level significantly more complicated to define and maintain? Are not authorization and integrity constraints more complicated to specify?

If it turns out that fansets have to be *inessential* (perhaps because it is not possible to support a relational external view on essential fansets), then their role at the conceptual level must once again be questioned.

It is interesting to note, incidentally, that Bachman himself in his Turing Award lecture [1] suggests that fansets are fundamentally inessential and are intended primarily for improving performance: ". . . The field named department code appears in both the department record and the employee record. . . . The use of the same data value as a primary key for one record and as a secondary key for a set of records is the basic concept upon which data structure sets are declared and maintained." And later: "The joint usage of the department code by both [department and employee] records and the declaration of a set based upon this data key provide the basis for the creation and maintenance of the set relationship between a department record and all the records representing employees of that department. [A benefit of this construct is] the significant improvement in performance that

---

*These questions were originally raised by Codd in reference [8], and were republished as part of the reprinted version of that same paper in this book's predecessor. So far as I know, they have still never been answered in the open literature.

accrues from using the database sets in lieu of both primary and secondary [indexes] to gain access to all the records with a particular data key value."

6. CONCLUSION

Many papers have appeared over the past few years on the relative merits of different data structures and different ways of manipulating them [2, 3, 8, 10, 12, 15–20, 24]. In this paper, we have attempted to extract and present some of the most significant themes from those papers. In particular, we have tried to show the advantages of *n*-ary relations over CODASYL-like networks; however, for an opposing point of view, the reader is referred to certain of the original papers (particularly references [12] and [17]).

It seems appropriate to conclude with Codd's statement of objectives for the relational approach [8]. They are as follows:

1. To provide a high degree of data independence
2. To provide a community view of the data of spartan simplicity, so that a wide variety of users in an enterprise (ranging from the most computer-naive to the most computer-sophisticated) can interact with a common view (while not prohibiting superimposed user views for specialized purposes)
3. To simplify the potentially formidable job of the database administrator
4. To introduce a theoretical foundation (albeit modest) into database management (a field sadly lacking in solid principles and guidelines)
5. To merge the fact retrieval and file management fields in preparation for the addition at a later time of inferential services in the commercial world
6. To lift database application programming to a new level—a level in which sets (and more specifically relations) are treated as operands instead of being processed element by element

No one would claim that all these objectives have now been attained; much more work remains to be done. However, a strong foundation has been established, and there seems good reason to be optimistic about the eventual outcome.

REFERENCES AND BIBLIOGRAPHY

[Note: I have made a number of changes in the following. First, I have introduced some additional references, in order to make the paper reasonably self-contained

(the original had cross references to other chapters of the book in which it first appeared). Second, a few of the original references no longer seemed relevant, and I have therefore removed them. (In fact, I was tempted to remove several others also—the opinions expressed therein now seem a little quaint—but I eventually decided to retain them for their historical interest.) Third, I have edited the annotation in some cases to reflect more recent developments.]

1. C. W. Bachman, "The Programmer as Navigator," *Communications of the ACM* 16, No. 11 (November 1973).

   Contains the lecture that Bachman gave on the occasion of his receiving the 1973 ACM Turing Award.

2. C. W. Bachman, "The Data Structure Set Model," in reference [23].

   Presents arguments in favor of Bachman's view that the relational and network approaches are fundamentally compatible.

3. A. E. Bandurski and D. K. Jefferson, "Data Description for Computer-Aided Design," *Proc. 1975 ACM SIGMOD International Conference on Management of Data* (May 1975).

   Includes some interesting criticisms of both relations and networks.

4. E. F. Codd, "A Relational Model of Data for Large Shared Data Banks," *Communications of the ACM* 13, No. 6 (June 1970). Republished in *Communications of the ACM* 26, No. 1 (January 1983).

5. E. F. Codd, "Relational Completeness of Data Base Sublanguages," in *Data Base Systems,* Courant Computer Science Symposia Series, Vol. 6 (Englewood Cliffs, NJ: Prentice-Hall, 1972).

6. E. F. Codd, "Understanding Relations: Installment No. 4," *ACM SIGMOD Bulletin FDT* 6, No. 4 (1974).

   Includes a very clear description of the differences among the following concepts: (1) the domain concept; (2) comparability of attributes; (3) the association between a foreign key and a primary key; and (4) the CODASYL set or fanset. (The differences are important; the claim is frequently made that fansets are the CODASYL equivalent of one or other of the first three, and such is not the case.)

7. E. F. Codd, "Extending the Database Relational Model to Capture More Meaning," *ACM Transactions on Database Systems* 4, No. 4 (December 1979).

8. E. F. Codd and C. J. Date, "Interactive Support for Nonprogrammers: The Relational and Network Approaches," in reference [23]. Republished in C. J. Date, *Relational Database: Selected Writings* (Reading, MA: Addison-Wesley, 1986).

   As explained in this book's predecessor, this paper was really written by Codd (despite the attribution). It presents arguments in favor of Codd's view (with which of course I concur) that the relational and network approaches are fundamentally at odds. Section 5 of the present chapter draws heavily from this paper.

9. Data Base Task Group of CODASYL Programming Language Committee, Final Report (April 1971).

10. C. J. Date and E. F. Codd, "The Relational and Network Approaches: Comparison of the Application Programming Interfaces," in reference [23]. Republished in C. J. Date, *Relational Database: Selected Writings* (Reading, MA: Addison-Wesley, 1986).

    A companion paper to reference [8]. Somewhat unfair, in that it contrasts a relational set-at-a-time language (Codd's "Data Sublanguage ALPHA") with a network record-at-a-time language (the DML of CODASYL). *Note added* (1989): I was bending over backwards to appear impartial in this comment! Part of the argument in favor of relations vs. networks is precisely that relational languages are set-level, not record-level.

11. C. J. Date, "An Introduction to the Unified Database Language (UDL)," in C. J. Date, *Relational Database: Selected Writings* (Reading, MA: Addison-Wesley, 1986).

    Describes a language that supports both record- and set-level access to relational, hierarchic, and network databases in a uniform and consistent manner (and thus, not incidentally, provides a "level playing field" that can be used as a basis for systematic and unbiased comparisons among the different approaches).

12. C. P. Earnest, "A Comparison of the Network and Relational Data Structure Models," available from Computer Sciences Corporation, 650 N. Sepulveda Blvd., El Segundo, California 90245 (1973).

    Earnest's major conclusions are: "(1) The two models are in practice not very different; (2) the relational structures are somewhat simpler than networks; but (3) the price for this is that the network model has more structural power and *more,* not less, data independence than the relational, and is therefore likely to be a better basis for a standard."

13. Ronald Fagin, "Normal Forms and Relational Database Operators," *Proc. 1979 ACM SIGMOD Conference on Management of Data* (May/June 1979).

14. M. H. Kay, "An Assessment of the CODASYL DDL for Use with a Relational Subschema," in Douqué and Nijssen (eds.), *Data Base Description,* Proc. IFIP TC-2 Special Working Conference on Data Base Description, North-Holland (1975).

    An investigation into the question of supporting a relational subschema on top of a CODASYL schema. In general, such a subschema would be considerably more than just "a simple subset of the schema." The paper identifies some pertinent problems and criticizes the CODASYL schema DDL in the light of those problems.

15. W. C. McGee, "A Contribution to the Study of Data Equivalence," in Klimbie and Koffeman (eds.), *Data Base Management,* Proc IFIP TC-2 Working Conference on Data Base Management Systems, North-Holland (1974).

16. W. C. McGee, "On the Evaluation of Data Models," *ACM Transactions on Database Systems* 1, No. 4 (December 1976).

    Defines a set of criteria for choosing a particular view of data. The criteria are as follows: simplicity, elegance, logicalness, picturability, modeling directness, modeling uniqueness, provision of "structure schemas," overlap with coresi-

dent models, partitionability, consistent terminology, proximity to implementation base, and applicability of safe implementation techniques. Of course, some
of these criteria clash with others.

17. A. Metaxides, "Information-Bearing and Non-Information-Bearing Sets," in
Douqué and Nijssen (eds.), *Data Base Description,* Proc. IFIP TC-2 Special Working Conference on Data Base Description, North-Holland (1975).

> The terms "information-bearing" and "non-information-bearing" are unfor-
> tunately sometimes used in place of "essential" and "inessential." As Metax-
> ides quite rightly observes, the terms are misleading since essential and inessen-
> tial constructs both bear information. The paper claims that eliminating
> essential sets (a) provides no data independence benefits, (b) provides no integ-
> rity benefits, (c) does not really increase simplicity (simplification in the schema
> is achieved only at the expense of complication in programs), (d) reduces flexi-
> bility, and (e) leads to design and update problems.

> Metaxides was the chairman of the CODASYL Data Base Task Group at the
> time that group produced its final report, the so-called "CODASYL specifica-
> tions" for a DBMS [9].

18. A. S. Michaels, B. Mittman, and C. R. Carlson, "A Comparison of the Relational and CODASYL Approaches to Data Base Management," *ACM Computing
Surveys* 8, No. 1 (March 1976).

> Discusses the two approaches under the headings of data definition, data ma-
> nipulation (language level, complexity), data protection, data independence,
> and performance. The major conclusion is that no single approach to database
> management is desirable [sic] and no single approach is likely to emerge as
> dominant in the near future. *Note added* (1989): Events have shown otherwise.

19. G. M. Nijssen, "Data Structuring in DDL and the Relational Data Model," in
Klimbie and Koffeman (eds.), *Data Base Management,* Proc IFIP TC-2 Working
Conference on Data Base Management Systems, North-Holland (1974).

> Compares and contrasts the network and relational data structures, and pro-
> poses a discipline for network users. The "DDL" of the title is the CODASYL
> Data Description Language. It is interesting to compare the discipline suggested
> with another such discipline proposed in reference [8].

20. G. M. Nijssen, "Set and CODASYL Set or Coset," in Douqué and Nijssen
(eds.), *Data Base Description,* Proc. IFIP TC-2 Special Working Conference on
Data Base Description, North-Holland (1975).

> Considers the CODASYL DDL as a language for defining conceptual schemas,
> and suggests a number of improvements to the language with this aim in mind.
> The changes proposed include the following.

- All record types should include a primary key.
- All set types should be inessential.
- All ordering should be inessential.
- A set type should be allowed to have the same record type as both owner and
  member.

- A set type should not be allowed to have more than one type of member.

- The concept of membership class should be replaced by the ability to state whether the functional dependence of owners on members is total or partial, together with certain additional integrity constraints.

    The paper includes some good illustrations of why sets should not be essential. However, the author does not discuss the question (raised repeatedly in Section 5 of the present paper): "If sets must be inessential, what purpose are they really serving in the conceptual schema?"

21. G. Polya, *How to Solve It,* 2nd edition (Princeton: Princeton University Press: Princeton Paperback, 1971).

22. K. A. Robinson, "An Analysis of the Uses of the CODASYL Set Concept," in Douqué and Nijssen (eds.), *Data Base Description,* Proc. IFIP TC-2 Special Working Conference on Data Base Description, North-Holland (1975).
    Supports the contention of Section 5 that CODASYL sets should not appear at the conceptual level but might possibly be useful at the internal level.

23. R. Rustin (ed.), "Data Models: Data Structure Set vs. Relational," *Proc. 1974 ACM SIGMOD Workshop on Data Description, Access and Control,* Vol. II (May 1974).
    The proceedings of a debate held at the 1974 SIGMOD conference. Includes references [2,8,10], additional comments by D. C. Tsichritzis and J. R. Lucking, and the transcript of a panel-and-audience discussion.

24. T. B. Steel, Jr., "Data Base Standardization: A Status Report," in Douqué and Nijssen (eds.), *Data Base Description,* Proc. IFIP TC-2 Special Working Conference on Data Base Description, North-Holland (1975).
    An outline description of the ANSI/SPARC three-level architecture [25], with emphasis on the conceptual schema. The author argues strongly for his own conviction that the only acceptable formalism for the conceptual level is that of modern symbolic logic.

25. D. C. Tsichritzis and A. Klug (eds.), "The ANSI/X3/SPARC DBMS Framework: Report of the Study Group on Data Base Management Systems," *Information Systems* 3 (1978).

PART

THE SQL LANGUAGE

12

What's Wrong with SQL?

ABSTRACT

SQL is an industry phenomenon. Its level of acceptance, at least by vendors, is growing by leaps and bounds, and it has recently been adopted as a national standard by the American National Standards Institute (ANSI). Yet SQL is certainly not the panacea it is sometimes claimed to be. This paper explains why.

COMMENTS ON REPUBLICATION

An extensive criticism of SQL can be found in a previous paper of mine (reference [4]). I originally wrote that paper in 1983, however, well before SQL had become so widely available in the marketplace and well before it had become a standard. By contrast, the following paper, which may be regarded in part as a sequel to the previous one, differs from that earlier paper in that it focuses largely (though not exclusively) on the standard version of the language. It raises some points that were not addressed in the earlier paper. It is also much shorter! There is some overlap, but not

---

Originally published (in somewhat different form) in *Datamation* 33, No. 9 (May 1, 1987), under the title "Where SQL Falls Short." Reprinted by permission.

too much. I have taken the opportunity to make some minor revisions in order to bring the paper up to date, but otherwise it remains essentially as originally written.

I must make it clear that the paper is not intended to be exhaustive; SQL suffers from numerous additional deficiencies, over and above the ones identified herein. Some of those additional deficiencies are the subject of subsequent papers in this part of the book.

1. INTRODUCTION

By now, there cannot be many data processing professionals who are unaware that there is a new standard abroad in the DP field—the "Structured Query Language" (abbreviated SQL, usually pronounced "sequel"), which was recently adopted by the American National Standards Institute (ANSI) as a standard language for interacting with relational databases [1]. SQL is a hot topic; scarcely a week goes by without some SQL-related product announcement, either from IBM or from some other hardware or software vendor. Examples of such announcements have included:

- Brand new products in which SQL is the primary user language, such as SYBASE from Sybase Inc. and SQL/400 from IBM

- New SQL interfaces to existing products such as INGRES from Relational Technology Inc. and dBASE IV from Ashton-Tate

- Interfaces—sometimes with direct SQL pass-through facilities—from existing products, such as IDEAL from ADR (now part of Computer Associates Inc.) and FOCUS from Information Builders Inc., to one of IBM's own SQL-based mainframe DBMSs DB2 and SQL/DS

SQL products are now available on almost every kind of hardware, from the smallest micro to the largest mainframe; the total number of such products is close to 100 at the time of writing, and the end is not in sight.

Taken as a whole, then, the DP industry seems to have fallen in love with SQL. And as sometimes happens in a love affair, extravagant claims have been made, and still are being made, regarding the merits, attractions, compatibility, and general desirability of the love object—in this case, the SQL language. The purpose of this short paper is to try to inject a note of moderation into such claims. It can be seen as a continuation of my earlier paper "A Critique of the SQL Database Language" [4], which was originally published in ACM SIGMOD Record 14, No. 3 (November 1984), and later republished in my book *Relational Database: Selected Writings* (Addison-Wesley, 1986) and elsewhere.

Before getting into details, however, there are a couple of points that I would like to make absolutely clear right at the outset:

- First, the recent widespread acceptance of SQL of course stems from, and parallels, the corresponding widespread acceptance of relational database technology—and nobody could be more pleased than myself with the way that relational technology is finally having the impact it deserves. The criticisms that follow should very definitely *not* be taken as criticisms of the relational approach; they are criticisms of SQL per se, nothing more.

- Second, I do not want to be seen as being implacably opposed to SQL. On the contrary, I believe that SQL does have many admirable features. The thesis of this paper might be expressed: "SQL is great!—but it could have been so much better." SQL really *is* great, compared with older-style database languages such as DL/I, and there really have been some significant successes with it. The stories regarding ease of application development, ease of maintenance, improved productivity, etc., really do have a significant basis in fact. Nevertheless, the picture is not quite as rosy as some people have tried to paint it—and in this paper I would like to explain why.

The rest of the paper is divided into three main sections:

- What's wrong with the SQL language per se?
- What's wrong with the SQL standard?
- What about application portability?

2.   WHAT'S WRONG WITH SQL PER SE

In this section, I consider the SQL language purely *as* a language—more specifically, as a language that is intended as a concrete realization of the relational model. From this standpoint, SQL is deficient in at least three major respects:

- Missing relational features
- Lack of orthogonality
- Redundancy

    I consider each in turn.

Missing Relational Features

There are several aspects of the underlying relational model that SQL either does not support at all or else supports only indirectly—primary keys, foreign keys, the entity and referential integrity rules (also database-specific integrity rules), domains, certain of the relational operators, and so on.

These omissions mean extra work for users and lead to undesirably unsystematic behavior in many situations (e.g., in the area of view updating, which is disgracefully ad hoc—not to say incorrect—at present). Furthermore, adding proper support for such missing features at a later time is likely to be difficult, because of the need to remain compatible with the past.

In passing, it is only fair to mention that ANSI is currently at work on a set of proposed extensions to the standard [2] that address some (not all) of the foregoing omissions.

Lack of Orthogonality

Orthogonality means *independence.* Orthogonal language design means that distinct language concepts are cleanly separated, not bundled together. The advantage of orthogonal design is that it leads to a language that is *coherent*—one that possesses a simple, clean, and consistent structure (both syntactic and semantic), and hence one that is easy for the user to grasp and the vendor to implement. If a language is coherent, users are able (perhaps without consciously realizing the fact) to build a simple mental model of its behavior, from which they can make extrapolations and predictions with confidence. There are no exceptions or special cases or unpleasant surprises for the user to have to deal with.

Unfortunately, SQL in its present form is extremely *un*orthogonal. It is chock full of apparently arbitrary restrictions, exceptions, and special rules. A few examples will serve to illustrate the point:

- INSERT, UPDATE, and DELETE statements cannot include a subquery that refers to the table to which the INSERT, UPDATE, or DELETE applies

- Updates via a cursor are not permitted if the cursor declaration includes ORDER BY

- UNION can be used in a SELECT statement or a cursor declaration but not in a view definition

- A SELECT clause cannot include the keyword DISTINCT more than once at any given level of nesting

- A FROM clause that references a "grouped view" is not allowed to reference any other table

- A SELECT operation against a grouped view cannot include a WHERE clause or a GROUP BY clause or a HAVING clause

- An operational expression such as $X + 1$ can appear in a SELECT clause or a WHERE clause or a SET clause but not in a VALUES clause

- SUM $(X + 1)$ is legal, and so is SUM (DISTINCT X), but SUM (DISTINCT X + 1) is not

And so on. Ironically (and paradoxically), such restrictions have the effect of simultaneously increasing the size of the language while decreasing its power or functionality.

Of course, it is possible to remove such restrictions at a later time, and no doubt they will be so removed. (Indeed, ANSI is—again—already at work on this problem [2].) However, the fact remains that the restrictions do currently exist, and they do currently cause difficulties. There was really no good excuse for including them in the first place. It is not as if SQL was defined 25 or 30 years ago. Orthogonality has been a well-established language design principle for many years; there was really no justification for ignoring it in a language that was first implemented (in product form) in the nineteen-*eighties*.

Redundancy

SQL is an extremely redundant language. By this I mean that all but the most trivial of problems can be expressed in SQL in a variety of different ways. For example, consider the query "Find supplier names for suppliers who supply part P2" (assuming the usual suppliers-and-parts database). This is a very simple problem, yet it is not difficult to find no less than eight formulations for it, all of them at least superficially distinct (see below). Of course, the differences would not be important if all formulations worked equally well, but that is unlikely. As a result, users are forced to spend time and effort trying to find the "best" formulation (i.e., the version that performs best)—which is exactly one of the things the relational model was trying to avoid in the first place.

```
1.  SELECT DISTINCT S.SNAME
    FROM    S
    WHERE   S.S# IN
          ( SELECT SP.S#
            FROM    SP
            WHERE   SP.P# = 'P2' ) ;

2.  SELECT DISTINCT S.SNAME
    FROM    S
    WHERE   S.S# =ANY
          ( SELECT SP.S#
            FROM    SP
            WHERE   SP.P# = 'P2' ) ;

3.  SELECT DISTINCT S.SNAME
    FROM    S
    WHERE   EXISTS
          ( SELECT *
            FROM    SP
            WHERE   SP.S# = S.S#
            AND     SP.P# = 'P2' ) ;
```

```
4.  SELECT  DISTINCT  S.SNAME
    FROM     S, SP
    WHERE    S.S# = SP.S#
    AND      SP.P# = 'P2' ;

5.  SELECT  DISTINCT  S.SNAME
    FROM     S
    WHERE    0 <
             ( SELECT  COUNT(*)
               FROM    SP
               WHERE   SP.S# = S.S#
               AND     SP.P# = 'P2' ) ;

6.  SELECT  DISTINCT  S.SNAME
    FROM     S
    WHERE    'P2' IN
             ( SELECT  SP.P#
               FROM    SP
               WHERE   SP.S# = S.S# ) ;

7.  SELECT  DISTINCT  S.SNAME
    FROM     S
    WHERE    'P2' =ANY
             ( SELECT  SP.P#
               FROM    SP
               WHERE   SP.S# = S.S# ) ;

8.  SELECT  S.SNAME
    FROM     S, SP
    WHERE    S.S# = SP.S#
    AND      SP.P# = 'P2'
    GROUP    BY S.SNAME ;
```

Incidentally, a major cause of SQL's high degree of redundancy is the following: When the language was first designed, it was specifically intended to be different from the relational calculus (and, I believe, from the relational algebra also). That goal was the motivation for the introduction of the "IN subquery" construct (see, e.g., the first of the eight formulations above). As time went by, however, it turned out that certain algebraic and calculus features were necessary after all, and the language grew to accommodate them. As a result, the situation now is that the entire "IN subquery" construct could be removed from the language with no loss of function at all! This fact is ironic, since it was that construct that was the justification for the "Structured" in the name "Structured Query Language" in the first place.

Unlike the two problems previously mentioned (missing relational features and lack of orthogonality), the redundancy problem is *not* easy to fix without major surgery.

Let me conclude this section on the SQL language per se by mentioning one thing that is *not* wrong with it—namely, its "mathematical and academic origins," which are sometimes the target of misguided attacks (see, e.g., reference [8]). To the extent that SQL does possess such origins, I would argue that they represent a significant strongpoint of the language. To suggest otherwise, as reference [8] does, "because most end users do not have a Ph.D. in mathematics and logic," is absurd. It is just such origins that provide the regularity, predictability, and coherence that are needed in a language if that language is to be truly usable (with all that that implies). The fact that relational systems are founded on a mathematical theory certainly does not mean that only theoreticians are capable of using (or understanding) such a system. On the contrary, the point of the theory (as has been publicly stated and emphasized many times) is that it enables us to build systems that are *100 percent practical* [6].

Of course, the foregoing paragraph should not be construed as saying that SQL is suitable for all categories of users, or that still higher-level interfaces (e.g., forms-based interfaces, natural language, etc.) built on top of SQL are not required—they certainly are, and vendors are providing them. In this latter connexion, however, I should mention another SQL shortcoming, namely that its lack of orthogonality and its redundancy make it a less than perfect *target* language also. In other words, it is not an ideal base on which to build such higher-level interfaces.

3.   WHAT'S WRONG WITH THE SQL STANDARD

I turn now to the official ANSI standard version of SQL [1]. The standard suffers from certain additional problems, over and above those sketched in the previous section. *Note:* The ANSI standard defines two language levels. Level 2 is the complete standard language; Level 1 is a subset of Level 2 (at least, that is the intent—but it does not necessarily follow that a Level 1 program will execute correctly under a Level 2 implementation). A few of the comments that follow apply strictly to Level 1, but most apply to both levels.

Functional Deficiencies

The standard has been characterized, perhaps a little unkindly, as "the intersection of existing implementations" [5]. This comment may not really be fair; however, it does highlight a general criticism, which is that the standard (at least in its initial form) seems more concerned with protecting existing vendor implementations than with establishing a truly solid foundation for the future. Partly as a consequence of this fact, the standard omits a number of features that are definitely useful in practice. Here is a short (and incomplete) list of such omitted features:

- All data types other than numbers and fixed-length strings
- REVOKE and DROP operations
- The SQL Communication Area
- Dynamic SQL (PREPARE, EXECUTE, etc.)
- ALTER TABLE
- CREATE and DROP INDEX
- Explicit locking facilities
- Data definition and data control statements in programs

As a result of such omissions, any commercial SQL implementation, even if it does support all the features of the standard, is certain to include a large number of implementation-defined extensions in addition. Consequently, it is virtually certain that no two SQL implementations will be precisely identical to each other, and no SQL implementation will be precisely identical to the standard. Even the IBM implementations in DB2 and SQL/DS are not 100 percent compatible (and neither one is a subset of the other).

Note added (1989): IBM now has *four* mutually incompatible SQL implementations, not just two [5]—DB2, SQL/DS, the OS/2 Extended Edition Database Manager, and the OS/400 Database Manager (SQL/400).

Implementation-Defined Aspects

The standard includes certain aspects that are explicitly stated to be implementation-defined. Here is a short (and incomplete) list of such aspects:

- SQLCODE values on error conditions
- Effect of certain operations on cursor positioning
- Precision of result of arithmetic expressions
- Character collating sequence
- Whether views are physically materialized
- Position of nulls in an ORDER BY sequence
- Effect on the database if an error occurs in the middle of an operation (Level 1 only)
- Whether two nulls are considered equal for purposes of GROUP BY (Level 1 only)
- Whether a given cursor permits updates (Level 1 only)

As a result of such considerations, two SQL implementations can both conform to the standard and yet still be incompatible with each other.

Static Schema

A major advantage of genuinely relational products is that they support *dynamic data definition;* in other words, data definition operations are dynamically executable, and they can be invoked both interactively and from within an application program. In the standard, by contrast, such operations can appear only within the context of a "schema"; and while the standard does not actually specify how a schema is entered into the system, it does seem as if the definitional interface is something distinct from both a conventional interactive interface and a conventional programming interface. In fact, it seems to be rather static. By comparison with the dynamic facilities *already implemented* in most existing relational products, this static approach represents a major step backward. It is a throwback to the inflexibility of prerelational systems. From a relational standpoint, in fact, the whole idea of drawing a sharp dividing line between data definition and data manipulation, as the standard does, is an archaic one—one that is wholly inappropriate to the relational environment.

Now, it is true that (as mentioned above) the standard does not specify the mechanism for making a schema known to the system, and hence that the possibility of a genuinely dynamic interface is not totally ruled out. But this point is a subtle one and is likely to escape the attention of many people. There should really be *no hint* in the standard that separate languages are needed for data definition and data manipulation. It is even conceivable that such a separation could eventually lead (as it did with CODASYL) to the establishment of two separate standards committees, one for data definition and one for data manipulation, with all the attendant horrors of such an arrangement.

Undefined Aspects

A few aspects of standard SQL are (presumably unintentionally) left undefined. For example, the standard does not appear to specify how operations on views are to be processed, at least not in any direct fashion. At a more detailed level, the standard also does not specify whether literals are considered to have the NOT NULL property (the point is significant, given the restrictions on the UNION operation; see the standard definition for details). Again, therefore, it is entirely possible that two implementations could both be "conforming" and yet be incompatible with one another.

4. APPLICATION PORTABILITY

Application portability is of course the primary justification for the existence of the standard in the first place. Once again, however, some words of caution are appropriate. First, of course, the shortcomings identified in the previous section mean that (as already pointed out) it is probable that no two SQL implementations will be precisely identical to one another, and no SQL implementation will be precisely identical to the standard. For example, it is possible to identify well over 50 points of difference (some of them very major) between the standard and DB2—and on the whole I would say that DB2 SQL is fairly close to ANSI SQL! Thus, all claims on the part of vendors to the effect that their product supports "the standard SQL language" or is "compatible with IBM's DB2 product" should be treated with suspicion, to say the least.

It is perhaps worth spelling out the ANSI rules for standard conformance here. Of course, a conforming implementation must support, either at Level 1 or at Level 2, all of the standard data definition and data manipulation operations. However, a conforming implementation is also explicitly permitted:

- To provide support for additional facilities not specified in the standard
- To provide options to process conforming SQL language in a nonconforming manner
- To provide options to process nonconforming SQL language

It follows that, just because two implementations do both conform to the standard, there is no guarantee that a SQL program that operates successfully on one of those implementations will also do so on the other.

In addition, there are a number of more specific points to be made on this general topic.

SQL Is Only a Database Sublanguage

It must of course be understood that SQL by itself is not a full programming language, nor was it ever intended to be. On the contrary, it is what Codd (in reference [3]) originally called a *data sublanguage*. As a consequence, SQL statements must be embedded in some host language such as COBOL in order to gain access to those facilities (e.g., conditional branching, terminal I/O, screen handling, etc.) that SQL itself does not provide. The portability of a given program will thus depend on the portability of the surrounding host language as well as on the portability of SQL per se.

Data Types

A major question regarding portability has to do with data types. Different host languages support different data types, and conversion among those data types is a notoriously difficult problem. In fact, the SQL standard defines different database data types for each host language!—in other words, there is no guarantee that (e.g.) a database created for and populated by a COBOL program will be accessible from a PL/I program. Furthermore, such matters as (default) numeric precision and scale and string length are all left as implementation-defined, with the result that (e.g.) a "standard" application that operates successfully on a DEC VAX may very well not do so on an IBM machine (etc.).

In this regard it is perhaps as well to point out that there is more to compatibility than just *syntactic* compatibility. Just because two implementations both support a data type called FLOAT (for example) certainly does not guarantee that a given program will be able to operate unchanged and produce the same output on both systems.

Catalog

The SQL standard does not include any specification for a standard catalog structure (and indeed it is difficult to see how it could have done so, given that the catalog tends to be somewhat implementation-dependent). Nevertheless, the unfortunate fact is that *generalized* applications, at least, do frequently need to read and interpret catalog information, precisely because of their generalized nature. (An example of such a generalized application is IBM's Query Management Facility QMF, which is an ad hoc query and report-writing frontend for DB2 and SQL/DS.) The lack of a standard catalog structure is likely to impose severe limitations on the portability of such applications.

It is worth pointing out, incidentally, that "third-party" software products tend (for obvious reasons) to be, exactly, generalized applications in the foregoing sense.

Dynamic SQL

[*Note:* This point is related to the previous one.]

The standard also does not include a dynamic SQL facility (i.e., the facility to construct SQL statements dynamically at run time and then have those statements executed). Again, it is hard to see how such a facility could possibly have been included, since it is likely to be somewhat implementation-dependent. Nevertheless, the fact is (once again) that generalized applications are likely to make extensive use of such a facility, precisely because of their generalized nature; hence the omission is likely (once again) to impair the portability of such applications severely.

Distributed Database

Another argument in favor of the SQL standard is that it could provide a basis whereby distinct systems (i.e., distinct SQL implementations) might all be able to cooperate as equal partners in a distributed database system.

From one point of view, such a system can be regarded as an environment in which application portability is *the* problem *par excellence*. Here I would only add that, in addition to the problems already identified in this section (and indeed throughout this paper)—all of which apply to such an environment—certain additional problems present themselves also. Examples of such additional problems include different physical data representations, different communication protocols, and different commit protocols. Some of these problems will be addressed in a forthcoming paper. *Note added* (1989): The "forthcoming paper" was "What Is a Distributed Database System?" [7], which can be found elsewhere in the present volume.

5. CONCLUSIONS

There is really little that needs to be said by way of conclusion except "Caveat emptor!" The purpose of the paper is very definitely NOT to suggest that investment in a SQL system would be an unwise move—on the contrary, I believe the opposite quite strongly. However, would-be purchasers and users of such products are urged to study the problems discussed above, to decide for themselves how significant those problems are in their own environment, to balance the costs against the undoubted benefits that a SQL system can provide, and above all to approach vendor claims regarding compatibility, portability, and the like with a healthy degree of skepticism.

ACKNOWLEDGMENTS

I am grateful to Ted Codd and Sharon Weinberg for their helpful comments on an earlier draft of this paper.

REFERENCES AND BIBLIOGRAPHY

1. American National Standards Institute (ANSI), Database Language SQL. Document ANSI X3.135-1986 (1986). Also available as International Standards Organization (ISO) Document ISO/TC97/SC21/WG3 N117 (1987).

2. ISO/IEC JTC1/SC21/WG3 / ANSI X3H2, ISO-ANSI (working draft) Database Language SQL2. Document ISO DBL CPH-2b / ANSI X3H2-88-210 (April 1988).

3. E. F. Codd, "A Relational Model of Data for Large Shared Data Banks," *Communications of the ACM* 13, No. 6 (June 1970). Republished in *Communications of the ACM* 26, No. 1 (January 1983).

4. C. J. Date, "A Critique of the SQL Database Language," in C. J. Date, *Relational Database: Selected Writings* (Reading, MA: Addison-Wesley, 1986). Republished in revised form in reference [5].

5. C. J. Date, *A Guide to the SQL Standard,* 2nd edition (Reading, MA: Addison-Wesley, 1989).

6. C. J. Date, "Why Relational?" (in this volume).

7. C. J. Date, "What Is a Distributed Database System?" (in this volume).

8. Stephen Gerrard, "SQL Scrutinized," *Computerworld* (September 22, 1986).

13

EXISTS Is Not "Exists"! (Some Logical Flaws in SQL)

ABSTRACT

SQL is not sound.

COMMENTS ON PUBLICATION

It was late in 1987 or early in 1988 that I first explicitly realized that SQL had a problem over the EXISTS function, in that invocations of that function always returned *true* or *false,* never *unknown* (and hence that earlier claims in this book's predecessor *Relational Database: Selected Writings* (Addison-Wesley, 1986) and elsewhere regarding the mapping of all-or-any comparisons into existence tests were in fact incorrect). Also, I had already known for some years that scalar comparisons with a subquery in SQL did not correctly handle the case in which the subquery returns an empty set. A telephone call on such matters from an old acquaintance, Don Slutz of

Previously unpublished.

the SQL group at Tandem, in November 1988 set me thinking about the problem more deeply. I came to the conclusion that the matter was quite serious, and so decided to try and pull the various points together and present them in a coherent manner. This paper was the result.

Incidentally, an interesting sidelight on the issue is the following: When I demonstrated the problem to people skilled in SQL, their reaction was typically not to appreciate the gravity of the problem, but rather to try to show me how to reformulate the examples so that SQL would produce the right answer!

1. INTRODUCTION

We assume for the purposes of this paper that DBMS support for nulls [1,2,3] is required and desirable. We also assume all the necessary consequences of this base assumption—sets must be allowed to contain nulls,* the system must support three-valued logic, support for a MAYBE operator (or equivalent) is required, etc., etc. [9].

Now, SQL does provide some support for nulls, of course, though it is well known that the support in question is incomplete and is subject to certain anomalies in (e.g.) the way nulls are treated by the aggregate functions [7]. The purpose of this paper is to demonstrate that SQL additionally suffers from certain *logical* flaws in this area, and hence that SQL cannot be said to be "sound"—that is, it is possible, using SQL, to derive a contradiction from the database.

The basic problem can be stated very simply, and is as follows:

■   In a formal system based on three-valued logic, truth-valued expressions have three possible values (in general), namely *true, false,* and *unknown* (which we abbreviate to just *unk*). In SQL, however, there is one particular kind of truth-valued expression, namely an EXISTS function reference, that always returns *true* or *false,* never *unk,* even when *unk* is the logically correct response.

As a consequence, the EXISTS function in SQL is not a faithful representation of the existential quantifier ("there exists") of three-valued predicate logic. This fact accounts for the somewhat tongue-in-cheek title of the paper, of course.

Let us consider a simple example. Suppose we have a set Z containing just the values 1, 2, and null:

---

*Actually, sets per se do *not* have to be allowed to contain nulls; rather, *tables* must be allowed to contain *rows* in which one or more components—possibly all components—are null [9]. For the purposes of the present paper, however, it is convenient to ignore this refinement. The resultant simplification does not invalidate any of the arguments.

```
Z = ( 1, 2, null )
```

Let *v* be a variable that ranges over the set Z. In three-valued logic, then, the existentially quantified expression

```
EXISTS v ( v > 5 )
```

will evaluate to *unk,* because it is not known whether the condition $v > 5$ evaluates to *true* for any *v* in Z. More precisely, the expression EXISTS *v* ($v > 5$) is defined to be equivalent to the following "iterated OR" expression [1,9]:

```
( 1 > 5 )  OR  ( 2 > 5 )  OR  ( null > 5 )
```

—i.e., "*false* OR *false* OR *unk,*" which reduces to *unk.* (The truth tables for three-valued logic can be found in many places; see, e.g., reference [9].)

However, the SQL version of the foregoing looks something like the following:

```
EXISTS ( SELECT DISTINCT V.*
         FROM   Z V
         WHERE  V.N > 5 )
```

(we assume that Z is regarded as a table of one column, with column name N; V is a range variable that ranges over that table). The parenthesized SELECT-expression here evaluates to the empty set, because SELECT in SQL is defined to select only the values for which the expression in the WHERE clause evaluates to *true,* not to *false* and not to *unk.* As a result, the overall expression returns *false,* not *unk,* because EXISTS in SQL is defined to return *false* if its argument set is empty and *true* otherwise.

> *Note:* In this paper, we include the specification DISTINCT in all SELECT-expressions (even when that DISTINCT is logically unnecessary), simply in order to guarantee that all such expressions genuinely do evaluate to *sets,* without any duplicates. We also use *explicit range variables* throughout, for reasons of definiteness and clarity. See reference [10] for further discussion of these points.

As the example shows, the existential quantifier in predicate logic and the EXISTS function in SQL are indeed not the same thing.* We now proceed to examine some of the consequences of this fundamental flaw.

---

*In principle, the paper could stop right here; once it has been established that the EXISTS function is logically flawed, it is obvious that (as my colleague Nat Goodman puts it) "SQL will break"—i.e., problems will arise—and identifying specific places at which it does break— i.e., describing those problems in detail—might be regarded as just beating a dead horse. But some of the problems in question are so significant, and at the same time so subtle, that it does seem worthwhile, at least from a pedagogic standpoint, to examine them in some depth.

2.   AN EXAMPLE OF A CONTRADICTION

For our first example, we consider an extremely simple database—essentially a very much reduced version of the familiar suppliers-and-parts database—in which we have just one table SP (shipments), with values as shown in Fig. 1. The null in the row (S1,P1,*null*) is meant to be interpreted as "value unknown"—i.e., supplier S1 does supply part P1, we simply don't know the relevant quantity. The primary key for table SP is the composite column SP.(S#,P#).

```
SP   S#   P#   QTY
     --   --   ----
     S1   P1   null
     S2   P1   200
```

Fig. 1   Database for the first example

Now consider the query "Find supplier numbers for suppliers who do supply part P1, but not in a quantity of 1000"—meaning, of course, suppliers who are *known to the system* to supply part P1 but not in such a quantity. (We obviously cannot ask the system questions about the real world *per se*, only about its *knowledge* of the real world as represented by the values in the database [9].) Given the sample data shown above, the right answer to the query is clearly just the single supplier number S2; the system *does not know* whether supplier S1 supplies part P1 in a quantity of 1000, because of the null in the row (S1,P1,*null*).

The "obvious" formulation of the query in SQL would be:

```
SELECT  DISTINCT SPX.S#
FROM    SP SPX
WHERE   SPX.P# = 'P1'
AND     SPX.QTY <> 1000 ;
```

(*Note:* The symbol "< >" means "not equals.") This formulation is correct and does indeed return the right answer (supplier number S2); supplier S1 does not qualify, because for supplier S1 the expression in the WHERE clause becomes "*true* AND *unk*," which reduces to just *unk*.

This version of the query can be regarded as a "UNION" or "iterated OR" formulation—it examines the rows of table SP one at a time, extracts the supplier number from a given row if and only if the expression in the WHERE clause evaluates to *true* for that row, and returns the UNION of all supplier numbers so extracted. In other words, the formulation is effectively shorthand for an expanded formulation that might look something like this:

```
SELECT  DISTINCT SPX.S#
FROM    SP SPX
WHERE   SPX.S# = 'S1'          /* the "first" supplier number */
AND     SPX.P# = 'P1'
AND     SPX.QTY <> 1000
```

```
UNION

SELECT  DISTINCT SPX.S#
FROM    SP SPX
WHERE   SPX.S# = 'S2'           /* the "next" supplier number */
AND     SPX.P# = 'P1'
AND     SPX.QTY <> 1000

UNION

. . . . .

UNION

SELECT  DISTINCT SPX.S#
FROM    SP SPX
WHERE   SPX.S# = 'Sn'           /* the "last" supplier number */
AND     SPX.P# = 'P1'
AND     SPX.QTY <> 1000 ;
```

Here now is another formulation, one that logically *ought* to be equivalent to the previous "UNION" formulation:

```
SELECT  DISTINCT SPX.S#
FROM    SP SPX
WHERE   SPX.P# = 'P1'
AND     NOT EXISTS
        ( SELECT DISTINCT SPY.*
          FROM    SP SPY
          WHERE   SPY.S# = SPX.S#
          AND     SPY.P# = 'P1'
          AND     SPY.QTY = 1000 ) ;
```

("Select supplier numbers from shipments SPX such that the supplier in question does supply part P1, but there does not exist a shipment SPY saying that the same supplier supplies part P1 in a quantity of 1000"). Note, incidentally, that this second formulation would be the "obvious" formulation if there could be multiple rows having the same supplier number and same part number—i.e., if it could not be guaranteed that values of the composite column SP.(S#,P#) were unique.

Now consider how this expression is evaluated. First, suppose the range variable SPX takes on the value (S1,P1,*null*)—i.e., the "first" row of table SP. Then:

- The EXISTS argument logically becomes

```
( SELECT DISTINCT SPY.*
  FROM    SP SPY
  WHERE   SPY.S# = 'S1'
  AND     SPY.P# = 'P1'
  AND     SPY.QTY = 1000 )
```

which evaluates to the empty set, since there is no row (S1,P1,1000) in table SP.

- The EXISTS reference therefore evaluates to *false* (as explained earlier, EXISTS in SQL is defined to return *false* if its argument set is empty, *true* otherwise). The NOT EXISTS therefore evaluates to *true,* and the overall query logically becomes

```
SELECT DISTINCT SPX.S#
FROM    SP SPX
WHERE   SPX.P# = 'P1'
AND     true
```

and hence supplier number S1 appears in the final result (remember that range variable SPX currently represents the row for supplier S1). Error!

- (Supplier number S2 also appears in the final result, as the reader may care to confirm, but of course this is correct.)

So we see that two different methods of formulating the query, one (conceptually) via "UNION" or "iterated OR" and the other via EXISTS—two formulations that ought logically to be equivalent—can in fact return different results, and hence that (as claimed earlier) it is indeed possible to derive contradictions from a SQL-based DBMS.

Aside: By the way, the problem is not easy to fix! Consider the following:

- The root of the problem is that EXISTS in SQL is regarded as a *function* that takes a SELECT-expression as its argument, and of course SELECT-expressions by definition return values only where the expression in the WHERE clause evaluates to *true.* In other words, SQL is not really implementing the "iterated OR" definition of EXISTS at all.

- To correct the SQL definition of EXISTS would require recognition of the fact that the EXISTS argument ought *not* to be a SELECT-expression at all, but rather some new kind of linguistic construct that SQL currently does not support. (In fact, of course, EXISTS should not be thought of as a *function* in the usual programming sense at all. The "argument" to that "function" cannot really be evaluated in isolation, without paying attention to the context in which it appears. This is why it should *not* be a conventional SELECT-expression.)

- Furthermore, it would be highly desirable for that hypothetical new linguistic construct to have a syntax very different from the existing SELECT-expression syntax, precisely in order to avoid giving the impression that it *is* such an expression.

- The foregoing discussion shows why revising SQL to "do it right" would involve major surgery, and indeed would probably do a certain amount of violence to the spirit of the language. This is why we suggested above that the problem is not easy to fix.

■ Incidentally, the foregoing discussion additionally shows why extending SQL to provide support for the universal quantifier (FORALL)—an extension that would be very desirable in practice—would be a major undertaking also.

End of aside.

3. A PROBLEM OF INTERPRETATION

For our next example, we take a slightly more complicated version of the database with two tables, S (suppliers) and SP (shipments), with values as shown in Fig. 2. The primary keys for the two tables are S.S# and SP.(S#,P#), respectively.

```
S   S#   SNAME   STATUS   CITY         SP   S#   P#   QTY
    --   -----   ------   ------            --   --   ---
    S1   Smith       20   London            S1   P1   100
    S2   Jones       10   Paris
```

Fig. 2   Database for the "interpretation problem" example

Now consider the query "Find names of cities for suppliers who supply at least one part." A (correct) formulation of this query in SQL is as follows:

```
SELECT DISTINCT X.CITY
FROM    S   X
WHERE   EXISTS
      ( SELECT DISTINCT Y.P#
        FROM    SP  Y
        WHERE   Y.S# = X.S# ) ;
```

("Select cities for suppliers, X say, such that there exists at least one part that supplier X supplies"). This formulation does return the correct answer, which is a set containing just one city name, viz. London.

But suppose now that we have constructed another table SSP that is the *left outer natural join* [8] of table S and table SP over supplier numbers (refer to Fig. 3).

```
SSP   S#   SNAME   STATUS   CITY     P#     QTY
      --   -----   ------   ------   ----   ----
      S1   Smith       20   London   P1     100
      S2   Jones       10   Paris    null   null
```

Fig. 3   Left outer natural join of S and SP over S#

Note carefully that the nulls in table SSP must be interpreted as meaning, not that the shipments for supplier S2 are unknown, but rather that no such shipments exist. (This important point is discussed further in references [9] and [11].) Given this fact, a putative "equivalent" version of the previous SQL query that operates against table SSP might be:

```
SELECT  DISTINCT X.CITY
FROM    SSP  X
WHERE   EXISTS
      ( SELECT DISTINCT Y.P#
        FROM    SSP  Y
        WHERE   Y.S# = X.S# ) ;
```

(the difference between this formulation and the previous one is that all references to table S or table SP in that previous version have been replaced by references to table SSP). Now consider what happens when the range variable X takes as its value the row (S2,Jones,10,Paris,*null,null*):

- The inner SELECT-expression logically becomes

```
      ( SELECT DISTINCT Y.P#
        FROM    SSP  Y
        WHERE   Y.S# = 'S2' )
```

which evaluates to a set containing nothing except a null. *Note, however, that this set is not empty.* As a result, the SQL EXISTS reference returns *true*, and hence the city for supplier S2 (Paris) appears in the final result. Error!

The rationale for defining EXISTS to return *true* in such a case (i.e., the case where the argument set contains just one element and that element is null) is presumably that the null means "value unknown"—i.e., a value does exist to make the existence test *true,* we just don't know what that value is. But as pointed out above, null in the case at hand should *not* be interpreted as "value unknown" (again, see references [9] and [11] for further discussion of this point). This is why (as indicated in the title to this section) we regard this particular flaw as a *problem of interpretation.*

Aside: There is one more point to be made (a rather interesting one) before we leave the present discussion, namely as follows. In principle, it ought always to be possible to recast any query involving EXISTS into another query involving COUNT instead. This is because (again in principle):

(a) If S is a SELECT-expression, then (loosely speaking) the expression EXISTS (S) will evaluate to *false* if and only if the expression "COUNT (S)" evaluates to zero. (We show "COUNT (S)" in quotes here because COUNT in SQL has problems of its own [6]; specifically, its argument is *not* written as a SELECT-expression, though logically it ought to be.*

(b) Likewise, if we ignore nulls for the moment, the expression EXISTS (S) will evaluate to *true* if and only if the expression "COUNT (S)" evaluates to some integer *n,* where *n* is nonzero (more accurately, greater than zero).

The parallel between EXISTS and COUNT breaks down in SQL when nulls are taken into account, however, because "COUNT (S)" simply ignores any nulls in its argument set, whereas (as we have already seen) EXISTS (S) does not. But this discrepancy is precisely the point of the present aside. If we assume the existence of an improved "pseudoSQL" version of SQL in which "COUNT (S)" *is* legal syntax, the two EXISTS queries shown earlier in this section might be replaced by two COUNT versions, as follows:

```
SELECT  DISTINCT X.CITY              SELECT  DISTINCT X.CITY
FROM    S   X                        FROM    SSP  X
WHERE   COUNT                        WHERE   COUNT
        ( SELECT DISTINCT Y.P#               ( SELECT DISTINCT Y.P#
          FROM   SP  Y                         FROM   SSP  Y
          WHERE  Y.S# = X.S# ) > 0 ;           WHERE  Y.S# = X.S# ) > 0 ;
```

(we show the two pseudoSQL versions side by side, for ease of comparison; the query, to repeat, is "Find names of cities for suppliers who supply at least one part"). The interesting thing about these two formulations is that (unlike their EXISTS counterparts) they *both* return the right answer! Consider what happens in each case when the range variable X takes as its value the (unique) row for supplier S2:

(a) In the formulation on the left, the COUNT argument evaluates to the empty set (there are no part numbers in table SP for supplier S2); the COUNT reference therefore returns zero, and hence Paris does not appear in the final result (correct).

(b) In the formulation on the right, by contrast, the COUNT argument evaluates, not to the empty set, but to to a set containing just one element, namely a null. However, COUNT in SQL ignores nulls in its argument set (except for the special case of COUNT(*), which is not the case under consideration); the COUNT reference therefore again

---

*This is why the SQL COUNT function is not permitted in a WHERE clause, incidentally. The two "pseudoSQL" examples given subsequently show how SQL would be considerably improved if the syntax for COUNT did follow the same general style as that of EXISTS.

returns zero, and again Paris does not appear in the final result (correct).

For interest, we give a "genuine" SQL version of the pseudoSQL formulation shown on the right above:

```
SELECT DISTINCT X.CITY
FROM    SSP   X
GROUP   BY X.S#, X.CITY
HAVING COUNT ( DISTINCT X.P# ) > 0 ;
```

It is left as an exercise for the reader to determine that this formulation does indeed deliver the correct answer.

End of aside.

4. TRANSFORMING ALL-OR-ANY COMPARISONS INTO EXISTENCE TESTS

In an earlier paper [6], I made the claim that all-or-any comparisons (i.e., comparisons involving the quantified operators >ALL, <ANY, etc.) could always be recast as existence tests. I gave the following transformation rules. (*Warning:* These rules are *** INVALID ***!)

  1. The expression

```
x  $ANY  ( SELECT y FROM T WHERE p )
```

(where $ is any one of =, >, etc.) is equivalent to the expression

```
EXISTS ( SELECT * FROM T WHERE ( p ) AND x $ T.y )
```

  2. Likewise, the expression

```
x  $ALL  ( SELECT y FROM T WHERE p )
```

is equivalent to the expression

```
NOT EXISTS ( SELECT * FROM T WHERE ( p )
                          AND   NOT ( x $ T.y ) )
```

Now I find that I must eat my words. These transformations *ought* to be valid, but in my original paper I had overlooked the anomalous behavior of the SQL EXISTS function in the presence of nulls in its argument and/ or *unk* truth values in the conditional expression(s) defining that argument. The correct definition of all-or-any comparisons is as follows. First, the expression

```
x  $ANY  ( SELECT y FROM T WHERE p )
```

evaluates to *true* if the expression

    x   θ   (y)

evaluates to *true* for at least one value *y* in the result of evaluating the parenthesized SELECT-expression; it evaluates to *false* if the expression

    x   θ   (y)

evaluates to *false* for every value *y* in the result of evaluating that SELECT-expression (or if that result is empty); and it evaluates to *unk* otherwise. Second, the expression

    x   θALL   (SELECT y FROM T WHERE p)

evaluates to *true* if the expression

    x   θ   (y)

evaluates to *true* for every value y in the result of evaluating the parenthesized SELECT-expression (or if that result is empty); it evaluates to *false* if the expression

    x   θ   (y)

evaluates to *false* for at least one value *y* in the result of evaluating that SELECT-expression; and it evaluates to *unk* otherwise.

Returning now to the example of Section 2 ("Find supplier numbers for suppliers who do supply part P1, but not in a quantity of 1000"), here is another plausible SQL formulation:

```
SELECT  DISTINCT SPX.S#
FROM    SP SPX
WHERE   SPX.P# = 'P1'
AND     1000 <>ALL
      ( SELECT DISTINCT SPY.QTY
        FROM    SP SPY
        WHERE   SPY.S# = SPX.S#
        AND     SPY.P# = 'P1' ) ;
```

This formulation is in fact correct, but the reader should try to convince him- or herself of that fact before continuing. *Note:* The familiar SQL comparison operator "NOT IN" is just a different spelling for "< >ALL."

Explanation:

- First, suppose the range variable SPX takes on the value (S1,P1,*null*), i.e., the "first" row of table SP (refer back to Fig. 1 in Section 2). Then the expression following the < >ALL logically becomes

```
( SELECT DISTINCT SPY.QTY
  FROM    SP SPY
  WHERE   SPY.S# = 'S1'
  AND     SPY.P# = 'P1' )
```

which returns a set containing just one element, namely a null. The outer query thus logically becomes

```
SELECT DISTINCT SPX.S#
FROM    SP SPX
WHERE   SPX.P# = 'P1'           /* true for SPX = (S1,P1,null) */
AND     1000 <>ALL ( null ) ;
```

The comparison following the AND here returns *unk;* "*true* AND *unk*" returns *unk,* and so supplier S1 does *not* appear in the final result (which is of course correct).

- Now let the range variable SPX take on the value (S2,P1,200), i.e., the "second" row of table SP in Fig. 1. The expression following the <>ALL logically becomes

```
( SELECT DISTINCT SPY.QTY
  FROM    SP SPY
  WHERE   SPY.S# = 'S2'
  AND     SPY.P# = 'P1' )
```

which returns a set containing just the value 200. The outer query thus logically becomes

```
SELECT DISTINCT SPX.S#
FROM    SP SPX
WHERE   SPX.P# = 'P1'           /* true for SPX = (S2,P1,200) */
AND     1000 <>ALL ( 200 ) ;
```

The comparison following the AND returns *true,* and so supplier S2 does indeed appear in the final result, which is correct.

Hence (as claimed earlier), the formulation of the query involving <>ALL is indeed correct. However, suppose now that we transform that formulation into another "equivalent" version, using the pertinent (INVALID!) transformation rule given at the start of this section. We obtain the following formulation:

```
SELECT DISTINCT SPX.S#
FROM    SP SPX
WHERE   SPX.P# = 'P1'
AND     NOT EXISTS
        ( SELECT DISTINCT SPY.*
          FROM    SP SPY
          WHERE   SPY.S# = SPX.S#
          AND     SPY.P# = 'P1'
          AND     NOT ( 1000 <> SPY.QTY ) ) ;
```

And this formulation is readily seen to be equivalent to the version of the query already shown to be incorrect in Section 2 earlier. The example thus illustrates the point that the transformations given in reference [6] and repeated at the beginning of the present section are indeed invalid. My apologies to anyone who may have been led astray by my earlier claims to the contrary.

5. ANOTHER ANOMALY . . .

The discussions of the preceding section have paved the way for an explanation of another anomaly concerning quantification. This one has to do with the fact that, if the user knows that the parenthesized SELECT-expression following an all-or-any comparison operator should return exactly one value, then the ALL or ANY quantifier can be omitted (thus reducing the quantified operator to a simple scalar comparison such as $<$, $>$, etc.). Here is a simple example ("Find supplier numbers for suppliers who are located in the same city as supplier S1"):

```
SELECT DISTINCT SX.S#
FROM    S SX
WHERE   SX.CITY =
        ( SELECT DISTINCT SY.CITY
          FROM    S SY
          WHERE   SY.S# = 'S1' ) ;
```

Here we have abbreviated the more logically correct quantified comparison " $=$ ANY" to just " $=$ ". *Note:* The familiar SQL comparison operator "IN" is just a different spelling for " $=$ ANY".

Now consider the following rather complex query:

"Find supplier numbers for suppliers such that (a) they supply at least one part, and (b) if they supply part P1, they also supply some other part in a quantity greater than the quantity in which they supply part P1."

Suppose the database consists of just one table, namely table SP, with just one row (see Fig. 4).

```
SP   S#   P#   QTY
     --   --   ----
     S2   P2   400
```

Fig. 4 Database for the second contradiction example

Here is one possible SQL representation of the query (admittedly a trifle convoluted):

```
SELECT DISTINCT SPX.S#                           /* query Q1 */
FROM    SP SPX
WHERE   NOT ( SPX.QTY <=ANY
            ( SELECT DISTINCT SPY.QTY
              FROM    SP SPY
              WHERE   SPY.S# = SPX.S#
              AND     SPY.P# = 'P1' ) ) ;
```

("Select supplier numbers from shipments SPX such that it is not the case that the corresponding shipment quantity is less than or equal to some quantity in which the supplier in question supplies part P1"). Let us refer to this formulation as query Q1.

Noticing, however, that there should be at most one shipment for a given (S#,P#) combination, we can see that for a given value of the range variable SPX the nested SELECT-expression should return at most one value. We can therefore apply the SQL rule that allows us to drop the ANY, thus producing the following formulation (query Q2):

```
SELECT DISTINCT SPX.S#                           /* query Q2 */
FROM    SP SPX
WHERE   NOT ( SPX.QTY <=
            ( SELECT DISTINCT SPY.QTY
              FROM    SP SPY
              WHERE   SPY.S# = SPX.S#
              AND     SPY.P# = 'P1' ) ) ;
```

The only syntactic difference between the two versions is that the ANY quantifier of Q1 has been eliminated in Q2. But is there a semantic difference? Consider how Q1 is evaluated, given the sample data of Fig. 4:

- The range variable SPX takes on the value (S2,P2,400). The nested SELECT-expression thus logically becomes

```
            ( SELECT DISTINCT SPY.QTY
              FROM    SP SPY
              WHERE   SPY.S# = 'S2'
              AND     SPY.P# = 'P1' )
```

and evaluates to the empty set. The overall query thus logically becomes

```
SELECT DISTINCT SPX.S#
FROM    SP SPX
WHERE   NOT ( SPX.QTY <=ANY ( ) ) ;
```

(using "( )" to represent the empty set). The expression in the WHERE clause thus becomes "NOT (*false*)" (refer back to the definition of all-or-any comparisons in Section 4), which reduces to *true,* and so the final result does include the supplier number S2. (By the way, this result is correct!—perhaps a little surprisingly.)

Now consider query Q2:

- Once again, the range variable SPX takes on the value (S2,P2,400), and the nested SELECT-expression evaluates to the empty set, as before. The overall query thus logically becomes

```
SELECT DISTINCT SPX.S#
FROM    SP SPX
WHERE   NOT ( SPX.QTY <= ( ) ) ;
```

This time, however, the expression in the WHERE clause becomes "NOT (*unk*)," because SQL defines a "simple comparison" (of which the parenthesized expression following the NOT is an example) to return *unk* if the comparand on the right hand side is the empty set. The overall query thus logically becomes

```
SELECT DISTINCT SPX.S#
FROM    SP SPX
WHERE   unk ;
```

("NOT *unk*" is still *unk*), and so the final result does not include supplier number S2 in this case. Contradiction!

Aside: As an exercise, the reader might like to try using the concept of *logical implication* to come up with a formulation of this query that uses EXISTS instead of ALLs or ANYs. (See, e.g., reference [5] or reference [10] for an explanation of how to use logical implication in the construction of complex SQL queries.) *End of aside.*

6.   . . . AND ANOTHER

Yet another surprise can occur in SQL in connexion with quantification. By way of example, consider the comparison operator "<ANY". Intuitively speaking, if some value x is "less than any" value in some set (meaning, by the way, "less than *some*" value in that set!—there is a trap for the unwary here), then it is "obvious" that x must be less than the *maximum* value in that set. (Analogous remarks can also be made regarding most of the other all-or-any comparisons, of course [10].) And comparing a value with the maximum in some set is often intuitively easier to understand than comparing it with "any" (i.e., some) value in that set. The following "obvious" transformation rule thus suggests itself. (*Warning:* Once again, This rule is *** INVALID ***!)

- The expression

```
x  <ANY  ( SELECT y FROM T WHERE p )
```

is equivalent to the expression

```
x  <  ( SELECT MAX ( y ) FROM T WHERE p )
```

To see the fallacy, consider the following problem:

"Find supplier numbers for suppliers such that (a) they supply at least one part, and (b) it is not the case that they supply some part in a quantity less than that in which they supply some other part."

Here is one possible SQL formulation of the query:

```
SELECT DISTINCT SPX.S#
FROM    SP SPX
WHERE   NOT
        ( SPX.QTY <ANY
                ( SELECT DISTINCT SPY.QTY
                  FROM    SP SPY
                  WHERE   SPY.P# <> SPX.P# ) ) ;
```

And here is another formulation that is at least plausible, a formulation that is derived from the previous one by applying the "obvious" (INVALID!) transformation rule given above:

```
SELECT DISTINCT SPX.S#
FROM    SP SPX
WHERE   NOT
        ( SPX.QTY <
                ( SELECT DISTINCT MAX ( SPY.QTY )
                  FROM    SP SPY
                  WHERE   SPY.P# <> SPX.P# ) ) ;
```

But (surprise, surprise) this second formulation is not correct. Suppose table SP contains just the single row (S1,P1,100), as in Fig. 2 earlier in this paper. When the range variable SPX takes this row as its value, the expression

```
                ( SELECT DISTINCT SPY.QTY
                  FROM    SP SPY
                  WHERE   SPY.P# <> SPX.P# )
```

evaluates to the empty set; the expression

```
                ( SELECT DISTINCT MAX ( SPY.QTY )
                  FROM    SP SPY
                  WHERE   SPY.P# <> SPX.P# )
```

therefore evaluates to null (the MAX of an empty set is defined to be null in SQL); the overall conditional expression in the outermost WHERE clause in the second formulation (the one involving MAX) thus evaluates to *unk,* and hence supplier number S1 does not appear in the final result. Error!

(The first formulation, by contrast, is correct. It is left as an exercise for the reader to confirm that this is so.)

7. CONCLUSION

SQL is not sound. We have demonstrated a number of anomalies in its treatment of quantified operations under three-valued logic; as a consequence of such anomalies, expressions that logically ought to be equivalent can produce different results. Needless to say, this is not just an academic concern—there are definite implications for real-world applications. What is more, it is not easy to place bounds on the scope of the damage that might be caused in those applications. In fact, of course, there *are* no bounds: Medical treatments could be incorrect, bridges could collapse, spacecraft could fall out of the sky, . . .

The point, of course, is not just that *users* are likely to make mistakes—although they certainly are, even if they thoroughly understand three-valued logic (which the majority of users probably do not), because SQL's version of that logic is incorrect. At least as significant is the fact that *implementations* are likely to be incorrect also, because they may very well make internal query transformations that should theoretically be valid but in fact are not. It is virtually certain that some of the implementations currently available in the marketplace are incorrect in this sense. And even if a given implementation is "correct" (whatever "correct" means when the language itself is incorrect), there is still the point that the errors act as *optimization inhibitors,* because the optimizer is prevented from making certain transformations that are theoretically legal and could potentially improve performance.

Note too, incidentally, that users cannot simply avoid the problems by avoiding explicit nulls (i.e., by defining all columns to be NOT NULL or NOT NULL WITH DEFAULT, in SQL terms), because empty sets and nulls can be generated dynamically during query execution. However, it is probably true that avoiding explicit nulls will have the effect of reducing the error potential (though unfortunately not to zero). The only way to avoid the problem entirely—without making major changes to the SQL language—would be simply to eliminate from that language all aspects of its current support for three-valued logic. *Note:* A minor change would be required to the aggregate functions MAX, MIN, SUM, and AVG in order to handle the case of an empty argument set in some different manner than at present, but such a change does not appear to me to be a major hit.

In conclusion, pressure needs to be brought to bear on the SQL standards committees and the vendors to remedy the problems identified in this paper *as soon as possible* (though—as suggested earlier—those problems will not be easy to fix). In the meantime, users are urged to exercise EXTREME CAUTION when dealing with these aspects of the language.

ACKNOWLEDGMENTS

I am grateful to my reviewers Nagraj Alur, Hugh Darwen, Nat Goodman, and Colin White for their numerous helpful comments on earlier drafts of this paper. I am also grateful to Colin for checking out my SQL examples on his ORACLE system.

REFERENCES AND BIBLIOGRAPHY

1. E. F. Codd, "Extending the Database Relational Model to Capture More Meaning," *ACM Transactions on Database Systems* 4, No. 4 (December 1979).

2. E. F. Codd, "Missing Information (Applicable and Inapplicable) in Relational Databases," *ACM SIGMOD Record* 15, No. 4 (December 1986).

3. E. F. Codd, "More Commentary on Missing Information in Relational Databases (Applicable and Inapplicable Information)," *ACM SIGMOD Record* 16, No. 1 (March 1987).

4. E. F. Codd, "Fatal Flaws in SQL," Part I, *Datamation* 34, No. 16 (August 15, 1988); Part II, *Datamation* 34, No. 17 (September 1, 1988).

5. C. J. Date and Colin J. White, *A Guide to DB2,* 3rd edition (Reading, MA: Addison-Wesley, 1989).

6. C. J. Date, "A Critique of the SQL Database Language," in C. J. Date, *Relational Database: Selected Writings* (Reading, MA: Addison-Wesley, 1986). Republished in revised form in C. J. Date, *A Guide to the SQL Standard,* 2nd edition (Reading, MA: Addison-Wesley, 1989).

7. C. J. Date, "Null Values in Database Management," in C. J. Date, *Relational Database: Selected Writings* (Reading, MA: Addison-Wesley, 1986).

8. C. J. Date, "The Outer Join," in C. J. Date, *Relational Database: Selected Writings* (Reading, MA: Addison-Wesley, 1986).

9. C. J. Date, "NOT is Not "Not"! (Notes on Three-Valued Logic and Related Matters)" (in this volume).

10. C. J. Date, "SQL Dos and Don'ts" (in this volume).

11. Andrew Warden, "Into the Unknown" (in this volume).

14

Dates and Times
in IBM SQL:
Some Technical Criticisms

ABSTRACT

IBM has recently added date and time support to its SQL-based products
DB2 and SQL/DS [1,2]. While support for dates and times is generally to be
desired, the fact is that the specific support provided by IBM is exceedingly
complex—unnecessarily (even dangerously) so, in my opinion. Given the
degree of influence that IBM exerts on the database market (and hence,
indirectly, on society at large), this state of affairs is only to be deplored.
The purpose of the present paper is to expose some of the shortcomings
of the IBM approach—to expose them, moreover, to the widest possible
audience, so that (a) users can be warned of the potential pitfalls and can
try to steer clear of them, and (b) steps can be taken to avoid perpctuating
the mistakes of the IBM approach in any future version of the SQL standard.

Originally published (under a slightly different title) in *InfoDB* 3, No. 1 (Spring 1988). Reprinted by permission.

COMMENTS ON REPUBLICATION

The paper that follows is reasonably exhaustive; little further comment seems necessary at this time. One additional question that readers might like to ponder on, however, is the following: What would be involved in implementing some product on top of the SQL dialect described in the paper—say a natural language query product—if that product had to include date and time support that was comprehensible to end-users?

1.   INTRODUCTION

IBM has recently extended its dialect(s) of SQL to support dates and times and has implemented the extensions in DB2 Release 3 [1] and SQL/DS Version 2 Release 1 [2]. As indicated in the Abstract to this paper, it is my opinion that those extensions are far too complicated, and indeed misconceived in many respects. It is true that dates and times do suffer from certain inherent complexities, but the IBM support introduces numerous unnecessary difficulties, over and above the inherent ones—so much so, in fact, that IBM itself has produced at least one document [3] listing a number of "possible misunderstandings" of its support! Of course, "possible misunderstandings" translates into "mistakes easily made by users." And some of those mistakes will lead, not to system diagnostics, but rather to incorrect results and so to wrong business decisions—hence the claim in the Abstract that the IBM support can even be regarded as dangerous.

The aim of the present paper, therefore, is to document and expose some of the problems with the IBM support, in the hope that:

(a) Users can at least be made aware of the potential pitfalls and can take pains to avoid them; and

(b) The various bodies responsible for SQL standardization can take care not to repeat IBM's mistakes in the standard version of the language. (It would be monstrous if, thanks to its dominant position in the marketplace, IBM were to be allowed to foist its ill-conceived ideas on the rest of the community by forcing the standard to follow the same approach.)

Adding support for new data types such as dates and times to an existing language such as SQL is, of course, first and foremost, a problem of language design. Now, there are at least three sets of issues involved in language design, namely semantic, syntactic, and implementation issues [8], and it is generally desirable to keep these three aspects separate to the maximum extent possible. However, this goal of separation has not not been fully achieved in IBM's date/time extensions (in fact, an overall objection to the extensions is that they do not seem to have been formulated in accordance with well-established language design principles at all). The present paper therefore does not divide neatly into three separate discussions of semantic, syntactic, and implementation issues. Instead, it is structured into nine major sections, one on each of the following topics, and some at least of those nine sections include elements of all three aspects (semantics, syntax, implementation):

- Data types
- Literals
- Column definitions
- Conversions
- Durations
- Special registers
- Arithmetic operations
- Assignments
- Comparisons

Three further preliminary remarks:

1. The paper is not intended as a tutorial on IBM's date and time support, though it does necessarily include some tutorial explanation of the basic concepts. A comprehensive tutorial treatment of the material can be found in references [6] (for DB2) and [7] (for SQL/DS).

2. The paper is also not intended as a concrete proposal for a more systematic approach to the problem. Such a proposal can be found in reference [8]. The ISO and ANSI SQL committees are also at work on a proposal that (at least in its present form) is certainly more systematic than IBM's approach [9].

3. Last, a note on terminology: Throughout this paper, we use the term "date/time" to mean "date or time or timestamp" (see the next section for an explanation of these three terms in the present context). For example, the expression "date/time data types" means the three IBM data types DATE, TIME, and TIMESTAMP, considered collectively.

2.   DATA TYPES

(*Note:* This section is largely based on material from reference [8].)

   The first question to ask is: What fundamental data objects do we need? In the real world we are accustomed to regarding past, present, and future as forming a linear continuum, the *timeline*. For brevity, let us agree to refer to each point on the line as a *date,* even though it actually includes a time component (i.e., a date consists of year, month, day, hour, minute, second, etc., components, down to whatever precision is required, say microseconds). In order to provide a way of uniquely identifying individual dates, we choose some specific point on the line as the origin—typically midnight, December 31st, Year One B.C., GMT (this is the origin used by IBM). We can then refer to individual dates in terms of their relative position with respect to that origin.

Of course, facilities must be provided by which users who are not interested in precisions down to the microsecond—e.g., users who wish to deal only with the year/month/day components—can easily ignore the less significant portions of a given date. Facilities must also be provided for the extraction of individual components—in particular, the time components, either separately or en bloc—of a given date. Such aspects are discussed later in this paper.

Next, in order to be able to perform arithmetic on dates, we need the concept of an *interval,* so that we can (for example) add an interval to a date to obtain another date, or subtract two dates to obtain an interval. Intervals thus constitute the second fundamental data object (dates, in the "timeline" sense discussed above, constituting the first).

So the first criticism of the IBM support is that it does not identify the right fundamental data objects! Instead, it provides DATEs (year, month, and day), TIMEs (hour, minute, and second), and TIMESTAMPs (basically a concatenation of a DATE and a TIME, but to microsecond precision). DATEs and TIMESTAMPs are both "timeline" dates, but with different precisions; TIMEs are times of the day, such as "09.30.00" (meaning 9.30 AM). There is no interval data type at all. (*Note:* There are "durations," which are intended to represent intervals, but there is no duration data type per se. See later in this paper for an extensive discussion of this point and some of its consequences.) Hence the following suggested improvements [8]:

1. Collapse all three of DATE, TIME, and TIMESTAMP into a single "date" data type (actually identical to the existing TIMESTAMP), with appropriate mechanisms for ignoring components that are irrelevant in specific situations. *Note:* Compression techniques could be used on the disk if disk space is a concern (i.e., if it is argued that a full TIMESTAMP includes many components that are frequently irrelevant and hence is wasteful of space).

   Note: In fact, the existing TIMESTAMP data type could have been used in the above manner; IBM does provide functions—DATE, TIME, YEAR, HOUR, etc.—for extracting the date, time, year, hour, etc., components of a timestamp. Note in particular that the existing TIME data type could be simulated by a TIMESTAMP in which the year, month, day, and microsecond portions are all ignored. In other words, another criticism of the IBM approach is that it is very redundant.

2. Add an "interval" data type. (It is interesting to note, incidentally, that in a sense intervals are the more fundamental of the two basic objects; a date is really a special case of an interval, representing as it does a specific interval of time relative to the origin. See reference [8] for further discussion and elaboration of this point.)

Aside: It has been suggested that the reason IBM chose the data types DATE, TIME, and TIMESTAMP is that dates, times, and timestamps all appear (as control information) in the existing DB2 catalog. However, times never appear in the catalog without an accompanying date (i.e., the sole purpose of a time is to increase the precision of some date); times therefore do not really qualify as an independent kind of object. As for timestamps, they seem to be merely an internal representation of the combination of a date and a time, and hence do not really qualify as an independent kind of object either. Furthermore, dates, times, and timestamps in the catalog do not use the same internal representation as the DATE, TIME, and TIME-STAMP data types (in fact, they do not even have a *consistent* representation; dates, for example, are sometimes recorded in the form *yymmdd* and sometimes in the form *yyddd*). Basically, dates, times, and timestamps in the catalog are represented as character strings, while the DATE, TIME, and TIMESTAMP data types are represented as unsigned packed decimal integers. See reference [1] for more information. *End of aside.*

3. LITERALS

The second major criticism of the IBM support is that there is no proper support for literals at all! Instead, there are *interpreted character strings.* If a character string value—in particular, a character string literal, but more generally any character string expression—appears in a context that requires a date/time value, then that character string will be interpreted as a date/time value, provided of course that it is of the appropriate format. (A conversion error will occur if the format is incorrect. See below for a discussion of formats.) Here is an example:

```
UPDATE EMP
SET    HIREDATE = '1987-3-31'    /* ISO format -- see below */
WHERE  EMP# = ... ;
```

Let us agree to use the term "date/time string" to refer to a character string that represents a legal date/time value. By "legal" here, we mean that the value is of the appropriate format and is in the range of possible values (for example, it does not represent an impossible date such as "February 29th, 1987"). Several different date/time string formats are supported: United States (US), European (EUR), International Standards Organization (ISO), Japanese Industrial Standard Christian Era (JIS), and installation-defined (LOCAL). A variety of methods (installation options, etc.) are available for specifying the particular style to be used in a particular context. This paper uses ISO style throughout, for simplicity.

A remark in passing: One minor oddity of US time formats is that they do not include an explicit seconds component (an example would be "4:30 PM"). Of course, the internal representation of a time always does include such a component. What happens on conversion to US format if that component is not zero (error? rounding? truncation?) does not seem to be specified.

The fact that there are no proper date/time literals leads (among other things) to a rather complex set of coercion rules (i.e., rules for implicit data type conversion). For example, of the following expressions, the first three are legal but the fourth is not:

```
DATE ('1987-3-31') - DATE ('1987-2-28')
DATE ('1987-3-31') -      ('1987-2-28')
     ('1987-3-31') - DATE ('1987-2-28')
     ('1987-3-31') -      ('1987-2-28')
```

For explanation and more discussion, see the sections on "Conversions" and "Arithmetic Operations" later in this paper.

4. COLUMN DEFINITIONS

The only criticism under this heading is of the unsystematic way in which default values are assigned. (The criticism thus applies at the time of writing only to DB2, since SQL/DS does not currently support default values at all.) The basic point is that default values are not assigned in a consistent manner. If a date/time column is defined WITH DEFAULT, then:

- If the definition appears within a CREATE TABLE statement, then the default value is the value of CURRENT DATE or CURRENT TIME or CURRENT TIMESTAMP, as applicable (see Section 7, "Special Registers," later).

- If, on the other hand, the definition appears within an ALTER TABLE statement, then:

- For rows inserted into the table after the ALTER TABLE is executed, the CURRENT defaults apply (as in the CREATE TABLE case);
- For rows already existing in the table at ALTER TABLE time, however, the defaults are defined as follows:

```
DATE        --  '0001-01-01'

TIME        --  '00.00.00'

TIMESTAMP   --  '0001-01-01-00.00.00.000000'
```

The rationale for the inconsistent treatment is not clear—the reasons do not appear to be *logical* ones, but seem rather to have to do with implementation issues—and the differences are likely to cause difficulty for users.

5. CONVERSIONS

First, explicit conversions. IBM provides a number of scalar builtin functions for performing explicit conversions involving date/time data:

- YEAR, MONTH, DAY, HOUR, MINUTE, SECOND, and MICROSECOND, which extract the relevant portion of a specified date/time value (or duration) and convert it to a binary integer
- DATE, TIME, and TIMESTAMP, which convert a specified scalar value to a date/time value
  - Note, incidentally, that date/times themselves are scalar values. As a consequence, DATE and TIME can be used to "convert" some specified timestamp to a date or a time, i.e., to extract just the date or time portions of the given timestamp.
- CHAR, which converts a specified date/time value to its character string representation in a specified format (US format, European format, etc.)
- DAYS, which converts a specified date/time value to a binary integer, representing an absolute number of days since the origin point

Explicit conversions are generally to be preferred if unpleasant surprises are to be avoided, and the availability of explicit conversion functions is therefore to be welcomed. Nevertheless, I have a number of comments on the specific functions provided:

- (A small point.) Why exactly do YEAR, MONTH, etc., return a *binary* integer—especially as the external representation is a character string and the internal representation is a decimal integer? The likely result is surely to be a lot of additional conversion.

- (A more significant point.) It should be possible to *set* individual date/time components as well as extract them. For example, the following is not legal but should be:

```
UPDATE EMP
SET    MONTH (HIREDATE) = '3'
WHERE  EMP# = ... ;
```

(Though I would prefer something like the following—

```
UPDATE EMP
SET    MONTH (HIREDATE) = MONTH ('3')
WHERE  EMP# = ... ;
```

—for reasons of explicitness, as usual.)

- The "specified scalar value" argument to DATE, TIME, and TIMESTAMP can be a number as well as a date/time string. This fact can lead to some traps for the unwary. For instance:

```
DATE ('1987-3-31')  ===>    a date value representing March 3rd, 1987 (as
                            expected)

DATE ( 1987-3-31 )  ===>    a date value representing the 1,953rd day
                            after December 31st, Year One B.C.
```

Explanation: The argument in the second case is a numeric expression, $1987 - 3 - 31, = 1953$. Surprise!

- Consider the CHAR function reference

```
CHAR ( HIREDATE, EUR )
```

which will return the character string representation of the value of HIREDATE in European format ("EUR"). What kind of object is EUR, linguistically speaking? It is not a character string literal (no quotes), nor is it a database column name, nor is it a host program variable (etc.)—though of course it is a function argument. And note too that it is not possible to specify that argument by means of a variable (or general scalar expression), though of course it ought to be. And is EUR a reserved word?

- IBM has usurped a very general keyword (CHAR) for a very specific function. The user would naturally expect a CHAR function to convert *any* value (not just a date/time value) to its character string representation, just as (e.g.) the INTEGER function converts any (numeric) value to its integer representation.

- IBM provides a DAY duration and a DAYS duration (see later for a discussion of durations), and a DAY function and a DAYS function. It also provides a MONTH duration and a MONTHS duration, and a MONTH function—but it does *not* provide a MONTHS function. Similarly for years, hours, etc.; in fact, DAYS is the only plural duration keyword that does double duty as the name of a function. Symmetry would suggest that the other possibilities should be supported also.

- It should perhaps be mentioned that DAY and DAYS are synonymous when used in the context of durations but are certainly *not* synonymous when considered as function names. Is this good human factors?

- There are no "week" functions—e.g., to return the week of the year, the number of weeks in an interval, the day of the week, etc. Such functions are likely to be needed in practice; consider, for example, what is involved in defining a view to limit some user's access to some portion of the database to weekdays only. (Of course, such functions can always be added later.)

Now let us turn to the implicit conversions (coercions). IBM will perform implicit conversions in certain circumstances, but *not* in all circumstances in which such conversion might reasonably be expected. For example, this statement is legal—

```
SELECT *
FROM    EMP
WHERE   HIREDATE > '1987-01-01' ;
```

—but this one is not:

```
SELECT *
FROM    EMP
WHERE   HIREDATE LIKE '1987%' ;
```

(In the first case, the character string is coerced to a date value. In the second case, the date value is *not* coerced to a character string. The user might be forgiven for finding this state of affairs surprising, since both statements superficially have the same meaning.) Likewise, as mentioned earlier, the expression

```
DATE ('1987-3-31') - '1987-2-28'
```

is legal (the subtrahend—i.e., the second operand—is coerced to a date value), but the expression

```
'1987-3-31'  - '1987-2-28'
```

is not (character strings cannot be subtracted from one another). Note, therefore, that the expression "− string" (where "string" is a character string value) may or may not be legal, depending on context.

Surprises can also occur if the user attempts to use a numeric value to represent a duration and that numeric value is not of *exactly* the required data type, precision, and scale; IBM does not convert the value to the required format, although it might very reasonably be expected to. (Well, sometimes it does [at least in effect]; but in my opinion "sometimes" is worse than "never" in contexts like this. See Section 6, "Durations," below.)

To repeat, therefore: IBM will perform implicit conversions in some situations, but not in all cases in which such conversions might reasonably be expected. Furthermore, it does not seem easy to state exactly what the rules (as to when such conversions are performed) *are*. In fact, given SQL's tremendous lack of orthogonality [4,5], it seems quite likely that the rules as stated have holes in them; one of the problems with lack of orthogonality is precisely that it is very difficult to be sure, when trying to formulate some general rule, that all cases have been properly accounted for. It is certainly hard to discover, in the case of coercion specifically, exactly what the rules are from the IBM manuals.

One final surprise regarding coercion is that, contrary to what might have been expected, there are no implicit conversions between dates and timestamps or between times and timestamps.

6. DURATIONS

As indicated earlier in this paper, IBM does support "durations." A duration represents an interval of time, such as "3 years" or "90 days" or "5 minutes 30 seconds" (these examples are not intended to represent actual SQL syntax). However, there is no duration data type; instead, durations are *interpreted decimal integers*.

- A *date* duration is a signed decimal integer of 8 digits (*yyyymmdd*). Examples:

  ```
  00030000.    (3 years)
  00000090.    (90 days)
  ```

- A *time* duration is a signed decimal integer of 6 digits (*hhmmss*). Examples:

  ```
    000530.    (5 minutes 30 seconds)
  - 000099.    (minus 99 seconds)
  ```

(We include a decimal point in each of the foregoing examples in order to stress the fact that the values are of type DECIMAL, not IN-TEGER.)

The first surprise is that there is no such thing as a "timestamp duration." This omission is due to the following combination of facts:

1. Durations are intended primarily for use in date/time arithmetic;
2. Timestamps are represented as 20-digit decimal numbers with an assumed decimal point six digits from the right;
3. Operands in decimal arithmetic in IBM SQL are restricted to a maximum precision of 15 digits—i.e., IBM SQL cannot do decimal arithmetic on DECIMAL(20,6) operands (!).

(*Note:* Just to confuse matters further, IBM *can* perform certain limited arithmetic operations on timestamps, point 3 above notwithstanding. For example, it can add a date duration to a timestamp. See Section 8, "Arithmetic Operations," later.)

The second surprise is that there *is* such a thing as a "microsecond duration" (though—next surprise—it does not seem to have any official classifying name, and such a duration must be of the labeled variety—see further discussion below). A "microsecond duration" is a signed decimal integer of 6 digits (*nnnnnn*), representing a number of microseconds.

Note that a duration such as "90 days" or "25 hours" is (quite rightly) legal. However, since "duration" is not a data type:

- Nonsensical durations such as "1 month 99 days" are also legal (there is no proper integrity checking on the values that are assigned to a column or variable representing a duration).
- Nonsensical operations (e.g., multiplying two durations) are also legal, though the result will of course not be a duration (wrong precision).
- *Sensible* operations (e.g., adding two durations) can also be performed, but the result will not be a duration, even though it ought to be (wrong precision again).
- There is no such thing as a "duration literal." Instead, decimal literals (of the appropriate format) can be used, as in (e.g.) the expression

```
STARTTIME + 050000.
```

Note that the "duration literal" must be of *exactly* the right format (data type, precision, and scale). Thus the following are all incorrect (for various reasons):

```
STARTTIME +  50000.         /* literal is DECIMAL(5)   */

STARTTIME + 050000          /* literal is INTEGER      */

STARTTIME + 050000.00       /* literal is DECIMAL(8,2) */
```

Note: In certain very limited contexts, "labeled durations"—see below—can also play the role of "duration literals" (though this is not the only use for labeled durations).

Labeled Durations

A labeled duration is a special kind of scalar expression, whose value is a decimal integer that is to be interpreted as a duration (date or time or "microsecond"). Labeled durations take the form "n units", where "n" is any numeric expression (it is converted to a decimal integer if necessary), and "units" is one of the following:

```
YEAR[S]
MONTH[S]
DAY[S]
HOUR[S]
MINUTE[S]
SECOND[S]
MICROSECOND[S]
```

For example, the expressions "3 YEARS," "90 DAYS," "1 MINUTE," and "47 MICROSECONDS" are all labeled durations.

Some comments:

- "Labeled duration" is the DB2 term; the SQL/DS term is "simple duration." The reason for the discrepancy is not clear. "Simple duration" is actually a very bad term—the concept is actually very complicated, as will shortly become all too clear.

- Note that date durations in general involve years *and* months *and* days, but *labeled* date durations involve years *or* months *or* days (not a mixture). Similarly, time durations in general involve hours *and* minutes *and* seconds, but labeled time durations involve hours *or* minutes *or* seconds, not a mixture.

- In fact, "labeled date duration" is not an official IBM term at all; neither is "labeled time duration." Instead, IBM classifies durations differently, into date, time, and labeled durations; a labeled duration is not the same thing as either a date duration or a time duration. This classification seems perverse, however (and is certainly liable to cause confusion), since a labeled duration clearly does represent a date or time duration in the ordinary English sense. In this paper I will take the term "date duration" to include labeled date durations, and the term "time duration" to include labeled time durations.

- In (e.g.) the expression

```
3 MONTHS
```

   what kind of object is MONTHS, linguistically speaking? It might perhaps be argued that it is a precision (of a kind), but there is no data type for it to be a precision *of;* it cannot be *declared* as the precision of some database column or variable, it can only be introduced "on the fly," as it were, in the context of a date/time expression.

- (A VERY MAJOR FLAW, which incidentally is not obvious from the IBM manuals, at least in the case of DB2.) The *only* context in which a labeled duration can appear is in an expression involving infix " + " or " − ", in which one operand is the labeled duration in question and the other is a date/time value. (See Section 8, "Arithmetic Operations," later, for further discussion of this point.) Thus, for example, the following statement is legal:

```
SELECT  *
FROM    TRIPS
WHERE   ARRIVAL > DEPARTURE + 5 HOURS ;
```

   However, both of the following (intuitively reasonable) statements are illegal:

```
SELECT  *
FROM    TRIPS
WHERE   TRIPTIME > 5 HOURS ;

UPDATE TRIPS
SET     TRIPTIME = 5 HOURS
WHERE   TRIP# = ... ;
```

   What makes the situation even odder is that these two illegal statements can both be made legal by replacing the expression "5 HOURS" by the logically equivalent expression "5 HOURS + TIME ('00.00.00')" in each case:

```
SELECT  *
FROM    TRIPS
WHERE   TRIPTIME > 5 HOURS + TIME ('00.00.00') ;

UPDATE TRIPS
SET     TRIPTIME = 5 HOURS + TIME ('00.00.00')
WHERE   TRIP# = ... ;
```

7. SPECIAL REGISTERS

IBM supports a number of date/time "special registers," namely CURRENT DATE, CURRENT TIME, CURRENT TIMESTAMP, and CURRENT TIMEZONE. A reference to one of these registers returns the current date, time, timestamp, or timezone, as applicable. *Note:* The current timezone is a time duration, established by means of an installation parameter. The value returned by CURRENT DATE, CURRENT TIME, and CURRENT TIMESTAMP is based on a reading of the CPU clock, incremented in each case by the value of CURRENT TIMEZONE. In the case of Pacific Standard Time, for example, if the CPU clock is set to GMT and CURRENT TIMEZONE to "−8 hours," then CURRENT DATE, CURRENT TIME, and CURRENT TIMESTAMP would each return the true local value. If, on the other hand, the CPU clock is in fact set to the true local value, then CURRENT TIMEZONE should probably be set to zero.

Some comments:

- "Special register" is the DB2 term (it is based on conventional COBOL usage); the SQL/DS term is "keyword pair." The reason for the discrepancy is not clear. In any case, "zero-argument builtin scalar function" would be a more accurate term, though admittedly not so succinct.

- In normal circumstances it is illegal to add a time duration to a date. References to CURRENT DATE "bend" this rule, however, in that (as stated above) they return a value that is taken from the CPU clock but incremented by the value of CURRENT TIMEZONE. Just one more exception to a general rule that the user has to understand.

- Care will be needed in dealing with these special registers in the context of a distributed system.

8. ARITHMETIC OPERATIONS

The infix arithmetic operators " + " and " − " (only) can be used with date/times (i.e., in two-operand expressions in which at least one of the operands is a date/time value). For example, a date and a date duration can be added to yield another date. However, not all operations that would appear to make sense are in fact supported. Here is a complete list (extracted from references [6,7]) of the legal possibilities:

First operand	Operator	Second operand	Result
date	+	date duration	date
date duration	+	date	date
date	−	date	date duration
date	−	date duration	date
time	+	time duration	time
time duration	+	time	time
time	−	time	time duration
time	−	time duration	time
timestamp	+	duration	timestamp
duration	+	timestamp	timestamp
timestamp	−	duration	timestamp

Some comments:

- Note that it is not legal to add or subtract a time duration to or from a date, even though such an operation might reasonably be argued to make sense (e.g., "March 5th, 1988, plus 48 hours").

- Nor is it legal to subtract one timestamp from another. Again it might reasonably be argued that such an operation does make sense, and should yield a timestamp duration, but (as explained earlier) there is no such thing as a timestamp duration.

- The table lists all cases in which one operand is a date/time value. Operations such as the addition or subtraction (or even the multiplication or division) of two durations are also possible, though (again as explained earlier) the result will not be another duration.

- Note also that (once again as explained earlier) *labeled* durations are subject to an additional—and very major—constraint, namely as follows: They are permitted ONLY as operands of infix " + " or " − ", and ONLY if the other operand is a date/time value—NOT another duration (labeled or otherwise).

Here are some examples. Note that some of these examples are not legal; it is left as an exercise for the reader to determine why not. *Note:* STARTDATE is of type DATE; STARTTIME is of type TIME; WAITTIME is of type DECIMAL(6,0).

```
DATE ('1972-8-17') - DATE ('1969-10-28')
DATE ('1972-8-17') -      '1969-10-28'
     '1972-8-17'  - DATE ('1969-10-28')
     '1972-8-17'  -      '1969-10-28'        *** ILLEGAL ***
```

```
STARTDATE +   1 YEAR    +   6 MONTHS
1 YEAR    +   STARTDATE +   6 MONTHS
1 YEAR    +   6 MONTHS  +   STARTDATE              *** ILLEGAL ***
              1 YEAR    +   6 MONTHS               *** ILLEGAL ***
( STARTDATE +   1 YEAR ) +   6 MONTHS
STARTDATE +  ( 1 YEAR   +   6 MONTHS )            *** ILLEGAL ***
STARTDATE +    6 WEEKS                             *** ILLEGAL ***
STARTDATE +    4 HOURS                             *** ILLEGAL ***

STARTTIME + WAITTIME
STARTTIME + HOUR ( WAITTIME ) HOUR
STARTTIME + 120000                                *** ILLEGAL ***
STARTTIME + 120000.
TIME ('09.00.00')  + 120000.
       '09.00.00'  + 120000.                       *** ILLEGAL ***
       '09.00.00'  + 12 HOURS                       *** ILLEGAL ***
        9 HOURS    + 120000.                       *** ILLEGAL ***

CURRENT TIMESTAMP + 1 SECOND + 500000 MICROSECONDS
CURRENT TIME - CURRENT TIMEZONE
STARTTIME - ( CURRENT TIME - CURRENT TIMEZONE )
```

Date/time arithmetic is performed in accordance with the calendar and permissible date/time values. As a result, all kinds of surprises are possible. For instance:

```
DATE ('1987-3-31')  + 1 MONTH  + 1 MONTH   ===>   '1987-5-30'

DATE ('1987-3-31')  + 2 MONTHS             ===>   '1987-5-31'
```

And:

```
DATE ('1987-3-31')  + 1 MONTH  - 1 MONTH   ===>   '1987-3-30'

DATE ('1987-3-31')  + 2 MONTHS - 2 MONTHS  ===>   '1987-3-31'
```

The real problem with examples such as these is that date/time arithmetic uses the same *syntax* as ordinary arithmetic (i.e., it uses the same syntactic operators " + " and " − "), but it has different *semantics*.

Finally, a couple of miscellaneous oddities:

- To retrieve (e.g.) the current time, the user must execute (e.g.) the statement

```
SELECT CURRENT TIME
FROM    EMP ;
```

The actual table nominated in the FROM clause is arbitrary, of course (although presumably it must exist), but the syntax of SQL *requires* a FROM clause to be present. Note too that (a) it is probably a good idea to specify DISTINCT ("SELECT DISTINCT CURRENT TIME . . ."), for otherwise the SELECT will return *n* copies of the current time, where *n* is the number of rows in table EMP; (b) if table EMP happens to be empty (i.e., if *n* is zero), the SELECT will not return the current time at all but will instead return a null.

- If STARTTIME (data type TIME) and WAITTIME (a time duration) have the values "09.00.00" and 250000 (25 hours), respectively, then the expression

```
STARTTIME + WAITTIME
```

evaluates to "10.00.00"; the overflow in the hours position is ignored.

9. ASSIGNMENTS

Under this heading I simply repeat a couple of points made earlier. First, regarding date/time assignments: It should be possible to set individual date/time components as well as extract them (i.e., it should be possible to assign *to* them as well as *from* them); see Section 5, "Conversions" earlier. Second, regarding duration assignments: If DUR is a DECIMAL(6,0) column in the database and DUR1 and DUR2 are two time durations (not labeled), then which of the following are legal (in the context of an UPDATE statement)?

```
 1.  SET DUR = DUR1

 2.  SET DUR = 5 MINUTES

 3.  SET DUR = DUR1 - DUR2

 4.  SET DUR = 5 MINUTES - 1 MINUTE

 5.  SET DUR = DUR1 - 000100.

 6.  SET DUR = 5 MINUTES - 000100.

 7.  SET DUR = 000500

 8.  SET DUR = DUR1 - 1 MINUTE

 9.  SET DUR = 000500. - 000100.

10.  SET DUR = 5 MINUTES - 1

11.  SET DUR = 4
```

(*Answer:* The odd-numbered ones are legal, the even-numbered ones are illegal. I do not think the rules are particularly easy to remember.)

10. COMPARISONS

Did you know that 99 is greater than 100? Let T be a time and DUR99 and DUR100 time durations (not labeled), with values 99 and 100 respectively. Then:

```
DUR99       <   DUR100
```

(of course), but

```
DUR99 + T  >  DUR100 + T
```

(surprise!).

Next, let T1 and T2 be two times. Then the comparison

```
T1        > T2 + 1
```

is illegal, but the logically equivalent comparison

```
T1 - T2 >       1
```

is legal! Conversely, the comparison

```
T1       > T2 + 1 SECOND
```

is legal, but the logically equivalent comparison

```
T1 - T2 >       1 SECOND
```

is illegal. (Are we having fun yet?)

Next point: Note that equal durations does not necessarily mean equal *intervals*. For example:

```
DATE ('1987-3-1') - DATE ('1987-2-1')  ===>  100  [28 days]

DATE ('1987-4-1') - DATE ('1987-3-1')  ===>  100  [31 days]
```

It follows that, if FEB_1ST, MAR_1ST, and APR_1ST are each of data type DATE and have the obvious values (for some nonleap year, say 1987), then the comparison

```
( APR_1ST - MAR_1ST ) = ( MAR_1ST - FEB_1ST )

  [ i.e., 31 days ]        [ i.e., 28 days ]
```

evaluates to *true*! And note also that, whereas the following WHERE clause

```
WHERE  D1 - D2 = D3 - D4
```

(where D1, D2, D3, and D4 are dates) is syntactically legal, the following (logically equivalent?) one is not:

```
WHERE  D1 + D4 = D3 + D2
```

Note: If the observation made near the beginning of this paper is accepted—the observation, that is, that dates are really intervals—then adding two dates ought to be permitted, and should yield another date. For more discussion, see reference [8].

Another surprise regarding comparisons: The values "00.00.00" and "24.00.00" are both legal times—in fact, they both represent the same time, namely midnight—but they are not considered to be equal. This state of affairs is reminiscent of those early computer systems in which -0 and $+0$ were considered to be different.

11. SUMMARY AND CONCLUSION

The examples and discussions of this paper should serve to substantiate the claim made earlier that IBM's date and time support complicates the SQL interface enormously (and unduly). The fact that IBM itself considered it worth producing a document consisting mainly of "possible misconceptions" regarding its date/time support [3] seems to me a major indictment. In my opinion, in fact, the date/time support now constitutes one of the worst aspects of an already unsatisfactory language [4,5]—one that is liable to cause major practical difficulties in numerous areas: teaching, learning, understanding, remembering, debugging, etc.

Of course, it cannot be denied that there is a certain kind of mind that positively delights in "taking advantage"—perhaps I should say "taking *dis*advantage"—of anomalies such as the fact that, in certain circumstances, 99 is greater than 100. Here I will only remark that:

(a) Exploiting such anomalies leads to programs and databases that are a nightmare to maintain; and

(b) Once the vendor has implemented an interface in which (for example) 99 is greater than 100, it is committed to maintaining that interface, with all its anomalies, "for ever."

This is why it is so important to get languages right first time—because whatever is implemented first remains *the* language, warts and all, "for ever." And this is why IBM, with its current date/time support, has done us all a major disservice.

To summarize, therefore:

■ IBM's date/time support complicates the SQL language enormously (and unduly).

■ It does not provide all required function (it does not even support the right basic data objects and it does not provide all needed operators for the objects it does support).

■ It is rather redundant.

■ It is extremely unorthogonal and highly context-sensitive.

■ There are objects with no data type.

■ There are objects with no literal format.

- There are arithmetic operators that violate fundamental laws of arithmetic.

- There are comparison operators that violate fundamental laws of well-ordering.

- There are numerous miscellaneous anomalies and oddities.

Of course, it is tempting to point out that all of this is in accordance with well-established SQL tradition. But it is not the aim of this paper to indulge in criticisms of the SQL language per se; rather, the aim is to address the area of date and time support specifically. And in that connexion I have two major concerns:

1. I am concerned that if the existing date and time support can be taken as any indication, then before it has finished IBM will eventually have made DB2 (and SQL/DS) just as complicated as IMS ever was.

2. I am concerned that, because of its dominance in the marketplace, IBM will be allowed to foist its mistakes—in particular, its mistakes in the area of date and time support—on to the community at large, by influencing the direction taken by the SQL standard and by other vendors.

ACKNOWLEDGMENTS

I am grateful for comments on an earlier draft of this paper from my friends and colleagues Nagraj Alur, Ted Codd, Hugh Darwen, Sharon Weinberg, and Colin White.

REFERENCES AND BIBLIOGRAPHY

1. IBM Corporation, IBM DATABASE 2 SQL Reference, Release 3.0. IBM Document No. SC26-4346-3 (1987).

2. IBM Corporation, SQL/DS Application Programming for VM/SP, Version 2 Release 1. IBM Document No. SH09-8019 (1987).

3. IBM Corporation, "Looking Forward to SQL/DS Version 2.1." Slides from presentation by Dave Simpson, IBM Technical Support, Basingstoke, UK (December 1987).

4. C. J. Date, "A Critique of the SQL Database Language," in C. J. Date, *Relational Database: Selected Writings* (Reading, MA: Addison-Wesley, 1986). Republished in revised form in C. J. Date, *A Guide to the SQL Standard,* 2nd edition (Reading, MA: Addison-Wesley, 1989).

5. C. J. Date, "What's Wrong with SQL?" (in this volume).

6. C. J. Date and Colin J. White, *A Guide to DB2,* 3rd edition (Reading, MA: Addison-Wesley, 1989).

7. C. J. Date and Colin J. White, *A Guide to SQL/DS* (Reading, MA: Addison-Wesley, 1988).

8. C. J. Date, "Defining Data Types in a Database Language" (in this volume).

9. ISO/IEC JTC1/SC21/WG3 / ANSI X3H2, ISO-ANSI (working draft) Database Language SQL2. Document ISO DBL CPH-2b / ANSI X3H2-88-210 (April 1988).

15

SQL Dos and Don'ts

ABSTRACT

SQL-based systems are really beginning to take off. Nobody today can afford *not* to install such a system. The benefits have been widely touted—productivity, portability, connectivity, maintainability, etc., etc. But we live in an imperfect world: SQL really does not do a very good job of realizing the full potential of relational technology—it suffers from sins of both omission and commission—and moreover all SQLs are not created equal, a fact that has serious implications for the portability and connectivity objectives referred to above. So what should users do? This paper offers some practical advice on how to use SQL to avoid some of the potential pitfalls and to realize the maximum possible benefits.

COMMENTS ON PUBLICATION

This paper was originally prepared as the basis for a live presentation. This fact accounts for the informal tone and the slight marketing flavor—as evidenced by remarks such as "Nobody can afford not to install a SQL system." ("Nobody" here must be understood to mean "Nobody from the

---

Previously unpublished.

universe of potential DBMS purchasers," of course.) Despite the occasional shrill note, however, I do believe that the paper has a lot of sound advice to offer; hence its inclusion in this book.

1.   INTRODUCTION

In some respects this paper can be regarded as an experiment that failed. As the Abstract suggests, SQL-based DBMSs are now being installed at an ever-increasing rate; however, SQL is very far from being the perfect relational language, and moreover different SQL implementations vary widely in their capabilities. The idea behind the paper, therefore, was to attempt to provide some "recipes for success"—i.e., a set of recommendations that would enable users to avoid some of the known SQL pitfalls, to meet the widely advertised SQL objectives (especially the portability and connectivity objectives), and generally to achieve the maximum possible benefits from their use of the SQL language.

Now, when I first set out to pull the various recommendations together, I was optimistic that it would be possible to define a subset of SQL—a kind of "SQL kernel"—that would provide all of the necessary functionality and would be supported by all of the major implementations, and hence could safely be used as a basis for achieving the desired objectives of productivity, portability, connectivity, and all the rest. But I soon came to realize that matters were more complicated than I had previously thought.

- One problem was that different implementations varied more widely than I had realized hitherto. For example, no two of IBM's SQL-based DBMSs (DB2, SQL/DS, the OS/2 Extended Edition Database Manager, and the OS/400 Database Manager) support exactly the same SQL dialect, none of them supports exactly the official standard [1], and none of them even supports exactly IBM's own "Systems Application Architecture" (SAA) standard [22,23,24]. And the discrepancies between IBM and nonIBM implementations are typically just as extensive, if not even more so; see, e.g., reference [4], which contains a number of discussions of SQL differences between IBM's two mainframe products (DB2 and SQL/DS) and Oracle Corporation's ORACLE.

- Another problem was that, in attempting to define the desired "SQL kernel," I found that there were very few SQL features that could be eliminated entirely, owing mainly to the fact that the language is so very unorthogonal (i.e., independent concepts and constructs are mixed together in SQL in confusing ways). For example, consider the use of joins and subqueries in view definitions. There is no view that can be defined by means of the "IN subquery" construct that cannot be defined by means of a join, whereas there certainly *are* views that can be defined via joins and not via "IN subquery." However, "IN subquery" cannot (yet) be eliminated from the language, because a view in SQL that is defined using "IN subquery" might be updatable where the logically identical view defined using a join is not. (Of course, the rules of SQL are clearly at fault here, but the fact remains that this is the way the language is currently defined, at least in those implementations I am currently aware of.)

Despite the foregoing, however, I believe the recommendations that follow can still be useful, though they are perhaps not quite the "recipes for success" I had originally hoped they would be. They are offered from the perspective of one who is familiar with relational database theory (both the "what" and the "why"), with formal computer languages in general (to some extent), and with the SQL language in particular (both the official standard version and certain implemented dialects, in particular those of DB2 and SQL/DS).

Note: By and large the recommendations apply to the use of the SQL language no matter what the dialect, though certain suggestions (suitably identified) refer specifically to the official standard dialect and others to the IBM dialect as implemented in SQL/DS and/or DB2. My reason for occasionally concentrating on the IBM dialects, of course, is that the IBM products—especially DB2—do represent the de facto standard in the marketplace (even though there are some products that provide more SQL functionality than the IBM products do). The primary emphasis throughout is on SQL as used in application programs (i.e., embedded SQL); however, some of the recommendations apply to stored SQL queries and procedures also, and some apply to ad hoc, interactive queries as well.

2. ADVANTAGES AND BENEFITS

Let me begin by identifying some of the advantages that are usually claimed to accrue from the use of SQL-based systems. I assume that most of the advantages mentioned are generally accepted and do not require much additional discussion here. It is the thesis of this paper that users will stand a better chance of realizing those advantages if they abide by the recommendations that follow in subsequent sections.

First, there is a general objective of *compatibility*, meaning "conformance to [some] standard" (either the official SQL standard or the de facto "standard" that is the DB2 SQL dialect). Under that general heading we can identify the following subsidiary objectives, among others:

- Connectivity
- Portability
- Investment protection

The connectivity and portability objectives, in particular, are likely to become increasingly important in the years ahead as distributed database systems become increasingly widespread (I believe we are just beginning to see the tip of the distributed database iceberg at this time).

A second general objective is *productivity*. Under that heading we can identify the following:

- Clarity
- Maintainability
- Predictability
- Correctness
- Data independence

As indicated above, the recommendations that follow are intended to help users to realize all of the foregoing potential benefits.

3.   GENERAL RECOMMENDATIONS

This section is concerned with a few general principles or overall recommendations that set the tone for the detailed recommendations of the next three sections. Before getting into those general principles, however, a few preliminary remarks are in order:

- Generally speaking, the recommendations should be treated as guidelines, not unbreakable laws. There may well be occasions on which it is acceptable, or even essential, to violate some recommendation or other. There are bound to be situations that require a judgment call. The only point to be made in this connexion is (of course): "If you *must* break one of the guidelines, please be certain you know what you're doing."

- It is entirely possible that different recommendations may be in conflict on occasion. In such a case, you will find yourself in the situation of the previous paragraph—you will have to make a judgment call.

- Some people may find some of the recommendations a little unpalatable!—see, e.g., the comments immediately below regarding relational calculus. Palatable or otherwise, however, they should be taken in the spirit in which they are offered, which is one of the utmost sincerity.

Here then are the overall recommendations.

- *Adhere to relational principles*

If you are involved in any way with a relational DBMS, *you owe it to yourself to know the underlying theory* (i.e., the relational model). The theory is not difficult, but it *is* fundamental. Furthermore, it is not arbitrary; *every last detail of the theory has definite practical significance.* Users (and vendors and implementers) ignore that theory at their peril.* Thus, you should become familiar with relational principles, and you should adhere to those principles in your database and application systems. As a simple but fundamental example, you should ensure that every base table has a primary key (see Sections 4 and 5 below for further discussion of this particular point).

To elaborate on this first recommendation a little further: Relational theory can be regarded as an invaluable *mind tool;* it provides a precise notation for articulating problems and a precise way of thinking about how to solve those problems. In particular, *relational calculus* provides a systematic formalism—a much more systematic formalism than SQL, incidentally—in which (for example) queries, view definitions, and integrity constraints can all be formally and succinctly expressed. Thus, *users should have at least a basic familiarity with relational calculus.*†

Now, I am well aware that many people will react to this particular recommendation with some skepticism, or even horror; relational calculus has the reputation of being difficult and obscure and beyond the comprehension of ordinary mortals (and probably of no importance anyway, except to a few mathematicians). The truth is, however, that relational calculus is not really difficult at all. It does tend to use a rather esoteric set of symbols, like the "backwards E" (which means "there exists") and the "upside down A" (which means "for all")—but the *concepts* involved are not all that unfamiliar, and they are quite easy to understand, and they are very fundamental. It is quite possible to learn the notation of relational calculus and to become fairly adept at reading and writing relational calcu-

---

*It is my belief that many of the shortcomings of SQL products today can be traced back to a lack of theoretical knowledge on the part of the vendors and implementers of those products. It is certainly common, even today, to hear people decry theory—even people who really should know better. Such an attitude is particularly hard to understand in the database field, given the fact that relational DBMSs would not even exist if it were not for the original theoretical work done by Codd (and others) in the 1970s.

†I refer here to a version of the relational calculus that is extended beyond the one originally defined by Codd [6] to include (at least) simple scalar computational operators such as "+" and "−" and simple aggregate functions such as SUM and AVG.

lus expressions in a fairly short time, with practice. (Practice is important, of course.)

A thorough tutorial on the original relational model (including the relational calculus, both tuple and domain versions, and including also many examples, exercises, and answers) can be found in my book *An Introduction to Database Systems: Volume I* [9]. A discussion that includes a description of many recent extensions to the model can be found in Codd's book *The Relational Model for Database Management* [8].

- *Be explicit*

Another way of stating this recommendation is: *There should be no hidden assumptions.* As a general rule, it is always a good principle to state all syntax options explicitly, rather than relying on system defaults. For one thing, omitting information is poor documentation practice; for another, of course, there is always the possibility that the system default is not what you thought it was. For example, do you know what the default delete rule is in a foreign key specification in DB2? The answer is RESTRICT [15]; however, it is much clearer to state ON DELETE RESTRICT explicitly, if RESTRICT is what you want, rather than to obtain that option by default. (Even if you do know what the default is, the person reading your documentation might not.)

> *Note:* Actually, the recommendation to be explicit can be regarded just as one aspect of the more general recommendation, well known in programming circles, to *code defensively.*

An exception to the foregoing rule *might* possibly be made in the case where the default is "universally" understood. For example, the syntax of the SQL SELECT statement begins:

```
SELECT [ ALL | DISTINCT ] ...
```

However, "everybody knows" in this context that if neither ALL nor DISTINCT is specified explicitly, then ALL is deemed to have been specified implicitly; in other words, ALL is the default. Thus it *might* be acceptable to specify the ALL option implicitly in the context of a SELECT statement.* Even here, however, there is an argument in favor of being explicit, and that is that in a different (but analogous) SQL context—namely, in the context of UNION—ALL is *not* the default; UNION in SQL always eliminates duplicates unless ALL is stated explicitly.

---

*Except that we will recommmend subsequently in this paper (in Section 6) that the ALL option on a SELECT statement should never be specified anyway.

Aside: We are touching on another problem here, as follows. As the reader is probably aware, SQL unfortunately does not allow "DISTINCT"—as the alternative to ALL—to be stated explicitly *at all* in the context of UNION. It is a sad comment on the design of the SQL language that several options can be specified only by saying nothing explicit at all. For example, there is no direct way in SQL to specify that a given column has "nulls allowed"—such an option can be specified only by *not* saying NOT NULL for the column in question. This fact makes it very awkward even to talk about such a column ("a column that is not NOT NULL"?). The situation is even worse with DB2 and its system-defined default values; there, in order to talk about such a column, it is necessary to indulge in circumlocutions such as "a column that is not NOT NULL, with or without WITH DEFAULT." (What is more, it is impossible in DB2 for a column both to have a default value defined and to have nulls allowed. But this is an example of a different problem entirely, namely the problem of lack of orthogonality.)

Other options that cannot be explicitly stated in SQL (at least, not in standard SQL, though some products do provide system-specific extensions in some of these areas) include the following:

- "NONUNIQUE" (as part of a column or index specification)
- "ON UPDATE RESTRICT" (as part of a foreign key specification)
- "FOR FETCH" and "FOR DELETE" (on a cursor declaration)
- "ORDER BY SYSTEM" (on a cursor declaration, meaning that the order of rows is system-determined)
- "WITHOUT CHECK OPTION" (on a view definition)
- "WITHOUT GRANT OPTION" (on a GRANT statement)
- "START TRANSACTION" (COMMIT WORK is really "END TRANSACTION"; "START TRANSACTION" occurs implicitly when a recoverable action—e.g., an UPDATE operation—is performed and there is no transaction currently in progress)
- "WHERE *true*" (default WHERE clause). Actually, this last omission touches on yet another problem, which is that the expression in a WHERE clause (or HAVING clause) is of course a *truth-valued* expression, and as such returns a value of a data type that SQL does not explicitly support. Since there is no "truth value" data type, there is obviously no way to write a literal of that data type (which is what *true* is).

End of aside.

- *Use system facilities*

If the DBMS does provide support for some particular function, you should generally use that support, rather than attempting to implement the function yourself. As an example, don't hand code a join—get the system to do the join instead, by specifying it as part of an appropriate cursor declaration. As another example, don't write your own procedural code to enforce referential integrity—use the system declarative facilities instead (assuming, of course, that the system does provide such facilities).

The reasons for this recommendation are fairly obvious: Productivity, migratability, and performance will (or should) all be better if the system does the work; furthermore, the system will (or should) ensure that the implementation is *correct*—or, more precisely, if errors do occur, at least you will have someone to blame! *Note:* In the case of referential integrity specifically, if you decide to implement the function yourself via your own procedural code, then you should be aware that ensuring correctness is a very nontrivial task. See reference [5] for some idea of the complexities involved.

Of course, an exception to the foregoing guideline might be made if the system facilities are really bad; consider, for example, the system support for . . . . . in the product . . . . . (readers are invited to fill in the blanks for themselves).

- *Be careful with system-specific features*

Every DBMS supports its own dialect of SQL, and every SQL dialect includes its own extensions or features that are specific to the DBMS in question. Thus, it is virtually impossible to create an application that avoids the use of such system-specific features entirely, even though of course each such use does run counter to several of the objectives and recommendations already identified earlier in this paper. But before you decide to use a given system-specific extension, you should ask yourself the following questions:

1. First of all, *is* it an extension? To answer this question requires that you know the base SQL dialect that is (potentially) being extended—i.e., the official SQL standard, or the DB2 SQL dialect, or whatever other base dialect you are interested in being compatible with.

2. If it is an extension, then is it well thought out? For example, is it compatible with the proposed extensions to the standard known as "SQL2" [3]? (Not that such compatibility is necessarily a guarantee of "goodness," of course.) More important, does it adhere to relational principles? There are several examples of extensions in commercial SQL products today that very clearly violate this latter requirement. For example, there is at least one product in which certain queries generate a table in which the ordering of the rows carries meaning. Such a table

is not a relation, of course, and hence the product in question is clearly violating the relational closure principle.*

3. Do you really need to use the system-specific feature, or is there another way to achieve the desired function while staying within the base SQL dialect? For example, some systems support an explicit INTERSECT operator, and INTERSECT is not currently supported by either DB2 or the SQL standard—but the function of INTERSECT can be achieved equally well by means of either the EXISTS function or a join.

4. If you really must use the system-specific feature, then is it possible to isolate your use of that feature by placing it in its own separate subroutine or module? Such isolation will make it easier to replace the code at some future time, should such replacement ever become necessary or desirable.

- *Conform to the official standard*

Other things being equal, it is clearly desirable to conform to the official standard to the maximum extent possible. In this connexion, however, there are a number of points of which the reader needs to be aware:

1. First, the official standard per se is extremely weak; as I have mentioned elsewhere [22], it has been characterized, perhaps a little unkindly, as "the intersection of existing implementations." As a consequence (and as already indicated above), the objective of conforming to the standard is probably not achievable at the 100 percent level; applications will almost certainly have to stray outside the boundaries of the standard in particular areas.

2. Furthermore, the standard also includes numerous aspects (for example, character collating sequence, numeric expression precision, error return codes) that are explicitly stated to be "implementation-defined." As a consequence, two implementations could both legitimately claim to conform to the standard and yet be incompatible. (It is probably worth making yourself familiar with a list of those portions of the standard that are implementation-defined. Such a list—unfortunately for SQL2 rather than for the existing standard per se—is included in reference [3].)

3. The standard also includes certain *un*defined aspects!—both explicitly undefined aspects and implicitly undefined ones (of course, the latter are probably oversights). For example, if cursor C is in the "before"

---

*The fact that almost all known SQL-based DBMSs permit tables to contain duplicate rows is another major violation of relational principles, of course [18].

state (i.e., positioned "before" some given row) and a new row is inserted at that position, the effect on cursor C is explicitly undefined. Likewise, if table T is a view, the effect of performing a retrieval on T is *im*plicitly undefined (!). As a consequence, again, two implementations could both be conforming and yet still be incompatible. Again, reference [3] includes an appropriate list (for SQL2 rather than the existing standard, however).

4. As a result of the foregoing points, plus others already made earlier in this paper, it is probably true to say at the time of writing (early 1989) that no implementation actually supports exactly the official SQL standard, and furthermore that no two implementations support exactly the same SQL dialect. For example, even the various IBM implementations—DB2, SQL/DS, the OS/2 Extended Edition Database Manager, and the OS/400 Database Manager—are very far from being completely compatible with one another, as was already mentioned in Section 1 of this paper. As a result, all claims at this time by vendors to "support the SQL standard" or to be "compatible with IBM"—or worse, both!—should be regarded with EXTREME SKEPTICISM.

- *Worry about performance afterwards*

In the past, raw performance has all too often been *the* primary objective in database installations. All other considerations have been made subordinate to this overriding concern; such matters as understandability, stability, maintainability, portability, etc., have been sacrificed to the objective of squeezing the last ounce of performance out of the system. And raw performance is still the driving force in many installations, even today.

I would like to propose a different point of view. Performance is important, of course—a system that fails to perform satisfactorily is not an acceptable system—but I do not think performance should be treated as *the* one and only objective that outweighs all others. There is no point in going through complex machinations on a system that is handling 25 transactions per second to get a 10 percent improvement, or even a 100 percent improvement, if the installation only needs 20 transactions per second anyway. Thus, I would like to make the following concrete recommendations:

1. Get your logical design right first (both your database design and your application design), without even thinking about performance implications. Don't waste time up front on performance matters (e.g., in trying to decide which SQL formulation of a given query is the best performer). *Don't* corrupt your abstract logical design for performance reasons. Quite apart from anything else, such corruptions make most applications harder to write (this is a logical consideration, by the way, not a performance consideration!).

2. If you subsequently run into performance problems, then (and only then) is the time to react to them and to start tuning your design. Once again, "design" here means both your application design and your database design, in general, though any performance "fixes" should be limited to your application, if at all possible; it is still desirable not to have to corrupt the logical design of the database. (Tuning the physical design is acceptable, of course.)

Note: People sometimes claim that it *is* acceptable to change the logical database design if you know *exactly* the application(s) you are going to run on that database. My response to this argument is that I would agree with it, *if* you knew all the applications you are ever going to run—but you never do.

3. If you do find that you have to change your application design or logical database design (or both) for performance reasons, then:

(a) Try to minimize the degree to which you have to back off from the original clean abstract design.

(b) Document each and every departure from that clean design, so that you can later back the changes out again when some future release of the system makes them unnecessary.

(c) Where possible, make your "fixes" in such a manner that it is still the system that is doing the work, not the user. For example, suppose you need to search the employees table looking for all employees with salary greater than $20,000, and you want the search to be done by a sequential scan, not by means of the SALARY index (because you know that almost every employee's salary is greater than $20,000, and sequential scan is more efficient). Then there are two things you can do:

- Retrieve *all* employee rows and do the salary test yourself by program logic

- Let the system do the search, but write the WHERE clause in a form that will force it not to use the SALARY index (in DB2, for example, the formulation "WHERE SALARY + 0 > 20000" will have the desired effect, at least at the time of writing)

The second approach is obviously preferable (because it entails less work on the part of the user).

4. As an important specific instance of the recommendations of paragraph 3 above, try to resist temptations to "denormalize" your database (i.e., to depart from a fully normalized design, in which all tables are in the ultimate normal form). In other words, denormalize only if all else fails.

It is worth mentioning that one of the original objectives of the relational model was precisely to free users from having to worry about performance matters (the whole idea was to let the system do it). Most users do not have the time or the knowledge or the skills or the inclination to get involved in performance issues.

In the light of the foregoing, most of the rest of this paper will have little or nothing to say on performance matters—except in a few cases where the performance argument in fact serves to support and strengthen a recommendation that is being made for other reasons anyway.

4.   DATABASE DESIGN RECOMMENDATIONS

The overall purpose of this paper is to discuss SQL guidelines, not database design per se, so in this section I will content myself with simply stating a few design principles that are directly relevant to that overall purpose. (Note, however, that the boundary between database design and database definition is not entirely clearcut, so that some of the points that follow do have very immediate implications for SQL per se.) For further discussion and justification of the design principles summarized below, the reader is referred to reference [13].

- First, a general recommendation: Find a systematic design methodology—one that is not constrained by current implementation restrictions—and use it systematically. (One such methodology is described in reference [13].) Also, use a systematic approach for dealing with missing features in the target system (i.e., any such implementation restrictions).

  - For example, if the target system is DB2, do not allow yourself to be constrained at design time by the fact that DB2 does not currently support a CASCADE update rule on a foreign key specification [15,16]. When you reach the stage of implementing your design, of course, you will have to write your own procedural code to provide the missing function, but that code should be written in as generic a manner as possible and should probably be contained within its own separate module.

- Document all domains. For each domain, specify at least a name, an underlying data type (e.g., INTEGER), and any relevant domain level integrity constraints (e.g., upper and lower bounds on domain values [19]). For each column in each table (base table or view), identify the applicable underlying domain. In the case of views, note that these recommendations apply to "virtual" columns also (i.e., columns that are derived from something other than a simple column of the underlying table—for example, a column defined by means of an operational expression such as SALARY + COMMISSION).

- Ensure that every base table has exactly one primary key. *Note:* Enforcing this constraint will automatically enforce the constraint that no base table is ever allowed to contain any duplicate rows. We will discuss this latter point further in Section 6.

- Ensure that every view also has a primary key—i.e., ensure that the view definition is such as to prohibit duplicate rows—and document that primary key (it's part of the semantics of the view, after all).

- Likewise, document all alternate keys, in both base tables and views. (An alternate key is a candidate key that is not the primary key. Alternate keys can sometimes be more important than they might appear at first sight [17].)

- Document all foreign keys. Specify the nulls rule (nulls allowed or not allowed), the delete rule, and the update rule for each foreign key. Ensure that each foreign key references a primary key, not an alternate key. Ensure that each foreign key references exactly one target table.

  - In regard to this last recommendation, note that some people feel that it is acceptable, and even desirable, to permit a given foreign key to reference multiple target tables. My reasons for disagreeing with this position are explained in detail in reference [16], but in essence boil down to the following: A (perceived) need for multiple target tables usually means a bad database design—the designer has not identified the proper entities—and such designs lead to excessive complexity for the user.

    Note: An additional, pragmatic, reason in favor of this recommendation (quite apart from the philosophical reasons given in reference [16]) is simply that most DBMSs today provide little or no support for multiple target tables. Normally, of course, you should not allow such considerations to influence your design, but the point does seem worth mentioning in this particular context.

- For every composite primary key in your design, think very hard about whether you might not want to introduce another, noncomposite "surrogate" key in its place [7,13,16]. (If you do introduce such a surrogate key, of course, the original primary key will then become an alternate key.) If you decide to retain any composite primary keys, then:

  - Note first that a foreign key will be composite if and only if the primary key it refers to is composite also [16]; in other words, composite primary keys will frequently give rise to corresponding composite foreign keys.

- Generally, *treat composite keys*—both primary and foreign keys—*as if they were noncomposite* (except possibly for retrieval purposes). In particular:

  (a) Do not allow composite keys to overlap;

  (b) Do not allow composite foreign key values to be partly but not wholly null.

(See reference [16] for further explanation of these recommendations and for arguments in favor of them.) Incidentally, the second of these recommendations provides a reason (once again a rather pragmatic reason) for avoiding nulls in the first place (see the next paragraph below), namely as follows: If a given composite foreign key FK has nulls allowed, few DBMSs if any will provide any assistance to the user in ensuring that individual FK *values* are never partly but not wholly null—in other words, you will have to enforce this particular constraint yourself with your own procedural code. If you decide to avoid nulls entirely, on the other hand, then this problem will obviously not arise.

- Think very hard about whether you want to allow nulls to appear in your database at all. There are certainly very good reasons to prohibit them [12,20,21]. Of course, if you decide to avoid nulls entirely, then some of the previous recommendations become irrelevant, a fact that in itself can be regarded as an argument in favor of avoiding nulls in the first place.

- If you do decide to avoid nulls, you will presumably have to adopt some kind of "default value" scheme for dealing with missing information [12,21]. Some systems provide support for system-defined defaults, such as zero for a numeric column; others allow users to define their own defaults. User-defined defaults are to be preferred. Indeed, a user-defined default facility (albeit one that is less than fully satisfactory) is in the process of being added to the SQL standard [2].

- If you decide not to avoid nulls, then you should at least make yourself thoroughly familiar with the way they behave in SQL, for otherwise you may very easily misinterpret the answers you obtain from your database. The trouble is, making yourself familiar with the way nulls behave is not an easy task; SQL is so ad hoc in this area that it is hard to know when you have finished (finished learning, that is). In other words, no matter how well you think you know the subject, fresh surprises are always possible (as I know only too well, to my own cost).

- Document all known integrity constraints to which the database is subject (over and above the constraints already documented in the form of domain and key specifications as discussed above). Relational calculus is recommended as an appropriate formalism for this task (refer back to the discussion of this topic in the previous section; see also reference [19]).

- I will close the present section by repeating the overall design recommendation from Section 3 (because it is so important): Do not allow the purity of your clean logical design to be corrupted for physical performance reasons. In particular, resist temptations to "denormalize."

5.   DATA DEFINITION RECOMMENDATIONS

Now (at last) we are ready to turn to some specific SQL recommendations. This section is concerned with data definition and the next with data manipulation. Regarding data definition, the first point (of course) is that the database design recommendations discussed in the previous section have a number of obvious general consequences for SQL data definitions. The following recommendations are more specific, however, and are independent (for the most part) of the decisions that were made during the design process per se.

- *Domains*

By definition, the values that can legally appear in any given column are precisely the values in the applicable domain. This constraint needs to be enforced somehow. A few systems do provide support for such constraints, but most do not; in particular, the existing SQL standard does not include the domain concept at all. So what is to be done?

In the special case where the values in the domain can easily be enumerated, the system's foreign key support (if any) can be used to help in the task of enforcing the applicable constraint on relevant columns. For example, suppose in the usual suppliers-and-parts database [9] that the only legal city names are London, Paris, Athens, and Rome. Then the following code would serve to enforce the corresponding constraint for supplier cities in DB2:

```
CREATE TABLE CITIES                          /* pseudo domain */
     ( CITY   CHAR(15) NOT NULL,
       PRIMARY KEY ( CITY ) ) ;

CREATE UNIQUE INDEX XC ON CITIES ( CITY ) ;

INSERT INTO CITIES ( CITY ) VALUES ('London') ;
INSERT INTO CITIES ( CITY ) VALUES ('Paris') ;
INSERT INTO CITIES ( CITY ) VALUES ('Athens') ;
INSERT INTO CITIES ( CITY ) VALUES ('Rome') ;
```

```
CREATE TABLE S
     ( ... ,
       CITY CHAR(15),
       ... ,
       FOREIGN KEY SCFK ( CITY ) REFERENCES CITIES
                                 ON DELETE RESTRICT ) ;
```

Note, incidentally, that if the above technique is used to enforce a domain constraint for a column that happens to be a primary key, then any foreign keys that reference that primary key will a fortiori have their own domain constraints enforced automatically—assuming, of course, that the corresponding foreign key constraints are themselves enforced!

> *Aside:* The foregoing notwithstanding, please note carefully that a domain is *not* the same thing as a table of one column, and a domain constraint is *not* the same thing as a referential constraint. Indeed, I was somewhat uneasy about the idea of including the example in this paper in the first place, given that people do frequently confuse these matters; I do not want to be accused of compounding the confusion. I hope that readers will understand that the technique illustrated is merely a trick that might be useful in DB2 and systems like it, nothing more. *End of aside.*

In most cases, however, enforcing domain constraints will probably not be so easy. If the values in the domain cannot be easily enumerated, or if the system does not provide any foreign key support, then the constraints will probably have to be enforced by means of special-purpose procedural code.

> *Note:* The SQL standard is in the process of being extended to include a simple declarative facility (the CHECK clause [2]) that—among other things—will permit the enforcement of certain additional domain constraints without the need for any procedural code, and without the need for the foreign key trick illustrated above.* Such a facility is indeed already supported by several commercially available DBMSs, though not by DB2 or SQL/DS (at the time of writing).

- *Columns*

There are a number of specific recommendations that apply to column declarations. Numbers 2 and 5 are repeated from reference [13].

1. Name *all* columns explicitly, even in views—i.e., include an explicit list of column names in every CREATE VIEW statement, even if those names

---

*It would be more accurate to say that the CHECK clause permits the enforcement of *column* constraints [19], not domain constraints. However, column constraints can be used (with discipline) as a means of enforcing domain constraints.

are the ones that will "obviously" be inherited from the columns of the underlying table or tables. (Of course, columns in base tables *must* be named explicitly.)

2. Whenever possible, give each column the same name as the underlying domain (for clarity and for many other reasons). When it is not possible—which can be the case only if the same domain is used more than once within the same table, as in, e.g., a bill-of-materials structure—then give the column the name of the domain prefixed by some distinguishing qualifier to make it unique within its containing table. Thus, for example, use SNO or S_SNO or SP_SNO (etc.) as names of columns containing supplier numbers; do *not* use (e.g.) SNO in one table and SNUM in another and SNUMBER in a third (etc.).

> *Note 1:*   One reason for this recommendation is simply ease of recognition—users can tell at a glance when two columns are defined on the same domain and when not. Such a naming discipline also makes it possible to interrogate the system catalog regarding domains, even though the system probably does not support domains per se.

> *Note 2:*   It might perhaps be better in practice to give the domain name first (i.e., to distinguish uses of the same domain within the same table via suffixes rather than prefixes). This technique has the potential advantage that it might make it easier to group all uses of the same domain together when generating reports from the system catalog.

> *Note 3:*   One specific consequence of following this naming convention is that primary keys and matching foreign keys will usually have the same name. Since (a) the SQL standards committees are currently proposing support (in SQL2) for a name-based natural join [3]—which is a good idea, by the way—and (b) primary-to-foreign-key joins are a very common requirement in practice, there is the potential here for a significant reduction in source code (and other benefits also—see reference [25]).

> *Note 4:*   Observe that I did not give "S#" as a possible name for a supplier number column, even though I have used that name in most prior publications in which the suppliers-and-parts database appears (see, e.g., reference [9]). The reason is that "#" is not a valid character in an identifier in the SQL standard, and so should probably be avoided in such contexts in practice. In this paper, however, I will break this particular rule myself, in order to be consistent with my other publications.

3. If you decide that you want to avoid the use of nulls (see the previous section), you will have to specify NOT NULL explicitly for every (base table) column. Note, however, that NOT NULL (without WITH DEFAULT)

is not allowed for columns that are added to an existing base table via ALTER TABLE (on the other hand, NOT NULL WITH DEFAULT *is* allowed [in DB2]). More important, note that specifying NOT NULL (with or without WITH DEFAULT) for every column of every base table is *necessary but not sufficient* to achieve the overall objective of eliminating nulls entirely. See the further discussion of this topic in Section 6 below.

4. Regardless of your decision regarding the use of nulls in general, specify NOT NULL (probably without WITH DEFAULT) explicitly:

(a) For every (base table) column that participates in a primary key;

(b) For every (base table) column that participates in a foreign key, if and only if "nulls not allowed" was specified for that foreign key at design time.

5. When you reach the point at which it becomes necessary to specify the individual builtin (system-defined) data types for each column, specify those data types at the domain level and then follow a discipline by which each column inherits its data type from the corresponding domain. In this way you can guarantee that most run-time column comparisons—and therefore most joins, unions, etc.—will not involve the overhead of data type conversion. (Most DBMSs do permit such conversions, but it is obviously desirable to avoid them for performance reasons.)

6. *Data types:* One of our overall recommendations in Section 3 was "Use system facilities." However, another was "Be careful with system-specific features." Data types provide an example of where these two recommendations are likely to be in conflict. It is an unfortunate fact that almost all data types are somewhat system-specific, with the exception of fixed length character strings—and even in this latter case there are problems to do with character codes and collating sequences.

Here are some specific points to watch out for:

(a) The implementation of floating-point numbers tends to vary from system to system. Thus, just because two systems both support the SQL data type FLOAT, it does not necessarily mean that floating-point numbers are identical on those two systems.

(b) Different systems have different ways of handling varying length strings. For example, the comparison rules for VARCHAR are different in DB2 and SQL/DS.

(c) Several systems support "long strings," but those strings are typically subject to numerous restrictions (for example, it might not be possible to compare one long string with another). It might be better to represent what would otherwise be a long string of (say) 500 characters as two "short strings" of 250 characters each.

(d) Use the *right* data type (other things being equal). For example, consider the case of employee numbers (EMP#), which we suppose for the sake of the example to be five decimal digits. Now, employee numbers are not really *numbers*—we are not going to do any arithmetic on them—and so the specification (say) DECIMAL(5) is not really appropriate. On the other hand, CHAR(5) is not quite right either, because each character has only ten possible values, not 256. The "right" specification would be PICTURE 99999, but unfortunately most DBMSs today do not support a PICTURE data type. Given that PICTURE is not available, I would probably vote for CHAR(5). The argument that DECIMAL(5) takes less space on the disk would *not* persuade me to vote for it!—though other arguments might.

(e) Some systems support an uninterpreted byte string data type: DB2 and SQL/DS, for example, allow "FOR BIT DATA" to be specified as a qualifier on the various character string data types—CHAR, VARCHAR, etc.—and "FOR BIT DATA" really means that the data type is byte string. Byte strings should be used sparingly, however (quite apart from anything else, they are likely to violate our earlier recommendation to be explicit). In particular, byte strings should *not* be used as a means of subverting the system by (e.g.) hiding repeating groups in them (such a trick would violate both the recommendation to be explicit and the recommendation to adhere to relational principles).

7. *Dates and times:* Following on from the recommendations of paragraph 6 above, let us consider the specific case of dates and times. Dates and times are obviously very important in practice; unfortunately, no date and time support is included in the current SQL standard, even though it *is* included in most SQL products on the market today. The trouble is, the support is different in just about every product (indeed, the differences tend to be quite major). The IBM implementations in particular are not only different from all the rest (and from the current SQL2 proposals [3]), they are—in this writer's opinion—EXTREMELY BAD [14]. Thus, dates and times represent an area where you should at least *proceed with caution*. You may decide not to use the system facilities at all. If you do decide to use those facilities, then:

(a) At least be aware that you *are* using system-specific features, with all of the compatibility (etc.) problems implied by that fact;

(b) Consider limiting your use to the less esoteric aspects of those features. In the case of the IBM implementations, for example, consider doing all date arithmetic in terms of days only, in order to avoid some of the anomalies associated with (e.g.) adding and subtracting months [14].

- *Base tables*

As stated in Section 3, every base table should have exactly one primary key. Ideally, of course, the system will provide direct support for the primary key concept. Even if it does not, however, you should still enforce the primary key discipline for yourself (e.g., by maintaining a UNIQUE index on the column(s) that constitute the primary key and by specifying NOT NULL for the column(s) in question). No base table should ever be allowed to contain duplicate rows [18].

Some base tables might additionally have one or more alternate keys. You will almost certainly have to enforce any applicable alternate key constraints for yourself.

Note: The general rule regarding alternate keys is that they may or may not have nulls allowed. For a given alternate key (AK, say), if nulls are not allowed, then values of AK must be unique; if nulls are allowed, however, then *nonnull* values of AK must be unique, but any number of instances of AK may be null. Note, therefore, that UNIQUE indexes in SQL are not adequate for enforcing alternate key constraints (in general), because UNIQUE indexes permit *at most one* null—i.e., they support the constraint "unique, with at most one null," whereas what is required is the constraint "unique unless null." (Of course, this point will be irrelevant if you decide to avoid nulls entirely anyway.)

Many base tables will also contain one or more foreign keys. Ideally, of course, the system will provide the necessary support for enforcing foreign key constraints. If it does not, or if the support is deficient in some way, you will have to do at least some of the work yourself. References [5] and [13] give some idea of what is involved in "doing the work yourself," in the absence of appropriate support from the DBMS.

One last point regarding base tables: Some people feel that users should never operate directly on base tables anyway, but instead should always access the database through views (see the next subsection below). In other words, for every base table B, there should be a view V that is isomorphic to that base table, and users should operate in terms of V, not B. (Indeed, there is at least one product, namely Cincom's SUPRA, that explicitly enforces such a discipline.) From a conceptual standpoint, there is some merit to this position; at least it keeps the conceptual boundaries of the system clean and well-defined. From a more pragmatic standpoint, however, there may or may not be a genuine *operational* advantage, depending on the facilities available in the DBMS in question. In DB2, for example, there is no way to rename a column in a base table without dropping and recreating (and hence dumping and reloading) that table; however, for a user who accesses that base table via a view, the effect of a "column rename" operation can be achieved much less painfully by dropping and recreating the view.

- *Views*

The view mechanism in SQL is (unfortunately) extremely ad hoc at the present time—so much so, in fact, that its usefulness is very severely curtailed. Consider first the question of view updating (where by "updating," of course, we mean INSERT and/or UPDATE and/or DELETE operations). There are a number of considerations that apply specifically to views that you intend to be updatable:

1. First, you should ensure that each such view is updatable both from a theoretical standpoint (see paragraph 3 below) *and* in the system that you are actually using. (Some DBMSs actually do permit updates on views that are theoretically not updatable! For example, if T is a base table, a view that is defined as a projection of T but does not retain the primary key of T is not theoretically updatable at all [10]; however, under certain circumstances—details beyond the scope of this paper—DB2 will allow updates to be applied to such a view.)

2. Different DBMSs have different rules regarding which views they consider to be updatable. The rules in DB2 and the rules in the standard are different. (It is probably true that any view that is updatable in the standard is updatable in DB2, but the converse is certainly not. Also, the standard, like DB2, does permit updates on some views that ought not to be updatable at all.)

3. You should be aware of which views are theoretically updatable, at least in broad terms. Loosely speaking, if T is an updatable table, then the following views of T are theoretically updatable [10]:

   - Any restriction of T
   - A projection of T, if and only if it preserves the primary key of T
   - A natural join of T with some other table S, taken over the primary key of T and a matching foreign key in S, if and only if S is also updatable

(The foregoing is not intended to be an exhaustive list.) It goes without saying that no SQL system on the market today actually does permit updates on all views that are theoretically updatable—vendor claims to the contrary notwithstanding.

4. You may also decide to specify the "check option" (WITH CHECK OPTION) on certain updatable views, in order to enforce the constraint that INSERTs and UPDATEs on that view do not introduce any rows that fail to satisfy the view-defining condition. If you do, however, there are a number of additional points of which you need to be aware:

   - Not all systems support the check option (for example, SQL/DS does not).

- Even if the system in question does support it, it might not apply to all updatable views (in DB2, for example, it cannot be specified if the view definition includes a subquery).

- Since the definition of "updatable view" is different in DB2 and in the SQL standard, the check option might be (in fact, is) legal on some views in DB2 but not in the standard.

- If V is a view for which the check option is specified and W is a view defined on top of V, then the check option on V may or may not apply to updates performed via W also, depending on the system in question.

5.   One annoying aspect of the view updatability problem is that SQL suffers from a stupid limitation that a view whose definition involves DISTINCT cannot be updated, even if that DISTINCT is logically redundant and does not actually cause any duplicate elimination to occur. Thus, it is not possible to specify DISTINCT explicitly (in accordance with our recommendation from Section 3 to be explicit) and still have the view in question be updatable.

6.   Another annoying aspect is that it is possible to construct two view definitions that are semantically identical, and yet SQL will consider one of the two views to be updatable and the other not. One well-known example (mentioned in Section 1 of this paper) occurs when the two view definitions involve a join and a subquery respectively (see, e.g., reference [23]). Another would probably occur when one involves a UNION and the other involves OR. (I say "probably" here, because of course UNION is regrettably not allowed in a view definition at all in SQL at the time of writing. However, I venture to predict—on the basis of the way "cursor updatability" is defined in SQL today—that when it is allowed, a view whose definition includes a UNION will be defined to be nonupdatable in SQL, regardless of the semantics of the view in question.)

It can be seen that (as indicated earlier) the whole area of view updating is a mess in SQL at the present time. In fact, view *retrieval* is somewhat of a mess too! It is perhaps not as widely known as it ought to be that even retrieval operations sometimes fail on views in surprising ways (see, e.g., references [23] and [24]). What is more, different systems differ in this area also [23,24]. In particular, the rules in DB2 and the rules in the standard are different (though it is probably true that any retrieval that works in the standard will work in DB2).

In sum, the entire SQL view mechanism is disgracefully ad hoc at the present time. Cleaning it up is a problem that needs to be addressed with some urgency.

6. DATA MANIPULATION RECOMMENDATIONS

In this, the longest section of the paper, we turn to some recommendations that apply to the use of SQL data manipulation operations.

- *Adhere to relational principles*

This general recommendation from Section 3 has some specific aspects that apply to data manipulation operations in particular.

1. *Avoid duplicate rows.* Even if (as recommended earlier) every base table has a primary key, so that base tables never contain duplicate rows, it is still possible (in SQL) for duplicate rows to appear in *derived* tables (e.g., views or query results). For very good reasons (see reference [18]), the relational model does not recognize *any* table that permits duplicate rows as a "proper relational table," and so we need to avoid duplicate rows in derived tables also. *But users should not have to waste time and effort in trying to decide whether a given SQL expression can generate duplicate rows, or whether eliminating or not eliminating such duplicate rows can affect performance.* All such matters should be left to the DBMS. (In principle, performance matters should *always* be left to the DBMS, as explained in Section 3.)

Unfortunately, SQL was originally designed on the assumption that tables *can* have duplicate rows. It is therefore usually necessary to specify explicitly that duplicates *not* be retained (well, at least this is true for SELECT, though not for UNION). In order to save the user from having to waste time even thinking about the problem, therefore, I would like to recommend that duplicate elimination *always* be requested, and then leave it to the DBMS to figure out under what circumstances such a request either is a no-operation or can safely be ignored (a challenge for the optimizer, perhaps, though not I think a very difficult one). In other words:

- *Always* specify DISTINCT with SELECT, even in subqueries ("but be annoyed about it" [26])
- *Never* specify ALL with UNION.*

---

*The argument for specifying ALL on UNION is not really that users wish to retain duplicate rows in the output; rather, it is that they know that there are no duplicate rows in the input (the UNION is "disjoint"). In other words, it is a performance argument. If the system is really incapable of discovering such "disjointness" for itself, then I would argue that what is needed is a new *declarative* facility—actually part of a general declarative integrity facility [19]—whereby it could be specified as part of the database definition that the tables in question are in fact disjoint.

Some additional comments on these recommendations are in order, however.

- First, SQL suffers from numerous additional restrictions that mean that it is not always feasible to specify DISTINCT as suggested above. For example, as we have already seen, a view definition that includes DISTINCT will not permit updates. The same is true of cursor declarations. There are also various rules regarding the number of times that DISTINCT can appear within a certain syntactic scope—for example, "SELECT DISTINCT COUNT (DISTINCT . . .) . . ." is illegal. Be annoyed about all of these, too.

- Second, note that the recommendation "always specify DISTINCT" does not apply to the argument to aggregate functions such as SUM and AVG. The argument to such functions is *not* a set but a collection of values that in some cases can legitimately contain duplicates (consider, e.g., a request for "average salary"—two distinct employees may very well have the same salary). In such a context, either ALL or DISTINCT may legitimately be specified, depending on what the user wants. Whichever it is, of course, it should be stated explicitly!

2. *Use relational calculus.* Relational calculus includes certain very useful concepts—specifically, the concepts of *universal quantification* (FORALL) and *logical implication* (IF . . . THEN . . .)—that SQL does not directly support. As a consequence, many queries—certainly any queries that are a little more complex than the usual bread-and-butter examples given in vendor manuals—are frequently most easily expressed in SQL by formulating them in relational calculus first and then converting that formulation, more or less mechanically, into its SQL equivalent.

There are two logical transformation rules that the user needs to understand in order to be able to apply this technique, which we now explain. Let x be a range variable and let p and q be logical expressions, such as X > Y. (See later in this section for an explanation and further discussion of range variables.) Then:

(a) The expression

```
FORALL x ( p )
```

can be replaced by the expression

```
NOT EXISTS x ( NOT ( p ) )
```

For example, the statement "For all persons x, it is the case that x is mortal" is equivalent to the statement "There does not exist a person x such that x is not mortal."

(b) The expression

```
IF p THEN q
```

can be replaced by the expression

```
NOT ( p ) OR ( q )
```

For example, the statement "If it is raining, then the streets are getting wet" is equivalent to the statement "Either it is not raining or the streets are getting wet (or both)."

Example: The following rather complex query (based on the usual suppliers-and-parts database) is taken from references [23] and [24]: "Find supplier names for suppliers who supply at least all those parts supplied by supplier S2." We begin with a pidgin calculus formulation:

```
SX.SNAME WHERE FORALL PX ( IF   S2 supplies PX
                           THEN SX supplies PX )
```

("names of suppliers SX such that, for all parts PX, if supplier S2 supplies part PX, then supplier SX supplies part PX also"). SX and PX here are range variables ranging over the suppliers and parts tables S and P, respectively.

The first thing to do is to tighten up the expressions "S2 supplies PX" and "SX supplies PX":

```
SX.SNAME WHERE FORALL PX
               ( IF    EXISTS SPX ( SPX.S# = 'S2'
                                    AND
                                    SPX.P# = PX.P# )
                 THEN EXISTS SPY ( SPY.S# = SX.S#
                                    AND
                                    SPY.P# = PX.P# ) )
```

(SPX and SPY here are range variables, both of which range over the shipments table SP.) Applying the two transformation rules given above, we obtain the following expression:

```
SX.SNAME WHERE NOT EXISTS PX ( NOT
               ( NOT ( EXISTS SPX ( SPX.S# = 'S2'
                                    AND
                                    SPX.P# = PX.P# ) )
                 OR   ( EXISTS SPY ( SPY.S# = SX.S#
                                    AND
                                    SPY.P# = PX.P# ) ) ) )
```

Now the expression involves only operators such as NOT and EXISTS that SQL does directly support. It can therefore be converted into SQL form:

```
SELECT DISTINCT SX.SNAME
FROM    S SX
WHERE   NOT EXISTS
      ( SELECT DISTINCT PX.*
        FROM    P PX
        WHERE   NOT
              ( NOT  ( EXISTS
                     ( SELECT DISTINCT SPX.*
                       FROM    SP SPX
                       WHERE   SPX.S# = 'S2'
                       AND     SPX.P# = PX.P# ) )
                OR   ( EXISTS
                     ( SELECT DISTINCT SPY.*
                       FROM    SP SPY
                       WHERE   SPY.S# = SX.S#
                       AND     SPY.P# = PX.P# ) ) ) ) ;
```

Note that an expression such as (e.g.) "EXISTS PX" in the calculus formulation becomes "EXISTS (SELECT DISTINCT PX.* FROM P PX)" in the SQL version.

Finally, we can simplify the SQL version slightly:

```
SELECT DISTINCT SX.SNAME
FROM    S SX
WHERE   NOT EXISTS
      ( SELECT DISTINCT PX.*
        FROM    P PX
        WHERE   EXISTS
              ( SELECT DISTINCT SPX.*
                FROM    SP SPX
                WHERE   SPX.S# = 'S2'
                AND     SPX.P# = PX.P# )
        AND     NOT EXISTS
              ( SELECT DISTINCT SPY.*
                FROM    SP SPY
                WHERE   SPY.S# = SX.S#
                AND     SPY.P# = PX.P# ) ) ;
```

("names of suppliers SX such that there does not exist a part PX such that (a) there exists a shipment SPX saying that supplier S2 supplies part PX but (b) there does *not* exist a shipment SPY saying that supplier SX supplies part PX also"). In this final simplification step, we have made use of the well known fact that the expression

```
NOT ( p OR q )
```

can be replaced by the expression

```
NOT ( p ) AND NOT ( q )
```

Two NOTs cancel out in the simplified form—i.e., the expression NOT (NOT(EXISTS(. . .))) becomes simply EXISTS(. . .). We have also eliminated some obviously redundant parentheses.

End of example.

The foregoing discussion gives some idea of how the concepts of relational calculus can be useful in the formulation of certain rather complex queries in SQL. The contention is that expressing such queries in SQL directly, without going through the relational calculus step first, is a rather difficult thing to do. Furthermore, the resulting SQL expression is frequently not all that easy to understand directly; however, we *know* it is correct, because of the systematic manner in which we have derived it.

For further discussion of the foregoing technique, see reference [23].

Note: There is unfortunately one fly in the ointment, however, which really ought to be mentioned before we leave this topic. The problem is that EXISTS in SQL is not a truly faithful implementation of the existential quantifier of relational calculus [20]. Specifically, EXISTS in SQL can return the wrong answer if the evaluation of the subquery that represents the EXISTS argument either

(a) produces a set that includes a null, or

(b) involves the elimination of a candidate value from that set because the condition in the applicable WHERE or HAVING clause evaluates, not to *true* or *false* but to *unk* ("unknown"), for that candidate value.

This fact can be seen as yet another argument in favor of avoiding nulls entirely, of course. If nulls are avoided, EXISTS in SQL will work correctly—I think—and the foregoing technique can be applied with impunity (logical impunity, at any rate!—performance may be another matter).

- *Redundancy*

SQL is a highly redundant language—that is, it often provides several different ways of formulating the same query. Now, it is hard to understand why this should be so, given that the redundancy in question helps neither the user nor the implementer (nor even the language definer); however, the fact remains that it *is* so. Thus, it would be nice (as suggested in Section 1 of this paper) to be able to identify a "SQL kernel," i.e., a set of *canonical forms* for SQL queries—in other words, a proper subset of all possible SQL queries, with the property that every SQL query is semantically identical to exactly one query in that subset (the *canonical representation* of the query under consideration). If such a kernel could be identified, then users could simply ignore all aspects of SQL lying outside that kernel.

Unfortunately, trying to identify such a kernel is a somewhat hopeless task (as was also mentioned in Section 1). The fact is, the SQL language was not designed in a particularly systematic manner. As a consequence, it seems to be the case that, although most queries can be expressed in numerous different ways, it is always possible to find *some* particular query that can be expressed only in one particular way, and just about every construct in the language appears to be needed to express *some* particular query. Instead of identifying the desired SQL kernel, therefore, the best that seems to be possible is to offer a few general guidelines (an open-ended list), as follows:

1. Don't use the "IN subquery" construct when EXISTS or a join can be used to achieve the same effect.

There is no query, loosely speaking, that can be formulated using "IN subquery" that cannot be formulated using EXISTS or a join instead, whereas there very definitely are queries that can be formulated using EXISTS or a join that cannot be formulated using "IN subquery." What is more, in some systems at least, the "IN subquery" construct is a significant optimization inhibitor. Personally, I would like to eliminate subqueries from the language entirely; unfortunately, it is not yet possible to remove them totally, owing to such things as SQL's rules regarding which views are updatable. See Section 5 of this paper.

2. Don't use the quantified comparisons ">ALL," "<ANY," etc., when EXISTS or a join can be used to achieve the same effect.

The rationale for this particular recommendation is essentially the same as that given for the recommendation above to avoid the "IN subquery" construct. There is also the point that all-or-any comparisons are error-prone. See the next subsection ("Avoid all-or-any comparisons") for further discussion.

3. Don't use the quantified comparisons ">ALL," "<ANY," etc., when simple comparisons together with MAX or MIN can be used to achieve the same effect.

Again, see the next subsection for further discussion.

4. Don't use COUNT where EXISTS would be more logically correct.

For example, don't say "The number of suppliers who supply part P2 is greater than zero" when what you mean is "There exists a supplier who supplies part P2." The first formulation suggests that the system must first count the relevant suppliers—which could take a long time, if there are a million of them. The second allows the system to stop searching as soon as it finds just one. Thus, quite apart from anything else, there is a strong possibility that the COUNT version will not perform as well as the EXISTS version.

Note: As the example suggests, the temptation to use COUNT instead of EXISTS arises from the fact that, loosely speaking, EXISTS returns *true* if and only if the COUNT is nonzero [20]. Programmers (as opposed to end users)—especially unreconstructed CODASYL, IMS, etc. programmers—tend to be especially prone to this particular misuse.

5. Don't use UNION when OR can be used to achieve the same effect.

Actually, this is not a particularly hard-and-fast recommendation. The rationale for making it is simply that using OR is likely to lead to more succinct formulations. On the other hand, there are some queries that can be expressed in SQL using UNION that cannot be expressed using OR. In some systems, there are performance implications also (in DB2, for example, the optimizer will sometimes use an index on a UNION query but not on a logically equivalent OR query).

6. Don't use "~ =" or "~ <" or "~ >" (use "< >" or "> =" or "< =" instead).

The operators "~ =", "~ <", and "~ >" are not included in the SQL standard.

7. Don't use "<" or ">" or BETWEEN or SUBSTR in a scalar string comparison when LIKE can be used to achieve the same effect.

For example, given a CITIES table that includes a CITY column ("city name"), the following SELECT—

```
SELECT DISTINCT CX.CITY
FROM    CITIES CX
WHERE   CX.CITY LIKE 'L%' ;
```

—is preferable to all of the following as a representation of the query "Find all cities whose name begins with L":

```
SELECT DISTINCT CX.CITY
FROM    CITIES CX
WHERE   CX.CITY > 'K' AND CX.CITY < 'M' ;

SELECT DISTINCT CX.CITY
FROM    CITIES CX
WHERE   SUBSTR ( CX.CITY, 1, 1 ) = 'L' ;

SELECT DISTINCT CX.CITY
FROM    CITIES CX
WHERE   CX.CITY BETWEEN 'K' AND 'M' ;
```

Aside: It is always advisable to exercise caution in the use of BETWEEN, for at least two reasons. First, do you know whether the range of values in a BETWEEN condition is inclusive or exclusive? The answer is that it is *in*clusive—which means that the last example above is incorrect! (Did you spot the error?) A correct version would be:

```
SELECT DISTINCT CX.CITY
FROM    CITIES CX
WHERE   CX.CITY BETWEEN 'L  ' AND 'LZZ' ;
```

The second problem is that BETWEEN does not mean the same as "between" in ordinary English. For example, what is the output from the following query?

```
SELECT DISTINCT CX.CITY
FROM    CITIES CX
WHERE   CX.CITY BETWEEN 'San Francisco' AND 'New York' ;
```

Hint: What is the expanded form of this BETWEEN condition as a pair of simple comparisons "ANDed" together?

End of aside.

- *Avoid all-or-any comparisons*

As indicated above, the quantified comparisons ">ALL", "<ANY", etc., are very largely superfluous; most queries that can be expressed in terms of them can usually be expressed in some different and much clearer manner. Moreover, the all-or-any comparisons are confusing and (in this writer's opinion) dangerously error-prone. For instance, consider the following example (based on one given in references [23] and [24]):

```
SELECT DISTINCT SX.S#
FROM    S SX
WHERE   SX.CITY <>ANY
      ( SELECT DISTINCT PX.CITY
        FROM    P PX ) ;
```

Appearances to the contrary notwithstanding, this statement does *not* retrieve supplier numbers for suppliers whose city is "not equal to any" part city. The corresponding EXISTS formulation makes the correct interpretation clear:

```
SELECT DISTINCT SX.S#
FROM    S SX
WHERE   EXISTS
      ( SELECT DISTINCT PX.CITY
        FROM    P PX
        WHERE   PX.CITY <> SX.CITY ) ;
```

("Select supplier numbers for suppliers such that there exists some part city that is different from the supplier city"). The natural intuitive interpretation of "<>ANY" as "not equal to any" is both incorrect and very misleading. Analogous criticisms apply to all of the ANY and ALL operators.

The example shows how queries involving all-or-any comparisons can frequently be transformed into equivalent queries involving EXISTS instead. They can also frequently be transformed into equivalent queries involving MAX or MIN instead, rather than EXISTS. This is because if (for example) some value x is greater than *all* values in some set, it must certainly be the case that x is greater than the *maximum* value in that set, and vice versa. And comparisons involving MAX and MIN are usually easier to understand, intuitively speaking, than comparisons involving all-or-any operators.

The following table (which is meant to be self-explanatory) is intended to be helpful in applying such transformations.

	ANY	ALL
=	IN	
< >		NOT IN
<	< MAX	< MIN
< =	< =MAX	< =MIN
>	> MIN	> MAX
> =	> =MIN	> =MAX

By way of example, consider the query "Find supplier numbers for suppliers who supply part P1 in a quantity greater than or equal to that in which they supply every other part." One possible SQL formulation is:

```
SELECT DISTINCT SPX.S#
FROM    SP SPX
WHERE   SPX.P#  = 'P1'
AND     SPX.QTY >=ALL
      ( SELECT DISTINCT SPY.QTY
        FROM    SP SPY
        WHERE   SPY.S# = SPX.S# ) ;
```

The table shows that this query can be transformed into the following, arguably clearer, version:

```
SELECT DISTINCT SPX.S#
FROM    SP SPX
WHERE   SPX.P#  = 'P1'
AND     SPX.QTY >=
      ( SELECT MAX ( SPY.QTY )
        FROM    SP SPY
        WHERE   SPY.S# = SPX.S# ) ;
```

A couple of additional points regarding the all-or-any operators:

- First, note that the comparison =ANY is just a different spelling for the familiar SQL operator IN. However, the comparison < >ANY ("not equal to any") is *not* a different spelling for NOT IN!—rather, it is < >ALL that is equivalent to NOT IN. There is an obvious trap for the unwary here.
- As the table suggests, the comparisons =ALL and < >ANY do not possess any simpler equivalent.

Note: There is unfortunately—once again—a fly in the ointment, however, namely as follows: The transformations suggested by the table (i.e., the transformations that replace all-or-any queries by MAX/MIN queries) are *not* guaranteed to be correct if any nulls are involved. This is not the place to go into details (once again, a detailed discussion can be found in reference [20]), but of course we have here yet another argument in favor of avoiding nulls entirely.

- *Be explicit*

This is another general recommendation from Section 2 that has specific application to certain aspects of data manipulation operations in particular.

1. *Don't use "SELECT *"*. The problem with "SELECT *" is that the meaning of "*" can change. Generally speaking, the star or asterisk is shorthand for a list of all column names in the table(s) identified in the FROM clause, in the left-to-right order in which those columns were defined in the relevant CREATE (or ALTER) TABLE statement(s). The notation is convenient (and acceptable) in interactive queries, because it saves keystrokes. However, it is potentially dangerous in stored queries or application programs (i.e., in embedded SQL), because the meaning of the "*" can change—e.g., if another column is added to the table. In other words, a program might execute perfectly correctly for many years and then one day suddenly fail—a very unfortunate state of affairs.

For essentially analogous reasons:

(a) Don't use "SELECT *" in a view definition.

(b) Don't use INSERT without an explicit list of column names.

Note: "COUNT(*)" is acceptable, however; so is "SELECT *" in the special context of an EXISTS function reference—see earlier in this section for several examples.*

2. *Always qualify column references.* In general, references to a specific column in SQL can always be qualified by the name of the appropriate table (more accurately, by the name of the appropriate range variable—see paragraph 3 below). However, SQL allows the qualifier to be omitted if no ambiguity results from such omission, i.e., if the relevant *implicit* qualifier is well defined. But:

(a) The SQL rules for defining the implicit qualifier are not all that easy to understand, and may very well be different in different systems (indeed, the DB2 rules and the SQL standard rules are different); hence it is not always clear what a particular unqualified name refers to.

---

*Even in the context of EXISTS, "SELECT primary-key" might be preferable to "SELECT *", for performance reasons if for no other.

(b) What is unambiguous today may very easily become ambiguous tomorrow (e.g., if new columns are added to an existing table).

(c) Earlier in this paper we recommended that columns be given the same name as the underlying domain whenever possible. If followed, that recommendation implies that unqualified column names will frequently be ambiguous anyway.

Our overall recommendation, therefore, is: *Always qualify.**

> *Aside:* There are a few potential traps here—qualified column names are not allowed in SQL in certain specific contexts. The contexts in question are those in which the column name refers to the column per se, rather than to the data value(s) currently contained in the column. In other words, qualified names are not permitted:
>
> - In a column declaration in CREATE (or ALTER) TABLE
> - In a column specification in CREATE INDEX
> - In a column specification in a PRIMARY KEY or FOREIGN KEY clause
> - In the list of view column names in CREATE VIEW
> - In a COMMENT or LABEL statement
> - In a column specification in an UPDATE privilege in a GRANT statement (the same applies to the REFERENCES privilege in the standard and SQL/DS, but not in DB2; DB2 does not support the REFERENCES privilege)
> - In the INTO clause on INSERT
> - On the left hand side of a SET assignment on UPDATE
>
> The reader is cautioned to take note of the last two of these exceptions in particular. *End of aside.*

One more point regarding name qualification: The discussions above were concerned specifically with qualifying column references by the name of the relevant table (or appropriate range variable). The recommendation "Always qualify" should *not* be construed to mean that higher-level qualifiers (authorization IDs, database names, etc.) should be explicitly shown as

---

In fact, as the reader will have noticed from the example discussed earlier under the recommendation to "Use relational calculus," it is possible—and generally desirable—to qualify not only column names but "" references also. (At least, such qualification is possible in DB2 but not in the SQL standard, owing presumably to an oversight on the part of the standard committees [22]. Also, in DB2, such qualification is—annoyingly—permitted in "SELECT *" but not in "COUNT(*)".) Of course, we have already suggested that "SELECT *" should appear only within EXISTS function references anyway.

well. On the contrary, such higher-level qualifiers should normally *not* be hardcoded into programs; to do so makes the programs in question unnecessarily inflexible.

- In DB2, for example, the full name of a table T that has been created by user U (more precisely, under authorization ID U) is "U.T". However, references to that table by user U can (and normally do) omit the "U." portion. References to that table by any other user should be handled via the system's synonym facility. In other words, the only place the qualified name "U.T" should appear is in CREATE SYNONYM and similar statements.

3. *Use explicit range variables.** This one is perhaps more of a suggestion than a hard recommendation; personally, I find that range variables aid clarity, but I know some people find them confusing.

Range variables are specified in the SQL SELECT statement in the FROM clause, immediately following the relevant table name. For example:

```
SELECT DISTINCT SX.S#
FROM    S SX
WHERE   SX.CITY = 'Paris' ;
```

SX here is a range variable that "ranges over" table S; in other words, its permitted values are rows of table S. You can think of the query as being executed as follows. First, the range variable takes on one of its permitted values; let us suppose that that value is the row for supplier S1. Is the city value in that row equal to "Paris"? If it is, then supplier number S1 will appear in the output. Next, the range variable moves on to another row of table S, say the row for supplier S2; again, if the city value in that row is "Paris," then the relevant supplier number is added to the output. And so on, exhaustively, until variable SX has successively taken all of its permitted values.

Note: It might help to think of the range variable as a kind of *loop control variable* for the implicit loop that the system has to execute in order to respond to the query.

Whether you decide to use explicit range variables or not, however, you should at least be aware of the following points:

- From an abstract point of view, SQL *always* requires queries to be formulated in terms of range variables. If no range variables are spec-

---

*Range variables go by a variety of different names: They are called "tuple variables" in (the tuple version of) relational calculus, "correlation names" in DB2 and the SQL standard ("correlation variables" would be better), "join variables" (among other things) in SQL/DS, etc., etc.

ified explicitly, SQL assumes the existence of implicit variables with the same name(s) as the corresponding table(s). For example, the query

```
SELECT DISTINCT S#
FROM    S
WHERE   CITY = 'Paris' ;
```

is treated by SQL as if it had been expressed as follows:

```
SELECT DISTINCT S.S#
FROM    S S
WHERE   S.CITY = 'Paris' ;
```

The "S" here in "S.S#" and "S.CITY" and the second "S" in the FROM clause do *not* denote "table S"; rather, they denote a range variable called S that ranges over the table with the same name.

- DB2 supports the use of explicit range variables in UPDATE and DELETE as well as SELECT; the standard unfortunately does not. For example, the following is legal in DB2 but not in the standard:

```
DELETE
FROM    SP SPX
WHERE   SPX.QTY < 100 ;
```

- The DB2 rules for binding range variables to their corresponding tables are different from those in the standard (and are in fact incorrect) in certain "tricky" cases. For instance, the behavior of DB2 is unpredictable (in general) in all of the following examples:

```
SELECT ...
FROM    T, T
 ...      ;

SELECT ...
FROM    T1 T2, T1
 ...      ;

SELECT ...
FROM    T1 T2, T2 T1
 ...      ;
```

The moral is obvious, of course: Avoid such usages!

4. *Use colons to mark host variables.* DB2 (but not SQL/DS, and not the SQL standard) provides an option by which the colon marker on host variable references can be omitted in contexts where no ambiguity can be caused by such omission (essentially contexts in which SQL column names cannot appear—e.g., in the INTO clause on a FETCH statement). This option is confusing at best and should not be exercised.

5. *Use parentheses to indicate operator precedence.* This recommendation is perhaps more directly applicable to conditional expressions than to (e.g.)

simple arithmetic expressions. The default precedence order for arithmetic operators is well established by familiar convention; few people are likely to misconstrue (e.g.) the expression

```
A + B * C
```

—though of course it is not wrong to show the implied parentheses explicitly:

```
A + ( B * C )
```

In fact, even with arithmetic expressions, "unnecessary" parentheses can be a good idea, especially if the expression involves any exponentiation operators ("**"). (Of course, exponentiation is not included in the SQL standard, nor is it supported by DB2 and SQL/DS, but it *is* supported by several other commercially available products.) For example, what is the meaning of the following expression?

```
X ** Y ** Z
```

Matters get a little more confusing in the case of conditional expressions. Suppose, for example, that *p, q,* and *r* are simple comparisons such as "A > B". Consider the expression

```
NOT p OR NOT q AND r
```

In DB2 and the standard, this means:

```
( NOT ( p ) ) OR ( ( NOT ( q ) ) AND r )
```

Do you know what it means in *your* DBMS?

6. *Use explicit conversions.* By and large, data type conversions should be avoided if possible. If it is not possible, then it is probably better to perform them explicitly by means of the builtin conversion functions (provided in DB2 though not in the standard) INTEGER, DECIMAL, FLOAT, etc. In this way you might be able to exert more direct control on (e.g.) the precision and scale of the result of the conversion. Note, incidentally, that DB2 allows an "approximate numeric" value (FLOAT, REAL, or DOUBLE PRECISION) to be assigned to an "exact numeric" object (SMALLINT, INTEGER, or DECIMAL), whereas the standard does not.

A related question is that of the data type of literals and the results of operational expressions. There are some more traps for the unwary here. For example:

- String literals are considered to be fixed length in the standard but varying length in DB2.

- Note that the literal (e.g.) "4" is of type SMALLINT whereas the literal "4." is of type DECIMAL(1,0). (At least, this is true for DB2; in the standard they are both "exact numeric," with precision and scale (1,0).)

- In DB2, if X and Y are both of integer data type (INTEGER or SMALLINT), then dividing X by Y yields a result of type INTEGER (i.e., the remainder, or equivalently the fractional part of the result, is lost). For example, in DB2, the expression "2/3" evaluates to zero! The standard states that the precision and scale of the result of such a division are "implementation-defined," so DB2 is within its rights here, but the net effect could be a surprise for the user. Analogous remarks apply to the AVG function, by the way.

- Indeed, the standard gives "implementation-defined" for the precision and scale of the result of almost every kind of arithmetic expression, so it is quite likely that different systems will display different behavior in this general area.

- The standard is silent on the question of whether the results of operational expressions are considered to have the NOT NULL property. This omission is unfortunate, given the criticality of such matters in certain contexts, e.g., in a UNION.*

7. *Always use indicator variables.* Every target host variable in a FETCH (or singleton SELECT) should have an associated indicator variable, even if you have decided to avoid nulls entirely! (In DB2, at any rate, there are situations in which the system actually generates nulls, if a data type conversion error occurs on input, for example. And in any case, a column that is defined to be NOT NULL today might possibly have nulls allowed at some future time.)

8. *Close cursors explicitly.* COMMIT and ROLLBACK automatically close all open cursors, but closing them explicitly is good coding practice. Occasionally it might lead to slightly better performance also (if it means releasing system resources earlier).

9. *Don't rely on implicit ordering.* Suppose you have defined a cursor to run through the set of all employees. You might "know" that there is an index on employee number (EMP#) and that the optimizer is going to use that index, and hence that employee rows will be delivered to you in ascending EMP# order. However, do not rely on this hidden assumption in your

---

*Presumably such expressions in fact have "nulls allowed," since they may in fact evaluate to null if any of the operands is null.

program logic. If the ordering is important to you, specify an appropriate explicit ORDER BY clause. (Unfortunately, of course, that ORDER BY clause will have the effect of making the cursor "nonupdatable." See the further discussion of this topic under point 11 below.)

10. *Use explicit COMMITs and ROLLBACKs.* If a program completes execution without issuing either COMMIT or ROLLBACK, some transaction managers assume that COMMIT is implied and others ROLLBACK. The standard has nothing to say on the matter. Explicit COMMITs and ROLL-BACKs are obviously desirable. *Note:* Of course, some transaction managers do not permit COMMIT and ROLLBACK statements to appear at all, but instead provide the corresponding function by means of special statements of their own. Explicit operations are still to be recommended, however, even if they are nonstandard.

Note also that the standard *requires* the keyword WORK to appear in COMMIT and ROLLBACK (it is required in SQL/DS also but optional in DB2).

11. *Be careful with "side-operations."* As a general rule, it is a good idea to avoid having multiple cursors open on the same (or overlapping) data at the same time. Equally, it is a good idea to avoid performing an "out of the blue" (noncursor) operation on data that you are simultaneously accessing through a cursor. The reason for avoiding such situations is, of course, that the effects are unpredictable; they are certainly not specified in the standard, and it is a safe bet that different systems will display different behavior in this area.

Unfortunately, there is at least one situation in which it is impossible to abide by the preceding recommendations, namely as follows. First, the reader will be aware that SQL has a rule to the effect that if a cursor declaration includes an ORDER BY clause, then "positioned" UPDATEs and DELETEs (i.e., UPDATE and DELETE . . . WHERE CURRENT operations) cannot be performed via that cursor. In other words, it is not possible to retrieve a set of rows via a cursor in some specified order *and* UPDATE or DELETE some of those rows via that same cursor at the same time. The following is thus *** ILLEGAL *** (pseudocode):

```
FETCH cursor INTO input area ;
IF row in input area needs updating THEN
    UPDATE ...
    SET    ...
    WHERE  CURRENT OF cursor ;
```

Instead, when the user decides that the "current row of the cursor" needs to be updated, he or she has to perform a *side-operation*—that is, issue an

"out of the blue" update, identifying the row by its primary key value.*
The following pseudocode illustrates the technique:

```
FETCH cursor INTO input area ;
IF row in input area needs updating THEN
    DO ;
        extract primary key value from row in input area ;
        UPDATE ...
        SET    ...
        WHERE  primary key = extracted value ;
    END ;
```

Note, therefore, that SQL *forces* you not to be explicit here. At least you
should include some appropriate comments in your code. But that is not
the main point I want to make. Rather, the point is that issuing side-
operations in this manner is "living dangerously." *There is no guarantee
that the row retrieved via the FETCH operation is in fact the genuine data
row.* Instead, it is possible that the ORDER BY on the cursor declaration
caused the system to construct a temporary (sorted) copy of the data—
indeed, this is precisely why UPDATE and DELETE CURRENT operations
are not allowed in the first place. If the FETCH is in fact retrieving a copy
of the real row, then the real row might not be locked at the time of the
FETCH, and so there can be no guarantee that the "out of the blue" update will succeed (the real row might not even exist any longer).

There are a number of possible approaches to this problem. The first
is to lock the real data explicitly before opening the cursor. This approach
has several drawbacks, however:

- First, the standard does not provide any explicit locking facilities at
  all; thus, you are immediately entering the realm of DBMS-specific
  extensions with this approach.

- Second, DB2 at any rate provides explicit locking facilities only at
  the level of the entire table (via its LOCK TABLE statement), and
  indeed in some cases physically locks even more than that; concurrency is thus likely to suffer significantly, and the chances of deadlock are increased also. (This criticism might not apply to a system
  that provides a means of locking individual rows, of course.)

- Third, LOCK TABLE in DB2 (and SQL/DS) applies only to base
  tables, not to views, which means that the user has to be more aware
  of the physical realities of the database, and data independence suffers.

---

*Naturally we assume that the row in question in fact does have a primary key value!

A second possible approach is to perform an explicit check that the row has not changed before doing the update. This approach will require an explicit retrieval of the real data row at the appropriate time (thereby acquiring a lock on that row at that time). The following pseudocode illustrates this approach.

```
FETCH cursor INTO input area ;
IF row in input area needs updating THEN
    DO ;
        extract primary key value from row in input area ;
        SELECT ...
        INTO   ...
        FROM   ...
        WHERE  primary key = extracted value ;
        IF row just retrieved = row in input area THEN
            UPDATE ...
            SET    ...
            WHERE  primary key = extracted value ;
        ELSE ROLLBACK WORK (?) ;
    END ;
```

This approach also has certain drawbacks:

- First, it assumes that "repeatable read" (RR) isolation level is in effect.* If instead the isolated level is "cursor stability" (CS), there is still no guarantee that the SELECTed row will be locked by the time of the UPDATE. In this case, the user should retrieve the desired row by means of another cursor instead of via SELECT. (Note too, incidentally, that isolation level is another area where SQL forces you not to be explicit, since it is specified outside the program code, at least in DB2.)

     Aside: The standard supports isolation level RR only, and that only implicitly. *End of aside.*

- Second, it is complicated. It relies very heavily on the user doing the right thing.
- Third, it is not very explicit. It relies on the assumption that retrieval operations *implicitly* lock the data they read.

A third possible approach (for which I am indebted to Gabrielle Wiorkowski) is to get the system itself to do the check, by making it part of the condition in the WHERE clause on the UPDATE. Pseudocode:

---

*Actually, if RR is in effect—and if it is properly implemented!—then the system *will* have locked the real row, even if the FETCH operates on a copy. The check described above is thus strictly unnecessary in the RR case (at least in principle).

```
FETCH cursor INTO input area ;
IF row in input area needs updating THEN
    DO ;
        UPDATE ...
        SET     ...
        WHERE   column-1 = column-1 in input area
        AND     column-2 = column-2 in input area
        AND     ...
        AND     column-1 = column-1 in input area ;
        IF SQLCODE = +100 THEN
        /*  no row found to satisfy WHERE clause --  */
        /*  therefore original row must have been    */
        /*  UPDATEd or DELETEd -- so user's UPDATE   */
        /*  has had no effect                        */
        ROLLBACK WORK (?) ;
    END ;
```

Here we are assuming that column-1, column-2, . . . , column-n together constitute all of the columns of the relevant table. The drawback to this approach is that it rapidly becomes very tedious to code as the number of columns increases. Note too that it is not guaranteed to work if the table in question permits duplicate rows!

12. *Be careful with "side-operations"* (*continued*). Analogous remarks to those in point 11 above apply also when, for example, the user is simultaneously using two distinct views over the same data. Consider, for example, the structure of a program that scans and prints all suppliers and also updates (and is authorized to update) just some of them—say, suppliers in Paris—as it goes; two views will be needed, one for all suppliers (with SELECT privileges only) and one for suppliers in Paris (with SELECT and UPDATE privileges). *Note:* This example is elaborated in references [23] and [24].

■ *Avoid nulls* (?)

I have suggested several times in this paper already that it might very well be a good idea to avoid nulls in SQL entirely. It is certainly undeniable that nulls in SQL can be the source of a lot of problems, and in fact it can be shown that SQL's treatment of nulls is fundamentally unsound [20,21]. However, it is not my intention to rehearse all of the various "antinull" arguments here; rather, I simply want to draw the reader's attention to a couple of points that have to with data manipulation operations specifically.

The main point is that (as indicated in Section 5) it is not sufficient just to specify NOT NULL for every column in every base table. Such specifications will of course prevent nulls from ever appearing in those base tables per se; however, nulls can still appear (in the absence of a suitable discipline) in *derived* tables (e.g., in a view or a final query result or an intermediate result), as follows.

1. First, some systems support certain operations—in particular, certain forms of *outer join*—that are defined to generate nulls in their result [11].

2. Second, the aggregate functions SUM, AVG, MAX, and MIN are defined to return a null if their argument evaluates to the empty set. (This is a flaw in SQL, in my opinion [21].)

3. Third, the IBM products DB2 and SQL/DS actually generate nulls as a response to certain kinds of error—for example, if the user tries to FETCH the value of some expression, say "A divided by B," and B happens to be zero, then the result is automatically set to null [23,24].

However, some systems do also provide a means for replacing nulls by some nonnull value. For example, ORACLE provides a function called NVL, and DB2 and SQL/DS both provide a function called VALUE. Each of these functions can be used to eliminate nulls "as soon as they appear," i.e., before they have a chance to do any further damage. For instance, consider the query

```
SELECT DISTINCT SX.S#
FROM    S SX
WHERE   1000 >
        ( SELECT SUM ( SPX.QTY )
          FROM    SP SPX
          WHERE   SPX.S# = SX.S# ) ;
```

("supplier numbers of suppliers for whom the corresponding total shipment quantity is less than 1000"). This query, counterintuitively, will *not* include in its output supplier numbers of suppliers for whom there are no shipments at all, i.e., suppliers for whom the total quantity is zero. (*Exercise for the reader:* Why not?) A correct formulation (or at least one that is intuitively superior, in that it does include such supplier numbers in its output), using the DB2 VALUE function, is as follows:

```
SELECT DISTINCT SX.S#
FROM    S SX
WHERE   1000 >
        ( SELECT VALUE ( SUM ( SPX.QTY ), 0 )
          FROM    SP SPX
          WHERE   SPX.S# = SX.S# ) ;
```

If the SUM function returns a null for some particular supplier, the VALUE function will effectively replace that null by a zero (the second argument to the VALUE function reference). In general, VALUE takes a sequence of any number of arguments and returns either the value of the first nonnull argument in the sequence, or null if the arguments are all null. *Recommendation:* In any invocation of the VALUE function, make sure that at least one of the arguments is definitely nonnull. (In practice, this recommendation is likely to mean that at least one of those arguments will be a [nonnull] literal.)

For further discussion of the problems that nulls can cause in SQL, see references [12,20,21].

■ *Isolate the use of system-specific facilities*

As indicated earlier, it is impossible in practice to avoid the use of non-standard (i.e., system-specific) facilities entirely. However, it might be a good idea to isolate the use of such facilities by placing them in their own sections of code (subroutines or modules), in order to simplify subsequent maintenance and possible replacement. (We note in passing that the SQL INCLUDE statement, which might be used to incorporate such modules into the overall program, is not part of the standard either!)

Here is a short (and open-ended) list of items that might be candidates for such isolation:

- Any SQL statements (such as FETCH or INSERT) that include references to host structures or arrays instead of just references to scalar variables (the standard deals in terms of scalar variables only)
- Any code that depends on the structure of the SQL Communication Area and/or on specific SQLCODE values (all of which, except zero and +100, are "implementation-defined" in the standard)
- Any code that uses dynamic SQL facilities (PREPARE, EXECUTE, DESCRIBE, the SQL Descriptor Area, etc.)
- Any code that depends on the structure of the system catalog
- Any code that relies on a system-specific extension that *clearly* has no chance of ever making it into the official standard, because it is not well designed (readers can supply their own examples here)
- Any code that provides a generic function (such as support for a CASCADE update rule on a foreign key specification) that probably *will* be included in the official standard at some future time

■ *Miscellaneous points*

Finally, a few fairly obvious miscellaneous suggestions and recommendations:

1. Follow every executable SQL statement with a test on SQLCODE (possibly via WHENEVER). Provide an exception-handling routine for (at least) the most commonly occurring exceptions—e.g., data not found, uniqueness violation, referential constraint violation, deadlock, etc.—together with a catchall routine for other exceptions. If WHENEVER is used and the exception-handling routine itself includes any SQL statements, watch out for the possibility of an infinite loop.

2. Prefer static SQL to dynamic SQL wherever possible. Dynamic SQL is much harder to write and debug and maintain. In the case of DB2 in

particular, it also causes security and administration problems. Furthermore, there are significant performance implications (a lot of catalog access—and locking—is involved).

3. Don't write code that relies on quirks of thc system optimizer. You are bound to get a surprise in the next release (or the one after that, or the one after that, or . . .).

4. Avoid SQL constructs that are known to be optimization inhibitors, if possible. In DB2, for example, avoid the use of the "IN subquery" construct (as already recommended earlier in this paper for different reasons).

5. Don't use null indicator variables in WHERE or HAVING clauses. They are permitted in the standard (though not in some implementations), but they don't do what you might expect them to do. In fact, they don't do anything useful at all. (Once again, of course, this particular piece of advice will be irrelevant if you decide to avoid nulls entirely.)

6. In addition to its primary function (supporting access to the database per se), SQL also allows you to do things like retrieving the time of day or performing simple calculations. Unfortunately, however, the structure of the language is such that such things can only be done by SELECTing whatever it is that you want FROM some table. . . . It is therefore probably a good idea to have a dummy table in your database, say DUMMY, with just one column and one row (the data content is irrelevant). Then you can do things like:

```
SELECT 2 + 2 FROM DUMMY ;

SELECT CURRENT TIME FROM DUMMY ;
```

In such contexts DISTINCT and explicit range variables would genuinely be obtrusive and can safely be omitted. (Note, however, that the dummy table *must* contain exactly one row, otherwise a variety of unpleasant surprises are likely to occur.)

7. CONCLUSION

It can be seen that the recommendations sketched and illustrated in the foregoing sections are not really the unequivocal "recipes for success" that I had hoped they would be when I embarked on this paper. Nor do I claim that they constitute any kind of exhaustive list; there must surely exist additional guidelines, both ones that are relevant to specific implementations and others of a more general nature. At least some potential pitfalls have been identified, however, and I do believe that the positive advice can be useful in many practical situations. Meanwhile, we must hope that the problems of SQL as it is currently defined will eventually be fixed and that the discrepancies among various implementations will eventually disappear, so that the potential for compatibility and productivity inherent in relational technology can one day truly be realized.

ACKNOWLEDGMENTS

I am grateful to my friends and colleagues Nagraj Alur, Mike Ferguson, Diann Trautwein, Gabrielle Wiorkowski, Colin White, and Ed Wrazen for their numerous helpful comments on earlier drafts of this paper.

REFERENCES AND BIBLIOGRAPHY

1. ANSI, Database Language SQL. Document ANSI X3.135-1986. Also available as ISO Document ISO/TC97/SC21/WG3 N117.

2. ISO/TC97/SC21/WG3 / ANSI X3H2, Database Language SQL Addendum-1. Document ISO DBL AMS-10 / ANSI X3H2-87-205 (1987).

3. ISO/IEC JTC1/SC21/WG3 / ANSI X3H2, ISO-ANSI (working draft) Database Language SQL2. Document ISO SYD-2 / ANSI X3H2-88-259 (July 1988).

4. Oracle Corporation, SQL*Connect User's Guide. Oracle Part No. 774 (1988).

5. Nagraj Alur, "IBM DATABASE 2 and Referential Integrity," *InfoDB* 3, No. 1 (Spring 1988).

6. E. F. Codd, "Relational Completeness of Data Base Sublanguages," in *Data Base Systems,* Courant Computer Science Symposia Series 6 (Englewood Cliffs, NJ: Prentice-Hall, 1972).

7. E. F. Codd, "Extending the Database Relational Model to Capture More Meaning," *ACM Transactions on Database Systems* 4, No. 4 (December 1979).

8. E. F. Codd, *The Relational Model for Database Management* (Reading, MA: Addison-Wesley, 1989).

9. C. J. Date, *An Introduction to Database Systems: Volume I,* 4th edition (Reading, MA: Addison-Wesley, 1986).

10. C. J. Date, "Updating Views," in C. J. Date, *Relational Database: Selected Writings* (Reading, MA: Addison-Wesley, 1986).

11. C. J. Date, "The Outer Join," in C. J. Date, *Relational Database: Selected Writings* (Reading, MA: Addison-Wesley, 1986).

12. C. J. Date, "Null Values in Database Management," in C. J. Date, *Relational Database: Selected Writings* (Reading, MA: Addison-Wesley, 1986).

13. C. J. Date, "A Practical Approach to Database Design," in C. J. Date, *Relational Database: Selected Writings* (Reading, MA: Addison-Wesley, 1986).

14. C. J. Date, "Dates and Times in IBM SQL: Some Technical Criticisms" (in this volume).

15. C. J. Date, "Primary and Foreign Key Support in DB2," *InfoDB* 3, No. 3 (Fall 1988).

16. C. J. Date, "Referential Integrity and Foreign Keys. Part I: Basic Concepts; Part II: Further Considerations" (in this volume).

17. C. J. Date, "A Note on One-to-One Relationships" (in this volume).

18. C. J. Date, "Why Duplicate Rows Are Prohibited" (in this volume).

19. C. J. Date, "A Contribution to the Study of Database Integrity" (in this volume).

20. C. J. Date, "EXISTS Is Not "Exists"! (Some Logical Flaws in SQL)" (in this volume).

21. C. J. Date, "NOT Is Not "Not"! (Notes on Three-Valued Logic and Related Matters)" (in this volume).

22. C. J. Date, *A Guide to the SQL Standard,* 2nd edition (Reading, MA: Addison-Wesley, 1989).

23. C. J. Date and Colin J. White, *A Guide to DB2,* 3rd edition (Reading, MA: Addison-Wesley, 1989).

24. C. J. Date and Colin J. White, *A Guide to SQL/DS* (Reading, MA: Addison-Wesley, 1988).

25. Andrew Warden, "In Praise of Marriage" (in this volume).

26. Andrew Warden, "The Keys of the Kingdom" (in this volume).

PART **IV**

DATABASE DESIGN

16

A Note on
One-to-One Relationships

ABSTRACT

The problem of one-to-one relationships in database design is examined.
The problem turns out to be not quite as trivial as it might sound. Some
recommendations are made and some interesting questions raised.

COMMENTS ON REPUBLICATION

This paper could probably have been included in Part I of this book with
equal justification. I decided to include it in Part IV (on database design)
because it is of course primarily concerned with a database design problem
(albeit a very specific one), but there are strong ties between it and the two-
part paper on foreign keys in Part I (Chapters 5 and 6). The paper on general database integrity in Part I (Chapter 9) is also relevant.

Originally published in *InfoDB* 3, No. 4 (Winter 1988/89). Reprinted by permission.

1. INTRODUCTION

The entity and relationship concepts are part of the database designer's stock-in-trade. Informally, we can say that an entity is simply any identifiable thing (it can be as concrete or as abstract as we please), and a relationship is a special kind of entity that serves to connect two or more other entities together. Those other entities are not necessarily all distinct, of course—think of the familiar "parts contain parts" relationship that arises in the bill-of-materials application.

Before going any further, let me stress that I do feel strongly that relationships are best regarded as entities in their own right, not as some totally different kind of object [2]; in other words, all relationships are entities, but some entities are not relationships. However, this paper is concerned only with relationships, and with a special kind of relationship at that.

In general, of course, a given relationship can involve any number of entities. For simplicity, however, let us agree to limit our attention to relationships of degree two—i.e., relationships that relate exactly two entities, or in other words binary relationships; the discussions that follow extend in an obvious manner to relationships of higher degree. Now, it is usual to classify binary relationships into three kinds, namely one-to-one, many-to-one (or one-to-many), and many-to-many relationships. Of these three kinds, many-to-one and many-to-many relationships have been extensively discussed in the literature, but one-to-one relationships do not seem to have received very much attention. However, one-to-one relationships do raise certain interesting questions that do not apply to the other two cases. The purpose of this paper is to address some of those questions.

One further preliminary remark: In the interests of precision, we ought really never to use the unqualified term "entity," but always the qualified terms "entity *type*" and "entity *instance*" (as appropriate) instead. Likewise, we ought not to use the term "relationship," but rather the terms "relationship type" and "relationship instance" (again as appropriate). However, repeated use of these qualified terms tends to start sounding rather pedantic, and certainly makes for very tedious reading. In this paper, therefore, I will generally use the unqualified terms only, relying on context to show which interpretation is intended; I will, however, occasionally use the qualified terms if emphasis or clarity so dictates.

2. WHAT DOES "ONE-TO-ONE" MEAN ?

The first thing we need to do is to pin down exactly what is meant by the term "one-to-one" (perhaps surprisingly, it is open to several possible, or at least plausible, distinct interpretations). Suppose we have a one-to-one relationship between two entity types A and B. Possible interpretations include the following:

1. For a given A there is *exactly one* corresponding B (but many A's may have the same corresponding B).

   - For example, a given employee has exactly one corresponding department (but many employees have the same department).

Here, even if the relationship from A to B is considered to be one-to-one, the inverse relationship from B to A is clearly not; rather, it is one-to-many. In the case of departments and employees, for example, one department has many employees (or possibly no employees at all; note that it is conventional for the term "many" to include the zero case). It thus seems obviously better to regard the relationship from A to B as many-to-one, not one-to-one. For the remainder of this paper I will not consider this case as "one-to-one" in any sense at all.

2. For a given A there is *at most one* corresponding B (but again many A's may have the same corresponding B).

   - For example, a given employee has at most one corresponding department (but some employees have no department at all).

The relationship here is best regarded as "many-to-(zero-or-one)"—many A's have the same B (or perhaps no B at all), each B has many A's (where again the term "many" includes the zero case). Again, for the remainder of this paper I will not consider this case as "one-to-one" in any sense at all.

3. For a given A there is *exactly one* corresponding B and for a given B there is *at most one* corresponding A (but some B's may have no corresponding A at all).

   - For example, a given department has exactly one manager (i.e., employee who manages the department)—and a given manager manages exactly one department—but some employees are not managers at all.

This case would more accurately be characterized as "(zero-or-one)-to-one"—for one A there is one B, for one B there is either one A or no A at all. Such a relationship frequently arises in the context of subtypes and supertypes, incidentally, though the example above does not illustrate this point. For example, "manager" might be a subtype of the "employee" supertype: Every manager is an employee—for one instance of the "manager" subtype there is one instance of the "employee" supertype (representing, of course, exactly the same entity)—but the converse is not true. Thus, the relationship from manager to employee is (zero-or-one)-to-one.

I will discuss (zero-or-one)-to-one relationships further in the next section. *Note:* If the relationship from A to B is (zero-or-one)-to-one, the relationship from B to A is obviously one-to-(zero-or-one). Thus, everything regarding "(zero-or-one)-to-one" in what follows applies equally to "one-to-(zero-or-one)," mutatis mutandis.

4. For a given A there is *at most one* corresponding B and for a given B there is *at most one* corresponding A (but some A's may have no corresponding B at all, and vice versa).

- For example, a given man has at most one wife and a given woman has at most one husband (assuming no bigamy), but some men have no wife and some women have no husband.

I will refer to this case as "(zero-or-one)-to-(zero-or-one)." Again I will discuss it further later in the paper.

5. For a given A there is *exactly one* corresponding B and for a given B there is *exactly one* corresponding A.

- For example, a given shipment has exactly one invoice and a given invoice has exactly one shipment.

This last case might be described as a "genuine" one-to-one relationship (in fact, this is the *only* case that is recognized as truly one-to-one in mathematics, which is of course where the "one-to-one" terminology comes from in the first place). Once again I will discuss it further later in the paper. Indeed, this case is in many respects the most interesting case of all.

We can summarize the foregoing by means of the matrix shown in Fig. 1. (*Note:* "N" in that figure means "many," where "many" is taken to include the zero case.) The matrix is obviously symmetric—for example, as indicated above, one-to-(zero-or-one) and (zero-or-one)-to-one are really the same case. Also, we are not concerned in this paper with the many-to-one and many-to-many cases. Thus, there are essentially three cases left to discuss, represented by the shaded portions of the matrix:

- (Zero-or-one)-to-one, also known as one-to-(zero-or-one)
- (Zero-or-one)-to-(zero-or-one)
- "Genuine" one-to-one

These three cases are discussed in the next three sections.

B⟍ A	0 or 1	1	N
0 or 1	(0-or-1) -to- (0-or-1)	(0-or-1)-to-1	(0-or-1)-to-N
1	1-to-(0-or-1)	"genuine" 1-to-1	1-to-N
N	N-to-(0-or-1)	N-to-1	N-to-N

Fig. 1 Types of relationship

3. THE (ZERO-OR-ONE)-TO-ONE CASE

I will begin by considering the "departments and managers" example (refer to Fig. 2; the arrow in that figure from MGR_EMP# in the DEPT table to EMP# in the EMP table represents a referential constraint [4,5]). We can represent this example as follows, using the (deliberately rather wordy and repetitive) "pseudoSQL" syntax of reference [4]. *Note:* The syntax is similar but not identical to the actual syntax used in the IBM products DB2 and SQL/DS [5,6]. It is intended to be broadly self-explanatory.

```
DEPT ( DEPT#, ..., MGR_EMP#, ... )
     PRIMARY KEY ( DEPT# )
     ALTERNATE KEY ( MGR_EMP# )
                    NULLS NOT ALLOWED
     FOREIGN KEY ( MGR_EMP# ) REFERENCES EMP
                   NULLS NOT ALLOWED
                   DELETE OF EMP RESTRICTED
                   UPDATE OF EMP.EMP# CASCADES

EMP  ( EMP#, ... )
     PRIMARY KEY ( EMP# )
```

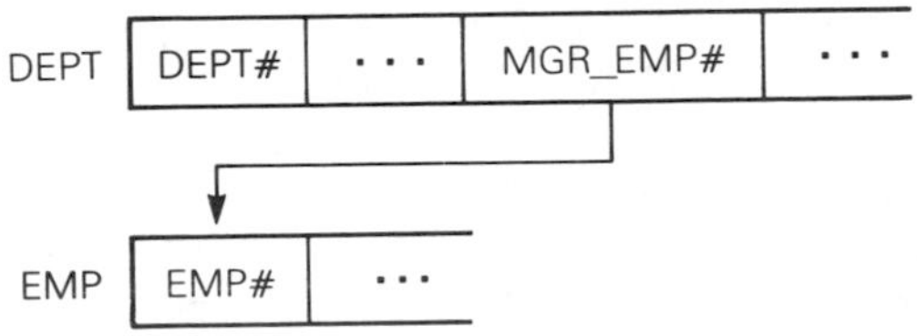

Fig. 2 Departments and managers

Points arising:

1. Note first that column MGR_EMP# ("employee number of the department manager") is an alternate key for the DEPT table. (An alternate key is a candidate key that is not the primary key. See, e.g., reference [4] for further discussion of alternate keys.) The fact that MGR_EMP# has been specified as an alternate key (via the ALTERNATE KEY clause) enforces the constraint that every manager manages exactly one department. The fact that the alternate key has NULLS NOT ALLOWED enforces the constraint that every department has a manager. (Note that alternate keys, unlike primary keys, must sometimes be permitted to accept nulls, though most of the alternate keys discussed in the present paper in fact do not.)

2. The alternate key MGR_EMP# is of course also a foreign key, referencing the EMP table. The FOREIGN KEY clause enforces the constraint that every manager is an employee. The delete and update rules in that clause are basically arbitrary (except that they cannot be NULLIFIES, because MGR_EMP# has NULLS NOT ALLOWED).

3. The only additional point—a fairly obvious one—that seems worth making in connexion with this example is that including the MGR_EMP# foreign key in the DEPT table is the right thing to do, instead of including (say) a MGD_DEPT# ("managed department") foreign key in the EMP table. (In other words, the foreign key should go in the smaller table— where "smaller" means "smaller cardinality." I am indebted to Paul Winsberg for this observation.) The reasons for this recommendation are as follows:

(a) First, MGD_DEPT# would have to have NULLS ALLOWED, and presumably would actually be null in the majority of EMP rows (most employees are not managers). Avoiding nulls if possible is generally to be recommended [2].

(b) Second, the constraint that every department must have a manager would now have to be enforced via application code instead of declaratively.

Note too that MGD_DEPT# would have to be specified as an alternate key for table EMP, in order to enforce the constraint that every manager manages exactly one department. (What is more, this constraint would have to be maintained by application code, at least in the IBM products DB2 and SQL/DS, since (a) as explained above, MGD_DEPT# must have NULLS ALLOWED and will actually be null in many EMP rows, and (b) the IBM mechanism for enforcing uniqueness, namely the UNIQUE index, will permit *at most one* null in the column concerned.)

Now let us turn to the "managers and employees" example, the subtype-supertype example (refer to Fig. 3). The pseudoSQL looks like this:

```
MGR    ( EMP#, ... )
       PRIMARY KEY ( EMP# )
       FOREIGN KEY ( EMP# ) REFERENCES EMP
                   NULLS NOT ALLOWED
                   DELETE OF EMP CASCADES
                   UPDATE OF EMP.EMP# CASCADES

EMP    ( EMP#, ... )
       PRIMARY KEY ( EMP# )
```

The only formal difference between this example and the previous one is that the foreign key in the referencing table—MGR.EMP# in the example—is actually the primary key of that table, not an alternate key. As a consequence of this fact, it is not necessary to state NULLS NOT ALLOWED explicitly (in our pseudoSQL syntax, that is, though it would still be necessary in DB2 and SQL/DS). Also, RESTRICTED delete and update rules probably do not make sense. Again, it is obviously better to have the foreign key where it is instead of in the other table, for essentially the same reasons as before.

Note 1: It might possibly be argued that, since a row in the MGR table and the corresponding row in the EMP table do in fact represent the same entity in the real world, deleting a MGR row should "cascade back" to delete the corresponding EMP row. However, I would take the position that such an argument is incorrect, in that it is imputing the wrong semantics to the operation of deleting a subtype row. Rather, I feel that such an operation should be regarded as *removing the subtype role* from the relevant entity, not as deleting the entity altogether. Deleting a row from the MGR table, for example, should be interpreted as a demotion (i.e., the removal of the employee in question from his or her managerial position), not as the deletion of that employee from the database entirely.

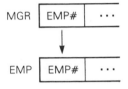

Fig. 3 Managers and employees

Note 2:   If we combine the two examples discussed in this section ("departments and managers" and "managers and employees") as indicated in Fig. 4, we obtain a situation in which:

(a) The subtype-supertype relationship from MGR to EMP is still (zero-or-one)-to-one, as before;

(b) The "managed by" relationship from DEPT to EMP, which was (zero-or-one)-to-one, is replaced by a *genuine* one-to-one relationship between DEPT and MGR (every department has one manager, every manager has one department). The interesting thing about this particular one-to-one relationship is that the DEPT# for a given MGR row—i.e., the field value that references the department of the manager in question—will probably be found in the (unique) EMP row corresponding to that MGR row, not directly in that MGR row per se. The example thus illustrates the point that the "genuine" case does have some novel and complicated aspects of its own that do not apply to the other cases. As already stated, the genuine one-to-one case will be discussed in detail later in the paper.

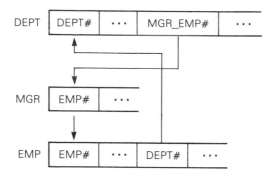

Fig. 4   Combining the first two examples

From the foregoing examples and discussions, we can draw the following conclusions regarding the treatment of the (zero-or one)-to-one case. Let the entities involved be A and B respectively (i.e., for each A there is exactly one B, for each B there is at most one A). Then:

▪   Include a foreign key in table A referencing table B.

▪   That foreign key will be the primary key for table A in the subtype-supertype case (table A represents the subtype), an alternate key for table A otherwise. Either way, it should have NULLS NOT ALLOWED, either explicitly or implicitly.

- The delete and update rules must be CASCADES in the subtype-supertype case, CASCADES or RESTRICTED otherwise.

4. THE (ZERO-OR-ONE)-TO-(ZERO-OR-ONE) CASE

Suppose now that we wish to design a database for the husband-and-wife example (in which, to repeat from Section 2, a given man has at most one wife and a given woman has at most one husband). Note first that if we attempt a single-table design along the following lines—

```
PEOPLE ( HUSBAND_NAME, WIFE_NAME, ... )
```

—where the single table is intended to list all relevant people, together with their spouse if any, then neither HUSBAND_NAME nor WIFE_NAME can serve as the primary key, because both must have NULLS ALLOWED. Thus, we would have to invent some artificial identifier (MARRIAGE#, say—except that some of the rows in the table would not correspond to any actual marriage in the real world!):

```
PEOPLE ( MARRIAGE#, HUSBAND_NAME, WIFE_NAME, ... )
       PRIMARY KEY ( MARRIAGE# )
       ALTERNATE KEY ( HUSBAND_NAME )
                   NULLS ALLOWED
       ALTERNATE KEY ( WIFE_NAME )
                   NULLS ALLOWED
```

The design of Fig. 5 (overleaf), which involves two tables, one to list all persons and the other to list all (actual) marriages, seems preferable. PseudoSQL:

```
PERSON   ( NAME, ... )
         PRIMARY KEY ( NAME )

MARRIAGE ( HUSBAND_NAME, WIFE_NAME, ... )
         PRIMARY KEY ( HUSBAND_NAME )
         ALTERNATE KEY ( WIFE_NAME )
                   NULLS NOT ALLOWED
         FOREIGN KEY ( HUSBAND_NAME ) REFERENCES PERSON
                   NULLS NOT ALLOWED
                   DELETE OF PERSON CASCADES
                   UPDATE OF PERSON.NAME CASCADES
         FOREIGN KEY ( WIFE_NAME ) REFERENCES PERSON
                   NULLS NOT ALLOWED
                   DELETE OF PERSON CASCADES
                   UPDATE OF PERSON.NAME CASCADES
```

The introduction of the PERSON table (together with the replacement of PEOPLE by the MARRIAGE table) has the effect of converting the (zero-or-one)-to-(zero-or-one) relationship into a combination of two (zero-or-one)-to-one relationships, both of them from MARRIAGE to PERSON. Each of those relationships can then be treated as discussed in the previous section.

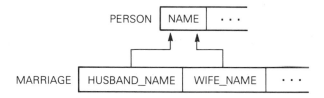

Fig. 5   Persons and marriages

Note 1:   The choice of primary key for the MARRIAGE table (between the candidate keys HUSBAND_NAME and WIFE_NAME) is of course arbitrary. There is an unfortunate asymmetry here.

Note 2:   It might be argued that the husband-and-wife example is somewhat atypical, involving as it does a relationship between two entities that are both of the same type (husbands and wives are both PERSONs). We could perhaps generalize the example as suggested in Fig. 6. PseudoSQL:

```
MAN         ( NAME, ... )
            PRIMARY KEY ( NAME )

WOMAN       ( NAME, ... )
            PRIMARY KEY ( NAME )

MARRIAGE ( HUSBAND_NAME, WIFE_NAME, ... )
            PRIMARY KEY ( HUSBAND_NAME )
            ALTERNATE KEY ( WIFE_NAME )
                        NULLS NOT ALLOWED
            FOREIGN KEY ( HUSBAND_NAME ) REFERENCES MAN
                        NULLS NOT ALLOWED
                        DELETE OF MAN CASCADES
                        UPDATE OF MAN.NAME CASCADES
            FOREIGN KEY ( WIFE_NAME ) REFERENCES WOMAN
                        NULLS NOT ALLOWED
                        DELETE OF WOMAN CASCADES
                        UPDATE OF WOMAN.NAME CASCADES
```

Each of MAN and WOMAN could then have their own properties, represented by different columns in the MAN and WOMAN tables. (I begin

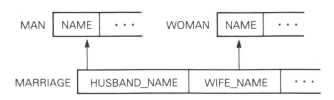

Fig. 6   The marriage example revisited

to get the feeling that I am straying into a minefield with this example. I will leave it to the reader to furnish his or her own suggestions for individual properties for the two entity types.) But there is one additional point that is worth discussing, namely as follows: The husband-and-wife example, precisely because it does involve a relationship between two entities of the same type, raises an interesting problem of *redundancy*. For instance, suppose we need to represent the property "address." Assume for the sake of the example that if A and B are a married couple, then A and B must have the same address. Then:

- For unmarried persons, there is no choice—the address property must clearly be represented by the value of a column (ADDR, say) in either the MAN or WOMAN table, as applicable.
- For married persons, on the other hand, the address property could be represented by an ADDR column in the MARRIAGE table. If instead it appears in the MAN and WOMAN tables, then if A and B are a married couple, their address will be given twice in the database.

Of course, this redundancy may or may not *hurt;* whether it does or not will presumably be a function of the application at hand. And placing ADDR in the MAN and WOMAN tables does at least have the advantage that it would permit a husband and wife to have different addresses at some time in the future, even if such a situation were not possible initially. But the "right" solution to problems like this one does not seem particularly obvious.

5. THE GENUINE ONE-TO-ONE CASE

Let us now turn—finally—to the "genuine" one-to-one case, which (as suggested earlier) in many ways represents the most interesting case of all. I will consider three examples.

The Suppliers Example

The first example is based on the familiar suppliers-and-parts database described in numerous books and papers. Suppose that for some reason—the reason is not important for the moment—suppliers are to be represented by two base tables, SX and SY say, where table SX gives the supplier name and city and table SY gives the supplier status (refer to Fig. 7). The data definitions will have to look something like this:

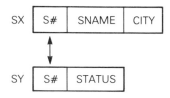

Fig. 7 Representing suppliers by two tables

```
SX ( S#, SNAME, CITY )
   PRIMARY KEY ( S# )
   FOREIGN KEY ( S# ) REFERENCES SY
                      CHECK AT COMMIT
                      NULLS NOT ALLOWED
                      DELETE OF SY CASCADES
                      UPDATE OF SY.S# CASCADES

SY ( S#, STATUS )
   PRIMARY KEY ( S# )
   FOREIGN KEY ( S# ) REFERENCES SX
                      CHECK AT COMMIT
                      NULLS NOT ALLOWED
                      DELETE OF SX CASCADES
                      UPDATE OF SX.S# CASCADES
```

Points arising:

1. Note first that the primary key in each of the two tables is also a foreign key that references the other. The NULLS NOT ALLOWED specifications ensure that every SX row does have a corresponding SY row and vice versa. (In fact, the foreign keys *must* have NULLS NOT ALLOWED, precisely because they are also primary keys.)

2. Observe also that the referential constraints form a cycle. As a result (and because both foreign keys have NULLS NOT ALLOWED in addition), it is necessary to specify deferred checking ("CHECK AT COMMIT") for at least one of the constraints, for otherwise it would never be possible to perform any INSERT operations on either table [4]. Purely for reasons of symmetry, I have specified deferred checking for both constraints.

> *Aside:* It is interesting to note that the IBM product DB2 does not support CHECK AT COMMIT and thus indeed never would allow INSERTs on either table [5]. (It would however allow the tables to be populated initially by means of the LOAD utility—details beyond the scope of this paper.) By contrast, the IBM product SQL/DS (DB2's "baby brother") does provide a way of deactivating, and later reactivating, individual referential constraints dynamically [6]. SQL/DS thus

would be able to support INSERTs on the two tables, by temporarily deactivating the constraints. *End of aside.*

3. If we assume that tables SX and SY "carry equal weight," in the sense that neither one can be regarded in any way as more important than the other, then the only delete rule that makes sense is CASCADES in both cases. If, however, we assume that one of the two tables is somehow subordinate to the other—if, for example, we regard SX as the "controlling" table—then we might specify DELETE CASCADES for the foreign key SY.S# but DELETE RESTRICTED for the foreign key SX.S#. With these specifications, deleting an SX row will automatically delete the corresponding SY row, but attempting to delete an SY row "directly" (i.e., via a direct DELETE on the SY table) will always fail.

Note, however, that at least one of the delete rules *must* be CASCADES, and the other must be either CASCADES or RESTRICTED; NULLIFIES obviously makes no sense in either case (because both foreign keys have NULLS NOT ALLOWED), and specifying RESTRICTED for both would mean that it would never be possible to delete anything at all.

> *Aside:* Neither DB2 nor SQL/DS would in fact be able to deal with the example in the manner suggested here, because they both suffer from an implementation restriction according to which *neither* of the two delete rules could be CASCADES [5,6,7]. *End of aside.*

4. The remarks above regarding delete rules apply to the update rules also, mutatis mutandis—except for the additional consideration that it might be quite reasonable to specify that the primary keys be nonupdatable [4], in which case any update rule for the corresponding foreign keys would be completely irrelevant and should not be specified at all.

> *Aside:* The only update rule supported in DB2 and SQL/DS (implicitly) is RESTRICTED [5,6,7]. As a consequence, the two primary keys would *have* to be nonupdatable in an IBM version of the two tables. (Though it is slightly unfortunate that the nonupdatability is thus enforced in a kind of "cart-before-the-horse" fashion. It ought to be possible, in general, to specify that *any* given column is nonupdatable, if appropriate, regardless of whether that column happens to be a primary key and—if it is a primary key—regardless of whether it happens to be the target of some foreign key.) *End of aside.*

5. I have argued elsewhere [4] that the two-table design for SX and SY as discussed above is in any case not particularly elegant, for reasons that are mostly beyond the scope of this paper. A better design would involve the introduction of a third table, S say, whose purpose is to serve as a kind of "master" for the other two tables (even if that master table were to contain nothing except the master list of all supplier numbers). Refer to Fig. 8.

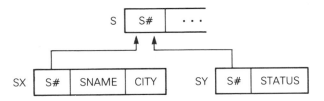

Fig. 8   A three-table design for suppliers

One effect of introducing the master table S is to simplify the referential constraints significantly:

```
S    ( S# )
     PRIMARY KEY ( S# )

SX   ( S#, SNAME, CITY )
     PRIMARY KEY ( S# )
     FOREIGN KEY ( S# ) REFERENCES S
               NULLS NOT ALLOWED
               DELETE OF S CASCADES
               UPDATE OF S.S# CASCADES

SY   ( S#, STATUS )
     PRIMARY KEY ( S# )
     FOREIGN KEY ( S# ) REFERENCES S
               NULLS NOT ALLOWED
               DELETE OF S CASCADES
               UPDATE OF S.S# CASCADES
```

In addition to all of the other advantages cited in reference [4], the foregoing structure has the advantage that it does permit an SX row to exist without a corresponding SY row (if desired), and vice versa. It also has the advantage that it can be handled by DB2 and SQL/DS without any problems. (In fact, the relationships from table SX to table S and from table SY to table S in the three-table design are very similar to the subtype supertype relationships discussed in Section 3 earlier in this paper.)

Note, however, that if we do wish to enforce the constraint that every SX row has a corresponding SY row and vice versa, then we still have the problem of maintaining a "genuine" one-to-one relationship between SX and SY. Indeed, if we also wish to enforce the constraint that every row in the master table S has a corresponding row in each of tables SX and SY, we have the problem of maintaining *two* "genuine" one-to-one relationships, one between S and SX and one between S and SY (the one-to-one relationship between SX and SY will then be maintained automatically, of course). In some respects, therefore, we are worse off than we were before!

6. Of course, even if suppliers are represented by two base tables SX and SY as discussed above, it would be possible to conceal that fact from the

user by defining a view that is the join of those two tables over supplier number. For example (now using genuine SQL syntax):

```
CREATE VIEW S ( S#, SNAME, STATUS, CITY )
    AS SELECT SX.S#, SX.SNAME, SY.STATUS, SX.CITY
       FROM   SX, SY
       WHERE  SX.S# = SY.S# ;
```

However, I choose not to discuss this possibility in any detail because:

(a) Presumably the whole point of the exercise is to allow the user (for some reason) to perceive suppliers as being represented by two separate tables.

(b) In most products today, including in particular the IBM products DB2 and SQL/DS, the join view would not be updatable.

(c) And even if it were updatable, all of the problems discussed under paragraphs 1–5 above would still apply to the underlying base tables (though it now *might* be possible to conceal those problems from the user of the view—*if* updates on a join view can be guaranteed by the system to be atomic; but it seems to me that there are some significant implementation problems here).

(d) Furthermore, if the database includes another table in which "supplier number" is a foreign key (e.g., the shipments table SP, in the usual suppliers-and-parts database), there is now a question as to whether a foreign key can be allowed to reference a view rather than a base table. While it might well prove desirable at some future time to permit foreign keys to reference views, I feel at this time that more research is required before all of the consequences of supporting such a possibility are fully understood.

7. (*A digression.*) Finally, let me briefly discuss a very different (and rather interesting) approach to the SX-SY problem, as follows. Instead of having two (or three) base tables as suggested above, it would be theoretically and logically cleaner to have just one base table S, containing all supplier properties, as follows:

```
S  ( S#, SNAME, STATUS, CITY )
   PRIMARY KEY ( S# )
```

(After all, there is really just one entity type involved, namely suppliers, and having one table per entity type does intuitively seem the right thing to do.) We could then define the SX and SY tables as views of this single table. For example (SQL):

```
CREATE VIEW SX ( S#, SNAME, CITY )
    AS SELECT S.S#, S.SNAME, S.CITY
        FROM   S ;

CREATE VIEW SY ( S#, STATUS )
    AS SELECT S.S#, S.STATUS
        FROM   S ;
```

(Note that this approach is in some respects the exact opposite of the approach described briefly in paragraph 6 above. Of course, this alternative might not be possible in practice, for a variety of reasons. For example, one of the reasons for going to two base tables in the first place might be that a single table would be too wide, in terms of either columns or bytes, to be handled by the DBMS in question. But to continue:)

This single-table design does enjoy several advantages over our previous two- and three-table versions. Those advantages include the following:

- First, note that each of the two views is logically updatable, because it is a primary-key-preserving projection view of the underlying table [3]. INSERTs, UPDATEs, and DELETEs can thus be directed to (either one of) those views.

- Any "foreign key" specifications now apply to the view level, not the base table level ("foreign key" in quotes, because they are no longer true foreign keys—precisely because they do apply to the view level). Such specifications might still be desirable for documentation purposes, but enforcing the corresponding constraints is trivial. Specifically:

  - Inserting a row into either view will automatically cause an appropriate corresponding row to be inserted into the other view. No deferred checking is needed.

    Aside: Of course, inserting a row into either one of the views will succeed only if the other column(s)—i.e., the column(s) not visible through that view—have "nulls allowed" or "defaults allowed." What is more, once a given row has successfully been inserted into one of the two views, an attempt to insert the corresponding row into the other will fail (primary key uniqueness violation). Instead, for example, inserting the supplier information

    ```
    S#  SNAME  STATUS  CITY
    --  -----  ------  ------
    S1  Smith      20  London
    ```

    must be done by (say) first inserting the row (S1,Smith,London) into view SX—which will cause the row (S1,*null*) to be inserted into view SY automatically—and then *updating* that latter row to (S1,20). *End of aside.*

- Deleting a row from either view will automatically cause the corresponding row to be deleted from the other view. No cascading is needed. (On the other hand, if one of the two entities "controls" the other, the necessary discipline of applying all DELETEs to the controlling view only will have to be imposed on the system from outside, instead of being enforced automatically from within.)
- Updating a supplier number in either view will automatically cause the corresponding change to be made in the other view. No cascading is necessary.
- Updating any other column in either view will (as required) *not* "cascade" to the other.

■ This design *will* work with the IBM products DB2 and SQL/DS. The delete rules *can* be CASCADES (logically speaking—at the view level, that is). The S# columns do *not* have to be nonupdatable.

■ Finally, as indicated above, this design (unlike the two- and three-table designs) does not obscure the fact that there is really only a single entity type involved.

Note, however, that—as suggested earlier—it is probable that the reasons for going to two or three tables in the first place were pragmatic, not logical, in nature, having to do with such matters as performance constraints or implementation restrictions, and hence the single-table design being recommended here might not be a viable option in practice.

(End of digression.)

The Invoices and Shipments Example

Let us now turn our attention to the "invoices and shipments" example mentioned briefly earlier in this paper, since that example does introduce some additional considerations of its own. First, unlike the suppliers example discussed above, this example really does involve two distinct entity types. The "right" design therefore "obviously" requires two base tables (refer to Fig. 9). PseudoSQL:

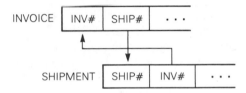

Fig. 9 Invoices and shipments

```
INVOICE ( INV#, SHIP#, INV_DETAILS )
        PRIMARY KEY ( INV# )
        ALTERNATE KEY ( SHIP# )
                    NULLS NOT ALLOWED
        FOREIGN KEY ( SHIP# ) REFERENCES SHIPMENT
                    CHECK AT COMMIT
                    NULLS NOT ALLOWED
                    DELETE OF SHIPMENT CASCADES
                    UPDATE OF SHIPMENT.SHIP# CASCADES

SHIPMENT ( SHIP#, INV#, SHIP_DETAILS )
        PRIMARY KEY ( SHIP# )
        ALTERNATE KEY ( INV# )
                    NULLS NOT ALLOWED
        FOREIGN KEY ( INV# ) REFERENCES INVOICE
                    CHECK AT COMMIT
                    NULLS NOT ALLOWED
                    DELETE OF INVOICE CASCADES
                    UPDATE OF INVOICE.INV# CASCADES
```

Points arising:

1. Note first that each of the two tables includes the primary key of the other as an *alternate* key (this example is therefore different in kind from the SX-SY example discussed above). The ALTERNATE KEY clauses ensure that no two invoices have the same shipment and no two shipments have the same invoice. The NULLS NOT ALLOWED specifications in those clauses ensure that every invoice does have a shipment and every shipment does have an invoice.

2. Next, each of the alternate keys is of course also a foreign key, and the constraints again form a cycle (a good example of one, incidentally). The remarks above under the discussion of the SX-SY example regarding INSERTs, UPDATEs, and DELETEs (paragraphs 2, 3, and 4) apply here also, mutatis mutandis.

3. Note that the approach suggested in paragraph 5 under the SX-SY discussion above is not appropriate here: There is no obvious "master" table that can be introduced, since INVOICE and SHIPMENT are really distinct entity types and do not have any properties in common. The approach suggested (briefly) in paragraph 6 under the SX-SY example is also not appropriate, for essentially the same reason (not to mention the reasons already discussed in that paragraph).

4. However, there is a problem with the foregoing design, as follows. Clearly, the database is required to satisfy the constraint that if the INVOICE table shows invoice *i* as corresponding to shipment *s,* then the SHIPMENT table must show shipment *s* as corresponding to invoice *i,* and vice versa; in other words, the (INV#,SHIP#) pair (*i,s*) must appear in table INVOICE if and only if the (SHIP#,INV#) pair (*s,i*) appears in table SHIPMENT. But the design shown above does not capture or enforce this

constraint. For example, the following configuration of values is permitted by that design and yet violates the constraint:

```
INVOICE  INV#  SHIP#          SHIPMENT  SHIP#  INV#
         ----  -----                    -----  ----
         i1    s1                       s1     i2
         i2    s2                       s2     i1
```

This constraint therefore needs to be separately stated and separately enforced. For example (using a slightly simplified form of the hypothetical integrity language described in reference [1]):

```
CREATE INTEGRITY RULE INV_SHIP_1
    AT COMMIT CHECK
    FORALL INVOICE
        ( EXISTS SHIPMENT
                ( SHIPMENT.SHIP# = INVOICE.SHIP# AND
                  SHIPMENT.INV#  = INVOICE.INV#  ) )
    AND
    FORALL SHIPMENT
        ( EXISTS INVOICE
                ( INVOICE.INV#   = SHIPMENT.INV#  AND
                  INVOICE.SHIP#  = SHIPMENT.SHIP# ) ) ;
```

Ideally, of course, this constraint would be enforced by the system, not by application code (though for most products today this ideal is mere wishful thinking).

5. Last, note that (as the previous paragraph indicates) this example— again unlike the SX-SY example—involves some *redundancy:* Every pair of (INV#,SHIP#) values appearing in either one of the two tables also necessarily appears in the other. If instead we go for a single-table design, along the lines discussed for the SX-SY example above (paragraph 7), we can avoid this redundancy:

```
INV_SHIP ( INV#, SHIP#, INV_DETAILS, SHIP_DETAILS )
         PRIMARY KEY ( INV# )
         ALTERNATE KEY ( SHIP# ) NULLS NOT ALLOWED
```

We can define the INVOICE and SHIPMENT tables as (projection) views:

```
CREATE VIEW INVOICE ( INV#, SHIP#, INV_DETAILS )
    AS SELECT INV#, SHIP#, INV_DETAILS
       FROM   INV_SHIP ;

CREATE VIEW SHIPMENT ( SHIP#, INV#, SHIP_DETAILS )
    AS SELECT SHIP#, INV#, SHIP_DETAILS
       FROM   INV_SHIP ;
```

Again, each of these views preserves the primary key (and alternate key, incidentally) of the underlying table, and so is updatable. The primary keys of the views are INV# (for INVOICE) and SHIP# (for SHIPMENT); IN-

VOICE.SHIP# and SHIPMENT.INV# are alternate keys, with NULLS NOT ALLOWED in each case.

Once again, this single-table design does enjoy several advantages over the previous two-table version. Those advantages include all the ones that applied in the SX-SY case; in addition, the single-table design avoids the redundancy of the two-table version (at the base table level, that is; there is still redundancy—logically speaking—at the *view* level, but that redundancy does not hurt). There is no longer any need to state or enforce the complex integrity constraint INV_SHIP_1 shown earlier.

On the other hand, there are some disadvantages also. Suppose that:

(a) We choose INV# as the primary key for the INV_SHIP base table, as shown above. (Note the unpleasant asymmetry here, incidentally—the choice of which of the candidate keys INV# and SHIP# is to be the primary key is basically arbitrary.)

Suppose also that:

(b) Shipments have certain "characteristics" (i.e., dependent entities [2]) that invoices do not; e.g., suppose that shipments are containerized, each shipment involving multiple containers. Then a new CONTAINER base table is needed (see Fig. 10).

PseudoSQL (first attempt):

```
CONTAINER   ( CONT#, SHIP#, ... )
            PRIMARY KEY ( CONT# )
            FOREIGN KEY ( SHIP# ) REFERENCES INV_SHIP ...
                        /* warning : this is INVALID */
```

The problem is that column SHIP# in the INV_SHIP table is an *alternate* key, not the primary key. The syntax shown above is thus not legal: Column SHIP# in the CONTAINER table cannot be a foreign key referencing table INV_SHIP, because foreign keys in the relational model are required—for very good reasons [4]—to reference primary keys, not alternate keys. What is more, it would be extremely undesirable to have to give up

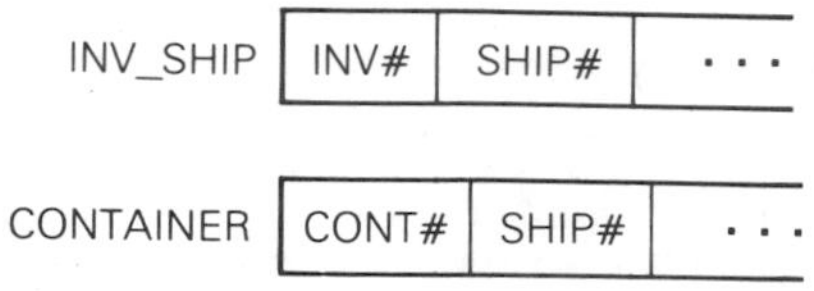

Fig. 10 Shipments and containers

on such a basic principle, especially just in order to cater for such a comparatively esoteric kind of situation. Hence we are faced with the following possibilities:

(a) We could replace SHIP# by INV# in the CONTAINER table. However, this design seems very artificial (containers have nothing to do with invoices per se), and moreover introduces an unpleasant level of indirection into the design (the shipment for a given container can only be found via the corresponding invoice).

(b) We could leave the design as it is (without the foreign key specification), but add an explicit statement of the constraint that every SHIP# value in the CONTAINER table must also appear in the INV_SHIP table:

```
CREATE INTEGRITY RULE INV_SHIP_2
   CHECK
   FORALL CONTAINER
      ( EXISTS INV_SHIP
            ( INV_SHIP.SHIP# = CONTAINER.SHIP# ) ) ;
```

Again, of course, this constraint would ideally be enforced by the system, not by application code.

(c) We could introduce a "surrogate" primary key for INV_SHIP (IS#, say), and use that as the foreign key in the CONTAINER table—which still involves a level of indirection, as in case (a) above, but does at least reintroduce the symmetry that was lost when we arbitrarily chose INV# as the primary key for INV_SHIP.

(Actually, the surrogate solution has certain other arguments in its favor also [2,4]. However, no system today—so far as I am aware—provides any direct support for surrogates; as a consequence, the surrogates in the example would have to be managed by application code and would probably have to be exposed to the user, for update operations at least, if not for retrieval operations as well.)

Another disadvantage of the single-table design in this example is that it tends to conceal the fact that there really are two distinct entity types (because it bundles them both into a single base table). It is true that the two entity types are highly interdependent, but nevertheless "one base table for one entity type" does generally seem to be a good design principle. (Note that this principle itself can be regarded as another good example of a "genuine" one-to-one relationship!) The loss of symmetry referred to above (in the solution not involving surrogates)—arising from the arbitrariness of the choice between INV# and SHIP# as the primary key for the INV_SHIP table—can be seen as yet another disadvantage.

So what is the "right" solution to this problem? I tend to feel that it is better to have a clean logical design—i.e., to have two separate base tables

INVOICE and SHIPMENT at the logical level. Unfortunately, I am not aware of any existing DBMS that provides adequate support for such a design; implementation restrictions, in every DBMS I know, effectively mandate a less than fully clean solution. Finding a good way to provide support for the clean design—perhaps by mapping the two tables to a single (prejoined) file at the physical level?—can be regarded as a new challenge for DBMS architects and implementers.

The Departments and Managers Example

For my final example of a genuine one-to-one relationship, I return to the "departments and managers" example discussed briefly toward the end of Section 3, in which there are three tables as follows (refer back to Fig. 4):

```
DEPT  ( DEPT#, ..., MGR_EMP#, ... )
      PRIMARY KEY ( DEPT# )
      ALTERNATE KEY ( MGR_EMP# )
                  NULLS NOT ALLOWED
      FOREIGN KEY ( MGR_EMP# ) REFERENCES MGR
                  CHECK AT COMMIT
                  NULLS NOT ALLOWED
                  DELETE OF MGR RESTRICTED
                  UPDATE OF MGR.EMP# CASCADES

MGR   ( EMP#, ... )
      PRIMARY KEY ( EMP# )
      FOREIGN KEY ( EMP# ) REFERENCES EMP
                  NULLS NOT ALLOWED
                  DELETE OF EMP CASCADES
                  UPDATE OF EMP.EMP# CASCADES

EMP   ( EMP#, ... , DEPT#, ... )
      PRIMARY KEY ( EMP# )
      FOREIGN KEY ( DEPT# ) REFERENCES DEPT
                  NULLS NOT ALLOWED
                  DELETE OF DEPT RESTRICTED
                  UPDATE OF DEPT.DEPT# CASCADES
```

Points arising:

1. Once again we have a cycle of referential constraints, this time involving three tables. Deferred checking must be specified for at least one of the three constraints. I have specified CHECK AT COMMIT for the constraint from DEPT to MGR only, on the grounds that this particular relationship is likely to be fairly stable in practice, and hence that the presumed inefficiency of deferred checking is unlikely to constitute much of a problem.

Aside: This latter consideration is admittedly "only" a performance matter. As a general principle, it is a bad idea to allow "mere" performance considerations to corrupt the logical design. In the example, there may very well be other (as yet unknown) reasons for requesting deferred checking on one or both of the other two constraints instead of or as well as on the constraint from DEPT to MGR. *End of aside.*

2. As explained earlier in this paper (Section 3), the relationship between DEPT and MGR is a "genuine" one-to-one relationship; in other words, for one DEPT row there is one corresponding MGR row and vice versa. Enforcing the constraint from DEPT to MGR is handled by enforcing the foreign key constraint on DEPT.MGR_EMP#. However, enforcing the constraint from MGR to DEPT is not quite so straightforward, because (again as explained in Section 3) there is no direct foreign key in MGR that refers to DEPT. But if the system enforces both

(a) the foreign key constraint on MGR.EMP# (from MGR to EMP)

and

(b) the foreign key constraint on EMP.DEPT# (from EMP to DEPT),

then the constraint from MGR to DEPT will be enforced automatically. In fact, the constraint from MGR to DEPT is *transitive* (via EMP); it is not even necessary to state the constraint explicitly (though it will probably still be desirable to document it in the form of a comment, at least). Transitive constraints are discussed in more detail in reference [4].

6. CONCLUSIONS

From the discussions in the body of this paper, a number of conclusions can be drawn:

- One-to-one relationships present a set of design problems that are not quite as trivial as they might appear at first sight and require rather careful treatment.

- The (zero-or-one)-to-(zero-or-one) case and the "genuine" one-to-one case both raise certain problems of data redundancy whose solution is far from obvious.

- System support for alternate keys is more important than it might appear at first sight.

- The "genuine" one-to-one case, at least, suggests some directions in which DBMSs might be extended to support additional flexibility in the mapping between base tables and physical storage. Lack of such facilities in present-day systems—in particular, in the IBM products DB2 and SQL/DS—is likely to lead to a variety of unfortunate design compromises.

ACKNOWLEDGMENTS

I am grateful to an attendee at one of my seminars, Afranio Rocha, for first drawing my attention to some of the special problems of one-to-one relationships. This paper grew directly out of my attempts to answer his questions in this area. I am also grateful to Nagraj Alur for helpful technical discussions and to Nagraj, Nat Goodman, Colin White, and Paul Winsberg, all with Codd and Date, for their comments on earlier drafts of this paper.

REFERENCES AND BIBLIOGRAPHY

1. C. J. Date, "A Contribution to the Study of Database Integrity" (in this volume).

2. C. J. Date, "A Practical Approach to Database Design," in C. J. Date, *Relational Database: Selected Writings* (Reading, MA: Addison-Wesley, 1986).

3. C. J. Date, "Updating Views," in C. J. Date, *Relational Database: Selected Writings* (Reading, MA: Addison-Wesley, 1986).

4. C. J. Date, "Referential Integrity and Foreign Keys. Part I: Basic Concepts; Part II: Further Considerations" (in this volume).

5. C. J. Date, "Primary and Foreign Key Support in DB2," *InfoDB* 3, No. 3 (Fall 1988).

6. Nagraj Alur, "Primary and Foreign Key Support in SQL/DS," *InfoDB* 3, No. 3 (Fall 1988).

7. IBM Corporation, IBM DATABASE 2 Referential Integrity Usage Guide, IBM Document No. GG24-3312-0 (June 1988).

PART V

ADVENTURES IN RELATIONLAND

Andrew Warden

An Introduction
by C. J. Date

The papers in this part of the book were originally written as a series for *The Relational Journal,* starting with the third issue (March 1988). They are reprinted here with permission. By way of introduction, I cannot do better than repeat what I wrote in that March 1988 issue:

> "[This issue of *The Relational Journal*] contains the first of a welcome series of articles by a newcomer to the relational literature, Andrew Warden. In his own peculiar—and deceptively light—style, Warden exposes some of the fundamental errors pervading the most popular relational products today (notably those based on SQL). He uses simple examples to demonstrate the practical problems that arise from such errors, and shows how much more genuinely useful (and how much more genuinely relational) products would be if those errors were corrected. He also provides much sound practical advice. Gradually, he builds up to a vision of the way that relational products can and must evolve over the next several years.

"It is a privilege and an honor for me to introduce Warden's articles in this way: They deserve the widest possible circulation among users, vendors, and indeed anyone who has relational interests at heart. I recommend the entire series wholeheartedly."

I hope readers of this book will enjoy the articles as much as I did when I first read them.

These chapters are lovingly dedicated to
the **California Gray Whale,**
a Prince among Monsters

Preface

The metaphorical style I have chosen for these chapters perhaps needs a little explanation, and an apology to those who might otherwise be offended by the use of gender necessitated by that style—I cannot rewrite our traditional mythology!

Monsters are database management systems that purport to be relational but do not properly adhere to the Relational Model of Data—those that support SQL, for instance.

Princes are database management systems (regrettably hypothetical at the time of writing) that do adhere to the Relational Model and are thus able to perform **Chivalrous Deeds** that are beyond the capabilities of the Monsters.

Beautiful Maidens are users of database management systems.

Wise Old Men are people who have studied the Relational Model in depth, are frustrated by the pervasiveness of the Monsters, and feel sorry for the Beautiful Maidens who are thus not getting anything like the amount of Chivalry they deserve.

Please do not infer that I think that wisdom, princeliness, monstrosity, and the ability to use database management systems are exclusive to either sex.

In spite of my personal distaste for the language, my examples do use the style of SQL (albeit often considerably modified) wherever possible. My extensions, illustrating how the Chivalry might be provided, have not been thoroughly researched for syntactical soundness. I use " = " as an operator to introduce names for column or table expressions, rather than the "AS" (or nothing at all) preferred by most SQL dialects.

I base much of my technical discussion and examples on the Relational Algebra, with which I am much more at home than the Calculus. I assume that my readers are familiar with the operators **restriction** (also known as selection), **projection, Cartesian product, natural join, union, intersection,** and **difference.** For completeness, I need four extensions to the original algebra as given by E. F. Codd, which are defined informally below. The first three are already accepted by most authorities.

RENAME

This returns its input table, with one or more columns renamed. It is used to avoid duplicate column names in the results of joins.

Example, given the table SP(S#,P#):

```
R1 = RENAME ( SP, SA = S# ) ;
R2 = RENAME ( SP, SB = S# ) ;
```

R1 could now be joined with R2 to give R3(SA,SB,P#), showing pairs of suppliers who supply the same part, and R3 could then be restricted to eliminate suppliers paired with themselves.

EXTENSION

This "adds" one or more (named) columns to a table. For each added column a formula is given, defining the value to be placed in that column in each row of the result. The formula can refer to columns of the input table. The cardinality (number of rows) of the result is the same as that of the input table.

Example:

```
EXTEND ( EMP, PAY = SALARY + COMMISSION )
```

Or, in a style more like SQL's:

```
SELECT *, PAY = SALARY + COMMISSION
FROM    EMP ;
```

The result contains all the columns of EMP, plus the computed column PAY.

SUMMARIZE

This is similar to extension, except that the formulas for calculations involve **aggregating** functions, optionally within defined **groups.** In fact, it can be thought of as an extension of a projection over the "grouping columns."

Example:

```
SUMMARIZE ( EMP, GROUP_BY ( DEPT# ), AVESAL = AVG ( SALARY ) )
```

Or, in SQL style:

```
SELECT DEPT#, AVESAL = AVG ( SALARY )
FROM    EMP
GROUP   BY DEPT# ;
```

EMP is projected over DEPT#, and the projection is extended by a column called AVESAL, which contains the average salary for each department. If no grouping columns are specified, the average salary for the whole company is obtained. If EMP is empty, so is the result.

The available aggregating functions typically include SUM, AVG, MAX, and MIN. COUNT, if available, is the same as SUM(1). Additional functions, such as STDEV (standard deviation), can easily be defined. If the DBMS supports a Boolean data type (as it really should), then further possibilities include the functions ALL and ANY, which return TRUE if a given predicate is true for all or any, respectively, of the rows contributing to each group. ALL and ANY can be used to show, e.g., which departments employ only people earning more than a certain salary, or which departments employ any programmers.

GENERALIZED DIVISION

The usual example given for division is the query "Find supplier numbers for suppliers who supply all parts," which is done by dividing the shipments table SP(S#,P#) by the projection of the parts table P over P#.

This form of division requires all of the columns of the divisor to have corresponding columns in the dividend. A generalization, for which I am grateful to Stephen Todd, allows division to be defined for **any two tables,** and also generalizes the kinds of queries for which it can be used.

Suppose we have the tables CHILDOF(PARENT,CHILD) and ATTENDS(CHILD,SCHOOL). The original division would allow us to ask the ridiculous questions "Which parents are parents of all the children?" and "Which schools are attended by all the children?" (though in both cases we would have to project one of the given tables over CHILD before performing the division).

In the generalized division, CHILDOF can be divided by ATTENDS or ATTENDS can be divided by CHILDOF. In both cases, the result is a binary relation over PARENT and SCHOOL. If CHILDOF is divided by ATTENDS, the result shows schools whose pupils all have the same parents, and who those parents are (still perhaps a little ridiculous). If ATTENDS is divided by CHILDOF, the result shows parents whose children all attend the same school, and which those schools are (which is not ridiculous at all).

More generally, given R(A,C) and S(B,C), where C is the set of columns common to R and S, A is the other columns of R, and B is the other columns of S, dividing R by S gives pairs (a,b) such that for every (b,c) in S there exists an (a,c) in R. Any of the sets of columns A, B, C can be empty. If B is empty, the operation degencrates to the original division of R by S. If A is empty, the operation degenerates to the original division of S by R. If C is empty, the operation degenerates to the Cartesian product of R and S.

In Chapter 20, "In Praise of Marriage," I further define a commonly accepted special case of **natural join,** choosing to call it **marriage.**

ACKNOWLEDGMENTS

Above all, I must acknowledge the fine work of the team at the IBM United Kingdom Scientific Centre (now located in Winchester, England) in ironing out so many aspects of the implementation of a system based firmly on E. F. Codd's Relational Algebra. In the early seventies, when the Centre was in Peterlee, they devised the Peterlee Relational Test Vehicle (PRTV), including its data language Information Systems Base Language (ISBL), which is the origin of many of the ideas I express in these chapters. Those in "The Naming of Columns" and "In Praise of Marriage" can be found in:

- "An Algebra of Relations for Machine Computation," by Patrick Hall and Stephen Todd, in the *Conference Record of the 2nd ACM Symposium on Principles of Programming Languages,* Palo Alto, California (January 1975)
- "Relations and Entities," by Patrick Hall, John Owlett, and Stephen Todd, in G. M. Nijssen (ed.), *Modelling in Database Management Systems,* North-Holland (1976)
- "The Peterlee Relational Test Vehicle—A System Overview," by Stephen Todd, in the *IBM Systems Journal* 15, No. 4, 285–308 (1976)

These ideas found their way into Business System 12,* too, and I am particularly indebted to **Stephen Todd** for the many useful discussions we have had over the years.

I must mention my colleague **Brian Rastrick,** who, as a joint planner for Business System 12, accompanied me on a wonderful voyage of discovery into the relational world in 1978.

Two other IBM colleagues, **Geoff Butler** (a coworker on Business System 12, and the chief designer of its language) and **Adrian Larner,** have also contributed enormously to the straightening out of my own thinking and writing.

I hope that all the other colleagues who worked on Business System 12, too many to mention individually, will forgive me for singling out the late **Jim Hobbs,** with whom I had an exhilarating time developing the first version of Business System 12's optimizer. Sadly, Jim died of cancer, while still in his thirties, in 1987.

Chris Date taught me the Relational Model in 1972, and thus initiated the love affair to which I confess in "The Naming of Columns." He has also reviewed all of my articles and provided much vital encouragement and support, especially on my occasional trips to California. The dedication of my part of this book results from one of those trips, when we made an unforgettable visit to Point Lobos and I saw my first Gray Whales.

My indebtedness to **E. F. Codd,** the originator of the Relational Model, goes without saying. Dr. Codd reviewed my first three *Relational Journal* articles and made many useful comments.

My thanks, too, to **Phil Jones,** managing director of Codd and Date Ltd. and editor of *The Relational Journal,* for publishing my articles in the first place and for permission to reproduce them here.

My wife, **Lindsay Darwen,** has done much more than tolerate the frequent mental and physical absences occasioned by my work in the Relational field. She pointed out some dreadful extravagances in the early drafts of my articles and persuaded me to correct them. My son **Jamie Darwen** also reviewed the drafts and found some technical errors.

Warwick, England   Andrew Warden
1989

---

*The product I worked on in the early 1980s, for use by subscribers to IBM's "Bureau Service."

17

The Naming of Columns

In this first chapter, I vow my allegiance to the **Relational Model of Data,** *and introduce my theme. I open my technical discussion by reasserting the importance of properly formed* **headings** *in tables—that is, every column in every table, whether a base table or a query result, should have a simple, regularly-formed, unique name.*

I show how support for this requirement would permit a system to begin to deliver an orthogonal query language, devoid of some of the restrictions we see in, for instance, SQL.

Listen to this everybody: **I'm IN LOVE!**

I'm in love with my wife and children. I'm in love with the music of Beethoven. And I'm in love with **the Relational Model of Data.**

Like all love affairs, this last one has given me cause to weep at times. Real tears. Sometimes the tears of unbounded joy, sometimes the tears of sorrow and despair. And I'm weeping now, as I write this.

Well, you weren't expecting an introduction like that, when the title of this chapter caught your eye, were you? The fact is, my love affair with the Relational Model has been going on for a long time. During that time I have not only been able to acquire a deep understanding of the Model and its implications, but I have also been in the privileged position of actually being able to use, and to help others to use, a really-and-truly faithful Relational DBMS.

I have been **all the way** with the Relational Model.

Think what that means. I have seen Ted Codd's ideas **come true!** Let me assure you, everybody, they **do** work; his promises are **not** in vain.

I say "privileged," because I suspect that precious few of you can say you've had an experience anything like that; for the truth is that no such DBMSs have yet surfaced to the marketplace to reach a wide public. The one I used made a brief, shining appearance in a small scene, and was then abruptly and brutally murdered by a monstrous, grotesque parody of itself.

Unfortunately, this Monster has remarkable powers of self-replication,* and threatens to engulf the planet. However, all is not lost, for the Monster, like all good monsters, has a **kind heart**, and just a few Magic Words, from a Beautiful Maiden, will turn him and all his clones into Handsome Princes, strutting and wooing and vying for the place in the Maiden's heart.

But, and here's the glitch, the words do have to come from a Beautiful Maiden. **The Monster doesn't listen to Wise Old Men.** The Wise Old Men have to teach the Beautiful Maiden the Magic Words, take her by the hand, lead her to the Monster's Lair, and trust to luck.

End of Emotional Introduction. Tears wiped away.

Start of Real Business.

Ted Codd and Chris Date have shown you the Relational Model, how it works and why it works well. They have also shown you how and why the current DBMSs don't match up to it, and Codd has given you a comprehensive set of criteria by which you can judge to what extent any particular offering adheres to the model, the correct assumption being: The more faithful the adherence, the more useful the product.

What I want to do is to build on some of Codd's criteria by giving real, meaningful, practical tests that you can easily apply for yourself. If your DBMS fails any of my tests, you can be sure that it consequently fails to meet one or more of Codd's criteria. I hope you will also be able to judge the importance of my tests in your own business. And above all I hope you will feel sufficiently well-armed to confront your Vendor with this thing your DBMS can't do, and why it can't do it, and why it needs to be able to.

This brings me to:

Warden's Test Number 1

Does the system allow you to phrase, in a single expression, the query "For each employee, show his or her name, salary, and average salary for his or her department"?

---

*Not true replication, for the clones do tend to have their warts in different places.

More generally, can the system combine aggregate results, such as totals and averages, with the details from which the aggregates were computed?

This is a very common requirement indeed. Think of all those reports that computers have been producing since the Year Dot, showing details, grouped typically by "department" or "branch" or "customer" or whatever, with the group totals on a special line at the end of each group.

A "relational" DBMS that can't give you that information in a single result is a very poor relation indeed!

It is true that a relational DBMS can't give you the report formatted as I have described. Report formatting isn't its job. But it should at least be able to give you the data, in one go, from which you can easily make that report (with a friendly report generator, of course).

Of course, I'm sure you'd prefer to ask the question "Can **any query**, no matter how complicated, be expressed in a single statement?" Well, Warden's Test Number 1 gets you off to a very good start in probing such a question, and here's why:

When we try to break the "name, salary, average salary" query down using Relational Algebra,* we find it has three components. Two of these use the well-known **project** and **natural join** operators. The third is an operation that provides the vital function expressed, in part, by the GROUP BY clause of SQL. I shall call this function SUMMARIZE, and I'll express that part of the query by:

```
SUMMARIZE ( EMP, GROUP_BY ( DEPT# ), AVESAL = AVG ( SALARY ) )
```

The three arguments to SUMMARIZE are:

1. The table from which the summary is to be made, denoted by the simple name EMP in the example
2. The set of columns (just one column, DEPT#, in the example) to be used to determine the groups inside which aggregating will be done
3. The aggregate calculations to be done within each group

The result is a table, with two columns (in our example), one containing department numbers, the other containing the average salary for each corresponding department number. There is one row for each department, and the primary key is DEPT#.

Note that both columns have a name. Remember the title of this chapter?

---

*As Chris Date says, programmers like the algebra, end-users the calculus. Sorry, I'm a programmer!

- The name of the department number column is DEPT#, inherited from the table EMP.

- The name of the average salary column is AVESAL. It's a brand new column, and I gave it that name by associating thc name with the formula for calculating the value. I used an equals sign to perform this association—many languages use an equals sign for such purposes, don't they?

For convenience, I'll give a name to the above table expression. I'll call it DEPTAVE.

Now I can depart from this syntax of my own invention and go into one that will almost certainly be more familiar to you. I need to join each row resulting from the expression called DEPTAVE to each row in the EMP table that has the same value in DEPT# (department number). I could express this join by:

```
SELECT *
FROM    EMP, DEPTAVE
WHERE   EMP.DEPT# = DEPTAVE.DEPT# ;
```

We're very close to the answer we want now. We merely have to throw away the columns from EMP and DEPTAVE that contain information we weren't asked for:

```
SELECT ENAME, SALARY, AVESAL
FROM    EMP, DEPTAVE
WHERE   EMP.DEPT# = DEPTAVE.DEPT# ;
```

I've merely replaced the "*" in the SELECT clause by a list of the **names** of the columns I want in the answer.

Now, Warden's Test Number 1 demands that the query be expressible in a **single** statement. So far, it looks as if we might have to have two statements, one to define the intermediate result DEPTAVE, another to finish things off. However, we could combine the two steps into a single expression, albeit using a rather strange, concocted syntax, like this:

```
SELECT ENAME, SALARY, AVESAL
FROM    EMP,
        DEPTAVE = SUMMARIZE ( EMP, GROUP_BY ( DEPT# ),
                                    AVESAL = AVG ( SALARY ) )
WHERE   EMP.DEPT# = DEPTAVE.DEPT# ;
```

All I've done, you see, is replace the simple reference to the name DEPTAVE by its definition, using an equals sign, again, to associate the name with the table expression it stands for. Note that I have to preserve the name, because I need to use it in the WHERE clause.*

---

*In some languages, this name would be called a "correlation name."

Points to note:

1. Every column in the "final" result has a **simple, regularly-formed, unique name:** ENAME, SALARY, AVESAL.

2. I was only able to ask for these three columns because (a) every column in the base table EMP has a simple, regularly-formed, unique name and (b) every column in the table representing the calculated departmental averages has a simple, regularly-formed, unique name too! If I had not given AVG(SALARY) a name, I wouldn't have been able to ask for it to appear in the final answer.

3. Because of point 1, the expression defining the "final" result could, if required, be used as a subexpression in some even more complicated query. Perhaps what I really wanted to find out was the managers of all employees whose salary exceeds the department average by a certain amount, because the company's having a purge on prima donnas.

4. Two column names used inside the overall expression, EMP.DEPT# and DEPTAVE.DEPT#, are unique but not simple. Fortunately, I was able to throw them away because they weren't required in the final answer. But they are indeed a problem, and I'll show you how a respectable DBMS should tackle this one in the next chapter.

Do you see, then, that I am pointing toward a way by which a DBMS might achieve **full orthogonality?** Perhaps the most important test for orthogonality in any system is:

Can a table expression be used anywhere a table name can be used?

In other words, **a table name is merely the trivial case of a table expression!**

Would you tolerate a programming language (say a dialect of FORTRAN) in which you didn't have complete freedom to use a numeric formula of arbitrary complexity anywhere a number is required?

Why the title of this chapter?

That wonderful property of true algebras (such as the Relational Algebra) that guarantees that results are the same kind of thing as the operands is called **closure.** I'm merely reemphasizing a point in the Model, as it seems to have been forgotten by so many vendors of DBMSs that are claimed to be relational, that requires that the closure property be satisfied for the **heading** of a table as well as for its **body.** (The heading of a table is its set of column names, the body is its set of rows.)

Does your DBMS make sure every column has a simple, regularly-formed, unique name? No? Then I'm certain it fails Warden's Test Number 1. And I'm certain it can't answer queries of arbitrary complexity. And I'm certain it's not suitable as a target for the Natural Language Query products that we are all expecting to see in the "fifth generation."

End of Real Business. Return of wistful tears.

Well, Beautiful Maiden, will you hold my hand? Please do, if you've stayed with me up to now, for the fact is, we're a long way toward the Monster's Lair already. Remember the Magic Words I've taught you thus far, and go over them again and again. There are more to come, and you are going to have to remember **everything** when I leave you to that part of our dread mission that is yours, and yours alone, to undertake.

18

In Praise of Marriage

In this chapter, I extol the virtues of the "Natural Join" relational operator, in particular the special case to which I affectionately refer as "marriage," and suggest how this operator might usefully be implemented in a query language that espouses the principle laid down in "The Naming of Columns."

I show also how this principle can form the basis for implementation of other operators in the query language.

"Let me not to the marriage of true tables* admit impediments."

Now, my Beautiful Maiden, today we will talk about marriage. Oh no, my dear, not you and I. That might have been (*sigh*) but it's far too late now! Besides, you are betrothed to the Monster, aren't you? And we must turn him into a Handsome Prince for you, mustn't we?

No. Rather, we are going to study "the marriage of true tables," and any let or hindrance thereto that you should look out for.

You haven't forgotten the Magic Words I've already taught you, have you? You **must** remember them, because they are intimately connected with the new ones you will learn today.

Let's get down to business straight away, then, and consider:

---

*Some scholars think the Bard wrote "minds" here. He didn't. And even if he did, it was only for the scansion. He **meant** tables.

467

Warden's Test Number 2

Can you, with a single command, make a copy of any arbitrary result?

For instance, you might want to take a snapshot of some result, for further analysis; or you might be reorganizing your database, splitting or joining the current base tables, horizontally or vertically.

A possible syntax for the command* is:

```
COPY table-expression INTO table-name [, REPLACING ] ;
```

where:

- "table-expression" is an arbitrary expression, defining the result to be copied;

- "table-name" is the name of the table to which the result is to be copied (the target table). **This table is not required to exist already;** its definition is **implied by the table expression whose result (value) is to be copied.**

- "REPLACING" means "If a base table with this name already exists, I'm happy for it to be overwritten."

For example:

```
COPY ( SELECT * FROM S, SP WHERE S.S# = SP.S# ) INTO S_SP ;
```

This would copy the "equijoin" of S (suppliers) and SP (shipments) on S# (supplier number) to a new table called S_SP.

You can probably see already why this example cannot possibly work, but let's first consider those features of the Relational Model that would allow a really-and-truly faithful Relational DBMS to support such a COPY command.

According to the model, the definition of a base table comprises:

1. The name of the table

2. The name and underlying domain† of each column

3. The **primary key** (a subset of the column names)

---

*In fact, this is the "Relational Assignment" operation insisted on in E. F. Codd's evaluation criteria for relational DBMSs. It is probably better implemented as two distinct commands, "CREATE TABLE table-name LIKE table-expression" and "INSERT table-expression INTO table-name," thus separating the action of defining the new table from the action of populating it. See further discussion in Chapter 20.

†The underlying domain might be just a builtin data type such as NUMBERS.

For our COPY command to work, therefore, each column in the result of our table expression must have a simple, unique name, in accordance with the column naming rules for base tables, and the result must have an **implied primary key,** which will become the primary key for S_SP.

In other words, the **heading** of a result must be of the same form as the heading of a base table ("**closure**"—we've already seen the importance of this, in Warden's Test Number 1), including, for each column, its underlying domain and whether or not it participates in the primary key.

Forget about the primary key, for now. I'll come back to that in the next chapter. Here, I am concerned only with the problem of naming the columns in the target table, having stated that those names should be implied by the expression defining the result to be copied.

The table resulting from the table expression in our example has two columns, S.S# and SP.S#, that do not have proper (i.e., simple) column names. These qualified names cannot be used as column names in a base table. Furthermore, changing the column naming rules to allow such names in a base table is not a workable solution to the problem, for then the specter of multiply-qualified names (such as X.SP.S#) would start to rear its head, and there would be no limit to the length of column names. And the problem is more far-reaching than that: Suppose your DBMS passes Warden's Test Number 1 and allows nested table expressions in queries. Then we would have multiply-qualified column names (such as X.SP.S#) arising from subexpressions, and complex queries would become more and more difficult to express.

The first part of the solution to this problem is merely to **disallow** duplicate column names! In other words, whenever the query involves a **product** of two or more tables, as implied by "FROM S, SP" in our example, we insist that no column of any operand has the same name as any other column of any operand.

Then, so long as any calculated columns are also properly named, **all** the columns of the result have unique, simple names, eligible for use in the definition of a base table. In other words, table **headings** are **closed** under all the operations of our manipulative language.

At first sight this rule against duplicated column names might seem to impose enormous restrictions, for of course it is essential to be able to join **any** two tables. Furthermore, it is both natural and correct for the supplier number columns in tables S and SP to have the same name and the same underlying domain, and the **natural join** of S and SP over supplier numbers is bound to occur very commonly in queries against this database.

The solution is simple, elegant, obvious, natural, and charming:

The DBMS **must** provide natural join as an **explicit operator** in its query language.*

A DBMS that does not provide such an operator makes some of the commonest joins well-nigh impossible to express, for the following reason:

"SELECT * FROM S, SP WHERE S.S# = SP.S#" is not a natural join; it is only an equijoin. It omits the essential final step of a natural join, the removal of one of the (duplicated) sets of joining columns.

To achieve that removal, we have to replace the "*" in the SELECT clause by a list of column names that includes the common columns (just S#, in the example) once only, all the other columns of table S, and all the other columns of table SP.

Thus, natural join in such a DBMS is restricted to those users who happen to know all the column names and who have the time and energy to type them all in. **This is an unbearable restriction.**†

Furthermore, a natural join that is thus "handcoded" is vulnerable to changes in the database schema. The **meaning** of the natural join of suppliers and shipments does not change, just because the joining column changes its name or becomes composite.

Let's now study the natural join operator, and see what a huge difference it makes to our lives. I'll express it in the following syntax:

```
MARRIAGE ( table-expression-1, table-expression-2 )
```

We can consider the wonderful union achieved by this operator to take place as follows:

First, there is the **tender foreplay,** in which the columns of both operands are examined to see which, if any, have the same name. Those that have the same name are called "common columns," and a common column must have the same domain, as well as the same name, in both operands.‡

---

*A note for the purist: I am deliberately limiting my use of the term "natural join" to the case that is far and away the most important in practice—namely, natural join based on **common column names.**

†A considerable improvement is obtained if, in the SELECT clause (or your equivalent thereof), you can specify the columns to be **excluded**—perhaps "SELECT * EXCEPT columns"—but the operation would still be restricted to those users who know the names of the common columns and have the time and energy to write them all out **three** times!

‡If the names are the same but the domains are different, it is (usually) an error. See Chapter 2.

Second, we have the **coupling,** in which the matching rows of the two operands (rows that have identical values in all the common columns) are joined together.

Finally, and most important of all, we have the grand climax in which one set of common columns (it doesn't matter which) is **ejaculated,** along with those dreaded correlation names.

And the child of this union is as complete and perfect an individual as you could wish for! Every characteristic is inherited from one or other of its parents, yet there isn't a single blemish to betray the mechanism of this inheritance or the origin of any particular characteristic.

The benefits of Marriage are huge and wide-ranging:

- It is a very succinct way of asking for a natural join, and in real life the vast majority of the joins you want to do are natural ones.

- Applications using it are immune to many changes in the database schema. For example, the Database Administrator might want to change the name of a common column, or to add a new common column (such changes often arise during refinement of referential integrity constraints, for instance).

- There is no longer any need for correlation names. Every column can be identified just by a simple name.

- If the system also makes sure that all calculated columns in results have proper simple names, a table expression can be used immediately as a model for the creation of a new table. So we can do the "copy" that Warden's Test Number 2 asks for. Furthermore, headings are closed under the manipulative operations, and the language has a chance to be **orthogonal.**

- If the DBMS supports **user-defined** relational functions, the definition of such a function could, for instance, include an expression of the marriage of the two arbitrary tables given as arguments to the function, without having to be told the names of the common columns.*

The detractors of Marriage will say "What about those occasions when I want to do a nonnatural join of tables that have common columns?" and, more importantly, "What about when the tables I want to join have common columns that are not intended to be joining columns?" For

---

*This was exactly how **division** was delivered to users of Business System 12, though certain other system-provided operators, based on the same principle as Marriage, were also needed.

instance, some queries require a table to be joined to itself (I call such a join a **reflex join**).

A DBMS that embraces natural join and disallows duplicate column names must also provide a **column rename** operator, for use in query expressions.

For an example of a nonnatural join, suppose that you want to see a list of all the employees who were hired before employee E39, and the answer is to include the date on which E39 was hired. You might start with:

```
SELECT HIREDATE
FROM    EMP
WHERE   EMP# = 'E39' ;
```

This will deliver a table with a single row and a single column, HIREDATE. You now need to join that result with EMP, retaining only those joined rows whose HIREDATE is before E39's. The trouble is, you don't want (and shouldn't be able to have) two columns both called HIREDATE in the result. The solution is to rename one of the HIREDATE columns. For example:

```
SELECT E39_HIREDATE, EMP#, HIREDATE
FROM    ( SELECT E39_HIREDATE = HIREDATE
          FROM    EMP
          WHERE   EMP# = 'E39'),
        EMP
WHERE   HIREDATE < E39_HIREDATE ;
```

The expression "E39_HIREDATE = HIREDATE" is an example of the use of the column rename operator.

For my second example, a natural join of tables with a common column that is not the column to be joined on, suppose my personnel file, a table called EMP, includes NAME, SALARY, and MANAGER, where MANAGER is the NAME of somebody else in the file. If I wanted to see everybody's salary and manager's salary, I might have to write

```
SELECT NAME, SALARY, MANAGER_SALARY
FROM    EMP, ( SELECT MANAGER_NAME = NAME, MANAGER_SALARY = SALARY
               FROM    EMP )
WHERE   MANAGER = MANAGER_NAME ;
```

The inner SELECT here delivers a table that has no column names in common with EMP, even though it derives its result from EMP. Of course, the above join is in fact a natural join, so we might instead have written something like the following:

```
SELECT NAME, SALARY, MANAGER_SALARY
FROM    MARRIAGE ( EMP,
                   ( SELECT MANAGER = NAME, MANAGER_SALARY = SALARY
                     FROM    EMP ) ) ;
```

Now MANAGER is the common column for the join. On one side of the join it is the original MANAGER column, on the other side it is a new name for the NAME column.

Other points about Marriage:

- The operation is **associative,** so it can be extended to support any number of arguments N (N > 0). It is also **commutative,** though the order of the operands might be used to determine the order in which the columns of the result are presented to the outside world. Associativity and commutativity are very important properties for an optimizer to be aware of.

- When there are no common columns, the operation degenerates to an ordinary Cartesian product, because it is true for all possible couplings of rows from the two operands that they have the same combined value (a combination of no values at all) in the common columns (of which there are none).

Other Ways of Combining Tables

The Relational Algebra includes versions of the well-known set operators **union, intersection,** and **difference.**

We can apply any of these operators to any two tables that are **union-compatible.** Union-compatibility requires there to be a one-to-one correspondence between the columns of the two operands; each column of the first operand must have exactly one corresponding column in the second, and vice versa. A row in the first operand is equal in value to a row in the second if the corresponding values in all columns are equal. Of course, the domains of corresponding columns must also be compatible (see Chapter 2).

But how shall we determine the corresponding columns? Domains are insufficient, for two columns in the same table might have the same domain. Column number is distasteful, for the Relational Model insists that column position (left to right) carries no meaning and that operations on tables are unaffected by column position.

The marriage principle supplies the answer. Columns correspond if and only if they have the same **name.** In other words, union compatible tables have the same **heading,** * and that heading is also the heading of the result of a union, intersection, or difference of those tables. *Note:* If we have two

---

*They may, however, have different primary keys.

tables whose bodies are union-compatible, but not their headings, we can use our column rename operator to bang their heads together.

So column names aren't just pretty adornments that remind us what we have where. They are absolutely fundamental to the definition of a decent, orthogonal, query language.

Now, my Beautiful Maiden, you have all the Magic Words that are to do with being able to express any query, however complicated:

- *Name All Columns*

  Within any table, whether a base table or the result of a table expression, every column must have a simple, regularly-formed, unique name.

- *Eschew Duplicate Column Names*

  When two or more tables are joined together, do not allow multiple distinct columns of the same name, from different operands, to appear in the result.

- *Espouse Marriage*

  Support **natural join** (and other polyadic operators that can be defined around the notion of column correspondence by name) as explicit operators in the query language. And don't forget the all-important **column rename** operator!

- *Support Nests*

  Allow a table expression to be used in place of a table name everywhere in the language where it is reasonable to do so (especially in the FROM clause of a SELECT statement, or your equivalent thereof).

You see, it wasn't just that we wanted to be able to do Warden's Tests Numbers 1 and 2. We wanted to soften the Monster's very heart, so that he can do not only those tests but also lots of other lovely, chivalrous things, when he becomes your Prince.

Now that we've got our **headings** straight, in the next chapter I'll give you the Magic Words for the **body,** for that needs attention too, before we can do whatever we will with the results of our queries. Then, at last, we'll be in Relationland, where I hope you'll stay with me a little longer before I take you to the Monster's Lair. We'll have some adventures together that will make sure you remember forever the Magic Words, and hold them true as your sure defense against any Monsters there might ever again be.

19

The Keys of the Kingdom

In this chapter I discuss the principle of **primary key inheritance,** *whereby query results have implied primary keys, derived from those of the base tables and from the semantics of the algebraic operations expressed or implied in the queries.*

I also address some of the inconveniences that are sometimes perceived by users who are compelled to define primary keys for all base tables, and I show what the system could do to relieve them.

Yes, my Beautiful Maiden, the keys of the Kingdom of Relationland are **primary** keys. I know you know about primary keys already, for their fundamental importance has been clearly expounded in the Original Wisdom you and I have already received. But some Monsters, and some Maidens, have failed to take primary keys fully to heart, in the mistaken belief that they are sometimes a nuisance. We need to explode this myth and thus complete the Magic Words that, uttered by you, will make the Monster become your Prince.

Princes, you see, must deal only in **tables.** There is no other viable currency. And a thing is not a table unless it has:

- A regularly-formed **heading,** comprising a set of regularly formed **column names.** I have already given you the Magic Words for this.

- A regularly-formed **body**—a **set** of regularly-formed **rows,** each one containing a single value in each column.

- A **primary key**—a **set** of **column names** (a subset of the heading), such that no two rows have identical values in the indicated set of columns.

A DBMS that deals in any other currency, even if it does deal in proper tables when asked to, is creating unnecessary confusion and complication. What is worse, if it tries to use improper objects in operations that are designed to be operations on tables, then it is very likely to deliver nasty things like **incorrect answers.**

Let us look at an application that might try to take "advantage" of such a DBMS's support for *not-proper-tables.*

There is some process, perhaps computerized, perhaps manual, that measures something at regular times. Every time it takes a measure, it adds that number to a list kept in a not-proper-table called MEASURES. This not-proper-table has a single column, called AMOUNT, and no primary key. At the end of the agreed period, various statistical analyses are done on MEASURES, using the DBMS's query language.

Before these analyses are done, it is agreed that the highest and lowest amounts are to be discarded, to cater for aberrations in the measuring process. If two or more amounts are equal to the highest or lowest, then only one of them will be discarded.

Now it is time to introduce

Warden's Test Number 3

Can you delete any particular row?

If the three highest amounts are all 1,234,567, how do you delete just one of them, without deleting the other two as well?* Delete all three, then reinsert two of them? How do you know how many such duplicates there are?

Even the solution of changing one of them to some impossible amount, such as −1, then deleting that, is not available. If you have no means of identifying a particular row (and that's one of the things primary keys are for), you can neither delete it nor update any of its column values.

The trouble is, the **correct** way of doing this application is probably distasteful, if it involves your having to make the effort of choosing some new, unique value for the key of every new measure you add to the table. But that's because the Monster doesn't know about **chivalry.**

You are quite happy to manage things like personnel numbers, customer numbers, supplier numbers, etc., and use them in primary keys. They

---

*I discount solutions such as SQL's CURRENT OF CURSOR, which is available only to computer programs. I want a command that the end-user could "type in."

arc intimately connected with the way you manage your business. But you really don't want all that kind of fuss to assign a new measure number every time you add a new amount to the MEASURES table.

The Prince will do this **for** you! He'll let you say, when you create the table, that a column called MEASURE_TIME is the primary key, and that when no value is specified on INSERT, he is to generate a new value himself, according to an algorithm called TIME_NOW.*

Then you would be able to delete just one of the 1,234,567s, perhaps by nominating (arbitrarily) the row whose key is "just after 3 o'clock in the afternoon, yesterday."

Other possible algorithms for the generation of unique key-column values include:

SERIAL   This delivers the number 1 when a row is inserted into an empty table. Otherwise it delivers an integer that is equal to the highest previously used, plus one. It can be qualified by reference to some other component of a composite key. For instance, the table called ORDER_DETAILS is often keyed on ORDER# and LINE#, each row describing a particular item (product number, price, quantity, discount) on a particular order. Order numbers are generated by some external process, but you would like line numbers to be generated by the DBMS according to the algorithm "SERIAL within ORDER#."

USERID   This delivers the user ID of the user inserting the row. In some circumstances the user ID is enough, in combination with the other key-column values, to ensure uniqueness.

So you can, after all, eat your cake **and** have it. You can have a proper table called MEASURES, with a primary key called MEASURE_TIME and a single additional column called AMOUNT, and it is just as easy to add a new measure to the table as it was to add one to the not-proper-table.

And there's icing, too!

Suppose you wanted to have a separate base table of measures for each day of the week, and suppose you wanted to do your statistical analysis on the whole week's worth. Now the relational operation called **union** can be safely used to combine all the rows of all seven tables into a single set. By choosing a timestamp as our primary key, we guarantee that no row in any

---

*Perhaps this algorithm delivers the elapsed time, in femtoseconds, since the creation of the universe.

of the tables will be identical to any other row in any other table,* and none of our measures will be "lost" in the union.

Union could not be used when we were working with not-proper-tables, as it would have removed duplicate values, and our statistical analyses would have been incorrect. We would have needed some other, nonrelational, operation, perhaps called *concatenate,* to do the job.†

Two final remarks about not-proper-tables:

1. None of the operations in the query language should ever deliver a not-proper-table. If you have to use a qualifying word such as UNIQUE or DISTINCT to obtain a true relational table, do not fail to do so, but be annoyed about it.

2. No respectable DBMS should let anybody deal in not-proper-tables, for there is no requirement for them; all objections to proper tables can be handled without deviating from the Relational Model.

Any DBMS that has already made the mistake of "supporting" not-proper-tables should now correct the error, without impairing existing applications that take "advantage" of them, by providing new catalog information to help you sort out the sheep from the goats.

The high-level languages we are expecting in the "fifth generation" will need a firm relational base to work on, and will only be able to avoid accidents if the DBMS is able to tell them which tables are proper and which are not.

Now we can address the business outstanding from Warden's Test Number 2, which was:

Can you, with a single command, make a copy of any arbitrary result?

To repeat from Chapter 18, a possible syntax for the command is:

```
COPY table-expression INTO table-name [, REPLACING ] ;
```

where:

- "table-expression" is an arbitrary expression, defining the result to be copied;

- "table-name" is the name of the table to which the result is to be copied (the target table). **That table is not required to exist already;** its definition is **implied by the table expression whose result (value) is to be copied.**

---

*So it is a union of **disjoint sets.**

†I know a DBMS that lets you do unions of not-proper-tables. You get strange effects like: A UNION A is not equal to A; nor is A UNION *empty*; and A UNION B can be smaller than both A and B!

- "REPLACING" means "If a base table with this name already exists, I'm happy for it to be overwritten."

The important thing is that the result of the table expression must be a proper table, so that it can be used as a model for the creation of the target table. I have already shown (in Chapters 17 and 18) how the DBMS can make sure the heading of the result contains only regular column names. But a proper table, as we have seen, has to have a primary key, too. What is to be done about that?

We must assume that the DBMS knows the primary keys of all the base tables (does **your** DBMS know them?), and that the DBMS's query language is mappable to the Relational Algebra (is yours?).

Then we can consider the operations in the Relational Algebra, and specify for each one a rule that determines the primary key of its result:

- **Rename**

  The primary key of the result is the same as that of the operand, bearing in mind that some of the columns of this key might have new names.

- **Restriction**

  The primary key of the result is the same as that of its operand.

  A further refinement is possible if the defining condition for the restriction implies that, in the result, some component of the primary key is of constant value, or always equal to some other component of the primary key. In such cases, that component can be eliminated from the primary key of the result.*

- **Projection**

  If the result includes the primary key of the operand, that is the primary key of the result. Otherwise, the primary key is the combination of all of the columns.†

- **Natural Join (including Cartesian Product)**

  Let C be the set of common columns ("joining columns").

  Let Ka be the primary key of either of the operands and Kb the primary key of the other.

---

*This raises the interesting possibility that a primary key might be the empty set, a notion I will discuss in Chapter 22, "TABLE_DEE and TABLE_DUM."

†I do not consider here any special knowledge the DBMS might have to help it detect any other candidate key.

Let Kr be the primary key of the result.

Kr is given by the following rules, taking the cases in the given order.

1. If Ka and Kb are both subsets of C, either Ka or Kb may be taken as Kr (take the one with fewer columns, if possible, otherwise make an arbitrary choice).

2. If just one of Ka and Kb is a subset of C, take the other as Kr.

3. If C is a subset of just one of Ka and Kb and is disjoint from (i.e., has no columns in common with) the other, take (Ka *union* Kb) *difference* C as Kr.

4. Otherwise, take Ka *union* Kb as Kr.

   Note that, if C is empty, the natural join degenerates to Cartesian product, and Ka and Kb are disjoint. Case 3 applies, but degenerates to Case 4.

- **Union**

   The primary key is the combination of all the columns.

- **Intersection**

   The primary key of either operand may be chosen.

- **Difference**

   The primary key of the result is the primary key of the first operand.

- **Summarize**

   The primary key of the result is the set of grouping columns.

- **Extension**

   The primary key of the operand is preserved.

- **Generalized Division**

   Let the dividend and divisor be R(A,C) and S(B,C), respectively, where C is the set of common columns, A is the other columns of R, and B is the other columns of S. The primary key of the result is the union of the primary key of the projection of R on A and the primary key of the projection of S on B.

Thus, any system in which (a) primary keys are required in base tables (as indeed they should be) and (b) the data manipulation language is mappable into the Relational Algebra (as indeed it should be) could support this aspect of closure (as indeed it should) and could let you make copies easily.

There is just one fly in the ointment:

If your DBMS provides a special mechanism for recording unknown or missing values (sometimes referred to as "nulls"), the above scheme falls over when every column in the result is permitted to contain unknown values, for a primary key value in a base table is not permitted to have an unknown component (this is Codd's **entity integrity** rule). Such a result can arise, for example, when the query involves a projection over a column for which nulls are allowed.

A table that cannot be stored in the database is surely not a proper table, and we can regard this fact as further evidence that a satisfactory systematic treatment of unknowns has not yet been delivered by the research world, and that DBMSs in the meantime would be better advised to implement the "default values" scheme proposed by Date.*

So now at last, my Beautiful Maiden, you have all the Magic Words for turning your Monster into a Prince:

- *Name All Columns*

  Within any table, whether a base table or the result of a table expression, every column must have a simple, regularly-formed, unique name.

- *Eschew Duplicate Column Names*

  When two or more tables are joined together, do not allow multiple distinct columns of the same name, from different operands, to appear in the result.

- *Espouse Marriage*

  Support **natural join** (and other polyadic operators that can be defined around the notion of column correspondence by name) as explicit operators in the query language. And don't forget the all-important **column rename** operator!

- *Support Nests*

  Allow a table expression to be used in place of a table name everywhere in the language where it is reasonable to do so (especially in the FROM clause of a SELECT statement, or your equivalent thereof).

- *Deal Only in Proper Tables*

  Not-proper tables, containing duplicate rows, serve no purpose and give rise to ill-defined operations and traps for the unwary. Allow primary keys to be system-generated in appropriate cases.

---

*See Chapter 8, Appendix A.

- *Spurn Unknowns*

  Yes, this advice is somewhat spurious—I know you can't avoid the problem of "missing data." But please avoid unknowns wherever possible, look askance at current systems that provide "support" for "nulls" or "unknowns" (and criticize them where you find them to be unsound and to deliver traps), and watch carefully for results of new research in this field.

  Of course, there are still many Chivalrous Deeds to be done by the Prince, and I'll show you some of them next time—you do want to stay with me a while, before you visit the Lair, don't you?
  The Prince will be well equipped to rise to the challenge.
  Monsters don't know about chivalry!

20

Chivalry

I have now given some **Magic Words** *for converting* **Monsters** *into* **Princes.**

I have also described two acts of **chivalry** *that a Prince might undertake—the use of a query expression as a model for the creation of a new table, and the system-generation of primary key values to help with certain otherwise awkward applications.*

In this chapter I relate further chivalrous deeds that an intrepid but well-equipped Prince might venture to undertake.

Well, my Beautiful Maiden, here we are, in Relationland at last!

Do you remember, my dear, the Magic Words that got us here, that will turn the Monster into your Handsome Prince? Let's just go over them once again—you chant the Words (in italics), and I'll do the recitatives that accompany them:

- *Name All Columns*

    Within any table, whether a base table or the result of a table expression, every column must have a simple, regularly formed, unique name.

- *Eschew Duplicate Column Names*

    When two or more tables are joined together, do not allow multiple distinct columns of the same name, from different operands, to appear in the result.

- *Espouse Marriage*

  Support **natural join,** and its relatives, as explicit operators in the query language. And don't forget the all-important **column rename** operator!

- *Support Nests*

  Allow a table expression to be used in place of a table name everywhere in the language where it is reasonable to do so (especially in the FROM clause of a SELECT statement, or your equivalent thereof). With reasonable support for "updating through views," table expressions would also be usable as targets for commands like INSERT, UPDATE, and DELETE.

- *Deal Only in Proper Tables*

  Not-proper tables, containing duplicate rows, serve no purpose and give rise to ill-defined operations and traps for the unwary. Allow primary keys to be system-generated in appropriate cases.

- *Spurn Unknowns*

  At least, avoid them wherever you can, and be very wary of the support for "nulls" that is found in some current systems. Watch carefully for results of new research in this field.

Very good! I did notice a little hesitation over the last one, and I sympathize. I just hope that, when the Wise Old Men finally come up with a good approach to missing values, I won't have to spend so much time with you, protecting you from new Monsters.

Now, I've already shown you two chivalrous deeds of which our Prince is capable:

CHIVALROUS DEED NUMBER 1
COPYING QUERY RESULTS

This is also known as "Relational Assignment." Because every table resulting from a query expression has a proper heading, and a primary key, any query expression can be used as a model for the creation of a new table. You don't have to write out the definition of the new table all over again. The new table might be used to contain a snapshot, or it might be part of a reorganization of the database.

All of our Magic Words are important here!

For simplicity, I previously suggested a COPY command for this purpose. Much better is:

```
CREATE TABLE table-name LIKE table-expression [ optional extras ] ;
```

This would create a new, empty table, modeled on the given table expression. The optional extras allow you to override some of the characteristics that would otherwise be inherited from the expression. For instance, if the expression involves a UNION, the system might be unable to derive a better primary key than the entire heading, whereas you, knowing your data, might want to specify a suitable subset of the heading.

When you actually want to populate the snapshot,

```
INSERT table-expression INTO table-name ;
```

would be available, but the Prince will very likely give you a variant of CREATE LIKE that both creates the table and populates it, to save you having to type the table expression twice:

```
CREATE TABLE table-name = table-expression [ optional extras ] ;
```

CHIVALROUS DEED NUMBER 2
SYSTEM-GENERATED KEY VALUES

In Chapter 19, I showed how the Prince helps out when you don't want the bother of working out new primary key values yourself, every time you have to add a new row to a table.

He does this because he doesn't want you ever to feel that any aspect of his dogma is an encumbrance. He knows that, with just a little extra effort on his part, he can help without ever deviating from his principles.

Of course, you would only take advantage of the Prince's automatic key generation in certain special cases. For things like personnel numbers, part numbers, supplier numbers, and customer numbers, you would want to continue managing the scheme yourself.

Now, here are some other things your Prince will do. I leave it to you to judge how well your Monster does them, if at all.

CHIVALROUS DEED NUMBER 3
NAMING AN EXPRESSION

For nontrivial queries, you will very often want to take advantage of nested table expressions. Let's have another look at the example given with Warden's Test Number 1 in Chapter 17. I'll make the question a little more complicated than I did then:

"For each employee whose salary is greater than the average salary in his or her department, show employee name, number, salary, department, average salary for that department, and the amount by which the employee's salary exceeds that departmental average."

Here is that query in a new dialect of SQL that I have just invented, adhering to the Magic Words:

```
SELECT ENAME, EMP#, SALARY, DEPT#, DEPTAVE,
       SURPLUS - ( SALARY - DEPTAVE )
FROM   MARRIAGE ( EMP,
          /        ( SELECT DEPT#, DEPTAVE = AVG (SALARY)
                     FROM    EMP
                     GROUP   BY DEPT# ) )
WHERE   SALARY > DEPTAVE ;
```

I had to do a lot of analytical thinking to arrive at that! And I had to write the first two lines, which refer to results of the inner lines, *before* I had worked out what to write inside!

Actually, the Prince sprang to my rescue, by giving me a special command to assign names to expressions (or subexpressions). The syntax of this command is perhaps:

```
SUPPOSE temporary-name = table-expression ;
```

and the result is a name I can subsequently use in place of the expression, anywhere in the language. The name disappears at the end of my session, and is unique during that session. For convenience, it might take precedence over any base table of the same name.

This, then, is how I set about developing my complex query, using a DISPLAY command to show results for verification purposes on my screen:

```
/* Preliminary calculation of department averages: */

SUPPOSE T1 =
        SELECT DEPT#, DEPTAVE = AVG(SALARY)
        FROM   EMP
        GROUP  BY DEPT# ;

DISPLAY T1 ;    /* check Step 1 */

/* Combine averages with original table: */

SUPPOSE T2 =
        MARRIAGE ( EMP, T1 )     /* Natural Join on DEPT# ! */

DISPLAY T2 ;    /* check Step 2 */

/* Concentrate on high earners: */

SUPPOSE T3 =
        T2   WHERE   SALARY > DEPTAVE ;

DISPLAY T3 ;    /* check that too */

/* Perform final column selection and calculation: */

SUPPOSE ANSWER =
        SELECT ENAME, EMP#, SALARY, DEPT#, DEPTAVE,
               SURPLUS = ( SALARY - DEPTAVE )
        FROM   T3 ;

DISPLAY ANSWER ;    /* check final answer */
```

We hope that one day good natural language query products will obviate the need for this kind of work. In the meantime, the Prince will at least help you to break down a complex query into easier bits and pieces, checking out each one on the way.

Note, in the definitions of T2 and T3, that I assume the Prince won't insist on an inoperative prefix such as "SELECT * FROM."

When you are happy that ANSWER is indeed the right answer, there are several things you could do next. For instance:

```
CREATE TABLE SNAPSHOT_OF_HIGH_EARNERS LIKE ANSWER ;
INSERT ANSWER INTO SNAPSHOT_OF_HIGH_EARNERS ;
```

The primary key of the snapshot is EMP#. The Prince arrived at this conclusion by applying the algorithms for key inheritance through Summarize, Natural Join, Restriction, Projection, and Extension, as given in Chapter 19, "The Keys of the Kingdom."

Another possibility:

```
SUPPOSE PRIMA_DONNAS =
        ANSWER WHERE SURPLUS > 5000 ;
DISPLAY PRIMA_DONNAS ;
```

And another:

```
CREATE VIEW HIGH_EARNERS = ANSWER ;
```

Note that the view HIGH_EARNERS is a permanent object, remaining intact when you finish your session even though the names (T1 and so on) used to build it disappear. That's because the saved view retains the complete expression, resolving the temporary names at the time you create the view.

There are some problems that cannot reasonably be solved without temporary names. Occasionally, for example, your query might include some subexpression that is used more than once, amd writing it out several times is tedious and error-prone.

While we're on the subject of temporary things, there's a chivalrous subdeed you'll be pleased with:

That snapshot you made with the help of the Prince's first and third deeds (and his understanding of primary key inheritance)—you won't want to keep it for very long. Very likely you need it only for the duration of your current session, while you complete the various reports you have to make from it.

Well, you could have told the Prince about this, when you gave the CREATE TABLE command for it. Then he will delete it automatically when you log off (unless you change your mind).

CHIVALROUS DEED NUMBER 4
GIVING USEFUL INFORMATION

Your DBMS no doubt provides a system catalog, special tables that you can query to find out about the structure of your database, authorizations, and so on.

The Prince will provide much more than just the catalog. He'll give you lots of useful builtin functions, answering common questions that arise during your day-to-day work with the database. Of course, every answer will be in the form of a proper table, so that the query language can be used to formulate ever more specific questions.

Here are some of those builtin functions. As usual, the syntax is my own invention, only for this book. If they were available in SQL, you would probably have to incant "SELECT * FROM" in front of each one.

at tables do I have?

```
LES ( MINE )
```

result is a table in which each row describes some table that was ted by you. The primary key is "table name."

it other tables can I access?

```
.ES ( OTHERS )
```

The result is a table in which each row describes some table that was created by somebody else who has given you some authority to access it. The primary key is the combination of owner ID and table name.

A WHERE clause could be included if you want to see what some particular user has shared with you.

If TABLES(MINE) includes a column for "owner ID," the union of TABLES(MINE) and TABLES(OTHERS) will show absolutely everything you can access.

▪ What about my temporary definitions?

You sometimes want to see a list of all the temporary names that you have defined with the help of Chivalrous Deed Number 3.

```
NAMES ( TEMPORARY )
```

Each row in the result shows a definition name and the associated expression. The primary key is "definition name."

▪ What columns do I have in some table I'm interested in?

```
COLUMNS ( table-expression )
```

Each row in the result describes a column that occurs in the would-be result of the given table expression. The primary key is "column name."

If a simple base table name is given, the answer is derived directly from the system catalog.

When the table expression includes derived columns, such as AVESAL = AVG(SALARY), the Prince works out a suitable lookalike of a catalog entry, for orthogonality. The domain of such a column (if numeric) would probably be given as just NUMBERS, and the "remarks" (for the Prince's catalog certainly includes these) would give the expression used to derive the column.

Note that COLUMNS(COLUMNS(table-expression)) is a rather neat object. Its cardinality is equal to its degree (sorry, my dear, I mean it has as many rows as it has columns), and its value is constant, regardless of what table expression you specify. The column names in the heading are the same as the primary key values down the side. It contains useful tutorial information, answering the question: "What information does this system require in order to describe a column?"

Other builtin functions let you see exactly what authorizations you have in connexion with any table you can access, what authorizations you have given other users for accessing your own tables, what messages other users have sent you or the Prince has sent on their behalf (warnings about dropped or altered tables, for instance), and any other information the Prince would like you to be able to find out.

As a particularly generous subdeed, the Prince will let you **update,** within reason, the tables delivered by his builtin information functions.

For instance, you could insert a row into TABLES(MINE) as an alternative to using the system's CREATE TABLE command! The table thus created—let's call it NEW_ONE—wouldn't have any columns, of course, but you could define these by inserting rows into COLUMNS(NEW_ONE).

No, don't scoff at that idea! I know a single CREATE TABLE command is much easier than a bunch of INSERTs, but suppose you have been equipped with a nice, friendly, general-purpose data entry tool for use at your workstation—one that can be used to "edit" the result of **any** table expression and send your changes back to the database?

The makers of such a tool would be very grateful not to have to make special versions for special cases such as column definition. But they would need a Prince and all his Chivalrous Deeds to be able to meet such an objective. You could use this editor to insert the new row into TABLES(MINE). Then, using the same tool, you could edit COLUMNS(NEW_ONE) to build the column descriptions. Finally, you could use the editor again to enter some rows into NEW_ONE itself.

CHIVALROUS DEED NUMBER 5
EXTENDING THE MARRIAGE PRINCIPLE

Here's a common sort of question that is awkward to ask of Monsters:

"Which departments currently have no employees at all?"

Using just the primitive operators of the Relational Algebra, you have to:

1. Project the departments table, DEPT, over DEPT#. Call the one-column result A1.
2. Project the employees table, EMP, over DEPT#. Call the one-column result A2.
3. Take the set difference A1 − A2. Call the result D.
4. Take the natural join (marriage) of D with DEPT.

In SQL, the solution is perhaps more intelligible, but involves a subquery:

```
SELECT  *
FROM    DEPT
WHERE   DEPT# NOT IN
      ( SELECT DEPT#
        FROM    EMP ) ;
```

Not too difficult, but it gets more and more tricky the more columns are involved in the "matching" process, and in any case you do have to know the names of those columns.

The Prince, having already *embraced marriage,* extends the principle to cater for searches for unmatched things as well as for the matches that occur in joins.

For instance, he might let you write:

```
SELECT  *
FROM    UNMATCHED ( DEPT, EMP ) ;
```

The common columns of the two tables involved (in this case just the single DEPT# column) are implicitly used as the matching columns. The result has the same heading as DEPT, and contains a subset of the rows thereof.

Of course, if you replaced UNMATCHED by MATCHED, you would be asking for those departments that have at least one employee. Some people call this operation (based on *intersection,* where UNMATCHED is based on *difference*) **semijoin,** because it involves approximately half of the steps by which Join is described.

If the question is a little more probing, say:

"Which departments employ no prima donnas?"

then we merely replace the table name EMP by the table expression that delivers just those employees whose salaries exceed their departmental average by the amount agreed for the definition of "prima donna."

On the few occasions when the column names are not suitable for implicit matching, you can resort to the Prince's **column rename** operator, or choose a more long-winded method of expressing the query.

CHIVALROUS DEED NUMBER 6
BATCHED UPDATES

The Prince really takes marriage seriously, in all spheres of his activity, not just in queries.

Suppose you are the manager of some department, and you are planning the annual salary increments for those of your employees who deserve any.

You prepare a table called RAISES, keyed on EMP#, and containing one other column, PERCENT_RAISE.

The day comes when it's at last time to dish out the goodies. Do you have to write a computer program, with a main loop reading rows from RAISES, matching each row with its corresponding row in the EMP table, calculating the new salary and updating the EMP row? No, you don't, for here comes the Prince:

```
UPDATE    EMP
USING     RAISES
CHANGING  SALARY TO SALARY * PERCENT_RAISE / 100 ;
```

The Prince applies the Marriage Principle (using columns of the same name to connect tables, as in the Marriage operator itself) to interpret and execute this simple command.

The "USING table" (RAISES) must have one or more columns in common with the target table (EMP), and this set of common columns **must include the primary key of the target table.** This is the case in our example, for RAISES includes a column, EMP#, that is the primary key of EMP (it is also the primary key of RAISES, but that doesn't matter).

For each row in RAISES, the Prince looks up the matching row in EMP and changes the SALARY value according to the given formula. If there are any rows in RAISES with no matching row in EMP, they are reported as errors (and you could have asked for the whole transaction to be canceled in such an eventuality, of course).

The common columns might include more than the target's primary key. In any case, matching is done on all common columns, just as in Marriage, and you are not allowed to change any common column in the target table.

If the USING table can have more than one row matching the same row in the target table—when your transactions represent stock movements, for instance—you might want to tell the Prince to be sure to process the transactions in the right order, by adding an ORDER BY clause to your UPDATE command.

THE LAST CHIVALROUS DEED
JUST BEING CHIVALROUS

You can breathe again, my Beautiful Maiden—I only said "last" to frighten you. Sorry.

There really is no end to your Prince's chivalry. Because he took to heart the fundamental principles enshrined in the Original Wisdom, he'll have no trouble with all the other things I know are on your mind.

His stock of scalar functions, for use in derived column expressions, is infinitely extendable. For instance, if you happen to like Rexx's wonderful armory of string-handling functions, you'll get them.

When new Wisdom arrives, for outstanding problems like "bill of materials" and "missing values," the Prince will take it to heart too, and his heart's already in the right place.

The Wisdom for Distributed Databases is now available. Will the Monster take heed? You'd be safer, I think, with the Prince. Perhaps, therefore, it is now time for all Beautiful Maidens to approach the Lair and chant the Magic Words. When you've done so, come back to me, and bring your new Prince with you. Then we'll have some adventures, together in Relationland.

21

A Constant Friend

In this chapter, I introduce readers to one of my special friends in **Relation-land,** *a country inhabited only by Princes and Happy Maidens.*

Hello again, my dear. Did you visit the Lair? And chant the Magic Words? And did the Monster turn into a Prince? And did the Prince promise to do those Chivalrous Deeds?

Oh, he said it would take a little time? Yes, I was afraid of that. It's not that the naming of columns, the Marriage Principle, and primary key inheritance are difficult for him. It's having to undo all the damage he did when he was a Monster.

Never mind, I am still allowed to give you some further glimpses into the glorious future made possible by what you did at the Lair, and today I would like to introduce you to the first of some very special people that I hope you will meet in Relationland.

In fact, here he comes—that very long, thin fellow, trotting over the horizon. He's called **TABLE_NUM**—yes, he's actually a **table,** and a very proper one, of course! The reason why he looks so emaciated is that he has only one column, called **N.** And the reason why he's so long is that N contains every possible **integer** that your computer can think of.*

---

*Fortunately, no computer can think of *all* the integers, so we don't have to worry about the awesome prospect of infinite relations, which are expressly excluded from the Relational Model.

TABLE_NUM is a tabular representation of the **domain** of integers. He has a proper heading, comprising the single column, N, a body containing a very large but finite number of rows, and a primary key, N (which is the same as his heading, of course).

So far, so good, but TABLE_NUM does possess one property that makes him a little peculiar from the Model's point of view:

> His value, the set of recordable integers, is constant. The Model deals explicitly in **time-varying** relations, but only to emphasize its applicability to real-life databases. Constant relations, while less useful in general, are easily accommodated.

In fact, TABLE_NUM is a **constant friend,** by which I mean a table whose constant value can be computed algorithmically and thus does not need to be stored in the database.

What's the use of TABLE_NUM?

I'll come to that in a minute. First, I want to suggest a convenient shorthand for specifying proper subsets of TABLE_NUM, for we will invariably want to do that when we make use of him. And this gives me the opportunity to tell you, by way of an aside, about yet another **Chivalrous Deed,** for I didn't have time to tell you all of them at our last meeting.

Suppose, for instance, that we want a one-column table of the integers from 1 to 100. If our query language is SQL, we can express this by:

```
SELECT  N
FROM    TABLE_NUM
WHERE   N >= 1 AND N <= 100 ;
```

You would much rather be able to say just this:

```
INTEGERS (1:100)
```

and the Prince will surely let you do so, for he is only too pleased (Chivalrous Deed coming up . . .) to entertain the notion of **builtin functions that return tables,** a simple extension of **views,** supporting **arguments.**

The argument to the Prince's INTEGERS function happens to be a **range-expression.** It takes advantage of the ordering property of the natural numbers, letting you specify a subset by giving the lowest and highest numbers of a particular range. The underlying definition of the function might be given by:

```
CREATE VIEW INTEGERS (!low:!high) =
       SELECT  N
       FROM    TABLE_NUM
       WHERE   N >= !low AND N <= !high ;
```

I have invented a simple syntax (let us not argue about its soundness) for specifying the argument, using names beginning with exclamation marks for its two components, which must be separated by a colon.

Aside: If you are thinking about some existing language with a CREATE VIEW command somewhat like the above but not supporting arguments, you will remember that the parentheses serve a different purpose there—they delimit the list of names of columns of the view. The Prince, of course, doesn't need to do this, because result columns are always named in the SELECT clause. *End of aside.*

This syntax shows how INTEGERS could be a **user-defined** function, though in practice it should be system-defined, so that its result can be delivered quickly, without a mechanical search through the whole of TABLE_NUM.

So, our INTEGERS function is merely a shorthand for expressing a relational **restriction** on TABLE_NUM. In fact, we no longer need to refer to the name TABLE_NUM, except for definitional purposes. The primary key of any table delivered by INTEGERS is N, according to the key inheritance rule for restriction (this fact being intuitively obvious).

What's the use of the INTEGERS function?

Well, I shall give two examples. These are necessarily rather complicated queries that are proverbially difficult to express in current languages such as SQL, and I will need to introduce some new builtin scalar functions. Furthermore, my uses of these functions have the savor of programming tricks, so I do not mind their being used only for definitional purposes, in a language that delivers higher-level functions to satisfy the kinds of requirement I have in mind.

Example 1

Suppose I have a table called SALES, recording the monthly sales figures for each product in the previous year:

P#	JAN	FEB	MAR	APR	MAY	JUN	JUL	AUG	SEP	OCT	NOV	DEC
P1	93	101	14	92	89	105	93	93	99	86	93	157
P2	0	0	0	0	0	0	0	0	0	1	1	1
P3	9	9	9	9	8	6	0	9	9	9	4	0
.	.	.	.	.	.	.	.	.	.	.	.	.

The table is keyed on product number, P#—this is the significance of the double underlining in the heading—and has 12 other columns, one for each month. A row in the table thus represents the sales volume for each month of some specific product.

The query I want to present is:

"For each product, show me its most successful month(s)."

If the table had been organized differently, with a separate row for each month for each product (keyed on the combination of product number and month number, with a single sales column called VOLUME), it would have looked like this:

```
P#   MONTH   VOLUME
==   =====   ------
P1      1        93
P1      2       101
P1      3        14
P1      4        92
P1      5        89
P1      6       105
P1      7        93
P1      8        93
P1      9        99
P1     10        86
P1     11        93
P1     12       157
P2      1         0
P1      2         0
 .      .         .
```

With this table, the query would have been moderately easy:

```
SELECT X.P#,  X.MONTH
FROM   X = SALES
WHERE  X.VOLUME =
       ( SELECT MAX_VOL = MAX ( VOLUME )
         FROM   Y = SALES
         WHERE  X.P# = Y.P# ) ;
```

If we can therefore find a way, using our query language, of deriving the long, three-column table from the given, short, 13-column one, we can consider the job done.*

The first step is, for each of the rows in the given table SALES, to derive twelve "replicas," each distinguished from the rest by a unique tag obtained from INTEGERS(1:12):

```
SUPPOSE T1 =
        SELECT SALES.*, MONTH = M.N
        FROM   SALES, M = INTEGERS(1:12) ;
```

T1 would look like this:

---

*Assuming, of course, that our DBMS adheres to the Magic Words "Name all columns" and "Support nests."

P#	JAN	FEB	MAR	APR	MAY	JUN	JUL	AUG	SEP	OCT	NOV	DEC	MONTH
==	---	---	---	---	---	---	---	---	---	---	---	---	=====
P1	93	101	14	92	89	105	93	93	99	86	93	157	1
P1	93	101	14	92	89	105	93	93	99	86	93	157	2
P1	93	101	14	92	89	105	93	93	99	86	93	157	3
P1	93	101	14	92	89	105	93	93	99	86	93	157	4
P1	93	101	14	92	89	105	93	93	99	86	93	157	5
P1	93	101	14	92	89	105	93	93	99	86	93	157	6
P1	93	101	14	92	89	105	93	93	99	86	93	157	7
P1	93	101	14	92	89	105	93	93	99	86	93	157	8
P1	93	101	14	92	89	105	93	93	99	86	93	157	9
P1	93	101	14	92	89	105	93	93	99	86	93	157	10
P1	93	101	14	92	89	105	93	93	99	86	93	157	11
P1	93	101	14	92	89	105	93	93	99	86	93	157	12
P2	0	0	0	0	0	0	0	0	0	1	1	1	1
P2	0	0	0	0	0	0	0	0	0	1	1	1	2
.	.	.	.	.	.	.	.	.	.	.	.	.	.

The primary key of this intermediate result is the combination of P# and MONTH, as given by the key inheritance rule for Cartesian product.

Associated with each (P#,MONTH) combination, we now have all twelve sales volumes. We need to reduce these to a single column, containing the sales volume for the particular month identified by our new MONTH column (throwing away the other eleven months).

Now I introduce two new scalar functions. The first is a very useful string operator, available in some programming languages today:

```
WORD ( string, n )
```

This function delivers the nth word in a string of words separated by blanks. For instance, the expression

```
WORD ( "I'd like to see that done on paper", 4 )
```

delivers the string "see".

The second allows a column **name,** in an expression, to vary from row to row. It is called "the Column Whose Name Is," CWNI for short:

```
CWNI ( string-expression )
```

This function returns the scalar **value** in the column whose name is given by its (possibly variable) operand.

Now, assuming the definition for T1 given above, we can say:

```
SUPPOSE T2 =
        SELECT P#, MONTH,
               VOLUME = CWNI ( WORD ( "JAN FEB MAR APR MAY JUN
                                       JUL AUG SEP OCT NOV DEC"
                                       MONTH ) )
        FROM    T1 ;
```

And T2 is exactly the table we need to do the query of Example 1! For each row in T1, the WORD function delivers the month name corresponding to the month number in the MONTH column (a number we originally obtained from INTEGERS(1:12)), and the CWNI function delivers the sales figure for that particular month, which we place in a new column called VOLUME. For instance, consider the row in T1 identified by P# = "P1" and MONTH = 3. The WORD expression in the definition of T2 becomes

```
WORD ( "JAN FEB MAR APR MAY JUN JUL AUG SEP OCT NOV DEC", 3 )
```

which in turn yields "MAR". CWNI("MAR") then returns the value in the column named MAR, which is 14.

Similarly, for the row identified by P# = "P1" and MONTH = 4, the value of VOLUME is 92.

The primary key of T2 is (P#,MONTH), as determined by the key inheritance rules for projection and extension.

The query that transforms T2 back into the original table, SALES, is left as an exercise for the reader. It requires eleven joins, and I don't think it can be done in SQL, unless you can use the column rename operator, and have query expressions in the FROM clause (Magic Words: "Name all columns" and "Support nests").

Example 2

Here's another problem where TABLE_NUM comes to the rescue.

I wrote a book. My publisher asked me to provide an index showing, for each interesting word I used in the book, the numbers of the pages on which that word could be found.

I managed to import the text of the book into a table (BOOK), keyed on page number (PAGE#), the other column (TEXT) containing the text of each page.

Fortunately, I have another table, called BORING_WORDS, listing all the words (like "the") that should never appear in an index for any of my books, in its single column, WORD (which is therefore the primary key for BORING_WORDS—sorry, I cannot bring myself ever to describe a table without mentioning its primary key).

To create the index, I use the WORD function defined above, and also the function

```
WORDS ( string-expression )
```

which delivers the number of words in its operand (which must be a string of words separated by blanks). For example, the expression

```
WORDS ( "The sixth sick sheik's sixth sheep's sick." )
```

delivers the answer 7.

Now:

```
1. SUPPOSE INDEX =
2.          SELECT WORD = WORD ( B.TEXT, I.N ), B.PAGE#
3.          FROM    B = BOOK,
4.                  I = INTEGERS ( 1 : SELECT MW = MAX (WORDS(TEXT))
5.                                      FROM    BOOK )
6.          WHERE   I.N <= WORDS ( B.TEXT )
7.          AND     WORD NOT IN
8.                ( SELECT WORD
9.                  FROM    BORING_WORDS ) ;
```

Line 1 asserts that the rest of the expression defines the answer I want. This is indeed the case, because:

- Lines 3–5 "replicate" each page in my book, as many times (MW) as there are words in the longest page in the book ("longest" here means "containing most words"). Such replicas are distinguished from one another by a unique value in the column called N, obtained from the table delivered by the invocation of the INTEGERS function.

- Line 6 throws away rows in which a page of text is associated with a value of N greater than the number of words on that page.

  Suppose page 109 contained the text "This page intentionally left blank." Part of the result of this step now looks like this:

```
PAGE#  N  TEXT
=====  =  --------------------------------------------------------
  .    .   . . .
  .    .   . . .
 109   1  This page intentionally left blank
 109   2  This page intentionally left blank
 109   3  This page intentionally left blank
 109   4  This page intentionally left blank
 109   5  This page intentionally left blank
  .    .   . . .
  .    .   . . .
```

Other pages would be similarly repeated as many times as their numbers of words.

- Line 2 isolates each Nth word in each page into a column called WORD, simultaneously eliminating duplicate occurrences of the same word on the same page,* producing (from our sample page):

```
PAGE#  WORD
=====  ===================
  .     . . .
  .     . . .
 109   This
 109   page
 109   intentionally
 109   left
 109   blank
  .     . . .
  .     . . .
```

---

*I am fondly imagining that the Prince will not require the word DISTINCT to be written here, though you'd need it in SQL, which would otherwise deliver a useless, not-proper table.

- Lines 7–9 eliminate boring words from the index.

The primary key of INDEX is its heading, (WORD,PAGE#).

Of course, we don't want to print the index as it appears in this table, even if we order it on PAGE# within WORD. Since what I **really** wanted was an ordered list of page numbers, separated by commas, associated with each word, I'll just have to invent a new aggregate function for use in conjunction with GROUP BY. I'll call this function COMMACAT_IN_ORDER. What it does is to concatenate all the values in a column, in ascending order, separated by commas, into a single string. When the column values are numbers, they are implicitly converted to string format. Then I can say:

```
SUPPOSE WHAT_I_REALLY_WANTED =
        SELECT WORD, PAGE_NUMBERS = COMMACAT_IN_ORDER ( PAGE# )
        FROM    INDEX
        GROUP   BY WORD ;
```

Now I only have to add ORDER BY WORD when I send the result of WHAT_I_REALLY_WANTED to my printer. For example:

```
WORD        PAGE_NUMBERS
==========  --------------------------------
aardvark    93, 204
antimony    3, 39, 204
  ...          ...
relational  1, 2, 3, 4, 5, 6, 7, 8, 9, 10, ...
  ...          ...
zymotic     131
```

The primary key of WHAT_I_REALLY_WANTED is WORD, as determined by the key inheritance rule for GROUP BY (more correctly, Summarize), and associated with each word is the required list of page numbers, such as "19, 45, 301."

I hope you agree that the further refinements needed to eliminate punctuation marks and words that turn out to be just numbers, and to ignore case differences, could easily be incorporated.

Phew! He's rather heavy, TABLE_NUM, even though so skinny. By way of contrast, when we next meet I'll introduce you to my lightweight friends, TABLE_DEE and TABLE_DUM.

22

Table_Dee and Table_Dum

In this chapter we meet two other **constant friends** *to be encountered in Relationland. These two little chaps cement the bond between the Relational Model and the first-order predicate logic on which it is based.*

Oh, it's you again. No, no, no, of course I'm not too busy, and of course I'm delighted to see you again, my dear. In fact, I was rather worried you'd never come back to me again, after all those complicated things I showed you last time!

How's the Prince? Still working on the Chivalrous Deeds? Ah well, we did ask for some more, after you had met TABLE_NUM, didn't we? So we can't really blame him.

Never mind, there's plenty of time, and besides, you haven't met TABLE_DEE and TABLE_DUM yet, have you? In fact, look, here they are.

DEE! DUM! How wonderful to bump into you again! Meet my new friend, the Beautiful Maiden. DEE: Beautiful Maiden, Beautiful Maiden: DEE.

"Yes" (in a hoarse whisper)

And you, DUM. DUM: Beautiful Maiden, Beautiful Maiden: DUM.

Silence

You must forgive their apparent rudeness, my dear. They have not mastered the gentle art of conversation, for they have hardly any vocabulary with which to do it. Let me explain.

TABLE_DEE has only one row. Furthermore, he's so thin that you can't even see him—even thinner than this: |

TABLE_DUM is even smaller, for he has no rows at all—something like this: .

You see, these impoverished twins, poor things, are utterly devoid of any **columns!**

Do they mean anything? Indeed they do. They have the most powerful meanings imaginable. TABLE_DEE means "something is **TRUE**," and TABLE_DUM means "nothing is **TRUE**." Unequivocally.

When mathematicians discover rules that seem to hold true for any value of *n,* they detest it if $n = 0$ turns out to be an exception. So do computer programmers, for whom the undefined division-by-zero is a famous bête noire, and who don't like having to use a language that has forgotten to support, for instance, arrays with zero elements.

— We would like to confirm, therefore, that the theory of *n*-ary relations, the backbone of our Relational Model of Data, holds true even when $n = 0$. And, having confirmed it, we would like the Princes to reassure us that they won't overlook the matter. And then we'd like to investigate the usefulness of $n = 0$.

TABLE_DEE and TABLE_DUM are the only possible instances of the only possible example of an *n*-ary relation with $n = 0$. This relation is called the **nullary relation.**

The heading of the nullary relation is the empty set. We have already implied this fact by stating that the relation has no columns.

The body of an instance of the nullary relation contains zero or one 0-tuples (rows with no column-values at all). If it contains zero 0-tuples, it is TABLE_DUM. If it contains one, it is TABLE_DEE. It can't contain more than one, because all 0-tuples are identical.

The primary key of any table is (among other things) a subset of the table's heading. The only subset of the empty set is the empty set itself, and this is indeed the primary key of TABLE_DEE and TABLE_DUM.

It is not very useful, to say the least, for a **base** table to be the nullary relation. That may be why none of the Monsters lets you have one, but more likely it is because they forgot to let you. When I create my table of employees, EMP, with columns EMP#, DEPT#, and SALARY, keyed on EMP#, I am asserting that the set of rows in this table represents that subset of all possible (EMP#,DEPT#,SALARY) combinations for which the predicate

"EMP# identifies an employee, working in the department identified by DEPT#, and earning the salary identified by SALARY" is true. (Logicians refer to such a predicate as an "open sentence.") Table EMP is said to "model" this predicate. Loosely speaking, the predicate is what the table **means.**

When I put a row into this table, I am asserting that a particular employee exists, identified by a particular employee number, working in a particular department, and earning a particular salary. When I leave one out, I am asserting that no employee exists with that employee number and that collection of properties.

If I create a table with no columns, I am modeling the predicate TRUE. If I insert a row into this table, I am asserting only that something (I don't say, or even need to know, what) is true. If I delete that row, I am retracting that assertion.

So far, perhaps, we might see no use for the twins, except to maintain the orthogonality of our DBMS's language,* and for the sheer elegance and delight in being able to say that zero is no exception.

But there is a little more to them than that.

Consider queries that require no more than "Yes" or "No" as the answer, such as: "Do I have any suppliers in Paris?" Here is how you might express this query in a Princely version of SQL:†

```
SELECT ANSWER = "Yes"
FROM    S
WHERE   CITY = "Paris" ;
```

You would see "Yes," if that were the answer, but you wouldn't see "No." Breaking the query down into primitive operations in the Relational Algebra, we find:

1. A **restriction** of S, where CITY = "Paris"
2. A **projection** of the result of 1, over **no columns at all**
3. An **extension** of the result of 2, with a column containing the constant value "Yes"

The final result contains a single column. It contains a single row if the result of Step 2 is TABLE_DEE, and that row shows the word "Yes." It is empty if the result of Step 1 is empty (in which case the result of Step 2 is TABLE_DUM).

For completeness, we really ought to be allowed to have TABLE_DEE and TABLE_DUM as final results of query expressions. Why not just:

---

*Orthogonality means having no arbitrary, unexpected restrictions.

†SQL2, rather less monstrous than existing SQL, supports an "AS" operator for giving names to result columns, but would still require that obnoxious DISTINCT to be included.

```
SELECT
FROM    S
WHERE   CITY = "Paris" ;
```

After all, adding "Yes" only helps in the case where "Yes" is the actual answer. We thereby convert the nullary result to a unary relation, by extension, but uselessly when the answer is "No." DEE, on his own, can just about whisper "Yes"; poor DUM can manage no more than an apologetic shake of the head!

Various behaviors of TABLE_DEE and TABLE_DUM, under the operations of the Relational Algebra, help us to feel more comfortable about the theory. For instance, just as the number 1 is the **identity** under multiplication in arithmetic (in other words, $n * 1 = n$ for all values of n), so TABLE_DEE is the identity under Cartesian product (and natural join) in the Relational Algebra. In other words,

```
SELECT *
FROM    T, TABLE_DEE ;
```

and

```
SELECT *
FROM    MARRIAGE ( T, TABLE_DEE ) ;
```

both deliver the same result as

```
SELECT *
FROM    T ;
```

whatever table, base or derived, that T represents.

The Cartesian product of any table, T, with TABLE_DUM has the columns of T but is empty (as is any Cartesian product involving an empty table).

Clearly, the only relation that is union-compatible with the nullary relation is the nullary relation itself. The results of union, intersection, and difference operations involving TABLE_DEE and TABLE_DUM are intimately related to the truth tables, in logic, for OR, AND, and NAND:

- DEE union DEE = DEE
- DEE union DUM = DEE
- DUM union DEE = DEE
- DUM union DUM = DUM
- DEE intersection DEE = DEE
- DEE intersection DUM = DUM
- DUM intersection DEE = DUM
- DUM intersection DUM = DUM

- DEE difference DEE = DUM
- DEE difference DUM = DEE
- DUM difference DEE = DUM
- DUM difference DUM = DUM

Furthermore, we can note:

- Any restriction of DEE yields either DEE or DUM.
- Any restriction of DUM yields DUM.
- Projection of any table over no columns yields DUM if the original table is empty, DEE otherwise. In particular, projection of DEE or DUM, necessarily over no columns, returns its input.
- Summarizing DEE or DUM, necessarily over no grouping columns, with p assignments of aggregate results to new columns, generates a p-ary relation with the same cardinality as its input table (DEE or DUM). For instance,

  SUMMARIZE (TABLE_DEE, GROUP_BY ( ), FIVE = SUM (5))

  yields a unary relation with a single row, containing the value 5 in its single column FIVE.
- Any table, T, divided by DEE, yields T.*
- Any table, T, divided by DUM, yields an empty table with the columns of T.
- DEE, divided by any table, T, yields T.
- DUM, divided by any table, T, yields an empty table with the columns of T.
- Any nonempty table, T, divided by itself, yields DEE. An empty table divided by itself yields DUM.
- Extension that adds p columns to DEE yields a p-ary relation of cardinality 1.
- Extension that adds p columns to DUM yields an empty p-ary relation.

Extension of the nullary relation is of some further interest, for we now have to consider the primary key of the result.

According to our key inheritance rules, the primary key of an extension is the same as that of its operand. The primary key of the nullary relation is the empty set. It follows that the primary key of any extension of the

---

*I mean here the generalized division as defined in my Preface.

nullary relation is also the empty set. And it follows therefore that it is quite in order for the primary key of a table of any degree to be the empty set!

As the empty set is a subset of every set there is, this assertion remains consistent with the rule that the primary key of a table is some subset of the heading.

A table with the empty set as primary key can clearly never contain more than one row. The values of the keys of any two candidate rows are both what we might call "the empty value" (in fact, the value of the 0-tuple), and thus necessarily equal.

It might be **very useful** to be able to have such a table, as a **base** table, thus enforcing some rule in the real world that should be expressed in the database by the assertion: "This table must never have more than one row."

Such an assertion is equivalent to saying that the empty set is a **candidate** key. Now, the Relational Model includes a "minimality" rule in its definition of "candidate key." This rule asserts that, if the set C is a candidate key, then no proper superset of C (C plus one or more other columns) is a candidate key.

The Model also asserts that the primary key of any table must be some candidate key of that table. Therefore, if the empty set is a candidate key, it **must** be the **only** candidate key, and therefore the primary key.

If the Prince supports **nullary**—i.e., empty—**primary keys,** his natural enforcement of primary key uniqueness would be enough to guarantee that the table in fact never did have more than one row—no other fancy assertion would need to be expressed.

By the way, an example of a table that very definitely does have a nullary primary key is that given by:

```
SUMMARIZE ( EMP, GROUP_BY ( ), AVESAL = AVG ( SALARY ) )
```

Furthermore, if a table T1 can have a nullary primary key, we must also consider what it means for some other table T2 to include a matching **foreign key** (which by definition would have to be nullary also). The referential constraint from T2 to T1—which involves matching two nullary key values—would be satisfied whenever T1 is nonempty, and violated whenever T1 is empty but T2 is nonempty. In other words, you cannot delete the row in T1 unless T2 is empty, and you cannot insert a row into T2 if T1 is empty.

This rule, too, might be very useful in practice. If T1 is a one-row table containing certain global values, perhaps some parameters to be used in formatting results for presentation, you might want every table in your database to include an appropriate nullary foreign key, in order to guarantee the existence of those formatting parameters for every state of the database other than complete emptiness.

In conclusion, perhaps TABLE_DEE and TABLE_DUM (and TABLE_NUM) are only figments of our imagination. But they need to be firmly planted in the Prince's imagination, too, if he is to aspire to the greatest heights of chivalry we might demand of him.

Now, my Beautiful Maiden, I must take my leave of you, temporarily, I hope. There is a Journey that I have to undertake alone. Do you remember the Magic Words "Spurn unknowns"? I know you didn't care for them much, for they left the Big Problem unsolved. Unfortunately, it was all we could do, for now, because not spurning them seems to create more problems than it solves.

My Journey will take me to the dread Land of the Unknown, and its offshore forbidden islands of Outer Join and Outer Union, all surrounded by the storm-ridden Sea of Nulls. I do not expect to return unscathed, but I'll try to tell you what I find there.

Goodbye, my dear, and wish me luck!

23

Into the Unknown

Having previously cautioned readers to "Spurn unknowns," in this chapter I examine the concept of "nulls," the method by which many database languages, notably SQL, attempt to handle the problem of missing values. I find the same flaws and traps that have been noted by other investigators before me, and perhaps some more.

Memo

From: AW

To: BM

Subject: My journey to the Land of the Unknown, and what I found there

    I first had to make my way through **Database Jungle.**

    There, I encountered many **Happy Tables.** These simple folk hadn't a care in the world, for every row they ever contained had something factual to say in every column, and was thus a straightforward assertion. Questions involving Happy Tables could always be expressed reliably in one of the Princes' query languages, firmly founded in the Relational Algebra or the Relational Calculus, and many Beautiful Maidens successfully based many Important Decisions on the answers.

    But I also found large numbers of **Unhappy Tables,** typically skulking in dark hollows or lurking behind trees. Scattered over their rows were nasty blemishes, like carbuncles, called **nulls,** purporting to represent various cases where it was not possible to record a firm, true fact. A particularly unhappy table, EMP (a table of information about employees, keyed on EMP#), told me some of the ways this happened to him.

EMP	EMP#	ENAME	JOBCODE	SALARY	COMMISSION	PHONE	DEPT#
	E1	Smith	33	5500	null	671	D5
	E2	Jones	33	5600	null	672	D5
	E3	Brown	34	null	null	490	D6
	E4	Green	33	4900	null	673	D7
	E5	White	49	7300	3314	321	D4
	E6	Black	49	6900	2512	324	null
	E7	Pink	null	null	null	null	D5

- Employees other than salespeople didn't earn commission. A zero value in the COMMISSION column indicated that the employee was eligible for commission, but didn't actually earn any in the previous month. The commission for ineligible employees was therefore recorded as null, not zero.

- For some new recruits, not all of the information had been obtained yet. They had been temporarily given nulls in such columns as JOBCODE, SALARY, and PHONE.

- Some employees had not been assigned to any department, so they had nulls in their DEPT# column.

- EMP had a close friend called DEPT. DEPT was a table of information about departments, keyed on DEPT#. It was this common column, DEPT#, that sealed her vow of friendship with EMP. But when EMP had a null in DEPT#, DEPT felt betrayed, and this made **her** unhappy.

- Maidens sometimes wanted to see the information about each department, along with all the information about all the employees in that department. They did this by sending DEPT and EMP, in separate parcels, express mail, to a place called **Outer Join.** The single parcel returned from Outer Join did indeed show the departments together with their employees. When a department had five employees, its row from DEPT came back five times, each time joined with one of EMP's rows. But some rows from DEPT represented departments to which no employees at all had been assigned. These came back joined with nulls in all of EMP's columns, including EMP#. This confused the Maidens no end, and made EMP and DEPT even more unhappy.

When questions were asked involving Unhappy Tables, the answers were sometimes confusing, and the Maidens searched in vain for different ways of asking them. At other times, the answers seemed clear enough, but were not true answers to the questions the Maidens thought they were asking. Then the Maidens made Bad Decisions—satellites crashed, moonshots missed, wars broke out, and the results of football matches were badly predicted.

I took note of the complaints of these Unhappy Tables, and proceeded on my journey.

By and by, I came to a dark and forbidding mangrove swamp. I found a raft, and made my way through it, beset by crabs, snakes, spiders, and the insufferable stench of hydrogen sulfide. Eventually the dank fog cleared, to reveal the storm-ridden Sea of Nulls. In the distance, I could see the gray mass of the Land of the Unknown, and its offshore islands, Outer Join and Outer Union. The sea itself swarmed with the dorsal fins of what I knew to be fearsome nulls.

Somehow my raft withstood the storms, and the gnashing teeth of the nulls, and I eventually reached the shores of the Land of the Unknown. The path from the beach led me up a steep hill to a small castle, whose owner and sole occupant was a pathetically sad and grisly creature called Sauron.

"But you can call me Sorry—everybody else does, these days," he told me. "You are very welcome. Have you come to buy some of my lovely nulls?"

"Well, I'm not sure," I replied, cautiously. "I'd like to have a look at them first, and ask a few questions."

That Sorry was a worried man was plain to see, and I soon discovered the cause. Nulls, you see, were an essential ingredient in Sorry's Query Language. Subscribers, on payment of a fee, were allowed to catch them and put them in their tables. Business went very well to begin with, but one day there arrived in the Sea of Nulls a certain Wizard, disguised as a turtle. This turtle was armed with a small magic dagger, his defense against the voracious attacks of the nulls. Whenever a null approached, he would give it a small stab, just behind the gills. This didn't kill the null. It just made it rather ill, so it didn't always work properly in Sorry's Query Language. This made the tables unhappy.

I told Sorry the sad tale of EMP and DEPT. "The first problem," I said, "is that all your nulls look awfully alike. Some of them were put in EMP's COMMISSION column, some of them in his SALARY column. The ones in COMMISSION were supposed to mean inapplicable (employee not eligible for commission), while the ones in SALARY were supposed to mean the salary was not yet determined. When I say SALARY + COMMISSION, to compute the total pay, I correctly get a null result when SALARY is null. But I also get a null result when SALARY is nonnull and COMMISSION is null. With some query languages I might get around this problem by asking for COMMISSION to be treated as zero in calculations, when it is null, but surely the system should **know** that anyway?''

"Hmm," pondered Sorry. "Tell you what, here's a good wheeze. How about using **male** nulls for COMMISSION, **female** ones for SALARY. And get the system to understand the difference between the sexes."

"That sounds wonderful, Sorry. Many thanks!" Then I thought of something. "Oh, but hang on a minute . . . Sometimes they have to put a null in the JOBCODE column, because they don't even know, yet, what sort of job the new recruit will be doing. Do they then put a male null, or a female one, in COMMISSION?''

"A female one, of course."

"But a female null means 'missing, but applicable,' so that's the one they'd put to mean 'eligible for commission, but the value is not available,' which does sometimes happen. Seems to me they need a third kind of null, to mean 'missing, and we don't know for which reason.'''

"Sorry," said Sorry. "I don't have any of those."

"OK, next question: Sometimes the Maidens like to see which departments use which job codes. They do this by projecting EMP over DEPT# and JOBCODE. The result of the query is a binary relation, a table with two columns, looking something like this:

```
DEPT#   JOBCODE
-----   -------
D5          33
D5          34
D3          33
D3          37
D3         null
null        33
null        34
null       null
D7          49
  .          .
```

and so on. Now, in EMP, there are actually two employees in department D3 with a null job code. How did the system know that these were not two distinct DEPT#-JOBCODE pairings?''

"Ah," said Sorry. "In projections, the system treats null as equal to null, rather than it being unknown as to whether they are equal or not. The only alternative would be to treat them as unequal, and then you'd see (D3,null) twice in the result, and they would look like duplicate rows, which aren't allowed, as you very well know."

"But we don't really know whether they are duplicates or not, so neither treatment seems to be correct."

"What do you want, then?" Sorry was beginning to sound exasperated. "Should we just give an apologetic message, instead of an answer?''

I stuck to my guns. "No, I want an answer that is an accurate and reliable expression of the underlying truths."

"Sorry," said Sorry, "I can't do that."

"Anyway," I continued, "that result's supposed to be a **relation,** isn't it? All relations have **primary keys,** don't they? What's the primary key of this one?"

"That's easy—it's the combination (DEPT#,JOBCODE), the entire heading—your own rule for primary keys of projections handles that."

"But primary keys can't contain nulls—*you* know *that*!"

"Oh yes they can—in derived tables."

"But if we have to distinguish between two types of table, base and derived, we have lost that wonderful property, **closure,** which guarantees that the result of any operation in our algebra is the same kind of thing as the operands.* Indeed, you can't even call it an algebra unless the closure property is satisfied."†

"Er, you do seem to have a point there."

"And there's another point. If we join any row in the result of a projection back to the table from which it was derived, we expect to see again those rows that gave rise to it. For instance, joining the row (D5,33) back to EMP will show all the employees who work in department D5 with job code 33. What do we see if we join the row (D3,null) back to EMP? Or the row (null,33)? Or the row (null,null)?"

"I suppose that depends on whether you do a straight join or a 'maybe' join."

"The straight join must give an empty result, because null is deemed not to be equal to anything, not even another null. On the other hand, the 'maybe' join of (D3,null) with EMP would show all the employees in department D3, regardless of their job codes; and the same join for (null,null) would show all the employees! In other words, if I take a subset of my projection and join that subset back to EMP, no matter how I do the join I will not necessarily see the answer I intuitively expect."

"Sorry," said Sorry.

The foundations were beginning to crumble. Already many of the wonderful facets of the Relational Model I had once learned, and upon which I had based my understanding, my acceptance of its reliability and usability, and my delight in its **closure** properties, were ceasing to glitter.

"Oh dear," Sorry consoled. "I can see you're not happy about my

---

*And here I must admit to being somewhat at odds with the Relational Model, which does permit derived tables to have primary keys containing nulls. I see this permission as no more than a condoning of projections such as this one, and as leaving my question unanswered.

†And you certainly cannot satisfy Warden's Test Number 2, discussed in Chapters 18 and 19.

nulls. Tell you what, to cheer you up I'll take you to one of my special tourist attractions, the isle of **Outer Join.** Bring those copies of EMP and DEPT with you.''

During the journey, Sorry was in his element. Shoals of nulls congregated on his side of the boat, and every now and again one or two would rise out of the water and lick him, lovingly, on the cheeks. A large turtle appeared briefly on my side, carrying something shiny in its beak. I took this as a reminder to be on my defenses.

When we got there, Sorry first showed me the Left Outer Join of EMP with DEPT. The result looked like this, the columns to the left of DEPT# originating from EMP, the one on the right from DEPT (we agreed not to use all the columns from both tables, just enough to illustrate what was happening):

```
EMP#    JOBCODE    DEPT#    LOCATION
====    -------    -----    --------
E1          33     D5       Newtown
E2          33     D5       Newtown
E3          34     D6       null
E4          33     D7       null
E5          49     D4       Oldplace
E6          49     null     null
E7        null     D5       Newtown
  .           .       .        . . .
```

and so on.

"Look," said Sorry. "Isn't that beautiful? And don't come that primary key business with me this time—as you can see, it's got a very respectable one, EMP#. Each row from EMP is merely extended with appropriate DEPT information.''

"That's very good. Well done, Sorry! But you agree that we'd better just have a little closer look at all those nulls, just to be on the safe side, don't you?'' Sorry paled somewhat, but reluctantly concurred.

"I understand the one for E7's job code—it was like that in EMP, and merely means that we don't know what kind of job E7 does. I guess that's a female null. And the one for E6's location—that must have got there because E6 hasn't been put in a department yet. It must be of the same sex as the one E6's DEPT#.''

"You're beginning to get the hang of it,'' encouraged Sorry. But something was bothering me.

"The annoying thing is, they do actually know that E6 works at Oldplace; they just don't know which department in Oldplace. It seems a shame to know something and not be able to record it.''

"You could put LOCATION in EMP,'' suggested Sorry.

"But then EMP wouldn't be in third normal form,* and EMP is un-happy enough as it is."

"Sorry," said Sorry.

"Never mind—just so long as we know where we stand. In any case, that particular problem isn't **your** fault, Sorry, and I can't imagine any reasonable solution. Now, what about those other two nulls in LOCATION, for E3 and E4. What sex are they?"

Sorry scrutinized them closely. "Both female, I think."

"So they both mean the same thing, then?" "Of course."

"But take a look at table DEPT. The row for department D6 is there all right; it just happens to have a null in LOCATION—presumably they haven't yet decided where to site department D6, even though they know at least one employee who will work there. On the other hand, DEPT doesn't even have a row for department D7. I didn't ask why they weren't enforcing **referential integrity,** but presumably they had a good reason. Perhaps department D7 is a secret one. So those two nulls, both female, don't mean the same thing after all."

"Really, how particular you are," scolded Sorry. "What does it matter?"

"Well, if I make further queries against this result, the system might well treat those two nulls as the same thing, when in reality they are not. So the Maidens could get misleading answers, and if, as I suspect, department D7 really is to do with counterespionage, war might break out."

"Sorry," said Sorry.

So we reached another impasse. I then gave Sorry another chance to show his colors. "How about the left outer join the other way around, of DEPT with EMP? That should show me all the departments, each one joined repeatedly to each employee in that department."

"That's right," said Sorry, "and we can do that one, too!"

This was the result:

EMP#	JOBCODE	DEPT#	LOCATION
E1	33	D5	Newtown
E2	33	D5	Newtown
E3	34	D6	null
E5	49	D4	Oldplace
E7	null	D5	Newtown
null	null	D9	Oldplace
.	.	.	...

and so on.

---

*Unless the DEPT# column were excluded from EMP, but then we would be unable to deter-mine the department of any employee.

I quickly spotted the obvious differences between this and our previous join. Department D7 correctly didn't show, for there was no record of department D7 in table DEPT. Employee E6 didn't show, because employee E6 was not assigned to a department. The new row, for department D9, puzzled me at first—we had not seen that one previously.

"That," explained Sorry, "must be because nobody works in department D9." A quick glance into EMP revealed that this was indeed the case.

"Tell me then, Sorry, what kind of nulls are those in department D9's EMP# and JOBCODE columns?"

"Female," he replied. "No, sorry, hang on . . . I think they're male."

"I see. Now, when we used male nulls for the COMMISSION of ineligible employees, we meant that it was inapplicable to talk about **the** commission of such employees, right?"

"Yes—but why stress the definite article?"

"Well, I deduce that as we have male nulls in department D9's EMP# and JOBCODE, it must be inapplicable to talk about **the** EMP# and JOBCODE of department D9. But that doesn't make sense. We don't ever talk about **the** EMP# and JOBCODE of a department. A typical department has lots of EMP#s, each bringing a JOBCODE with it. The number of EMP#s in department D9 just happens to be zero. In fact, we have used a male null when what we really meant was that the **set** of EMP#s belonging to department D9 is **empty** (as is the set of JOBCODEs)."

"Er, it looks like you need yet another kind of null, and I've still only two. I really am awfully sorry," said Sorry.

I didn't bother to point out to him that the result of this one-to-many* outer join had no candidate key, and therefore no primary key.† I must have felt sorry for him.

In a last-ditch effort to appease me, Sorry took me to his other island, Outer Union. Some Maidens, I knew, were displeased with the amount of repetitive information that appeared when they did joins. By way of illustration, Sorry conjured up a couple of new tables for us to play with, SKILLS and COURSES. SKILLS showed which employees were skilled in which subjects, and was keyed on the combination of its two columns, EMP# and SUBJECT. COURSES showed which employees had been on which courses, and was also keyed on the combination of its two columns, EMP# and COURSE#.

In order to get a list of everything known about every employee, we married together these two tables, and EMP itself, using the old-fashioned

---

*A many-to-one outer join is not so bad—it inherits the primary key of its left operand.
†See the first footnote on page 513.

but reliable **natural inner join** (i.e., the "Marriage" operator defined in Chapter 18), to see:

EMP#	JOBCODE	DEPT#	SUBJECT	COURSE#
E1	33	D5	Latin	C3
E1	33	D5	Latin	C4
E1	33	D5	Latin	C5
E1	33	D5	Greek	C3
E1	33	D5	Greek	C4
E1	33	D5	Greek	C5
E1	33	D5	Cookery	C3
E1	33	D5	Cookery	C4
E1	33	D5	Cookery	C5
E2	33	D5	Greek	C31
E2	33	D5	Greek	C13
.	.	.	...	.

and so on. The primary key was the combination of the columns EMP#, SUBJECT, and COURSE#.

The repetition was obvious. Even when an employee, such as E1, had only three skills and had been on only three courses, the job code and department number were shown as many as nine times. For older employees, the explosion was horrendous. Besides, what was the point in saying that employee E1 was good at Latin, and had attended course C3 (which happens to be a cookery course), in the same row?

Furthermore, employees who had no skills, or had been on no courses, didn't show at all, even though there was some information about them in the database.

Sorry's outer union of the three tables was his attempt to get round these problems. In the outer union, each row from each table was shown only once, extended with nulls in its "extra" columns:

EMP#	JOBCODE	DEPT#	SUBJECT	COURSE#
E1	33	D5	null	null
E1	null	null	Latin	null
E1	null	null	Greek	null
E1	null	null	Cookery	null
E1	null	null	null	C3
E1	null	null	null	C4
E1	null	null	null	C5
E2	33	D5	null	null
E2	null	null	null	C13
.	.	.	...	.

and so on.

"See," said Sorry, proudly. "JOBCODE and DEPT# shown only once, and only 7 rows for employee E1 instead of 9."

Indeed, the reduction in the number of rows for the older employees was much more dramatic. One, who had 13 skills and had been on 49 courses, now showed only 63 times instead of 637. But I felt completely beset by nulls. I asked Sorry what they all meant, and which sex they were, but neither of us could find any answers. We weren't even sure if they had the same meaning as **any** we had previously encountered. They seemed even to contradict each other. The first row shown in the above extract seems to say that employee E1 doesn't have any skills and hasn't been on any courses. The next three say that E1 does have some skills after all, and reassert that E1 has been on no courses; and the three after that retract the information about skills at the same time as telling us about courses we were beginning to conclude he or she had not attended.

Do we have to see these rows in a particular **order,** to work out what the table is supposed to mean, I wondered. But the Relational Model explicitly eschews any meaning associated with order—and, in any case, which columns would I ask the system to "order by"?

"I suppose you're going to ask me what the primary key is, too," sobbed Sorry.

"'Fraid so," I inevitably and relentlessly replied.*

I also spent some time trying to work out the **predicate** that would describe this result—i.e., an **open sentence,** as logicians call it (see Chapter 22), equally applicable to every row. It was extremely difficult, and made me feel even more uncomfortable about using the result as the basis for further queries.

While I was thinking about the logical foundations of the Relational Model, I suddenly remembered my friends TABLE_DEE and TABLE_DUM, those funny little tables with no columns at all, modeling the predicate TRUE. TABLE_DEE means "something is TRUE" and TABLE_DUM means "nothing is TRUE." Bearing in mind that Sorry was advocating the use of logic with three (or more) values, such as TRUE, FALSE, and MAYBE, it occurred to me that neither TABLE_DEE nor TABLE_DUM correctly represents the conclusion "nothing is definitely TRUE, but something **might** be TRUE." So I fired my final shot:

"Who or what, pray tell me, in any system where predicates can evaluate to MAYBE (or any other meaning arising from your nulls), as well as to the time-honored TRUE and FALSE, are TABLE_DUM's **other brothers?"**

That proved to be the end of the matter,† though perhaps it should have been the beginning, too, obviating the need for any further discussion.

---

*See the first footnote on page 513.

†I mean it was the end so far as my conversation with Sorry was concerned. Really, however, the question is offered for logicians (and others) to ponder over. I have already been deeply impressed by the inability of several experts I have consulted to grapple with it, and this fact alone seems a fair enough indictment of nulls to me.

"All right," moaned Sorry. "I give up. You're right—*spurn unknowns* is the only thing you can say to the Maidens and Princes, for the time being. Oh, to think of all those Unhappy Tables and the mishaps they cause, just because of my nulls. I am so dreadfully, dreadfully **sorry!**"

AFTERNOTE

I should mention that there have been some recent developments in research* concerning the possibility of recording **sets** (in particular, "nested relations") as column values in rows within tables. Such developments are thought by some researchers to provide a possible basis for a solution to many (not all) of the problems surrounding "missing values." Such solutions would stay firmly within the framework of the Relational Model, without stepping beyond the bounds of our familiar two-valued logic, and, above all, without introducing any such awkward and ill-understood concept as "null values."

---

*See, for instance, Mark A. Roth, Henry F. Korth, and Abraham Silberschatz, "Extended Algebra and Calculus for Nested Relational Databases," *ACM Transactions on Database Systems* 13, No. 4 (December 1988).

Is SQL Getting There?

I wrote my first three chapters before I became involved with the committee working on the proposed extended version of the SQL standard called SQL2.

The problems I describe in "The Naming of Columns" are partially addressed by a new operator, AS, which allows a result column optionally to be named or renamed. Since derived tables are now permitted in the FROM clause, SQL2 can be considered to pass "Warden's Test Number 1," but failure to use the new AS operator will still cause problems.

The incorporation of NATURAL JOIN into the query syntax meets some of the requirements expressed in "In Praise of Marriage," as do the various uses of the new CORRESPONDING operator.

The new PRIMARY KEY clause of CREATE TABLE starts to address the matters of "The Keys of the Kingdom," but there is still no notion of inherited primary keys for derived tables, and no support for system-generated-key columns. For these and several other reasons, SQL2 still does not provide any of the useful functions suggested in "Chivalry."

TABLE_DEE and TABLE_DUM are still xenophobically shunned by SQL2, as is TABLE_NUM, and poor old Sorry's **nulls** still flash their fins and gnash their teeth.

Index

A-mark, 220
abstract data type, 50
addressing
  positional, *see* positional addressing
  relational model, 88, 137
all-or-any comparisons, 348ff, 406, 408–410
alternate key, 116, 148, 240, 398, 444
Alur, Nagraj, 97, 127, 167, 168, 356, 376, 423, 450
application development, 17–18
assertion, 141
atomic value, 35
atomicity (statement), 121
automatic navigation, 7

Bachman, C. W., 316, 318
bag, 95

Bandurski, A. E., 318
baseset, 309
Batory, D., 53
Beautiful Maidens, 456
Beethoven, 461
BETWEEN, 407
bill of materials, 105, 253–255
Bontempo, C. J., 97, 167, 243

candidate key, 116
  minimality, 117
Carey, M. J., 53
Carlson, C. R., 320
Casanova, Marco A., 97
catalog, 488
Chamberlin, D. D., 129, 169, 186, 215
CHECK option, 190, 399–400
closure, 8, 94, 308, 469, 513
CODASYL, 4, 5, 13, 14, 140, 167,

CODASYL (*cont.*)
    254, 257, 259, 260, 307, 309,
    310, 313, 314, 318
Codd, E. F., *passim*
coercion, 44, 67
component selector function, 35
conceptual schema, 302ff
coordinator (two-phase commit),
    288
cursor stability (CS), 418

Darwen, Hugh, 52, 93, 97, 167,
    243, 356, 376
data independence, 15–17
  logical, 16
  physical, 15
data type, 59ff, 396–397
  see also domain
database design, 20, 31, 36, 187,
    390–393, 427ff
Date, C. J., *passim*
dates and times, 59ff, 397
  IBM, 357ff, 387, 401
dBASE IV, 326
DBTG, *see* CODASYL
De Morgan's laws, 232
DEE, 501ff
default values, 245, 392
deferred constraint, 206–207
  foreign keys, 123
delete rule (foreign key), 120, 124
delete-connected, 146
dictionary, 20–21, 41, 257–258
  see also catalog
distributed database, 21–22, 267ff
domain, 27ff, 393–394
  composite, 34
  simple, 34
domain check override, 31, 41–42,
    47
domain-based access path, 52

dual-mode principle, 14–15
DUM, 501ff
duplicate rows, 83ff
  as optimization inhibitors, 92
duplicates (in presence of nulls),
    224, 229, 243
duration, 366
  labeled, 368
dynamic data definition, 18–19,
    333
dynamic SQL, 335, 421

E-relation, 109
Earnest, C. P., 319
entity integrity rule, 118
entity subtype, *see* subtypes and
    supertypes
entity supertype, *see* subtypes and
    supertypes
entity/relationship approach, 263
essential ordering, 314–315
essentiality, 308
Eswaran, K. P., 129, 169, 186, 215
EXISTS (SQL), 339ff
EXTEND, 457
extendability, 23–24
extended data type, *see* user-de-
    fined data type

Fagin, Ronald, 53, 97, 215, 319
fanset, 309
Ferguson, Mike, 423
first normal form, 35
FOCUS, 326
Fogg, D., 81
foreign key, 99ff, 133ff
  benefits, 125
  data independence, 256–257
  definition, 117
  not a pointer, 140–141

not partly null, 148ff
overlapping, 152ff
rules, 119ff
fragmentation, 280
fragmentation independence, 281
fragmentation transparency, *see*
    fragmentation independence

gateway, 292ff
generalized division, 458
Gerrard, Stephen, 337
Goodman, Nathan, 52, 97, 167,
    214, 243, 244, 341, 356, 450
Guttman, Antonin, 81

Hall, Patrick, 459
Held, Gerald, 265

I-mark, 220
IDEAL, 326
identifiability, 85
immediate constraint, 206–207
    foreign key, 123
IMS, 254, 259, 294–295, 309
IN subquery, 381, 406
inclusion constraint, 92
indicator variable, 415
Information System Base Lan-
    guage, 459
INGRES, 268, 269, 291ff, 326
INGRES/STAR, 268, 269, 270,
    277, 278, 290
"insert rule" (foreign key), 122
integrity, 185ff
    vs. concurrency, 189
    vs. recovery, 189
    vs. security, 189–90
integrity constraint, 185ff
    domain, 38

integrity rule, 190ff
    aggregate function, 204
    classification scheme, 194
    classification scheme (Codd),
        212–214
    database-specific, 214
    domain, 194
    immediate vs. deferred, 206
    metarules, 203
    multi-row, 200
    single-row, 197
    SQL/DS, 207
    state vs. transition, 205
    "user-defined," 213
interval, 63
ISBL, *see* Information System Base
    Language

Jefferson, D. K., 318

Kay, M. H., 313, 319
key
    composite, 159ff
    overlapping, 152ff
    see also alternate key; foreign
        key; primary key
Klug, Anthony, 266, 321
Korth, Henry F., 53, 519
Kreps, Peter, 265

labeled duration, *see* duration
LIKE, 407
local autonomy, 274
location independence, 277
location transparency, *see* location
    independence
logical implication, 402
Lorence, Linda, 97

Magic Words, 483–484
Maier, David, 53
manual navigation, 8
mark, 219
MAYBE, 226
MAYBE operations, 231
McCord, Rob, 297
McGee, W. C., 319
Metaxides, A., 320
Michaels, A. S., 320
minimality (candidate key), *see*
    candidate key
missing information, *see* null
Mittman, B., 320
mixed-mode expression, 44
Monsters, 456
multiset, *see* bag

nested relations, 519
Nijssen, G. M., 320
normalization, 212, 258–259
normalized relation, 35
null, 217ff, 509ff
    kinds, 219–223
nullary keys, 506
nullary relation, 502
nulls rule (foreign key), 120

object-oriented database, 50
objectives for relational model, 317
one-to-one relationship, 427ff
Ong, J., 81
operator precedence, 413
optimization
    inhibitor, 92, 355
    semantic, 127
optimizer, 22, 92
ORACLE, 268, 291ff, 356, 380
ordering, 86
orthogonality, 74, 94, 328, 385, 465

outer join, 221, 241, 514
outer union, 221, 516
Owlett, John, 459

Papadimitriou, Christos H., 97
participant (two-phase commit),
    288
performance, 22–23, 388–389
    see also optimization
Peterlee Relational Test Vehicle,
    459
Polya, G., 305, 321
portability, 334
positional addressing, 86
primary domain, 107
primary key, 88, 93, 101
    definition, 116
    exactly one per table, 136
    inheritance, 93, 479
    not null, 147
Princes, 456
Principle of Cautious Design, 134
PRTV, *see* Peterlee Relational Test
    Vehicle

qualified names, 410–411
quantification, 402
    see also EXISTS

R*, 269, 285, 287
range variable, 412–413
redundancy (database design), 437,
    445
redundancy (SQL), 329ff, 405ff
referenced row, 101
referenced table, 101
REFERENCES privilege, 166
referencing table, 101
referential constraint, 102

referential cycle, 105, 123, 448
referential integrity, 99ff, 133ff
  DB2, 146, 172ff
  recovery implications, 166
  rule, 119
  SQL standard, 170–171
  SQL/DS, 178, 184
referential path, 103
  conterminous, 143ff
referential structure, 166
relational assignment, 484
relational calculus, 383, 402ff
RENAME, 457, 472
repeatable read (RR), 418
replication, 282
replication independence, 284
replication transparency, *see* replication independence
RM/T, 109, 302
Robinson, K. A., 321
Roth, Mark A., 53, 519
Rubinstein, Brad, 81

Sawyer, Tom, 25
scalar, 35
Schmitt, Joseph W., 129, 169
Schueler, B.-M., 129, 169
SELECT *, 410
self-referencing table, 104
semantic optimization, *see* optimization
semantic override, *see* domain check override
semijoin, 491
side-operations, 416ff
Silberschatz, Abraham, 53, 519
Slutz, Don, 339
snapshot, 284
special registers, 370
SQL/400, 326
SQL*STAR, 268, 277

SQL kernel, 405
SQL standard, 10, 331ff, 387
SQL2, 387, 521
Steel, T. B., Jr., 321
Stein, Jacob, 53
Stonebraker, Michael, 53, 81, 265, 297
strict homogeneity assumption, 271
strong typing, 47
subquery, 320
  see also IN subquery
subtypes and supertypes, 106, 433
SUMMARIZE, 458, 463
surrogates, 137, 140, 162–163, 391, 447
Sweet, Frank, 266
SYBASE, 326
symmetric exploitation, 308
synonyms, 137

TABLE_DEE, *see* DEE
TABLE_DUM, *see* DUM
target row, *see* referenced row
target table, *see* referenced table
  multiple, 163ff
tautology, 232
third normal form, 259
three-schema architecture, 261
three-valued logic, 223ff
Tierney, Pete, 267
Todd, Stephen, 459
transaction, 287
Trautwein, Diann, 423
trigger, 141
  see also triggered procedure
triggered procedure, 203
triggering event, 203
Tsichritzis, D. C., 266, 321
two-phase commit, 288

UDL, 223
unk, 224
UNK, 223
unnormalized relation, 36
UNSPEC, 48
update rule (foreign key), 121, 124
    CASCADES (need for), 181ff
user-defined data type 43ff
    vs. extended, 54ff
    see also domain

van Wijngaarden, A., 53
view, 11–12, 399–400
    retrieval, 400
    updating, 399
virtual table, *see* view

Walker, Adrian, 214
Warden, Andrew, 53, 82, 97, 138,
    218, 244, 356, 424
Warden's Test Number 1, 462

Warden's Test Number 2, 468
Warden's Test Number 3, 476
weak identifier, 137, 148
Weinberg, Sharon B., 167, 249,
    265, 297, 336, 376
well-formed formula, 191
wff, *see* well-formed formula
White, Colin J., 81, 82, 129, 167,
    169, 215, 265, 297, 298, 356,
    376, 423, 424, 450
Whitener, Theresa, 129, 169
Williams, R., 298
Willmot, Richard B., 266
Winsberg, Paul, 432, 450
Wiorkowski, Gabrielle K., 418, 423
Wise Old Men, 456
Wong, E., 265
Wrazen, Ed, 423

XDB, 97

Yost, Bob, 297